CompTIA Security+ Study Guide, 5th Edition

Exam SY0-301 Exam Objectives

OBJECTIVE	CHAPTER

1.0 Network Security

1.1 Explain the security function and purpose of network devices and technologies — 2, 3, 7

Firewalls; Routers; Switches; Load Balancers; Proxies; Web security gateways; VPN concentrators; NIDS and NIPS (Behavior based, signature based, anomaly based, heuristic); Protocol analyzers; Sniffers; Spam filter, all-in-one security appliances; Web application firewall vs. network firewall; URL filtering, content inspection, malware inspection

1.2 Apply and implement secure network administration principles — 5, 11

Rule-based management; Firewall rules; VLAN management; Secure router configuration; Access control lists; Port Security; 802.1x; Flood guards; Loop protection; Implicit deny; Prevent network bridging by network separation; Log analysis

1.3 Distinguish and differentiate network design elements and compounds — 1, 2, 5

DMZ; Subnetting; VLAN; NAT; Remote Access; Telephony; NAC; Virtualization; Cloud Computing: Platform as a Service; Software as a Service; Infrastructure as a Service)

1.4 Implement and use common protocols — 2

IPSec; SNMP; SSH; DNS; TLS; SSL; TCP/IP; FTPS; HTTPS; SFTP; SCP; ICMP; IPv4 vsIPv6

1.5 Identify commonly used default network ports — 2

FTP; SFTP; FTPS; TFTP; TELNET; HTTP; HTTPS; SCP; SSH; NetBIOS

1.6 Implement wireless network in a secure manner — 12

WPA; WPA2; WEP; EAP; PEAP; LEAP; MAC filter; SSID broadcast; TKIP; CCMP; Antenna Placement; Power level controls

2.0 Compliance and Operational Security

2.1 Explain risk related concepts — 1

Control types (Technical; Management; Operational); False positives; Importance of policies in reducing risk (Privacy policy; Acceptable use; Security policy; Mandatory vacations; Job rotation; Separation of duties; Least privilege); Risk calculation (Likelihood; ALE; Impact); Quantitative vs. qualitative; Risk-avoidance, transference, acceptance, mitigation, deterrence; Risks associated to Cloud Computing and Virtualization

2.2 Carry out appropriate risk mitigation strategies — 1, 14

Implement security controls based on risk; Change management; Incident management; User rights and permissions reviews; Perform routine audits; Implement policies and procedures to prevent data loss or theft

Sybex®
An Imprint of
WILEY

Sybex®
An Imprint of
WILEY

CompTIA® Security+™
Study Guide
Fifth Edition

CompTIA® Security+™
Study Guide
Fifth Edition

Emmett Dulaney

WILEY

Wiley Publishing, Inc.

Senior Acquisitions Editor: Jeff Kellum
Development Editor: Denise Lincoln
Technical Editors: Michael Gregg, Billy Haines
Production Editor: Liz Britten
Copy Editor: Linda Recktenwald
Editorial Manager: Pete Gaughan
Production Manager: Tim Tate
Vice President and Executive Group Publisher: Richard Swadley
Vice President and Publisher: Neil Edde
Media Project Manager 1: Laura Moss-Hollister
Media Associate Producer: Josh Frank
Media Quality Assurance: Marilyn Hummel
Book Designer: Judy Fung, Bill Gibson
Compositor: Craig Woods, Happenstance Type-O-Rama
Proofreader: Word One, New York
Indexer: Nancy Guenther
Project Coordinator, Cover: Katie Crocker
Cover Designer: Ryan Sneed

Copyright © 2011 by Wiley Publishing, Inc., Indianapolis, Indiana

Published simultaneously in Canada

ISBN: 978-1-118-01473-8

ISBN: 978-1-118-11370-7 (ebk)

ISBN: 978-1-118-11371-4 (ebk)

ISBN: 978-1-118-11369-1 (ebk)

Dear Reader,

Thank you for choosing *CompTIA Security+ Study Guide, Fifth Edition* from Sybex, a proud Authorized Gold Partner in the CompTIA Authorized Partner Program (CAPP) for content developers. The learning material in this book, which meets the exacting standards of CompTIA's content assurance program, was written by an outstanding author who combines practical experience with a passion for teaching.

Sybex was founded in 1976. More than 30 years later, we're still committed to producing consistently exceptional books. With each of our titles, we're working hard to set a new standard for the industry. From the paper we print on, to the authors we work with, our goal is to bring you the best books available.

I hope you see all that reflected in these pages. I'd be very interested to hear your comments and get your feedback on how we're doing. Feel free to let me know what you think about this or any other Sybex book by sending me an email at nedde@wiley.com. If you think you've found a technical error in this book, please visit http://sybex.custhelp.com. Customer feedback is critical to our efforts at Sybex.

Best regards,

Neil Edde
Vice President and Publisher
Sybex, an Imprint of Wiley

Wiley Publishing, Inc.

For Karen, Kristin, Evan, and Spencer

Acknowledgments

This book would not exist were it not for Mike Pastore, the author of the first edition. He took a set of convoluted objectives for a broad exam and wrote the foundation of the study guide you now hold in your hands. This, the fifth edition, is indebted to his hard work and brilliance so early on.

Thanks are also due to Jeff Kellum, one of the best acquisitions editors in the business, and all of those at Wiley Publishing who worked on this title.

About the Author

Emmett Dulaney is a professor at Anderson University and the former director of training for Mercury Technical Solutions. He is a columnist for *CertCities* and the author of more than 30 books on certification and cross-platform integration. Emmett can be reached at eadulaney@comcast.net.

Contents at a Glance

Contents

Table of Exercises

Foreword

CompTIA.

CompTIA Security+:

- Designed for IT professionals focused on system security.

- Covers network infrastructure, cryptography, assessments, and audits.

- Security+ is mandated by the U.S. Department of Defense and is recommended by top companies such as Microsoft, HP, and Cisco

It Pays to Get Certified

In a digital world, digital literacy is an essential survival skill.   Certification proves you have the knowledge and skill to solve business problems in virtually any business environment.

Certification makes you more competitive and employable.   Research has shown that people who study technology get hired. In the competition for entry-level jobs, applicants with high school diplomas or college degrees who included IT coursework in their academic load fared consistently better in job interviews—and were hired in significantly higher numbers. If considered a compulsory part of a technology education, testing for certification can be an invaluable competitive distinction for professionals.

How Certification Helps Your Career

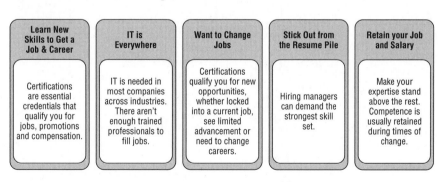

Learn New Skills to Get a Job & Career	IT is Everywhere	Want to Change Jobs	Stick Out from the Resume Pile	Retain your Job and Salary
Certifications are essential credentials that qualify you for jobs, promotions and compensation.	IT is needed in most companies across industries. There aren't enough trained professionals to fill jobs.	Certifications qualify you for new opportunities, whether locked into a current job, see limited advancement or need to change careers.	Hiring managers can demand the strongest skill set.	Make your expertise stand above the rest. Competence is usually retained during times of change.

Why CompTIA?

Global Recognition   CompTIA is recognized globally as the leading IT non-profit trade association and has enormous credibility among government and industry organizations. Plus, CompTIA's certifications are technology and vendor-neutral and offer proof of foundational knowledge that translates across technologies.

Valued by Hiring Managers   Hiring managers value CompTIA certification because it is vendor and technology independent validation of your technical skills.

Recommended or Required by Government and Businesses   Many government organizations and corporations either recommend or require technical staff to be CompTIA certified. (e.g. Dell, Sharp, Ricoh, the US Department of Defense and many more)

Three CompTIA Certifications ranked in the top 10.   In a study by DICE of 17,000 technology professionals, certifications helped command higher salaries at all experience levels.

CompTIA Career Pathway

CompTIA offers a number of credentials that form a foundation for your career in technology and allow you to pursue specific areas of concentration. Depending on the path you choose to take, CompTIA certifications help you build upon your skills and knowledge, supporting learning throughout your entire career.

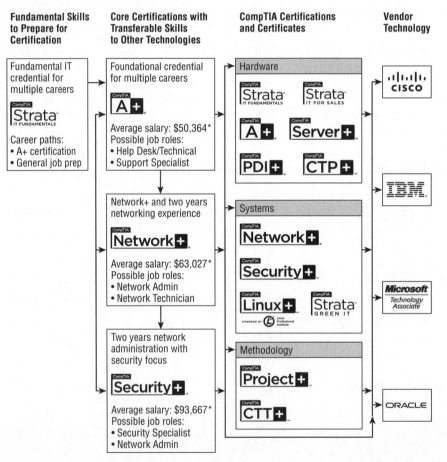

4 Steps to Getting Certified

Step 1. Review Exam Objectives   Review the Certification objectives to make sure you know what is covered in the exam `www.comptia.org/certifications/testprep/examobjectives.aspx`.

Step 2. Practice for the Exam   After you have studied for the certification, take a free assessment and sample test to get an idea what type of questions might be on the exam. `www.comptia.org/certifications/testprep/practicetests.aspx`.

Step 3. Purchase an Exam Voucher   Purchase exam vouchers on the CompTIA Marketplace, which is located at: `www.comptiastore.com`.

Step 4. Take the Test!   Select a certification exam provider and schedule a time to take your exam. You can find exam providers at the following link: `ww.comptia.org/certifications/testprep/testingcenters.aspx`.

Join the IT Professional Community

The free IT Pro online community provides valuable content to students and professionals.

- Career IT Job Resources
    - Where to start in IT
    - Career Assessments
    - Salary Trends
    - US Job Board
- Forums on Networking, Security, Computing and Cutting Edge Technologies
- Access to blogs written by Industry Experts
- Current information on Cutting Edge Technologies
- Access to various industry resource links and articles related to IT and IT careers

Content Seal of Quality

This text bears the seal of CompTIA Approved Quality Content. This seal signifies this content covers 100% of the exam objectives and implements important instructional design principles. CompTIA recommends multiple learning tools to help increase coverage of the learning objectives. Look for this seal on other materials you use to prepare for your certification exam.

How to Obtain More Information

- Visit us online at www.comptia.org to learn more about getting a CompTIA certification. And while you're at it, take a moment to learn a little more about CompTIA. We're the voice of the world's IT industry. Our membership includes companies on the cutting edge of innovation.

- To contact CompTIA with any questions or comments, please call 866-835-8020, ext. 5 or email: questions@comptia.org.

- Social Media. Find us on:
    - Facebook
    - LinkedIn
    - Twitter
    - YouTube

Terry Erdle
Executive Vice President, Skills Certification,
CompTIA

Introduction

If you're preparing to take the Security+ exam, you'll undoubtedly want to find as much information as you can concerning computer and physical security. The more information you have at your disposal and the more hands-on experience you gain, the better off you'll be when attempting the exam. This study guide was written with that in mind. The goal was to provide enough information to prepare you for the test, but not so much that you'll be overloaded with information that's outside the scope of the exam.

This book presents the material at an intermediate technical level. Experience with and knowledge of security concepts, operating systems, and application systems will help you get a full understanding of the challenges you face as a security professional.

I've included review questions at the end of each chapter to give you a taste of what it's like to take the exam. If you're already working in the security field, I recommend that you check out these questions first to gauge your level of expertise. You can then use the book mainly to fill in the gaps in your current knowledge. This study guide will help you round out your knowledge base before tackling the exam.

If you can answer 90% or more of the review questions correctly for a given chapter, you can feel safe moving on to the next chapter. If you're unable to answer that many correctly, reread the chapter and try the questions again. Your score should improve.

> Don't just study the questions and answers! The questions on the actual exam will be different from the practice questions included in this book and on the CD. The exam is designed to test your knowledge of a concept or objective, so use this book to learn the objectives behind the questions.

Before You Begin the CompTIA Security+ Certification Exam

Before you begin studying for the exam, it's imperative that you understand a few things about the Security+ certification. Security+ is a certification from CompTIA (an industry association responsible for many entry-level certifications) granted to those who obtain a passing score on a single entry-level exam. In addition to adding Security+ to your resume as a stand-alone certification, you can use it as an elective in many vendor-certification tracks.

> At the time of this writing, CompTIA is in the process of creating an advanced security certification that builds on Security+ and authenticates knowledge at a higher level. The CompTIA Advance Security Practitioner (CASP) certification is designed for those with up to 10 years of security experience.

When you're studying for any exam, the first step in preparation should always be to find out as much as possible about the test; the more you know up front, the better you can plan your course of study. The current exam, and the one this book is written for, is the 2011 update. While all variables are subject to change, as this book is being written, the exam consists of 100 questions. You have 90 minutes to take the exam, and the passing score is based on a scale from 100 to 900. Both Pearson VUE and Prometric testing centers administer the exam throughout the United States and several other countries.

The exam is multiple choice with short, terse questions usually followed by four possible answers. Don't expect lengthy scenarios and complex solutions. This is an entry-level exam of knowledge-level topics; you're expected to know a great deal about security topics from an overview perspective rather than implementation. In many books, the Glossary is filler added to the back of the text; this book's Glossary (located on the companion CD) should be considered necessary reading. You're likely to see a question on the exam about what a Trojan horse is, not how to identify it at the code level. Spend your study time learning the different security solutions and identifying potential security vulnerabilities and where they would be applicable. Don't get bogged down in step-by-step details; those are saved for certification exams beyond the scope of Security+.

You should also know that CompTIA is notorious for including vague questions on all its exams. You might see a question for which two of the possible four answers are correct—but you can only choose one. Use your knowledge, logic, and intuition to choose the best answer, and then move on. Sometimes the questions are worded in ways that would make English majors cringe—a typo here, an incorrect verb there. Don't let this frustrate you; answer the question, and go to the next. Although we haven't intentionally added typos or other grammatical errors, the questions throughout this book make every attempt to re-create the structure and appearance of the real exam questions. CompTIA offers a page on study tips for their exams at `http://certification.comptia.org/resources/test_tips.aspx`, and it is worth skimming. (Also, read the section later in this Introduction titled "Tips for Taking the Security+ Exam.")

CompTIA frequently does what is called *item seeding,* which is the practice of including unscored questions on exams. It does that to gather psychometric data, which is then used when developing new versions of the exam. Before you take it, you are told that your exam may include unscored questions. So if you come across a question that does not appear to map to any of the exam objectives—or for that matter, does not appear to belong in the exam—it is likely a seeded question.

As you study, you need to know that the exam you'll take was created at a certain point in time. You won't see a question about the new virus that hit your systems last week, but you'll see questions about concepts that existed when this exam was created. Updating the exam is a difficult process and results in an increment in the exam number.

Why Become Security+ Certified?

There are a number of reasons for obtaining a Security+ certification. These include the following:

It Provides Proof of Professional Achievement.   Specialized certifications are the best way to stand out from the crowd. In this age of technology certifications, you'll find hundreds of thousands of administrators who have successfully completed the Microsoft and Cisco certification tracks. To set yourself apart from the crowd, you need a little bit more. The Security+ exam is part of the CompTIA certification track that includes A+, Network+, and other vendor-neutral certifications such as Linux+, Project+, and more. This exam will help you prepare for more advanced certifications because it provides a solid grounding in security concepts and will give you the recognition you deserve.

It Increases Your Marketability.   Almost anyone can bluff their way through an interview. Once you're Security+ certified, you'll have the credentials to prove your competency. And, certifications can't be taken from you when you change jobs—you can take that certification with you to any position you accept.

It Provides Opportunity for Advancement.   Individuals who prove themselves to be competent and dedicated are the ones who will most likely be promoted. Becoming certified is a great way to prove your skill level and show your employer that you're committed to improving your skill set. Look around you at those who are certified: They are probably the people who receive good pay raises and promotions.

It Fulfills Training Requirements.   Many companies have set training requirements for their staff so that they stay up-to-date on the latest technologies. Having a certification program in security provides administrators with another certification path to follow when they have exhausted some of the other industry-standard certifications.

It Raises Customer Confidence.   As companies discover the CompTIA advantage, they will undoubtedly require qualified staff to achieve these certifications. Many companies outsource their work to consulting firms with experience working with security. Firms that have certified staff have a definite advantage over firms that don't.

How to Become a Security+ Certified Professional

As this book goes to press, there are two Security+ exam providers: Prometric and Pearson VUE. The following table contains all the necessary contact information and exam-specific details for registering. Exam pricing might vary by country or by CompTIA membership.

Vendor	Website	Phone Number
Prometric	securereg3.prometric.com	U.S. and Canada: 800-977-3926
Pearson VUE	www.vue.com/comptia	U.S. and Canada: 877-551-PLUS (7587)

When you schedule the exam, you'll receive instructions regarding appointment and cancellation procedures, ID requirements, and information about the testing center location. In addition, you'll receive a registration and payment confirmation letter. Exams can be scheduled up to six weeks out or as late as the next day (or, in some cases, even the same day).

 Exam prices and codes may vary based on the country in which the exam is administered. For detailed pricing and exam registration procedures, refer to CompTIA's website at www.comptia.com.

After you've successfully passed your Security+ exam, CompTIA will award you a certification. Within four to six weeks of passing the exam, you'll receive your official CompTIA Security+ certificate and ID card. (If you don't receive these within eight weeks of taking the test, contact CompTIA directly using the information found in your registration packet.)

Who Should Read This Book?

If you want to acquire a solid foundation in computer security and your goal is to prepare for the exam by learning how to develop and improve security, this book is for you. You'll find clear explanations of the concepts you need to grasp and plenty of help to achieve the high level of professional competency you need in order to succeed in your chosen field.

If you want to become certified as a certification holder, this book is definitely what you need. However, if you just want to attempt to pass the exam without really understanding security, this study guide isn't for you. It's written for people who want to acquire hands-on skills and in-depth knowledge of computer security.

 In addition to reading this book, you might consider downloading and reading the white papers on security that are scattered throughout the Internet.

Tips for Taking the Security+ Exam

Here are some general tips for taking your exam successfully:

- Bring two forms of ID with you. One must be a photo ID, such as a driver's license. The other can be a major credit card or a passport. Both forms must include a signature.

- Arrive early at the exam center so you can relax and review your study materials, particularly tables and lists of exam-related information. After you are ready to enter the testing room, you will need to leave everything outside; you won't be able to bring any materials into the testing area.

- Read the questions carefully. Don't be tempted to jump to an early conclusion. Make sure you know exactly what each question is asking.

- Don't leave any unanswered questions. Unanswered questions are scored against you.

- There will be questions with multiple correct responses. When there is more than one correct answer, a message at the bottom of the screen will prompt you to either "Choose two" or "Choose all that apply." Be sure to read the messages displayed to know how many correct answers you must choose.

- When answering multiple-choice questions you're not sure about, use a process of elimination to get rid of the obviously incorrect answers first. Doing so will improve your odds if you need to make an educated guess.

- On form-based tests (nonadaptive), because the hard questions will take the most time, save them for last. You can move forward and backward through the exam.

- For the latest pricing on the exams and updates to the registration procedures, visit CompTIA's website at www.comptia.org.

How to Use This Book and the CD

We've included several testing features in the book and on the CD-ROM. These tools will help you retain vital exam content as well as prepare you to sit for the actual exam:

Assessment Test   At the end of this Introduction is an Assessment Test that you can use to check your readiness for the exam. Take this test before you start reading the book; it will help you determine the areas you might need to brush up on. The answers to the Assessment Test questions appear on a separate page after the last question of the test. Each answer includes an explanation and a note telling you the chapter in which the material appears.

Chapter Review Questions   To test your knowledge as you progress through the book, there are review questions at the end of each chapter. As you finish each chapter, answer the review questions and then check your answers—the correct answers appear on the page following the last review question. You can go back to reread the section that deals with each question you got wrong to ensure that you answer correctly the next time you're tested on the material.

Sybex Test Engine   The CD contains the Sybex Test Engine. Using this custom software, you can identify up front the areas in which you are weak and then develop a solid studying strategy using each of these robust testing features. The ReadMe file walks you through the installation process.

In addition to taking the assessment test and the chapter review questions in the test engine, you'll find practice exams. Take these practice exams just as if you were taking the actual exam (without any reference material). When you've finished the first exam, move on to the next one to solidify your test-taking skills. If you get more than 90 percent of the answers correct, you're ready to take the certification exam.

Electronic Flashcards   You'll find flashcard questions on the CD for on-the-go review. These are short questions and answers. You use them for quick and convenient reviewing.

PDF of Glossary of Terms   The Glossary of Terms is on the CD in PDF format.

Exam Objectives

CompTIA goes to great lengths to ensure that its certification programs accurately reflect the IT industry's best practices. They do this by establishing committees for each of its exam programs. Each committee comprises a small group of IT professionals, training providers, and publishers who are responsible for establishing the exam's baseline competency level and who determine the appropriate target-audience level.

Once these factors are determined, CompTIA shares this information with a group of hand-selected Subject Matter Experts (SMEs). These folks are the true brainpower behind the certification program. In the case of this exam, they are IT-seasoned pros from the likes of Microsoft, Sun Microsystems, VeriSign, and RSA Security, to name just a few. The SMEs review the committee's findings, refine them, and shape them into the objectives that follow this section. CompTIA calls this process a job task analysis (JTA).

Finally, CompTIA conducts a survey to ensure that the objectives and weightings truly reflect the job requirements. Only then can the SMEs go to work writing the hundreds of questions needed for the exam. And in many cases, they have to go back to the drawing board for further refinements before the exam is ready to go live in its final state. So, rest assured the content you're about to learn will serve you long after you take the exam.

Exam objectives are subject to change at any time without prior notice and at CompTIA's sole discretion. Visit the certification page of CompTIA's website at www.comptia.org for the most current listing of exam objectives.

CompTIA also publishes relative weightings for each of the exam's objectives. The following table lists the six Security+ objective domains and the extent to which they are represented on the exam. As you use this study guide, you'll find that I have administered just the right dosage of objective knowledge by tailoring coverage to mirror the percentages that CompTIA uses.

Domain	% of Exam
1.0 Network Security	21%
2.0 Compliance and Operational Security	18%
3.0 Threats and Vulnerabilities	21%
4.0 Application, Data and Host Security	16%
5.0 Access Control and Identity Management	13%
6.0 Cryptography	11%
Total	100%

1.0 Network Security

1.1 Explain the security function and purpose of network devices and technologies (covered in Chapters 2, 3, and 7)

- Firewalls
- Routers
- Switches
- Load Balancers
- Proxies
- Web security gateways
- VPN concentrators
- NIDS and NIPS (Behavior based, signature based, anomaly based, heuristic)
- Protocol analyzers
- Sniffers
- Spam filter, all-in-one security appliances
- Web application firewall vs. network firewall
- URL filtering, content inspection, malware inspection

1.2 Apply and implement secure network administration principles (covered in Chapters 5 and 11)

- Rule-based management
- Firewall rules
- VLAN management
- Secure router configuration
- Access control lists
- Port Security
- 802.1x
- Flood guards
- Loop protection
- Implicit deny
- Prevent network bridging by network separation
- Log analysis

1.3 Distinguish and differentiate network design elements and compounds (covered in Chapters 1, 2, and 5)

- DMZ
- Subnetting

- VLAN
- NAT
- Remote Access
- Telephony
- NAC
- Virtualization
- Cloud Computing
    - Platform as a Service
    - Software as a Service
    - Infrastructure as a Service

1.4   Implement and use common protocols (covered in Chapter 2)

- IPSec
- SNMP
- SSH
- DNS
- TLS
- SSL
- TCP/IP
- FTPS
- HTTPS
- SFTP
- SCP
- ICMP
- IPv4 vs. IPv6

1.5   Identify commonly used default network ports (covered in Chapter 2)

- FTP
- SFTP
- FTPS
- TFTP
- TELNET
- HTTP
- HTTPS
- SCP

- SSH
- NetBIOS

1.6   Implement wireless network in a secure manner (covered in Chapter 12)

- WPA
- WPA2
- WEP
- EAP
- PEAP
- LEAP
- MAC filter
- SSID broadcast
- TKIP
- CCMP
- Antenna Placement
- Power level controls

2.0 Compliance and Operational Security

2.1   Explain risk related concepts (covered in Chapter 1)

- Control types
  - Technical
  - Management
  - Operational
- False positives
- Importance of policies in reducing risk
  - Privacy policy
  - Acceptable use
  - Security policy
  - Mandatory vacations
  - Job rotation
  - Separation of duties
  - Least privilege

- Risk calculation
    - Likelihood
    - ALE
    - Impact
- Quantitative vs. qualitative
- Risk-avoidance, transference, acceptance, mitigation, deterrence
- Risks associated to Cloud Computing and Virtualization

2.2 Carry out appropriate risk mitigation strategies (covered in Chapters 1 and 14)

- Implement security controls based on risk
- Change management
- Incident management
- User rights and permissions reviews
- Perform routine audits
- Implement policies and procedures to prevent data loss or theft

2.3 Execute appropriate incident response procedures (covered in Chapter 13)

- Basic forensic procedures
    - Order of volatility
    - Capture system image
    - Network traffic and logs
    - Capture video
    - Record time offset
    - Take hashes
    - Screenshots
    - Witnesses
    - Track man hours and expense
- Damage and loss control
- Chain of custody
- Incident response: first responder

2.4 Explain the importance of security related awareness and training (covered in Chapter 6)

- Security policy training and procedures
- Personally identifiable information
- Information classification: Sensitivity of data (hard or soft)
- Data labeling, handling and disposal

- Compliance with laws, best practices, and standards
- User habits
- Password behaviors
- Data handling
- Clean desk policies
- Prevent tailgating
- Personally owned devices
- Threat awareness
- New viruses
- Phishing attacks
- Zero days exploits
- Use of social networking and P2P

2.5   Compare and contrast aspects of business continuity (covered in Chapter 13)

- Business impact analysis
- Removing single points of failure
- Business continuity planning and testing
- Continuity of operations
- Disaster recovery
- IT contingency planning
- Succession planning

2.6   Explain the impact and proper use of environmental controls (covered in Chapter 10)

- HVAC
- Fire suppression
- EMI shielding
- Hot and cold aisles
- Environmental monitoring
- Temperature and humidity controls
- Video monitoring

2.7   Execute disaster recovery plans and procedures (covered in Chapter 13)

- Backup / backout contingency plans or policies
- Backups, execution and frequency
- Redundancy and fault tolerance
  - Hardware
  - RAID

- Clustering
- Load balancing
- Servers
- High availability
- Cold site, hot site, warm site
- Mean time to restore, mean time between failures, recovery time objectives and recover point objectives

2.8   Exemplify the concepts of confidentiality, integrity and availability (CIA) (covered in Chapters 2 and 8)

3.0 Threats and Vulnerabilities

3.1   Analyze and differentiate among types of malware (covered in Chapter 4)

- Adware
- Virus
- Worms
- Spyware
- Trojan
- Rootkits
- Backdoors
- Logic bomb
- Botnets

3.2   Analyze and differentiate among types of attacks (covered in Chapters 4, 5, and 6)

- Man-in-the-middle
- DDoS
- DoS
- Replay
- Smurf attack
- Spoofing
- Spam
- Phishing
- Spim
- Vishing
- Spear phishing

- Xmas attack
- Pharming
- Privilege escalation
- Malicious insider threat
- DNS poisoning and ARP poisoning
- Transitive access
- Client-side attacks

3.3 Analyze and differentiate among types of social engineering attacks (covered in Chapters 4 and 6)

- Shoulder surfing
- Dumpster diving
- Tailgating
- Impersonation
- Hoaxes
- Whaling
- Vishing

3.4 Analyze and differentiate among types of wireless attacks (covered in Chapter 12)

- Rogue access points
- Interference
- Evil twin
- War driving
- Bluejacking
- Bluesnarfing
- War chalking
- IV attack
- Packet sniffing

3.5 Analyze and differentiate among types of application attacks (covered in Chapters 3, 6, and 7)

- Cross-site scripting
- SQL injection
- LDAP injection
- XML injection
- Directory traversal/command injection
- Buffer overflow

- Zero day
- Cookies and attachments
- Malicious add-ons
- Session hijacking
- Header manipulation

3.6 Analyze and differentiate among types of mitigation and deterrent techniques (covered in Chapters 3, 7, 10, and 11)

- Manual bypassing of electronic controls
  - Failsafe/secure vs. failopen
- Monitoring system logs
  - Event logs
  - Audit logs
  - Security logs
  - Access logs
- Physical security
  - Hardware locks
  - Mantraps
  - Video surveillance
  - Fencing
  - Proximity readers
  - Access list
- Hardening
  - Disabling unnecessary services
  - Protecting management interfaces and applications
  - Password protection
  - Disabling unnecessary accounts
- Port security
  - MAC limiting and filtering
  - 802.1x
  - Disabling unused ports
- Security posture
  - Initial baseline configuration
  - Continuous security monitoring
  - Remediation

- Reporting
  - Alarms
  - Alerts
  - Trends
- Detection controls vs. prevention controls
  - IDS vs. IPS
  - Camera vs. guard

3.7 Implement assessment tools and techniques to discover security threats and vulnerabilities (covered in Chapters 1, 3, and 11)

- Vulnerability scanning and interpret results
- Tools
  - Protocol analyzer
  - Sniffer
  - Vulnerability scanner
  - Honeypots
  - Honeynets
  - Port scanner
- Risk calculations
  - Threat vs. likelihood
- Assessment types
  - Risk
  - Threat
  - Vulnerability
- Assessment technique
  - Baseline reporting
  - Code review
  - Determine attack surface
  - Architecture
  - Design reviews

3.8 Within the realm of vulnerability assessments, explain the proper use of penetration testing versus vulnerability scanning (covered in Chapter 11)

- Penetration testing
  - Verify a threat exists
  - Bypass security controls

- Actively test security controls
- Exploiting vulnerabilities
- Vulnerability scanning
  - Passively testing security controls
  - Identify vulnerability
  - Identify lack of security controls
  - Identify common misconfiguration
- Black box
- White box
- Gray box

4.0 Application, Data and Host Security

4.1 Explain the importance of application security (covered in Chapters 3 and 7)

- Fuzzing
- Secure coding concepts
  - Error and exception handling
  - Input validation
- Cross-site scripting prevention
- Cross-site Request Forgery (XSRF) prevention
- Application configure baseline (proper settings)
- Application hardening
- Application patch management

4.2 Carry out appropriate procedures to establish host security (covered in Chapters 2, 7, and 10)

- Operating system security and settings
  - Anti-malware
  - Anti-virus
  - Anti-spam
  - Anti-spyware
  - Pop-up blockers
  - Host-based firewalls
- Patch management

- TACACS+
- Kerberos
- LDAP
- XTACACS

5.2   Explain the fundamental concepts and best practices related to authentication, authorization, and access control (covered in Chapters 5, 10, and 14)

- Identification vs. authentication
- Authentication (single factor) and authorization
- Multifactor authentication
- Biometrics
- Tokens
- Common access card
- Personal identification verification card
- Smart card
- Least privilege
- Separation of duties
- Single sign on
- ACLs
- Access control
- Mandatory access control
- Discretionary access control
- Role/rule-based access control
- Implicit deny
- Time of day restrictions
- Trusted OS
- Mandatory vacations
- Job rotation

5.3   Implement appropriate security controls when performing account management (covered in Chapter 14)

- Mitigates issues associated with users with multiple account/roles
- Account policy enforcement
  - Password complexity
  - Expiration

- - Recovery
  - Length
  - Disablement
  - Lockout
- Group based privileges
- User assigned privileges

6.0 Cryptography

6.1 Summarize general cryptography concepts (covered in Chapter 8)
- Symmetric vs. asymmetric
- Fundamental differences and encryption methods
  - Block vs. stream
- Transport encryption
- Non-repudiation
- Hashing
- Key escrow
- Steganography
- Digital signatures
- Use of proven technologies
- Elliptic curve and quantum cryptography

6.2 Use and apply appropriate cryptographic tools and products (covered in Chapter 8)
- WEP vs. WPA/WPA2 and preshared key
- MD5
- SHA
- RIPEMD
- AES
- DES
- 3DES
- HMAC
- RSA
- RC4
- One-time-pads

- CHAP
- PAP
- NTLM
- NTLMv2
- Blowfish
- PGP/GPG
- Whole disk encryption
- TwoFish
- Comparative strengths of algorithms
- Use of algorithms with transport encryption
- SSL
- TLS
- IPSec
- SSH
- HTTPS

6.3 Explain the core concepts of public key infrastructure (covered in Chapter 8)

- Certificate authorities and digital certificates
  - CA
  - CRLs
- PKI
- Recovery agent
- Public key
- Private key
- Registration
- Key escrow
- Trust models

6.4   Implement PKI, certificate management and associated components (covered in Chapter 9)

- Certificate authorities and digital certificates
  - CA
  - CRLs
- PKI
- Recovery agent
- Public key
- Private keys
- Registration
- Key escrow
- Trust models

Assessment Test

1. Which type of audit can be used to determine whether accounts have been established properly and verify that privilege creep isn't occurring?

    A. Privilege audit

    B. Usage audit

    C. Escalation audit

    D. Report audit

2. What kind of physical access device restricts access to a small number of individuals at one time?

    A. Checkpoint

    B. Perimeter security

    C. Security zones

    D. Mantrap

3. Which of the following is a set of voluntary standards governing encryption?

    A. PKI

    B. PKCS

    C. ISA

    D. SSL

4. Which protocol is used to create a secure environment in a wireless network?

    A. WAP

    B. WEP

    C. WTLS

    D. WML

5. An Internet server interfaces with TCP/IP at which layer of the DOD model?

    A. Transport layer

    B. Network layer

    C. Process layer

    D. Internet layer

6. You want to establish a network connection between two LANs using the Internet. Which technology would best accomplish that for you?

    A. IPSec

    B. L2TP

    C. PPP

    D. SLIP

7. Which design concept limits access to systems from outside users while protecting users and systems inside the LAN?

   A. DMZ

   B. VLAN

   C. I&A

   D. Router

8. In the key recovery process, which key must be recoverable?

   A. Rollover key

   B. Secret key

   C. Previous key

   D. Escrow key

9. Which kind of attack is designed to overload a particular protocol or service?

   A. Spoofing

   B. Back door

   C. Man in the middle

   D. Flood

10. Which component of an IDS collects data?

    A. Data source

    B. Sensor

    C. Event

    D. Analyzer

11. What is the process of making an operating system secure from attack called?

    A. Hardening

    B. Tuning

    C. Sealing

    D. Locking down

12. The integrity objective addresses which characteristic of information security?

    A. Verification that information is accurate

    B. Verification that ethics are properly maintained

    C. Establishment of clear access control of data

    D. Verification that data is kept private and secure

13. Which mechanism is used by PKI to allow immediate verification of a certificate's validity?

    A. CRL

    B. MD5

    C. SSHA

    D. OCSP

14. Which of the following is the equivalent of a VLAN from a physical security perspective?

    A. Perimeter security

    B. Partitioning

    C. Security zones

    D. Physical barrier

15. A user has just reported that he downloaded a file from a prospective client using IM. The user indicates that the file was called `account.doc`. The system has been behaving unusually since he downloaded the file. What is the most likely event that occurred?

    A. Your user inadvertently downloaded a virus using IM.

    B. Your user may have a defective hard drive.

    C. Your user is hallucinating and should increase his medication.

    D. The system is suffering from power surges.

16. Which mechanism or process is used to enable or disable access to a network resource based on an IP address?

    A. NDS

    B. ACL

    C. Hardening

    D. Port blocking

17. Which of the following would provide additional security to an Internet web server?

    A. Changing the port address to 80.

    B. Changing the port address to 1019.

    C. Adding a firewall to block port 80.

    D. Web servers can't be secured.

18. What type of program exists primarily to propagate and spread itself to other systems?

    A. Virus

    B. Trojan horse

    C. Logic bomb

    D. Worm

19. An individual presents herself at your office claiming to be a service technician. She wants to discuss your current server configuration. This may be an example of what type of attack?

   A. Social engineering

   B. Access control

   C. Perimeter screening

   D. Behavioral engineering

20. Which of the following is a major security problem with FTP servers?

   A. Password files are stored in an unsecure area on disk.

   B. Memory traces can corrupt file access.

   C. User IDs and passwords are unencrypted.

   D. FTP sites are unregistered.

21. Which system would you install to provide active protection and notification of security problems in a network connected to the Internet?

   A. IDS

   B. Network monitoring

   C. Router

   D. VPN

22. The process of verifying the steps taken to maintain the integrity of evidence is called what?

   A. Security investigation

   B. Chain of custody

   C. Three As of investigation

   D. Security policy

23. What encryption process uses one message to hide another?

   A. Steganography

   B. Hashing

   C. MDA

   D. Cryptointelligence

24. Which policy dictates how computers are used in an organization?

   A. Security policy

   B. User policy

   C. Use policy

   D. Enforcement policy

25. Which algorithm is used to create a temporary secure session for the exchange of key information?

    A. KDC

    B. KEA

    C. SSL

    D. RSA

26. You've been hired as a security consultant for a company that's beginning to implement hand-held devices, such as PDAs. You're told that the company must use an asymmetric system. Which security standard would you recommend it implement?

    A. ECC

    B. PKI

    C. SHA

    D. MD

27. Which of the following backup methods will generally provide the fastest backup times?

    A. Full backup

    B. Incremental backup

    C. Differential backup

    D. Archival backup

28. You want to grant access to network resources based on authenticating an individual's retina during a scan. Which security method uses a physical characteristic as a method of determining identity?

    A. Smart card

    B. I&A

    C. Biometrics

    D. CHAP

29. Which access control method is primarily concerned with the role that individuals have in the organization?

    A. MAC

    B. DAC

    C. RBAC

    D. STAC

30. The process of investigating a computer system for clues into an event is called what?

    A. Computer forensics

    B. Virus scanning

    C. Security policy

    D. Evidence gathering

Answers to Assessment Test

1. **A.** A privilege audit is used to determine that all groups, users, and other accounts have the appropriate privileges assigned according to the policies of an organization. For more information, see Chapter 5.

2. **D.** A mantrap limits access to a small number of individuals. It could be, for example, a small room. Mantraps typically use electronic locks and other methods to control access. For more information, see Chapter 10.

3. **B.** Public-Key Cryptography Standards is a set of voluntary standards for public-key cryptography. This set of standards is coordinated by RSA. For more information, see Chapter 8.

4. **B.** Wired Equivalent Privacy (WEP) is designed to provide security equivalent to that of a wired network. WEP has vulnerabilities and isn't considered highly secure. For additional information, see Chapter 12.

5. **C.** The Process layer interfaces with applications and encapsulates traffic through the Host-to-Host or Transport layer, the Internet layer, and the Network Access layer. For more information, see Chapter 3.

6. **B.** L2TP (Layer 2 Tunneling Protocol) is a tunneling protocol that can be used between LANs. L2TP isn't secure, and you should use IPSec with it to provide data security. For more information, see Chapter 3.

7. **A.** A DMZ (demilitarized zone) is an area in a network that allows restrictive access to untrusted users and isolates the internal network from access by external users and systems. It does so by using routers and firewalls to limit access to sensitive network resources. For more information, see Chapter 3.

8. **C.** A key recovery process must be able to recover a previous key. If the previous key can't be recovered, then all the information for which the key was used will be irrecoverably lost. For more information, see Chapter 9.

9. **D.** A flood attack is designed to overload a protocol or service by repeatedly initiating a request for service. This type of attack usually results in a DoS (denial of service) situation occurring because the protocol freezes or excessive bandwidth is used in the network as a result of the requests. For more information, see Chapter 4.

10. **B.** A sensor collects data from the data source and passes it on to the analyzer. If the analyzer determines that unusual activity has occurred, an alert may be generated. For additional information, see Chapter 11.

11. **A.** Hardening is the term used to describe the process of securing a system. This is accomplished in many ways, including disabling unneeded protocols. For additional information on hardening, see Chapter 7.

12. **A.** To meet the goal of integrity, you must verify that information being used is accurate and hasn't been tampered with. Integrity is coupled with accountability to ensure that data is accurate and that a final authority exists to verify this, if needed. For more information, see Chapter 8.

13. D. Online Certificate Status Protocol (OCSP) is the mechanism used to immediately verify whether a certificate is valid. The Certificate Revocation List (CRL) is published on a regular basis, but it isn't current once it's published. For additional information, see Chapter 9.

14. B. Partitioning is the process of breaking a network into smaller components that can each be individually protected. The concept is the same as building walls in an office building. For additional information, see Chapter 3.

15. A. IM and other systems allow unsuspecting users to download files that may contain viruses. Due to a weakness in the file extension naming conventions, a file that appears to have one extension may actually have another extension. For example, the file `account.doc.vbs` would appear in many applications as `account.doc`, but it's actually a Visual Basic script and could contain malicious code. For additional information, see Chapter 4.

16. B. Access control lists (ACLs) are used to allow or deny an IP address access to a network. ACL mechanisms are implemented in many routers, firewalls, and other network devices. For additional information, see Chapter 5.

17. B. The default port for a web server is port 80. By changing the port to 1019, you force users to specify this port when they are using a browser. This action provides a little additional security for your website. Adding a firewall to block port 80 would secure your website so much that no one would be able to access it. For more information, see Chapter 3.

18. D. A worm is designed to multiply and propagate. Worms may carry viruses that cause system destruction, but that isn't their primary mission. For more information, see Chapter 4.

19. A. Social engineering is using human intelligence methods to gain access or information about your organization. For additional information, see Chapter 6.

20. C. In most environments, FTP sends account and password information unencrypted. This makes these accounts vulnerable to network sniffing. For additional information, see Chapter 11.

21. A. An intrusion detection system (IDS) provides active monitoring and rule-based responses to unusual activities on a network. A firewall provides passive security by preventing access from unauthorized traffic. If the firewall were compromised, the IDS would notify you based on rules it's designed to implement. For more information, see Chapter 11.

22. B. The chain of custody ensures that each step taken with evidence is documented and accounted for from the point of collection. Chain of custody is the Who, What, When, Where, and Why of evidence storage. For additional information, see Chapter 13.

23. A. Steganography is the process of hiding one message in another. Steganography may also be referred to as electronic watermarking. For additional information, see Chapter 8.

24. C. The use policy is also referred to as the usage policy. It should state acceptable uses of computer and organizational resources by employees. This policy should outline consequences of noncompliance. For additional information, see Chapter 14.

25. B. The Key Exchange Algorithm (KEA) is used to create a temporary session to exchange key information. This session creates a secret key. When the key has been exchanged, the regular session begins. For more information, see Chapter 9.

26. A. Elliptic Curve Cryptography (ECC) would probably be your best choice for a PDA. ECC is designed to work with smaller processors. The other systems may be options, but they require more computing power than ECC. For additional information, see Chapter 8.

27. B. An incremental backup will generally be the fastest of the backup methods because it backs up only the files that have changed since the last incremental or full backup. See Chapter 15 for more information.

28. C. Biometrics is the authentication process that uses physical characteristics, such as a palm print or retinal pattern, to establish identification. For more information, see Chapter 11.

29. C. Role-based access control (RBAC) is primarily concerned with providing access to systems that a user needs based on the user's role in the organization. For more information, see Chapter 5.

30. A. Computer forensics is the process of investigating a computer system to determine the cause of an incident. Part of this process would be gathering evidence. For additional information, see Chapter 13.

Chapter

1

Measuring and Weighing Risk

THE FOLLOWING COMPTIA SECURITY+ EXAM OBJECTIVES ARE COVERED IN THIS CHAPTER:

✓ **1.3 Distinguish and differentiate network design elements and compounds.**

  ▪ Cloud computing: Platform as a Service; Software as a Service; Infrastructure as a Service

✓ **2.1 Explain risk related concepts.**

  ▪ Control types: Technical; Management; Operational

  ▪ False positives

  ▪ Importance of policies in reducing risk: Privacy policy; Acceptable use; Security policy; Mandatory vacations; Job rotation; Separation of duties; Least privilege

  ▪ Risk calculation; Likelihood; ALE; Impact

  ▪ Quantitative vs. Qualitative

  ▪ Risk avoidance, transference, acceptance, mitigation, deterrence

  ▪ Risk associated to Cloud Computing and Virtualization

✓ **2.2 Carry out appropriate risk mitigation strategies.**

  ▪ Implement security controls based on risk

  ▪ Change management

  ▪ Incident management

  ▪ User rights and permission reviews

  ▪ Perform routine audits

✓ **3.7 Implement assessment tools and techniques to discover security threats and vulnerabilities.**

  ▪ Risk calculations: Threat vs. likelihood

✓ **4.3 Explain the importance of data security.**

  ▪ Cloud computing

As an administrator, you know that there are risks involved in working with data. You know that data can become corrupt, can be accessed by those who shouldn't see it, can have values changed, and so on. If you think that being armed with this knowledge is enough to enable you to take the steps to keep any harm from happening, however, you'll be sadly mistaken. One of the possible actions administrators can take to potential threats is to simply accept that they will happen. If the cost of preventing a particular risk from becoming a reality exceeds the value of the harm that could be caused by the event, then a cost/benefit risk calculation dictates that the risk should remain.

Most risk calculations weigh a potential *threat* against the *likelihood* of it occurring. As frustrating as it may seem, you should always be able to accept the fact that sometimes some risks must remain. This chapter focuses on risk and various ways of dealing with it, all of which you will need to understand fully for the Security+ exam.

Risk Assessment

Risk assessment is also known as *risk analysis*. It deals with the threats, vulnerabilities, and impacts of a loss of information-processing capabilities or information itself. Each risk that can be identified should be outlined, described, and evaluated for the likelihood of it occurring. The key is to think out of the box. Conventional threats/risks are often too limited when considering risk assessment.

The key components of a risk-assessment process are outlined here:

Risks to Which the Organization Is Exposed   This component allows you to develop scenarios that can help you evaluate how to deal with these risks if they occur. An operating system, server, or application may have known risks in certain environments. You should create a plan for how your organization will best deal with these risks and the best way to respond.

Risks That Need Addressing   The risk-assessment component also allows an organization to provide a reality check on which risks are real and which aren't likely. This process helps an organization focus on its resources as well as on the risks that are most likely to occur. For example, industrial espionage and theft are likely, but the risk of a pack of wild dogs stealing the entire contents of the payroll file is very low. Therefore, resources should be allocated to prevent espionage or theft as opposed to the latter possibility.

Coordination with BIA   The risk-assessment component, in conjunction with the BIA (Business Impact Analysis) which is discussed in Chapter 13, provides an organization with an accurate picture of the situation facing it. It allows an organization to make intelligent decisions about how to respond to various scenarios.

 Real World Scenario

Conducting a Risk Assessment

You've been asked to do a quick assessment of the risks your company faces from a security perspective. What steps might you take to develop an overview of your company's problems?

1. Interview the department heads and the owners to determine what information they feel needs additional security and what the existing vulnerabilities are from their perspectives.

2. Evaluate the servers to determine their known vulnerabilities and how you might counter them.

3. Make sure you do a physical assessment of the facility to evaluate what physical risks you must counter.

Armed with this information, you have a place to start, and you can determine which measures may be appropriate for the company from a risk perspective.

Computing Risk Assessment

When you're doing a risk assessment, one of the most important things to do is to prioritize. Not everything should be weighed evenly because some events have a greater likelihood of happening; in addition, a company can live with some risks, whereas others would be catastrophic. One method of measurement to consider is *annualized rate of occurrence (ARO)*. This is the likelihood, often drawn from historical data, of an event occurring within a year. This measure can be used in conjunction with a monetary value assigned to data to compute *single loss expectancy (SLE)* and *annual loss expectancy (ALE)* values.

When you're computing risk assessment, remember this formula:

SLE × ARO = ALE

Thus, if you can reasonably expect that every SLE, which is equal to asset value (AV) times exposure factor (EF), will be equivalent to $1,000 and that there will be seven occurrences a year (ARO), then the ALE is $7,000. Conversely, if there is only a 10 percent chance of an event occurring in a year (ARO = .1), then the ALE drops to $100.

In Exercise 1.1, we'll walk through some risk-assessment computations.

Real World Scenario

Risk-Assessment Computations

As a security professional, you should know how to compute SLE, ALE, and ARO. Given any two of the numbers, it's possible to calculate the third. Following are three separate scenarios detailing a hypothetical risk assessment situation followed by details for how to figure out the ALE. They are intended to give you experience working scenarios similar to those you may find on the Security+ exam. For this exercise, compute the missing values:

1. You're the administrator of a web server that generates $25,000 per hour in revenue. The probability of the web server failing is estimated to be 25 percent, and a failure would lead to three hours of downtime and cost $5,000 in components to correct. What is the ALE?

    The SLE is $80,000 ($25,000 × 3 hours + $5,000), and the ARO is .25. Therefore the ALE is $20,000 ($80,000 × .25).

2. You're the administrator for a research firm that works on only one project at a time and collects data through the Web to a single server. The value of each research project is approximately $100,000. At any given time, an intruder could commandeer no more than 90 percent of the data. The industry average for ARO is .33. What is the ALE?

    The SLE equals $90,000 ($100,000 × .9), and the ARO is .33. Therefore, the ALE is $29,700 ($90,000 × .33).

3. You work at the help desk for a small company. One of the most common requests you must respond to is to help retrieve a file that has been accidentally deleted by a user. On average, this happens once a week. If the user creates the file and then deletes it on the server (about 60 percent of the incidents), then it can be restored in moments from the shadow copy, and there is rarely any data lost. If the user creates the file on their workstation and then deletes it (about 40 percent of the incidents), and if it can't be recovered and it takes the user an average of two hours to re-create it at $12 an hour, what is the ALE?

    The SLE is $24 ($12 × 2), and the ARO is 20.8 (52 weeks × .4). Therefore the ALE equals $499.20 ($24 × 20.8).

Key to any risk assessment is identifying both assets and threats. You first have to identify what you want to protect and then what possible harms could come to those assets. You then analyze the risks in terms of either cost or severity.

Risk assessment can be either *qualitative* (opinion-based and subjective) or *quantitative* (cost-based and objective), depending upon whether you are focusing on dollar amounts or not. The formulas for single loss expectancy (SLE), annual loss expectancy (ALE), and annualized rate of occurrence (ARO) are all based on doing assessments that lead to dollar amounts and are thus quantitative.

To understand the difference between quantitative and qualitative, it helps to use a simplistic example. Imagine that you get an emergency call to help a small company that you have never even heard from before. It turns out that their one and only server has crashed and their backups are useless. One of the files lost was the only copy of the company history. This file detailed the company from the day it began to the present day and had the various iterations of the mission statement as they changed over time. As painful a loss as this file represents to the company culture, it has nothing to do with filling orders and keeping customers happy and its loss represents a qualitative loss.

Another loss was the customer database. This held customer contact information as well as a history of all past orders, charge numbers, and so on. The company cannot function without this file and it needs to be re-created by pulling all the hard copy invoices from storage and re-entering them into the system. This loss can be calculated by the amount of business lost and the amount of time it takes to find/re-enter all the data, and thus it is a quantitative loss.

Acting on Your Risk Assessment

Once you've identified and assessed the risks that exist, for the purpose of the exam, you have five possible actions you can choose to follow:

Risk Avoidance   *Risk avoidance* involves identifying a risk and making the decision to no longer engage in the actions associated with that risk. For example, a company could decide that many risks are associated with email attachments and choose to forbid any email attachments from entering the network.

Risk Transference   *Risk transference*, contrary to what the name may imply, does not mean that you shift the risk completely to another entity. What you do instead is share some of the burden of the risk with someone else, such as an insurance company. A typical policy would pay you a cash amount if all the steps were in place to reduce risk and your system still was harmed.

Risk Mitigation   *Risk mitigation* is accomplished anytime you take steps to reduce the risk. This category includes installing antivirus software, educating users about possible threats, monitoring the network traffic, adding a firewall, and so on. In Microsoft's Security Intelligence Report, Volume 9, they list the following suggestions for mitigating risk:

- Keep security messages fresh and in circulation.
- Target new employees and current staff members.
- Set goals to ensure a high percentage of the staff is trained on security best practices.
- Repeat the information to raise awareness.

Risk Deterrence   *Risk deterrence* involves understanding something about the enemy and letting them know the harm that can come their way if they cause harm to you. This can be as simple as posting prosecution policies on your login pages and convincing them that you have steps in place to identify intrusions and act on them.

Risk Acceptance   *Risk acceptance* is often the choice you must make when the cost of implementing any of the other four choices exceeds the value of the harm that would occur if the risk came to fruition. To truly qualify as acceptance, it cannot be a risk that the administrator/management does not know exists; it has to be an identified risk for which those involved understand the potential cost/damage and agree to accept.

It can often be helpful to create sagacious examples to help in understanding or memorizing various lists, and this works well for the five possible risk actions. Imagine that you are a junior administrator for a large IT department and you believe that one of the older servers should be replaced with a new one. There are no signs of failure now, but it would be prudent to upgrade before anything disastrous happens. The problem, however, is that all spending requires approval from your superior, who is focused on saving the company as much money as possible in order to be considered for a promotion, and he does not want anyone finding ways to spend money. You know him well enough to fear that if a problem does occur, he will not hesitate to put all the blame on you in order to save his own career. Table 1.1 shows how you would apply each of the possible risk actions to this scenario.

TABLE 1.1   Risk actions for the scenario

Risk Action	Application
Risk avoidance	You begin moving services from the older server to other servers and remove the load to avoid the risk of any services being affected by its demise.
Risk transference	You write up the possibility of the server failing along with details of what you think should be done to prevent it and submit it to your boss while keeping a copy for yourself. If the server does fail, you have proof that you documented this possibility and made the appropriate parties aware of the situation.
Risk mitigation	You write up the possibility of failure and submit it to your boss while also moving crucial services from that server to others.
Risk deterrence	You write up the possibility of the server failing along with details of what you think should be done to prevent it and submit it not only to your boss but also to his boss. Use quantitative analysis to show the logic in replacing the server before it fails rather than after.
Risk acceptance	You know the server could fail but pray that it doesn't. You don't write and submit reports because you don't want to rock the boat and make your boss unhappy with you. With luck, you'll have transferred to coding before the server ever goes down.

Risks Associated with Cloud Computing

The term *cloud computing* has grown in popularity recently, but few agree on what it truly means. For the purpose of the Security+ exam, cloud computing means using the Internet to host services and data instead of hosting it locally. Some examples of this include running Office-like applications from the Web (such as Google Docs) instead of having the applications installed on each workstation, storing data on server space rented from Amazon, using sites such as Salesforce.com, and so on.

From an exam standpoint, there are three ways of implementing cloud computing:

Platform as a Service   The Platform as a Service (PaaS) model is also known as cloud platform services. In this model, vendors allow apps to be created and run on their infrastructure. Two well-known models of this implementation are Amazon Web Services and Google Code.

Software as a Service   The Software as a Service (SaaS) model is the one often thought of when users generically think of cloud computing. In this model, applications are remotely run over the Web. The big advantage is that no local hardware is required (other than to obtain web access) and no software applications need be installed on the machine accessing the site. The best known model of this is Salesforce.com. Costs are usually computed on a subscription basis.

Infrastructure as a Service   The Infrastructure as a Service (IaaS) model utilizes virtualization, and clients pay an outsourcer for resources used. Because of this, this model closely resembles the traditional utility model used by electric, gas, and water providers. GoGrid is a well-known example of this implementation.

A number of organizations have examined risk-related issues that can be associated with cloud computing. These issues include the following:

Regulatory Compliance   Depending upon the type and size of your organization, there are any number of regulatory agency's rules with which you must comply. If your organization is publically traded, for example, then you must adhere to Sarbanes-Oxley's demanding and exacting rules—which can be difficult to do when the data is not located on your servers. Make sure whoever hosts your data takes privacy and security as seriously as you do.

User Privileges   Enforcing user privileges can be fairly taxing. If the user does not have least privilege (addressed later in this chapter), then their escalated privileges could allow them to access data they otherwise would not be able to and cause harm to it, whether intentional or not. Be cognizant of the fact that you won't have the same control over user accounts in the cloud as you did locally, and when someone locks their account by giving the wrong password too many times in a row, you/they could be at the mercy of the hours the technical staff is available at the provider.

Data Integration/Segregation   Just as web-hosting companies usually put more than one company's website on a server in order to be profitable, data-hosting companies can put more than one company's data on a server. In order to keep this from being problematic, you should use encryption to protect your data. Be cognizant of the fact that your data is only as safe as the data it is integrated with. As an overly simplistic example, assume that your client database is hosted on a server that another company is also using to test an application they are creating. If their application obtains root level at some point (such as to change passwords) and crashes at that point, then the user running the application could be left with root permissions and conceivably be able to see data on the server beyond what they should see (such as your client database). Data segregation is crucial; keep your data on secure servers.

Data integration is equally important—making certain your data is not comingled beyond your expectations. It is not uncommon in an extranet to pull information from a number of databases in order to create a report. Those databases can be owned by anyone connected to the extranet, and it is important to make certain the permissions on your databases are set properly to keep other members from accessing more information that you intended to share.

 Among the groups focused on cloud security issues, one worth paying attention to is the Cloud Security Alliance (http://www.cloudsecurityalliance .org). As of this writing, they have published "Top Threats to Cloud Computing" and "Security Guidance for Critical Areas of Focus in Cloud Computing," which are both highly recommended reading for security administrators.

Risks Associated with Virtualization

If cloud computing has grown in popularity, *virtualization* has become the technology du jour. Virtualization—allowing one set of hardware to host multiple virtual machines—is in use at most large corporations and becoming more common at smaller businesses as well.

Some of the security risks that are possible with virtualization include the following:

Breaking Out of the Virtual Machine   If a malcontent could break out of the virtualization layer and be able to access the other virtual machines, they could access data they should never have access to.

Network and Security Controls Can Intermingle   The tools used to administer the virtual machine may not have the same granularity as those used to manage the network. This could lead to privilege escalation and a compromise of security.

Most virtualization-specific threats focus on the *hypervisor*. The hypervisor is the virtual machine monitor —the software that allows the virtual machines to exist. If the hypervisor can be successfully attacked, the attacker can gain root-level access to all virtual systems. While this is a legitimate issue, and one that has been demonstrated to be possible in most systems (including VMware, Xen, and Microsoft Virtual Machine), it is one that has been patched each time it has reared. The solution to most virtualization threats is to always apply the most recent patches and keep the system(s) up to date.

Developing Policies, Standards, and Guidelines

The process of implementing and maintaining a secure network must first be addressed from a policies, standards, and guidelines perspective. This sets the tone, provides authority, and gives your efforts the teeth they need to be effective. Policies and guidelines set a standard of expectation in an organization. The process of developing these policies will help everyone in an organization become involved and invested in making security efforts successful. You can think of policies as providing the big picture on issues. Standards tell people what is expected, and guidelines provide specific advice on how to accomplish a given task or activity.

The next sections discuss the policies, standards, and guidelines you need to establish in order for your security efforts to be successful.

Implementing Policies

Policies provide the people in an organization with guidance about their expected behavior. Well-written policies are clear and concise, and they outline consequences when they aren't followed. A good policy contains several key areas besides the policy itself:

Chapter 14 also discusses policies, and you will find an expanded discussion there of many of the topics introduced in this section.

Scope Statement   A good policy has a scope statement that outlines what the policy intends to accomplish and which documents, laws, and practices the policy addresses. The scope statement provides background to help readers understand what the policy is about and how it applies to them.

The scope statement is always brief—usually not more than a single sentence in length.

Policy Overview Statement   A policy overview statement provides the goal of the policy, why it's important, and how to comply with it. Ideally, a single paragraph is all you need to provide readers with a sense of the policy.

Policy Statement   Once the policy's readers understand its importance, they should be informed of what the policy is. A policy statement should be as clear and unambiguous as possible. The policy may be presented in paragraph form, as bulleted lists, or as checklists.

The presentation will depend on the policy's target audience as well as its nature. If the policy is intended to help people determine how to lock up the building at the end of the business day, for example, it might be helpful to provide a specific checklist of the steps that should be taken.

Accountability Statement   The policy should address who is responsible for ensuring that it is enforced. This statement provides additional information to the reader about who to contact if a problem is discovered. It should also indicate the consequences of not complying with the policy.

 The accountability statement should be written in words the reader can understand. If the accountability statement is to be read by the users, then it must be written in such a way as to leave no room for misinterpretation.

Exception Statement   Sometimes even the best policy doesn't foresee every eventuality. The exception statement provides specific guidance about the procedure or process that must be followed in order to deviate from the policy. This may include an escalation contact, in the event that the person dealing with a situation needs to know whom to contact.

The policy development process is sometimes time consuming. The advantage of this process, though, is that the decisions can be made in advance and can be sent to all involved parties so the policy doesn't have to be restated over and over again. In fact, formally developing policies saves time and provides structure: Instead of using valuable time trying to figure out what to do, employees will know what to do.

Incorporating Standards

A *standard* deals with specific issues or aspects of a business. Standards are derived from policies. A standard should provide enough detail that an audit can be performed to determine if the standard is being met. Standards, like policies, have certain structural aspects in common.

The following five points are the key aspects of standards documents:

Scope and Purpose   The standards document should explain or describe the intention. If a standard is developed for a technical implementation, the scope might include software, updates, add-ins, and any other relevant information that helps the implementer carry out the task.

Roles and Responsibilities   This section of the standards document outlines who is responsible for implementing, monitoring, and maintaining the standard. In a system configuration, this section would outline what the customer is supposed to accomplish and what the installer is supposed to accomplish. This doesn't mean that one or the other can't exceed those roles; it means that in the event of confusion, it's clear who is responsible for accomplishing which tasks.

Reference Documents   This section of the standards document explains how the standard relates to the organization's different policies, thereby connecting the standard to the underlying policies that have been put in place. In the event of confusion or uncertainty, it also allows people to go back to the source and figure out what the standard means. You'll encounter many situations throughout your career where you're given a standard that doesn't make sense. Frequently, by referring to the policies, you can figure out why the standard was written the way it was. Doing so may help you carry out the standard or inform the people responsible for the standard of a change or problem.

Performance Criteria   This part of the standards document outlines how to accomplish the task. It should include relevant baseline and technology standards. Baselines provide a minimum or starting point for the standard. Technology standards provide information about the platforms and technologies. Baseline standards spell out high-level requirements for the standard or technology.

 An important aspect of performance criteria is benchmarking. You need to define what will be measured and the metrics that will be used to do so.

If you're responsible for installing a server in a remote location, for example, the standards spell out what type of computer will be used, what operating system will be installed, and any other relevant specifications.

Maintenance and Administrative Requirements   These standards outline what is required to manage and administer the systems or networks. For instance, in the case of a physical security requirement, the frequency with which locks or combinations are changed would be addressed.

As you can see, the standards documents provide a mechanism for both new and existing standards to be evaluated for compliance. The process of evaluation is called an *audit*. Increasingly, organizations are being required to conduct regular audits of their standards and policies.

Following Guidelines

Guidelines are slightly different from either policies or standards. Guidelines help an organization implement or maintain standards by providing information on how to accomplish the policies and maintain the standards.

Guidelines can be less formal than policies or standards because their nature is to help users comply with policies and standards. An example might be an explanation of how to install a service pack and what steps should be taken before doing so.

Guidelines aren't hard-and-fast rules. They may, however, provide a step-by-step process to accomplish a task. Guidelines, like standards and policies, should contain background information to help a user perform the task.

The following four items are the minimum contents of a good guidelines document:

Scope and Purpose   The scope and purpose provide an overview and statement of the guideline's intent. It is not uncommon to see the heading "Purpose and Scope" or "Scope and Purpose" at the beginning of a document followed by verbiage to the effect: "This document contains the guidelines and procedures for the assignment and use of *xyz* and establishes the minimum requirements for governing the acceptable use of…"

Where the scope and purpose are two separate headings, the information beneath the "Purpose" section states why it exists (i.e., "This policy establishes guidelines and minimum requirements governing…") and the "Scope" section tells who it applies to (i.e., "This policy applies to any employee who…").

Roles and Responsibilities   This section of the guidelines identifies which individuals or departments are responsible for accomplishing specific tasks. This may include implementation, support, and administration of a system or service. In a large organization, it's likely that the individuals involved in the process will have different levels of training and expertise. From a security perspective, it could be disastrous if an unqualified technician installed a system without guidelines.

Guideline Statements   These statements provide the step-by-step instructions on how to accomplish a specific task in a specific manner. Again, these are guidelines—they may not be hard-and-fast rules.

Operational Considerations   A guideline's operational considerations specify and identify what duties are required and at what intervals. This list might include daily, weekly, and monthly tasks. Guidelines for systems backup, for example, might provide specific guidance as to which files and directories must be backed up and how frequently.

Guidelines help an organization in three different ways. First, if a process or set of steps isn't performed routinely, experienced support and security staff will forget how to do them; guidelines will help refresh their memory. Second, when you're trying to train someone to do something new, written guidelines can improve the new person's learning curve. Third, when a crisis or high-stress situation occurs, guidelines can keep you from coming unglued.

Business Policies

Business policies also affect the security of an organization. They address organizational and departmental business issues as opposed to corporate-wide personnel issues. When developing your business policy, you must consider these primary areas of concern:

- Separation of duties
- Due care
- Physical access control
- Document disposal and destruction
- Privacy policy
- Acceptable use
- Security policy
- Mandatory vacations
- Job rotation
- Least privilege

The following sections discuss these areas.

Separation of Duties Policies

Separation of duties policies are designed to reduce the risk of fraud and prevent other losses in an organization. A good policy will require more than one person to accomplish key processes. This may mean that the person who processes an order from a customer isn't the same person who generates the invoice or deals with the billing.

Separation of duties helps prevent various problems, such as an individual embezzling money from a company. To successfully embezzle funds, an individual would need to recruit others to commit an act of *collusion* (an agreement between two or more parties established for the purpose of committing deception or fraud). Collusion, when part of a crime, is also a criminal act in and of itself.

In addition, separation-of-duties policies can help prevent accidents from occurring in an organization. Let's say you're managing a software development project. You want someone to perform a quality assurance test on a new piece of code before it's put into production. Establishing a clear separation of duties prevents development code from entering production status until quality testing is accomplished.

Many banks and financial institutions require multiple steps and approvals to transfer money. This helps reduce errors and minimizes the likelihood of fraud.

 Very small attacks are often called salami attacks. In banking, various forms of salami attacks can occur, such as shaving a few cents from many accounts, rounding to whole numbers and compiling the remainder into one account, and so on.

Due Care Policies

Due care policies identify the level of care used to maintain the confidentiality of private information. These policies specify how information is to be handled. The objectives of due care policies are to protect and safeguard customer and/or client records. The unauthorized disclosure of this information creates a strong potential for liability and lawsuits. Everyone in an organization must be aware of and held to a standard of due care with confidential records.

 It's easy to say that everyone else should adhere to policies and then overlook the importance of doing so yourself. As an administrator, you have access to a great deal of personal information, and you need to be as careful with it, if not more careful, as anyone else in the organization. In many cases, something as simple as a printed list of user information sitting in plain view on your desk can violate rules of disclosure.

One of the leading ways to handle due care policies is to implement *best practices*. Best practices are based on what is known in the industry and how others would respond to similar situations.

Physical Access Control Policies

Physical access control policies refer to the authorization of individuals to access facilities or systems that contain information. Implementing a physical access control policy helps prevent theft and unauthorized disclosure of information and keeps other problems from cropping up. Many organizations limit office hours of employees to prevent them from accessing computer systems during odd hours. (This may not be appropriate for some positions, but it may be essential in others.) What would happen in your company if a payroll clerk decided to give herself a raise? In all probability, she wouldn't do this under the supervision of the payroll manager—she would do it when no one was around. By limiting access to the physical premises and computer systems, you reduce the likelihood that an individual will be tempted to commit a crime.

Document Disposal and Destruction Policies

Document disposal and destruction policies define how information that is no longer needed is handled. According to Microsoft's Security Intelligence Report, Volume 9, "Improper disposal of business records is the second largest source of breach incidents related to negligence, and the third largest source of incidents overall."

You should ensure that financial, customer, and other sensitive information is disposed of properly when it's no longer needed. Most organizations use mountains of paper, and much of it needs to be shredded or destroyed to prevent unauthorized access to sensitive information. Investigate the process that your organization uses to dispose of business records; it may need to be reevaluated.

Many large cities have businesses that do nothing but destroy paper for banks and other institutions. Using a truck that resembles a mobile shredder on wheels, they will come to your site and guarantee that the paper is destroyed. If your organization works with data of a sensitive nature, you should investigate the possibility of using such a service.

Privacy Policies

Privacy policies define what controls are required to implement and maintain the sanctity of data privacy in the work environment. Many of the restrictions regarding privacy are addressed in legislation and covered in Chapter 6. For now, however, think of the privacy policy as a legal document that outlines how data collected is secured. A great example of a privacy policy is Google's (see `http://www.google.com/privacy/privacy-policy.html`), which outlines exactly what information the company collects, choices you have based on your account, information sharing of the data that is done with other parties, security measure in place, and enforcement. The last paragraph of the policy should appear in every policy and addresses the fact that the policy may change. The verbiage, as currently written, is succinct and clear: "Please note that this Privacy Policy may change from time to time. We will not reduce your rights under this Privacy Policy without your explicit consent. We will post any Privacy Policy changes on this page and, if the changes are significant, we will provide a more prominent notice (including, for certain services, email notification of Privacy Policy changes). We will also keep prior versions of this Privacy Policy in an archive for your review."

Acceptable Use Policies

Acceptable use policies (AUPs) describe how the employees in an organization can use company systems and resources: both software and hardware. This policy should also outline the consequences for misuse. In addition, the policy (also known just as a *use policy*) should address installation of personal software on company computers and the use of personal hardware such as USB devices. When portable devices are plugged directly into a machine, they bypass the network security measures (such as firewalls) and allow data to be copied in what is known as *pod slurping*.

Even secure workstations that contain no traditional media devices (CD, DVD, and so forth) usually contain USB ports. Unless those ports are disabled, a user can easily connect a flash drive and copy files to and from it. Not only should you make every attempt to limit USB ports, but you should also have the use of such devices spelled out in the acceptable use policy to circumvent the "I didn't know" defense.

 Real World Scenario

The Trouble with Not Having a Policy

A few years ago, an employee in a large company was using corporate computer systems to run a small accounting firm he had started. He was using the computers on his own time. When this situation was discovered, he was immediately fired for the misuse of corporate resources. He sued the company for wrongful discharge and won the case. The company was forced to hire him back and pay his back wages, and he was even awarded damages. The primary reason the company lost the case was that its acceptable use policy didn't say he couldn't use the company computers for personal work, only that he couldn't use them for personal work during work hours. The company wasn't able to prove that he did the personal work during work hours.

Every acceptable use policy today should include a section on cell phone usage (and even presence) within the workplace. While a cell phone can be convenient for employees (they can now more easily take personal calls at work), it can be a headache for the security administrator. Most cell phones can store files the same as any USB device and can be used to copy files to and from the workstation. Additionally, the camera feature of most phones makes it possible for a user to take pictures of such things as documents, your servers, your physical security implementation, and many other things you probably don't want to share. For this reason, most secure facilities have stringent restrictions on the presence of cell phones within the vicinity.

Make sure your acceptable use policies provide you with adequate coverage regarding all acceptable uses of corporate resources.

Security Policies

Security policies define what controls are required to implement and maintain the security of systems, users, and networks. This policy should be used as a guide in system implementations and evaluations. Security policies will be discussed throughout the book, and you should be aware of their key aspects.

Mandatory Vacations

A *mandatory vacation policy* requires all users to take time away from work and refresh. As contradictory as it may seem, an employee who doesn't take their vacation time can be detrimental to the health not only of the employee but of the company as well. If the company becomes too dependent on one person, they can end up in a real bind if something should happen to that person. Not only does the mandatory vacation give the employee a chance to refresh, but it also gives the company the chance to make sure others can fill in any gaps in skills and satisfy the need to have replication/duplication at all levels. The mandatory vacations also provide an opportunity to discover fraud.

Job Rotation

A *job rotation policy* defines intervals at which employees must rotate through positions. Similar in purpose to mandatory vacations, it helps to ensure that the company does not become too dependent on one person (who then has the ability to do enormous harm). Rotate jobs on a frequent enough basis so that you are not putting yourself—and your data—at the mercy of any one administrator. Just as you want redundancy in hardware, you want redundancy in abilities.

When one person fills in for another, such as for mandatory vacations, it provides an opportunity to see what the person is doing and potentially uncover any fraud.

Least Privilege

A *least privilege policy* should be used when assigning permissions. Give users only the permissions they need to do their work and no more. For example, a temporary employee should never have the right to install software, a receptionist does not need the right to make backups, and so on. Every operating system includes the ability to limit users based on groups and individual permissions, and your company should adhere to the policy of always applying only those permissions users need and blocking all others.

Understanding Control Types, False Positives, and Change and Incident Management

Risk assessment/analysis involves calculating potential risks and making decisions based on the variables associated with those risks (likelihood, ALE, impact, etc.). Once you've identified risks that you want to address with actions other than avoidance, you put controls in place to address the risks.

The U.S. Department of Energy Cyber Security Program places controls into various types. The *control types* fall into three categories: Management, Operational, and

Technical, as defined in the Management, Operational, and Technical Controls Guidance (`http://www.ornl.gov/doe/doe_oro_dmg/TMR/TMRs/CS01%20Final%20Controls%20070706 .pdf`). Table 1.2 shows the various controls and the classification type they fall under.

 While risk assessment was discussed in this chapter, most of the other controls are addressed in subsequent chapters.

TABLE 1.2 Control Types and Controls

Control Type	Controls
Management	Risk Assessment
Management	Planning
Management	System and Services Acquisition
Management	Certification, Accreditation, and Security Assessment
Operational	Personnel Security
Operational	Physical and Environmental Protection
Operational	Contingency Planning
Operational	Configuration Management
Operational	Maintenance
Operational	System and Information Integrity
Operational	Media Protection
Operational	Incident Response
Operational	Awareness and Training
Technical	Identification and Authentication
Technical	Access Control
Technical	Audit and Accountability
Technical	System and Communication Protection

In addition to the U.S. Department of Energy Cyber Security Program controls, another worth looking at is NIST 800-53, which is used by government
and industry and viewed more as a global standard (http://csrc.nist.gov/
publications/nistpubs/800-53-Rev3/sp800-53-rev3-final_updated-
errata_05-01-2010.pdf).

After you have implemented security controls based on risk, you must routinely perform
routine audits. Those audits should include reviews of user rights and permissions as well
as events that occur. You should pay particular attention to false positives, change management, and incident management.

False positives are events that aren't really incidents. Event flagging is often based on
established rules of acceptance (deviations from which are known as *anomalies*) and such
things as attack signatures. If the rules aren't set up properly, normal traffic may set off the
analyzer and generate an event. You don't want to declare an emergency unless you're sure
you have one.

The audits should address *change management*—the structured approach that is followed
to secure the company's assets—and *incident management*—the steps followed when events
occur. Details here should include the controls that are in place to prevent unauthorized access
to, and changes of, all IT assets.

Summary

Risk assessment is the process of evaluating and cataloging the threats, vulnerabilities,
and weaknesses that exist in the systems being used. The risk assessment should tie in
with BCP to ensure that all bases are covered.

Security models begin with an understanding of the business issues an organization is
facing. The following business issues must be evaluated:

- Policies
- Standards
- Guidelines

A good policy design includes scope statements, overview statements, accountability
expectations, and exceptions. Each of these aspects of a well-crafted policy helps set the
expectation for everyone in a company. For a policy to be effective, it needs the unequivocal
support of the senior management or decision makers in an organization.

Exam Essentials

Know the three categories of control types.   The three types of controls that can be administered are Technical, Management, and Operational.

Know how to calculate risk.   Risk can be calculated either qualitatively (subjective) or quantitatively (objective). Quantitative calculations assign dollar amounts, and the basic formula is SLE × ARO = ALE where SLE is the single loss expectancy, ARO is the annualized rate of occurrence, and ALE is the annual loss expectancy.

Know the five different approaches to risk.   The five risk strategies are avoidance (don't engage in that activity), transference (think insurance), mitigation (take steps to reduce the risk), deterrence (warn of harm to others if they affect you), and acceptance (be willing to live with the risk).

Know the importance of policies, standards, and guidelines.   The process of implementing and maintaining a secure network must first be addressed from a policies, standards, and guidelines perspective. Policies and guidelines set a standard of expectation in an organization. Standards tell people what is expected, and guidelines provide specific advice on how to accomplish a given task or activity.

Know the principles of cloud computing.   Cloud computing can be implemented three ways: Platform as a Service, Software as a Service, and Infrastructure as a Service. Each provides a different set of threats that administrators must be cognizant of.

Review Questions

1. You're the chief security contact for MTS. One of your primary tasks is to document everything related to security and create a manual that can be used to manage the company in your absence. Which documents should be referenced in your manual as the ones that identify the methods used to accomplish a given task?

    A. Policies

    B. Standards

    C. Guidelines

    D. BIA

2. Consider the following scenario: The asset value of your company's primary servers is $2 million and they are housed in a single office building in Anderson, Indiana. You have field offices scattered throughout the United States, so the servers in the main office account for approximately half the business. Tornados in this part of the country are not uncommon, and it is estimated one will level the building every 60 years.

    Which of the following is the SLE for this scenario?

    A. $2 million

    B. $1 million

    C. $500,000

    D. $33,333.33

    E. $16,666.67

3. Refer to the scenario in question 2. Which of the following is the ALE for this scenario?

    A. $2 million

    B. $1 million

    C. $500,000

    D. $33,333.33

    E. $16,666.67

4. Refer to the scenario in question 2. Which of the following is the ARO for this scenario?

    A. 0.0167

    B. 1

    C. 5

    D. 16.7

    E. 60

5. Which of the following strategies involves identifying a risk and making the decision to no longer engage in the action?

   A. Risk acceptance

   B. Risk avoidance

   C. Risk deterrence

   D. Risk mitigation

   E. Risk transference

6. Which of the following policy statements may include an escalation contact, in the event that the person dealing with a situation needs to know whom to contact?

   A. Scope

   B. Exception

   C. Overview

   D. Accountability

7. Which of the following policies are designed to reduce the risk of fraud and prevent other losses in an organization?

   A. Separation of duties

   B. Acceptable use

   C. Least privilege

   D. Physical access control

8. What is the term used for events that mistakenly were flagged and aren't truly events to be concerned with?

   A. Fool's gold

   B. Non-incidents

   C. Error flags

   D. False positives

9. Which of the following is the structured approach that is followed to secure the company's assets?

   A. Asset management

   B. Incident management

   C. Change management

   D. Skill management

10. Which of the following strategies involves sharing some of the burden of the risk with someone else such as an insurance company?

    A. Risk acceptance

    B. Risk avoidance

    C. Risk deterrence

    D. Risk mitigation

    E. Risk transference

11. The risk-assessment component, in conjunction with the _____, provides the organization with an accurate picture of the situation facing it.

A. RAC

B. ALE

C. BIA

D. RMG

12. Which of the following policy statements should address who is responsible for ensuring that it is enforced?

A. Scope

B. Exception

C. Overview

D. Accountability

13. Which of the following strategies is accomplished anytime you take steps to reduce the risk?

A. Risk acceptance

B. Risk avoidance

C. Risk deterrence

D. Risk mitigation

E. Risk transference

14. If you calculate SLE to be $4,000 and that there will be 10 occurrences a year (ARO), then the ALE is:

A. $400

B. $4,000

C. $40,000

D. $400,000

15. Which of the following policies describes how the employees in an organization can use company systems and resources, both software and hardware?

A. Separation of duties

B. Acceptable use

C. Least privilege

D. Physical access control

16. Separation of duties helps prevent an individual from embezzling money from a company. To successfully embezzle funds, an individual would need to recruit others to commit an act of _____ (an agreement between two or more parties established for the purpose of committing deception or fraud).

A. Misappropriation

B. Misuse

C. Collusion

D. Fraud

17. Which of the following strategies involves understanding something about the enemy and letting them know the harm that can come their way if they cause harm to you?

A. Risk acceptance

B. Risk avoidance

C. Risk deterrence

D. Risk mitigation

E. Risk transference

18. If you calculate SLE to be $25,000 and that there will be one occurrence every four years (ARO), then what is the ALE?

A. $6,250

B. $12,500

C. $25,000

D. $100,000

19. Which of the following policies should be used when assigning permissions, giving users only the permissions they need to do their work and no more?

A. Separation of duties

B. Acceptable use

C. Least privilege

D. Physical access control

20. Which of the following strategies necessitates an identified risk that those involved understand the potential cost/damage and agree to accept?

A. Risk acceptance

B. Risk avoidance

C. Risk deterrence

D. Risk mitigation

E. Risk transference

Answers to Review Questions

1. C. Guidelines help clarify processes to maintain standards. Guidelines tend to be less formal than policies or standards.

2. B. SLE (single loss expectancy) is equal to asset value (AV) times exposure factor (EF). In this case, asset value is $2 million and exposure factor is 1/2.

3. E. ALE (annual loss expectancy) is equal to SLE times the annualized rate of occurrence. In this case, SLE is $1 million and the ARO is 1/60.

4. A. ARO (annualized rate of occurrence) is the frequency (in number of years) the event can be expected to happen. In this case, ARO is 1/60 or 0.0167.

5. B. Risk avoidance involves identifying a risk and making the decision to no longer engage in the actions associated with that risk.

6. B. The exception policy statement may include an escalation contact, in the event that the person dealing with a situation needs to know whom to contact.

7. A. The separation of duties policies are designed to reduce the risk of fraud and prevent other losses in an organization.

8. D. False positives are events that mistakenly were flagged and aren't truly events to be concerned with.

9. C. Change management is the structured approach that is followed to secure the company's assets.

10. E. Risk transference involves sharing some of the burden of the risk with someone else such as an insurance company.

11. C. The risk-assessment component, in conjunction with the BIA (Business Impact Analysis), provides the organization with an accurate picture of the situation facing it.

12. D. The accountability policy statement should address who is responsible for ensuring that it is enforced.

13. D. Risk mitigation is accomplished anytime you take steps to reduce the risk.

14. C. If you calculate SLE to be $4,000 and that there will be 10 occurrences a year (ARO), then the ALE is $40,000 ($4,000 × 10).

15. B. The acceptable use policies describe how the employees in an organization can use company systems and resources, both software and hardware.

16. C. Collusion is an agreement between two or more parties established for the purpose of committing deception or fraud. Collusion, when part of a crime, is also a criminal act in and of itself.

17. C. Risk deterrence involves understanding something about the enemy and letting them know the harm that can come their way if they cause harm to you.

18. A. If you calculate SLE to be $25,000 and that there will be one occurrence every four years (ARO), then the ALE is $6,250 ($25,000 × .25).

19. C. The principle of least privilege should be used when assigning permissions. Give users only the permissions they need to do their work and no more.

20. A. Risk acceptance necessitates an identified risk that those involved understand the potential cost/damage and agree to accept.

Chapter

2

Infrastructure and Connectivity

THE FOLLOWING COMPTIA SECURITY+ EXAM OBJECTIVES ARE COVERED IN THIS CHAPTER:

✓ **1.1 Explain the security function and purpose of network devices and technologies.**

- Firewalls
- Routers
- Switches
- Load Balancers
- Proxies
- Web security gateways
- VPN concentrators
- Spam filter, all-in-one security appliances
- Web application firewall vs. network firewall

✓ **1.3 Distinguish and differentiate network design elements and compounds.**

- DMZ
- Subnetting
- VLAN
- NAT
- Remote Access
- Telephony
- Virtualization

✓ **1.4 Implement and use common protocols.**

- IPSec
- SNMP
- SSH
- DNS
- TLS
- SSL
- TCP/IP
- FTPS
- HTTPS
- SFTP
- SCP
- ICMP
- IPv4 vs. IPv6

✓ **1.5 Identify commonly used default network ports.**

- FTP
- SFTP
- FTPS
- TFTP
- TELNET
- HTTP
- HTTPS
- SCP
- SSH
- NetBIOS

✓ **2.8 Exemplify the concepts of confidentiality, integrity, and availability (CIA).**

✓ **4.2 Carry out appropriate procedures to establish host security.**

- Virtualization

This chapter introduces the hardware used within the network. Your network is composed of a variety of *media* and devices that both facilitate communications and provide security. Most of these devices (such as routers, modems, and PBX systems) provide external connectivity from your network to other systems and networks. To provide reasonable security, you must know how these devices work and how they provide, or fail to provide, security.

This chapter deals with issues of infrastructure, network ports, and common protocols. They're key components of the Security+ exam, and it's necessary that you understand them to secure your network. Like many certification exams, though, the Security+ test requires you to know not only current technologies but some legacy components as well.

Mastering TCP/IP

TCP/IP has been a salvation for organizations that need to connect different systems together to function as a unified whole. Unfortunately, a downside that comes with an easy-to-use, well-documented network that has been around for many years is numerous holes. You can easily close most of these holes in your network, but you must first know about them.

You need to have a good understanding of the processes TCP/IP uses in order to know how attacks on TCP/IP work. The emphasis in this section is on the types of connections and services. If you're weak in those areas, you'll do well to supplement your study with basic networking information that can be found on the Web.

The following sections delve into issues related to TCP/IP and security. Many of these issues will be familiar to you if you've taken the Network+ or Server+ exam from CompTIA. If there are any gaps in your knowledge of the topics, however, be sure to read these sections carefully.

When discussing networking, most refer to the seven-layer OSI model—long considered the foundation for how networking protocols should operate. TCP/IP precedes the creation of the OSI model, and that is why it carries out the same operations but does so with four layers instead of seven.

Working with the TCP/IP Suite

The TCP/IP suite is broken into four architectural layers:

- Application layer

- Host-to-Host or Transport layer

- Internet layer

- Network Access layer (also known as the Network Interface layer or the Link layer)

Computers using TCP/IP use the existing physical connection between the systems. TCP/IP doesn't concern itself with the network topology, or physical connections. The network controller that resides in a computer or host deals with the physical protocol, or topology. TCP/IP communicates with that controller and lets the controller worry about the network topology and physical connection.

In TCP/IP parlance, a computer on the network is a *host*. A host is any device connected to the network that runs a TCP/IP protocol suite, or stack. Figure 2.1 shows the four layers in a TCP/IP protocol stack. Notice that this drawing includes the physical, or network, topology. Although it isn't part of TCP/IP, the topology is essential to conveying information on a network.

FIGURE 2.1   The TCP/IP architecture layers

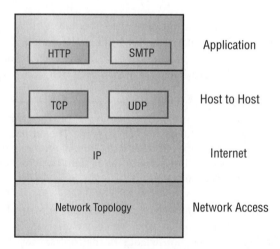

The four layers of TCP/IP have unique functions and methods for accomplishing work. Each layer talks to the layers that reside above and below it. Each layer also has its own rules and capabilities.

The following sections discuss the specific layers of TCP/IP as well as the common protocols used in the stack and how information is conveyed between the layers. I also discuss some of the more common methods used to attack TCP/IP-based networks.

Encapsulation, the process used to pass messages between the layers in TCP/IP, is briefly discussed in the next section after the layers have been covered.

The Application Layer

The *Application layer* is the highest layer of the suite. It allows applications to access services or protocols to exchange data. Most programs, such as web browsers, interface with TCP/IP at this level. The most commonly used Application layer protocols are as follows:

Hypertext Transfer Protocol   *Hypertext Transfer Protocol (HTTP)* is the protocol used for web pages and the World Wide Web. HTTP applications use a standard language called *Hypertext Markup Language (HTML)*. HTML files are normal text files that contain special coding that allows graphics, special fonts, and characters to be displayed by a web browser or other web-enabled applications.

HTTP Secure   *HTTP Secure (HTTPS)* is the protocol used for "secure" web pages that a user should see when they must enter personal information such as credit card numbers, passwords, and other identifiers. It combines HTTP with SSL/TLS to provide encrypted communication. The default port is 443 and the URL begins with https:// instead of http://. The protocol was originally created by Netscape for use with their browser and became a finalized standard with RFC 2818 (which can be found at: http://www.ietf.org/rfc/rfc2818.txt).

File Transfer Protocol   *File Transfer Protocol (FTP)* is an application that allows connections to FTP servers for file uploads and downloads. FTP is a common application used to transfer files between hosts on the Internet but is inherently insecure. A number of options have been released to try to create a more secure protocol including *FTP over SSL (FTPS)*, which adds support for SSL cryptography, and *SSH File Transfer Protocol (SFTP)*, which is also known as Secure FTP.

An alternative utility for copying files is *Secure Copy (SCP)*, which combines an old remote copy program (RCP) from the first days of TCP/IP with SSH. On the opposite end of the spectrum, from a security standpoint, is the *Trivial File Transfer Protocol (TFTP)*, which can be configured to transfer files between hosts without any user interaction (unattended mode) and should be avoided at all costs.

Simple Mail Transfer Protocol   *Simple Mail Transfer Protocol (SMTP)* is the standard protocol for email communications. SMTP allows email clients and servers to communicate with each other for message delivery.

Telnet   *Telnet* is an interactive terminal emulation protocol. It allows a remote user to conduct an interactive session with a Telnet server. This session can appear to the client as if it were a local session.

Domain Name System   *Domain Name System (DNS)* allows hosts to resolve hostnames to an Internet Protocol (IP) address. IP is discussed in the section on the Internet layer.

Routing Information Protocol   *Routing Information Protocol (RIP)* allows routing information to be exchanged between routers on an IP network.

Simple Network Management Protocol   *Simple Network Management Protocol (SNMP)* is a management tool that allows communications between network devices and a management console. Most routers, bridges, and intelligent hubs can communicate using SNMP.

Post Office Protocol   *Post Office Protocol (POP)* is a protocol used in many email systems. It allows for advanced features and is a standard interface in many email servers. POP is used for receiving email.

> One of the key things to know when securing any network is that you are running only the protocols needed for operations. Make certain that *antiquated protocols*—those once needed but now no longer used—are removed. If you do not remove them, you are leaving an opening for an attacker to access your system through weaknesses in that protocol.

The Host-to-Host or Transport Layer

The *Host-to-Host layer*, also called the *Transport layer*, provides the Application layer with session and datagram communications services. The *Transmission Control Protocol (TCP)* and *User Datagram Protocol (UDP)* operate at this layer. These two protocols provide a huge part of the functionality of the TCP/IP network:

TCP   TCP is responsible for providing a reliable, one-to-one, connection-oriented session. TCP establishes a connection and ensures that the other end receives any packets. Two hosts communicate packet results to each other. TCP also makes sure that packets are decoded and sequenced properly. This connection is persistent during the session. When the session ends, the connection is torn down.

UDP   UDP provides an unreliable connectionless communication method between hosts. UDP is considered a best-effort protocol, but it's considerably faster than TCP. The sessions don't establish a synchronized session like the kind used in TCP, and UDP doesn't guarantee error-free communications. The primary purpose of UDP is to send small packets of information. The application is responsible for acknowledging the correct reception of the data.

The Internet Layer

The *Internet layer* is responsible for routing, IP addressing, and packaging. The Internet layer protocols accomplish most of the behind-the-scenes work in establishing the ability to exchange information between hosts. Here are the four standard protocols of the Internet layer:

Internet Protocol   *Internet Protocol (IP)* is a routable protocol that is responsible for IP addressing. IP also fragments and reassembles message packets. IP only routes information; it doesn't verify it for accuracy. Accuracy checking is the responsibility of TCP. IP determines if a destination is known and, if so, routes the information to that destination. If the destination is unknown, IP sends the packet to the router, which sends it on.

Address Resolution Protocol   *Address Resolution Protocol (ARP)* is responsible for resolving IP addresses to Network Interface layer addresses, including hardware addresses. ARP can resolve an IP address to a *Media Access Control (MAC)* address. MAC addresses are used to identify hardware network devices such as a network interface card (NIC).

You'll notice the acronym *MAC* used a lot. It's also used to identify *Mandatory Access Control*, which defines how access control operates in an authentication model. You'll also see *MAC* used in cryptography, where it stands for *Message Authentication Code*. This MAC verifies that an algorithm is accurate.

Internet Control Message Protocol   *Internet Control Message Protocol (ICMP)* provides maintenance and reporting functions. It's used by the Ping program. When a user wants to test connectivity to another host, they can enter the PING command with the IP address, and the user's system will test connectivity to the other host's system. If connectivity is good, ICMP will return data to the originating host. ICMP will also report if a destination is unreachable. Routers and other network devices report path information between hosts with ICMP.

Internet Group Management Protocol   *Internet Group Management Protocol (IGMP)* is responsible primarily for managing IP multicast groups. IP multicasts can send messages or packets to a specified group of hosts. This is different from a broadcast, which all users in a network receive.

The Network Access Layer

The lowest level of the TCP/IP suite is the *Network Access (or Interface) layer*. This layer is responsible for placing and removing packets on the physical network through communications with the network adapters in the host. This process allows TCP/IP to work with virtually any type of network topology or technology with little modification. If a new physical network topology were installed—say, a 10GB Fiber Ethernet connection—TCP/IP would only need to know how to communicate with the network controller in order to function properly. TCP/IP can also communicate with more than one network topology simultaneously. This allows the protocol to be used in virtually any environment.

IPv4 vs. IPv6

The TCP/IP protocol suite in use today has been around since the earliest days of the Internet—prior to it even being known by that name. The remarkable fact that it has been able to scale to the level it is used at today is testament to the forward thinking of those involved in its creation.

Several years back, however, a panic arose amid fears that there would not be enough IP addresses to assign to every host needing to connect. The current numbering system, known as IP version 4 (IPv4) even though there really weren't publically released prior versions, is what is described throughout this chapter and still widely used today. IP version 6 (IPv6) was introduced several years ago to replace IPv4 but has failed to do so, and most systems currently support both at the Internet layer.

Key things to know for the exam are that IPv6 supports 128-bit addresses, while IPv4 supports 32-bit addresses (see "Network Address Translation" later in this chapter), and IPv6 includes mandatory IPSec security (see "Internet Protocol Security" later in this chapter).

Understanding Encapsulation

One of the key points in understanding this layering process is the concept of *encapsulation*. Encapsulation allows a transport protocol to be sent across the network and utilized by the equivalent service or protocol at the receiving host. Figure 2.2 shows how email is encapsulated as it moves from the application protocols through the transport and Internet protocols. Each layer adds header information as the email moves down the layers.

FIGURE 2.2 The encapsulation process of an email message

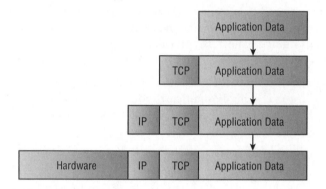

Transmission of the packet between the two hosts occurs through the physical connection in the network adapter. Figure 2.3 illustrates this process between two hosts. What's shown in the figure isn't comprehensive but illustrates the process of message transmission.

FIGURE 2.3 An email message that an email client sent to an email server across the Internet

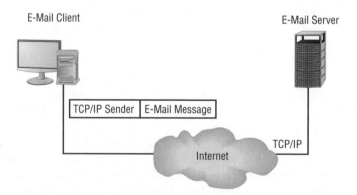

After it is encapsulated, the message is sent to the server. Notice that in Figure 2.3 the message is sent via the Internet; it could have just as easily been sent locally. The email client doesn't know how the message is delivered, and the server application doesn't care how the

message got there. This makes designing and implementing services such as email possible in a global or Internet environment.

Working with Protocols and Services

It's imperative that you have a basic understanding of protocols and services to pass this exam. Although it isn't a requirement, CompTIA recommends that you already hold the Network+ certification before undertaking this exam. In case you're weak in some areas, the following sections will discuss in more detail how TCP/IP hosts communicate with each other. I'll discuss the concepts of ports, handshakes, and application interfaces. The objective isn't to make you an expert on this subject but to help you understand what you're dealing with when attempting to secure a TCP/IP network.

> The majority of the discussion in this book focuses on TCP/IP as the networking protocol since it is used in almost every implementation. Know, however, that TCP/IP is not the only networking protocol and Microsoft's implementation of *NetBIOS* (Network Basic Input Output System) was a default in early versions of Windows. Since then, NetBIOS has been adapted to run on top of TCP/IP and is still widely used for name resolution and registration in Windows-based environments.

Well-Known Ports

Simply stated, *ports* identify how a communication process occurs. Ports are special addresses that allow communication between hosts. A port number is added from the originator, indicating which port to communicate with on a server. If a server has a port defined and available for use, it will send back a message accepting the request. If the port isn't valid, the server will refuse the connection. The *Internet Assigned Numbers Authority (IANA)* has defined a list of ports called *well-known ports*.

> You can see the full description of the ports defined by IANA on the following website: www.iana.org/assignments/port-numbers. Many thousands of ports are available for use by servers and clients.

A port is nothing more than a bit of additional information added to either the TCP or UDP message. This information is added in the header of the packet. The layer below it encapsulates the message with its header.

Many of the services you'll use in the normal course of utilizing the Internet use the TCP port numbers identified in Table 2.1. Table 2.2 identifies some of the more common, well-known UDP ports. You will note that some services utilize both TCP and UDP ports, while many use only one or the other.

TABLE 2.1 Well-known TCP ports

TCP Port Number	Service
20	FTP (data channel)
21	FTP (control channel)
22	SSH and SCP
23	Telnet
25	SMTP
49	TACACS authentication service
80	HTTP (used for the World Wide Web)
110	POP3
115	SFTP
119	NNTP
137	NetBIOS name service
138	NetBIOS datagram service
139	NetBIOS session service
143	IMAP
389	LDAP
443	HTTPS (used for secure web connections)
989	FTPS (data channel)
990	FTPS (control channel)

TABLE 2.2 Well-known UDP ports

UDP Port Number	Service
22	SSH and SCP
49	TACACS authentication service

UDP Port Number	Service
53	DNS name queries
69	Trivial File Transfer Protocol (TFTP)
80	HTTP (used for the World Wide Web)
137	NetBIOS name service
138	NetBIOS datagram service
139	NetBIOS session service
143	IMAP
161	SNMP
389	LDAP
989	FTPS (data channel)
990	FTPS (control channel)

The early documentation for these ports specified that ports below 1024 were restricted to administrative uses. However, enforcement of this restriction has been voluntary and is creating problems for computer security professionals. As you can see, each of these ports potentially requires different security considerations, depending on the application it's assigned for. All the ports allow access to your network; even if you establish a firewall, you must have these ports open if you want to provide email or web services.

In Exercise 2.1, I'll show you how to view the active TCP and UPD ports.

EXERCISE 2.1

View the Active TCP and UDP Ports

As an administrator, you should know what ports are active on your server. To view the active TCP and UDP ports, follow these steps:

1. Go to a command prompt. To do this in Windows, enter **CMD** at the Run prompt. On a Linux server, open a command window.

2. Enter the command **netstat**.

3. Few items should appear. Now enter the command **netstat -a**. The –a parameter tells the netstat command to display all the information.

4. Note the ports that are listed.

5. View the services file (*systemroot*\system32\drivers\etc\services in Windows or /etc/services in Linux). Although the file is not actively read by the system, this file lists the services and the ports used for the most common network operations.

TCP Three-Way Handshake

TCP, which is a *connection-oriented protocol*, establishes a session using a *three-way hand-shake*. A host called a *client* originates this connection. The client sends a TCP segment, or message, to the server. This client segment includes an *Initial Sequence Number (ISN)* for the connection and a window size. The server responds with a TCP segment that contains its ISN and a value indicating its buffer, or window size. The client then sends back an acknowledgment of the server's sequence number.

Figure 2.4 shows this three-way handshake occurring between a client and a server. When the session or connection is over, a similar process occurs, using four steps, to close the connection.

FIGURE 2.4   The TCP connection process

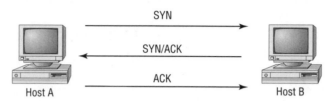

A web request uses the TCP connection process to establish the connection between the client and the server. After this occurs, the two systems communicate with each other; the server uses TCP port 80. The same thing occurs when an email connection is made, with the difference being that the client (assuming it's using POP3) uses port 110.

In this way, a server can handle many requests simultaneously. Each session has a different sequence number even though all sessions use the same port. All the communications in any given session use this sequence number to keep from confusing the sessions.

Application Programming Interface

Interfacing to TCP/IP is much simpler than interfacing to earlier network models. A well-defined and well-established set of *Application Programming Interfaces (APIs)* is available from most software companies. APIs allow programmers to create interfaces to the protocol. When a programmer needs to create a web-enabled application, they can call or use one of these APIs to make the connection, send or receive data, and end the connection. The APIs are prewritten, and they make the job considerably easier than manually coding all of the connection information.

Microsoft uses the *Windows Sockets (Winsock)* API to interface to the protocol. It can access either TCP or UDP protocols to accomplish the needed task. Figure 2.5 illustrates how Winsock connects to the TCP/IP protocol suite.

FIGURE 2.5   The Winsock interface

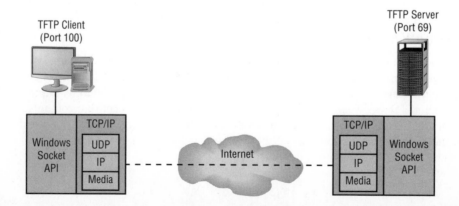

Distinguishing between Security Topologies

The *security topology* of your network defines the network design and implementation from a security perspective. Unlike a network topology, here we're concerned with access methods, security, and technologies used. Security topology covers four primary areas of concern:

- Design goals
- Security zones
- Technologies
- Business requirements

Setting Design Goals

When setting design goals for a security topology, you must deal with issues of confidentiality, integrity, availability, and accountability, all four of which are discussed continually throughout this book as they apply to various topics. Addressing these four issues as an initial part of your network design will help you ensure tighter security. You'll often see confidentiality, integrity, and availability referred to as the *CIA* of network security, but the accountability component is equally important—design goals must identify who is responsible for the various aspects of computer security. The next few sections introduce these four security components.

Confidentiality

Meeting the goal of *confidentiality* is to prevent or minimize unauthorized access to and disclosure of data and information. In many instances, laws and regulations require specific information confidentiality. For example, Social Security records, payroll and employee records, medical records, and corporate information are high-value assets. This information could create liability issues or embarrassment if it fell into the wrong hands. Over the last few years, there have been a number of cases in which bank account and credit card numbers were published on the Internet. The costs of these types of breaches of confidentiality far exceed the actual losses from the misuse of this information.

Confidentiality entails ensuring that data expected to remain private is seen only by those who should see it. Confidentiality is implemented through authentication and access controls.

If you address confidentiality issues early in the design phase, the steps that must be taken to minimize this exposure will become clear.

Integrity

Meeting the goal of *integrity* involves making sure that the data being worked with is the correct data. Information integrity is critical to a secure topology. Organizations work with and make decisions using the data they have available. If this information isn't accurate or is tampered with by an unauthorized person, the consequences can be devastating.

Take the case of a school district that lost all the payroll and employment records for the employees in the district. When the problem was discovered, the school district had no choice but to send out applications and forms to all the employees, asking them how long they had worked in the school district and how much they were paid. Integrity was jeopardized because the data was vulnerable and then lost.

> You can think of integrity as the level of confidence you have that the data is what it's supposed to be—untampered with and unchanged. *Authentic, complete,* and *trustworthy* are often used to describe integrity in terms of data.

Availability

To meet the goal of *availability*, you must protect data and prevent its loss. Data that can't be accessed is of little value. If a mishap or attack brings down a key server or database, that information won't be available to the people who need it. This can cause havoc in an organization. Your job is to provide maximum availability to your users while ensuring integrity and confidentiality. The hardest part of this process is determining the balance you must maintain between these three aspects to provide acceptable security for the organization's information and resources.

> The key to availability is that the data must be available when it's needed and accessible by those who need it.

Accountability

The final and often overlooked goal of design concerns *accountability*. Many of the resources used by an organization are shared among departments and individuals. If an error or incident occurs, who is responsible for fixing it? Who determines whether information is correct?

It's a good idea to be clear about who owns the data or is responsible for making sure that it's accurate. You should also be able to track and monitor data changes to detect and repair the data in the event of loss or damage. Most systems will track and store logs on system activities and data manipulation, and they will also provide reports on problems.

Real World Scenario

Compute Availability

Availability is often expressed in terms of *uptime*. High availability strives for 99.9999% uptime over the course of the year (24 hours a day, 7 days a week, 365 days a year). For this exercise, compute how long data wouldn't be available over the course of the year with the following availability percentages. For example, with 98% uptime, there is a 2% downtime of 525,600 minutes in a year. That means the data would be down for 10,512 minutes, or 71/3 days! Try your math on the following:

1. 99%

2. 99.9%

3. 99.99%

4. 99.999%

5. 99.9999%

The increments may seem small, but over the course of a year, they represent a significant difference in the amount of time data is and isn't available. Answers: (1.) 5,256 minutes, which is more than 87 hours or 3.5 days; (2.) 525 minutes, or a little less than 9 hours; (3.) 52.56 minutes; (4.) 5.25 minutes; (5.) about half a minute.

Creating Security Zones

Over time, networks can become complex beasts. What may have started as a handful of computers sharing resources can quickly grow to something resembling an electrician's nightmare. The networks may even appear to have lives of their own. It's common for a network to have connections among departments, companies, countries, and public access using private communication paths and through the Internet.

Not everyone in a network needs access to all the assets in the network. The term *security zone* describes design methods that isolate systems from other systems or networks. You can isolate networks from each other using hardware and software. A router is a good example of a hardware solution: You can configure some machines on the network to be in a certain address range and others to be in a different address range. This separation makes the two networks invisible to each other unless a router connects them. Some of the newer data switches also allow you to partition networks into smaller networks or private zones.

When discussing security zones in a network, it's helpful to think of them as rooms. You may have some rooms in your house or office that anyone can enter. For other rooms, access is limited to specific individuals for specific purposes. Establishing security zones is a similar process in a network: Security zones allow you to isolate systems from unauthorized users. Here are the four most common security zones you'll encounter:

- Internet
- Intranet
- Extranet
- Demilitarized zone (DMZ)

 Real World Scenario

Accountability Is More than a Catchphrase

Accountability, like common sense, applies to every aspect of information technology. Several years ago, a company that relied on data that could never be re-created wrote shell scripts to do backups early in the morning when the hosts were less busy. Operators at those machines were told to insert a tape in the drive around midnight and check back at 3:00 a.m. to make certain that a piece of paper had been printed on the printer, signaling the end of the job. If the paper was there, they were to remove the tapes and put them in storage; if the paper was not there, they were to call for support.

The inevitable hard drive crash occurred on one of the hosts one morning, and an IT "specialist" was dispatched to swap it out. The technician changed the hard drive and then asked for the most recent backup tape. To his dismay, the data on the tape was two years old. The machine crash occurred before the backup operation ran, he reasoned, but the odds of rotating exactly two years' worth of tapes was highly unlikely. Undaunted, he asked for the tape from the day before, and found that the data on it was also two years old.

Beginning to sweat, he found the late shift operator for that host and asked her if she was making backups. She assured him that she was and that she was rotating the tapes and putting them away as soon as the paper printed out. Questioning her further on how the data could be so old, she said she could verify her story because she also kept the pieces of paper that appeared on the printer each day. She brought out the stack and handed them to him. They all reported the same thing—*tape in drive is write protected*.

Where did the accountability lie in this true story? The operator was faithfully following the procedures given to her and going through the procedures to back up the company's information each night. She thought the fact that the tape was protected represented a good thing. It turned out that all the hosts had been printing the same message, but the operator lacked the information she needed to realize there was a problem, leading to the company not having any backups for two years.

The problem lay not with the operator but with the training she was given. Had she been shown what correct and incorrect backup completion reports looked like, the data would never have been lost.

The next few sections identify the topologies used to create security zones to provide security, as well as designing them. The Internet has become a boon to individuals and to businesses, but it creates a challenge for security. By implementing intranets, extranets, and DMZs, you can create a reasonably secure environment for your organization.

The Internet

The *Internet* is a global network that connects computers and individual networks together. It can be used by anybody who has access to an Internet portal or an Internet service provider (ISP). In this environment, you should have a low level of trust in the people who use the Internet. You must always assume that the people visiting your website may have bad intentions; they may want to buy your product or hire your firm, or they may want to bring your servers to a screaming halt. Externally, you have no way of knowing until you monitor their actions. Because the Internet involves such a high level of anonymity, you must always safeguard your data with the utmost precautions.

Figure 2.6 illustrates an Internet network and its connections.

FIGURE 2.6   A typical LAN connection to the Internet

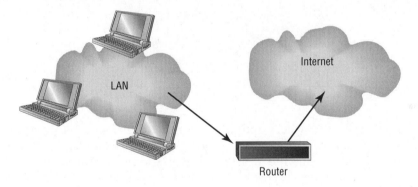

 Sometimes the data leaving a network can be as much a sign of trouble as the data entering it. Examining data leaving the network for signs of malicious traffic is a fairly new field of computer security and is known as *extrusion*.

Intranets

Intranets are private networks implemented and maintained by an individual company or organization. You can think of an intranet as an Internet that doesn't leave your company; it's internal to the company, and access is limited to systems within the intranet. Intranets use the same technologies used by the Internet. They can be connected to the Internet but can't be accessed by users who aren't authorized to be part of them; the anonymous user of the Internet is instead an authorized user of the intranet. Access to the intranet is granted to trusted users inside the corporate network or to users in remote locations.

Figure 2.7 displays an intranet network.

FIGURE 2.7   An intranet network

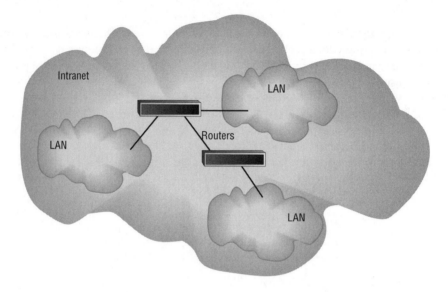

Extranets

Extranets extend intranets to include outside connections to partners. The partners can be vendors, suppliers, or similar parties who need access to your data for legitimate reasons. An extranet allows you to connect to a partner via a private network or a connection using a secure communications channel across the Internet. Extranet connections involve connections between trustworthy organizations.

An extranet is illustrated in Figure 2.8. Note that this network provides a connection between the two organizations. The connection may be through the Internet; if so, these networks would use a tunneling protocol to accomplish a secure connection.

FIGURE 2.8   A typical extranet between two organizations

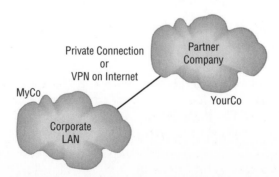

Demilitarized Zone

A *demilitarized zone (DMZ)* is an area where you can place a public server for access by people you might not trust otherwise. By isolating a server in a DMZ, you can hide or remove access to other areas of your network. You can still access the server using your network, but others aren't able to access further network resources. This can be accomplished using firewalls to isolate your network.

When establishing a DMZ, you assume that the person accessing the resource isn't necessarily someone you would trust with other information. Figure 2.9 shows a server placed in a DMZ. Notice that the rest of the network isn't visible to external users. This lowers the threat of intrusion in the internal network.

FIGURE 2.9   A typical DMZ

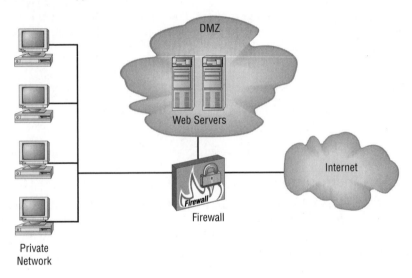

 Anytime you want to separate public information from private information, a DMZ is an acceptable option.

The easiest way to create a DMZ is to use a firewall that can transmit in three directions:

- to the internal network
- to the external world (Internet)
- to the public information you're sharing (the DMZ)

From there, you can decide what traffic goes where; for example, HTTP traffic would be sent to the DMZ, and email would go to the internal network.

 A host that exists outside the DMZ and is open to the public is often called a *bastion host*. Routers and firewalls, because of where they must exist, often constitute bastion hosts.

Designing Security Zones

Security zone design is an important aspect of computer security. You can use many different approaches to accomplish a good solid design. Some of the design trade-offs involve risk and money. You can create layers of security to protect systems from less-secure connections, and you can use Network Address Translation (NAT) (discussed later) to hide resources. New methods and tools to design secure networks are being introduced on a regular basis. It's important to remember that after you have a good security design, you should revisit it on a regular basis based on what you learn about your security risks.

Working with Newer Technologies

One of the nice things about technology is that it's always changing. One of the bad things about technology is that it's always changing. Several relatively new technologies have become available to help you create a less-vulnerable system. The four technologies this section will focus on are:

- virtualization
- virtual local area networks (VLANs)
- Network Address Translation
- tunneling

These technologies allow you to improve security in your network at little additional cost.

Virtualization Technology

Virtualization is easily the technology du jour, with VMware, one of the largest vendors of such technology, counting 100 percent of the Fortune 100 as part of their customer base. In addition to proprietary solutions, there are open source solutions as well, with Xen and VirtualBox being the best-known examples.

Virtualization technology allows you to take any single physical device and hide its characteristics from users—in essence allowing you to run multiple items on one device and make them appear as if they are stand-alone entities. For example, workstations can run only one operating system at a time. Using virtualization, it is possible for a workstation running Windows 7 to also be running Fedora, Red Hat, Windows Server 2008, and any number of other operating systems within virtual windows. The developer working on code can move between windows, cutting and pasting if they choose, and do all they need to do on one machine without having to run four different workstations. Thanks to virtualization, the workstation can run multiple operating systems, multiple versions of the same operating system, multiple applications, and so on.

Just as a workstation can be virtualized, so too can a server. A single server can host multiple logical machines. By using one server to do the functions of many, you can immediately gain cost savings in terms of hardware, utility, infrastructure, and so on.

As wonderful as virtualization is, from a security standpoint it can present challenges. A user accessing the system could have access to everything on the system (not just within their logical machine) if they could override the physical layer protection. As of this writing, the threat of that occurring has been far more rumored than performed, but with virtualization growing in popularity, it is a safe bet that virtual machines will become a popular target of miscreants in coming years.

Virtual Local Area Networks

A *virtual local area network (VLAN)* allows you to create groups of users and systems and segment them on the network. This segmentation lets you hide segments of the network from other segments and thereby control access. You can also set up VLANs to control the paths that data takes to get from one point to another. A VLAN is a good way to contain network traffic to a certain area in a network.

Think of a VLAN as a network of hosts that act as if they're connected by a physical wire even though there is no such wire between them.

On a LAN, hosts can communicate with each other through broadcasts, and no forwarding devices, such as routers, are needed. As the LAN grows, so too does the number of broadcasts. Shrinking the size of the LAN by segmenting it into smaller groups (VLANs) reduces the size of the broadcast domains. The advantages of doing this include reducing the scope of the broadcasts, improving performance and manageability, and decreasing dependence on the physical topology. From the standpoint of this exam, however, the key benefit is that VLANs can increase security by allowing users with similar data sensitivity levels to be segmented together.

Figure 2.10 illustrates the creation of three VLANs in a single network.

Network Address Translation

Network Address Translation (NAT) creates a unique opportunity to assist in the security of a network. Originally, NAT extended the number of usable Internet addresses. Now it allows an organization to present a single address to the Internet for all computer connections. The NAT server provides IP addresses to the hosts or systems in the network and tracks inbound and outbound traffic.

A company that uses NAT presents a single connection to the network. This connection may be through a router or a NAT server. The only information that an intruder will be able to get is that the connection has a single address.

NAT effectively hides your network from the world, making it much harder to determine what systems exist on the other side of the router. The NAT server effectively operates as a firewall for the network. Most new routers support NAT; it provides a simple, inexpensive firewall for small networks.

It's important to understand that NAT acts as a proxy between the local area network (which can be using private IP addresses) and the Internet. Not only can NAT save IP addresses, but it can also act as a firewall.

FIGURE 2.10   A typical segmented VLAN

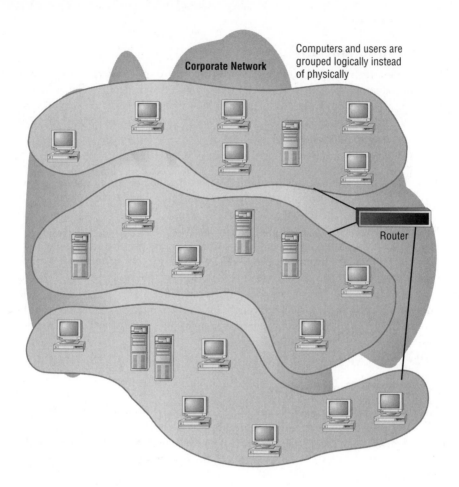

Most NAT implementations assign internal hosts private IP address numbers and use public addresses only for the NAT to translate to and communicate with the outside world. The private address ranges, all of which addresses are non-routable, are as follows:

10.0.0.0–10.255.255.255

172.16.0.0–172.31.255.255

192.168.0.0–192.168.255.255

Figure 2.11 shows a router providing NAT services to a network. The router presents a single address for all external connections on the Internet.

FIGURE 2.11 A typical Internet connection to a local network

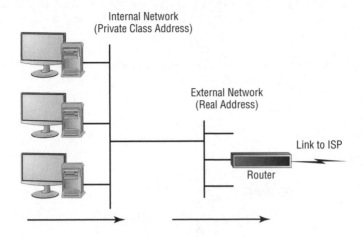

Internal Network
(Private Class Address)

External Network
(Real Address)

Link to ISP

Router

 In addition to NAT, Port Address Translation (PAT) is possible. Whereas NAT can use multiple public IP addresses, PAT uses a single one and shares the port with the network. Because it is using only a single port, PAT is much more limited and typically used only on small and home-based networks. Microsoft's Internet Connection Sharing is an example of a PAT implementation.

 IP addressing is a subject on the Network+ exam, as opposed to Security+, but CompTIA still expects you to know the basics. In addition to understanding the concept behind NAT, you should know that subnetting is how networks are divided. RFCs 1466 and 1918 detail subnetting and can be found at http://www.faqs.org/rfcs/.

Tunneling

Tunneling refers to creating a virtual dedicated connection between two systems or networks. You create the tunnel between the two ends by encapsulating the data in a mutually agreed-upon protocol for transmission. In most tunnels, the data passed through the tunnel appears at the other side as part of the network.

Tunneling protocols usually include data security as well as encryption. Several popular standards have emerged for tunneling, with the most popular being the Layer 2 Tunneling Protocol (L2TP).

Tunneling sends private data across a public network by placing (encapsulating) that data into other packets. Most tunnels are virtual private networks (VPNs).

Figure 2.12 shows a connection being made between two networks across the Internet. To each end of the network, this appears to be a single connection.

FIGURE 2.12   A typical tunnel

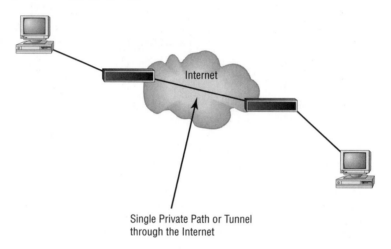

Single Private Path or Tunnel
through the Internet

Telephony

When telephone technology is married with information technology, the result is known as *telephony*. A breach in your telephony infrastructure is just as devastating as any other violation and can lead to the loss of valuable data.

With the exodus from land lines to Voice over IP (VoIP) in order for companies to save money in full swing, it is imperative that you treat this part of the network the same as you would any other. VOIP can be easily sniffed with tools such as Cain & Abel (http://www.oxid.it/) and is susceptible to Denial of Service (DoS) attacks because it rides on UDP. There is also the outage issue with VoIP in cases where the data network goes down and you lose the telephony as well.

As an example of some of the information available, SecureLogix markets a voice firewall (http://www.securelogix.com/ip-telephony-security.html), and Cisco has published a white paper titled "IP Telephony Security in Depth" (http://www.cisco.com/warp/public/cc/so/cuso/epso/sqfr/safip_wp.pdf).

From a security standpoint, the biggest problem with VoIP and data being on the same line is that they are then both vulnerable in the event of a PBX (private branch exchange) attack. For more information about PBX, see http://www.pbxinfo.com/.

Working with Business Requirements

The final component of security design is working with business requirements. A number of chapters in this book focus on the issue of understanding business requirements and working with policies and standards. For this discussion, simply know that there is no one-size-fits-all solution as straightforward as the other three areas (design goals, security zones, and technology) may seem, because every company will have different business requirements, including a different level of risk they are willing to accept and different regulations they must adhere to.

Understanding Infrastructure Security

As the name implies, an *infrastructure* is the basis for all the work occurring in your organization. *Infrastructure security* deals with the most basic aspect of how information flows and how work occurs in your network and systems. When discussing infrastructures, keep in mind that this includes servers, networks, network devices, workstations, and the processes in place to facilitate work.

To evaluate the security of your infrastructure, you must examine the hardware and its characteristics as well as the software and its characteristics. Each time you add a device, change configurations, or switch technologies, you're potentially altering the fundamental security capabilities of your network. Just as a chain is no stronger than its weakest link, it can also be said that a network is no more secure than its weakest node.

Networks are tied together using the Internet and other network technologies, thereby making them vulnerable to any number of attacks. The job of a security professional is to eliminate the obvious threats, to anticipate how the next creative assault on your infrastructure might occur, and to be prepared to neutralize it before it happens.

The following sections deal with the hardware and software components that make up a network.

Working with Hardware Components

Network hardware components include physical devices such as routers, servers, firewalls, workstations, and switches. Figure 2.13 depicts a typical network infrastructure and some of the common hardware components in the environment. From a security perspective, this infrastructure is much more than just the sum of all its parts. You must evaluate your network from the standpoint of each and every device within it. It cannot be overstated: The complexity of most networks makes securing them extremely complicated. To provide reasonable security, you must evaluate every device to determine its unique strengths and vulnerabilities.

Notice in this figure that the network we'll be evaluating has Internet connections. Internet connections expose your network to the highest number of external threats. These threats can come from virtually any location worldwide.

FIGURE 2.13 A typical network infrastructure

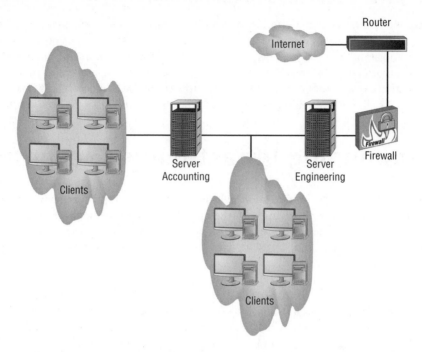

 Real World Scenario

Updating Your Infrastructure List

As an administrator, you have to deal with a variety of devices every day. Not only must you attend to the needs of the servers, but you must also maintain Internet access, manage a plethora of users and workstations, and keep everything running smoothly. You can have firewall after firewall in place, but if you're allowing a salesperson to dial in from the road with minimal safeguards, that connection becomes the baseline of your security.

Keeping track of your organization's hardware is therefore a fairly important task, which is why you should survey your network and compile an infrastructure list. If you've already done this in the past, now is a great time to update that list. While doing this, make a note of all the devices that are connected—permanently or intermittently—to your network. Here are some questions you should try to answer:

1. How many servers are there? What is the function of each, and what level of security applies to each?

2. How many workstations are there? What operating systems are they running? How do they connect to the network (cabling, wireless, dial-in)?

3. How does data leave the network (routers, gateways)? How secure is each of those devices? Are firewalls or other devices impeding traffic?

4. What else is connected to the network (modems and so on) that can be used to access it?

In all honesty, this information should already exist and be readily accessible. If your organization is like most others, though, the information doesn't exist, and devices are added as needed with the intent of creating documentation at some future point in time. There is no better time than the present to create it.

One issue to watch out for is the "It can't happen to me/us!" attitude many seem to have. Be prepared to handle it by explaining that it can indeed happen and actively doing all you can to prevent it.

Working with Software Components

Hardware exists to run software. The software is intended to make the hardware components easy to configure and easy to support. To a certain extent, however, that software can also make the hardware easy to bypass.

The network infrastructure illustrated at the beginning of the chapter in Figure 2.1 includes servers, workstations running operating systems, a router, a firewall (and there may be some that run as applications on servers), and dedicated devices that have their own communications and control programs. This situation leaves networks open to attacks and security problems because many of these systems work independently.

Many larger organizations have built a single area for network monitoring and administrative control of systems. This centralization lets you see a larger overall picture of the network, and it lets you take actions on multiple systems or network resources if an attack is under way. Such a centralized area is called a *network operations center (NOC)*. Using a NOC makes it easier to see how an attack develops and to provide countermeasures. Unfortunately, a NOC is beyond the means of most medium-sized and small businesses. NOCs are expensive and require a great deal of support: factors beyond the economy or scale of all but the largest businesses. After a NOC is developed and implemented, the job doesn't stop there—the NOC must be constantly evaluated and changed as needed.

If your organization does not employ a dedicated security professional but you still need to implement security measures, one approach is to outsource to a *managed security service provider (MSSP)*. MSSPs offer overall security services to small companies and can be more cost effective than adding a dedicated individual to the payroll.

AT&T Wireless NOCs

AT&T Wireless maintains a huge NOC for each of the cell centers it manages. These centers provide 24/7 real-time monitoring of all devices in the cellular and computer network they support. The operators in the NOC can literally reach out and touch any device in the network to configure, repair, and troubleshoot it. A single NOC has dozens of people working around the clock to keep on top of the network. When an AT&T Wireless center goes down, it effectively takes down the cell-phone service for an entire region. As you can imagine, this is horrendously expensive, and the company doesn't let it happen often. There are several NOC facilities in the United States, and one region can support or take over operations for another region if that center becomes inoperable.

Understanding the Different Network Infrastructure Devices

Connecting all these components requires physical devices. Large multinational corporations, as well as small and medium-sized corporations, are building networks of enormous complexity and sophistication. These networks work by utilizing miles of both wiring and *wireless technologies*. If the network is totally wire and fiber based or totally wireless, the method of transmitting data from one place to another opens vulnerabilities and opportunities for exploitation. Vulnerabilities appear whenever an opportunity exists to intercept information from the media.

The devices briefly described here are the components you'll typically encounter in a network.

 Many network devices contain firmware that you interact with during configuration. For security purposes, you must authenticate in order to make configuration changes and do so initially by using the default account(s). Make sure the default password is changed after the installation on any network device; otherwise you are leaving that device open for anyone recognizing the hardware to access it using the known factory password.

Firewalls

Firewalls are one of the first lines of defense in a network. There are different types of firewalls, and they can be either stand-alone systems or included in other devices such as routers or servers. You can find firewall solutions that are marketed as hardware only and others that are software only. Many firewalls, however, consist of add-in software that is available for servers or workstations.

 Although solutions are sold as "hardware only," the hardware still runs some sort of software. It may be hardened and in ROM to prevent tampering, and it may be customized—but software is present nonetheless.

The basic purpose of a firewall is to isolate one network from another. Firewalls are becoming available as appliances, meaning they're installed as the primary device separating two networks. *Appliances* are freestanding devices that operate in a largely self-contained manner, requiring less maintenance and support than a server-based product.

 To understand the concept of a firewall, it helps to know where the term comes from. In days of old, dwellings used to be built so close together that if a fire broke out in one, it could easily destroy a block or more before it could be contained. To decrease the risk of this happening, firewalls were built between buildings. The firewalls were huge brick walls that separated the buildings and kept a fire confined to one side. The same concept of restricting and confining is true in network firewalls. Traffic from the outside world hits the firewall and isn't allowed to enter the network unless otherwise invited.

The firewall shown in Figure 2.14 effectively limits access from outside networks, while allowing inside network users to access outside resources. The firewall in this illustration is also performing proxy functions, discussed later.

FIGURE 2.14 A proxy firewall blocking network access from external networks

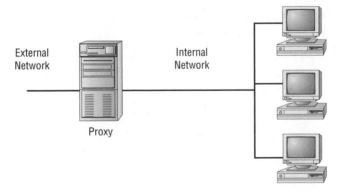

Firewalls function as one or more of the following:

- Packet filter
- Proxy firewall
- Stateful inspection firewall

Although firewalls are often associated with outside traffic, you can place a firewall anywhere. For example, if you want to isolate one portion of your internal network from others, you can place a firewall between them.

Packet Filter Firewalls

A firewall operating as a *packet filter* passes or blocks traffic to specific addresses based on the type of application. The packet filter doesn't analyze the data of a packet; it decides whether to pass it based on the packet's addressing information. For instance, a packet filter may allow web traffic on port 80 and block Telnet traffic on port 23. This type of filtering is included in many routers. If a received packet request asks for a port that isn't authorized, the filter may reject the request or simply ignore it. Many packet filters can also specify which IP addresses can request which ports and allow or deny them based on the security settings of the firewall.

Packet filters are growing in sophistication and capability. A packet filter firewall can allow any traffic that you specify as acceptable. For example, if you want web users to access your site, then you configure the packet filter firewall to allow data on port 80 to enter. If every network were exactly the same, firewalls would come with default port settings hard-coded, but networks vary, so the firewalls don't include such settings.

Decide Which Traffic to Allow Through

As an administrator, you need to survey your network and decide which traffic should be allowed through the firewall. What traffic will you allow in, and what will you block at the firewall?

The following is a list of only the most common TCP ports. Check the boxes indicating whether you'll allow data using this port through the firewall.

TCP Port Number	Service	Yes	No
20	FTP (data channel)	❏	❏
21	FTP (control channel)	❏	❏
23	Telnet	❏	❏
25	SMTP	❏	❏
49	TACACS authentication service	❏	❏
80	HTTP (used for World Wide Web)	❏	❏

TCP Port Number	Service	Yes	No
110	POP3	❏	❏
119	NNTP	❏	❏
137, 138, and 139	NetBIOS session service	❏	❏
143	IMAP	❏	❏
389	LDAP	❏	❏
443	HTTPS (used for secure web connections)	❏	❏
636	LDAP (SSL)	❏	❏

Proxy Firewalls

A *proxy firewall* can be thought of as an intermediary between your network and any other network. Proxy firewalls are used to process requests from an outside network; the proxy firewall examines the data and makes rule-based decisions about whether the request should be forwarded or refused. The proxy intercepts all the packages and reprocesses them for use internally. This process includes hiding IP addresses.

 When you consider the concept of hiding IP addresses, think of Network Address Translation (NAT) as it is discussed in the section "Working with Newer Technologies."

The proxy firewall provides better security than packet filtering because of the increased intelligence that a proxy firewall offers. Requests from internal network users are routed through the proxy. The proxy, in turn, repackages the request and sends it along, thereby isolating the user from the external network. The proxy can also offer caching, should the same request be made again, and can increase the efficiency of data delivery.

A proxy firewall typically uses two network interface cards (NICs). This type of firewall is referred to as a *dual-homed firewall*. One of the cards is connected to the outside network, and the other is connected to the internal network. The proxy software manages the connection between the two NICs. This setup segregates the two networks from each other and offers increased security. Figure 2.15 illustrates a dual-homed firewall segregating two networks from each other.

FIGURE 2.15   A dual-homed firewall segregating two networks from each other

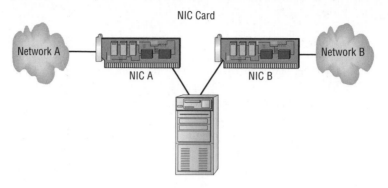

Make sure routing or IP
forwarding is disabled in
the operating system.

 Real World Scenario

Dual-Homed Proxy Firewall

You're the network administrator of a small network. You're installing a new firewall
server. After you complete the installation, you notice that the network doesn't appear
to be routing traffic through the firewall and that inbound requests aren't being blocked.
This situation presents a security problem for the network because you've been getting
unusual network traffic lately.

The most likely solution to this problem deals with the fact that the server offers the ability
to use IP forwarding in a dual-homed server. IP forwarding bypasses your firewall and uses
the server as a router. Even though the two networks are effectively isolated, the new router
is doing its job well, and it's routing IP traffic.

You'll need to verify that IP forwarding and routing services aren't running on this server.

 Anytime you have a system that is configured with more than one
IP address, it can be said to be *multihomed*.

The proxy function can occur at either the application level or the circuit level.

Application-level proxy functions read the individual commands of the protocols that are being served. This type of server is advanced and must know the rules and capabilities of the protocol used. An implementation of this type of proxy must know the difference between GET and PUT operations, for example, and have rules specifying how to execute them. A *circuit-level proxy* creates a circuit between the client and the server and doesn't deal with the contents of the packets that are being processed.

A unique application-level proxy server must exist for each protocol supported. Many proxy servers also provide full *auditing, accounting,* and other usage information that wouldn't normally be kept by a circuit-level proxy server.

Stateful Inspection Firewalls

The last section on firewalls focuses on the concept of stateful inspection. In order to understand the terminology, it helps to know that what came before was referred to as *stateless.* Stateless firewalls make decisions based on the data that comes in—the packet, for example—and not based on any complex decisions.

Stateful inspection is also referred to as *stateful packet filtering.* Most of the devices used in networks don't keep track of how information is routed or used. After a packet is passed, the packet and path are forgotten. In stateful inspection (or stateful packet filtering), records are kept using a state table that tracks every communications channel. Stateful inspections occur at all levels of the network and provide additional security, especially in connectionless protocols such as User Datagram Protocol and Internet Control Message Protocol. This adds complexity to the process. Denial-of-Service attacks present a challenge because flooding techniques are used to overload the state table and effectively cause the firewall to shut down or reboot.

For the exam, remember that pure packet filtering has no real intelligence. It allows data to pass through a port if that port is configured and otherwise discards it—it doesn't examine the packets. Stateful packet filtering, however, has intelligence in that it keeps track of every communications channel.

Hubs

One of the simplest devices in a network is a hub. Although it's possible to load software to create a managed hub, in its truest sense, a *hub* is nothing more than a device allowing many hosts to communicate with each other through the use of physical ports. Broadcast traffic can traverse the hub, and all data received through one port is sent to all other ports. This arrangement creates an extremely unsecure environment should an intruder attach to a hub and begin intercepting data.

Broadcasts are messages sent from a single system to the entire network. *Multicasting* sends a message to multiple addresses. *Unicasts* are oriented at a single system.

Some of the more expensive hubs do allow you to enable *port security*. If this is enabled, each port takes note of the first MAC address it hears on that port. If the MAC address changes, the hub disables the port. Port security increases the level of security on the LAN, but it can also increase the administrator's workload if you reconfigure your environment often.

 For exam purposes, think of hubs as, by default, being unsecure LAN devices that should be replaced with switches for security and increased throughput.

Modems

A *modem* is a hardware device that connects the digital signals from a computer to an analog telephone line. It allows the signals to be transmitted over longer distances than are normally possible. The word *modem* is an amalgam of the words *modulator* and *demodulator*, which are the two functions that occur during transmission.

Modems present a unique set of challenges from a security perspective. Most modems answer any call made to them when connected to an outside line. After the receiving modem answers the phone, it generally synchronizes with a caller's modem and makes a connection. A modem, when improperly connected to a network, can allow instant unsecured access to the system's or network's data and resources. If a physical security breach occurs, a modem can be used as a remote network connection that allows unrestricted access. This can occur with no knowledge on the part of the system's owner or the network administrators.

While modems are not used as much as they once were, many PCs being built and delivered today still come with internal modems. Unless the modems are specifically needed, they should be disabled or removed from network workstations. If this isn't possible, they should be configured not to auto-answer incoming calls. In other words, you must eliminate as many features of the modem as possible in order to increase security.

Many preconfigured administrative systems provide modem connections for remote maintenance and diagnostics. These connections should either be password protected or have a cut-off switch so they don't expose your network to security breaches.

Remote Access Services

Remote Access Services (RAS) refers to any server service that offers the ability to connect remote systems. The current Microsoft product for Windows-based clients is called *Routing and Remote Access Services (RRAS),* but it was previously known as Remote Access Services (RAS). Because of this, you'll encounter the term *RAS* used interchangeably to describe both the Microsoft product and the process of connecting to remote systems.

Figure 2.16 depicts a dial-up connection being made from a workstation to a network using a RAS server on the network. In this case, the connection is being made between a Windows-based system and a Windows server using *plain-old telephone service (POTS)* and a modem.

FIGURE 2.16   A RAS connection between a remote workstation and a Windows server

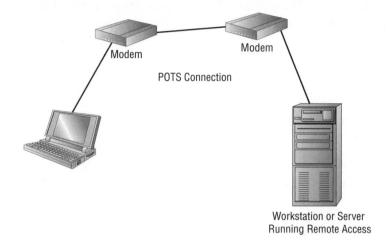

The RAS connection is accomplished via dial-up or network technologies such as VPNs, ISDN, DSL, and cable modems. RAS connections may be secure or in the clear, depending on the protocols that are used in the connection.

A popular method of remote access is through the use of PC Anywhere and similar remote connection/virtual network programs. A major issue with Virtual Network Computing (VNC) is that you are leaving a door into the network open that anyone may stumble upon. By default, most of these programs start the server service automatically, and it is running even when it is not truly needed. It is highly recommended that you configure the service as a manual start service and launch it *only* when needed to access the host. At all other times, that service should be shut down.

Routers

The primary instrument used for connectivity between two or more networks is the *router*. Routers work by providing a path between the networks. A router has two connections that are used to join the networks. Each connection has its own address and appears as a valid address in its respective network. Figure 2.17 illustrates a router connected between two LANs.

FIGURE 2.17   Router connecting two LANs

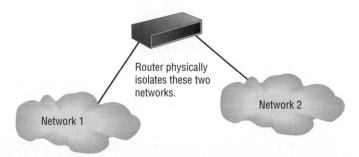

Routers are intelligent devices, and they store information about the networks to which they're connected. Most routers can be configured to operate as packet-filtering firewalls. Many of the newer routers also provide advanced firewall functions.

Routers, in conjunction with a Channel Service Unit/Data Service Unit (CSU/DSU), are also used to translate from *LAN framing* to *WAN framing* (for example, a router that connects a 100BaseT network to a T1 network). This is needed because the network protocols are different in LANs and WANs. Such routers are referred to as *border routers*. They serve as the outside connection of a LAN to a WAN, and they operate at the border of your network. Like the border patrols of many countries, border routers decide who can come in and under what conditions.

Dividing internal networks into two or more subnetworks is a common use for routers. Routers can also be connected internally to other routers, effectively creating *zones* that operate autonomously. Figure 2.18 illustrates a corporate network that uses the combination of a border router for connection to an ISP and internal routers to create autonomous networks for communications. This type of connection keeps local network traffic off the backbone of the corporate network and provides additional security to internal users.

 Because broadcasts don't traverse routers, network segmentation decreases traffic.

FIGURE 2.18   A corporate network implementing routers for segmentation and security

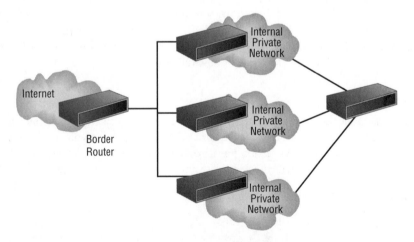

Routers establish communication by maintaining tables about destinations and local connections. A router contains information about the systems connected to it and where to send requests if the destination isn't known. These tables grow as connections are made through the router.

Routers usually communicate routing and other information using one of three standard protocols. Routing can occur interior to the network or exterior, and the three protocols in question are defined here:

Routing Information Protocol (RIP)   RIP is a simple protocol that is part of the TCP/IP protocol suite. Routers that use RIP routinely broadcast the status and routing information of known routers. RIP also attempts to find routes between systems using the smallest number of hops or connections. Multiple versions of RIP are available, with version 2 being the most used today.

Border Gateway Protocol (BGP)   BGP allows groups of routers to share routing information.

Open Shortest Path First (OSPF)   OSPF allows routing information to be updated faster than with RIP.

In the Cisco world, *Interior Gateway Routing Protocol (IGRP)* and *Enhanced Interior Gateway Routing Protocol (EIGRP)* are commonly used. These are distance vector protocols that automatically/mathematically compute routes and choose the best one.

Routers are your first line of defense, and they must be configured to pass only traffic that is authorized by the network administrators. In effect, a router can function as a firewall if it's configured properly. The best approach is layered; a router shouldn't take the place of a firewall but simply augment it.

The routes themselves can be configured as static or dynamic. If they are static, then they are edited manually and stay that way until changed. If they are dynamic, then they learn of other routers around them and use information about those to build their routing tables.

Switches

Switches are multiport devices that improve network efficiency. A switch typically has a small amount of information about systems in a network. Using switches improves network efficiency over hubs because of the virtual circuit capability. Switches also improve network security because the virtual circuits are more difficult to examine with network monitors. You can think of a switch as a device that has some of the best capabilities of routers and hubs combined.

The switch maintains limited routing information about systems in the internal network and allows connections to systems like a hub. Figure 2.19 shows a switch in action between two workstations in a LAN. The connection isn't usually secure or encrypted; however, it doesn't leave the switched area and become part of the overall broadcast traffic as typically happens on a star-based or bus-based LAN.

FIGURE 2.19   Switching between two systems

Load Balancers

Load balancing refers to shifting a load from one device to another. Most often the device in question is a server, but the term could be used for a hard drive, a CPU, or almost any device that you want to avoid overloading. Using a server as the device in question, balancing the load between multiple servers instead of relying on only one reduces the response time, maximizes throughput, and allows better allocation of resources.

A *load balancer* can be implemented as a software or hardware solution and is usually associated with a device—a router, a firewall, NAT, and so on. Under the most common implementation, the load balancer splits the traffic intended for a website into individual requests that are then rotated to redundant servers as they become available (if a server that should be available is busy or down, it is taken out of the rotation).

Telecom/PBX Systems

Telecommunications (or *telecom*) capabilities have undergone radical changes in the last 10 years. The telephone systems and technologies available to deal with communications have given many small businesses fully integrated voice and data services at reasonable prices.

These changes have complicated the security issues that must be handled. One of the primary tools in communications systems is the *private branch exchange (PBX)* system. PBX systems now allow users to connect voice, data, pagers, networks, and almost any other conceivable application into a single telecommunications system. In short, a PBX system allows a company to be its own phone company.

The technology is developing to the point where all communications occur via data links to phone companies using standard data transmission technologies, such as T1 or T3. This means that both voice and data communications are occurring over the same network connection to a phone company or a provider. This allows a single connection for all communications to a single provider of these services.

Potentially, your phone system is a target for attack. Figure 2.20 shows a PBX system connected to a phone company using a T1 line. The phone company, in this illustration, is abbreviated *CO* (for central office). The phone company systems that deal with routing and switching of calls and services are located at the CO.

FIGURE 2.20   A modern digital PBX system integrating voice and data onto a single network connection

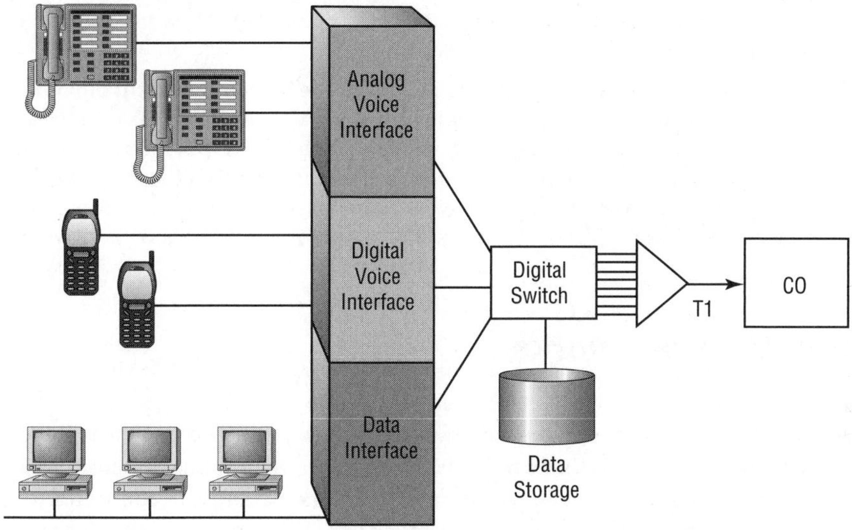

If your phone system is part of your data communications network, an attack on your network will bring down your phone system. This event can cause the stress level in a busy office to increase dramatically.

Find the Holes

The United States Department of Commerce, in conjunction with the National Institute of Standards and Technology, has posted an excellent article titled "PBX Vulnerability Analysis: Finding Holes in Your PBX Before Someone Else Does" at http://csrc.nist.gov/publications/nistpubs/800-24/sp800-24pbx.pdf. This document walks through system architecture, hardware, maintenance, and other issues relevant to daily administration as well as exam study.

The security problems in this situation also increase because you must work to ensure security for your voice communications. At the time the exam questions were written, there were no incidents you needed to be aware of involving phone systems being attacked by malicious code. Since then, some Voice over IP attacks have been reported, and such attacks will probably become a greater concern in the near future.

For the exam, know that because a PBX has many of the same features as other network components, it's subject to the same issues, such as leaving TCP ports open. The PBX should be subject to audit and monitoring like every other network component.

Imagine that someone left a voice message for the president of your company. A *phreaker* (someone who abuses phone systems, as opposed to data systems) might intercept this message, alter it, and put it back. The result of this prank could be a calamity for the company (or at least for you). Make sure the default password is changed on the maintenance and systems accounts for a PBX after its installation, as you would for any network device.

Virtual Private Networks

A *virtual private network (VPN)* is a private network connection that occurs through a public network. A private network provides security over an otherwise unsecure environment. VPNs can be used to connect LANs together across the Internet or other public networks. With a VPN, the remote end appears to be connected to the network as if it were connected locally. A VPN requires either special hardware to be installed or a VPN software package running on servers and workstations.

VPNs typically use a tunneling protocol such as Layer 2 Tunneling Protocol, IPSec, or Point-to-Point Tunneling Protocol (PPTP). Figure 2.21 shows a remote network being connected to a LAN using the Internet and a VPN. This connection appears to be a local connection, and all message traffic and protocols are available across the VPN.

FIGURE 2.21 Two LANs being connected using a VPN across the Internet

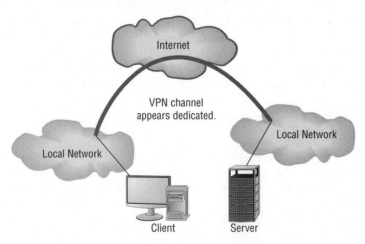

VPNs are becoming the connection of choice when establishing an extranet or intranet between two or more remote offices. The major security concern when using a VPN is encryption. PPTP offers some encryption capabilities, although they're weak. IPSec

offers higher security, and it's becoming the encryption system used in many secure VPN environments.

 Even though a VPN is created through the Internet or other public network, the connection logically appears to be part of the local network. This is why a VPN connection used to establish a connection between two private networks across the Internet is considered a private connection or an extranet.

As mentioned earlier, VPNs are used to make connections between private networks across a public network, such as the Internet. These connections aren't guaranteed to be secure unless a tunneling protocol (such as PPTP) and an encryption system (such as IPSec) are used. A wide range of options, including proprietary technologies, is available for VPN support. Many of the large ISPs and data communications providers offer dedicated hardware with VPN capabilities. Many servers also provide software VPN capabilities for use between two networks.

VPN systems can be dedicated to a certain protocol, or they can pass whatever protocols they see on one end of the network to the other end. A pure VPN connection appears as a dedicated wired connection between the two network ends.

A *VPN concentrator* is a hardware device used to create remote access VPNs. The concentrator creates encrypted tunnel sessions between hosts, and many use two-factor authentication for additional security. Cisco models often incorporate *Scalable Encryption Processing (SEP)* modules to allow for hardware-based encryption and/or redundancy.

Web Security Gateway

One of the newest buzzwords is *web security gateway*, which can be thought of as a proxy server (performing proxy and caching functions) with web protection software built in. Depending on the vendor, the "web protection" can range from a standard virus scanner on incoming packets to also monitoring outgoing user traffic for red flags.

Potential red flags the gateway can detect/prohibit include inappropriate content, trying to establish a peer-to-peer connection with a file-sharing site, instant messaging, and unauthorized tunneling. You can configure most web security gateways to block known HTTP/HTML exploits, strip ActiveX tags, strip Java applets, and block/strip cookies.

Spam Filters

Spam filters can be added to catch unwanted email and filter it out before it gets delivered internally. The filtering is done based on rules that are established (block email coming from certain IP addresses, email that contains particular words in the subject line, and the like).While spam filters are usually used to scan incoming messages, they can also be used to scan outgoing as well and thus act as a quick identifier of internal PCs that may have contracted a virus.

It is estimated that over 90 percent of the incoming email to many organizations is spam. SpamAssassin is one of the best known open source spam filters, and you can find more information on it at `http://spamassassin.apache.org/`.

 A number of vendors make all-in-one security devices that combine spam filters with firewalls, load balancers, and a number of other services.

Understanding Remote Access

One of the primary purposes for having a network is the ability to connect systems. As networks have grown, many technologies have come on the scene to make this process easier and more secure. A key area of concern relates to the connection of systems and other networks that aren't part of your network. The following sections discuss the more common protocols used to facilitate connectivity among remote systems.

 Any authentication done for a remote user is known as *remote authentication*. This authentication is commonly done using TACACS or RADIUS (which are discussed in Chapter 5).

Using Point-to-Point Protocol

Introduced in 1994, *Point-to-Point Protocol (PPP)* offers support for multiple protocols including AppleTalk, IPX, and DECnet. PPP works with POTS, Integrated Services Digital Network (ISDN), and other faster connections such as T1. PPP doesn't provide data security, but it does provide authentication using *Challenge Handshake Authentication Protocol (CHAP)*.

Figure 2.22 shows a PPP connection over an ISDN line. In the case of ISDN, PPP would normally use one 64Kbps B channel for transmission. PPP allows many channels in a network connection (such as ISDN) to be connected or bonded together to form a single virtual connection.

PPP works by encapsulating the network traffic in a protocol called *Network Control Protocol (NCP)*. Authentication is handled by *Link Control Protocol (LCP)*. A PPP connection allows remote users to log on to the network and have access as though they were local users on the network. PPP doesn't provide for any encryption services for the channel.

As you might have guessed, the unsecure nature of PPP makes it largely unsuitable for WAN connections. To counter this issue, other protocols have been created that take advantage of PPP's flexibility and build on it. A dial-up connection using PPP works well because it isn't common for an attacker to tap a phone line. You should make sure all your PPP connections use secure channels, dedicated connections, or dial-up connections.

FIGURE 2.22   PPP using a single B channel on an ISDN connection

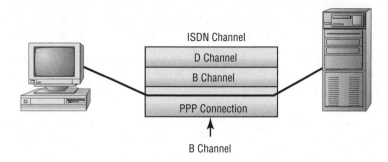

Remote users who connect directly to a system using dial-up connections don't necessarily need to have encryption capabilities enabled. If the connection is direct, the likelihood that anyone would be able to tap an existing phone line is relatively small. However, you should make sure that connections through a network use an encryption-oriented tunneling system.

Working with Tunneling Protocols

Tunneling protocols add a capability to the network: the ability to create tunnels between networks that can be more secure, support additional protocols, and provide virtual paths between systems. The best way to think of tunneling is to imagine sensitive data being encapsulated in other packets that are sent across the public network. Once they're received at the other end, the sensitive data is stripped from the other packets and recompiled into its original form.

The most common protocols used for tunneling are as follows:

Point-to-Point Tunneling Protocol   *Point-to-Point Tunneling Protocol (PPTP)* supports encapsulation in a single point-to-point environment. PPTP encapsulates and encrypts PPP packets. This makes PPTP a favorite low-end protocol for networks. The negotiation between the two ends of a PPTP connection is done in the clear. After the negotiation is performed, the channel is encrypted. This is one of the major weaknesses of PPTP. A *packet-capture device*, such as a sniffer, that captures the negotiation process can potentially use that information to determine the connection type and information about how the tunnel works. Microsoft developed PPTP and supports it on most of the company's products. PPTP uses port 1723 and TCP for connections.

Layer 2 Forwarding   *Layer 2 Forwarding (L2F)* was created by Cisco as a method of creating tunnels primarily for dial-up connections. It's similar in capability to PPP and shouldn't be used over WANs. L2F provides authentication, but it doesn't provide encryption. L2F uses port 1701 and TCP for connections.

Layer 2 Tunneling Protocol   Relatively recently, Microsoft and Cisco agreed to combine their respective tunneling protocols into one protocol: *Layer 2 Tunneling Protocol (L2TP)*. L2TP is a hybrid of PPTP and L2F. It's primarily a point-to-point protocol. L2TP supports multiple network protocols and can be used in networks besides TCP/IP. L2TP works over IPX, SNA, and IP, so it can be used as a bridge across many types of systems. The major problem with L2TP is that it doesn't provide data security: The information isn't encrypted. Security can be provided by protocols such as IPSec. L2TP uses port 1701 and UDP for connections.

Secure Shell   *Secure Shell (SSH)* is a tunneling protocol originally designed for Unix systems. It uses encryption to establish a secure connection between two systems. SSH also provides alternative, security-equivalent programs for such Unix standards as Telnet, FTP, and many other communications-oriented applications. SSH is now available for use on Windows systems as well. This makes it the preferred method of security for Telnet and other cleartext-oriented programs in the Unix environment. SSH uses port 22 and TCP for connections.

Internet Protocol Security   *Internet Protocol Security (IPSec)* isn't a tunneling protocol, but it's used in conjunction with tunneling protocols. IPSec is oriented primarily toward LAN-to-LAN connections, but it can also be used with dial-up connections. IPSec provides secure authentication and encryption of data and headers; this makes it a good choice for security. IPSec can work in either Tunneling mode or Transport mode. In Tunneling mode, the data or payload and message headers are encrypted. Transport mode encrypts only the payload.

 Real World Scenario

Connecting Remote Network Users

Your company wants to support network connections for remote users. These users will use the Internet to access desktop systems and other resources in the network. What would you advise the company to consider?

You should advise your organization to implement a tunneling protocol that supports security. A good solution would be a VPN connection that uses IPSec. You might also want to explore protocols like SSL, TLS, and SSH as alternatives. All of these protocols offer security as a part of their connection process.

Summary

In this chapter, I covered the key elements of the network infrastructure and the various components involved in networking. Your infrastructure is the backbone and key to all the security capabilities of your network.

Your infrastructure includes the hardware and software necessary to run your network. The key elements used in security are routers and firewalls. Proper configuration is the key to providing services the way your network needs them. If your network security devices are improperly configured, you may be worse off than if you didn't have them at all. It's a dangerous situation when you think you're secure but in actuality you aren't.

Networks are becoming more complicated, and they're being linked to other networks at an accelerated speed. Several tools are available to help you both link and secure your networks:

- VPNs
- Tunneling protocols
- Remote access

The connections you make using TCP/IP are based primarily on IP addresses. When coupled with a port, these addresses form a socket. Sockets are the primary method used to communicate with services and applications such as the Web and Telnet. Most services have standard sockets that operate by default. Sockets are changeable for special configurations and additional security. Changing default ports requires that users know which ports provide which services.

Exam Essentials

Be able to describe the various components and the purpose of an infrastructure. Your network's infrastructure is the backbone of your systems and network operations. The infrastructure includes all the hardware, software, physical security, and operational security methods in place. The key components of your infrastructure include devices such as routers, firewalls, switches, modems, telecommunications systems, and the other devices used in the network.

Know the characteristics of the connectivity technologies available to you and the security capabilities associated with each. Remote access, PPP, tunneling protocols, and VPNs are your primary tools. PPTP and L2TP are two of the most common protocols used for tunneling. IPSec, although not a tunneling protocol, provides encryption to tunneling protocols; it's often used to enhance tunnel security.

Familiarize yourself with the technologies used by TCP/IP and the Internet. IP addresses and port numbers are combined to create an interface called a socket. Most TCP and UDP protocols communicate using this socket as the primary interface mechanism. Clients and servers communicate using ports. Ports can be changed to enhance security. Web services use HTML and other technologies to allow rich and animated websites. These technologies potentially create security problems because they may have individual vulnerabilities. Verify the problems that exist from a security perspective before enabling these technologies on your systems.

Review Questions

1. Which of the following devices is the most capable of providing infrastructure security?

   A. Hub

   B. Switch

   C. Router

   D. Modem

2. Upper management has decreed that a firewall must be put in place immediately, before your site suffers an attack similar to one that struck a sister company. Responding to this order, your boss instructs you to implement a packet filter by the end of the week. A packet filter performs which function?

   A. Prevents unauthorized packets from entering the network

   B. Allows all packets to leave the network

   C. Allows all packets to enter the network

   D. Eliminates collisions in the network

3. Which device stores information about destinations in a network?

   A. Hub

   B. Modem

   C. Firewall

   D. Router

4. As more and more clients have been added to your network, the efficiency of the network has decreased significantly. You're preparing a budget for next year, and you specifically want to address this problem. Which of the following devices acts primarily as a tool to improve network efficiency?

   A. Hub

   B. Switch

   C. Router

   D. PBX

5. Which device is used to connect voice, data, pagers, networks, and almost any other conceivable application into a single telecommunications system?

   A. Router

   B. PBX

   C. Hub

   D. Server

6. Most of the sales force have been told that they should no longer report to the office on a daily basis. From now on, they're to spend the majority of their time on the road calling on customers. Each member of the sales force has been issued a laptop computer and told to connect to the network nightly through a dial-up connection. Which of the following protocols is widely used today as a transport protocol for Internet dial-up connections?

   A. SMTP

   B. PPP

   C. PPTP

   D. L2TP

7. Which protocol is unsuitable for WAN VPN connections?

   A. PPP

   B. PPTP

   C. L2TP

   D. IPSec

8. You've been given notice that you'll soon be transferred to another site. Before you leave, you're to audit the network and document everything in use and the reason why it's in use. The next administrator will use this documentation to keep the network running. Which of the following protocols isn't a tunneling protocol but is probably used at your site by tunneling protocols for network security?

   A. IPSec

   B. PPTP

   C. L2TP

   D. L2F

9. A socket is a combination of which components?

   A. TCP and port number

   B. UDP and port number

   C. IP and session number

   D. IP and port number

10. You're explaining protocols to a junior administrator shortly before you leave for vacation. The topic of Internet mail applications comes up, and you explain how communications are done now as well as how you expect them to be done in the future. Which of the following protocols is becoming the newest standard for Internet mail applications?

   A. SMTP

   B. POP

   C. IMAP

   D. IGMP

11. Which protocol is primarily used for network maintenance and destination information?

    A. ICMP

    B. SMTP

    C. IGMP

    D. Router

12. You're the administrator for Mercury Technical. A check of protocols in use on your server brings up one that you weren't aware was in use; you suspect that someone in HR is using it to send messages to multiple recipients. Which of the following protocols is used for group messages or multicast messaging?

    A. SMTP

    B. SNMP

    C. IGMP

    D. L2TP

13. IPv6, in addition to having more bits allocated for each host address, also has mandatory requirements built in for which security protocol?

    A. TFTP

    B. IPSec

    C. SFTP

    D. L2TP

14. Which ports are, by default, reserved for use by FTP? (Choose all that apply.)

    A. 20 and 21 TCP

    B. 20 and 21 UDP

    C. 22 and 23 TCP

    D. 22 and 23 UDP

15. Which of the following services use only TCP ports and not UDP? (Choose all that apply.)

    A. IMAP

    B. LDAP

    C. FTPS

    D. SFTP

16. Which of the following can be implemented as a software or hardware solution and is usually associated with a device—a router, a firewall, NAT, and so on—and used to shift a load from one device to another?

    A. Proxy

    B. Hub

    C. Load balancer

    D. Switch

17. Which of the following are multiport devices that improve network efficiency?

    A. Switches

    B. Modems

    C. Gateways

    D. Concentrators

18. Which service(s), by default, use TCP and UDP port 22? (Choose all that apply.)

    A. SMTP

    B. SSH

    C. SCP

    D. IMAP

19. What protocol, running on top of TCP/IP, is often used for name registration and resolution with Windows-based clients?

    A. Telnet

    B. SSL

    C. NetBIOS

    D. TLS

20. How many bits are used for addressing with IPv4 and IPv6, respectively?

    A. 32, 128

    B. 16, 64

    C. 8, 32

    D. 4, 16

Answers to Review Questions

1. C. Routers can be configured in many instances to act as packet-filtering firewalls. When configured properly, they can prevent unauthorized ports from being opened.

2. A. Packet filters prevent unauthorized packets from entering or leaving a network. Packet filters are a type of firewall that blocks specified port traffic.

3. D. Routers store information about network destinations in routing tables. Routing tables contain information about known hosts on both sides of the router.

4. B. Switches create virtual circuits between systems in a network. These virtual circuits are somewhat private and reduce network traffic when used.

5. B. Many modern PBX (private branch exchange) systems integrate voice and data onto a single data connection to your phone service provider. In some cases, this allows an overall reduction in cost of operations. These connections are made using existing network connections such as a T1 or T3 network.

6. B. PPP can pass multiple protocols and is widely used today as a transport protocol for dial-up connections.

7. A. PPP provides no security, and all activities are unsecure. PPP is primarily intended for dial-up connections and should never be used for VPN connections.

8. A. IPSec provides network security for tunneling protocols. IPSec can be used with many different protocols besides TCP/IP, and it has two modes of security.

9. D. A socket is a combination of IP address and port number. The socket identifies which application will respond to the network request.

10. C. IMAP is becoming the most popular standard for email clients and is replacing POP protocols for mail systems. IMAP allows mail to be forwarded and stored in information areas called stores.

11. A. ICMP is used for destination and error reporting functions in TCP/IP. ICMP is routable and is used by programs such as Ping and Traceroute.

12. C. IGMP is used for group messaging and multicasting. IGMP maintains a list of systems that belong to a message group. When a message is sent to a particular group, each system receives an individual copy.

13. B. The implementation of IPSec is mandatory with IPv6. While it is widely implemented with IPv4, it is not a requirement.

14. A. FTP uses TCP ports 20 and 21. FTP does not use UDP ports.

15. D. SFTP uses only TCP ports. IMAP, LDAP, and FTPS all use both TCP and UDP ports.

16. C. A load balancer can be implemented as a software or hardware solution, and is usually associated with a device—a router, a firewall, NAT, and so on. As the name implies, it is used to shift a load from one device to another.

17. A. Switches are multiport devices that improve network efficiency. A switch typically has a small amount of information about systems in a network.

18. B, C. Port 22 is used by both SSH and SCP with TCP and UDP.

19. C. NetBIOS is used for name resolution and registration in Windows-based environments. It runs on top of TCP/IP.

20. A. IPv4 uses 32 bits for the host address, while IPv6 uses 128 bits for this.

Chapter

3

Protecting Networks

THE FOLLOWING COMPTIA SECURITY+ EXAM OBJECTIVES ARE COVERED IN THIS CHAPTER:

✓ **3.1 Explain the security function and purpose of network devices and technologies.**

- NIDS and NIPS (Behavior based, signature based, anomaly based, heuristic)
- Protocol analyzers
- Sniffers

✓ **3.5 Analyze and differentiate among types of application attacks.**

- Cross-site scripting
- Buffer overflow
- Cookies and attachments
- Malicious add-ons

✓ **3.6 Analyze and differentiate among types of mitigation and deterrent techniques.**

- Detection controls vs. prevention controls
  - IDS vs. IPS

✓ **3.7 Implement assessment tools and techniques to discover security threats and vulnerabilities.**

- Tools
  - Protocol analyzer
  - Sniffer
  - Honeypots
  - Honeynets
  - Port scanner

✓ **4.1 Explain the importance of application security.**

- ▪ Secure coding concepts
  - ▪ Error and exception handling
  - ▪ Input validation
- ▪ Cross-site scripting prevention

While the first chapter looked at various forms of risk and how to calculate them, the second chapter looked at the technology the network is built upon and some devices that can help mitigate some of the risk. The focus of this chapter is on identifying security-related problems when they do occur.

Intrusion detection and intrusion prevention, whether network based or local, provide key methods of identifying intrusions and notifying administrators when responses are needed. In addition to these monitors, you can create traps for those who violate security, by building honeypots and honeynets that fool the intruders and allow you to track them or catch them.

Lastly, this chapter looks at some of the key concepts in application security and problems to be aware of.

Monitoring and Diagnosing Networks

It is important to monitor the network and make sure the traffic on it belongs there. In this section, we'll explore basic network monitors as well as intrusion detection systems.

Network Monitors

Network monitors, otherwise called *sniffers*, were originally introduced to help troubleshoot network problems. Simple network configuration programs like IPCONFIG don't get down on the wire and tell you what is physically happening on a network. Instead, examining the signaling and traffic that occurs on a network requires a network monitor. Early monitors were bulky and required a great deal of expertise to use. Like most things in the computer age, they have gotten simpler, smaller, and less expensive. Network monitors are now available for most environments, and they're effective and easy to use.

Today, a network-monitoring system usually consists of a PC with a NIC (running in *promiscuous mode*) and monitoring software. The monitoring software is menu driven, is easy to use, and has a big help file. The traffic displayed by sniffers can become overly involved and require additional technical materials; you can buy these materials at most bookstores, or you can find them on the Internet for free. With a few hours of work, most people can make network monitors work efficiently and use the data they present.

Windows Server products include a service called Network Monitor that you can use to gain basic information about network traffic. A more robust, detailed version of Network Monitor is included with Systems Management Server (SMS). When it comes to third-party products, Wireshark, available for most platforms, is a market leader (see http://www.wireshark.org/ for more information).

Sniffer is a trade name, like Kleenex. It's the best-known network monitor, so everyone started calling network-monitoring hardware *sniffers*.

Intrusion Detection Systems

An intrusion detection system (IDS) is software that runs on either individual workstations or network devices to monitor and track network activity. By using an IDS, a network administrator can configure the system to respond just like a burglar alarm. IDSs can be configured to evaluate system logs, look at suspicious network activity, and disconnect sessions that appear to violate security settings.

Many vendors have oversold the simplicity of these tools. They're quite involved and require a great deal of planning and maintenance to work effectively. Many manufacturers are selling IDSs with firewalls, and this area shows great promise. Firewalls by themselves will prevent many common attacks, but they don't usually have the intelligence or the reporting capabilities to monitor the entire network. An IDS, in conjunction with a firewall, allows both a reactive posture with the firewall and a preventive posture with the IDS.

Figure 3.1 illustrates an IDS working in conjunction with a firewall to increase security.

In the event the firewall is compromised or penetrated, the IDS can react by disabling systems, ending sessions, and even potentially shutting down your network. This arrangement provides a higher level of security than either device provides by itself. A section exploring IDS in more detail appears later in this chapter.

FIGURE 3.1   An IDS and a firewall working together to secure a network

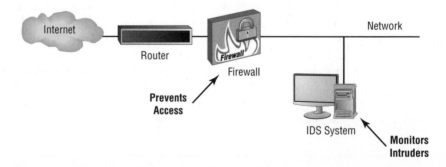

Understanding Intrusion Detection Systems

In the original *Walking Tall* movies, the sheriff puts small strips of clear tape on the hood of his car. Before getting in the vehicle, he would check the difficult-to-detect tape to see if it was broken—if it was, it tipped him off that someone had been messing beneath the hood, and that saved his life. Do you have clear tape on your network?

Intrusion detection systems (IDSs) are becoming integral parts of network monitoring. IDS is a relatively new technology, and it shows a lot of promise in helping to detect network intrusions. *Intrusion detection (ID)* is the process of monitoring events in a system or network to determine if an intrusion is occurring. An *intrusion* is defined as any activity or action that attempts to undermine or compromise the confidentiality, integrity, or availability of resources. Firewalls, as you may recall, were designed to prevent access to resources by an attacker. An IDS reports and monitors intrusion attempts.

Know the Resources Available in Linux

Security information is readily found at a number of Linux-related sites. The first to check, and stay abreast of, is always the distribution vendor's site. Its pages usually provide an overview of Linux-related security issues with links to other relevant pages. You should also keep abreast of issues and problems posted at www.cert.org and www.linuxsecurity.com.

You can also find information on any Linux command through a number of utilities inherent in Linux:

- The man tool offers pages on each utility. For example, to find information about the setfacl tool, you can type **man setfacl**.

- Most utilities have the built-in option of –help to offer information. From the command line, you can type **setfacl –help** to see a quick list of available options.

- The info utility shows the man pages as well.

- The whatis utility can show if there is more than one set of documentation on the system for the utility.

- The whereis utility lists all the information it can find about locations associated with a file.

- The apropos utility uses the whatis database to find values and returns the short summary information.

It should be inherently understood that every network, regardless of size, should utilize a firewall. On a home-based network, a personal software firewall can be implemented to provide protection against attacks.

Several key terms are necessary to explain the technology behind intrusion detection, as follows:

Activity   An *activity* is an element of a data source that is of interest to the operator. This could include a specific occurrence of a type of activity that is suspicious. An example might be a TCP connection request that occurs repeatedly from the same IP address.

Administrator   The *administrator* is the person responsible for setting the security policy for an organization and is responsible for making decisions about the deployment and configuration of the IDS. The administrator should make decisions regarding alarm levels, historical logging, and session-monitoring capabilities. They're also responsible for determining the appropriate responses to attacks and ensuring that those responses are carried out.

Most organizations have an escalation chart. The administrator is rarely at the top of the chart but is always expected to be the one doing the most to keep incidents under control.

Alert   An *alert* is a message from the analyzer indicating that an event of interest has occurred. The alert contains information about the activity as well as specifics of the occurrence. An alert may be generated when an excessive amount of *Internet Control Message Protocol (ICMP)* traffic is occurring or when repeated logon attempts are failing. A certain level of traffic is normal for a network. Alerts occur when activities of a certain type exceed a preset threshold. For instance, you might want to generate an alert every time someone from inside your network pings the outside using the Ping program.

Analyzer   The *analyzer* is the component or process that analyzes the data collected by the sensor. It looks for suspicious activity among all the data collected. Analyzers work by monitoring events and determining whether unusual activities are occurring, or they can use a rule-based process that is established when the IDS is configured.

Data Source   The *data source* is the raw information that the IDS uses to detect suspicious activity. The data source may include audit files, system logs, or the network traffic as it occurs.

Event   An *event* is an occurrence in a data source that indicates that a suspicious activity has occurred. It may generate an alert. Events are logged for future reference. They also typically trigger a notification that something unusual may be happening in the network. An IDS might begin logging events if the volume of inbound email connections suddenly spiked; this event might be an indication that someone was probing your network. The event might trigger an alert if a deviation from normal network traffic patterns occurred or if an activity threshold was crossed.

Manager   The *manager* is the component or process the operator uses to manage the IDS. The IDS console is a manager. Configuration changes in the IDS are made by communicating with the IDS manager.

Notification   *Notification* is the process or method by which the IDS manager makes the operator aware of an alert. This might include a graphic display highlighting the traffic or an email sent to the network's administrative staff.

Operator   The *operator* is the person primarily responsible for the IDS. The operator can be a user, administrator, and so on, as long as they're the primary person responsible.

Sensor   A *sensor* is the IDS component that collects data from the data source and passes it to the analyzer for analysis. A sensor can be a device driver on a system, or it can be an actual black box that is connected to the network and reports to the IDS. The important thing to remember is that the sensor is a primary data collection point for the IDS.

The IDS, as you can see, has many different components and processes that work together to provide a real-time picture of your network traffic. Figure 3.2 shows the various components and processes working together to provide an IDS. Remember that data can come from many different sources and must be analyzed to determine what's occurring. An IDS isn't intended as a true traffic-blocking device, though some IDSs can also perform this function; it's intended to be a traffic-auditing device.

FIGURE 3.2   The components of an IDS working together to provide network monitoring

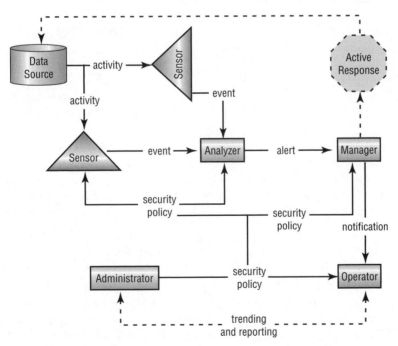

IDSs use four primary approaches:

Behavior-Based-Detection IDS   A *behavior-based system* looks for variations in behavior such as unusually high traffic, policy violations, and so on. By looking for deviations in behavior, it is able to recognize potential threats and respond quickly.

Signature-Based-Detection IDS   A *signature-based system*, also commonly known as *misuse-detection IDS (MD-IDS)*, is primarily focused on evaluating attacks based on attack signatures and audit trails. Attack signatures describe a generally established method of attacking a system. For example, a TCP flood attack begins with a large number of incomplete TCP sessions. If the MD-IDS knows what a TCP flood attack looks like, it can make an appropriate report or response to thwart the attack.

Figure 3.3 illustrates a signature-based IDS in action. Notice that this IDS uses an extensive database to determine the signature of the traffic. This process resembles an antivirus software process.

FIGURE 3.3   A signature-based IDS in action

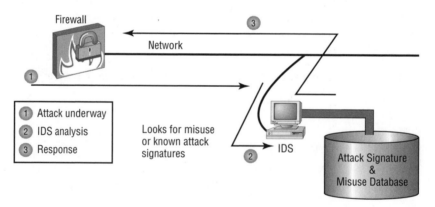

Anomaly-Detection IDS   An *anomaly-detection IDS (AD-IDS)* looks for anomalies, meaning it looks for things outside of the ordinary. Typically, a training program learns what the normal operation is and then can spot deviations from it. An AD-IDS can establish the baseline either by being manually assigned values or through automated processes that look at traffic patterns. One method is *behavior-based*, which looks for unusual behavior and then acts accordingly.

Heuristic IDS   A *heuristic system* uses algorithms to analyze the traffic passing through the network. As a general rule, heuristic systems require more tweaking and fine-tuning than the other types of detection systems to prevent false positives in your network.

IDSs are primarily focused on reporting events or network traffic that deviate from historical work activity or network traffic patterns. For this reporting to be effective, administrators should develop a baseline or history of typical network traffic. This baseline activity provides a stable, long-term perspective on network activity. An example might be a report generated when a higher-than-normal level of ICMP responses is received in a specified time period. Such activity may indicate the beginning of an ICMP flood attack. The system may also report when a user who doesn't normally access the network using a VPN suddenly requests administrative access to the system. Figure 3.4 demonstrates an AD-IDS tracking and reporting excessive traffic in a network. The AD-IDS process frequently uses artificial intelligence or expert system technologies to learn about normal traffic for a network.

FIGURE 3.4   AD-IDS using expert system technology to evaluate risks

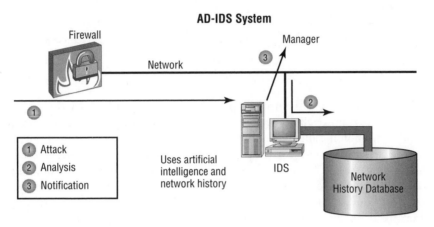

 Whenever there is an attack, there is almost always something created that identifies it—an entry in the login report, an error in a log, and so forth. Those items represent intrusion signatures, and you can learn from them and instruct an IDS to watch for and prevent repeat performances of those items.

MD-IDS and AD-IDS are merging in most commercial systems. They provide the best opportunity to detect and thwart attacks and unauthorized access. Unlike a firewall, the IDS exists to detect and report unusual occurrences in a network, not block them.

The next sections discuss network-based and host-based implementations of IDS and the capabilities they provide. I'll also introduce honeypots and incident response.

Working with a Network-Based IDS

A *network-based IDS (NIDS)* approach to IDS attaches the system to a point in the network where it can monitor and report on all network traffic. This can be in front of or behind the firewall, as shown in Figure 3.5.

 The best solution to creating a secure network is to place the IDS in front of and behind the firewall. This double security provides as much defense as possible.

FIGURE 3.5 NIDS placement in a network determines what data will be analyzed.

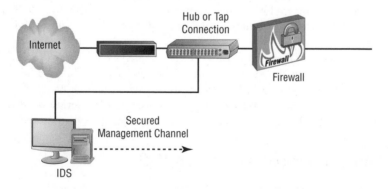

Placing the NIDS in front of the firewall provides monitoring of all network traffic going into the network. This approach allows a huge amount of data to be processed, and it lets you see all the traffic coming into the network. Putting the NIDS behind the firewall only allows you to see the traffic that penetrates the firewall. Although this approach reduces the amount of data processed, it doesn't let you see all the attacks that might be developing.

The NIDS can be attached to a switch or a hub, or it can be attached to a tap. Many hubs and switches provide a monitoring port for troubleshooting and diagnostic purposes. This port may function in a manner similar to a tap. The advantage of the tap approach is that the IDS is the only device that will be using the tap. Figure 3.6 illustrates a connection to the network using a hub or tap.

FIGURE 3.6 A hub being used to attach the NIDS to the network

Port spanning, also known as *port mirroring,* copies the traffic from all ports to a single port and disallows bidirectional traffic on that port. Cisco's Switched Port Analyzer (SPAN) is one example of a port-spanning implementation.

In either case, the IDS monitors and evaluates all the traffic to which it has access.

Two basic types of responses can be formulated at the network level: passive and active. They're briefly explained in the following sections.

 Real World Scenario

Working with Network Audit Files

You're the network administrator of a relatively busy network. Your company has gone through a couple of cutbacks, and your staffing is limited. You want to make sure that your network stays as secure as you can make it. What can you do to ease your workload?

You have three possibilities. There are two you should consider to protect your network: Either install an IDS or reduce the logging levels of your network audit files. An alternative is to install an audit log-collection system with filtering.

You might be able to reduce the amount of logged traffic in your audit files by changing the settings that determine what you audit. However, changing audit rules would prevent you from seeing what's happening on your network because most events wouldn't be logged.

Installing an IDS would allow you to establish rules that would provide a higher level of automation than you could achieve by reviewing audit files. Your best solution might be to convince your company to invest in an IDS. An IDS could send you an email or alert you when an event is detected.

Implementing a Passive Response

A *passive response* is the most common type of response to many intrusions. In general, passive responses are the easiest to develop and implement. The following list includes some passive response strategies:

Logging   *Logging* involves recording that an event has occurred and under what circumstances it occurred. Logging functions should provide sufficient information about the nature of the attack to help administrators determine what has happened and to assist in evaluating the threat. This information can then be used to devise methods to counter the threat.

Notification   *Notification* communicates event-related information to the appropriate personnel when an event has occurred. This includes relaying any relevant data about the event to help evaluate the situation. If the IDS is manned full time, messages can be displayed on the manager's console to indicate that the situation is occurring.

Shunning   *Shunning* or ignoring an attack is a common response. This might be the case if your IDS notices an Internet Information Server (IIS) attack occurring on a system that's running another web-hosting service, such as Apache. The attack won't work because Apache doesn't respond the same way that IIS does, so why pay attention to it? In a busy network, many different types of attacks can occur simultaneously. If you aren't worried about an attack succeeding, why waste energy or time investigating it or notifying someone about it? The IDS can make a note of it in a log and move on to other more pressing business.

Remember that passive responses are the most commonly implemented. They are the least costly and the easiest to put into practice.

Implementing an Active Response

An *active response* involves taking an action based on an attack or threat. The goal of an active response is to take the quickest action possible to reduce an event's potential impact. This type of response requires plans for how to deal with an event, clear policies, and intelligence in the IDS in order to be successful. An active response will include one of the reactions briefly described here:

Terminating Processes or Sessions   If a flood attack is detected, the IDS can cause the subsystem, such as TCP, to force resets to all the sessions that are under way. Doing so frees up resources and allows TCP to continue to operate normally. Of course, all valid TCP sessions are closed and will need to be reestablished—but at least this will be possible, and it may have little effect on the end users. The IDS evaluates the events and determines the best way to handle them. Figure 3.7 illustrates TCP being directed to issue RST commands from the IDS to reset all open connections to TCP. This type of mechanism can also terminate user sessions or stop and restart any process that appears to be operating abnormally.

Network Configuration Changes   If a certain IP address is found to be causing repeated attacks on the network, the IDS can instruct a border router or firewall to reject any requests or traffic from that address. This configuration change can remain in effect permanently or for a specified period. Figure 3.8 illustrates the IDS instructing the firewall to close port 80 for 60 seconds to terminate an IIS attack.

If the IDS determines that a particular socket or port is being attacked, it can instruct the firewall to block that port for a specified amount of time. Doing so effectively eliminates the attack but may also inadvertently cause a self-imposed DoS situation to occur by eliminating legitimate traffic. This is especially true for port 80 (HTTP or web) traffic.

Deception   A *deception* active response fools the attacker into thinking the attack is succeeding while the system monitors the activity and potentially redirects the attacker to a system that is designed to be broken. This allows the operator or administrator to gather data about how the attack is unfolding and the techniques being used in the attack. This process is referred to as *sending them to the honeypot*, and it's described later in the section "Utilizing Honeypots." Figure 3.9 illustrates a honeypot where a deception has been successful.

The advantage of this type of response is that all activities are watched and recorded for analysis when the attack is completed. This is a difficult scenario to set up, and it's dangerous to allow a hacker to proceed into your network, even if you're monitoring the events.

FIGURE 3.7 IDS instructing TCP to reset all connections

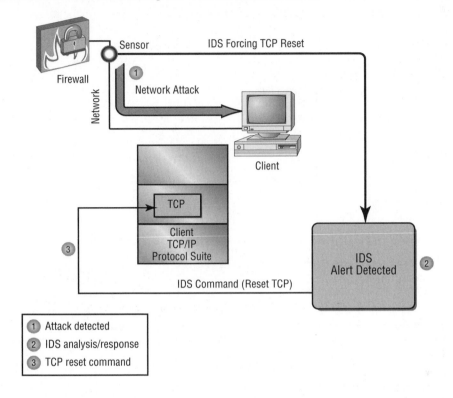

This approach is frequently used when an active investigation is under way by law enforcement and they're gathering evidence to ensure a successful prosecution of the attacker. Deception allows you to gather documentation without risking live data.

 Remember that active responses are the least commonly implemented. Those that are the most effective are the most costly and the hardest to put into practice, not to mention the trouble you can get into following a we-attack-those-who-attack-us strategy.

Working with a Host-Based IDS

A *host-based IDS (HIDS)* is designed to run as software on a host computer system. These systems typically run as a service or as a background process. HIDSs examine the machine logs, system events, and applications interactions; they normally don't monitor incoming network traffic to the host. HIDSs are popular on servers that use encrypted channels or channels to other servers.

FIGURE 3.8   IDS instructing the firewall to close port 80 for 60 seconds to thwart an IIS attack

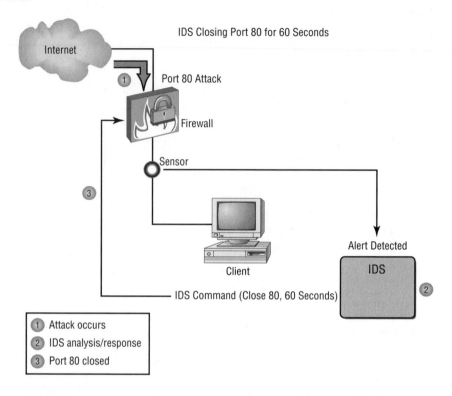

1 Attack occurs
2 IDS analysis/response
3 Port 80 closed

FIGURE 3.9   A network honeypot deceives an attacker and gathers intelligence.

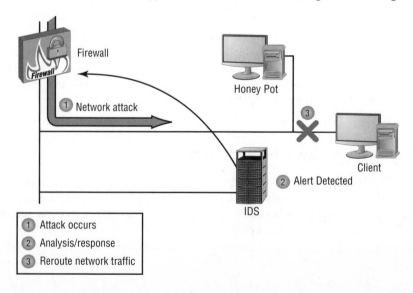

1 Attack occurs
2 Analysis/response
3 Reroute network traffic

Figure 3.10 illustrates an HIDS installed on a server. Notice that the HIDS interacts with the logon audit and kernel audit files. The kernel audit files are used for process and application interfaces.

FIGURE 3.10   A host-based IDS interacting with the operating system

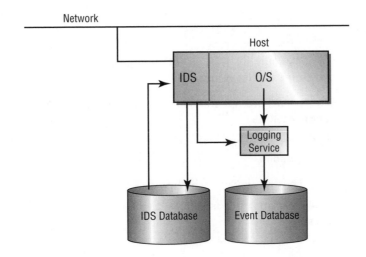

Two major problems with HIDS aren't easily overcome. The first problem involves a compromise of the system. If the system is compromised, the log files the IDS reports to may become corrupt or inaccurate. This may make fault determination difficult or the system unreliable. The second major problem with HIDS is that it must be deployed on each system that needs it. This can create a headache for administrative and support staff.

One of HIDS's major benefits is the potential to keep checksums on files. These checksums can be used to inform system administrators that files have been altered by an attack. Recovery is simplified because it's easier to determine where tampering has occurred.

Host-based IDSs typically respond in a passive manner to an incident. An active response would theoretically be similar to those provided by a network-based IDS.

Working with NIPS

As opposed to *Network Intrusion Detection Systems (NIDSs),* Network Intrusion Prevention Systems (NIPSs) focus on *prevention.* These systems focus on signature matches and then take a course of action. For example, if it appears as if an attack might be under way, packets can be dropped, ignored, and so forth. In order to be able to do this, the NIPS must be able to *detect* the attack occurring, and thus it can be argued that NIPS is a subset of NIDS.

The line continues to blur between technologies. For example, NIST now refers to its releases as IDPS. While it is important to stay current on the terminology in the real world, know that the exam is frozen in time and you should be familiar with the older terminology for the questions you will face on it.

Log Files in Linux

There are a number of logs to check for entries that might indicate an intrusion. The primary ones you should examine are listed here:

/var/log/faillog   Open a shell prompt and use the `faillog` utility to view a list of users' failed authentication attempts.

/var/log/lastlog   Open a shell prompt and use the `lastlog` utility to view a list of all users and when they last logged in.

/var/log/messages   Use grep, or a derivative thereof, to find login-related entries in this file.

/var/log/wtmp   Open a shell prompt and use the `last` command to view a list of users who have authenticated to the system.

Utilizing Honeypots

A *honeypot* is a computer that has been designated as a target for computer attacks. The best way to visualize a honeypot is to think of Winnie the Pooh and the multiple times the character has become stuck while trying to get the honey out of the jugs it is stored in. By getting stuck, he has incapacitated himself and become an easy target for anyone trying to find him.

Two of the most popular honeypots for Linux are honeyd (http://honeyd .org) and Tiny Honeypot (thp) (http://freshmeat.net/projects/thp/).

The purpose of a honeypot is to allow itself to succumb to an attack. During the process of "dying," the system can be used to gain information about how the attack developed and what methods were used to institute the attack. The benefit of a honeypot system is that it draws attackers away from a higher-value system or allows administrators to gain intelligence about an attack strategy. See Figure 3.9 for a diagram of a honeypot implementation.

Honeypots aren't normally secured or locked down. If they come straight out of the box with an operating system and applications software, they may be configured as is. Elaborate honeypot systems can contain information and software that might entice an attacker to probe deeper and take over the system. If not configured properly, a honeypot system can be used to launch attacks against other systems.

There are several initiatives in the area of honeypot technology. One of the more interesting involves the Honeynet Project, which created a synthetic network that can be run on a single computer system and is attached to a network using a normal network interface card (NIC). The system looks like an entire corporate network, complete with applications and data, all of which are fake. As part of the Honeynet Project, the network was routinely scanned, worms were inserted, and attempts were made to contact other systems to infest them—all over the course of a three-day period. At the end of day three, the system had been infected by no fewer than three worms. This infestation happened without any advertising by the Honeynet Project.

Additional information is available on the Honeynet Project at `http://www.honeynet.org/`.

Before you even consider implementing a honeypot or a honeynet-type project, you need to understand the concepts of *enticement* and *entrapment*:

Enticement   *Enticement* is the process of luring someone into your plan or trap. You might accomplish this by advertising that you have free software, or you might brag that no one can break into your machine. If you invite someone to try, you're enticing them to do something that you want them to do.

Entrapment   *Entrapment* is the process in which a law enforcement officer or a government agent encourages or induces a person to commit a crime when the potential criminal expresses a desire not to go ahead. Entrapment is a valid legal defense in a criminal prosecution.

While enticement is legally acceptable, entrapment isn't. Your legal liabilities are probably small in either case, but you should seek legal advice before you implement a honeypot on your network. You may also want to contact law enforcement or the prosecutor's office if you want to pursue legal action against attackers.

Some security experts use the term *tar pit* in place of honeypot. The two terms are interchangeable.

Understanding Protocol Analyzers

The terms *protocol analyzing* and *packet sniffing* are interchangeable. They refer to the process of monitoring the data that is transmitted across a network. The software that performs the operation is called either an *analyzer* or a *sniffer*, as mentioned in the "Network Monitors" section at the beginning of this chapter. Sniffers are readily available on the Internet. These tools were initially intended for legitimate network-monitoring processes, but they can also be used to gather data for illegal purposes.

IM traffic, for example, uses the Internet and is susceptible to packet-sniffing activities. Any information contained in an IM session is potentially vulnerable to interception. Make sure users understand that sensitive information should not be sent using this method.

One of the best-known tools for analyzing network traffic in real time is Snort (`http://www.snort.org`). Exercise 3.1 walks through the installation of this tool.

EXERCISE 3.1

Install Snort in Linux

The de facto standard for intrusion detection in Linux is Snort. To install the package on a SuSE server, follow these steps:

1. Log in as root and start YaST.

2. Choose Software and then Install And Remove Software. Search for **snort**.

3. Check the box when the package appears.

4. Click Accept. If any dependency messages appear, click Continue to add them as well.

5. Swap CDs as prompted and exit YaST upon completion.

To use the Snort utility, open a terminal session and type **snort**. This generates an error message that lists all the options that you can use with the utility.

Securing Workstations and Servers

Workstations are particularly vulnerable in a network. Most modern workstations, regardless of their operating systems, communicate using services such as file sharing, network services, and applications programs. Many of these programs have the ability to connect to other workstations or servers.

Because a network generally consists of a minimal number of servers and a large number of workstations, it's often easier for a hacker to find an unsecure workstation and enter there first. Once the hacker has gained access to the workstation, it becomes easier to access the network since they're now inside the firewall.

These connections are potentially vulnerable to interception and exploitation. The process of making a workstation or a server more secure is called *platform hardening*. The process of hardening the operating system is referred to as *OS hardening*. (OS hardening is part of platform hardening, but it deals only with the operating system.) Platform hardening procedures can be categorized into three basic areas:

- Remove unused software, services, and processes from the workstations (for example, remove the server service from a workstation). These services and processes may create opportunities for exploitation.

- Ensure that all services and applications are up-to-date (including available service and security packs) and configured in the most secure manner allowed. This may include assigning passwords, limiting access, and restricting capabilities.

- Minimize information dissemination about the operating system, services, and capabilities of the system. Many attacks can be targeted at specific platforms once the platform has been identified. Many operating systems use default account names for administrative access. If at all possible, these should be changed. During a new installation of Windows 7 or Windows Vista, the first user created is automatically added to the Administrators group. Windows then goes one step further and automatically disables the actual administrator account once another account belonging to the Administrators group has been created. Earlier versions of Windows did not do this and the account was enabled. In Linux, the root user account is automatically created during installation as well.

One way to prevent users from making changes in Microsoft operating systems is to lock their configuration settings. This is possible with Windows clients through the use of group policies.

Most modern server products also offer workstation functionality. In fact, many servers are virtually indistinguishable from workstations. Linux functions as both a workstation and a server in most cases.

Most successful attacks against a server will also work against a workstation, and vice versa. Additionally, servers run dedicated applications, such as SQL Server or a full-function web server.

An early version of Internet Information Services (IIS) included a default mail system as a part of its installation. This mail system was enabled unless specifically disabled. It suffered from most of the vulnerabilities to virus and worm infections discussed in Chapter 4. Make sure your system runs only the services, protocols, and processes you need. Turn off or disable things you don't need.

When you're looking for ways to harden a server, never underestimate the obvious. You should always apply all patches and fixes that have been released for the operating system. Additionally, you should make certain you aren't running any services that aren't needed on the machine.

Real World Scenario

Users Installing Unauthorized Software

Members of your Information Systems (IS) department are upset about the amount of unauthorized software that is being installed on many of the Windows clients on your network. They come to you for advice on how to minimize the impact of this software. What do you tell them?

All newer Windows clients allow permissions to be established to prevent software installation. You should evaluate the capabilities of the settings in the workstations for security. This process is referred to as *locking down* a desktop. You can lock down most desktops to prevent the installation of software. Yet although this may sound like a great solution, remember that doing so may also prevent users from automatically upgrading software and may create additional work for the IS department. You'll need to evaluate both issues to determine the best approach to take and then make your recommendation to the IS department.

Real World Scenario

Finding Ways to Harden Your Servers

Armed with a list of the different types of servers on your network, look for ways in which they can be hardened by answering the following questions:

1.   Are there services running on them that aren't needed?

2.   Have the latest patches and fixes been applied?

3.   Are there known issues with this operating system?

4.   Are there known issues with the services or applications that are running?

One of the first tasks you should do is to go to a search engine and enter the word *hardening* along with the exact operating system you're running.

Securing Internet Connections

The Internet is perhaps the area of largest growth for networks. The technology started as a research project funded by the Department of Defense and has grown at an enormous rate. Within a few years, virtually every computer in the world is expected to be connected to the Internet. This situation creates a security nightmare and is one of the primary reasons the demand for professionals trained in information and computer security is expected to grow exponentially.

The following sections describe ports and sockets and then some of the more common protocols, including email, web, and FTP, that you should be familiar with for the exam.

Working with Ports and Sockets

As we've already discussed, the primary method of connection between systems using the Internet is TCP/IP. This protocol establishes connections and circuits using a combination of the IP address and a port. A *port* is an interface that is used to connect to a device. *Sockets* are a combination of the IP address and the port. For example, if you attempt to connect to a remote system with the IP address 192.168.0.100, which is running a website, you'll use port 80 by default. The combination of these two elements gives you a socket. The full address and socket description would then be 192.168.0.100:80.

IP is used to route the information from one host to another through a network. The four layers of TCP/IP encapsulate the information into a valid IP packet that is then transmitted across the network. Figure 3.11 illustrates the key components of a TCP packet requesting the home page of a website. The data will be returned from the website to port 1024 on the originating host.

FIGURE 3.11   A TCP packet requesting a web page from a web server

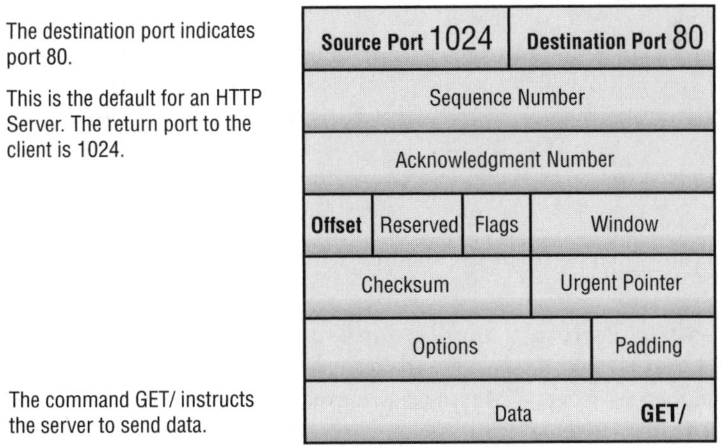

The destination port indicates port 80.

This is the default for an HTTP Server. The return port to the client is 1024.

Source Port 1024	Destination Port 80
Sequence Number	
Acknowledgment Number	

Offset	Reserved	Flags	Window

Checksum	Urgent Pointer
Options	Padding
Data	**GET/**

The command GET/ instructs the server to send data.

The source port is the port that is addressed on the destination. The destination port is the port to which the data is sent. In the case of a web application, the data for both port addresses would contain 80. A number of the fields in this packet are used by TCP for verification and integrity, and you need not be concerned with them at this time.

However, the data field contains the value Get/. This value requests the home or starting page from the web server. In essence, this command or process requested the home page of the site 192.168.0.100 port 80. The data is formed into another data packet that is passed down to IP and sent back to the originating system on port 1024.

The connections to most services using TCP/IP are based on this port model. Many of the ports are well documented, and the protocols to communicate with them are well known. If a vendor has a technological weakness or implements security poorly, the vulnerability will become known and exploited in a short time.

Working with Email

Email is one of the most popular applications in use on the Internet. Several good email servers and clients are available. Figure 3.12 demonstrates the process of transferring an email message.

FIGURE 3.12 Email connections between clients and a server

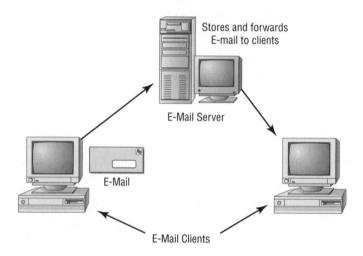

The most common email systems use the following protocols, which use TCP for session establishment:

Simple Mail Transport Protocol *Simple Mail Transport Protocol (SMTP)* is a mail delivery protocol that is used to send email between an email client and an email server as well as between email servers. Messages are moved from client to server to client via the Internet. Each email message can take a different path from the client to the server. In the case of Figure 3.12, the clients are on two different email servers; they could both be on the same server, and the process would appear transparent to the user. SMTP uses port 25 and TCP for connections.

Post Office Protocol *Post Office Protocol (POP)* is a newer protocol that relies on SMTP for message transfer to receive email. POP provides a message store that can be used to store and forward messages. If a server isn't operating, the originating server can store a message and try to resend it later. POP3, the newest version of POP, allows messages to be transferred from the waiting post office to the email client. The current POP standard uses port 109 for POP2 and 110 for POP3. POP uses TCP for connections.

Internet Message Access Protocol   *Internet Message Access Protocol (IMAP)* is the newest player in the email field, and it's rapidly becoming the most popular. Like POP, IMAP has a store-and-forward capability. However, it has much more functionality. IMAP allows messages to be stored on an email server instead of being downloaded to the client. It also allows messages to be downloaded based on search criteria. Many IMAP implementations also allow connections using web browsers. The current version of IMAP (IMAP 4) uses port 143 and TCP for connections.

> *S/MIME* and *PGP* are two of the more popular methods of providing security for emails. We discuss these in Chapter 8.

Working with the Web

When two hosts communicate across the Web, data is returned from the host using *Hypertext Markup Language (HTML)*. HTML is nothing more than a coding scheme to allow text and pictures to be presented in a specific way in a web browser. HTML can be created any number of ways, including via manual coding and in graphical design programs. HTML files are read, interpreted by your browser, and displayed on your system. If you want to see what HTML looks like, you can set your browser to view source code—you'll see things similar to word-processor coding for virtually every characteristic of the web page you're viewing.

Websites are collections of these pages, which are called into your browser when you click a link or scroll through the pages. Most developers want more than the ability to display pages and pages of colored text on your computer. To make creative and sophisticated websites possible, web browsers have become more complicated, as have web servers. Current browsers include audio, visuals, animations, live chats, and almost any other feature you can imagine.

Figure 3.13 illustrates some of the content that can be delivered over the Internet via a web server.

This ability to deliver content over the Web is accomplished in one of several ways. The most common approach involves installing applications that talk through the server to your browser. The applications require additional ports to be opened through your firewall and routers. Unfortunately, doing so inherently creates security vulnerabilities.

> Each port you leave open in your network increases your vulnerability. For instance, if you open the ports necessary to use the popular program Net-Meeting, you're exposing your users to additional opportunities for attack. NetMeeting, like many other programs, has had a number of security vulnerabilities in the past, and it will probably have more in the future.

FIGURE 3.13 A web server providing streaming video, animation, and HTML data to a client

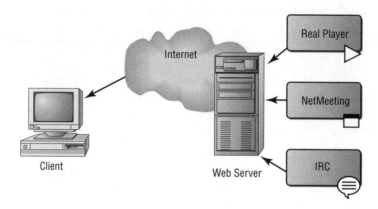

Each of the popular web services is now offered in conjunction with web-enabled programs such as Flash and Java. These services use either a socket to communicate or a program that responds to commands through the browser. If your browser can be controlled by an application, your system is at great risk of being coerced into giving attackers information you don't want them to have. Servers are also vulnerable to this issue because they must process requests from browsers for information or data. A little research into the vulnerabilities of a proposed new service may save you a lot of time later should you become the target of an attack.

While HTML remains popular, *Extensible Markup Language (XML)* has also been adopted by many. Although it's not a replacement for HTML, XML offers many capabilities that HTML does not. These include the ability to describe the information (and not just display it). By being able to describe the data, it can display it across several platforms, systems, and so forth.

The best solution for many of the vulnerabilities that exist on the Web is to implement secure web connections—the topic of our next section.

Secure Web Connections

There are two common ways to provide secure connections between a web client and a web server:

Secure Sockets Layer and Transport Layer Security *Secure Sockets Layer (SSL)* and *Transport Layer Security (TLS)* are two common protocols used to convey information between a web client and a server. The SSL protocol uses an encryption scheme between the two systems. The client initiates the session, the server responds, indicating that encryption is needed, and then they negotiate an appropriate encryption scheme. TLS is a newer protocol that merges SSL with other protocols to provide encryption. TLS supports SSL connections for compatibility, but it also allows other encryption protocols, such as Triple DES, to be used. SSL/TLS uses port 443 and TCP for connections.

HTTP/S   *HTTP Secure (HTTP/S)* is a protocol that is used for secure connections between two systems that use the Web. It protects the connection, and all traffic between the two systems is encrypted. HTTP/S uses SSL or TLS for connection security, and it uses port 443 and TCP for connections.

> Don't confuse Secure HTTP (S-HTTP) with HTTP/S. S-HTTP is a different protocol that lets systems negotiate an encryption connection between each other. S-HTTP can provide some of the capabilities of HTTP/S, but it isn't as secure and is rarely used in practice, but it makes for an excellent exam question.

Vulnerabilities of Web Add-ins

The growth of the Web and demands from users for more features have spurred the creation of a new set of vulnerabilities that must be evaluated and managed. Increasingly, web browsers and other web-enabled technologies allow servers to send instructions to the client to provide multimedia and other capabilities. This is creating a problem for security professionals because these protocols offer potential weaknesses.

The following sections discuss the more common web-based applications, such as JavaScript and applets, and the vulnerabilities you should be aware of. These vulnerabilities can include malicious code, viruses, and exploitations.

ActiveX

ActiveX is a technology that was implemented by Microsoft to customize controls, icons, and other features, which increases the usability of web-enabled systems. ActiveX runs on the client. It uses a method called *Authenticode* for security. Authenticode is a type of certificate technology that allows ActiveX components to be validated by a server.

ActiveX components are downloaded to the client hard disk, potentially allowing additional security breaches. Web browsers can be configured so that they require confirmation to accept an ActiveX control. However, many users don't understand these confirmation messages when they appear, and they automatically accept the components. Automatically accepting an ActiveX component or control creates the opportunity for security breaches on a client system when the control is used because an ActiveX control contains programming instructions that can contain malicious code or create vulnerabilities in a system.

> It's highly recommended that browsers be configured so that they do not allow ActiveX to run without prompting the user because of the potential security hole that could be opened.

Buffer Overflows

Buffer overflows occur when an application receives more data than it's programmed to accept. This situation can cause an application to terminate or to write data beyond the end of the allocated space. Termination may leave the system sending the data with temporary access to privileged levels in the attacked system, while overwriting can cause important data to be lost. This exploitation is usually a result of a programming error in the development of the software.

Buffer overflows, while a less-common source of exploitation than in the past, are still quite common and far from a small problem.

Common Gateway Interface

Common Gateway Interface (CGI) is an older form of scripting that was used extensively in early web systems. CGI scripts were used to capture data from a user using simple forms. They aren't widely used in new systems and are being replaced by Java, ActiveX, and other technologies.

CGI scripts run on the web server and interact with the client browser. CGI is often frowned upon in new applications because of its security issues, but it's still widely used in older systems. Vulnerabilities in CGI are the result of its inherent ability to do what it is told. If a CGI script is written to wreak havoc (or carries extra code added to it by a miscreant) and it is executed, your systems will suffer. The best protection against any weaknesses is to not run applications written in CGI but rather to opt for those written in the newer languages where possible.

Cookies

Cookies are text files that a browser maintains on the user's hard disk in order to provide a persistent, customized web experience for each visit. A cookie typically contains information about the user. For example, a cookie can contain a client's history to improve customer service. If a bookstore wants to know your buying habits and what types of books you last viewed at its site, it can load this information into a cookie on your system. The next time you return to that store, the server can read your cookie and customize what it presents to you. Cookies can also be used to time-stamp a user to limit access. A financial institution may send your browser a cookie once you've authenticated. The server can read the cookie to determine when a session is expired.

Obviously, cookies are considered a risk because they have the potential to contain your personal information, which could get into the wrong hands, and are highly treasured by advertisers today. A new breed of cookie known as *evercookie* writes data to multiple locations to make it next to impossible to ever remove it completely (see `http://samy.pl/evercookie/`).

If security is your utmost concern, the best protection is to not allow cookies to be accepted. Almost every browser offers the option of enabling or disabling cookies. If you enable them, you can usually choose whether to accept/reject all or only those from an originating server.

Cross-Site Scripting

Using a client-side scripting language, it is possible for a ne'er-do-well to trick a user into visiting their site and have code then execute locally. When this is done, it is known as *cross-site scripting (XSS)*. As an example, UserA may get a message telling him that he needs to make changes to his XYZ account, but the link in the message is not really to the XYZ site (a phishing ploy). When he clicks the link, a JavaScript routine begins to run on his machine. Since the script is running on UserA's system, it has his permissions and can begin doing such things as running malevolent routines to send/delete/alter data.

The best protection against cross-site scripting is to disable the running of scripts.

Input Validation

Anytime a user must supply values in a session, the data entered should be validated. Many vendors, however, have fallen prey to *input validation* vulnerabilities within their code. In some instances, empty values have been accepted, while others have allowed privilege escalation if certain backdoor passwords were used.

The best protection against input-validation vulnerabilities is for developers to follow best practices and always validate all values entered. As an administrator, when you learn of an input-validation vulnerability with any application on your system, you should immediately stop using it until a patch has been released and installed.

Java Applets

A *Java applet* is a small, self-contained Java script that is downloaded from a server to a client and then run from the browser. The client browser must have the ability to run Java applets in a virtual machine on the client. Java applets are used extensively in web servers today, and they're becoming one of the most popular tools used for website development.

Java-enabled applications can accept programmed instructions (Java scripts) from a server and control certain aspects of the client environment. Java requires you to download a virtual machine in order to run the Java applications or applets. Java scripts run on the client.

The applets run in a restricted area of memory called the *sandbox*. The sandbox limits the applet's access to user areas and system resources. An applet that runs in the sandbox is considered *safe*, meaning it won't attempt to gain access to sensitive system areas. Errors in the Java virtual machine that runs in the applications may allow some applets to run outside the sandbox. When this occurs, the applet is unsafe and may perform malicious operations. Attackers on client systems have exploited this weakness. From a user's standpoint, the best defense is to make certain you run only applets from reputable sites you're familiar with. From an administrator's standpoint, you should make certain programmers adhere to programming guidelines when creating the applets.

JavaScript

JavaScript is a programming language that allows access to system resources of the system running a script. A JavaScript script is a self-contained program that can be run as an executable file in many environments. These scripts can interface with all aspects of an operating system, just as programming languages such as the C language can. This means that JavaScript scripts, when executed, can potentially damage systems or be used to send information to unauthorized persons. JavaScript scripts can be downloaded from a website and executed.

Popups

While not technically an add-in, *popups* (also known as pop-ups) are both frustrating and chancy. Whenever a user visits a website and another instance (either another tab or another browser window) is opened in the foreground, it is called a popup; if it opens in the background, it is called a popunder. Both popups and popunders open pages or sites that the user did not specifically request and may only display ads, but they might bring up undesirable applets.

Popup blockers are used to prevent both popups and popunders from appearing. While older browsers did not incorporate an option to block popups, most newer browsers now have that capability built in.

Signed Applets

Signed applets are similar to Java applets, with two key differences: A signed applet doesn't run in the Java sandbox, and it has higher system access capabilities. Signed applets aren't usually downloaded from the Internet; this type of applet is typically provided by in-house or custom-programming efforts. These applets can also include a digital signature to verify authenticity. If the applet is verified as authentic, it will be installed. Users should never download a signed applet unless they're sure the provider is trusted. A signed applet from an untrustworthy provider has the same security risks as an unsigned applet.

A vulnerability reveals itself when an applet is always assumed to be safe because it is signed. Being signed, it may have the ability to do things outside the realm of normal applets, such as execute programs. A disgruntled programmer can create a malicious signed applet and wreak havoc until stopped.

Most web browsers have settings that can be used to control Java access. This allows clients to control resource access using Java applets or scripts.

SMTP Relay

SMTP relay is a feature designed into many email servers that allows them to forward email to other email servers. Initially, the SMTP relay function was intended to help bridge traffic between systems. This capability allows email connections between systems across the Internet to be made easily.

Unfortunately, this feature has been used to generate a great deal of spam on the Internet. An email system that allows this type of forwarding to occur is referred to as an *open relay*. Unscrupulous individuals can use open relays to send advertisements and other messages through open relay servers, and they can post your mail server on lists for others to use (which could lead to your server being blacklisted). SMTP relaying should be disabled on your network unless it's limited to the email servers in your domain.

Working with File Transfer Protocol

File Transfer Protocol (FTP) was the most common protocol used to transfer files between systems on the Internet for many years, and it's available on most major server environments.

🌐 Real World Scenario

SMTP Relaying in Action

You've just received a call from a client indicating that their email server is acting peculiarly. When you arrive at the site, you notice that there are more than 20,000 emails in the outbound mail folder and that the system has no disk space available. When you shut down the email software, you delete these files and restart the email server. You see that the outbound mail folder begins to fill up again. What problem could this server be encountering?

E-marketers may be using the server as a relay. This hijacking will continue until you disable the SMTP relay capabilities in the server. Many older systems don't allow SMTP relaying to be turned off; such servers must be upgraded or replaced to prevent this from continuing.

The Internet has replaced many of the functions FTP served in the past. FTP is still commonly used, but it's becoming less popular as other methods of file downloading are made available. Most popular browsers allow an FTP site to be accessed as a website, and HTTP supports file transfer capabilities. A browser provides a graphical interface that users can use without having to be exposed to the command structure that FTP uses by default.

The following sections discuss FTP, its vulnerabilities, and ways to secure it.

Blind/Anonymous FTP

Early FTP servers didn't offer formal security—security was based on the honor system. In most cases, the honor system was used strictly for downloading files from an FTP server to a client; a client couldn't upload files without using a different logon ID. In some cases, the opposite situation existed, and a client could "blindly" upload files for others but could not download—or even see—any files.

Most logons to an FTP site used the anonymous logon; by convention, the logon ID was anonymous, and the password was the user's email address. This honor system is still used in systems that want to allow public access to files, and it simplifies administration because only one account is used.

The cost of this implementation, however, is the risk that is taken on. In this situation, the only security offered is what is configured by the operating system.

Secure FTP

Secure FTP (S/FTP or SFTP) is accomplished using a protocol called *Secure Shell (SSH)*—a type of tunneling protocol that allows access to remote systems in a secure manner. As discussed earlier, SSH allows connections to be secured by encrypting the session between the client and the server. SSH is available for Unix and other systems that provide capabilities similar to FTP.

Sharing Files

File sharing is accomplished by storing files at an assigned location on the server or workstation. When files are stored on a workstation, the connection is referred to as a *peer-to-peer connection*. The assigned location is typically a subdirectory located on one of the disk drives on the server or another workstation.

In an FTP connection, you can upload a file from a client using the PUT command. You download using the GET command. Most modern servers and applications allow an application program to access shared files at the record level. This type of sharing allows multiuser applications, such as databases, to function. Web browsers typically accept files from a web server by downloading them from the server. These downloaded files are then processed through the browser and displayed to the user.

FTP's Vulnerability

FTP has a major flaw: The user ID and password aren't encrypted and are subject to packet capture. This creates a major security breach—especially if you're connecting to an FTP server across the Internet. There is also a problem if you're allowing the use of the anonymous version of FTP: *Trivial File Transfer Protocol (TFTP)*. TFTP is a UDP-based service and has no username or password and can be used to transfer files in unattended mode.

 Real World Scenario

Remote File Transfers

Your organization has a large number of remote users who transfer files to your system across the Internet. These file transfers are an essential part of your business, and they must be allowed to continue. You want to provide additional security to your users so that information won't be compromised. How might you accomplish this?

You could implement SSH or other secure protocols for FTP file transfers. Doing so would allow information to be sent across the Internet in a secure manner. You may also be able to use TLS, SSL, or another secure format.

Understanding Network Protocols

Your network may have network protocols running in addition to TCP/IP, and each of these protocols may be vulnerable to outside attack. Some protocols (such as NetBEUI, DLC, and other more primitive protocols) aren't routable and, therefore, aren't subject to attack. Of course, there is a great big "unless": If your router or firewall is configured to pass them, some of these protocols can be imbedded in TCP/IP and may be passed to other systems.

The major protocols used by TCP/IP for maintenance and other activities include those discussed in the following list:

Simple Network Management Protocol   TCP/IP uses *Simple Network Management Protocol (SNMP)* to manage and monitor devices in a network. Many copiers, fax machines, and other smart office machines use SNMP for maintenance functions. This protocol travels through routers quite well and can be vulnerable to attack. Although such an attack might not be dangerous, think about what could happen if your printer suddenly went online and started spewing paper all over the floor.

SNMP was upgraded as a standard to SNMPv2, which provides security and improved remote monitoring. SNMP is currently undergoing a revision; although a new standard (SNMPv3) is out, most systems still use SNMPv2.

Internet Control Message Protocol   TCP/IP uses *Internet Control Message Protocol (ICMP)* to report errors and reply to requests from programs such as Ping and Traceroute. ICMP is one of the favorite protocols used for DoS attacks. Many businesses have disabled ICMP through the router to prevent these types of situations from occurring.

 Real World Scenario

Disabling ICMP to Deal with Smurf Attacks

Your organization has been repeatedly hit by smurf attacks (an attack that uses IP spoofing and broadcasting to send a ping to a group of hosts in a network). These attacks have caused a great deal of disruption, and they must be stopped. What could you suggest to minimize these attacks?

You should recommend disabling ICMP traffic at the point where your network connects to the Internet. You can do this by disabling the protocol on your router and blocking this traffic in firewall systems. Doing so won't completely eliminate the problem, but it will greatly reduce the likelihood of a successful attack occurring using ICMP. This step will also prevent people from gaining information about your network because any programs (such as Ping) that request information from your network systems will no longer function.

Internet Group Management Protocol   TCP/IP uses *Internet Group Management Protocol (IGMP)* to manage group or multicasting sessions. It can be used to address multiple recipients of a data packet: The sender initiates broadcast traffic, and any client who has broadcasting enabled receives it. (*Broadcasts* are messages sent from a single system to the entire network—the systems could be inside your network or throughout the world.) This process, called *multicasting*, can consume huge amounts of bandwidth in a network and possibly create a DoS situation. Most network administrators disable the reception of broadcast and multicast traffic from outside their local network.

A *unicast* is IGMP traffic that is oriented at a single system. TCP/IP primarily uses a unicast method of communication: A message is sent from a single system to another single system.

Every one of these major protocols used by TCP/IP presents a potential problem for security administrators. Make sure you use what you need and disable what you don't.

Summary

In this chapter, I covered ports and sockets. Sockets are the primary method used to communicate with services and applications. Sockets are changeable for special configurations and additional security.

Network monitors are primarily troubleshooting tools, and they can be used to eavesdrop on networks. Intrusion detection systems take an active role and can control traffic and systems. IDSs use extensive rule-based procedures to check audit files and network traffic, and they can make decisions based on those rules. In conjunction with a firewall, an IDS can offer high levels of security.

Exam Essentials

Familiarize yourself with the technologies used by TCP/IP and the Internet.   IP addresses and port numbers are combined to create an interface called a socket. Most TCP and UDP protocols communicate using this socket as the primary interface mechanism. Clients and servers communicate using ports. Ports can be changed to enhance security. Web services use HTML and other technologies to allow rich and animated websites. These technologies potentially create security problems because they may have individual vulnerabilities. Verify the problems that exist from a security perspective before enabling these technologies on your systems.

Be able to describe the primary methods used for network monitoring.   The primary methods used for network monitoring are sniffers and IDSs. Sniffers are passive and can provide real-time displays of network traffic. They're intended to be used primarily for troubleshooting purposes, but they're one of the tools used by attackers to determine what protocols and systems you're running. IDSs are active devices that operate to alert administrators of attacks and unusual events. This is accomplished by automatically reviewing log files and system traffic and by applying rules that dictate how to react to events. An IDS, when used in conjunction with firewalls, can provide excellent security for a network.

Be able to identify and describe the two types of intrusion detection systems in use. The two types of IDSs in use are host-based (HIDS) and network-based (NIDS). Host-based IDS works strictly on the system on which it's installed. Network-based IDS monitors the entire network.

Be able to identify and explain the terms and functions in an IDS environment. These terms include *activity*, *administrator*, *alert*, *analyzer*, *data source*, *event*, *manager*, *notification*, *operator*, and *sensor*. For simplicity's sake, some of these systems are combined in IDSs, but they're all functions that must be performed to be effective.

Know the difference between an active response and a passive response. An active response allows an IDS to manage resources in the network if an incident occurs. Passive responses involve notification and reporting of attacks or suspicious activities.

Be able to explain the purpose of a honeypot. A honeypot is a system that is intended to be used to gather information or designed to be broken. Honeypot systems are used to gather evidence in an investigation and to study attack strategies.

Review Questions

1. In order for network monitoring to work properly, you need a PC and a network card running in what mode?

   A. Launch

   B. Exposed

   C. Promiscuous

   D. Sweep

2. Which Linux utility can show if there is more than one set of documentation on the system for a command you are trying to find information on?

   A. Lookaround

   B. Howmany

   C. Whereall

   D. Whatis

3. In intrusion detection system parlance, which account is responsible for setting the security policy for an organization?

   A. Supervisor

   B. Administrator

   C. Root

   D. Director

4. Which of the following IDS types looks for things outside of the ordinary?

   A. Incongruity-based

   B. Variance-based

   C. Anomaly-based

   D. Difference-based

5. Which of the following copies the traffic from all ports to a single port and disallows bidirectional traffic on that port?

   A. Port spanning

   B. Socket blending

   C. Straddling

   D. Amalgamation

6. Which of the following implies ignoring an attack and is a common response?

   A. Eschewing

   B. Spurning

   C. Shirking

   D. Shunning

7. Which IDS system uses algorithms to analyze the traffic passing through the network?

    A. Arithmetical

    B. Algebraic

    C. Statistical

    D. Heuristic

8. Which of the following utilities can be used in Linux to view a list of users' failed authentication attempts?

    A. `badlog`

    B. `faillog`

    C. `wronglog`

    D. `killlog`

9. Which of the following is the process in which a law enforcement officer or a government agent encourages or induces a person to commit a crime when the potential criminal expresses a desire not to go ahead?

    A. Enticement

    B. Entrapment

    C. Deceit

    D. Sting

10. The IDS console is known as what?

    A. Manager

    B. Window

    C. Dashboard

    D. Screen

11. Sockets are a combination of the IP address and which of the following?

    A. Port

    B. MAC address

    C. NIC setting

    D. NetBIOS ID

12. Which type of active response fools the attacker into thinking the attack is succeeding while the system monitors the activity and potentially redirects the attacker to a system that is designed to be broken?

    A. Pretexting

    B. Shamming

    C. Deception

    D. Scamming

13. Which device monitors network traffic in a passive manner?

    A. Sniffer

    B. IDS

    C. Firewall

    D. Web browser

14. Security has become the utmost priority at your organization. You're no longer content to act reactively to incidents when they occur—you want to start acting more proactively. Which system performs active network monitoring and analysis and can take proactive steps to protect a network?

    A. IDS

    B. Sniffer

    C. Router

    D. Switch

15. Which of the following can be used to monitor a network for unauthorized activity? (Choose two.)

    A. Network sniffer

    B. NIDS

    C. HIDS

    D. VPN

16. You're the administrator for Acme Widgets. After attending a conference on buzzwords for management, your boss informs you that an IDS should be up and running on the network by the end of the week. Which of the following systems should be installed on a host to provide IDS capabilities?

    A. Network sniffer

    B. NIDS

    C. HIDS

    D. VPN

17. Which of the following is an active response in an IDS?

    A. Sending an alert to a console

    B. Shunning

    C. Reconfiguring a router to block an IP address

    D. Making an entry in the security audit file

18. A junior administrator bursts into your office with a report in his hand. He claims that he has found documentation proving that an intruder has been entering the network on a regular basis. Which of the following implementations of IDS detects intrusions based on previously established rules that are in place on your network?

  A. MD-IDS

  B. AD-IDS

  C. HIDS

  D. NIDS

19. Which IDS function evaluates data collected from sensors?

  A. Operator

  B. Manager

  C. Alert

  D. Analyzer

20. What is a system that is intended or designed to be broken into by an attacker called?

  A. Honeypot

  B. Honeybucket

  C. Decoy

  D. Spoofing system

Answers to Review Questions

1. C. In order for network monitoring to work properly, you need a PC and a network card running in promiscuous mode.

2. D. In Linux, the `whatis` utility can show if there is more than one set of documentation on the system for a command you are trying to find information on.

3. B. The administrator is the person/account responsible for setting the security policy for an organization.

4. C. An anomaly-detection IDS (AD-IDS) looks for anomalies, meaning it looks for things outside of the ordinary.

5. A. Port spanning (also known as port mirroring) copies the traffic from all ports to a single port and disallows bidirectional traffic on that port.

6. D. Shunning, or ignoring an attack, is a common response.

7. D. A heuristic system uses algorithms to analyze the traffic passing through the network.

8. B. Use the `faillog` utility in Linux to view a list of users' failed authentication attempts.

9. B. Entrapment is the process in which a law enforcement officer or a government agent encourages or induces a person to commit a crime when the potential criminal expresses a desire not to go ahead.

10. A. The IDS console is known as the manager.

11. A. Sockets are a combination of the IP address and the port.

12. C. A deception active response fools the attacker into thinking the attack is succeeding while the system monitors the activity and potentially redirects the attacker to a system that is designed to be broken.

13. A. Sniffers monitor network traffic and display traffic in real time. Sniffers, also called network monitors, were originally designed for network maintenance and troubleshooting.

14. A. An IDS is used to protect and report network abnormalities to a network administrator or system. It works with audit files and rule-based processing to determine how to act in the event of an unusual situation on the network.

15. A, B. Network sniffers and NIDSs are used to monitor network traffic. Network sniffers are manually oriented, whereas an NIDS can be automated.

16. C. A host-based IDS (HIDS) is installed on each host that needs IDS capabilities.

17. C. Dynamically changing the system's configuration to protect the network or a system is an active response.

18. A. By comparing attack signatures and audit trails, a misuse-detection IDS determines whether an attack is occurring.

19. D. The analyzer function uses data sources from sensors to analyze and determine whether an attack is under way.

20. A. A honeypot is a system that is intended to be sacrificed in the name of knowledge. Honeypot systems allow investigators to evaluate and analyze the attack strategies used. Law enforcement agencies use honeypots to gather evidence for prosecution.

Chapter

4

Threats and Vulnerabilities

THE FOLLOWING COMPTIA SECURITY+ EXAM OBJECTIVES ARE COVERED IN THIS CHAPTER:

✓ **3.1 Analyze and differentiate among types of malware.**

- Adware
- Virus
- Worms
- Spyware
- Trojan
- Rootkits
- Backdoors
- Logic bomb
- Botnets

✓ **3.2 Analyze and differentiate among types of attacks.**

- Man-in-the-middle
- DDoS
- DoS
- Replay
- Smurf attack
- Spoofing
- Spam
- Phishing
- Spim
- Spear phishing

- Xmas attack

- Pharming

- Privilege escalation

- DNS poisoning and ARP poisoning

✓ **3.3 Analyze and differentiate among types of social engineering attacks.**

- Hoaxes

As we discussed in the first chapter, everywhere you turn there are risks; they begin the minute you first turn a computer on and grow exponentially the moment the network card becomes active. While Chapter 1 discussed how to measure and weigh risks, and Chapters 3 and 4 looked at network dangers, this chapter will focus on two particular types of risks: malware and attacks.

In the case of malware, you are exposed to situations because of software that is running on your system—sometimes not intentionally creating vulnerabilities, but there nevertheless. In the case of attacks, someone is purposely targeting your system(s) and trying to do you harm.

In this chapter, we'll look at malware and several different types of attacks, as well as some of the reasons your network may be vulnerable. This list is far from inclusive because new variants of each are being created by miscreants on a regular basis. The list is thorough, however, on two counts: It includes everything CompTIA expects you to know for the exam, and many of the new malware and attack variants are simply newer modifications, or implementations, of those listed here.

Understanding Software Exploitation

The term *software exploitation* refers to attacks launched against applications and higher-level services. They include gaining access to data using weaknesses in the data access objects of a database or a flaw in a service or application. This section briefly outlines common exploitations that have been successful in the past. The following exploitations can be introduced using viruses, as in the case of the Klez32 virus, or by using access attacks:

Database Exploitation Many database products allow sophisticated access queries to be made in the client/server environment. If a client session can be hijacked or spoofed, the attacker can formulate queries against the database that disclose unauthorized information. For this attack to be successful, the attacker must first gain access to the environment through one of the attacks outlined later in this chapter.

Application Exploitation The macro virus is another example of software exploitation. A macro virus is a set of programming instructions in a language such as VBScript that commands an application to perform illicit actions. Users want more powerful tools, and manufacturers want to sell users what they want. The macro virus takes advantage of the power offered by word processors, spreadsheets, or other applications. This exploitation is inherent in the product, and all users are susceptible to it unless they disable all macros.

Email Exploitation Hardly a day goes by without another email virus being reported. This is a result of a weakness in many common email clients. Modern email clients offer many shortcuts, lists, and other capabilities to meet user demands. A popular exploitation of email clients involves accessing the client address book and propagating viruses. There is virtually nothing a client user can do about these exploitations, although antivirus software that integrates with your email client does offer some protection. To be truly successful, the software manufacturer must fix the weaknesses—an example is Outlook's option to protect against access to the address book. This type of weakness isn't a bug, in many cases, but a feature that users wanted.

Teach users to exercise discretion when opening any email attachment.

Spyware *Spyware* differs from other malware in that it works—often actively—on behalf of a third party. Rather than self-replicating, like viruses and worms, spyware is spread to machines by users who inadvertently ask for it. The users often do not know they have asked for it but have acquired it by downloading other programs, visiting infected sites, and so on.

The spyware program monitors the user's activity and responds by offering unsolicited pop-up advertisements (which fit into the category described next known as *adware*), gathers information about the user to pass on to marketers, or intercepts personal data such as credit card numbers. One thing separating spyware from most other malware is that it almost always exists to provide commercial gain. The operating systems from Microsoft are the ones most affected by spyware, and Microsoft released Microsoft AntiSpyware (now known as Windows Defender) to combat the problem as well as set up the SpyNet community. In Exercise 4.1, I'll show you how to join the Microsoft SpyNet using Windows Defender.

EXERCISE 4.1

Join Microsoft SpyNet Using Windows Defender

Versions of Windows from XP on have included, or had available, Windows Defender. This spyware/adware interface works similar to most antivirus programs and uses a definition file that must be updated regularly to locate malware. It provides a number of options, including the ability to join Microsoft SpyNet, a community devoted to stopping spyware infections.

The exercise walks through the steps of using Windows Defender to join the community:

1. Click the Windows Start button.

2. Type **Windows Defender** in the Start Search box, and choose it from the programs that appear. If it is not currently running, click the link to turn it on.

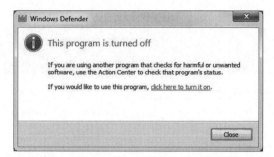

3. In Windows Defender, click Tools.

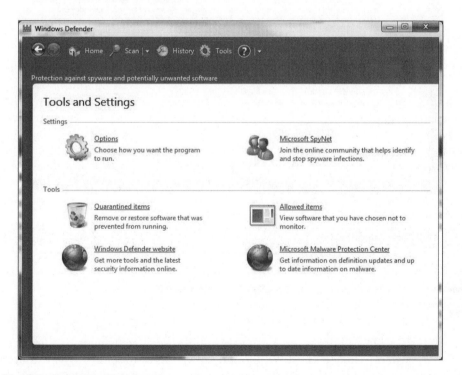

4. Click Microsoft SpyNet.

EXERCISE 4.1 *(continued)*

5. If Join With A Basic Membership or Join With An Advanced Membership is not already selected, read the options and make the choice you are comfortable with.

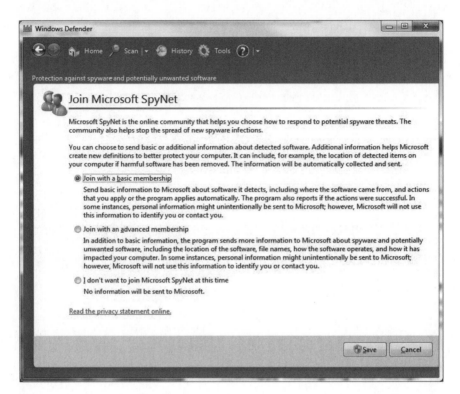

6. Click Save.

7. Exit Windows Defender.

 IPv4 and IPv6 were discussed in Chapter 2.

Adware   If the primary purpose of a spyware application is to deliver ads, then it is classified as adware. Make no mistake about it, adware is a subset of spyware and thus can have the same qualities, but the primary purpose in this case is to display ads and generate revenue for the creator. Because spyware and adware share the same features, Windows Defender (available for operating systems from Windows XP on) can be used as a first line of defense.

New Attacks on the Way

The discussion of attacks in this chapter isn't comprehensive. New methods for dealing with and counteracting attacks are being developed even as you read this book. Your first challenge when confronting an attack is to recognize that you're fighting the battle on two fronts:

- The first front involves the inherent open nature of TCP/IP and its protocol suite. TCP/IP is a robust and rich environment. This richness allows many opportunities to exploit the vulnerabilities of the protocol suite.

- The second front of this battle involves the implementation of TCP/IP by various vendors. A weak TCP/IP implementation will be susceptible to all forms of attacks, and there is little you'll be able to do about it except to complain to the software manufacturer.

Fortunately, most of the credible manufacturers are now taking these complaints seriously and doing what they can to close the holes they have created in your systems. Keep your updates current because this is where most of the corrections for security problems are implemented.

Rootkits   Recently, *rootkits* have become the software exploitation program du jour. Rootkits are software programs that have the ability to hide certain things from the operating system. With a rootkit, there may be a number of processes running on a system that do not show up in Task Manager or connections established or available that do not appear in a `netstat` display—the rootkit masks the presence of these items. The rootkit is able to do this by manipulating function calls to the operating system and filtering out information that would normally appear. Theoretically, rootkits could hide anywhere there is enough memory to reside: video cards, PCI cards, and the like. In Exercise 4.2, I'll show you how to view running processes on a Windows-based machine, and in Exercise 4.3, I'll do the same on a Linux-based machine.

Unfortunately, many rootkits are written to get around antivirus and antispyware programs that are not kept up-to-date. The best defense you have is to monitor what your system is doing and catch the rootkit in the process of installation.

EXERCISE 4.2

View Running Processes on a Windows-Based Machine

As an administrator, you need to know what processes are running on a machine at any given time. In addition to the programs that a user may be using, there are always many others that are required by the operating system, the network, or other applications.

All recent versions of Windows include Task Manager to allow you to see what is running. To access this information, follow these steps:

1. Right-click an empty location in the Windows Taskbar.

2. Choose either Task Manager or Start Task Manager (depending on the Windows version you are running) from the pop-up menu that appears.

3. The Task Manager opens to Applications by default and shows what the user is actually using. Click the Processes tab. Information about the programs that are needed for the running applications is shown, as well as all other processes running.

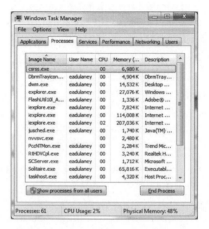

4. If the Show Processes From All Users check box appears beneath this tab, click it. Many of the names of the processes appear cryptic, but definitions for most (good and bad) can be found at http://www.liutilities.com/products/wintaskspro/processlibrary.

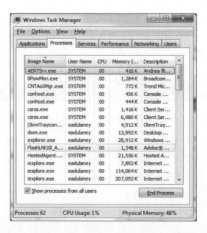

EXERCISE 4.2 *(continued)*

5. Examine the list and look for anything out of the ordinary. After doing this a few times, you will become familiar with what is normally there and will be able to spot oddities quickly.

6. Notice the values in the CPU column. Those values will always total 100, with System Idle Processes typically making up the bulk. High numbers on another process can indicate that there is a problem with it. If the numbers do not add up to 100, it can be a sign that a rootkit is masking some of the display.

7. If you are running Windows Vista, click the button Show Processes From All Users. The UAC will ask you to confirm the action; click Continue.

8. Click the top of the second column where it says User Name to order the list alphabetically by this field.

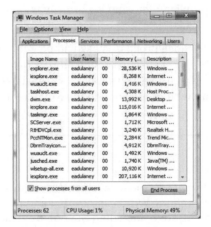

9. Scroll to where the SYSTEM entries begin and look for anything suspicious there.

10. Close Task Manager.

EXERCISE 4.3

View Running Processing on a Linux-Based Machine

Most versions of Linux include a graphical utility to allow you to see the running processes. Those utilities differ based on the distribution of Linux you are using and the desktop that you have chosen.

EXERCISE 4.3 *(continued)*

All versions of Linux, however, do offer a command line and the ability to use the ps utility. Because of that, this method is employed in this exercise. To access this information, follow these steps:

1. Open a shell window, or otherwise access a command prompt.

2. Type **ps −ef | more**.

3. The display shows the processes running for all users. The names of the processes appear in the rightmost column, and the processor time will be in the column closest to it. The names are cryptic, but definitions for most can be found by using the **man** command followed by the name of the process. Those that are application specific can usually be found through a web search.

4. Examine the list and look for anything out of the ordinary. After doing this a few times, you will become familiar with what is normally there and will be able to spot oddities quickly.

5. Pay particular attention to those processes associated with the root user (the user appears in the first column). Because the root user has the power to do anything, only necessary daemons and processes should be associated with that user. You can look only at those running with association to the root user by typing **ps −u root**.

6. Exit the shell.

As these new threats have developed, so have some excellent programs for countering them. Within any search engine, you can find a rootkit analyzer for your system, including Spybot, Spyware Doctor, and Ad-Aware. There are also a number of products that specialize in integrity verification, such as those from Tripwire (http://www.tripwire.com).

One of the most important measures you can take to proactively combat software attacks is to know common file extensions and the applications they're associated with. For example, the .scr filename extension is used for screensavers, and viruses are often distributed through the use of these files. No legitimate user should be sending screensavers via email to your users, and all attachments with the .scr filename extension should be banned from entering the network.

Table 4.1, while not comprehensive, contains the most common filename extensions for files that should and should not, as a general rule, be allowed into the network as email attachments.

TABLE 4.1   Common filename extensions for email attachments

Should Be Allowed	Should *Not* Be Allowed
.doc/docx	.bat
.pdf	.com
.txt	.exe
.xls/xlsx	.hlp
.zip	.pif
	.scr

If there is any one file extension that belongs in both columns in Table 4.1, it is .pdf. For years, .pdf files have been preferred over most others since they essentially hold a snapshot of the documents created with other programs and have been thought to be safer than the original files (which could be stuffed with macros). As the complexity of Adobe Acrobat has increased, however, so has the ability to create malware .pdf files; one example of this is the GhostRat Trojan, which allows attackers to take advantage of the Remote Administration Tool (see http://www.symantec.com/connect/blogs/rise-pdf-malware).

Surviving Malicious Code

Malicious code refers to a broad category of software threats to your network and systems, including viruses, Trojan horses, logic bombs, and worms.

Your users depend on you to help keep them safe from harm and to repulse these attacks. When successful, these attacks can be devastating to systems, and they can spread through an entire network. One such incident involved the Conficker worm that spread rapidly through PCs running Microsoft operating systems in late 2008. This is considered the largest worm infestation to date, and variants of it are still propagating through the Internet.

The following sections will briefly introduce you to the types of malicious code you'll encounter. I'll also explain the importance of antivirus software.

Viruses

A *virus* is a piece of software designed to infect a computer system. Under the best of circumstances, a virus may do nothing more than reside on the computer, but it may also damage the data on your hard disk drive (HDD), destroy your operating system, and possibly spread to other systems. Viruses get into your computer in one of three ways:

- On contaminated media (DVD, USB drive, or CD-ROM)

- Through email and social networking sites

- As part of another program

    Viruses can be classified as:

    Polymorphic—those that change form in order to avoid detection

    Stealth—those that attempt to avoid detection by masking themselves from applications

    Retroviruses—attacks or bypasses the antivirus software installed on a computer

    Multipartite—attacks your system in multiple ways

    Armored—one that is designed to make itself difficult to detect or analyze

    Companion—attaches itself to legitimate programs and then creates a program with a different filename extension

    Phage—one that modifies and alters other programs and databases

    Macro viruses—those that exploit the enhancements made to many application programs, which are used by programmers to expand the capability of applications

    Each type of virus has a different attack strategy and different consequences.

 Estimates for losses due to viruses are in the billions of dollars. These losses include financial loss as well as lost productivity.

The following sections will introduce the general symptoms of a virus infection, explain how a virus works, and describe the types of viruses you can expect to encounter and how they generally behave. I'll also discuss how a virus is transmitted through a network and look at a few hoaxes.

Symptoms of a Virus Infection

Many viruses will announce that you're infected as soon as they gain access to your system. They may take control of your system and flash annoying messages on your screen or destroy your hard disk. When this occurs, you'll know that you're a victim. Other viruses will cause your system to slow down, cause files to disappear from your computer, or take over your disk space.

You should look for some of the following symptoms when determining if a virus infection has occurred:

- The programs on your system start to load more slowly. This happens because the virus is spreading to other files in your system or is taking over system resources.

- Unusual files appear on your hard drive, or files start to disappear from your system. Many viruses delete key files in your system to render it inoperable.

- Program sizes change from the installed versions. This occurs because the virus is attaching itself to these programs on your disk.

- Your browser, word processing application, or other software begins to exhibit unusual operating characteristics. Screens or menus may change.

- The system mysteriously shuts itself down or starts itself up and does a great deal of unanticipated disk activity.

- You mysteriously lose access to a disk drive or other system resources. The virus has changed the settings on a device to make it unusable.

- Your system suddenly doesn't reboot or gives unexpected error messages during startup.

This list is by no means comprehensive but is a good start to determining if your computer has been infected.

How Viruses Work

A virus, in most cases, tries to accomplish one of two things: render your system inoperable or spread to other systems. Many viruses will spread to other systems given the chance and then render your system unusable. This is common with many of the newer viruses.

If your system is infected, the virus may try to attach itself to every file in your system and spread each time you send a file or document to other users. Figure 4.1 shows a virus spreading from an infected system either through a network or by removable media. When you give removable media to another user or put it into another system, you then infect that system with the virus.

FIGURE 4.1 Virus spreading from an infected system using the network or removable media

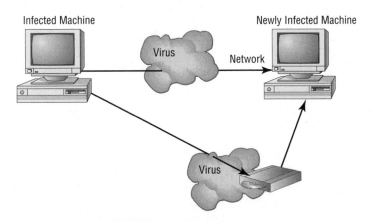

Many viruses spread using email. The infected system attaches a file to any email that you send to another user. The recipient opens this file, thinking it's something you legitimately sent them. When they open the file, the virus infects the target system. The virus might then attach itself to all the emails the newly infected system sends, which in turn infects the recipients of the emails. Figure 4.2 shows how a virus can spread from a single user to literally thousands of users in a very short time using email.

FIGURE 4.2 An email virus spreading geometrically to other users

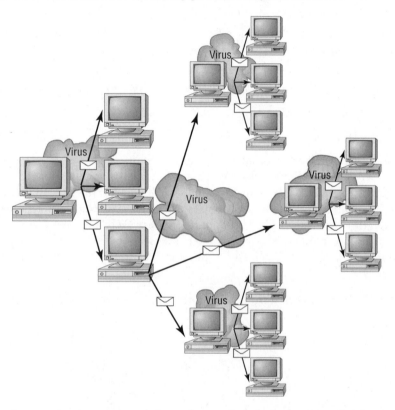

Quite a few newer viruses spread through USB thumb drives. An employee may see one lying about and plug it into a machine without realizing that it could contain a virus. This is such a problem that the Department of Defense has banned the use of thumb drives.

 For more information on thumb drives and viruses, see http://www.tomshardware.com/news/usb-flash-virus-secure,6564.html.

Types of Viruses

Viruses take many different forms. The following sections briefly introduce these forms and explain how they work. These are the most common types, but this isn't a comprehensive list.

The best defense against a virus attack is up-to-date antivirus software installed and running. The software should be on all workstations as well as the server.

Armored Virus   An *armored virus* is designed to make itself difficult to detect or analyze. Armored viruses cover themselves with protective code that stops debuggers or disassemblers from examining critical elements of the virus. The virus may be written in such a way that some aspects of the programming act as a decoy to distract analysis while the actual code hides in other areas in the program.

From the perspective of the creator, the more time it takes to deconstruct the virus, the longer it can live. The longer it can live, the more time it has to replicate and spread to as many machines as possible. The key to stopping most viruses is to identify them quickly and educate administrators about them—the very things that the armor intensifies the difficulty of accomplishing.

Companion Virus   A *companion virus* attaches itself to legitimate programs and then creates a program with a different filename extension. This file may reside in your system's temporary directory. When a user types the name of the legitimate program, the companion virus executes instead of the real program. This effectively hides the virus from the user. Many of the viruses that are used to attack Windows systems make changes to program pointers in the Registry so that they point to the infected program. The infected program may perform its dirty deed and then start the real program.

Macro Virus   A *macro virus* exploits the enhancements made to many application programs, which are used by programmers to expand the capability of applications such as Word and Excel. Word, for example, supports a mini-BASIC programming language that allows files to be manipulated automatically. These programs in the document are called *macros*. For example, a macro can tell your word processor to spell-check your document automatically when it opens. Macro viruses can infect all the documents on your system and spread to other systems via email or other methods. Macro viruses are the fastest-growing exploitation today.

Multipartite Virus   A *multipartite virus* attacks your system in multiple ways. It may attempt to infect your boot sector, infect all of your executable files, and destroy your application files. The hope here is that you won't be able to correct all the problems and will allow the infestation to continue. The multipartite virus in Figure 4.3 attacks your boot sector, infects application files, and attacks your Microsoft Word documents.

Phage Virus   A *phage virus* modifies and alters other programs and databases. The virus infects all of these files. The only way to remove this virus is to reinstall the programs that are infected. If you miss even a single incident of this virus on the victim system, the process will start again and infect the system once more.

Polymorphic Virus   *Polymorphic viruses* change form in order to avoid detection. These types of viruses attack your system, display a message on your computer, and delete files on your system. The virus will attempt to hide from your antivirus software.

Frequently, the virus will encrypt parts of itself to avoid detection. When the virus does this, it's referred to as *mutation*. The mutation process makes it hard for antivirus software to detect common characteristics of the virus. Figure 4.4 uses a phrase to illustrate how the polymorphic virus changes characteristics to avoid detection. Like the phrase, small things within the virus are changed. In this example, the virus changes a signature to fool antivirus software.

FIGURE 4.3   A multipartite virus commencing an attack on a system

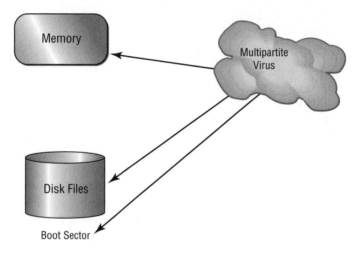

FIGURE 4.4   The polymorphic virus changing its characteristics

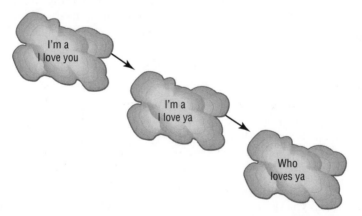

Retrovirus   A *retrovirus* attacks or bypasses the antivirus software installed on a computer. You can consider a retrovirus to be an anti-antivirus. Retroviruses can directly attack your antivirus software and potentially destroy the virus definition database file. Destroying this

information without your knowledge would leave you with a false sense of security. The virus may also directly attack an antivirus program to create bypasses for itself.

Stealth Virus   A *stealth virus* attempts to avoid detection by masking itself from applications. It may attach itself to the boot sector of the hard drive. When a system utility or program runs, the stealth virus redirects commands around itself in order to avoid detection. An infected file may report a file size different from what is actually present in order to avoid detection. Figure 4.5 shows a stealth virus attaching itself to the boot sector to avoid detection. Stealth viruses may also move themselves from fileA to fileB during a virus scan for the same reason.

An updated list of the most active viruses and spyware is on the Panda Software site at http://www.pandasecurity.com/homeusers/security-info/default.aspx?lst=ac.

FIGURE 4.5   A stealth virus hiding in a disk boot sector

This is a disk

Boot Record | Virus

Present Virus Activity

New viruses and threats are released on a regular basis to join the cadre of those already in existence. From an exam perspective, you need only be familiar with the world as it existed at the time the questions were written. From an administration standpoint, however, you need to know what is happening today. This book is current for virus activity up to the date of writing, but you should stay up to date on what has happened since then.

To find this information, visit the CERT/CC Current Activity web page at http://www .us-cert.gov/current/current_activity.html. Here you'll find a detailed description of the most current viruses as well as links to pages on older threats.

Identifying Virus Hoaxes

Network users have plenty of real viruses to worry about. Yet some people find it entertaining to issue phony threats to keep people on their toes. Some of the more popular hoaxes that have been passed around are the Good Time and the Irina viruses. Millions of users received emails about these two viruses, and the symptoms sounded awful.

Both of these viruses claimed to do things that are impossible to accomplish with a virus. When you receive a virus warning, you can verify its authenticity by looking on the website of the antivirus software you use, or you can go to several public systems. One of the more helpful sites to visit to get the status of the latest viruses is the CERT organization (`www.cert .org`). CERT monitors and tracks viruses and provides regular reports on this site.

> Though the names are similar, there is a difference between `cert.org` and `us-cert.gov`. While the latter is a government site for the United States Computer Emergency Readiness Team, the former is a federally funded research and development center at Carnegie Mellon University.

When you receive an email you suspect is a hoax, check the CERT site before forwarding the message to anyone else. The creator of the hoax wants to create widespread panic, and if you blindly forward the message to coworkers and acquaintances, you're helping the creator accomplish this task. For example, any email that says "forward to all your friends" is a candidate for hoax research. Disregarding the hoax allows it to die a quick death and keeps users focused on productive tasks. Any concept that spreads quickly through the Internet is referred to as a *meme*.

> Symantec and other vendors maintain pages devoted to bogus hoaxes (`www.symantec.com/business/security_response/threatexplorer/ risks/hoaxes.jsp`). You can always check there to verify whether an email you've received is indeed a hoax.

Managing Spam to Avoid Viruses

While *spam* is not truly a virus or a hoax, it is one of the most annoying things an administrator can contend with. Spam is defined as any unwanted, unsolicited email, and not only can the sheer volume of it be irritating, but it can also often open the door to larger problems. For instance, some of the sites advertised in spam may be infected with viruses, worms, and other unwanted programs. If users begin to respond to spam by visiting those sites, then viruses and other problems will multiply in your system.

> There are numerous antispam programs available and they can be run by users as well as administrators. One of the biggest problems with many of these applications is false positives: They will occasionally flag legitimate email as spam and stop it from being delivered. You should routinely check your spam folders and make sure legitimate email is not being flagged and held there.

Just as you can, and must, install good antivirus software programs, you should also consider similar measures for spam. Filtering the messages out and preventing them from ever entering the network is the most effective method of dealing with the problem. Recently, the word *spam* has found its way into other forms of unwanted messaging beyond email, giving birth to the acronyms SPIM (spam over Instant Messaging) and SPIT (spam over Internet Telephony).

Trojan Horses

Trojan horses are programs that enter a system or network under the guise of another program. A Trojan horse may be included as an attachment or as part of an installation program. The Trojan horse could create a backdoor or replace a valid program during installation. It would then accomplish its mission under the guise of another program. Trojan horses can be used to compromise the security of your system, and they can exist on a system for years before they're detected.

Trojans Today

An area in which Trojan horses have been cropping up recently is with social networking. The Boonana Trojan began cropping up in Facebook and affecting both Mac OS X and Windows-based systems in 2010. A message would appear asking the user if it was them in a video and including a link. Clicking to run the video triggered a Java applet that would then redirect legitimate requests to known malware servers.

Another successful Trojan of recent years is Ghost Rat, which exploits the remote administration feature in Windows-based operating systems (the "Rat" stands for Remote Administration Tool) and allows miscreants to record audio and video remotely.

The best preventive measure for Trojan horses is to not allow them entry into your system. Immediately before and after you install a new software program or operating system, back it up! If you suspect a Trojan horse, you can reinstall the original programs, which should delete the Trojan horse. A port scan may also reveal a Trojan horse on your system. If an application opens a TCP or UDP port that isn't regularly used in your network, you can notice this and begin corrective action.

Is a Trojan horse also a virus? A Trojan horse is anything that sneaks in under the guise of something else. Given that general definition, it's certainly possible that a virus can (and usually does) sneak in, but this description most often fits the definition of a companion virus. The primary distinction, from an exam perspective, is that with a Trojan horse you always intentionally obtained something (usually an application) and didn't know an unpleasant freeloader was hidden within. An example is spyware, which is often installed (unknown to you) as part of another application.

Logic Bombs

Logic bombs are programs or snippets of code that execute when a certain predefined event occurs. A bomb may send a note to an attacker when a user is logged on to the Internet and is using a word processor. This message informs the attacker that the user is ready for an attack.

Figure 4.6 shows a logic bomb in operation. Notice that this bomb doesn't begin the attack but tells the attacker that the victim has met the needed criteria or state for an attack to begin. Logic bombs may also be set to go off on a certain date or when a specified set of circumstances occurs.

FIGURE 4.6   A logic bomb being initiated

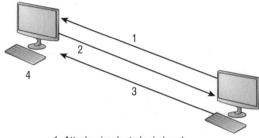

1. Attacker implants logic bomb.
2. Victim reports installation.
3. Attacker sends attack message.
4. Victim does as logic bomb indicates.

In the attack depicted in Figure 4.6, the logic bomb sends a message back to the attacking system that it has loaded successfully. The victim system can then be used to initiate an attack such as a DDoS attack, or it can grant access at the time of the attacker's choosing.

Worms

A *worm* is different from a virus in that it can reproduce itself, it's self-contained, and it doesn't need a host application to be transported. Many of the so-called viruses that have made the papers and media were, in actuality, worms and not viruses. However, it's possible for a worm to contain or deliver a virus to a target system.

> The Melissa virus (which was actually a worm) spread itself to more than 100,000 users in a relatively short period when it first came out, according to CERT. One site received more than 32,000 copies of the Melissa virus in a 45-minute period.

Worms by their nature and origin are supposed to propagate and will use whatever services they're capable of to do that. Early worms filled up memory and bred inside the RAM of the target computer. Worms can use TCP/IP, email, Internet services, or any number of means to reach their target.

Antivirus Software

The primary method of preventing the propagation of malicious code involves the use of *antivirus software*. Antivirus software is an application that is installed on a system to protect it and to scan for viruses as well as worms and Trojan horses. Most viruses have characteristics that are common to families of virus. Antivirus software looks for these characteristics, or fingerprints, to identify and neutralize viruses before they impact you. Most of the newer antivirus packages will now look for problems with cookies as well, as shown in the Norton Security Suite example in Figure 4.7.

FIGURE 4.7   Antivirus programs often look for problems with much more than just viruses.

More than 60,000 known viruses, worms, logic bombs, and other malicious code have been defined. New ones are added all the time. Your antivirus software manufacturer will usually work very hard to keep the definition database files current. The definition database file contains all of the known viruses and countermeasures for a particular antivirus software product. You probably won't receive a virus that hasn't been seen by one of these companies. If you keep the virus definition database files in your software up-to-date, you probably won't be overly vulnerable to attacks.

The best method of protection is to use a layered approach. Antivirus software should be at the gateways, at the servers, and at the desktop. If you want to go one step further, you can use software at each location from different vendors to make sure you're covered from all angles.

The second method of preventing viruses is education. Teach your users not to open suspicious files and to open only those files that they're reasonably sure are virus free. They need to scan every disk, email, and document they receive before they open them. You should also verify that security settings are high within the applications your users are using. Figure 4.8, for example, shows the macro settings that can be applied to Microsoft Word 2010.

FIGURE 4.8   In Microsoft Office 2010 applications, choose to disable macros to increase security.

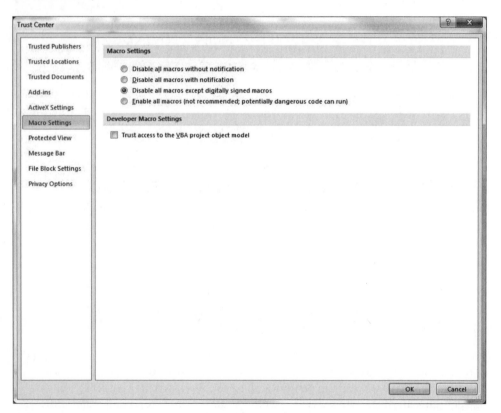

Using Microsoft Word 2010 as an example, in addition to the macro settings shown in Figure 4.8, the Protected View settings allow you to choose to open "potentially dangerous files" in protected view to minimize threats. The File Block Settings are where you define which file types qualify for opening in that Protected View. These settings are reached by choosing Options from the Word menu, choosing Trust Center, and then clicking the Trust Center Settings button.

 Real World Scenario

How to Stop A Virus/Worm That Is Out of Control

A large private university has over 30,000 students taking online classes. These students use a variety of systems and network connections. The instructors of this university are being routinely hit with the Klez32 virus. Klez32 (specifically, in this case, the W32/Klez.mm virus) is a well-known and documented virus. It uses Outlook or Outlook Express to spread. It grabs a name randomly from the address book and uses that name in the header. The worm part of it then uses a mini-mailer and mails the virus to all the people in the address book. When one of these users opens the file, the worm attempts to disable their antivirus software and spread to other systems. Doing so opens the system to an attack from other viruses, which might follow later.

You've been appointed to the IT department at this school, and you've been directed to solve this problem. Take a moment to ponder what you can do about it.

If you think the best solution would be to install antivirus software that scans and blocks all emails that come through the school's servers, you are right. You should also inspect outgoing email and notify all internal users of the system when they attempt to send a virus-infected document using the server.

These two steps—installing antivirus scanners on the external and internal connections and notifying unsuspecting senders—would greatly reduce the likelihood that the virus could attack either student or instructor computers.

Calculating Attack Strategies

In computing, a lot of the terminology used comes from other fields, such as the military. That seems to be particularly true when it comes to security. Using that line of logic, an *attack* occurs when an unauthorized individual or group of individuals attempts to access, modify, or damage your systems or environment. These attacks can be fairly simple and unfocused, or they can appear to be almost blitzkrieg-like in their intensity.

One main reason for the differences in attacks is that they occur in many ways and for different reasons. Regardless of how they occur, they are generally used to accomplish one or more of these three goals:

Access attack—This occurs when someone who does not have permission to access resources attempts to gain access.

Modification and repudiation attack—This occurs when someone wants to modify information in your systems.

Denial-of-service (DoS) attack—This is an attempt to disrupt your network and services. When your system becomes so busy responding to illegitimate requests, it can prevent authorized users from having access.

Attackers have various reasons for initiating an attack. Here are a few:

- They might be doing it for the sheer fun of it.
- They might be criminals attempting to steal from you.
- They might be individuals or groups who are using the attack to make a political statement or commit an act of terrorism.

Regardless of their motive, your job is to protect the people you work with from these acts of aggression. You are, in many cases, the only person in your organization charged with the responsibility of repulsing these attacks.

The following sections deal with the general types of attacks you'll experience.

The attacks described in the following sections are considered attack strategies. We'll look at the specific attacks—each of which will fall within one or more of these strategies—later in this chapter in the section titled "Recognizing Common Attacks."

Understanding Access Attack Types

The goal of an *access attack* is straightforward. An access attack is an attempt to gain access to information that the attacker isn't authorized to have. These types of attacks focus on breaching the confidentiality of information. They occur either internally or externally; they might also occur when physical access to the information is possible. Following are some commonly used methods for creating an access attack.

Dumpster Diving

Dumpster diving is a common physical access method. Companies normally generate a huge amount of paper, most of which eventually winds up in dumpsters or recycle bins. Dumpsters may contain information that is highly sensitive in nature. In high-security and government environments, sensitive papers are either shredded or burned. Most businesses don't do this. In addition, the advent of "green" companies has created an increase in the amount of recycled paper, which can often contain all kinds of juicy information about a company and its individual employees; make sure your employees appreciate the importance of using a shredder to destroy the paper's content before it leaves the premise.

Capturing Information en Route

A second common method used in access attacks is to capture information en route between two systems; rather than paper, data is found in such attacks. There are several common types of access attacks using this method:

Eavesdropping *Eavesdropping* is the process of listening in on or overhearing parts of a conversation, including listening in on your network traffic. This type of attack is generally passive. For example, a coworker might overhear your dinner plans because your speakerphone is set too loud or you're yelling into your cell phone. The opportunity to overhear a conversation is coupled with the carelessness of the parties in the conversation.

Snooping *Snooping* occurs when someone looks through your files hoping to find something interesting. The files may be either electronic or on paper. In the case of physical snooping, people might inspect your Dumpster, recycling bins, or even your file cabinets; they can look under the keyboard for Post-it notes or look for scraps of paper tacked to your bulletin board. Computer snooping, on the other hand, involves someone searching through your electronic files trying to find something interesting.

Interception *Interception* can be either an active or a passive process. In a networked environment, a passive interception would involve someone who routinely monitors network traffic. Active interception might include putting a computer system between the sender and receiver to capture information as it's sent. The process is usually covert. The last thing a person on an intercept mission wants is to be discovered. Intercept missions can occur for years without the knowledge of the parties being monitored.

Government agencies routinely run intercept missions to gather intelligence about the capabilities and locations of enemies. For instance, the FBI has several products that they install on ISPs' systems to gather and process email, looking for keywords. These keyword searches become the basis of an investigation.

The major difference between these types of attacks is how they're accomplished. The ultimate objective is to gain unauthorized access to information.

As an administrator, you've no doubt heard countless horror stories of data being accessed as a result of carelessness. Users write their passwords on scraps of paper and tape them to the monitor because the length/complexity requirements have made the passwords too difficult to remember. Other users go home without logging out and never return; the terminal stays logged in indefinitely, allowing an attacker to sit at it and copy key files. These stories may sound too unrealistic to believe, but they are actually fairly common.

> ### 🌐 Real World Scenario
>
> #### Survey Your Surroundings
>
> Imagine that you're an outsider wanting to find any sliver of data that can be used to allow you to gain access to a network. That sliver of data could be a user's password, the name and location of a data file, or anything else of a sensitive nature. From that perspective, see if you can answer these questions:
>
> - How often do users change their passwords, and how do they go about memorizing their new ones for the first few days? Do they write them down and carry them in their belongings? Do they stick a piece of paper in a drawer (and if so, is it locked)?
>
> - What happens to sensitive information that's printed? Is it shredded or just tossed in the wastebasket? Who collects the trash—a contracted service provider or the city?
>
> - Is crucial data, such as backup sets, stored offsite? Would it be easier to break in and get that data than to break into the network? How many people know where the backup sets are located?
>
> Putting yourself into the mind of a potential attacker allows you to ask the questions you must ask as an administrator in order to keep your data safe. Your answers can help you determine whether you need to make the workplace more secure. Throughout this book, I'll introduce topics for you to think about and apply to your own environment.

Recognizing Modification and Repudiation Attacks

Modification attacks involve the deletion, insertion, or alteration of information in an unauthorized manner that is intended to appear genuine to the user. These attacks can be hard to detect. They're similar to access attacks in that the attacker must first get to the data on the servers, but they differ from that point on. The motivation for this type of attack may be to plant information, change grades in a class, fraudulently alter credit card records, or something similar. Website defacements are a common form of modification attack; they involve someone changing web pages in a malicious manner.

A variation of a modification attack is a *repudiation attack*. Repudiation attacks make data or information appear to be invalid or misleading (which can be even worse). For example, someone might access your email server and send inflammatory information to others under the guise of one of your top managers. This information might prove embarrassing to your company and possibly do irreparable harm. Repudiation attacks are fairly easy to accomplish because most email systems don't check outbound mail for validity. Repudiation attacks, like modification attacks, usually begin as access attacks.

The opposite of repudiation is *nonrepudiation*. When you purchase something from an online vendor, the vendor often asks for information—such as the CID/CVV (Card Identification Data/Card Verification Value) on the back of your credit card, not just the credit card number—to prove that you are in possession of the card, or your PIN number to prove you are who you say you are. By proving your identity or the physical presence of the card, the company has nonrepudiated evidence that the sale is valid.

A common type of repudiation attack involves a customer who claims that they never received a service for which they were billed. In this situation, the burden of proof that the information used to generate the invoice is accurate is on the company. If an external attacker has modified the data, verifying the information may be difficult.

Identifying Denial-of-Service and Distributed Denial-of-Service Attacks

Denial-of-service (DoS) attacks prevent access to resources by users authorized to use those resources. An attacker may attempt to bring down an e-commerce website to prevent or deny usage by legitimate customers. Most simple DoS attacks occur from a single system, and a specific server or organization is the target.

There isn't a single type of DoS attack but a variety of similar methods that have the same purpose. It's easiest to think of a DoS attack by imagining that your servers are so busy responding to false requests that they don't have time to service legitimate requests. Not only can the servers be physically busy, but the same result can occur if the attack consumes all the available bandwidth.

Several types of attacks can occur in this category. These attacks can do the following:

- Deny access to information, applications, systems, or communications.
- Bring down a website while the communications and systems continue to operate.
- Crash the operating system (a simple reboot may restore the server to normal operation).
- Fill the communications channel of a network and prevent access by authorized users.
- Open as many TCP sessions as possible; this type of attack is called a TCP SYN flood DoS attack.

Two of the most common types of DoS attacks are the *ping of death* and the *buffer overflow*. The ping of death crashes a system by sending Internet Control Message Protocol (ICMP) packets (think echoes) that are larger than the system can handle. Buffer overflow attacks, as the name implies, attempt to put more data (usually long input strings) into the buffer than it can hold. Code Red, Slapper, and Slammer are all attacks that took advantage of buffer overflows, and sPing is an example of a ping of death.

In a *null session attack*, a user logs into Windows-based computers as a null user (bypassing basic authentication). This type of access is often used to launch a DoS attack.

A *distributed denial-of-service (DDoS) attack* is similar to a DoS attack. A DDoS attack amplifies the concepts of a DoS attack by using multiple computer systems (often through botnets) to conduct the attack against a single organization. These attacks exploit the inherent weaknesses of dedicated networks such as DSL and cable. These permanently attached systems usually have little, if any, protection. An attacker can load an attack program onto dozens or even hundreds of computer systems that use DSL or cable modems. The attack program lies dormant on these computers until they get an attack signal from a master computer. The signal triggers the systems, which launch an attack simultaneously on the target network or system. DDoS attacks are common on the Internet, where they have hit large companies such as Amazon, Microsoft, and AT&T. These attacks are often widely publicized in the media.

Figure 4.9 shows an attack occurring and the master controller orchestrating the attack. The master controller may be another unsuspecting user. The systems taking direction from the master control computer are referred to as *zombies* or *nodes*. These systems merely carry out the instruction they've been given by the master computer.

FIGURE 4.9 Distributed denial-of-service attack

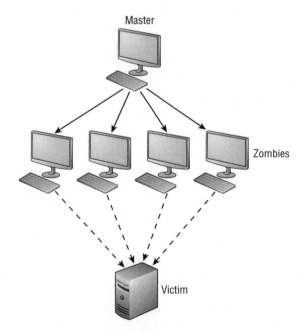

Remember that the difference between a DoS attack and a DDoS attack is that the latter uses multiple computers—all focused on one target. DDoS is far more common—and effective—today than DoS.

The nasty part of this type of attack is that the machines used to carry out the attack belong to normal computer users. The attack gives no special warning to those users. When the attack is complete, the attack program may remove itself from the system or infect the unsuspecting user's computer with a virus that destroys the hard drive, thereby wiping out the evidence.

Can You Prevent Denial Attacks?

In general, there is little you can do to prevent DoS or DDoS attacks. Many operating systems are particularly susceptible to these types of attacks. Fortunately, most operating system manufacturers have implemented updates to minimize their effects. Make sure your operating system and the applications you use are up-to-date.

Recognizing Botnets

Software running on zombie computers is often known as a *botnet*. Bots, by themselves, are but a form of software that runs automatically and autonomously (Google uses the Googlebot to find web pages and bring back values for the index), but *botnet* has come to be the word used to describe malicious software running on a zombie and under the control of a *bot-herder*.

The various denial of service attacks—DoS and DDoS—can be launched by botnets, as can many forms of adware, spyware, and spam (via *spambots*). Most bots are written to run in the background with no visible evidence of their presence. Many malware kits can be used to create botnets and modify existing ones.

There is not a universal approach to dealing with botnets, but knowing how to deal with the various types of them (all of which are described here) is key for exam preparation. Some can be easily detected by looking at a database of known threats, while others have to be identified through analysis of their behavior.

Botnets have become so common recently that Volume 9 of Microsoft's Security Intelligence Report (http://www.microsoft.com/security/sir) includes a special section titled "Battling Botnets for Control of Computers."

Recognizing Common Attacks

Most attacks are designed to exploit potential weaknesses, which can be in the implementation of programs or in the protocols used in networks. Many types of attacks require a high level of sophistication and are rare, but you need to know about them so that, should they occur, you can identify what has happened in your network.

In the following sections, we'll look at some common attacks more closely.

Backdoor Attacks

The term *backdoor attack* (known also as *back* door) can have two different meanings. The original term *backdoor* referred to troubleshooting and developer hooks into systems that often circumvented normal authentication. During the development of a complicated operating system or application, programmers add backdoors or maintenance hooks. Backdoors allow them to examine operations inside the code while the code is running. The backdoors are stripped out of the code when it's moved to production. When a software manufacturer discovers a hook that hasn't been removed, it releases a maintenance upgrade or patch to close the backdoor. These patches are common when a new product is initially released.

The second type of backdoor refers to gaining access to a network and inserting a program or utility that creates an entrance for an attacker. The program may allow a certain user ID to log on without a password or gain administrative privileges. Figure 4.10 shows how a backdoor attack can be used to bypass the security of a network. In this example, the attacker is using a backdoor program to utilize resources or steal information.

A backdoor attack is usually either an access or modification attack. A number of tools exist to create backdoor attacks on systems. One of the more popular is Back Orifice. Another popular backdoor program is NetBus. Fortunately, most conventional antivirus software will detect and block these types of attacks.

FIGURE 4.10   A backdoor attack in progress

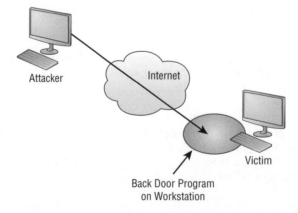

Back Orifice and NetBus are remote administration tools used by attackers to take control of Windows-based systems. These packages are typically installed using a Trojan horse program. Back Orifice and NetBus allow a remote user to take full control of systems on which they are installed. They run on all of the current Windows operating systems.

Spoofing Attacks

A *spoofing attack* is an attempt by someone or something to masquerade as someone else. This type of attack is usually considered an access attack. A common spoofing attack that was popular for many years on early Unix and other timesharing systems involved a programmer writing a fake logon program. It would prompt the user for a user ID and password. No matter what the user typed, the program would indicate an invalid logon attempt and then transfer control to the real logon program. The spoofing program would write the logon and password into a disk file, which was retrieved later.

The most popular spoofing attacks today are *IP spoofing*, ARP spoofing, and *DNS spoofing*. With IP spoofing, the goal is to make the data look as if it came from a trusted host when it didn't (thus spoofing the IP address of the sending host).

With ARP spoofing (also known as *ARP poisoning*), the MAC (Media Access Control) address of the data is faked. By faking this value, it is possible to make it look as if the data came from a network that it did not. This can be used to gain access to the network, to fool the router into sending data here that was intended for another host, or to launch a DoS attack. In all cases, the address being faked is an address of a legitimate user, and that makes it possible to get around such measures as allow/deny lists.

With DNS spoofing, the DNS server is given information about a name server that it thinks is legitimate when it isn't. This can send users to a website other than the one they wanted to go to, reroute mail, or do any other type of redirection wherein data from a DNS server is used to determine a destination. Another name for this is *DNS poisoning*.

 Always think of spoofing as fooling. Attackers are trying to fool the user, system, and/or host into believing they're something they aren't. Because the word *spoof* can describe any false information at any level, spoofing can occur at any level of network.

 Another DNS weakness is *domain name kiting*. When a new domain name is issued, there is a five-day grace period before you must technically pay for it. Those engaged in kiting can delete the account within the five days and re-register it—allowing them to have accounts that they never have to pay for.

Figure 4.11 shows a spoofing attack occurring as part of the logon process on a computer network. The attacker in this situation impersonates the server to the client attempting to log in. No matter what the client attempts to do, the impersonating system will fail the login. When this process is finished, the impersonating system disconnects from the client. The client then logs in to the legitimate server. In the meantime, the attacker now has a valid user ID and password.

FIGURE 4.11   A spoofing attack during logon

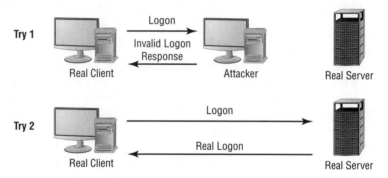

Attacker now has logon and password.

The important point to remember is that a spoofing attack tricks something or someone into thinking something legitimate is occurring.

Pharming Attacks

Pharming is a form of redirection in which traffic intended for one host is sent to another. This can be accomplished on a small scale by changing entries in the hosts file and on a large scale by changing entries in a DNS server (the poisoning mentioned earlier). In either case, when a user attempts to go to a site, they are redirected to another. An example of this would be Illegitimate Company ABC creating a site to look exactly like the one for Giant Bank XYZ. The pharming is done (using either redirect method), and users trying to reach Giant Bank XYZ are tricked into going to Illegitimate Company ABC's site, which looks enough like what they are used to seeing that they provide username and password data.

As soon as Giant Bank XYZ realizes that the traffic is being redirected, they will immediately move to stop it. Although Illegitimate Company ABC will be closed down, they were able to collect data for the length of time the redirection occurred, which could vary from minutes to days.

Phishing and Spear Phishing Attacks

Phishing is a form of social engineering (which is focused on in Chapter 6) in which you simply ask someone for a piece of information that you are missing by making it look as if it is a legitimate request. An email might look as if it is from a bank and contain some basic information, such as the user's name. In the email, it will often state that there is a problem with the person's account or access privileges. The user will be told to click a link to correct the problem. After they click the link—which goes to a site other than the bank's—they are asked for their username, password, account information, and so on. The person instigating the phishing can then use the values entered there to access the legitimate account.

One of the best counters to phishing is to simply mouse over the Click Here link and read the URL. Almost every time it is pointing to an adaptation of the legitimate URL as opposed to a link to the real thing.

Spear phishing is a unique form of phishing in which the message is made to look as if it came from someone you know and trust as opposed to an informal third party. For example, in a phishing attack, you would get a message that appears to be from Giant Bank ABC telling you that there is a problem with your account and you need to log in to rectify this right away; such a message from someone you've never heard of would run a high risk of raising suspicion and thus generate a lower than desired rate of return for the phishers. With spear phishing, you might get a message that appears to be from your boss telling you that there is a problem with your direct deposit account and you need to access this HR link right now to correct it.

Spear phishing works better than phishing because it uses information it can find about you from email databases, friends lists, and the like. It was this type of attack that was used against Google managers and employees in 2010 to open up an exploitation that factored heavily in the company's decision to pull out of China.

Man-in-the-Middle Attacks

Man-in-the-middle attacks tend to be fairly sophisticated. This type of attack is also an access attack, but it can be used as the starting point for a modification attack. The method used in these attacks clandestinely places a piece of software between a server and the user that neither the server administrators nor the user is aware of. The software intercepts data and then sends the information to the server as if nothing is wrong. The server responds to the software, thinking it's communicating with the legitimate client. The attacking software continues sending information on to the server, and so forth.

If communication between the server and user continues, what's the harm of the software? The answer lies in whatever else the software is doing. The man-in-the-middle software may be recording information for someone to view later, altering it, or in some other way compromising the security of your system and session.

A man-in-the-middle attack is an active attack. Something is actively intercepting the data and may or may not be altering it. If it's altering the data, the altered data masquerades as legitimate data traveling between the two hosts.

Figure 4.12 illustrates a man-in-the-middle attack. Notice how both the server and client assume that the system they're talking to is the legitimate system. The man in the middle appears to be the server to the client, and it appears to be the client to the server.

FIGURE 4.12 A man-in-the-middle attack occurring between a client and a web server

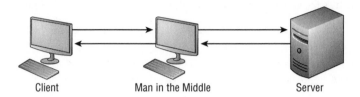

Client   Man in the Middle   Server

In recent years, the threat of man-in-the-middle attacks on wireless networks has increased. Because it's no longer necessary to connect to the wire, a malicious rogue can be outside the building intercepting packets, altering them, and sending them on. A common solution to this problem is to enforce a secure wireless authentication protocol such as WPA2.

An older term generically used for all man-in-the-middle attacks was *TCP/ IP hijacking*. TCP/IP hijacking is addressed in detail later in this chapter.

Replay Attacks

Replay attacks are becoming quite common. They occur when information is captured over a network. A replay attack is a kind of access or modification attack. In a distributed environment, logon and password information is sent between the client and the authentication system. The attacker can capture the information and replay it later. This can also occur with security certificates from systems such as Kerberos: The attacker resubmits the certificate, hoping to be validated by the authentication system and circumvent any time sensitivity.

Figure 4.13 shows an attacker presenting a previously captured certificate to a Kerberos-enabled system. In this example, the attacker gets legitimate information from the client and records it. Then the attacker attempts to use the information to enter the system. The attacker later relays information to gain access.

If this attack is successful, the attacker will have all the rights and privileges from the original certificate. This is the primary reason that most certificates contain a unique session identifier and a time stamp. If the certificate has expired, it will be rejected and an entry should be made in a security log to notify system administrators.

Password-Guessing Attacks

Password-guessing attacks occur when an account is attacked repeatedly. This is accomplished by utilizing applications known as *password crackers,* which send possible passwords to the account in a systematic manner. The attacks are initially carried out to gain passwords for an access or modification attack. There are two types of password-guessing attacks:

FIGURE 4.13   A replay attack occurring

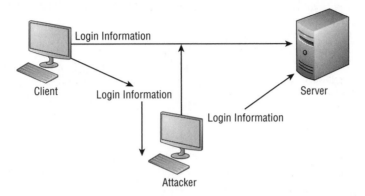

Login Information

Client   Login Information   Server

Login Information

Attacker

Brute-Force Attack   A *brute-force attack* is an attempt to guess passwords until a successful guess occurs. This type of attack usually occurs over a long period. To make passwords more difficult to guess, they should be much longer than two or three characters (six should be the bare minimum), be complex, and have password lockout policies.

Dictionary Attack   A *dictionary attack* uses a dictionary of common words to attempt to find the user's password. Dictionary attacks can be automated, and several tools exist in the public domain to execute them.

Not all attacks are only brute-force or dictionary based. A number of hybrids also exist that will try combinations of these two methods. One of the more common techniques involves using *rainbow tables*—values of hashes—to identify the *salt* (random bits added to the password) used in creating the stored value. By using values in an existing table of hashed passwords (think of taking a word and hashing it every way you can imagine), a rainbow table attack can reduce the amount of time needed to crack the password significantly.

Some systems will identify whether an account ID is valid and whether the password is wrong. Giving the attacker a clue as to a valid account name isn't a good practice. If you can enable your authentication to either accept a valid ID/password group or require the entire logon process again, you should.

Privilege Escalation

Privilege escalation can be the result of an error on an administrator's part in assigning too high a permission set to a user, but it's more often associated with bugs left in software. When creating a software program, developers will occasionally leave a backdoor in the program that allows them to become a root user should they need to fix something during the debugging phase.

After debugging is done and before the software goes live, these abilities are removed. If a developer forgets to remove the backdoor in the live version and the method of accessing it gets out, it leaves the ability for a miscreant to take advantage of the system.

To understand privilege escalation, think of cheat codes in video games. Once you know the game's code, you can enter it and become invincible. Similarly, someone might take advantage of a hidden cheat in a software application you are using to become root.

 Real World Scenario

Responding to an Attack

As a security administrator, you know all about the different types of attacks that can occur, and you're familiar with the value assigned to the data on your system. Now imagine that the log files indicate that an intruder entered your system for a lengthy period last week while you were away on vacation.

The first thing you should do is make a list of questions you should begin asking to deal with the situation, using your network as a frame of reference. The following list includes some of the questions you should be thinking of:

1. How can you show that a break-in really occurred?

2. How can you determine the extent of what was done during the entry?

3. How can you prevent further entry?

4. Whom should you inform in your organization?

5. What should you do next?

Answers to these questions will be addressed throughout this book. The most important question on the list, though, is whom you should inform in your organization. It's important to know the escalation procedures without hesitation and be able to act quickly.

One of the tools that can be used to look for holes is Microsoft Security Analyzer. This tool can scan a system and find missing updates and security misconfigurations. In Exercise 4.4, I'll show you how to use the Microsoft Security Analyzer to scan your system.

EXERCISE 4.4

Scanning with Microsoft Baseline Security Analyzer

The Microsoft Security Baseline Analyzer is a free tool downloadable from Microsoft that can scan a system and find security holes. As of this writing, version 2.2 is available and it runs on Windows 7, Windows Vista, Windows XP, Windows 2000, Windows Server 2008, and Windows Server 2003. During a scan, it will look for missing security updates, and operating system/software misconfigurations.

To scan a workstation with the Microsoft Security Baseline Analyzer, once it has been downloaded and installed, follow these steps:

1. Start the Microsoft Security Baseline Analyzer. With Windows 7 and Windows Vista, the UAC will prompt if you want to really run this. Choose Yes to continue.

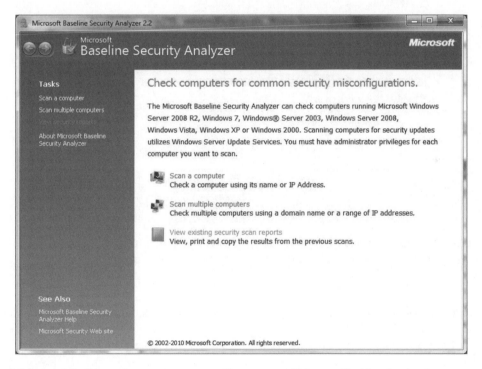

2. Make certain the updates are current—if not, you will be notified by the Analyzer.

EXERCISE 4.4 *(continued)*

3. Choose Scan A Computer. You are given a choice of which computer to scan (which can be specified by computer name or IP address), with the default being this one. Make sure all options are checked and click Start Scan.

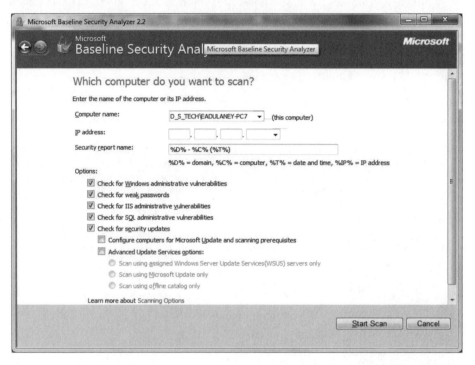

4. View the Report Details when the scan concludes. Items identified are classified in the various sections' vulnerabilities, with the worst offenses appearing first.

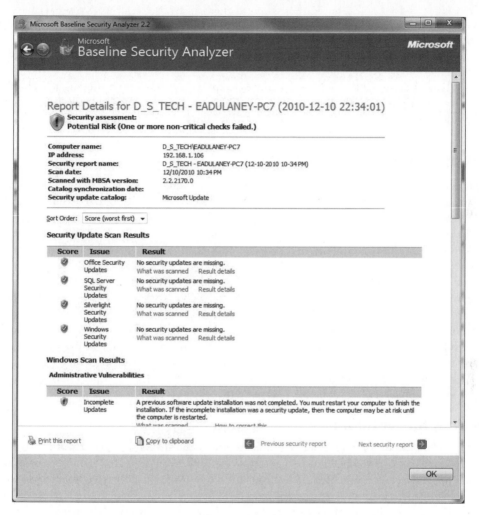

5. Look closely for any items appearing beneath Administrative Vulnerabilities. If an item has a link titled How To Correct This, click it and examine the issue, solution, and instructions.

6. Exit Microsoft Security Baseline Analyzer.

Identifying TCP/IP Security Concerns

One of your biggest problems as a security professional is working with TCP/IP. You could say that the ease of connectivity TCP/IP offers is one of the most significant difficulties we face. Virtually all large networks, including the Internet, are built on the TCP/IP protocol suite. It has become an international standard.

TCP/IP was designed to connect disparate computer systems into a robust and reliable network. It offers a richness of capabilities and support for many different protocols. After TCP/IP has been installed, it will generally operate reliably for years.

Recognizing TCP/IP Attacks

Attacks on TCP/IP usually occur at the host-to-host or Internet layer, although any layer is potentially vulnerable. TCP/IP is susceptible to attacks from both outside and inside an organization.

The opportunities for external attacks are somewhat limited by the devices in the network, including the router. The router blocks many of the protocols from exposure to the Internet. Some protocols, such as ARP, aren't routable and aren't generally vulnerable to outside attacks. Other protocols, such as SMTP and ICMP, pass through the router and form a normal part of Internet and TCP/IP traffic. TCP, UDP, and IP are all vulnerable to attack.

Your network is easily exposed to inside attacks. Any network-enabled host has access to the full array of protocols used in the network. A computer with a network card has the ability to act as a network sniffer with the proper configuration and software.

The following sections introduce you to the specific attacks that a TCP/IP-based network is susceptible to when off-the-shelf software or shareware is used.

Sniffing the Network

A *network sniffer*, or *scanner*, is a device that captures and displays network traffic. Your existing computers have the ability to operate as sniffers. Network cards usually pass information up to the protocol stack only if the information is intended for the computer on which they're installed; any network traffic not intended for that computer is ignored. Most NICs can be placed into what is called *promiscuous mode*, which allows the NIC to capture all information that it sees on the network. Devices such as routers, bridges, and switches are used to separate or segment networks within a larger network (known as virtual LANs, or VLANs). Any traffic in a particular segment is visible to all stations in that segment.

Adding a network sniffer such as the one included by Microsoft in its Systems Management Server (SMS) package allows any computer to function as a network sniffer. This software is widely available and is very capable. A number of public domain or shareware sniffers are also available online, such as Wireshark (http://www.wireshark.org).

By using a sniffer, an internal attacker can capture all the information transported by the network. Many advanced sniffers can reassemble packets and create entire messages, including user IDs and passwords. This vulnerability is particularly acute in environments where network connections are easily accessible to outsiders. For example, an attacker could put a laptop or a portable computer in your wiring closet and attach it to your network.

Scanning Ports

A TCP/IP network makes many of the ports available to outside users through the router. These ports respond in a predictable manner when queried. For example, TCP attempts synchronization when a session initiation occurs. An attacker can systematically query your network to determine which services and ports are open. This process is called *port scanning*, and it is part of fingerprinting a network; it can reveal a great deal about your systems. Port scans are possible both internally and externally. Many routers, unless configured appropriately, will let all protocols pass through them.

 Port scans help in identifying what services are running on a network.

Individual systems within a network might also have applications and services running that the owner doesn't know about. These services could potentially allow an internal attacker to gain access to information by connecting to the port associated with those services. Many users don't realize the weak security that some web server products offer. If all of the security patches were not installed during installation, attackers can exploit the weaknesses and gain access to information. This has been done in many cases without the knowledge of the owner. These attacks might not technically be considered TCP/IP attacks, but they are because the inherent trust of TCP is used to facilitate the attacks.

After they know the IP addresses of your systems, external attackers can attempt to communicate with the ports open in your network, sometimes simply by using Telnet.

Using Telnet to Check a Port

To check whether a system has a particular protocol or port available, all you have to do is use the `telnet` command and add the port number. For example, you can check to see if a particular server is running an email server program by entering **telnet www.youreintrouble.com** 25. This initiates a Telnet connection to the server on port 25. If the server is running SMTP, it will immediately respond with logon information. It doesn't take much to figure out how to talk to SMTP; the interface is well documented. If an email account didn't have a password, this system is now vulnerable to attack.

This process of port scanning can be expanded to develop a footprint of your organization. If your attacker has a single IP address of a system in your network, they can probe all the addresses in the range and probably determine what other systems and protocols your network is utilizing. This allows the attacker to gain knowledge about the internal structure of your network.

 In late 2005, a study done by the University of Maryland's A. James Clark School of Engineering found that 38 percent of attacks were preceded by vulnerability scans. The combination of port scans with vulnerability scans created a lethal combination that often led to an attack.

In addition to scanning, network mapping allows you to visually see everything that is available. The best-known network mapper is Nmap, which can run on all operating systems and is found at `http://nmap.org/`. One of the most popular attacks that utilizes Nmap is the *Xmas attack* (also more appropriately known as the *Xmas scan*). This is an advanced scan that tries to get around firewall detection and look for open ports. It accomplishes this by setting three flags (`FIN`, `PSH`, and `URG`); understanding the intricacies of this is beyond what you need to know for the Security+ exam, but you can find all you ever wanted to know at the nmap.org site in the reference guide.

TCP Attacks

TCP operates using synchronized connections. The synchronization is vulnerable to attack; this is probably the most common attack used today. As you may recall, the synchronization, or handshake, process initiates a TCP connection. This handshake is particularly vulnerable to a DoS attack referred to as a *TCP SYN flood attack*. The protocol is also susceptible to access and *modification attacks*, TCP sequence number attacks, and TCP/IP hijacking, which are briefly explained in the following sections.

TCP SYN or TCP ACK Flood Attack

The TCP SYN flood, also referred to as the *TCP ACK attack*, is common. The purpose is to deny service. The attack begins as a normal TCP connection: The client and server exchange information in TCP packets. Figure 4.14 illustrates how this attack occurs. Notice that the TCP client continues to send ACK packets to the server. The ACK packets tell the server that a connection is requested. The server responds with an ACK packet to the client. The client is supposed to respond with another packet accepting the connection, and a session is established.

In this attack, the client continually sends and receives the ACK packets but doesn't open the session. The server holds these sessions open, awaiting the final packet in the sequence. This causes the server to fill up the available sessions and deny other clients the ability to access the resources.

This attack is virtually unstoppable in most environments without working with upstream providers. Many newer routers can track and attempt to prevent this attack by setting limits on the length of an initial session to force sessions that don't complete to close out. This type of attack can also be undetectable. An attacker can use an invalid IP address, and TCP won't care because TCP will respond to any valid request presented from the IP layer.

FIGURE 4.14 TCP SYN flood attack

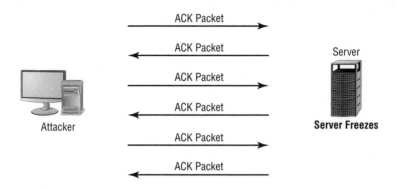

TCP Sequence Number Attack

TCP sequence number attacks occur when an attacker takes control of one end of a TCP session. This attack is successful when the attacker kicks the attacked end off the network for the duration of the session. Each time a TCP message is sent, either the client or the server generates a sequence number. In a TCP sequence number attack, the attacker intercepts and then responds with a *sequence number* similar to the one used in the original session. This attack can either disrupt or hijack a valid session. If a valid sequence number is guessed, attackers can place themselves between the client and server. Figure 4.15 illustrates a sequence number attack in process against a server. In this example, the attacker guesses the sequence number and replaces a real system with one of their own.

FIGURE 4.15 TCP sequence number attack

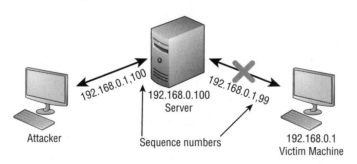

In this case, the attacker effectively hijacks the session and gains access to the session privileges of the victim's system. The victim's system may get an error message indicating that it has been disconnected, or it may reestablish a new session. In this case, the attacker gains the connection and access to the data from the legitimate system. The attacker then has access to the privileges established by the session when it was created.

This weakness is again inherent in TCP, and little can be done to prevent it. Your major defense against this type of attack is knowing that it's occurring. Such an attack is also frequently a precursor to a targeted attack on a server or network.

TCP/IP Hijacking

TCP/IP hijacking, also called *active sniffing*, involves the attacker gaining access to a host in the network and logically disconnecting it from the network. The attacker then inserts another machine with the same IP address. This happens quickly and gives the attacker access to the session and to all the information on the original system. The server won't know this has occurred and will respond as if the client is trusted. Figure 4.16 shows how TCP/IP hijacking occurs. In this example, the attacker forces the server to accept its IP address as valid.

FIGURE 4.16   TCP/IP hijacking attack

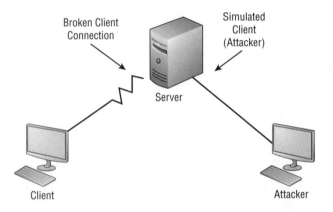

 It can be confusing, but know that when sniffing is performed on a switched network, it is known as active sniffing.

TCP/IP hijacking presents the greatest danger to a network because the hijacker will probably acquire privileges and access to all the information on the server. As with a sequence number attack, there is little you can do to counter the threat. Fortunately, these attacks require fairly sophisticated software and are harder to engineer than a DoS attack such as a TCP SYN attack.

UDP Attacks

A *UDP attack* attacks either a maintenance protocol or a UDP service in order to overload services and initiate a DoS situation. UDP attacks can also exploit UDP protocols.

One of the most popular UDP attacks is the ping of death discussed earlier in the section "Identifying Denial-of-Service and Distributed Denial-of-Service Attacks."

UDP packets aren't connection oriented and don't require the synchronization process described in the previous section. UDP packets, however, are susceptible to interception, and UDP can be attacked. UDP, like TCP, doesn't check the validity of IP addresses. The nature of this layer is to trust the layer below it, the IP layer.

The most common UDP attacks involve *UDP flooding*. UDP flooding overloads services, networks, and servers. Large streams of UDP packets are focused at a target, causing the UDP services on that host to shut down. UDP floods also overload the network bandwidth and cause a DoS situation to occur.

ICMP Attacks   *ICMP attacks* occur by triggering a response from ICMP to a seemingly legitimate maintenance request. From earlier discussions, you'll recall that ICMP is often associated with echoing.

ICMP supports maintenance and reporting in a TCP/IP network. It is part of the IP level of the protocol suite. Several programs, including Ping, use ICMP. Until fairly recently, ICMP was regarded as a benign protocol that was incapable of much damage. However, it has now joined the ranks of protocols used in common attack methods for DoS attacks. Two primary methods use ICMP to disrupt systems: *smurf attacks* and *ICMP tunneling*.

Smurf Attacks   *Smurf attacks* can create havoc in a network. A smurf attack uses IP spoofing and broadcasting to send a ping to a group of hosts in a network. An ICMP ping request (type 8) is answered with an ICMP ping reply (type 0) if the targeted system is up. Otherwise an unreachable message is returned. If a broadcast is sent to a network, all of the hosts will answer the ping. The result is an overload of the network and the target system.

Figure 4.17 shows a smurf attack under way in a network. The attacker sends a broadcast message with a legal IP address. In this case, the attacking system sends a ping request to the broadcast address of the network. The request is sent to all the machines in a large network. The reply is then sent to the machine identified with the ICMP request (the spoof is complete). The result is a DoS attack that consumes the network bandwidth of the replying system, while the victim system deals with the flood of ICMP traffic it receives.

The primary method of eliminating smurf attacks involves prohibiting ICMP traffic through a router. If the router blocks ICMP traffic, smurf attacks from an external attacker aren't possible.

ICMP Tunneling   ICMP messages can contain data about timing and routes. A packet can be used to hold information that is different from the intended information. This allows an ICMP packet to be used as a communications channel between two systems. The channel can be used to send a Trojan horse or other malicious packet. This is a relatively new opportunity to create havoc and mischief in networks.

FIGURE 4.17 A smurf attack under way against a network

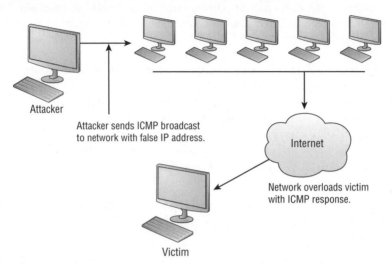

The countermeasure for ICMP attacks is to deny ICMP traffic through your network. You can disable ICMP traffic in most routers, and you should consider doing so in your network.

 Many of the newer SOHO router solutions (and some of the personal firewall solutions on end-user workstations) close down the ICMP ports by default. Keep this in mind, because it can drive you nuts when you are trying to see if a brand-new station/server/router is up and running.

Summary

This chapter focused on the various threats and vulnerabilities you'll encounter. We covered:

- Types of attacks
- Malicious code

Some of the attacks discussed are denial-of-service, distributed denial-of-service, back-door attacks, spoofing attacks, man-in-the-middle attacks, and replay attacks. These are just some of the attacks you may encounter. Each takes advantage of inherent weaknesses in the network technologies most commonly used today.

Common attacks on TCP include the SYN or ACK flood attack, TCP sequence number attack, and TCP/IP hijacking. UDP is vulnerable to flooding attacks. Flooding attacks are DoS attacks, and they're designed to prevent access by authorized users.

Malicious code describes an entire family of software that has nefarious intentions for your networks and computers. This includes viruses, Trojan horses, logic bombs, and worms. Viruses and worms are a major problem on the Internet.

Exam Essentials

Be able to describe the various types of attacks to which your systems are exposed. Your network is vulnerable to DoS attacks caused by either a single system or multiple systems. Multiple-system attacks are called DDoS. Your systems are also susceptible to access, modification, and repudiation attacks.

Be able to describe the methods used to conduct a backdoor attack. Backdoor attacks occur using either existing maintenance hooks or developmental tools to examine the internal operations of a program. These hooks are usually removed when a product is prepared for market or production. Backdoor attacks also refer to inserting into a machine a program or service that allows authentication to be bypassed and access gained.

Know how a spoofing attack occurs. Spoofing attacks occur when a user or system masquerades as another user or system. Spoofing allows the attacker to assume the privileges and access rights of the real user or system.

Be able to describe a man-in-the-middle attack. Man-in-the-middle attacks are based on the principle that a system can be placed between two legitimate users to capture or exploit the information being sent between them. Both sides of the conversation assume that the man in the middle is the other end and communicate normally. This creates a security breach and allows unauthorized access to information.

Be able to describe a replay attack. A replay attack captures information from a previous session and attempts to resend it to gain unauthorized access. This attack is based on the premise that if it worked once, it will work again. This is especially effective in environments where a user ID and password are sent in the clear across a large network.

Be able to describe a TCP/IP hijacking. TCP/IP hijacking occurs when an unauthorized system replaces the authorized system without being detected. This allows access privileges to be kept in the session. Hijacking attacks are hard to detect because everything appears to be normal except the hijacked system. Hijacking attacks take advantage of the sequencing numbers used in TCP sessions.

Be able to describe the methods used in password guessing. The methods used to guess passwords are brute force, dictionary, and hybrids. Brute-force attacks work by trying to randomly guess a password repeatedly against a known account ID. In a dictionary attack, a dictionary of common words is used to attempt to find a user's password. The best example of a hybrid attack uses a rainbow table of stored hash values to test against the password values.

Know how software exploitation occurs. Software exploitation involves using features or capabilities of a software product in a manner either unplanned for or unanticipated by the software manufacturer. In many cases, the original feature enhanced the functionality of the product but, unfortunately, creates a potential vulnerability.

Know the characteristics and types of viruses used to disrupt systems and networks. Several different types of viruses are floating around today. The most common ones are polymorphic viruses, stealth viruses, retroviruses, multipartite viruses, and macro viruses.

Be able to explain the characteristics of Trojan horses and logic bombs. Trojan horses are programs that enter a system or network under the guise of another program. Logic bombs are programs or snippets of code that execute when a certain predefined event occurs.

Know how worms operate. Worms attack systems and attempt to procreate and propagate. Worms spread using files, email, and physical media, such as a USB drive. A worm will also frequently contain a virus that causes the destruction of a system.

Be able to describe how antivirus software operates. Antivirus software looks for a signature in the virus to determine what type of virus it is. The software then takes action to neutralize the virus based on a virus definition database. Virus definition database files are regularly made available on vendor sites.

Review Questions

1. You are the senior administrator for a bank. A user calls you on the telephone and says they were notified to contact you but couldn't find your information on the company website. Two days ago, an email told them there was something wrong with their account and they needed to click a link in the email to fix the problem. They clicked the link and filled in the information, but now their account is showing a large number of transactions that they did not authorize. They were likely the victims of what type of attack?

    A. Spimming

    B. Phishing

    C. Pharming

    D. Escalating

2. As the security administrator for your organization, you must be aware of all types of attacks that can occur and plan for them. Which type of attack uses more than one computer to attack the victim?

    A. DoS

    B. DDoS

    C. Worm

    D. UDP attack

3. An alert signals you that a server in your network has a program running on it that bypasses authorization. Which type of attack has occurred?

    A. DoS

    B. DDoS

    C. Backdoor

    D. Social engineering

4. An administrator at a sister company calls to report a new threat that is making the rounds. According to him, the latest danger is an attack that attempts to intervene in a communications session by inserting a computer between the two systems that are communicating. Which of the following types of attacks does this constitute?

    A. Man-in-the-middle attack

    B. Backdoor attack

    C. Worm

    D. TCP/IP hijacking

5. You've discovered that an expired certificate is being used repeatedly to gain logon privileges. Which type of attack is this most likely to be?

   A. Man-in-the-middle attack

   B. Backdoor attack

   C. Replay attack

   D. TCP/IP hijacking

6. A junior administrator comes to you in a panic. After looking at the log files, he has become convinced that an attacker is attempting to use an IP address to replace another system in the network to gain access. Which type of attack is this?

   A. Man-in-the-middle attack

   B. Backdoor attack

   C. Worm

   D. TCP/IP hijacking

7. A server on your network will no longer accept connections using TCP. The server indicates that it has exceeded its session limit. Which type of attack is probably occurring?

   A. TCP ACK attack

   B. Smurf attack

   C. Virus attack

   D. TCP/IP hijacking

8. A smurf attack attempts to use a broadcast ping on a network; the return address of the ping may be a valid system in your network. Which protocol does a smurf attack use to conduct the attack?

   A. TCP

   B. IP

   C. UDP

   D. ICMP

9. A user calls you in a panic. He is receiving emails from people indicating that he is inadvertently sending viruses to them. Over 200 such emails have arrived today. Which type of attack has most likely occurred?

   A. SAINT

   B. Backdoor attack

   C. Worm

   D. TCP/IP hijacking

10. Which type of attack denies authorized users access to network resources?

   A. DoS

   B. Worm

   C. Logic bomb

   D. Social engineering

11. Your system has just stopped responding to keyboard commands. You noticed that this occurred when a spreadsheet was open and you dialed in to the Internet. Which kind of attack has probably occurred?

A. Logic bomb

B. Worm

C. Virus

D. ACK attack

12. You're explaining the basics of security to upper management in an attempt to obtain an increase in the networking budget. One of the members of the management team mentions that they've heard of a threat from a virus that attempts to mask itself by hiding code from antivirus software. What type of virus is he referring to?

A. Armored virus

B. Polymorphic virus

C. Worm

D. Stealth virus

13. What kind of virus could attach itself to the boot sector of your disk to avoid detection and report false information about file sizes?

A. Trojan horse virus

B. Stealth virus

C. Worm

D. Polymorphic virus

14. A mobile user calls you from the road and informs you that his laptop is exhibiting erratic behavior. He reports that there were no problems until he downloaded a tic-tac-toe program from a site that he had never visited before. Which of the following terms describes a program that enters a system disguised in another program?

A. Trojan horse virus

B. Polymorphic virus

C. Worm

D. Armored virus

15. Your system has been acting strangely since you downloaded a file from a colleague. Upon examining your antivirus software, you notice that the virus definition file is missing. Which type of virus probably infected your system?

A. Polymorphic virus

B. Retrovirus

C. Worm

D. Armored virus

16. Internal users are reporting repeated attempts to infect their systems as reported to them by pop-up messages from their virus-scanning software. According to the pop-up messages, the virus seems to be the same in every case. What is the most likely culprit?

    A. A server is acting as a carrier for a virus.

    B. You have a worm virus.

    C. Your antivirus software has malfunctioned.

    D. A DoS attack is under way.

17. Your system log files report an ongoing attempt to gain access to a single account. This attempt has been unsuccessful to this point. What type of attack are you most likely experiencing?

    A. Password-guessing attack

    B. Backdoor attack

    C. Worm attack

    D. TCP/IP hijacking

18. A user reports that he is receiving an error indicating that his TCP/IP address is already in use when he turns on his computer. A static IP address has been assigned to this user's computer, and you're certain this address was not inadvertently assigned to another computer. Which type of attack is most likely underway?

    A. Man-in-the-middle attack

    B. Backdoor attack

    C. Worm

    D. TCP/IP hijacking

19. You're working late one night, and you notice that the hard disk on your new computer is very active even though you aren't doing anything on the computer and it isn't connected to the Internet. What is the most likely suspect?

    A. A disk failure is imminent.

    B. A virus is spreading in your system.

    C. Your system is under a DoS attack.

    D. TCP/IP hijacking is being attempted.

20. You're the administrator for a large bottling company. At the end of each month, you routinely view all logs and look for discrepancies. This month, your email system error log reports a large number of unsuccessful attempts to log on. It's apparent that the email server is being targeted. Which type of attack is most likely occurring?

    A. Software exploitation attack

    B. Backdoor attack

    C. Worm

    D. TCP/IP hijacking

Answers to Review Questions

1. B. Sending an email with a misleading link to collect information is a phishing attack.

2. B. A DDoS attack uses multiple computer systems to attack a server or host in the network.

3. C. In a backdoor attack, a program or service is placed on a server to bypass normal security procedures.

4. A. A man-in-the-middle attack attempts to fool both ends of a communications session into believing the system in the middle is the other end.

5. C. A replay attack attempts to replay the results of a previously successful session to gain access.

6. D. TCP/IP hijacking is an attempt to steal a valid IP address and use it to gain authorization or information from a network.

7. A. A TCP ACK attack creates multiple incomplete sessions. Eventually, the TCP protocol hits a limit and refuses additional connections.

8. D. A smurf attack attempts to use a broadcast ping (ICMP) on a network. The return address of the ping may be a valid system in your network. This system will be flooded with responses in a large network.

9. C. A worm is a type of malicious code that attempts to replicate using whatever means are available. The worm may not have come from the user's system; rather, a system with the user's name in the address book has attacked these people.

10. A. A DoS attack is intended to prevent access to network resources by overwhelming or flooding a service or network.

11. A. A logic bomb notifies an attacker when a certain set of circumstances has occurred. This may in turn trigger an attack on your system.

12. A. An armored virus is designed to hide the signature of the virus behind code that confuses the antivirus software or blocks it from detecting the virus.

13. B. A stealth virus reports false information to hide itself from antivirus software. Stealth viruses often attach themselves to the boot sector of an operating system.

14. A. A Trojan horse enters with a legitimate program to accomplish its nefarious deeds.

15. B. Retroviruses are often referred to as anti-antiviruses. They can render your antivirus software unusable and leave you exposed to other, less-formidable viruses.

16. A. Some viruses won't damage a system in an attempt to spread into all the other systems in a network. These viruses use that system as the carrier of the virus.

17. A. A password-guessing attack occurs when a user account is repeatedly attacked using a variety of different passwords.

18. D. One of the symptoms of a TCP/IP hijacking attack may be the unavailability of a TCP/IP address when the system is started.

19. B. A symptom of many viruses is unusual activity on the system disk. This is caused by the virus spreading to other files on your system.

20. A. A software exploitation attack attempts to exploit weaknesses in software. A common attack attempts to communicate with an established port to gain unauthorized access. Most email servers use port 25 for email connections using SMTP.

Chapter

5

Access Control and Identity Management

THE FOLLOWING COMPTIA SECURITY+ EXAM OBJECTIVES ARE COVERED IN THIS CHAPTER:

✓ **1.2 Apply and implement secure network administration principles.**

- Firewall rules
- VLAN management
- Secure router configuration
- Access control lists
- Implicit deny

✓ **1.3 Distinguish and differentiate network design elements and compounds.**

- NAC

✓ **3.2 Analyze and differentiate among types of attacks.**

- Transitive access
- Client-side attacks

✓ **5.1 Explain the function and purpose of authentication services.**

- RADIUS
- TACACS
- TACACS+
- Kerberos
- LDAP
- XTACACS

✓ **5.2 Explain the fundamental concepts and best practices related to authentication, authorization, and access control.**

- Identification vs. authentication
- Authentication (single factor) and authorization
- Multifactor authentication
- Tokens
- Common access card
- Personal identification verification card
- Smart card
- Single sign on
- ACLs
- Access control
- Mandatory access control
- Discretionary access control
- Role/rule-based access control
- Implicit deny
- Trusted OS

While the previous chapters focused more on theoretical concepts than purchasable components, they created the foundation on which the topics in this chapter will build. In this chapter, the discussion moves more into the implementation of security features as opposed to focusing only on what potential problems exist. Bear in mind that even though a variety of products exist to satisfy every need of the market, none are as successful as they should be without education and training. One of your top priorities should always be to make certain your users understand every aspect of the security policies.

This chapter starts by looking at the basics of access control and then looks at remote access and authentication services. It concludes by examining access control implementation and best practices.

Access Control Basics

Quite simply, access control means allowing the correct users in (those who are authorized) and keeping the others out (those who are not authorized). You can employ a great many tools and technologies to make this happen—all of which are discussed in this chapter—but the fundamental principle remains the same: Let the right ones in.

In the following sections, we will look at the difference between identification and authentication, authentication and authorization, multifactor authentication, and operational security. We will also look at tokens and problems to watch for as well as issues to consider.

Identification vs. Authentication

Critical to correctly answering questions asked on the Security+ exam about access control is understanding the difference between identification and authentication. Identification requires a human to intercede and verify that someone is who they say they are. The human, often in the form of a guard or receptionist, can look at the credentials the user provides (think driver's license, employee ID card, etc.) and validate that they belong with the person possessing them.

Authentication is not as fail proof as identification because it removes the human element from the verification process and merely corroborates that the user has entered the correct values, such as the password provided going with the username entered. With authentication, the user may not be who they are supposed to be, but they have indeed given the correct combination of values (such as username and password, tokens, or biometrics) and thus they are authenticated.

For the exam, remember that authentication means someone has accurate information, while identification means the accurate information is proven to be in possession of the correct individual.

Authentication systems or methods are based on one or more of these three factors:

- Something you know, such as a password or PIN
- Something you have, such as a smart card, token, or an identification device
- Something physically unique to you, such as your fingerprints or retinal pattern

Systems authenticate each other using similar methods. Frequently, systems pass private information between each other to establish identity. Once authentication has occurred, the two systems can communicate in the manner specified in the design.

Several common methods are used for authentication, and they fall within the categories of either single factor or multifactor. Each offers something to security and should be considered when you're evaluating authentication schemes or methods.

Authentication (Single Factor) and Authorization

The most basic form of authentication is known as *single factor authentication (SFA)* because only one set of values is checked. SFA is most often implemented as the traditional username/password combination. A *username* and *password* are unique identifiers for a logon process. Here's a synopsis for how it works: When users sit down in front of a computer system, the first thing a security system requires is that they establish who they are. Identification is typically confirmed through a logon process. Most operating systems use a user ID and password to accomplish this. These values can be sent across the connection as plain text or can be encrypted.

The logon process identifies to the operating system, and possibly the network, that you are who you say you are. Figure 5.1 illustrates this logon and password process. Notice that the operating system compares this information to the stored information from the security processor and either accepts or denies the logon attempt. The operating system might establish privileges or permissions based on stored data about that particular ID.

Whenever two or more parties authenticate each other, this is known as *mutual authentication*. A client may authenticate to a server and a server authenticate to a client when there is a need to establish a secure session between the two and employ encryption. Mutual authentication ensures that the client is not unwittingly connecting and giving its credentials to a rogue server, which can then turn around and steal the data from the real server.

Commonly, mutual authentication will be implemented when the data to be sent during the session is of a critical nature, such as financial or medical records.

Multifactor Authentication

When two or more access methods are included as part of the authentication process, you're implementing a *multifactor* system. A system that uses smart cards and passwords is referred to as a *two-factor authentication* system. Two-factor authentication is shown in Figure 5.2. This example requires both a smart card and a logon password process.

FIGURE 5.1   A logon process occurring on a workstation

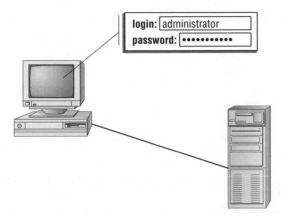

Logon or Security Server

FIGURE 5.2   Two-factor authentication

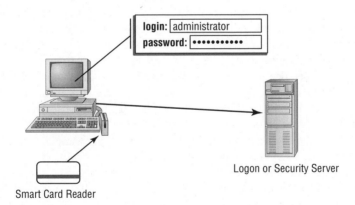

Smart Card Reader

Logon or Security Server

Both factors must be valid:
•User ID and Password
•Smart Card

A multifactor system can consist of a two-factor system, three-factor system, and so on. As long as more than one factor is involved in the authentication process, it is considered a multifactor system.

For obvious reasons, the two or more factors employed should not be from the same category. While you do increase difficulty in gaining system accessing by requiring the user to enter two sets of username/password combinations, it is much preferred to pair a single user-name/password combination with a biometric identifier or other check.

Operational Security

Operational security focuses on how an organization achieves its goals. It is also part of a security triad that includes physical and management security.

As such, operational security issues include *network access control (NAC)*, authentication, and security topologies after the network installation is complete. Issues include the daily operations of the network, connections to other networks, backup plans, and recovery plans. In short, operational security encompasses everything that isn't related to design or physical security in your network. Instead of focusing on the physical components where the data is stored, such as the server, the focus is now on the topology and connections.

 Some vendors use the acronym NAC to signify network *admission* control rather than the more commonly accepted network *access* control. Regardless of which word appears in the middle of the acronym, the concept is the same.

The issues you address in an operational capacity can seem overwhelming at first. Many of the areas you'll focus on are vulnerabilities in the systems you use or weak or inadequate security policies. For example, if you implement a comprehensive password expiration policy, you can require users to change their passwords every 30 or 60 days. If the system doesn't require password rotation, though (it allows the same passwords to be reused), you have a vulnerability that you may not be able to eliminate. A user can go through the motions of changing their password only to reenter the same value and keep it in use.

From an operational perspective, this type of system has weak password-changing capabilities. There is nothing you can do, short of installing a higher-security logon process or replacing the operating system. Either solution may not be feasible given the costs, conversion times, and possible unwillingness of an organization—or its partners—to make this switch.

Such dependence on a weak system usually stems from the fact that most companies use software that was developed by third parties in order to save costs or meet compatibility requirements. These packages may require the use of a specific operating system. If that operating system has significant security problems or vulnerabilities, your duties will be mammoth because you'll still be responsible for providing security in that environment. Your secure corporate network, for example, should never be connected to the Internet, where it can become subject to a seemingly endless number of potential vulnerabilities. You must install hardware and software solutions to improve security, and you must convince management that these measures are worth the cost to implement.

Tokens

Security tokens are similar to certificates. They contain the rights and access privileges of the token bearer as part of the token. Think of a token as a small piece of data that holds a sliver of information about the user. The term *claimant* is used for a subscriber to a credential service provider.

Many operating systems generate a token that is applied to every action taken on the computer system. If your token doesn't grant you access to certain information, then either that information won't be displayed or your access will be denied. The authentication system creates a token every time a user connects or a session begins. At the completion of a session, the token is destroyed. Figure 5.3 shows the security token process.

FIGURE 5.3   Security token authentication

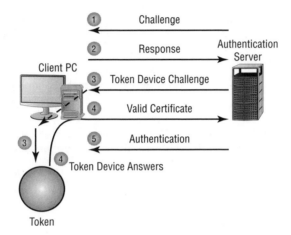

Potential Authentication and Access Problems

There are two problem areas you should know for the Security+ exam because they apply to authentication/access issues: transitive access and client-side attacks. Both of these are addressed in the sections that follow.

Transitive Access

The word *transitive* means involving transition, and it is necessary to understand this process in order to follow how transitive access problems occur. With *transitive access*, one party (A) trusts another party (B). If the second party (B) trusts another party (C), then a relationship can exist where the third party (C) is trusted by the first party (A).

In early operating systems, this process was often exploited. In current operating systems, such as Windows Server 2008, the problems with transitive access were solved by creating transitive trusts, which are a type of relationship that can exist between domains (the opposite is *nontransitive*). When the trust relationship is transitive, the relationship between party (A) and party (B) flows through as described earlier (i.e., A now trusts C). In all versions of Active Directory, the default is that all domains in a forest trust each other with two-way transitive trust relationships.

While this process makes administration much easier when you add a new child domain (no administrative intervention is required to establish the trusts), it leaves open the possibility of a hacker acquiring more trust than they should by virtue of joining the domain. In Exercise 5.1, we'll explore how to validate the trust relationship in Windows Server 2008—a step toward addressing this problem.

EXERCISE 5.1

Validate a Trust Relationship

As an administrator, you should know what trust relationships exist between domains. To validate a trust relationship in Windows Server 2008, follow these steps:

1. Open Active Directory Domains and Trusts.

2. Right-click your domain name and choose Properties from the menu.

3. Click the Trusts tab and select the name of the domain, or forest, that you want to validate.

4. Click Properties. The Properties dialog box for that trust appears.

5. Approximately two-thirds of the way down the dialog box, the Transitivity Of Trust item appears. Click Validate.

6. A confirmation message appears. Click OK.

7. Exit Active Directory Domains and Trusts.

Client-Side Attacks

A *client-side attack* is an attack that targets vulnerabilities in client applications that interact with a malicious server. A user accesses the trusted site—whether web, FTP, or almost anything else—and unwittingly downloads the rogue code (thinking they are downloading music, videos, etc.). The rogue code allows the miscreant to then install or execute programs on the affected machine remotely. What is relevant to the discussion on access is that the newly installed programs run with the privilege level of the individual who accessed the server.

If that user had elevated privileges—a junior administrator, for example—then the malware runs at that level. In most cases, the programs running try to reach beyond the workstation they are initially installed on and find their way to the server(s). Often data accessed along the way is pushed out across the Internet, using HTTPS to encrypt it and make it less likely to be detected. HTTPS and Secure HTTP are discussed in Chapter 8.

Authentication Issues to Consider

You can set up many different parameters and standards to force the people in your organization to conform. In establishing these parameters, it's important that you consider the capabilities of the people who will be working with these policies. If you're working in an environment where people aren't computer savvy, you may spend a lot of time helping them remember and recover passwords. Each organization has its own quirks, and many have had to reevaluate their security guidelines only after they've already invested great time and expense to implement high-security systems to accommodate them. Remember that it is always better to educate users—raise their awareness—than to lower security.

Setting authentication security, especially for supporting users, can become a high-maintenance activity for network administrators. On one hand, you want people to be able to authenticate themselves easily; on the other hand, you want to establish security that protects your company's resources. Here are some tips to making this process easier:

- Be wary of popular names or current trends that make certain passwords predictable. For example, every January, Super Bowl teams become likely passwords, as do variations on players' names and numbers. This can create a security problem for computer centers.

- Use *identity proofing* whenever an issue arises between identification and authentication. The identification process starts when a user ID or logon name is typed into a sign-on screen. Authentication is accomplished by challenging the claim about who is accessing the resource.

- Incorporate a second value—such as mother's maiden name—to prove a user's identity. This is helpful when identification proofing is invoked when a person claims they are the user but cannot be authenticated—such as when they lose their password.

 Real World Scenario

Multifactor Authentication and Security

The CEO of your company is becoming increasingly concerned about computer security and the laxness of users. She reports that users are regularly leaving the office at the end of the day without signing out of their accounts. The company is attempting to win a contract that involves working with the government and that will require additional security measures. What would you suggest?

First and foremost, you should recommend that the company implement a multifactor authentication system. This system could consist of a smart card and a logon/password process. Most smart card readers can be configured to require that the card remain inserted in the reader while the user is logged on. If the smart card is removed, say at the end of the day, the workstation will automatically log the user out. By requiring a logon/password process, you can still provide security if the smart card is stolen. This solution provides reasonable security, and it doesn't significantly increase security costs.

Other suggestions are to consider additional access controls, such as perimeter alarms and physical access control to sensitive areas. The government would probably require these anyway, although these measures won't force users to log out when they leave their workstations.

An inherent problem with many identity proofing implementations is that they ask questions that someone other than the user could easily guess or learn the value of (what color are your eyes?). To increase the difficulty of someone fraudulent proofing, you should use only questions that are more difficult to guess or implement biometrics such as voice identification. Under no circumstance should the person proofing be allowed access immediately—instead, their access information should be sent to their email account of record.

Understanding Remote Access Connectivity

One of the primary purposes for having a network is the ability to connect systems. As networks have grown, many technologies have come on the scene to make this process easier and more secure. A key area of concern relates to the connection of systems and other networks that aren't part of your network. The following sections discuss the more common protocols used to facilitate connectivity among remote systems.

Ancient History: the Serial Line Internet Protocol

Serial Line Internet Protocol (SLIP) is an older protocol that was used in early remote access environments and serves as the starting point for most remote discussions. SLIP was originally designed to connect Unix systems in a dial-up environment and supported only serial communications.

A very simple protocol, SLIP could only be used to pass TCP/IP traffic and wasn't secure or efficient. While some systems today still support SLIP, it is strictly there for legacy systems and should be avoided whenever possible.

Any authentication done for a remote user is known as *remote authentication*. This authentication is commonly done using TACACS or RADIUS.

Using the Point-to-Point Protocol

Introduced in 1994, the *Point-to-Point Protocol (PPP)* offers support for multiple protocols, including AppleTalk, IPX, and DECnet. PPP works with POTS, Integrated Services Digital Network (ISDN), and other faster connections such as T1. PPP doesn't provide data security, but it does provide authentication using the *Challenge Handshake Authentication Protocol (CHAP)*.

Figure 5.4 shows a PPP connection over an ISDN line. In the case of ISDN, PPP would normally use one 64Kbps B channel for transmission. PPP allows many channels in a network connection (such as ISDN) to be connected or bonded together to form a single virtual connection.

FIGURE 5.4   PPP using a single B channel on an ISDN connection

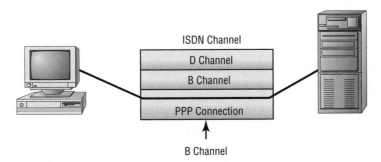

PPP works by encapsulating the network traffic in a protocol called the *Network Control Protocol (NCP)*. Authentication is handled by the *Link Control Protocol (LCP)*. A PPP connection allows remote users to log on to the network and have access as though they were local users on the network. PPP doesn't provide for any encryption services for the channel.

As you might have guessed, the unsecure nature of PPP makes it largely unsuitable for WAN connections. To counter this issue, other protocols have been created that take advantage of PPP's flexibility and build on it. You should make sure all your PPP connections use secure channels, dedicated connections, or high-speed connections.

Remote users who connect directly to a system don't necessarily need to have encryption capabilities enabled. If the connection is direct, the likelihood that anyone would be able to tap an existing phone line is relatively small. However, you should make sure that connections through a network use an encryption-oriented tunneling system.

Working with Tunneling Protocols

Tunneling protocols add a capability to the network: the ability to create tunnels between networks that can be more secure, support additional protocols, and provide virtual paths between systems. The best way to think of tunneling is to imagine sensitive data being encapsulated in other packets that are sent across the public network. Once they're received at the other end, the sensitive data is stripped from the other packets and recompiled into its original form.

The most common protocols used for tunneling are as follows:

Point-to-Point Tunneling Protocol   *Point-to-Point Tunneling Protocol (PPTP)* supports encapsulation in a single point-to-point environment. PPTP encapsulates and encrypts PPP packets. This makes PPTP a favorite low-end protocol for networks. The negotiation between the two ends of a PPTP connection is done in the clear. After the negotiation is performed, the channel is encrypted. This is one of the major weaknesses of PPTP. A *packet-capture device*, such as a sniffer, that captures the negotiation process can potentially use that information to determine the connection type and information about how the tunnel works. Microsoft developed PPTP and supports it on most of the company's products. PPTP uses port 1723 and TCP for connections.

Layer 2 Forwarding   *Layer 2 Forwarding (L2F)* was created by Cisco as a method of creating tunnels primarily for dial-up connections. It's similar in capability to PPP and shouldn't be used over WANs. L2F provides authentication, but it doesn't provide encryption. L2F uses port 1701 and TCP for connections.

Layer 2 Tunneling Protocol   Microsoft and Cisco agreed to combine their respective tunneling protocols into one protocol: *Layer 2 Tunneling Protocol (L2TP)*. L2TP is a hybrid of PPTP and L2F. It's primarily a point-to-point protocol. L2TP supports multiple network protocols and can be used in networks besides TCP/IP. L2TP works over IPX, SNA, and IP, so it can be used as a bridge across many types of systems. The major problem with L2TP is that it doesn't provide data security: The information isn't encrypted. Security can be provided by protocols such as IPSec. L2TP uses port 1701 and UDP for connections.

Secure Shell   *Secure Shell (SSH)* is a tunneling protocol originally designed for Unix systems. It uses encryption to establish a secure connection between two systems. SSH also provides alternative, security-equivalent programs for such Unix standards as Telnet, FTP, and many other communications-oriented applications. SSH is now available for use on Windows systems as well. This makes it the preferred method of security for Telnet and other cleartext-oriented programs in the Unix environment. SSH uses port 22 and TCP for connections.

Internet Protocol Security   *Internet Protocol Security (IPSec)* isn't a tunneling protocol, but it's used in conjunction with tunneling protocols. IPSec is oriented primarily toward LAN-to-LAN connections, but it can also be used with remote connections. IPSec provides secure authentication and encryption of data and headers; this makes it a good choice for security. IPSec can work in either Tunneling mode or Transport mode. In Tunneling mode, the data or payload and message headers are encrypted. Transport mode encrypts only the payload. IPSec is an add-on to IPv4 and built into IPv6.

Working with RADIUS

Remote Authentication Dial-In User Service (RADIUS) is a mechanism that allows authentication of remote and other network connections. Once intended for use on dial-up connections, it has moved far beyond that and has many modern features. The RADIUS protocol is an IETF standard, and it has been implemented by most of the major operating system manufacturers. A RADIUS server can be managed centrally, and the servers that allow access to a network can verify with a RADIUS server whether an incoming caller is authorized. In a large network with many connections, this allows a single server to perform all authentications.

Figure 5.5 shows an example of a RADIUS server communicating with an ISP to allow access to a remote user. Notice that the remote server is functioning as a client to the RADIUS server. This allows centralized administration of access rights.

FIGURE 5.5   The RADIUS client manages the local connection and authenticates against a central server.

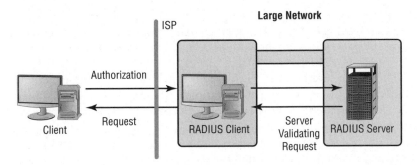

You should use RADIUS when you want to improve network security by implementing a single service to authenticate users who connect remotely to the network. Doing so gives you a single source for the authentication to take place. Additionally, you can implement auditing and accounting on the RADIUS server.

The major difficulty with a single-server RADIUS environment is that the entire network may refuse connections if the server malfunctions. Many RADIUS systems allow multiple servers to be used to increase reliability. All of these servers are critical components of the infrastructure, and they must be protected from attack.

TACACS/TACACS+/XTACACS

Terminal Access Controller Access-Control System (TACACS) is a client-server-oriented environment, and it operates in a manner similar to how RADIUS operates. Extended TACACS (XTACACS) replaced the original and combined authentication and authorization with logging to enable auditing.

The most current method or level of TACACS is TACACS+, and this replaces the previous two incarnations. TACACS+ allows credentials to be accepted from multiple methods, including Kerberos. The TACACS client/server process occurs in the same manner as the RADIUS process illustrated in Figure 5.5.

Cisco has widely implemented TACACS+ for connections. TACACS+ is expected to become widely accepted as an alternative to RADIUS.

   Remember, RADIUS and TACACS can be used to authenticate connections.

VLAN Management

A *virtual local area network (VLAN)* allows you to create groups of users and systems and segment them on the network. This segmentation lets you hide segments of the network from other segments and thereby control access. You can also set up VLANs to control the paths that data takes to get from one point to another. A VLAN is a good way to contain network traffic to a certain area in a network.

> Think of a VLAN as a network of hosts that act as if they're connected by a physical wire even though there is no such wire between them.

On a LAN, hosts can communicate with each other through broadcasts, and no forwarding devices, such as routers, are needed. As the LAN grows, so too does the number of broadcasts. Shrinking the size of the LAN by segmenting it into smaller groups (VLANs) reduces the size of the broadcast domains. The advantages of doing this include reducing the scope of the broadcasts, improving performance and manageability, and decreasing dependence on the physical topology. From the standpoint of this exam, however, the key benefit is that VLANs can increase security by allowing users with similar data sensitivity levels to be segmented together.

Figure 5.6 illustrates the creation of three VLANs in a single network.

FIGURE 5.6   A typical segmented VLAN

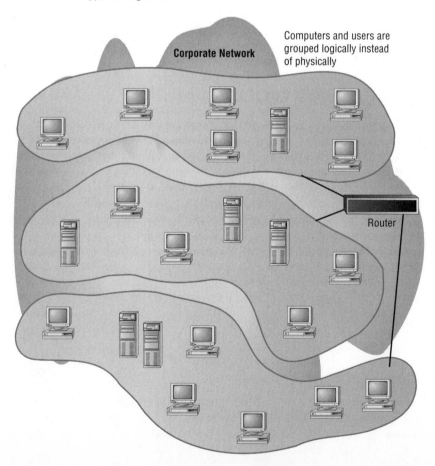

Understanding Authentication Services

Authentication services are the implementation of the technology in question. For this part of exam study, the focus is on LDAP and Kerberos, though many other possibilities exist, such as Internet Authentication Service (IAS) and Central Authentication Service (CAS), which are outside the scope of this exam. Single sign-on initiatives round out the discussion in this section.

LDAP

Lightweight Directory Access Protocol (LDAP) is a standardized directory access protocol that allows queries to be made of directories (specifically, pared-down X.500-based directories). If a directory service supports LDAP, you can query that directory with an LDAP client, but it's LDAP that is growing in popularity and is being used extensively in online white and yellow pages.

LDAP is the main access protocol used by Active Directory (discussed next). It operates, by default, at port 389. The LDAP syntax uses commas between names.

Kerberos

Kerberos is an authentication protocol named after the mythical three-headed dog that stood at the gates of Hades. Originally designed by MIT, Kerberos is very popular as an authentication method. It allows for a single sign-on to a distributed network.

Kerberos authentication uses a *key distribution center (KDC)* to orchestrate the process. The KDC authenticates the *principal* (which can be a user, a program, or a system) and provides it with a ticket. After this ticket is issued, it can be used to authenticate against other principals. This occurs automatically when a request or service is performed by another principal.

Kerberos is quickly becoming a common standard in network environments. Its only significant weakness is that the KDC can be a single point of failure. If the KDC goes down, the authentication process will stop. Figure 5.7 illustrates the Kerberos authentication process and the ticket being presented to systems that are authorized by the KDC.

The implementation of Kerberos is discussed in Chapter 9.

Single Sign-On Initiatives

One of the big problems that larger systems must deal with is the need for users to access multiple systems or applications. This may require a user to remember multiple accounts and passwords. The purpose of a *single sign-on (SSO)* is to give users access to all the applications and systems they need when they log on. This is becoming a reality in many environments, including Kerberos, Microsoft Active Directory, Novell eDirectory, and some certificate model implementations.

FIGURE 5.7   Kerberos authentication process

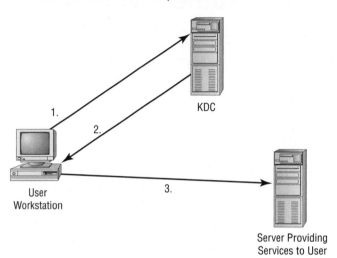

1. User requests access to service running on a different server.
2. KDC authenticates user and sends a ticket to be used between the user and the service on the server.
3. User's workstation sends a ticket to the service.

 Single sign-on is both a blessing and a curse. It's a blessing in that once the user is authenticated, they can access all the resources on the network and browse multiple directories. It's a curse in that it removes the doors that otherwise exist between the user and various resources.

In the case of Kerberos, a single token allows any "Kerberized" applications to accept a user as valid. The important thing to remember in this process is that each application that wants to use SSO must be able to accept and process the token presented by Kerberos.

Active Directory (AD) works off a slightly different method. A server that runs AD retains information about all access rights for all users and groups in the network. When a user logs on to the system, AD issues the user a globally unique identifier (GUID). Applications that support AD can use this GUID to provide access control.

Figure 5.8 illustrates this process in more detail. In this instance, the database application, email client, and printers all authenticate with the same logon. Like Kerberos, this process requires all the applications that want to take advantage of AD to accept AD controls and directives.

In this way, the user doesn't have to have separate sign-on, email, and application passwords. Using AD simplifies the sign-on process for users and lowers the support requirements for administrators. Access can be established through groups, and it can be enforced through group memberships.

FIGURE 5.8 AD validating a user

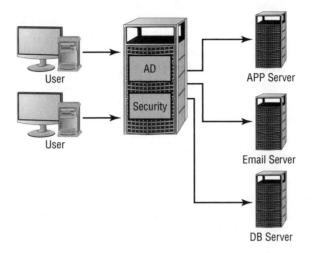

On a decentralized network, SSO passwords are stored on each server and can represent a security risk. It's important to enforce password changes and make certain passwords are updated throughout the organization on a frequent basis.

> While single sign-on is not the opposite of multifactor authentication, it is often mistakenly thought of that way. One-, two-, and three-factor authentication merely refers to the number of items a user must supply to authenticate. Authentication can be based on something they have (a smart card), something they know (a password), something unique (biometric), and so forth. After factor authentication is done, then single sign-on can still apply throughout the user's session.

Understanding Access Control

The three primary methods of access control are as follows:

Mandatory Access Control (MAC)   All access is predefined.

Discretionary Access Control (DAC)   Incorporates some flexibility.

Role-Based Access Control (RBAC)   Allows the user's role to dictate access capabilities.

A fourth method, Rule-Based Access Control (which also uses the RBAC acronym) is gaining in popularity. Each of these methods has advantages and disadvantages to the organization from a security perspective.

The method you choose will be greatly affected by your organization's beliefs about how information needs to be shared. In a high-security environment, the tendency would be to implement either a MAC or RBAC method. In a traditional business environment or school, the tendency would be to implement a DAC method. You should do some consulting within the organization to understand how a particular department and how the entire organization want to implement access control models. Doing so will allow you to gather input from all concerned parties regarding how access guidelines should be established and how security should be implemented.

In the following sections, we'll look at each of these methods from a business perspective.

Mandatory Access Control

Mandatory Access Control (MAC) is clearly an inflexible method for how information access is allowed. In a MAC environment, all access capabilities are predefined. Users can't share information unless their rights to share it were established by administrators; administrators must make any changes that need to be made. This process enforces a rigid model of security.

For a MAC model to work effectively, administrators and network designers must think relationships through carefully. The advantage of this model is that security access is well established and defined, making security breaches easier to investigate and correct. A well-designed MAC model can make the job of information control easier and can essentially lock down a network. The major disadvantages of this model are the lack of flexibility and the fact that its needs change over time. The inability of administrative staff to address these changes can sometimes make the model hard to keep up.

This model is used in environments where confidentiality is a driving force. It often employs government and military classifications (labels) such as Top Secret and others discussed in Chapter 6.

Discretionary Access Control

In a Discretionary Access Control (DAC) model, network users have some flexibility regarding how information is accessed. This model allows users to dynamically share information with other users. The method allows a more flexible environment, but it increases the risk of unauthorized disclosure of information. Administrators have a more difficult time ensuring that information access is controlled and that only appropriate access is given out.

A classic example of DAC is the permission structure that exists for "other" with files in the Unix/Linux environment. All permissions in this operating system fall within three groups of users: owner, group, and other. The permissions associated with the owner and the group the owner belongs to are based on their roles, but all of those who are not the owner, or a member of the owner's group, fall within the category of other.

The permissions for this group are set separate from the other two and with very few special exceptions are a combination of read, write, and execute. Within this environment, I can create a database and give myself (owner) permission to read and write, give other admins (group) only read permission, and not give any permission to those not in admin (other).

I could just as easily create a script file that cleans up log files and frees space on a work-station. I would give myself (owner) all rights, give other admins (group) the ability to read and execute, and give basic users (other) the right only to execute.

Role-Based Access Control

Role-Based Access Control (RBAC) models approach the problem of access control based on established roles in an organization. RBAC models implement access by job function or by responsibility. Each employee has one or more roles that allow access to specific information. If a person moves from one role to another, the access for the previous role will no longer be available. RBAC models provide more flexibility than the MAC model and less flexibility than the DAC model. They do, however, have the advantage of being strictly based on job function as opposed to individual needs.

Instead of thinking "Denise needs to be able to edit files," RBAC uses the logic "Editors need to be able to edit files" and "Denise is a member of the Editors group." This model is always good for use in an environment in which there is high employee turnover.

Rule-Based Access Control

Rule-Based Access Control (RBAC) uses the settings in preconfigured security policies to make all decisions. These rules can be to deny all but those who specifically appear in a list (an allow list) or deny only those who specifically appear in the list (a true deny list). Entries in the list may be actual usernames, IP addresses, hostnames, or even domains. Rule-Based models are often being used in conjunction with Role-Based to add greater flexibility.

The easiest way to implement RBAC is with access control lists (ACLs), discussed later in this chapter. The ACLs create the rules by which the access control model functions.

Implementing Access Control Best Practices

How you implement access control makes all the difference in how secure your systems are. In this section, we will look at smart cards, access control lists, trusted operating systems, and secure router configuration.

Smart Cards

Smart cards are generally used for access control and security purposes. The card itself usually contains a small amount of memory that can be used to store permissions and access information.

Smart cards are difficult to counterfeit, but they're easy to steal. Once a thief has a smart card, they have all the access the card allows. To prevent this, many organizations don't put any identifying marks on their smart cards, making it harder for someone to utilize them. A password or PIN is required to activate many modern smart cards, and encryption is employed to protect the contents. With many smart cards, if you enter the wrong pin number multiple times (usually three), the card will shut down to further enhance security.

Many European countries are beginning to use smart cards instead of magnetic-strip credit cards because they offer additional security and can contain more information.

When you think of a smart card, always remember that this tool can be used for authentication as well as storage. Not only can the card identify you, but it can hold relevant information as well. As an analogy, think of a smart card as a debit card that has an updated total of your bank account balance on it as opposed to a credit card that has only your account number.

 Real World Scenario

Working with Smart Cards

You've been asked to help troubleshoot a problem that is occurring in your school's computer lab. Students are complaining about viruses that are infecting the flash drives they bring to school. How can you help remedy this situation?

You should ensure that all the systems in your school lab computers are running antivirus software and that this software is kept up-to-date. Doing so will prevent known viruses from entering the school's system and being transferred to student files. You may also want to evaluate whether the school computers should have removable media installed on their systems. Several manufacturers now sell systems called *thin clients* that don't provide any disk storage or removable media on their workstations. Thin clients use dedicated servers to download applications, data, and any other information they need to have in order to run. This eliminates the danger of viruses being introduced from student disks.

There are two main types of smart cards, which we'll discuss in the following sections.

Common Access Card

One type of smart card is the *Common Access Card (CAC)*. These cards are issued by the Department of Defense as a general identification/authentication card for military personnel, contractors, and non-DoD employees. A picture appears on the front of the card with an integrated chip beneath and a barcode. On the back of the card, there is a magnetic strip and another barcode.

The CAC is used for access to DoD computers, signing email, and implementing PKI. In 2008, the most recent year for which numbers were available, it was stated that over 17 million cards had been issued. Current information on the CAC can be found at http://www.cac.mil.

Personal Identification Verification Card

What the CAC is for military employees, the *Personal Identity Verification (PIV)* (referenced by CompTIA as Personal Identification Verification Card) is to federal employees and contractors. Per Homeland Security Presidential Directive number 12 (HSPD-12), the PIV will eventually be required of all U.S. Government employees and contractors. It will be required to gain access (physical and logical) to government resources.

Access Control Lists

Access control lists (ACLs) enable devices in your network to ignore requests from specified users or systems or to grant them certain network capabilities. You may find that a certain IP address is constantly scanning your network, and you can block this IP address. If you block it at the router, the IP address will automatically be rejected any time it attempts to utilize your network.

ACLs allow a stronger set of access controls to be established in your network. The basic process of ACL control allows the administrator to design and adapt the network to deal with specific security threats.

The following sections look at approaches to ACLs, including implicit deny and firewall rules.

Implicit Deny

Within ACLs, there exists a condition known as *implicit deny*. An implicit deny clause is implied at the end of each ACL and it means that if the proviso in question has not been explicitly granted, then it is denied. The best way to think of this is to use an analogy: Suppose you're hosting a party at your home and have created a guest list and given it to a bouncer at the door. When each guest arrives, the bouncer looks sequentially down the list for their name; if the name is not found on the list, then they are denied entry. You don't have to tell the bouncer to not let in Evan or Kristin or Spencer—since their names do not appear on the list, they are implicitly denied access.

The same principle holds true in the ACL. The entity being denied because it does not appear on the list can be a source address, a destination address, a packet type, or almost anything else you want to deny access.

Firewall Rules

Firewall rules act like ACLs and are used to dictate what traffic can pass between the firewall and the internal network. Three possible actions can be taken based on the rule's criteria:

- Block the connection.
- Allow the connection.
- Allow the connection only if it is secured.

The rules can be applied to inbound traffic or outbound traffic and any type of network (LAN, wireless, BPN, remote access). On a regular basis, you should audit the firewall rules and verify that you are obtaining the results you wish and make any modifications needed.

Trusted OS

A *trusted operating system (TOS)* is any operating system that meets the government's requirements for security. The most common set of standards for security is *Common Criteria (CC)*. This document is a joint effort among Canada, France, Germany, the Netherlands, the United Kingdom, and the United States. The standard outlines a comprehensive set of evaluation criteria, broken down into seven *Evaluation Assurance Levels (EALs)*. EAL 1 to EAL 7 are discussed here:

 As of this writing, the latest version of the standard is 3.1 Release 3, and it's available for viewing at http://www.commoncriteriaportal.org. The website also maintains a registry of products certified by CC.

EAL 1   EAL 1 is primarily used when the user wants assurance that the system will operate correctly, but threats to security aren't viewed as serious.

EAL 2   EAL 2 requires product developers to use good design practices. Security isn't considered a high priority in EAL 2 certification.

EAL 3   EAL 3 requires conscientious development efforts to provide moderate levels of security.

EAL 4   EAL 4 requires positive security engineering based on good commercial development practices. It is anticipated that EAL 4 will be the common benchmark for commercial systems.

EAL 5   EAL 5 is intended to ensure that security engineering has been implemented in a product from the early design phases. It's intended for high levels of security assurance. The EAL documentation indicates that special design considerations will most likely be required to achieve this level of certification.

EAL 6   EAL 6 provides high levels of assurance of specialized security engineering. This certification indicates high levels of protection against significant risks. Systems with EAL 6 certification will be highly secure from penetration attackers.

EAL 7   EAL 7 is intended for extremely high levels of security. The certification requires extensive testing, measurement, and complete independent testing of every component.

EAL certification has replaced the Trusted Computer Systems Evaluation Criteria (TCSEC) system for certification, which was popular in the United States. It has also replaced the Information Technology Security Evaluation Criteria (ITSEC), which was popular in Europe. The recommended level of certification for commercial systems is EAL 4.

Currently, only a few operating systems have been approved at the EAL 4 level, and even though an operating system straight out of the box may be, that doesn't mean your own individual implementation of it is functioning at that level. If your implementation doesn't use the available security measures, then you're operating below that level.

Real World Scenario

Implementing a Secure Server Environment

You've been appointed to the panel that will make decisions regarding the purchase of a new server for your organization. The new server needs to be relatively secure and suitable for storing sensitive information. It will also be part of an e-commerce environment. How can you assist the panel?

You can be of real value to the panel by determining the operating systems that have been certified for the common criteria. You can visit the website http://www.commoncriteriaportal.org/products/?expand #OS to identify which operating systems and products have been EAL 4 certified. Encourage your IT staff members to make their decision based on the data available about security as opposed to vendor claims. Most vendors claim to have a secure environment when in fact they don't. The CC certification proves that an impartial third party did an evaluation.

As an administrator, you should know and thoroughly understand that just because the operating system you have is capable of being certified at a high level of security doesn't mean that your implementation is at that level.

Secure Router Configuration

One of the most important things you can do to secure your network is make sure you secure the router. As much common sense as it makes, it is too often overlooked in the hurry to get the router configuration finished and move on to the next job. To securely configure the router, you must do the following:

Change the Default Password.   The password for the administrator is set before the router leaves the factory. You have to assume that every miscreant wanting unauthorized access to your network knows the default passwords set by the factory. Employ good password principles (alphanumeric, more than 8 characters, etc.) and change it to a value that only those who must know do.

Walk through the Advanced Settings.   These settings will differ based on the router manufacturer and type but often include settings to block ping requests, perform MAC filtering, and so on. All of these issues are discussed elsewhere in this book and need to be applied to the router configuration the same as they would be applied elsewhere.

Keep the Firmware Upgraded.   Router manufacturers often issue patches when problems are discovered. Those patches need to be applied to the router to remove any security exploits that may exist.

Always remember to back up your router configuration before making any significant changes—in particular a firmware upgrade—to provide a fallback in case something goes awry.

 Cisco routers often utilize one of two different types of passwords for their accounts: Type 7 and MD5. Type 7 passwords use weak encryption and are considered only slightly above Type 0, which is cleartext. As such, Type 7 passwords are easily decrypted with readily available shareware/freeware and should be avoided. MD5 password encryption utilizes a one-way hash, and this is configured in IOS using the command **enable secret**.

Summary

The focus of this chapter was on access control and identity management. The key difference between authentication and identification is that authentication means someone has accurate information, while identification means the accurate information is proven to be in possession of the correct individual.

The most basic form of authentication is known as single factor authentication (SFA) because only one set of values is checked. To increase security, it is necessary to move to multifactor authentication, which involves two or more values that are checked.

This chapter examined the various types of authentication services in use, including RADIUS and different variations of TACACS. It also looked at tunneling protocols, smart cards, and other means of access control.

Security baselines provide a standardized method for evaluating the security capabilities of particular products. Never consider an operating system or application to be secured unless it has been certified using the EAL standard, which provides seven levels of certification. EAL 4 is the level recommended to provide reasonable security for commercial operating systems.

ACLs are being implemented in network devices and systems to enable the control of access to systems and users; ACLs allow individual systems, users, or IP addresses to be ignored.

Exam Essentials

Be able to describe the roles of access control.   The three primary roles are MAC, DAC, and RBAC. Mandatory Access Control (MAC) establishes rigid access control methods in the organization. Discretionary Access Control (DAC) allows for flexibility in access control. Role-Based Access Control (RBAC) is based on the role the individual or department has in the organization. In a fourth type, Rule-Based Access Control (RBAC), settings in preconfigured security policies are used to make all decisions.

Know the characteristics of the connectivity technologies available to you and the security capabilities associated with each.   Remote access, PPP, tunneling protocols, and VPNs are your primary tools. PPTP and L2TP are two of the most common protocols used for tunneling. IPSec, although not a tunneling protocol, provides encryption to tunneling protocols; it's often used to enhance tunnel security.

Know how ACLs work.   Access control lists (ACLs) are used to identify systems and specify which users, protocols, or services are allowed. ACL-based systems can be used to prevent unauthorized users from accessing vulnerable services.

Explain the relative advantages of the technologies available to you for authentication.   You have many tools available to establish authentication processes. Some of these tools start with a password and user ID. Others involve physical devices or the physical characteristics of the person who is requesting authentication.

Be able to identify the differences and characteristics of the technologies available to you.   A network can be segmented, and VLANs can be created to improve security. NAT presents only one Internet address to the world, hiding the other elements of the network. Tunneling allows you to make relatively secure connections to other networks using the Internet.

Review Questions

1. Most of your client's sales force have been told that they should no longer report to the office on a daily basis. From now on, they're to spend the majority of their time on the road calling on customers. Each member of the sales force has been issued a laptop computer and told to connect to the network nightly through a remote connection. Which of the following protocols is widely used today as a transport protocol for remote Internet connections?

   A. SMTP

   B. PPP

   C. PPTP

   D. L2TP

2. Which protocol is unsuitable for WAN VPN connections?

   A. PPP

   B. PPTP

   C. L2TP

   D. IPSec

3. You've been given notice that you'll soon be transferred to another site. Before you leave, you're to audit the network and document everything in use and the reason why it's in use. The next administrator will use this documentation to keep the network running. Which of the following protocols isn't a tunneling protocol but is probably used at your site by tunneling protocols for network security?

   A. IPSec

   B. PPTP

   C. L2TP

   D. L2F

4. The present method of requiring access to be strictly defined on every object is proving too cumbersome for your environment. The edict has come down from upper management that access requirements should be reduced slightly. Which access model allows users some flexibility for information-sharing purposes?

   A. DAC

   B. MAC

   C. RBAC

   D. MLAC

5. A newly hired junior administrator will assume your position temporarily while you attend a conference. You're trying to explain the basics of security to her in as short a period of time as possible. Which of the following best describes an ACL?

   A. ACLs provide individual access control to resources.

   B. ACLs aren't used in modern systems.

   C. The ACL process is dynamic in nature.

   D. ACLs are used to authenticate users.

6. LDAP is an example of which of the following?

   A. Directory access protocol

   B. IDS

   C. Tiered model application development environment

   D. File server

7. Upper management has suddenly become concerned about security. As the senior network administrator, you are asked to suggest changes that should be implemented. Which of the following access methods should you recommend if the method is to be one that is primarily based on preestablished access and can't be changed by users?

   A. MAC

   B. DAC

   C. RBAC

   D. Kerberos

8. Your office administrator is being trained to perform server backups. Which authentication method would be ideal for this situation?

   A. MAC

   B. DAC

   C. RBAC

   D. Security tokens

9. You've been assigned to mentor a junior administrator and bring him up to speed quickly. The topic you're currently explaining is authentication. Which method uses a KDC to accomplish authentication for users, programs, or systems?

   A. CHAP

   B. Kerberos

   C. Biometrics

   D. Smart cards

10. After a careful risk analysis, the value of your company's data has been increased. Accordingly, you're expected to implement authentication solutions that reflect the increased value of the data. Which of the following authentication methods uses more than one authentication process for a logon?

   A. Multifactor

   B. Biometrics

   C. Smart card

   D. Kerberos

11. You're the administrator for Mercury Technical. Due to several expansions, the network has grown exponentially in size within the past two years. Which of the following is a popular method for breaking a network into smaller private networks that can coexist on the same wiring and yet be unaware of each other?

   A. VLAN

   B. NAT

   C. MAC

   D. Security zone

12. Which technology allows a connection to be made between two networks using a secure protocol?

   A. Tunneling

   B. VLAN

   C. Internet

   D. Extranet

13. Your company provides medical data to doctors from a worldwide database. Because of the sensitive nature of the data you work with, it's imperative that authentication be established on each session and be valid only for that session. Which of the following authentication methods provides credentials that are valid only during a single session?

   A. Tokens

   B. Certificate

   C. Smart card

   D. Kerberos

13. Which of the following is the term used whenever two or more parties authenticate each other?

   A. SSO

   B. Multifactor authentication

   C. Mutual authentication

   D. Tunneling

15. Which of the following security areas encompasses network access control (NAC)?

  A. Physical security

  B. Operational security

  C. Management security

  D. Triad security

16. You have added a new child domain to your network. As a result of this, the child has adopted all the trust relationships with other domains in the forest that existed for its parent domain. What is responsible for this?

  A. LDAP access

  B. XML access

  C. Fuzzing access

  D. Transitive access

17. What is invoked when a person claims they are the user but cannot be authenticated—such as when they lose their password?

  A. Identity proofing

  B. Social engineering

  C. Directory traversal

  D. Cross-site requesting

18. Which of the following is a client-server-oriented environment that operates in a manner similar to RADIUS?

  A. HSM

  B. TACACS

  C. TPM

  D. ACK

19. What is implied at the end of each access control list?

  A. Least privilege

  B. Separation of duties

  C. Implicit deny

  D. Explicit allow

20. Which of the following is a type of smart card issued by the Department of Defense as a general identification/authentication card for military personnel, contractors, and non-DoD employees?

  A. PIV

  B. POV

  C. DLP

  D. CAC

Answers to Review Questions

1. B. PPP can pass multiple protocols and is widely used today as a transport protocol for remote connections.

2. A. PPP provides no security, and all activities are unsecure. PPP is primarily intended for remote connections and should never be used for VPN connections.

3. A. IPSec provides network security for tunneling protocols. IPSec can be used with many different protocols besides TCP/IP, and it has two modes of security.

4. A. DAC allows some flexibility in information-sharing capabilities within the network.

5. A. Access control lists allow individual and highly controllable access to resources in a network. An ACL can also be used to exclude a particular system, IP address, or user.

6. A. Lightweight Directory Access Protocol (LDAP) is a directory access protocol used to publish information about users. This is the computer equivalent of a phone book.

7. A. Mandatory Access Control (MAC) is oriented toward preestablished access. This access is typically established by network administrators and can't be changed by users.

8. C. Role-Based Access Control (RBAC) allows specific people to be assigned to specific roles with specific privileges. A backup operator would need administrative privileges to back up a server. This privilege would be limited to the role and wouldn't be present during the employee's normal job functions.

9. B. Kerberos uses a key distribution center (KDC) to authenticate a principal. The KDC provides a credential that can be used by all Kerberos-enabled servers and applications.

10. A. A multifactor authentication method uses two or more processes for logon. A two-factor method might use smart cards and biometrics for logon.

11. A. Virtual local area networks (VLANs) break a large network into smaller networks. These networks can coexist on the same wiring and be unaware of each other. A router or other routing-type device would be needed to connect these VLANs.

12. A. Tunneling allows a network to make a secure connection to another network through the Internet or other network. Tunnels are usually secure and present themselves as extensions of both networks.

13. A. Tokens are created when a user or system successfully authenticates. The token is destroyed when the session is over.

14. C. Whenever two or more parties authenticate each other, this is known as mutual authentication.

15. B. Operational security issues include network access control (NAC), authentication, and security topologies after the network installation is complete.

16. D. Transitive access exists between the domains and creates this relationship.

17. A. Identity proofing is invoked when a person claims they are the user but cannot be authenticated, such as when they lose their password.

18. B. Terminal Access Controller Access-Control System (TACACS) is a client-server-oriented environment, and it operates in a manner similar to how RADIUS operates.

19. C. An implicit deny clause is implied at the end of each ACL, and it means that if the proviso in question has not been explicitly granted, then it is denied.

20. D. One type of smart card is the Common Access Card (CAC). These cards are issued by the Department of Defense as a general identification/authentication card for military personnel, contractors, and non-DoD employees.

Chapter

6

Educating and Protecting the User

THE FOLLOWING COMPTIA SECURITY+ EXAM OBJECTIVES ARE COVERED IN THIS CHAPTER:

✓ **2.4 Explain the importance of security related awareness and training.**

- Security policy training and procedures
- Personally identifiable information
- Information classification: Sensitivity of data (hard or soft)
- Data labeling, handling, and disposal
- Compliance with laws, best practices, and standards
- User habits: Password behaviors; Data handling; Clean desk policies; Prevent tailgating; Personally owned devices
- Threat awareness: New viruses; Phishing attacks; Zero days exploits
- Use of social networking and P2P

✓ **3.2 Analyze and differentiate among types of attacks.**

- Vishing
- Malicious insider threat

✓ **3.3 Analyze and differentiate among types of social engineering attacks.**

- Shoulder surfing
- Dumpster diving
- Tailgating

- Impersonation

- Hoaxes

- Whaling

- Vishing

✓ **3.5 Analyze and differentiate among types of application attacks.**

- Zero day

Several years back, *InformationWeek* conducted a survey in partnership with Accenture. As part of the survey, the question "What are the biggest security challenges facing your company?" was asked. Multiple responses were allowed, and 58 percent of the respondents stated that managing the complexity of security was one of their biggest challenges, while 56 percent selected user awareness (http://www.verisign.com/static/DEV037173.pdf). As evident by this survey, managing security and educating users are major concerns for many organizations. Keeping computers and networks secure involves more than just the technical aspects of the systems and networks. The weakest link in many cases is the employee/user who has access to data and a less-than-full understanding of some of the security problems that they may encounter.

You, as a security professional, must address the issue of user weakness using a balanced response from both a technical perspective and a business perspective. It is your responsibility to keep the data safe and if that means training the users in addition to implementing tighter network security, then, as Lady Macbeth so eloquently put it, "Screw your courage to the sticking place, and we'll not fail."

This chapter will help you understand the complexities of managing security and the issues involved with users and their need for training and education. It also looks at some of the legal regulations governing data—those that you need to be aware of and that your users may as well. Lastly, it examines the growing issue of social engineering.

Understanding Security Awareness and Training

Security awareness and training are critical to the success of a security effort. They include explaining policies, procedures, and current threats to both users and management.

A security-awareness and training program can do much to assist in your efforts to improve and maintain security. Such efforts need to be ongoing, and they should be part of the organization's normal communications to be effective. The following sections discuss some of the things you can do as a security professional to address the business issues associated with training the people in your organization to operate in a manner that is consistent with organizational security goals.

Much of objective 3.3, "Analyze and differentiate among types of social engineering attacks," is covered in Chapter 4. Only those portions of it that are also relevant to social engineering appear in this chapter.

Communicating with Users to Raise Awareness

Communication and awareness help ensure that security information is conveyed to the appropriate people in a timely manner. Most users aren't aware of current security threats. If you set a process in place to concisely and clearly explain what is happening and what is being done to correct current threats, you'll probably find acceptance of your efforts to be much higher.

Communication methods that have proven to be effective for disseminating information include internal security websites, news servers, and emails. You might want to consider a regular notification process to convey information about security issues and changes. In general, the more you communicate about this in a routine manner, the more likely people will internalize the fact that security is everybody's responsibility.

Providing Education and Training

Your efforts in education and training must help users clearly understand prevention, enforcement, and threats. In addition to the efforts of the IT staff, the security department will also probably be responsible for a security-awareness program. Your organization's training and educational programs need to be tailored for at least three different audiences:

- The organization as a whole (the so-called rank and file employees)
- Management
- Technical staff

These three organizational roles have different considerations and concerns. For example, with organization-wide training, everyone understands the policies, procedures, and resources available to deal with security problems, so it helps ensure that all employees are on the same page. The following list identifies the types of issues that members of an organization should be aware of and understand.

Organization   Ideally, a security-awareness training program for the entire organization should cover the following areas:

- Importance of security
- Responsibilities of people in the organization
- Policies and procedures
- Usage policies
- Account and password-selection criteria
- Social engineering prevention

You can accomplish this training either by using internal staff or by hiring outside trainers. I recommend doing much of this training during new-employee orientation and staff meetings. To stay in their forefront of their minds, though, the training needs to be repeated periodically (once a year often works well). Also, don't forget to have the employees sign that they received the training and are aware of the policies.

Management Managers are concerned with more global issues in the organization, including enforcing security policies and procedures. Managers will want to know the hows and whys of a security program: how it works and why it is necessary. They should receive additional training or exposure that explains the issues, threats, and methods of dealing with threats. Management will also be concerned about productivity impacts, enforcement, and how the various departments are affected by security policies.

Technical Staff The technical staff needs special knowledge about the methods, implementations, and capabilities of the systems used to manage security. Network administrators will want to evaluate how to manage the network, best practices, and configuration issues associated with the technologies they support. Developers and implementers will want to evaluate the impact these measures have on existing systems and new development projects. The training that both administrators and developers need will be vendor specific; vendors have their own methods of implementing security.

Microsoft, Novell, and Cisco each offer certification programs to train administrators on their environments. All of these manufacturers have specific courseware on security implementations, and some offer security certification. You should implement security systems consistent with the manufacturer's suggestions and guidance. Implementing security in a non-standard way may leave your system unsecure.

Keep in mind that all of your efforts will be wasted if you don't make sure you reach an appropriate audience. Spending an hour preaching on backend database security will likely be an hour wasted if the only members of the audience are data-entry personnel who get paid by the keystroke to make weekly changes as quickly as possible.

Training Topics

It is said that knowledge is a powerful tool. Armed with it, you are more capable of tackling problems and avoiding pitfalls than without it. What is true for you is also true for the users with whom you work—the more they know about security issues, the better they are able to avoid pitfalls and recognize problems when they encounter them.

While it would be nice if you could get every user to fully understand security and stay current on the topic, this luxury exists in only a few workplaces. Given the limitations for educating the entire work staff, there are a number of topics that can be considered more important than others and on which you should focus user education, in no particular order:

Clean Desk Policy Information on a desk—in terms of printouts, pads of note paper, sticky notes, and the like—can be easily seen by prying eyes and often absconded. To protect data and your business, encourage having clean desks and keeping out only papers that are relevant to the project the user is working on at that moment. All sensitive information should be put away when the user is away from their desk.

Real World Scenario

Applying Education Appropriately

As a security administrator, you need to know the level of knowledge that is appropriate for the audience you're addressing and be able to understand the importance of speaking to them at that level. Imagine that you find yourself in each of the following situations, and think through your response. Remember that it's important to give the right message to the right people. When giving any presentation, you should always tailor it for the audience and be able to make your discussion relevant to them. Recommendations for how to handle each situation are provided after each scenario.

Scenario 1   You've been assigned the task of giving a one-hour briefing on the topic of security to management during their weekly luncheon (no other subtopics or specifics were given). Most of those in attendance will be upper management who know little about computers and tend to focus on financial sheets. What topics will you discuss and at what depth?

> **Recommendation**   Keep the talk at the overview level and focus on only the basics of security: why it's needed, how valuable data is, how to use good passwords, and so on.

Scenario 2   You've been told to meet with the developers of a new application that will soon be rolled out to all branch offices. The application will hold all human resource records as well as a small amount of client information. Your boss tells you that after the meeting, you're to sign off on the application as being okay to deploy. What type of security questions will you focus on?

> **Recommendation**   Push to test the application in a test environment first (nonproduction). You want to make certain that no back doors have been left in by the developers and that no negative interactions will occur between the new application and what is already running on your systems

Scenario 3   The annual company meeting is next month. Representatives, including those in IT, from all remote offices will arrive at headquarters for a three-day visit. You've been asked to speak about the importance of strong passwords throughout the organization. What will you say, and how will you make your one-hour presentation stay with them after they return to their offices?

> **Recommendation**   Give examples of security breaches that have been in the news recently. Talk about the impact such an event would have on your organization. Discuss how simple it is to prevent many attacks by implementing strong passwords; then give examples. Be sure to talk about how this affects their own jobs.

Compliance with Laws, Best Practices, and Standards   Users need to realize that working with data is the same as driving a car, owning a home, or almost anything else in that there are laws, practices, and standards they have to adhere to. Just as negligence fails to be an admissible excuse in other areas of the law, the same holds true when working with data. New regulations are passed regularly, and it is your job as an administrator to educate users on those that are applicable to your environment.

Regulations are discussed in greater detail at the end of this chapter.

Data Handling   Data should be accessed only by those users needing to work with it. While it is your job to implement safeguards to keep the data from being seen by those who should not, the users need to understand why those safeguards are there and abide by them. Plenty of examples of companies have suffered great financial loss when company information, trade secrets, and client information was leaked.

Dealing with Personally-Owned Devices   Empathize with the users who want to bring their gadgets from home, but make them comprehend why they cannot. You do not want them plugging in a flash drive, let alone a camera, phone, MP3 player, or other device on which company files could get intermingled with personal files. Allowing this to happen can create situations where data can leave the building that shouldn't as well as introduce malware to the system. There has been a rash of incidents in which data has been smuggled out of an organization through personal devices, with one of the most notorious being the 250,000 Top Secret documents that appeared on WikiLeaks (`http://www.dailymail .co.uk/news/article-1333982/WikiLeaks-US-Army-soldier-Bradley-Manning-prime-suspect-leaks-case.html`).

Employees should not sync unauthorized smartphones to their work systems. Some smartphones use multiple wireless spectrums and unwittingly open up the possibility for an attacker in the parking lot to gain access through the phone to the internal network.

Ban—and make sure the users know that you have done so—all social peer-to-peer (*P2P*) networking. These are common for sharing files such as movies and music, but you must not allow users to bring in devices and create their own little networks to share files, printers, songs, and so on. All networking must be done through administrators and not on a peer basis. The P2P ports should be listed on the company servers (either whitelisted or blacklisted), and an alert should be sent to you anytime anyone attempts any P2P activity. Vigilantly look for all such activity and put a stop to it immediately.

Personally Identifiable Information   Personally identifiable information (PII) is a catchall for any data that can be used to uniquely identify an individual. This data can be anything from the person's name to a fingerprint (think biometrics), credit card number, or patient record. The term became mainstream when the NIST (National Institute of Standards and Technology) began issuing guides and recommendations regarding it.

In April, 2010, the NIST published Special Publication 800-122, "Guide to Protecting the Confidentiality of Personally Identifiable Information (PII)," and it defines PII as "any information about an individual maintained by an agency, including (1) any information that can be used to distinguish or trace an individual's identity, such as name, social security number, date and place of birth, mother's maiden name, or biometric records; and (2) any other information that is linked or linkable to an individual, such as medical, educational, financial, and employment information." This document can be found at http:// csrc.nist.gov/publications/nistpubs/800-122/sp800-122.pdf

Users within your organization should understand PII and the reasons to safeguard their own data as well as respect the records of customers and other users. According to the NIST, "For PII protection, awareness methods include informing staff of new scams that are being used to steal identities, providing updates on privacy items in the news such as government data breaches and their effect on individuals and the organization, providing examples of how staff members have been held accountable for inappropriate actions, and providing examples of recommended privacy practices." To help users understand the significance of PII, explain that the SIM (Subscriber Identification Module) card in their smart phone contains PII information about them and they would not want it to fall into other hands.

Prevent Tailgating   *Tailgating* is the term used for someone being so close to you when you enter a building that they are able to come in right behind you without needing to use a key, a card, or any other security device. Many social engineering intruders needing physical access to a site will use this method of gaining entry. Educate users to beware of this and other social engineering ploys and prevent them from happening.

Sometimes the term *piggybacking* is used in place of *tailgating*, but there is a key difference between the two. In tailgating, the person in front does not give permission to the person behind, while with piggybacking, they do give permission.

Safe Internet Habits   As we discussed in Chapter 4, users should be familiar enough with phishing to comprehend that they should not click links or open attachments to files that they weren't expecting. They should appreciate that the best way to close pop-ups is to click the X in the upper-right corner and never by clicking OK or anything else in the pop-up.

Software should never be downloaded or installed from unknown sites. While the user may think they are saving the company money by finding a free version of software that promises to work just like an expensive package, the odds of malware accompanying the free program are considerable; administrators should contend with the high cost of software and not end users.

One of the most wicked phishing undertakings popular today is a fake security/antivirus program. A pop-up tells the user that their system is infected with a virus and to get rid of it they need to run a program that looks like an authorized cleanup tool but is actually itself the virus (http://www.microsoft.com/security/antivirus/rogue.aspx).

Smart Computing Habits   Every user should know that they should never introduce any stray media into their system regardless of how innocent they may think their actions. A flash drive found in the trashcan with "Pix of Chelsea" written on it can contain the Trojan needed to open a back door into the network.

Encourage reading of the EULA (End User License Agreement) on any third-party software. These can be more difficult to get through than a law school application form, but seeing what they are agreeing to can be an eye-opener for a user when they realize what limitations they are working with and what they're giving up. Discourage users from installing any third-party software without IT approval.

Social Networking Dangers   As of this writing, many companies allow full use of social media in the workplace believing that the marketing opportunities it holds outweigh any loss in productivity. What they are minimalizing are the threats that exist. Rather than being all new threats, the social networking/media threats tend to fall in the categories of the same old tricks used elsewhere but in a new format. A tweet can be sent with a shortened URL so that it does not exceed the 140-character limit set by Twitter; unfortunately, the user has no idea what the shortened URL leads to, and it can be to a phishing site, a downloadable Trojan, or just about anything else.

Educate users to exercise the same care and caution in social media as in any other environment. For an example of the dangers of this, read about "Cisco Fatty" (`http://www.msnbc`
`.msn.com/id/29901380/ns/technology_and_science-tech_and_gadgets/`).

The Need for All Computing to Be Safe   Many users work on data away from the office as well as in the office. They need to understand that the data is only as strong as the weakest place in which it is used, and they need to have security measures on their home computers that protect your company's data as well. While the home systems will never be as secure (most likely) as the business systems, at a minimum the home systems need to be running firewalls and updated virus scanners.

Since they need to be safe at home, educate them on the necessity to keep current on new threats. Those threats can come in the form of new viruses, new forms of phishing attacks, and new *zero day exploits*. The latter is the term used when a hole is found in a web browser or other software and miscreants begin exploiting it the very day it is discovered by the developer (bypassing the one-to-two-day response time many software providers need to put out a patch once the hole has been found).

 Zero day exploits are incredibly difficult to respond to. If attackers learn of the weakness the same day as the developer, then they have the ability to exploit it until a patch is released. Often, the only thing you as a security administrator can do between the discovery of the exploit and the release of the patch is to turn off the service. While this can be a costly undertaking in terms of productivity, it is the only way to keep the network safe. In 2010, Stuxnet was found to be using a total of four zero day vulnerabilities to spread (`http://www.symantec.com/connect/blogs/stuxnet-using-`
`three-additional-zero-day-vulnerabilities`).

The Value of Strong Passwords   Passwords are a common topic in this chapter and throughout this book. Users need to understand that the more difficult they make the password, the more difficulty they add to someone's attempt to crack it. They should be educated to use long passwords consisting of letters, numbers, and characters and to change them frequently.

They must also be educated that they cannot write their password down on a sticky note right after a change and post it under the keyboard, on the monitor, or anywhere else. The reasons for regularly changing passwords should be explained along with the requirement that you will make them do so at least every three months.

Microsoft has an online password checker that you can direct users to if they want to see how strong the value they are considering using for a password is. This can be found at https://www.microsoft.com/protect/fraud/passwords/checker.aspx.

Understanding Data Labeling and Handling   A great many users don't consider that there are different types of data and various values associated with them. They don't realize that a misplaced backup copy of the mission statement is not as great a loss from a financial standpoint as a misplaced backup copy of customer contacts.

As a security administrator, you should help users to realize that different types of data unique to your organization have different values and need to be labeled accordingly (the discussion of information models later in this chapter will help). Once it has been established and understood that there are signification differences, then you can address handling. The importance of protecting the data in all forms—online, backups, hard copies, and so on—should be covered as well as reasons why different groups cannot/should not access data outside of their permission category (again, the discussion of information models later in this chapter will help).

What to Do When Disposing of Old Media   Many users never think about data beyond the time that they are working with it. They don't realize that the old computer they toss out at home has copies of company-related files on the hard drive that could fall into the wrong hands. Or that the 256MB flash drive they finally toss away when they buy a new 32GB one also has files that should never be seen outside of the office. A good example of the importance of this is the tale of the U.S. missile data found on a hard drive purchased on eBay (http://www.independent.co.uk/news/world/americas/us-missile-data-found-on-ebay-hard-drive-1680529.html).

Teaching users the basics of *data disposal*—how to destroy media (such as by hammer, drill, or fire)—can be one of the most fun, and most memorable, training sessions of the year.

Responding to Hoaxes   In addition to all the different types of attacks that are present, there are also a plethora of hoaxes that exist. A *hoax* is defined as a deliberately fabricated falsehood. Just as the creator of a virus enjoys seeing his work do damage and knowing that he caused it, those who start hoaxes enjoy knowing that they caused a panic, and the Internet allows them to see the hoax spread with wild abandon. Most hoaxes are spread through email and alert the recipient to impending doom—their computer will crash if not turned off at 1:00 on Friday the 13th, they have been infected with the Lincoln virus if their hard drive has a file named WINWORD.EXE present, and so on. Software that tries to convince unsuspecting users that a threat exists is known as scareware. If it convinces them to pay money for protection from a fake threat, then the term rogueware is applied.

As a security administrator, you need to educate users that the best course of action when they receive such messages is to refuse to panic and to contact IT. Assure them that you will verify whether it is a hoax or a legitimate issue as quickly as possible and let them know. Under no circumstances, they should understand, are they to spread the warning and further propagate the alarm.

How security training is delivered—both in terms of method and frequency—will differ for most businesses. It is important, however, that new employees understand the importance of security on their first day at the job and that they be presented with a clearly articulated security policy that mentions the possible HR actions if they violate that policy.

As the administrator, you want to make certain you are taking a proactive stance and educating users on potential problems before they become real issues and revisit key topics often enough that they realize the importance of them.

Classifying Information

Information classification is a key aspect of a secure network. Again, the process of developing a classification scheme is both a technical and a human issue. The technologies you use must be able to support your organization's privacy requirements. People and processes must be in place and working effectively to prevent unauthorized disclosure of sensitive information.

 For this exam, CompTIA has an objective related to classifying data as "hard" or "soft." These are not standard industry terms for data classification. In general, however, anything "soft" is subject to adaptation, while anything "hard" is not. Soft mechanisms include policies and human elements, while hard mechanisms include alerts and system-driven events.

If you think about all the information your organization keeps, you'll probably find that it breaks down into three primary categories:

- Public use
- Internal use
- Restricted use

Figure 6.1 shows the typical ratios of how this information is broken down. Notice that 80 percent of the information in your organization is primarily for internal or private use. This information would include memos, working papers, financial data, and information records, among other things.

FIGURE 6.1 Information categories

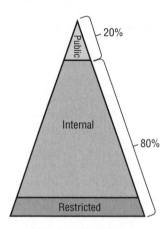

The following discussion looks at public information—and the various categories of it—and is followed by a discussion of private information.

Public Information

Public information is primarily information that is made available either to the larger public or to specific individuals who need it. Financial statements of a privately held organization might be information that is available publicly but only to individuals or organizations that have a legitimate need for it.

The important thing to keep in mind is that an organization needs to develop policies about what information is available and for what purposes it will be disseminated. It's also helpful to make sure that members of the organization know who has authorization to make these kinds of disclosures. There are organizations that gather competitive data for a fee; they often use social engineering approaches to gain information about a business. Good policies help prevent the accidental dissemination of sensitive information.

The following sections discuss the difference between limited and full distribution.

Limited Distribution

Limited distribution information isn't intended for release to the public. This category of information isn't secret, but it's private. If a company is seeking to obtain a line of credit, the information provided to a bank is of a private nature. This information, if disclosed to competitors, might give them insight into the organization's plans or financial health. If disclosed to customers, it might scare them and cause them to switch to a competitor.

Some End User License Agreements (EULAs) now limit the information that users can disclose about problems with their software. These new statements have not yet been challenged in court. Try to avoid being the test case for this new and alarming element of some software licenses; read the EULA before you agree to it.

These types of disclosures are usually held in confidence by banks and financial institutions. These institutions typically have privacy and confidentiality regulations as well as policies that must be followed by all employees of the institution.

Software manufacturers typically release early versions of their products to customers who are willing to help evaluate functionality. Early versions of software may not always work properly, and they often have features that aren't included in the final version. This version of the software is a *beta test*. Before beta testers are allowed to use the software, they're required to sign a nondisclosure agreement (NDA). The NDA tells the tester what privacy requirements exist for the product. The product being developed will change, and any problems with the beta version probably won't be a great secret. However, the NDA reminds the testers of their confidentiality responsibilities.

> NDAs are common in the technology arena. Make sure you read any NDA thoroughly before you sign it. You don't have to sign an NDA to be bound by it: If you agree that you'll treat the information as private and then receive the information, you have in essence agreed to an NDA. In most cases, this form of verbal NDA is valid for only one year.

Statements indicating privacy or confidentiality are common on limited-access documents. They should indicate that disclosure of the information without permission is a breach of confidentiality. This may help someone remember that the information isn't for public dissemination.

Full Distribution

Marketing materials are examples of information that should be available for *full distribution*. Annual reports to stockholders and other information of a public-relations nature are also examples of full-distribution materials.

The key element of the full-distribution classification involves decision-making responsibility. Who makes the decision about full disclosure? Larger organizations have a corporate communications department that is responsible for managing this process. If you aren't sure, it's a good idea to ask about dissemination of information. Don't assume that you know; this is the purpose of an information classification policy.

Private Information

Private information is intended only for use internally in the organization. This type of information could potentially embarrass the company, disclose trade secrets, or adversely affect personnel. Private information may also be referred to as *working documents* or *work product*. It's important that private information not be disclosed because it can potentially involve litigation if the disclosure is improper.

You'll learn about the difference between internal and restricted information in the following sections.

Internal Information

Internal information includes personnel records, financial working documents, ledgers, customer lists, and virtually any other information that is needed to run a business. This information is valuable and must be protected.

In the case of personnel and medical records, disclosure to unauthorized personnel creates liability issues. Many organizations are unwilling to do anything more than verify employment because of the fear of unauthorized disclosure.

A school views student information as internal. Schools can't release information about students without specific permission from the student.

Restricted Information

Restricted information could seriously damage the organization if disclosed. It includes proprietary processes, trade secrets, strategic information, and marketing plans. This information should never be disclosed to an outside party unless senior management gives specific authorization. In many cases, this type of information is also placed on a *need-to-know basis*—unless you need to know, you won't be informed.

Government and Military Classifications

The U.S. government and the military have slightly different sets of concerns relating to information classification. Governmental agencies are concerned about privacy and national security. Because of this, a unique system of classification and access controls has been implemented to protect information.

Following is a list of some of the types of government classifications:

Unclassified   This classification is used to indicate that the information poses no risk of potential loss due to disclosure. Anybody can gain access to this category of information. Many training manuals and regulations are unclassified.

Sensitive but Unclassified   This classification is used for low-level security. It indicates that disclosure of this information might cause harm but wouldn't harm national defense efforts. The amount of toilet paper a military base uses may be considered sensitive because this information might help an intelligence agency guess at the number of personnel on the base.

Confidential   This classification is used to identify low-level secrets; it's generally the lowest level of classification used by the military. It's used extensively to prevent access to sensitive information. Information that is lower than Confidential is generally considered Unclassified. The Confidential classification, however, allows information to be restricted for access under the Freedom of Information Act. The maintenance requirements for a machine gun may be classified as Confidential; this information would include drawings, procedures, and specifications that disclose how the weapon works.

Secret   Secret information, if disclosed, could cause serious and irreparable damage to defense efforts. Information that is classified as Secret requires special handling, training, and storage. This information is considered a closely guarded secret of the military or government. Troop movements, deployments, capabilities, and other plans would be minimally classified as Secret. The military views the unauthorized disclosure of Secret information as criminal and potentially treasonous.

Top Secret   The Top Secret classification is the highest classification level. There are rumored to be higher levels of classification, but the names of those classifications are themselves classified Top Secret. Releasing information that is classified as Top Secret poses a grave threat to national security, and therefore it must not be compromised. Information such as intelligence activities, nuclear war plans, and weapons systems development would normally be classified as Top Secret.

The government has also developed a process to formally review and downgrade classification levels on a regular basis. This process generally downgrades information based on age, sensitivity, and usefulness. There are methods of overriding this downgrade process to prevent certain information from being declassified; some secrets are best left secret.

The military also uses an additional method of classifying information and access, which has the effect of compartmentalizing information. For example, if you were a weapons developer, it isn't likely that you would need access to information from spy satellites. You would be given special access to information necessary for the specific project you were working on. When the project was finished, access to this special information would be revoked. This process allows information to be protected and access limited to a need-to-know basis.

The process of obtaining a security clearance either for the military, a federal office or lab, or a government contractor can be quite involved. The normal process involves investigating you, your family, and potentially anybody else who could put you in a compromised position. The process can take months, and it includes agents doing fieldwork to complete, or augment, the investigation.

Information Access Controls

Access control defines the methods used to ensure that users of your network can access only what they're authorized to access. The process of access control should be spelled out in the organization's security policies and standards. Several models exist to accomplish this. Regardless of the model you use, a few concepts carry over:

Implicit Denies   These are where you specifically lock certain users out. In Unix and Linux, for example, you can choose who can use the at service by configuring either an at.allow or an at.deny file. If you configure the at.allow file, then only those users specifically named can use the service and all others cannot. Conversely, if you configure the at.deny file, then only the users named in that file cannot use the service (you are implicitly denying them) and all others can.

Least Privilege   You should use this model when assigning permissions. Give users only the permissions they need to do their work and no more.

Job Rotation   Rotate jobs on a frequent enough basis that you are not putting yourself—and your data—at the mercy of any one administrator. Just as you want redundancy in hardware, you want redundancy in abilities. Web administrators, for example, can be moved to database administration and can become more valuable to the organization and themselves by gaining that skillset. Depending on the size of your organization, this may be easy or difficult to do, but it is highly recommended in all cases.

The following sections briefly explain the most common information models. A solid understanding of these will help you in the workplace as well as prepare you for the Security+ exam:

- Bell-LaPadula model
- Biba model
- Clark-Wilson model
- Information Flow model
- Noninterference model

Noninterference Bell-LaPadula Model

The *Bell-LaPadula model* was designed for the military to address the storage and protection of classified information. The model is specifically designed to prevent unauthorized access to classified information. The model prevents the user from accessing information that has a higher security rating than they're authorized to access. The model also prevents information from being written to a lower level of security.

For example, if you're authorized to access Secret information, you aren't allowed to access Top Secret information, nor are you allowed to write to the system at a level lower than the Secret level. This creates upper and lower bounds for information storage. This process is illustrated in Figure 6.2. Notice in the illustration that you can't *read up* or *write down*. This means that a user can't read information at a higher level than they're authorized to access. A person writing a file can't write down to a lower level than the security level they're authorized to access.

The process of preventing a write down keeps a user from accidentally breaching security by writing Secret information to the next lower level, Confidential. In our example, you can read Confidential information, but because you're approved at the Secret level, you can't write to the Confidential level. This model doesn't deal with integrity, only confidentiality. A user of Secret information can potentially modify other documents at the same level they possess.

FIGURE 6.2   The Bell-LaPadula model

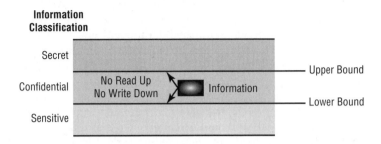

To see how this model works, think about corporate financial information. The chief financial officer (CFO) might have financial information about the company that needs to be protected. The Bell-LaPadula model would keep them from inadvertently posting information at an access level lower than their access level (writing down), thus preventing unauthorized or accidental disclosure of sensitive information. Lower-level employees wouldn't be able to access this information because they couldn't read up to the level of the CFO.

 The main thing to remember about the Bell-LaPadula model is that it interacts with every access—allowing it or disallowing it.

The Biba Model

The *Biba model* was designed after the Bell-LaPadula model. The Biba model is similar in concept to the Bell-LaPadula model, but its tenets are concentrated more on information integrity, an area that the Bell-LaPadula model doesn't address. In this model, there is no write up or read down. In short, if you're assigned access to Top Secret information, you can't read Secret information or write to any level higher than the level to which you're authorized. This keeps higher-level information pure by preventing less-reliable information from being intermixed with it. Figure 6.3 illustrates this concept in more detail. The Biba model was developed primarily for industrial uses, where confidentiality is usually less important than integrity.

FIGURE 6.3   The Biba model

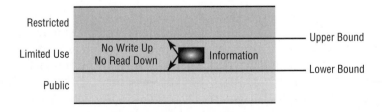

Think about the data that is generated by a researcher for a scientific project. The researcher is responsible for managing the results of research from a lower-level project and incorporating it into his research data. If bad data were to get into his research, the whole research project would be ruined. With the Biba model, this accident couldn't happen. The researcher wouldn't have access to the information from lower levels: That information would have to be promoted to the level of the researcher. This system would keep the researcher's data intact and prevent accidental contamination.

> The Biba model differs from Bell-LaPadula in the implementation of a lattice of integrity levels that allows information to flow downward but not upward. For the exam, think of the "I" in Biba as relating to integrity.

The Clark-Wilson Model

The *Clark-Wilson model* was developed after the Biba model. The approach, however, is a little different from either the Biba or the Bell-LaPadula method. In this model, data can't be accessed directly: It must be accessed through applications that have predefined capabilities. This process prevents unauthorized modification, errors, and fraud from occurring. If a user needs access to information at a certain level of security, a specific program is used. This program may allow only read access to the information. If a user needed to modify data, they would have to use another application. This allows a *separation of duties* in that individuals are granted access only to the tools they need. All transactions have associated audit files and mechanisms to report modifications. Figure 6.4 illustrates this process. Access to information is gained by using a program that specializes in access management; this can be either a single program that controls all access or a set of programs that control access. Many software-management programs work by using this method of security.

FIGURE 6.4 The Clark-Wilson model

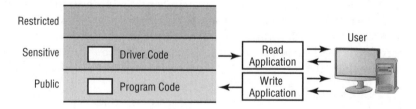

Let's say you are working on a software product as part of a team. You might need to access certain code to include in your programs. You aren't authorized to modify this code; you're merely authorized to use it. You would use a checkout program to get the code from the source library. Any attempt to put modified code back would be prevented. The developers of the code in the source library would be authorized to make changes. This process would ensure that only people authorized to change the code could accomplish the task.

The Clark-Wilson model focuses on business applications and consistency.

Information Flow Model

The *Information Flow model* is concerned with the properties of information flow, not only the direction of the flow. Both the Bell-LaPadula and Biba models are concerned with information flow in predefined manners; they're considered Information Flow models. However, this particular Information Flow model is concerned with all information flow, not just up or down. This model requires that each piece of information have unique properties, including operation capabilities. If an attempt were made to write lower-level information to a higher level, the model would evaluate the properties of the information and determine if the operation were legal. If the operation were illegal, the model would prevent it from occurring. Figure 6.5 illustrates this concept.

FIGURE 6.5   The Information Flow model

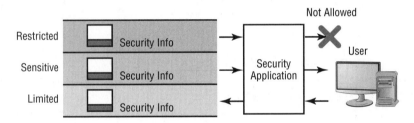

Let's use the previous software project as an example. A developer might be working with a version of the software to improve functionality. When the programmer had made improvements to the code, she would want to put that code back into the library. If the attempt to write the code were successful, the code would replace the existing code. If a subsequent bug were found in the new code, the old code would have been changed. The solution would be to create a new version of the code that incorporated both the new code and the old code. Each subsequent change to the code would require a new version to be created. While this process might consume more disk space, it would prevent things from getting lost, and it would provide a mechanism to use or evaluate an older version of the code.

Noninterference Model

The *Noninterference model* is intended to ensure that higher-level security functions don't interfere with lower-level functions. In essence, if a higher-level user were changing information, the lower-level user wouldn't know or be affected by the changes. This approach prevents the lower-level user from being able to deduce what changes are being made to the system. Figure 6.6 illustrates this concept. Notice that the lower-level user isn't aware that any changes have occurred above them.

FIGURE 6.6   The Noninterference model

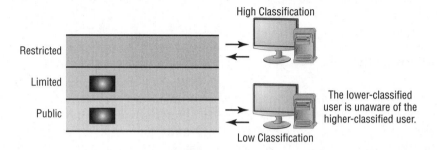

Let's take one last look at the software project with which we've been working. If a system developer were making changes to the library that was being used by a lower-level programmer, changes could be made to the library without the lower-level programmer being aware of them. This would allow the higher-level developer to work on prototypes without affecting the development effort of the lower-level programmer. When the developer finished the code, he could publish it to lower-level programmers. At this point, all users would have access to the changes, and they could use them in their programs.

Complying with Privacy and Security Regulations

An organization's security management policies don't exist in a vacuum. Regulatory and governmental agencies are key components of a security management policy. These agencies have made large improvements over the last several years to ensure the privacy of information; several laws have been passed to help ensure that information isn't disclosed to unauthorized parties. The following sections provide a brief overview of a few of these regulations. As a security professional, you must stay current with these laws because you're one of the primary agents to ensure compliance. Not only do you need to know them for the day-to-day grind, but CompTIA expects you to have a basic knowledge of them for the Security+ exam as well.

In addition to the federal laws, most states also have laws on computer crime. Check with your state attorney general's office for specific IT legislation that applies in your state.

The Health Insurance Portability and Accountability Act

The *Health Insurance Portability and Accountability Act (HIPAA)* is a regulation that mandates national standards and procedures for the storage, use, and transmission of personal medical information. Passed into law in 1996, HIPAA has caused a great deal of change in healthcare record keeping.

HIPAA covers three areas—confidentiality, privacy, and security of patient records—and was implemented in phases to make the transition easier. Confidentiality and privacy of patient records had to be implemented by a set date, followed by security of patient records. Standards for transaction codes in medical record transmissions had to be completed by a given date as well.

The penalties for HIPAA violations are very stiff: They can be as high as $250,000 based on the circumstances. Medical practices are required to appoint a security officer. All related parties, such as billing agencies and medical records storage facilities, are required to comply with these regulations.

For more information on HIPAA, you can visit `http://www.cms.hhs.gov/HIPAAGenInfo/`.

The Gramm-Leach-Bliley Act

The *Gramm-Leach-Bliley Act*, also known as the *Financial Modernization Act of 1999*, requires financial institutions to develop privacy notices and to notify customers that they are entitled to privacy. The act prohibits banks from releasing information to nonaffiliated third parties without permission. Many consumer groups have criticized the implementation of this act by financial institutions because of all the paperwork it has created.

Employees need to be trained on information security issues, and security measures must be put into place and tested to verify information privacy. The act includes a number of other provisions that allow banks and financial institutions to align and form partnerships.

The act requires banks to explain to individual consumers information-sharing policies. Customers have the ability to opt out of sharing agreements.

The act prohibits institutions from sharing account information for marketing purposes. It also prohibits the gathering of information about customers using false or fraudulent methods.

The law went into effect in July 2001. Financial officers and the board of directors can be held criminally liable for violations.

For more information on the Gramm-Leach-Bliley Act, visit `http://www.ftc.gov/privacy/privacyinitiatives/glbact.html`.

The Computer Fraud and Abuse Act

The *Computer Fraud and Abuse Act (CFAA)* was made into law in 1986. The original law was introduced to address issues of fraud and abuse that weren't well covered under existing statutes. The law was updated in 1994, in 1996, and again in 2001.

This act gives federal authorities, primarily the FBI, the ability to prosecute hackers, spammers, and others as terrorists. The law is primarily intended to protect government and financial computer systems from intrusion. Technically, if a governmental system, such as an Internet server, were used in the commission of the crime, virtually any computer user who could be shown to have any knowledge or part in the crime could be prosecuted.

The law is comprehensive and allows for stiff penalties, fines, and imprisonment of up to 10 years for convictions under this statute.

For more information on the Computer Fraud and Abuse Act, visit `http://cio.energy.gov/documents/ComputerFraud-AbuseAct.pdf`.

The Family Educational Rights and Privacy Act

The *Family Educational Rights and Privacy Act (FERPA)* dictates that educational institutions may not release information to unauthorized parties without the express permission of the student or, in the case of a minor, the parents of the student. This act also requires that educational institutions must disclose any records kept on a student when demanded by that student. This law has had a huge impact on privacy requirements of student records. It jeopardizes the federal funding of schools by government agencies if any violations occur.

For more information on FERPA, visit `http://www.ed.gov/policy/gen/guid/fpco/ferpa/index.html`. To view a database of losses involving personally identifiable information, visit `http://attrition.org/dataloss/`.

The Computer Security Act of 1987

The *Computer Security Act* requires federal agencies to identify and protect computer systems that contain sensitive information. This law requires agencies that keep sensitive information to conduct regular training and audits and to implement procedures to protect privacy. All federal agencies must comply with this act.

For more information on the Computer Security Act, visit `http://epic.org/crypto/csa/`.

The Cyberspace Electronic Security Act

The *Cyberspace Electronic Security Act (CESA)* was passed in 1999 and gives law enforcement the right to gain access to encryption keys and cryptography methods. The initial version of this act allowed federal law enforcement agencies to secretly use monitoring, electronic capturing equipment, and other technologies to access and obtain information. These provisions were later stricken from the act, although federal law enforcement agencies were given a large amount of latitude to conduct investigations relating to electronic information. This act is generating a lot of discussion about what capabilities should be allowed to law enforcement in the detection of criminal activity.

For more information on CESA, visit `http://epic.org/crypto/legislation/cesa/`.

The Cyber Security Enhancement Act

The *Cyber Security Enhancement Act* of 2002 allows federal agencies relatively easy access to ISPs and other data-transmission facilities to monitor communications of individuals suspected of committing computer crimes using the Internet. The act is also known as *Section 225 of the Homeland Security Act* of 2002.

For more information on the Cyber Security Enhancement Act, visit `http://www.usdoj.gov/criminal/cybercrime/homeland_CSEA.htm`.

The Patriot Act

The *Uniting and Strengthening America by Providing Appropriate Tools Required to Intercept and Obstruct Terrorism (USA PATRIOT) Act of 2001* was passed largely because of the World Trade Center attack on September 11, 2001. This law gives the U.S. government extreme latitude in pursuing criminals who commit terrorist acts. The definition of a terrorist act is broad.

The law provides for relief to victims of terrorism as well as the ability to conduct virtually any type of surveillance of a suspected terrorist. This act is constantly under review and portions of it are regularly being litigated. Portions of it relevant to IT security include the authority to intercept electronic communications.

For more information on the Patriot Act, one of the best sources is Wikipedia: `http://en.wikipedia.org/wiki/Patriot_act`.

Familiarizing Yourself with International Efforts

Many governments are now evaluating their current laws regarding cyberterrorism, cybercrime, and privacy. Among the agencies that are currently evaluating cyber laws are the European Union (EU) and the G20 (formerly G8).

The EU, which is a common governance agency that includes many member nations, is soon expected to enact tough legislation regarding computer use. In the next few years, the EU is likely to be formidable in its ability to pursue and prosecute cyber criminals.

The EU is adopting the strategy of looking at all EU member nations as a large "Information Society," and it will be passing laws and regulations regarding computer security and privacy among all members. It's also working on laws to protect computer systems and prevent cybercrime. The most all-encompassing law thus far is the Cybercrime Treaty, which makes all hacking illegal in Europe.

Understanding Social Engineering

Social engineering is the process by which intruders gain access to your facilities, your network, and even to your employees by exploiting the generally trusting nature of people. A social engineering attack may come from someone posing as a vendor, or it could take the form of an email from a (supposedly) traveling executive who indicates that they have forgotten how to log on to the network or how to get into the building over the weekend. It's often difficult to determine whether the individual is legitimate or has nefarious intentions.

> Occasionally, social engineering is also referred to as *wetware*. This term is used because it is a form of hacking that does not require software or hardware but rather the gray matter of the brain.

Social engineering attacks can develop subtly. They're also hard to detect. Let's look at some classic social engineering attacks.

Someone enters your building wearing a white lab jacket with a logo on it. He also has a toolkit. He approaches the receptionist and identifies himself as a copier repairman from a major local copier company. He indicates that he's here to do preventive service on your copier. In most cases, the receptionist will let him pass and tell him where the copier is. Once the "technician" is out of sight, the receptionist probably won't give him a second thought. Your organization has just been the victim of a social engineering attack. The attacker has now penetrated your first and possibly even your second layer of security. In many offices, including security-oriented offices, this individual would have access to the entire organization and would be able to pass freely anywhere he wanted. This attack didn't take any particular talent or skill other than the ability to look like a copier repairman. *Impersonation* can go a long way in allowing access to a building or network.

The next example is a true situation; it happened at a high-security government installation. Access to the facility required passing through a series of manned checkpoints. Professionally trained and competent security personnel manned these checkpoints. An employee decided to play a joke on the security department: He took an old employee badge, cut his picture out of it, and pasted in a picture of Mickey Mouse. He was able to gain access to the facility for two weeks before he was caught.

Social engineering attacks like these are easy to accomplish in most organizations. Even if your organization uses biometric devices, magnetic card strips, or other electronic measures, social engineering attacks are still relatively simple. A favorite method of gaining entry to electronically locked systems is to follow someone through the door they just unlocked, a process known as *tailgating*, which we discussed earlier in the chapter. Many people don't think twice about this event—it happens all the time.

> Famed hacker Kevin Mitnick wrote a book called *The Art of Deception: Controlling the Human Element of Security* (Wiley Publishing, Inc., 2002) in which 14 of the 16 chapters are devoted to social engineering scenarios that have been played out. If nothing else, the fact that one of the most notorious hackers known—who could write on any security subject he wants—chose to write a book on social engineering should emphasize the importance of the topic to you.

Types of Social Engineering Attacks

As an administrator, one of your responsibilities is to educate users on how to avoid falling prey to social engineering attacks. They should know the security procedures that are in place and follow them to a tee. You should also have a high level of confidence that the correct procedures are in place, and one of the best ways to obtain that confidence is to check your users on occasion.

Preventing social engineering attacks involves more than just training on how to detect and prevent them. It also involves making sure people stay alert. Here's a list of some of the most common attacks:

Shoulder Surfing   One form of social engineering is known as *shoulder surfing* and involves nothing more than watching someone when they enter their sensitive data. They can see you entering a password, typing in a credit card number, or entering any other pertinent information. The best defense against this type of attack is simply to survey your environment before entering personal data.

Dumpster Diving   *Dumpster diving* is a common physical access method. Companies normally generate a huge amount of paper, most of which eventually winds up in Dumpsters or recycle bins. Dumpsters may contain information that is highly sensitive in nature. In high-security and government environments, sensitive papers are either shredded or burned. Most businesses don't do this. In addition, the advent of "green" companies has created an increase in the amount of recycled paper, which can often contain all kinds of juicy information about a company and its individual employees.

Eavesdropping   *Eavesdropping* is the process of listening in on or overhearing parts of a conversation, including listening in on your network traffic. This type of attack is generally passive. For example, a coworker might overhear your dinner plans because your speakerphone is set too loud or you're yelling into your cell phone. The opportunity to overhear a conversation is coupled with the carelessness of the parties in the conversation.

Snooping   *Snooping* occurs when someone looks through your files hoping to find something interesting. The files may be either electronic or on paper. In the case of physical snooping, people might inspect your Dumpster (as in Dumpster diving), recycling bins, or even your file cabinets; they can look under the keyboard for Post-it notes or look for scraps of paper tacked to your bulletin board. Computer snooping, on the other hand, involves someone searching through your electronic files trying to find something interesting. This can happen onsite (using your physical computer) or through a remote attack into your system.

Interception   *Interception* can be either an active or a passive process. In a networked environment, a passive interception would involve someone who routinely monitors network traffic. Active interception might include putting a computer system between the sender and receiver to capture information as it's sent. The process is usually covert. The last thing a person on an intercept mission wants is to be discovered. Intercept missions can occur for years without the knowledge of the parties being monitored.

Government agencies routinely run intercept missions to gather intelligence about the capabilities and locations of enemies. For instance, the FBI has several products that they install on ISPs' systems to gather and process email, looking for keywords. These keyword searches become the basis of an investigation. The Computer and Internet Protocol Address Verifier (CIPAV), for example, is a data-gathering tool used by the FBI on suspects under electronic surveillance (`http://www.wired.com/threatlevel/2007/07/fbi-spyware-how/`).

Vishing   When you combine phishing with Voice over IP (VoIP), it becomes known as *vishing* and is just an elevated form of social engineering. While crank calls have been in existence since the invention of the telephone, the rise in VoIP now makes it possible for someone to call you from almost anywhere in the world, without the worry of tracing, caller ID, and other features of the land line, and pretend to be someone they are not in order to get data from you.

Spear Phishing   With *spear phishing*, the person conducting it uses information that the target would be less likely to question because it appears to be coming from a trusted source. As an example, instead of Wells Fargo sending you a message telling you to click here to fix a problem with your account, the message that comes in appears to be from your spouse and it says to click here to see that video of your children from last Christmas. Because it appears far more likely to be a legitimate message, it cuts through the user's standard defenses like a spear and has a higher likelihood of being clicked. Generating the attack requires much more work on the part of the miscreant and often involves using information from contact lists, friend lists from social media sites, and so on.

Whaling   *Whaling* is nothing more than phishing or spear phishing but for big users. Instead of sending out a To Whom It May Concern message to thousands of users, the whaler identifies one person from whom they can gain all the data they want—usually a manager or owner—and targets the phishing campaign at them.

Caller ID Spoofing   Many have come to rely on the caller ID display to inform them of who is calling and serve as a simple form of authentication. There are several programs available, however, that allow a miscreant to send fake values for both the phone number and the name display to a caller ID box. This is known as *caller ID spoofing* and, when coupled with other forms of social engineering, can help convince an insider that they are talking to someone trusted when the opposite is true.

The major difference between these types of attacks is how they're accomplished. The ultimate objective is to gain unauthorized access to information.

What Motivates an Attack?

Social engineering is easy to do, even with all of today's technology to prevent it at our disposal. Education is the one key that can help. Educate users on the reasons why someone would attempt to gain data and how the company can be negatively affected by it. Educate them on the simple procedures they can engage in, such as stopping tailgating and piggybacking, to increase security. It is surprising how helpful users can be once they understand the reasons why they're being asked to follow certain procedures.

Don't overlook the most common personal motivator of all: greed. It may surprise you, but people can be bribed to give away information, and one of the toughest challenges is someone on the inside who is displeased with the company and not afraid to profit from it. This is known as a *malicious insider threat* and can be far more difficult to contend with than any outside threat since they already have access—both physical and login—to your systems.

If someone gives out the keys, you won't necessarily know it has occurred. Those keys can be literal—as in the keys to the back door—or figurative—the keys to decrypt messages.

It is often a comforting thought to think that we cannot be bought. We look to our morals and standards and think that we are above being bribed. The truth of the matter, though, is that almost everyone has a price. Your price may be so high that for all practical purposes you don't have a price that anyone in the market would pay, but can the same be said for the other administrators in your company?

Social engineering can have a hugely damaging effect on a security system. Always remember that a social engineering attack can occur over the phone, by email, or by a visit. The intent is to acquire access information, such as user IDs and passwords.

Always think of a social engineering attack as one that involves people who are unwitting.

Social Engineering Attack Examples

Social engineering attacks are relatively low tech and are more akin to con jobs. Here are a few examples.

Your help desk gets a call at 4:00 a.m. from someone purporting to be the vice president of your company. She tells the help desk personnel that she is out of town to attend a meeting, her computer just failed, and she is sitting in a Kinko's trying to get a file from her desktop computer back at the office. She can't seem to remember her password and user ID. She tells the help desk representative that she needs access to the information right away or the company could lose millions of dollars. Your help desk rep knows how important this meeting is and gives the vice president her user ID and password over the phone instead of calling IT. You've been hit!

Another common approach is initiated by a phone call or email from someone claiming to be your software vendor, telling you that they have a critical fix that must be installed on your computer system. If this patch isn't installed right away, your system will crash, and you'll lose all your data. For some reason, you've changed your maintenance account password, and they can't log on. Your systems operator gives the password to the person instead of calling IT. You've been hit again.

 Users are bombarded with emails and messages on services such as Pay-Pal asking them to confirm the password they use. These attacks appear to come from the administrative staff of the network. The attacker already has the user ID or screen name; all they need to complete the attack is the password. Make sure your users never give their user IDs or passwords. Either case potentially completes an attack.

With social engineering, the villain doesn't always have to be seen or heard to conduct the attack. The use of email was mentioned earlier, and in recent years, the frequency of attacks via instant messaging has also increased thanks to social media. Attackers can send infected files over instant messaging (IM) as easily as they can over email, and this can occur in Facebook, MySpace, or anywhere else that IM is possible. A recent virus on the scene accesses a user's IM client and uses the infected user's friend list to send messages to other users and infect their machines as well.

In Exercise 6.1, I'll show you how to test social engineering in your environment.

EXERCISE 6.1

Test Social Engineering

In this exercise, you'll test your users to determine the likelihood of a social engineering attack. The following are suggestions for tests; you might need to modify them slightly to be appropriate at your workplace. Before doing any of them, make certain your manager knows that you're conducting such a test and approves of it:

1. Call the receptionist from an outside line. Tell them that you're a new salesperson and that you didn't write down the username and password the sales manager gave you last week. Tell them that you need to get a file from the email system for a presentation tomorrow. Do they direct you to the appropriate person?

EXERCISE 6.1 *(continued)*

2. Call the human resources department from an outside line. Don't give your real name, but instead say that you're a vendor who has been working with this company for years. You'd like a copy of the employee phone list to be emailed to you, if possible. Do they agree to send you the list, which would contain information that could be used to try to guess usernames and passwords?

3. Pick a user at random. Call them and identify yourself as someone who does work with the company. Tell them that you're supposed to have some new software ready for them by next week and that you need to know their password in order to finish configuring it. Do they do the right thing?

4. Look on Facebook for someone who works for the company and see what information they are posting. Are they talking about coworkers? About clients? Are there pictures posted from inside the workplace where it is possible to see doors/locks/servers?

The best defense against any social engineering attack is education. Make certain the employees of your company know how to react to the requests like these.

The only preventive measure in dealing with social engineering attacks is to educate your users and staff to never give out passwords and user IDs over the phone or via email or to anyone who isn't positively verified as being who they say they are. Social engineering is a recurring topic that will appear several times throughout this book as it relates to the subject being discussed.

 Real World Scenario

A Security Analogy

In this chapter, we discussed a number of access methods. Sometimes it can be confusing to keep them all straight. To put the main ones somewhat in perspective, think of the problem in terms of a stranger who wants to gain access to your house. Any number of types of individuals may want to get in your house without your knowing it:

▪   A thief wanting to steal any valuables you may have

▪   Teenagers wanting to do something destructive on a Saturday night

▪   Homeless people looking to get in out of the cold and find some food

▪   A neighbor who has been drinking and accidentally pulls in the wrong driveway and starts to come in, thinking it is their house

▪   A professional hit man wanting to lie in wait for you to come home

There are many more, but these represent a good cross-section of individuals, each of whom has different motives and motivational levels for trying to get in.

To keep the thief out, you could post security signs all around your house and install a home alarm. He might not know if you really have ABC Surveillance active monitoring, as the signs say, but he might not want to risk it and go away looking for an easier target to hit. In the world of computer security, encryption acts like your home alarm and monitoring software, alerting you (or your monitoring company) to potential problems when they arise.

The teenagers just want to do damage somewhere, and your house is as good as the next one. Installing motion lights above the doors and around the side of the house is really all you need to make them drive farther down the road. In the world of computer security, good passwords—and policies that are enforced—will keep these would-be intruders out.

The homeless also have no particular affection for your home as opposed to the next. You can keep them out by using locks on your doors and windows and putting a fence around your yard. If they can't get in the fence, they can't approach the house, and if they do manage that, they are confronted by the locks. Firewalls serve this purpose in the world of computer security.

The neighbor just made a legitimate error. That happens. I once went into the wrong person's tent when camping because they all look the same. To make yours look different, you can add banners and warnings to the login routines stating, for example, that this is ABC server and you must be an authorized user to access it.

This leaves the hit man. He has been paid to do a job, and that job entails gaining access to your home. No matter how good the locks are on your house, no matter how many motion lights you put up, if someone's sole purpose in life is to gain access to your house, they will find a way to do it. The same is true of your server. You can implement measures to keep everyone else out, but if someone spends their entire existence dedicated to getting access to that server, they will do it if it entails putting on a heating and air conditioning uniform and walking past the receptionist, pointing two dozen computers to hashing routines that will crack your passwords, or driving a tank through the side of the building. Your job is to handle all the reasonable risks that come your way. Some, however, you have to acknowledge have only a very slim chance of ever truly being risks, and some, no matter what precautions you take, will not go away.

When you combine phishing with Voice over IP (VoIP), it becomes known as *vishing* and is just an elevated form of social engineering. While crank calls have been in existence since the invention of the telephone, the rise in VoIP now makes it possible for someone to call you from almost anywhere in the world, without the worry of tracing, caller ID, and other features of the land line, and pretend to be someone they are not in order to get data from you.

Summary

In this chapter, I covered the key elements of security-related awareness and training, social engineering, regulations, and the user in the environment. Your job as a security professional includes keeping yourself up-to-date on current issues as well as informing affected parties of changes occurring in the industry and new threats.

The process of raising sensitivity about security is part of a security-awareness program. This program should include communications about the nature of the issues, education about policies and procedures, and clear support from management.

Information classification is the process of determining what information is accessible to what parties and for what purposes. Classifications in industry are usually based on cataloging information as *public* or *private*. Public information can be classified as either limited distribution or full distribution. Private information is usually classified for internal use or restricted.

Access control models exist to categorize the usage of sensitive information. Three of the more common models are the Bell-LaPadula model, the Biba model, and the Clark-Wilson model. Less common models include the Information Flow and Noninterference models.

By employing social engineering, attackers are able to gain a way to the data or the workplace through the employee. Many different types of social engineer attacks can occur, and this chapter examined those.

Exam Essentials

Be able to explain the process used to educate an organization about security issues. The four major aspects of a security management policy are communications, user awareness, education, and online resources. Communication should be ongoing and help the organization make decisions about security requirements and threats. A user-awareness program helps individuals in an organization understand how to implement policies, procedures, and technologies to ensure effective security. A wealth of online information is available to help you learn about current trends in the field. One of your primary responsibilities should be staying current on threats and trends.

Be able to describe the process of social engineering. Social engineering occurs when an unauthorized individual uses human or nontechnical methods to gain information or access to security information. Individuals in an organization should be trained to watch for these types of attempts, and they should report them to security professionals when they occur.

Be able to identify the main access control models. Three of the more common models are the Bell-LaPadula model, the Biba model, and the Clark-Wilson model. Less common models include the Information Flow and Noninterference models.

Know of the key legislation governing security.   At the federal level, IT is governed by HIPAA (which covers three areas—confidentiality, privacy, and security of patient records), the Gramm-Leach-Bliley Act (also known as the Financial Modernization Act of 1999), and several others. In addition to the federal laws, most states have laws on computer crime as well.

Know the importance of security awareness and training.   Security awareness and training are critical to the success of a security effort. They include explaining policies, procedures, and current threats to both users and management.

Review Questions

1. As part of your training program, you're trying to educate users on the importance of security. You explain to them that not every attack depends on implementing advanced technological methods. Some attacks, you explain, take advantage of human shortcomings to gain access that should otherwise be denied. What term do you use to describe attacks of this type?

    A. Social engineering

    B. IDS system

    C. Perimeter security

    D. Biometrics

2. Which classification of information designates that information can be released on a restricted basis to outside organizations?

    A. Private information

    B. Full distribution

    C. Restricted information

    D. Limited distribution

3. You've recently been hired by ACME to do a security audit. The managers of this company feel that their current security measures are inadequate. Which information access control model prevents users from writing information down to a lower level of security and prevents users from reading above their level of security?

    A. Bell-LaPadula model

    B. Biba model

    C. Clark-Wilson model

    D. Noninterference model

4. The Cyberspace Security Enhancement Act gives law enforcement the right to:

    A. Fine ISPs who host rogue sites

    B. Gain access to encryption keys

    C. Restrict information from public view

    D. Stop issuance of .gov domains

5. For which U.S. organization was the Bell-LaPadula model designed?

    A. Military

    B. Census Bureau

    C. Office of Management and Budget

    D. Executive Office of the President

6. Which of the following is another name for social engineering?

   A. Social disguise

   B. Social hacking

   C. Wetware

   D. Wetfire

7. The Clark-Wilson model must be accessed through applications that have predefined capabilities. This process prevents all except:

   A. Modification

   B. Spam

   C. Errors

   D. Fraud

8. There are two types of implicit denies. One of these can be configured so that only users specifically named can use the service and is known as:

   A. at.deny

   B. at.allow

   C. at.open

   D. at.closed

9. _____ information is made available to either large public or specific individuals, while _____ information is intended for only those internal to the organization.

   A. Private; Restricted

   B. Public; Private

   C. Limited distribution; Internal

   D. Public; Internal

10. Which of the following actions would *not* be allowed in the Bell-LaPadula model?

   A. General with Top Secret clearance writing at the Top Secret level

   B. Corporal with Confidential clearance writing at the Confidential level

   C. General with Top Secret clearance reading at the Confidential level

   D. General with Top Secret clearance writing at the Confidential level

11. Which of the following is the best description of tailgating?

   A. Following someone through a door they just unlocked

   B. Figuring out how to unlock a secured area

   C. Sitting close to someone in a meeting

   D. Stealing information from someone's desk

12. An NDA (nondisclosure agreement) is typically signed by?

  A. Alpha testers

  B. Customers

  C. Beta testers

  D. Focus groups

13. What is the form of social engineering in which you simply ask someone for a piece of information that you want by making it look as if it is a legitimate request?

  A. Hoaxing

  B. Swimming

  C. Spamming

  D. Phishing

14. Users should be educated in the correct way to close pop-up ads in the workplace. That method is to:

  A. Click the word Close

  B. Click the "X" in the top right

  C. Press Ctrl+Alt+Del

  D. Call IT

15. Which act mandates national standards and procedures for the storage, use, and transmission of personal medical information?

  A. CFAA

  B. HIPAA

  C. GLBA

  D. FERPA

16. When you combine phishing with Voice over IP, it is known as:

  A. Spoofing

  B. Spooning

  C. Whaling

  D. Vishing

17. Which of the following is the highest classification level in the government?

  A. Top Secret

  B. Secret

  C. Classified

  D. Confidential

18. `at.allow` is an access control that allows only specific users to use the service. What is `at.deny`?

   A. It does not allow users named in the file to access the system.

   B. It ensures that no one will ever be able to use that part of your system.

   C. It opens up the server only to intranet users.

   D. It blocks access to Internet users.

19. Which of the following is the best description of shoulder surfing?

   A. Following someone through a door they just unlocked

   B. Figuring out how to unlock a secured area

   C. Watching someone enter important information

   D. Stealing information from someone's desk

20. Which concept does the Bell-LaPadula model deal most accurately with?

   A. Integrity

   B. Trustworthiness

   C. Confidentiality

   D. Accuracy

Answers to Review Questions

1. A. Social engineering uses the inherent trust in the human species, as opposed to technology, to gain access to your environment.

2. D. Limited distribution information can be released to select individuals and organizations, such as financial institutions, governmental agencies, and creditors.

3. A. The Bell-LaPadula model is intended to protect confidentiality of information. This is accomplished by prohibiting users from reading above their security level and preventing them from writing below their security level.

4. B. The Cyberspace Security Enhancement Act gives law enforcement the right to gain access to encryption keys.

5. A. The Bell-LaPadula model was originally designed for use by the military.

6. C. Wetware is another name for social engineering.

7. B. The Clark-Wilson model must be accessed through applications that have predefined capabilities. This process prevents all the choices listed except spam.

8. B. `at.allow` configurations allow only users specifically named to use the service.

9. B. Public information is made available to either large public or specific individuals, while Private information is intended for only those internal to the organization.

10. D. The first three actions would be allowed since you can write to your level and read at your level (or below). The situation that would not be allowed is the General with Top Secret clearance writing at the Confidential level.

11. A. Tailgating is best defined as following someone through a door they just unlocked.

12. C. An NDA (nondisclosure agreement) is typically signed by beta testers.

13. D. Phishing is the form of social engineering in which you simply ask someone for a piece of information that you want by making it look as if it is a legitimate request.

14. B. Pop-up ads should be closed by clicking the "X" in the top right.

15. B. HIPAA mandates national standards and procedures for the storage, use, and transmission of personal medical information.

16. D. Vishing involves combining phishing with Voice over IP.

17. A. Top Secret is the highest classification level in the government.

18. A. The `at.deny` file does not allow users named in the file to access the system.

19. C. Shoulder surfing is best defined as watching someone enter important information.

20. C. The Bell-LaPadula model deals most accurately with confidentiality.

Chapter

7

Operating System and Application Security

THE FOLLOWING COMPTIA SECURITY+ EXAM OBJECTIVES ARE COVERED IN THIS CHAPTER:

✓ **1.1 Explain the security function and purpose of network devices and technologies.**

   ▪ URL filtering, content inspection, malware inspection

✓ **3.5 Analyze and differentiate among types of application attacks.**

   ▪ SQL injection

   ▪ LDAP injection

   ▪ XML injection

   ▪ Directory traversal/command injection

   ▪ Session hijacking

   ▪ Header manipulation

✓ **3.6 Analyze and differentiate among types of mitigation and deterrent techniques.**

   ▪ Hardening: Disabling unnecessary services; Protecting management interfaces and applications; Password protection; Disabling unnecessary accounts

✓ **4.1 Explain the importance of application security.**

   ▪ Fuzzing

   ▪ Cross-site Request Forgery (XSRF) prevention

   ▪ Application configuration baseline (proper settings)

   ▪ Application hardening

   ▪ Application patch management

✓ **4.2 Carry out appropriate procedures to establish host security.**

- Operating system security and settings

- Anti-malware: Anti-virus; Anti-spam; Anti-spyware; Pop-up blockers; Host-based firewalls

- Patch management

- Host software baselining

- Mobile devices: Screen lock; Strong password; Device encryption; Remote wipe/sanitation; Voice encryption; GPS tracking

✓ **4.3 Explain the importance of data security.**

- Data Loss Prevention (DLP)

- Data encryption: Full disk; Database; Individual files; Removable media; Mobile devices

- Hardware based encryption devices: TPM; HSM; USB encryption; Hard drive

The operating systems, applications, and network products you deal with are usually secure when they're implemented the way the manufacturer intends but differ in actual implementation. For example, once you start reducing security settings to increase interoperability with other operating systems or applications, you start introducing weaknesses that may be exploited. This chapter deals with the process of ensuring that the products you use are as secure as they can be.

The primary focus of this chapter is security hardening. *Hardening* refers to the process of reducing or eliminating weaknesses, securing services, and attempting to make your environment immune to attacks. Typically, when you install operating systems, applications, and network products, the defaults from the manufacturer are to make the product as simple to use as possible and allow it to work with your existing environment as effortlessly as possible. That isn't always the best scenario when it comes to security.

In this chapter, you'll learn the general process involved in securing the systems and applications that are typically found in a business. This chapter also touches on the concept of developing a security baseline.

Hardening the Operating System

Any network is only as strong as its weakest components, and it's your job as a security administrator to make certain that you find these. You must ensure that the operating systems running on the workstations and on the network servers are as secure as they can be.

Hardening an operating system (OS) refers to the process of making the environment more secure from attacks and intruders. The following sections discuss hardening an OS and the methods of keeping it hardened as new threats emerge.

The Basics of OS Hardening

Every operating system offers a unique set of tools and utilities that can be used for security and administrative purposes. Regardless of whether you are running Windows 7, Linux, Windows Server 2008, Apple OS X, or anything else, there are four universal categories of hardening to follow:

- Disabling unnecessary services

- Protecting the management interface (and applications)

- Adhering to solid authentication protection
- Disabling unnecessary accounts

Each of these will be explored in the sections that follow.

Disabling Unnecessary Services

The wonderful thing about servers is that they are able to run a plethora of services at the same time; if you are running a very small network, for example, your single server can act in many capacities. The terrible thing about servers is that they are able to run a plethora of services at the same time, and your network is only as strong as the weakest service. As a security administrator, you should regularly check all servers and make certain only necessary services are running on them. Here are some tips:

File and Print Servers These are primarily vulnerable to DoS and access attacks. DoS attacks can be targeted at specific protocols and overwhelm a port with activity. Make sure these servers run only the protocols needed to support the network.

Networks with PC-Based Systems In a network that has PC-based systems, make sure NetBIOS services are disabled on servers or that an effective firewall is in place between the server and the Internet. Many of the popular attacks that are occurring on systems today take place through the NetBIOS services, via ports 135, 137, 138, and 139. On Unix systems, make sure port 111, the Remote Procedure Call port, is closed.

Remote Procedure Call (RPC) is a programming interface that allows a remote computer to run programs on a local machine. It has created serious vulnerabilities in systems that have RPC enabled.

Directory Sharing Directory sharing should be limited to what is essential to perform systems functions. Make sure any root directories are hidden from browsing. It's better to designate a subfolder or subdirectory off the root directory and share it than to share a root directory. Figure 7.1 illustrates a network share connection. Notice that when a user connects to the network-shared directory, they aren't aware of where this share actually is in the hierarchy of the filesystem.

FIGURE 7.1 Network share connection

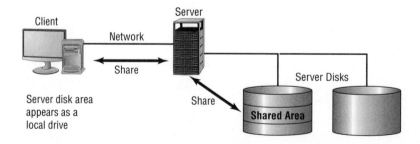

You should always apply the most restrictive access necessary for a shared directory.

Never share the root or parent directory of a disk drive. Doing so creates a potential vulnerability for every file on the system. Instead, share subdirectories.

Root Directories   If an attacker penetrates a root directory, all the subdirectories under that directory are vulnerable. If a subdirectory is penetrated, only the directories that reside below it are exposed—in most cases.

Protecting Management Interfaces and Applications

The ability to run the administrative interfaces within the operating system, and the applications associated with them, is often the difference between a standard user and an administrative user. The person running the administrative interfaces can make configuration changes to the system(s) and modify settings in ways that can have wide-sweeping consequences. For example, a user able to gain access to the administrative tools could delete other users, set their own ID equal to the root user, change passwords, or delete key files.

Even for administrators it is a good idea to log in as a user and then right-click and choose Run As Administrator when needed.

To protect against this, access to management/administrative interfaces should be restricted to only those administrators who need it. Not only should you protect server utilities, but you should even go so far as to remove users' access to workstation utilities that have administrative depth such as regedit and regedt32.

The System and Security applet (known just as Security in operating systems earlier than Windows 7), beneath the Control Panel, is the main interface for security features in Windows operating systems. From here, you can configure Windows Firewall, automatic scans of your computer, and Windows Defender.

The Microsoft security website is at http://www.microsoft.com/security/, and it is the first place to turn to for up-to-date information on operating system issues.

One of the best tools to use when looking for possible illicit activity on a workstation is *Performance Monitor* (known as *System Monitor* in previous operating systems). This utility can be used to examine activity on any counter, and excessive processor usage is one worth paying attention to if you suspect the workstation is affected or being illegitimately accessed. Exercise 7.1 explores how to use it.

EXERCISE 7.1

Using Performance Monitor

This tool is a subcomponent (a snap-in) in the Performance Console. To access it, follow these steps:

1. Choose Start and in the Search box type **perfmon.msc**.

2. Choose Performance Monitor. By default, the monitor comes up showing one counter: % Processor Time.

3. To add more counters, right-click in the right pane and choose Add Counters from the pop-up menu.

With a Group Policy, you create restrictions that will apply to workstations when users authenticate. Upon each authentication, those restrictions are then applied as Registry settings, providing an efficient way to manage a large number of computers.

The restrictions you set come from choices within template files and can be as simple as not allowing the user to access the game Solitaire, to removing their ability to access the other networks. *Security templates* are those template files that hold Registry setting choices that relate to security settings.

The Microsoft Windows Group Policy FAQ, which can be found at http:// technet2.microsoft.com/windowsserver/en/technologies/featured/ gp/faq.mspx, is highly recommended reading for real-world answers and solutions.

Not every configuration setting needs to be downloaded through the domain. Every current Microsoft operating system also includes *local policies*—settings that apply to the workstation when the user has yet to authenticate with the network. The purpose of these policies is to restrict the user locally, just as you would across the network, when they have yet to log into the domain. To see the local polices, choose Start ≻ Run and type **secpol.msc**.

You should routinely monitor the settings made throughout your network in local and Group Policies and tweak them as needed.

Two other tools that are useful for this purpose are secedit.exe and the Security and Configuration Analysis (SCA) console. Both tools perform the exact same function, but secedit is a command-line utility, while SCA runs in the graphical interface. Typing **secedit** without parameters at a command prompt will show you what options are available with the command. To start the Security and Configuration Analysis console, follow these steps:

1. Choose Start and in the Run box type **mmc /s**.

2. Choose File ≻ Add/Remove Snap-in.

3. From the list of available snap-ins, choose Security Configuration and Analysis and click Add.

4. Click OK.

5. If you have a security template to use, then right-click Security Configuration and Analysis and choose Open Database from the menu. At the prompt, enter a new database name, such as **example1**.

6. Click Open. Choose an INF file and click Open.

7. You can now right-click Security Configuration and Analysis and choose Analyze Computer Now to generate a log file comparing current settings to those in the template.

The security templates that existed in previous versions of Windows do not ship with Windows 7. If you have access only to Windows 7 workstations, skip this discussion.

Most operating systems today also include *Data Execution Prevention (DEP)* features. The sole purpose of this feature is to make sure that applications do not run in non-executable memory regions. By restricting the possibility of this happening, the OS limits its exposure to the buffer overflow issues discussed in Chapter 4.

Password Protection

Passwords should always be as long and as complicated as possible. Most vendors recommend that you use nonalphabetic characters such as #, $, and % in your password, and some go so far as to require it. You should know, however, that the more stringent you make the password requirements, the more you are increasing the likelihood that users will need to write down their password following a change. This is a tradeoff, because on the one hand easy passwords allow an attacker to break in more quickly, and on the other hand tough passwords increase the number of slips of paper an attacker may find with the password written on it, thus simplifying the job of breaking in.

Chapter 8 provides an in-depth discussion on passwords.

Regardless of the balance you strike between easy and tough passwords, it is an administrator's responsibility to make certain the values remain closely guarded on the system. The folders in which password files are stored must be protected and made available only by those who are permitted access to this information. The backups, which contain copies of those same files, must be securely stored and protected at all costs.

Disabling Unnecessary Accounts

Enabled accounts that are not needed on a system provide a door in which attackers can gain access. No matter how minimal the permissions of that user may be, they still provide a first stop from which the attacker can begin to gather information about the system and begin looking for ways to access with elevated privileges.

You should disable all accounts that are not needed immediately—on servers and workstations alike. Following are some types of accounts you should disable:

Employees Who Have Left the Company Be sure to immediately disable accounts for any employee who has left the company. This should be done the minute employment is terminated.

Temporary Employees It is not uncommon to create temporary accounts for short periods of access by temporary employees, and these also need to be disabled the moment they are no longer needed.

Default Guest Accounts In many operating systems, a guest account is created during installation and intended for use by those only needing limited access and lacking their own account on the system. This account presents a door into the system that should not be there, and its existence is known by all who have worked with the operating system, thus making it a likely target for attackers.

In Exercise 7.2, I'll show you how to turn off the Guest account in Windows 7.

EXERCISE 7.2

Turning a Guest Account Off

The Guest account is automatically created in Windows with the intent that it is to be used when someone must access a system but lacks a user account on that system. Since it is so widely known to exist, it is recommended that you not use this default account and create another one for the same purpose if you truly need one. The Guest account leaves a security risk at the workstation and should be disabled to prevent it from being accessed by those attempting to gain unauthorized access. To turn off the Guest account, follow these steps:

1. Click the Start button ➢ Control Panel.

2. From Control Panel, choose Add Or Remove User Accounts beneath the User Accounts And Family Safety options.

3. At the prompt to choose the account you would like to change, click Guest.

EXERCISE 7.2 *(continued)*

4. Click the option Turn Off The Guest Account.

 Depending on your installation, the Guest account may already be turned off. If that is the case, and you wish to do the exercise, you can turn it on first and then off.

5. You will be returned to the Manage Accounts dialog box, and the text beneath Guest should state that the account is off.

6. Exit Control Panel.

Parental Controls

Note that you can also block what programs users can execute—as well as limit the times when they are allowed to use the computers and what games they can play—using the Parental Controls. Parental Controls cannot be applied to an administrative user, but they can be applied to any standard user.

Hardening Filesystems

Several filesystems are involved in the operating systems we've discussed, and, from a network perspective, they have a high level of interoperability between them. Through the years, different vendors have implemented their own sets of file standards. Some of the more common filesystems in Windows are listed here:

Microsoft FAT   Microsoft's earliest filesystem was referred to as the *File Allocation Table (FAT)*. FAT is designed for relatively small disk drives. It was upgraded first to FAT-16 and finally to FAT-32. FAT-32 allows large disk systems to be used on Windows systems. FAT allows only two types of protection: share-level and user-level access privileges. If a user has Write or Change Access permission to a drive or directory, they have access to any file in that directory. This is very unsecure in an Internet environment.

It is rare to find FAT used in the corporate world these days, but you should still know about it for the exam.

Microsoft NTFS   The *New Technology Filesystem (NTFS)* was introduced with Windows NT to address security problems. Before Windows NT was released, it had become apparent to Microsoft that a new filing system was required to handle growing disk sizes, security concerns, and the need for more stability. NTFS was created to address those issues.

Although FAT was relatively stable if the systems that were controlling it kept running, it didn't do so well when the power went out or the system crashed unexpectedly. One of the benefits of NTFS was a transaction-tracking system, which made it possible for Windows NT to back out of any disk operations that were in progress when Windows NT crashed or lost power.

With NTFS, files, directories, and volumes can each have their own security. NTFS's security is flexible and built in. Not only does NTFS track security in access control lists (ACLs), which can hold permissions for local users and groups, but each entry in the ACL can specify what type of access is given—such as Read-Only, Change, or Full Control. This allows a great deal of flexibility in setting up a network. In addition, special file-encryption programs were developed to encrypt data while it was stored on the hard disk drive (HDD).

Microsoft strongly recommends that all network shares be established using NTFS. As Microsoft has continued to refine NTFS, the versions have incremented, with 3.1 being the most commonly used today. To see the version on a particular workstation, at the command prompt with administrative privileges type **fsutil fsinfo ntfsinfo C:**, and the second line shown will be the NTFS version.

Windows systems often have hidden administrative shares with names that end with a dollar sign character (C$, admin$, etc.). These are created for use in managing the computer on the network and can only be permanently disabled through Registry edits. You can temporarily disable them with the Computer Management console, but they will return on reboot. For the purpose of this exam, simply know they exist and are needed for full network functionality.

Make sure you periodically review the manufacturers' support websites and other support resources that are available to apply current updates and security patches to your systems. Doing this on a regular basis will lower your exposure to security risks.

Although Windows is the focus here, know that other operating systems have their own filesystems. In Linux, for example, common choices include ext3, ext4, and XFS. Macs used HFS (Hierarchical File System) and replaced it with HFS Plus (also known as HFS Extended). For the exam, your focus should be on Windows-based filesystems.

Updating Your Operating System

Operating system manufacturers typically provide product updates. For example, Microsoft provides a series of regular updates for Windows (a proprietary system) and other applications. However, in the case of public source systems (such as Linux), the updates may come from a newsgroup, the manufacturer of the version you're using, or a user community.

In both cases, public and private, updates help keep operating systems up to the most current revision level. Researching updates is important to stay protected from newly discovered threats; when possible, so is getting feedback from other users before you install an update so you can learn form their experiences what difficulties may be encountered. In a number of cases, a service pack or update has rendered a system unusable. Make sure your system is backed up before you install updates.

Be sure to test updates on test systems before you implement them on production systems.

Three different types of updates are discussed here: hotfixes, service and support packs, and patches.

Hotfixes

Hotfixes are used to make repairs to a system during normal operation, even though they might require a reboot. A hotfix may entail moving data from a bad spot on the disk and remapping the data to a new sector. Doing so prevents data loss and loss of service. This type of repair may also involve reallocating a block of memory if, for example, a memory problem occurred. This allows the system to continue normal operations until a permanent repair can be made. Microsoft refers to a bug fix as a *hotfix*. It involves the replacement of files with an updated version.

Service Packs and Support Packs

A *service pack* or *support pack* (depending upon the vendor) is a comprehensive set of fixes consolidated into a single product. A service pack may be used to address a large number of bugs or to introduce new capabilities in an OS. When installed, a service pack usually contains a number of file replacements.

Make sure you check related websites to verify that the service pack works properly. Sometimes a manufacturer will release a service pack before it has been thoroughly tested.

An untested service pack can cause extreme instability in an operating system or, even worse, render it inoperable.

One large OS manufacturer released a service pack for a popular server product three times before getting it right. When installed, this service pack caused many systems to become inoperable. The service pack took down the entire server farm of a large ISP. Many users lost their servers for several days while everything was being sorted out and repaired.

Patches

A *patch* is a temporary or quick fix to a program. Patches may be used to temporarily bypass a set of instructions that have malfunctioned. Several OS manufacturers issue patches that can either be manually applied or applied using a disk file to fix a program.

When you're working with customer support on a technical problem with an OS or applications product, customer service may have you go into the code and make alterations to the binary files that run on your system. Double-check each change to prevent catastrophic failures due to improperly entered code.

Patches fix problems, but they also add the potential for new problems. Most manufacturers would rather release a new program than patch an existing program. A new release can repair multiple problems.

When more data is known about the problem, a service pack or hotfix may be issued to fix the problem on a larger scale. Patching is becoming less common, but it's still very much a way of life for many vendors and administrators.

Application Hardening

As we've explained, a good way to begin securing a network is to make sure every system in the network is up-to-date and to verify that only the protocols you need are enabled. Unfortunately, these steps aren't enough. Your servers and workstations also run applications and services. Server services (especially web, email, and media servers) are particularly vulnerable to exploitation and attack. These applications must also be hardened to make them as difficult as possible to exploit.

The following sections deal with hardening your applications, both on the desktop and at the server, to provide maximum security.

Fuzzing

Most applications that are written to accept input expect a particular type of data to be given—string values, numerical values, and so on. Sometimes, it is possible to enter unexpected values and cause the application to crash. When that happens, it may be possible for the user to be left with elevated privileges or access to values they should not have. *Fuzzing* is the technique of providing unexpected values as input to an application to try to make it crash. Those values can be random, invalid, or just unexpected, and a common method is to flood the input with a stream of random bits.

The best way to prevent fuzzing from being an exploit possible on your systems is to do *fuzz testing* to find and fix the problems first.

Cross-Site Request Forgery

Cross-Site Request Forgery, also known as *XSRF*, *session riding*, and *one-click attack*, involves unauthorized commands coming from a trusted user to the website. This is often done without the user's knowledge and employs some type of social networking to pull it off.

For example, assume that Evan and Spencer are chatting through Facebook. Spencer sends Evan a link to what he purports is a funny video that will crack him up. Evan clicks the link, but it actually brings up Evan's bank account information in another browser tab, takes a screenshot of it, closes the tab, and sends the information to Spencer. The reason the attack is possible is because Evan is a trusted user with his own bank. In order for it to work, Evan would need to have recently accessed that bank's website and have a cookie that had yet to expire.

Facebook is but an example of where this could happen. With the increased usage of *Internet Relay Chat (IRC)*, this type of attack can happen anywhere one user can talk and interact with other users. Characteristics common to these attacks include ascertaining a user's identity, exploiting their trust (often by trickery), and using HTTP requests.

XSRF attacks can be easily confused with other types of attacks, such as phishing, but the key is that they always involve a site that relies on a user's identity and take advantage of the fact that the user being tricked is a trusted user on that site. The major limitation of this attack is that the victim must be lured in; header checking can stop it cold.

Application Configuration Baselining

Baselining always involves comparing performance to a metric. That metric is a historical measurement that you can point to and identify as being before a configuration change, before the site became busy, before you added new services, and so on. Baselining can be done with any metric, such as network performance or CPU usage, as well as with applications.

It is advisable to do baselining with key applications prior to major configuration changes. Make certain that applications have proper settings to work at their optimal values and provide security protection as well.

Application Patch Management

Just as you need to keep the operating system patches current, because they often fix security problems that are discovered with the OS, you need to do the same with application patches for the same purpose. Once an exploit in an application becomes known, an attacker can take advantage of it to enter or harm a system. Most vendors post patches on a regular basis, and you should routinely scan for any that are available.

A large number of attacks today are targeted at client systems for the simple reason that clients do not always manage application patching well. When you couple that with the fact that most clients have many applications running, you increase the odds of being able to find a weakness to exploit.

Making Your Network More Secure Through Hardening

To keep your network secure, you need to harden the individual components of it. In the sections that follow, we will look at hardening web servers, email servers, FTP servers, DNS servers, NNTP servers, and DHCP servers.

Hardening Web Servers

Web servers are favorite areas for attackers to exploit because of the reach they have. If an attacker can gain access to a popular web server and take advantage of a weakness there, they have the opportunity to reach thousands, if not hundreds of thousands, of users who access the site. By targeting a web server, the attacker can actually affect all the connections from users' web browsers and inflict harm far beyond the one machine they compromised.

Web servers were originally simple and were used primarily to provide HTML text and graphics content. Modern web servers allow database access, chat functionality, streaming media, and virtually every other type of service that can be contemplated. This diversity gives websites the ability to provide rich and complex capabilities to web surfers.

Every service and capability supported on a website is potentially a target for exploitation. Make sure they're kept to the most current software standards. You must also make certain that you're allowing users to have only the minimal permissions necessary to accomplish their tasks. If users are accessing your server via an anonymous account, then common sense dictates that you must make certain the anonymous account has only the permissions needed to view web pages and nothing more.

Two particular areas of interest with web servers are filters and controlling access to executable scripts. *Filters* allow you to limit the traffic that is allowed through. Limiting traffic to only that which is required for your business can help ward off attacks.

    A good set of filters can also be applied to your network to prevent users from accessing sites other than those that are business related. Not only does this increase productivity, but it also decreases the likelihood of users obtaining a virus from a questionable site.

Executable scripts, such as those written in PHP, Python, various flavors of Java, and Common Gateway Interface (CGI) scripts, often run at elevated permission levels. Under most circumstances this isn't a problem because the user is returned to their regular permission level at the conclusion of the execution. Problems arise, however, if the user can break out of the script while at the elevated level. From an administrator's standpoint, the best course of action is to verify that all scripts on your server have been thoroughly tested, debugged, and approved for use.

> On all web servers, one account is created when services are installed that is used to represent the anonymous user. Rights assigned to this account apply to all anonymous web users. With IIS, for example, that account is *IUSR_computername*, while in Apache it can be any account that you choose to assign as the anonymous user (often *webuser*).

Hardening Email Servers

Email servers provide the communications backbone for many businesses. They typically run either as an additional service on an existing server or as dedicated systems.

Putting an active virus scanner on email servers can reduce the number of viruses introduced into your network as well as prevent viruses from being spread by your email server. Figure 7.2 illustrates an email virus scanner being added to a server. In this implementation, the scanner filters incoming emails that are suspicious and informs email users of a potential system compromise. This feature is very effective in preventing the spread of viruses via email.

FIGURE 7.2   Email virus scanner on an email server

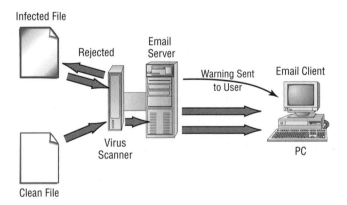

Several servers use data stores, or storage, to allow collaboration, meeting scheduling, conferencing, and other functions. The functionality and capabilities of these servers is increasing on a regular basis. Keep them up-to-date and current.

Real World Scenario

Using ACLs to Address Spam

You've been observing repeated attempts by a TCP/IP address to connect to your email server. These failed connection attempts appear in your email system logs. The intruder continually attempts to access port 25.

Email servers are being inundated by automated systems that attempt to use them to send spam. Most email servers have implemented measures to prevent this. However, the threats are becoming increasingly more sophisticated. You may be able to reduce these attempts to access your system by entering the TCP/IP addresses in your router's ACL Deny list. Doing so will cause your router to ignore connection requests from these IP addresses, effectively improving your security.

Hardening FTP Servers

File Transfer Protocol (FTP) servers aren't intended for high-security applications because of their inherent weaknesses. Most FTP servers allow you to create file areas on any drive on the system. You should create a separate drive or subdirectory on the system to allow file transfers. If possible, use virtual private network (VPN) or Secure Shell (SSH) connections for FTP-type activities. FTP isn't notable for security, and many FTP systems send account and password information across the network unencrypted. FTP is one of the tools frequently used to exploit systems.

From an operational security perspective, you should use separate logon accounts and passwords for FTP access. Doing so will prevent system accounts from being disclosed to unauthorized individuals. Also make sure that all files stored on an FTP server are scanned for viruses.

You should also *always* disable the anonymous user account. To make FTP usage easier, most servers default to allowing anonymous access. However, from a security perspective, the last thing you want is to allow anonymous users to copy files to and from your servers. Disabling anonymous access requires the user to be a known, authenticated user in order to access the FTP server.

As mentioned when discussing web access, an account is created on servers that offer FTP service for representing the anonymous user (for example, the IUSR_computername account is created in versions of IIS when services are installed). Rights assigned to this account apply to all anonymous users.

The best way to secure FTP is to replace it altogether. Instead of using FTP, the same functionality can be found in more secure services such as Secure File Transfer Protocol (SFTP), which was discussed in Chapter 3.

Hardening DNS Servers

Domain Name Service (DNS) servers resolve hostnames to IP addresses. This service allows a website name such as www.sybex.com to be resolved to an IP address such as 192.168.1.110.

> **NOTE**   A registrar manages your domain name, and most require an annual renewal fee. If these fees aren't paid, another company will be able to hijack your domain name. Such hijacking has embarrassed many organizations.

DNS servers can be used internally for private functions as well as externally for public lookups. DNS-related attacks aren't common, but they generally come in one of three types:

Domain Name Service Denial of Service Attacks   Domain Name Service Denial of Service (DNS DoS) attacks are primarily aimed at DNS servers. The intention is to disrupt the operations of the server, thereby making the system unusable. To address these attacks, make sure your DNS server software and the operating system software are kept up-to-date. Doing so will tend to minimize the impact of DNS DoS attacks.

Network Footprinting   *Footprinting* is the act of gathering data about a network in order to find ways someone might intrude. When you footprint, you're looking for vulnerabilities and any means of entry. A great deal of information about your network is stored in DNS servers. By using one of the common DNS lookup programs, such as NSLOOKUP, an attacker can learn about your network configuration. DNS entries typically include information pertaining to domain names and mail, web, commerce, and other key servers in your network. Keep the amount of information stored about your network in external DNS servers to a bare minimum.

> **TIP**   A good recommendation is to utilize two DNS servers: one on the internal network and one on the external network.

Compromising Record Integrity   DNS lookup systems usually involve either a primary or a primary and a secondary DNS server. If you make a change to a primary or secondary server, the change propagates to other trusted DNS servers. If a bogus record is inserted into a DNS server, the record will point to the location the attacker intends rather than to a legitimate site. Imagine the embarrassment to a corporation when its website visitors are redirected to a competitor or, even worse, to a porn site. Make sure all DNS servers require authentication before updates are made or propagated. Doing so will help ensure that unauthorized records aren't inserted into your servers.

As DNS was originally designed, it did not include security because it was never thought to be a possible weakness in the network. Once it was realized that DNS could be exploited, however, the Domain Name System Security Extensions (DNSSEC) were created by the IETF (Internet Engineering Task Force) to add security and maintain backward compatibility. DNSSEC checks digital signatures and can protect information by digitally signing records. More information on DNSSEC can be found at http://www.dnssec.net.

DNS poisoning is a problem that existed in early implementations of DNS. It hasn't been a serious problem for a while, but you should be aware of it for the exam. With DNS poisoning (also known as *cache poisoning*), a daemon caches DNS reply packets, which sometimes contain other information (data used to fill the packets). The extra data can be scanned for information useful in a break-in or man-in-the-middle attack.

A similar attack, *Address Resolution Protocol (ARP) poisoning,* tries to convince the network that the attacker's MAC address is the one associated with an IP address so that traffic sent to that IP address is wrongly sent to the attacker's machine.

Hardening NNTP Servers

Network News Transfer Protocol (NNTP) servers provide the capability for delivering network news messages. NNTP servers are also commonly used for internal communications in a company or community. These newsgroup servers should require authentication before accepting a posting or allowing a connection to be made.

NNTP servers in many public settings have become overwhelmed with junk mail. Moderators, as well as automated tools called *robots*, are usually used to screen as much of this junk as possible from subscribers. Newsgroups that don't use these types of approaches have become virtually useless as communication tools.

NNTP servers can become overwhelmed by spam and DoS attacks. Many newsgroups started out as small groups of users who shared a common interest. Typically, newsgroups use a moderator to ensure that spam messages aren't propagated to subscribers of the newsgroup. However, some newsgroups have grown to include tens of thousands of members worldwide, and the amount of traffic or messages on these servers has long since surpassed the level that moderators can manage.

Use caution when signing newsgroups with your main email account. Many spammers use this information to send junk mail, so you may be inundated with spam.

Several scanning programs are now available to help reduce the amount of junk mail these systems process. Of course, as with all good countermeasures, someone always comes up with a way to neutralize their effectiveness.

Hardening DHCP Services

Dynamic Host Configuration Protocol (DHCP) is used in many networks to automate the assignment of IP addresses to workstations. DHCP services can be provided by many different types of devices, including routers, switches, and servers. The DHCP process involves leasing a TCP/IP address to a workstation for a specified time. DHCP can also provide other network configuration options to a workstation.

In a given network or segment, only one DHCP server should be running. If more than one is running, they will clash with each other over which one provides the address. This can cause duplication of TCP/IP addresses and potentially lead to addressing conflicts.

DHCP-enabled clients can be serviced by a Network Address Translation (NAT) server. (See the section in Chapter 2, "Network Address Translation" for a discussion of NAT servers.) DHCP usage should be limited to workstation systems.

 Real World Scenario

Dealing with Strange IP Addresses

Some of your computer users have suddenly started calling you to indicate that after rebooting their systems, they can no longer access network services or the Internet. After investigating the situation, you discover that the IP addresses they're using are invalid for your network. The IP addresses are valid, but they aren't part of your network. You've inspected your DHCP server and can't find a reason for this. What should you investigate next?

You should investigate whether someone has configured another server or device in your network with an active DHCP server. If so, the illicit DHCP server is now leasing addresses to the users instead of the addresses coming from your server, or the systems can't reach your DHCP server and are getting an Automatic Private IP Addressing (APIPA) address.

This happens when administrators or developers are testing pilot systems. Make sure all test systems are isolated from your production network either by a router or by some other mechanism. These servers are referred to as *rogue servers,* and they can cause much confusion in a DHCP environment.

Many devices, such as routers and modems, have the ability to also act as DHCP servers. A user trying to skirt IT and adding their own wireless router into their cubicle could potentially add a rogue DHCP server to the network that an intruder could use to gain access. Use intrusion detection systems to look for rogue servers, and disable them immediately.

 An exception to having only one DHCP server running in the network would be if you are implementing redundant DHCP services without overlapping scopes.

Working with Data Repositories

Many of the systems that are being used in networks today rely heavily on stored data. The data is usually kept in servers that provide directory services and database services. These systems are referred to as *data repositories*. The following sections discuss some of the more common data repositories in use. Most data repositories are enabled by some form of database technology.

Directory Services

Directory services are tools that help organize and manage complex networks. They allow data files, applications, and other information to be quickly and easily relocated within a network. This greatly simplifies administrative tasks, and it allows programmers and developers to better utilize network resources. The more current methods treat data and other network resources as objects. This object-oriented approach allows information to be stored and accessed based on certain characteristics or attributes.

In addition to creating and storing data, directory services must publish appropriate data to users. Perhaps the best way to visualize this function is to think of it as a movie listing on Netflix. The movie needs to be visible in a list that's in alphabetical order. The movie also needs to appear in one or more categories in any genre directory. This type of appearing in multiple listings is what a directory can accomplish for you.

Most directory services have implemented a model of hierarchy similar to the one illustrated in Figure 7.3. This hierarchy allows an object to be uniquely identified to directory users.

Security for directory services is critical, and it's typically accomplished by using both authentication and access control. You wouldn't want your directory entry to show up just anywhere, would you?

The following sections briefly describe some of the directory services used in networking today. LDAP, Active Directory, X.500, and eDirectory are becoming more widely used and are sure to become even more targeted for misuse in the future.

Lightweight Directory Access Protocol

Lightweight Directory Access Protocol (LDAP) is a standardized directory access protocol that allows queries to be made of directories (specifically, pared-down X.500-based directories). If a directory service supports LDAP, you can query that directory with an LDAP client, but it's LDAP that is growing in popularity and is being used extensively in online white and yellow pages.

LDAP is the main access protocol used by Active Directory (discussed next). It operates, by default, at port 389. The LDAP syntax uses commas between names.

Active Directory

Microsoft implemented a directory service called *Active Directory (AD)* many years back with the release of Windows 2000. For Microsoft server products since then, AD is the backbone for all security, access, and network implementations. AD gives administrators full control of resources. It's a proprietary directory service that provides services for other directory services, such as LDAP. One or more servers manage AD functions; these servers are connected in a tree structure that allows information to be shared or controlled through the entire AD structure.

FIGURE 7.3   Directory structure showing unique identification of a user

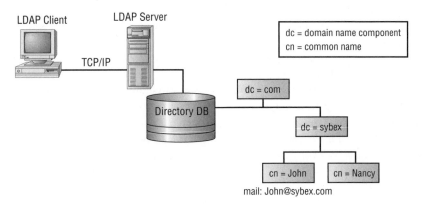

In conjunction with Active Directory, LDAP uses four different name types:

Distinguished Name   A *Distinguished Name (DN)* exists for every object in AD. These values can't be duplicates and must be unique. This is the full path of the object, including any containers.

Relative Distinguished Name   A *Relative Distinguished Name (RDN)* doesn't need to be a wholly unique value as long as there are no duplicates within the organizational unit (OU). As such, an RDN is the portion of the name that is unique within its container.

User Principal Name   A *User Principal Name (UPN)* is often referred to as a *friendly name*. It consists of the user account and the user's domain name and is used to identify the user (think of an email address).

Canonical Name   The *Canonical Name (CN)* is the DN given in a top-down notation.

X.500

The *International Telecommunications Union (ITU),* an international standards group for directory services in the late 1980s, implemented the *X.500 standard*, which was the basis for later models of directory structure such as LDAP. The major problem in the industry implementing a full-blown X.500 structure revolved around the complexity of the implementation. Novell was one of the first manufacturers to implement X.500 in its NetWare NDS product.

eDirectory

eDirectory is the backbone for new Novell networks. It stores information on all system resources and users and any other relevant information about systems attached to a NetWare server. eDirectory is an upgrade and replacement for NDS, and it has gained wide acceptance in the community.

Databases and Technologies

One key reason why computers are installed is for their ability to store, access, and modify data. The primary tool for data management is the database. Databases have become increasingly sophisticated, and their capabilities have grown dramatically over the last 10 years. This growth has created opportunities to view data in new ways; it has also created problems for both designers and users of these products.

This section briefly discusses database technologies and some of the common issues associated with vulnerabilities in database systems.

The *relational database* has become the most common approach to database implementation. This technology allows data to be viewed in dynamic ways based on the user's or administrator's needs. The most common language used to speak to databases is called *Structured Query Language (SQL)*. SQL allows queries to be configured in real time and passed to database servers. This flexibility causes a major vulnerability when it isn't implemented securely.

 Don't confuse the acronym *SQL* with Microsoft's database product *SQL Server*. SQL Server implements Structured Query Language, or SQL, as do most other databases.

For instance, you might want to get the phone numbers of all the customers who live in a certain geographic area and have purchased products from you in the last two years. In a manual system, you would first need to determine which customers live in the area you want. You would perform a manual search of customer records, and then you would identify which customers have made purchases. This type of process could be very involved and time consuming.

In a relational database environment, you could query the database to find all records that meet your criteria and then print them. The command to do this might be a single line of code, or it might require thousands of instructions. Obviously, the increase in productivity is a worthwhile investment.

Corporate or organizational data is one of an organization's most valuable possessions. It usually resides either in desktop systems or in large centralized database servers. This information makes the servers tempting targets for industrial espionage and damage.

Database servers suffer from all the vulnerabilities we've discussed to this point. Additionally, the database itself is a complex set of programs that work together to provide access to data.

Early database systems connected the end user directly to the data through applications programs. These programs were intended to allow easy data access and to allow transactions to be performed against the database. In a private network, physical security was usually all that was needed to protect the data.

As the Internet has grown, businesses have allowed customer access to data such as tracking orders, reviewing purchases, wiring funds, and virtually any other capabilities they want. This increased interoperability has added more coding, more software, and increased complexity to the database issue. Software manufacturers work hard to keep up with customer demands. Unfortunately, they frequently release software that is prone to security problems. The increase in demand for database-oriented systems and the security problems introduced by software developers and manufacturers have been the biggest areas of vulnerability for database servers.

 Databases need patching just like other applications. You should configure them to use access controls and provide their own levels of security.

To improve system performance, as well as to improve the security of databases, companies have implemented the tiered model of systems. Three different models are explained here:

One-Tier Model   In a *one-tier model*, or *single-tier environment,* the database and the application exist on a single system. This is common on desktop systems running a stand-alone database. Early Unix implementations also worked in this manner; each user would sign on to a terminal and run a dedicated application that accessed the data.

Two-Tier Model   In a *two-tier model*, the client PC or system runs an application that communicates with the database that is running on a different server. This is a common implementation, and it works well for many applications.

Three-Tier Model   The *three-tier model* effectively isolates the end user from the database by introducing a *middle-tier server.* This server accepts requests from clients, evaluates them, and then sends them on to the database server for processing. The database server sends the data back to the middle-tier server, which then sends the data to the client system. This approach is becoming common in business today. The middle server can also control access to the database and provide additional security.

These three models provide increasing capability and complexity. You must individually manage each system and keep it current for this system to provide security.

Injection Problems

One of the biggest issues with user input is the opportunity it creates for an attacker to enter values other than those expected. Doing so is called *injection*, and the following sections explore injection problems that can occur with SQL, LDAP, XML, and commands (also known as directory traversal).

SQL Injection

SQL (Structured Query Language) was discussed a bit earlier and is the de facto language used for communicating with online (and other relational) databases. With a *SQL injection attack* (also known as a *SQL insertion attack*), an attacker manipulates the database code to take advantage of a weakness in it. For example, if the interface is expecting the user to enter a string value, but it is not specifically coded that way, the attacker could enter a line of code and that code would then execute instead of being accepted as a string value.

Various types of exploits use SQL injection, and the most common fall beneath the following categories:

- Escape characters not filtered correctly
- Type handling not properly done
- Conditional errors
- Time delays

The best way to prevent SQL injection attacks is to make certain you type all parameters correctly and filter all user input. Additionally, make certain you keep your server current on all patches as they are released by the vendor.

LDAP Injection

Just as SQL injection attacks take statements input by users and exploit weaknesses within, an *LDAP injection attack* exploits weaknesses in LDAP (Lightweight Directory Access Protocol) implementations. This can occur when the user's input is not properly filtered, and the result can be executed commands, modified content, or results returned to unauthorized queries.

The best way to prevent LDAP injection attacks is to filter the user input and use a validation scheme to make certain queries do not contain exploits.

 Real World Scenario

LDAP Injection in Action

One of the most common uses of LDAP is associated with user information. Numerous applications exist—such as employee directories—where users find other users by typing in a portion of their name. These queries are looking at the cn value or other fields (those defined for department, home directory, etc.).

Someone attempting LDAP injection could feed unexpected values to the query to see what results are returned. All too often, finding employee information equates to finding usernames and values about those users that could be portions of their passwords.

XML Injection

When a web user takes advantage of a weakness with SQL by entering values they should not, it is known as a SQL injection attack. Similarly, when the user enters values that query

XML (known as XPath) with values that take advantage of exploits, it is known as an *XML injection attack*. XPath works similarly to SQL except that it does not have the same levels of access control, and taking advantage of weaknesses within can return entire documents.

The best way to prevent XML injection attacks is to filter the user's input and sanitize it to make certain it does not cause XPath to return more data than it should.

Directory Traversal/Command Injection

If an attacker is able to gain access to restricted directories (such as the root directory) through HTTP, it is known as a *directory traversal attack*. If the attacker can gain access to the root directory of a system (which is limited from all but administrative users), they can essentially gain access to everything on the system. Bear in mind that the root directory of a website is far from the true root directory of the server; an absolute path to the site's root directory is likely to something in IIS (Internet Information Server) such as `C:\inetpub\wwwroot`. If an attacker can get out of this directory and get to `C:\windows`, the possibility for inflicting harm is increased exponentially.

One of the simplest ways to perform directory traversal is by using a *command injection attack* that carries out the action. For example, exploiting a weak IIS implementation by calling up a web page along with the parameter `cmd.exe?/c+dir+c:\` would call the command shell and execute a directory listing of the root drive (`C:\`). With Unicode support, entries such as `%c%1c` and `%c0%af` can be translated into / and \ respectively.

The ability to perform command injection is rare these days. Most vulnerability scanners will check for weaknesses with directory traversal/command injection and inform you of their presence. To secure your system, you should run such a scanner and keep the web server software patched.

Host Security

It has been said before in this chapter but is worth repeating: The entire network should be considered only as strong as the weakest host. Given that, you should focus on keeping all hosts current in terms of malware protection and baselining—all areas of which are covered in the following sections.

Antimalware

To keep all hosts safe from malware, there are a number of things you should implement at a minimum:

Install Antivirus Software   Antivirus software, discussed in depth in Chapter 4, should be installed and definitions kept current on all hosts. Antivirus software should run on the server as well as on every workstation. In addition to active monitoring of incoming files, scans should be conducted regularly to catch any infections that have slipped through.

Install Antispam Filters   It is estimated that over 98 percent of all email is now spam. Spam filters are needed to keep the majority of this unwanted email from reaching the users.

Install Antispyware Software   Some antispyware software is combined with antivirus packages, while other programs are available as standalones. Regardless of the type you use, you must regularly look for spyware (often identified by the presence of tracking cookies) on hosts and remove those that get installed.

Utilize Pop-up Blockers   Pop-ups are not only irritating but also a security threat. Pop-ups (including pop-unders) represent unwanted programs running on the system and can jeopardize well-being. In Exercise 7.3, I'll show you how to configure Pop-up Blocker in Internet Explorer.

Employ Host-Based Firewalls   A firewall is the first line of defense against attackers and malware. Almost every current operating system includes a firewall, and most are turned on by default. In Exercise 7.4, I'll show you how to configure Windows Firewall in Windows 7 to notify when a program is blocked.

EXERCISE 7.3

Configuring Pop-up Blocker

Pop-ups represent a security risk that often bypasses other forms of security. To configure Pop-up Blocker in Internet Explorer, follow these steps:

1.   Within Internet Explorer, choose Tools ➢ Pop-up Blocker ➢ Pop-up Blocker Settings.

2. Add Google to the list of allowed pop-ups by entering the address **http://google.com** and clicking Add. This URL should now appear in the list of allowed sites as *.google.com.

3. Note the three possible settings for blocking levels:

    - Low allows pop-ups from sites considered secured.

    - Medium (the default) blocks most pop-ups.

    - High blocks all (but Ctrl+Alt will override).

    Click Close to exit the settings.

4. Go back to the Tools menu and choose Internet Options.

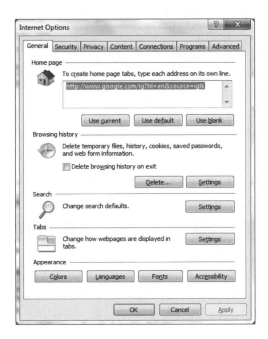

5. Click the Settings button beneath the Tabs option.

EXERCISE 7.3 *(continued)*

6. Beneath When A Pop-up Is Encountered, choose Let Internet Explorer Decide How Pop-ups Should Open.

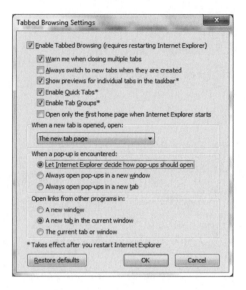

7. Click OK.

8. Click OK again to exit Internet Options.

EXERCISE 7.4

Configuring Windows Firewall

Windows Firewall is used to block access to a system from attackers and malware. You can configure it in a number of different ways, including to send a notification when a program is blocked. To configure Windows Firewall to send a notification, follow these steps:

1. Click Start ➢ Control Panel ➢ System and Security ➢ Windows Firewall.

2. Click Change Notification Settings. Beneath both the private and public location settings, check the box Notify Me When Windows Firewall Blocks A New Program.

3. Click OK. When a program is blocked, Windows Firewall will alert you (and give you the option to allow it).

4. Click Advanced Settings to bring up the Advanced Security dialog box.

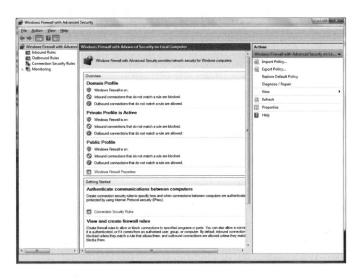

EXERCISE 7.4 *(continued)*

5.   Click Windows Firewall Properties to open the Properties dialog box.

6.   Click Customize next to Logging.

7.   From here you can configure the log file to be used and the size limit of that file.
     Increase the file size (if it is not already) to 4,096 KB.

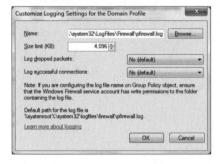

8.   Click OK. Click OK again to exit the properties. Exit the dialog boxes and Control Panel.

It should be noted that while software-based firewalls included with the operating system are a great defense, they should not be considered the only solution. A *Web Application Firewall (WAF)* can look at every request between a web client and a web server and identify possible attacks.

Host Software Baselining

One of the first steps in developing a secure environment is to develop a baseline of the minimum security needs of your organization. A *security baseline* defines the level of security that will be implemented and maintained. You can choose to set a low baseline by implementing next to no security or a high baseline that doesn't allow users to make any changes at all to the network or their systems. In practice, most implementations fall between the two extremes; you must determine what is best for your organization.

The security baseline, which can also be called a *performance baseline*, provides the input needed to design, implement, and support a secure network. Developing the baseline includes gathering data on the specific security implementation of the systems with which you'll be working.

Microsoft Baseline Security Analyzer is a free tool from Microsoft that can be downloaded and run on Windows to create security reports and scan for errors (`http://technet` `.microsoft.com/en-us/security/cc184923`). Figure 7.4 shows the interface for this tool.

FIGURE 7.4   The opening interface for Microsoft Baseline Security Analyzer

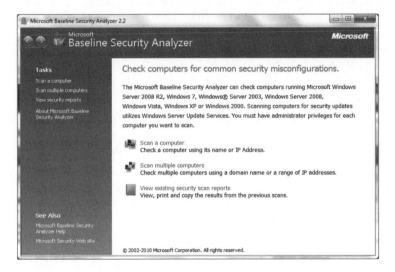

Mobile Devices

Mobile devices, such as laptops, net books, iPads, and smartphones, provide security challenges above those of desktop workstations, servers, and such in that they leave the office, and this increases the odds of their theft. In 2010, AvMed Health Plans, a Florida-based company, had two laptop computers stolen. Together, over one million personal customer records were on those computers, and this is but one of many similar stories that happen on a regular basis.

At a bare minimum, the following security measures should be in place on mobile devices:

Screen Lock   The display should be configured to time out after a short period of inactivity and the screen locked with a password. In order to be able to access the system again, the password must be given.

Strong Password   Passwords are always important, but even more so when you consider that the device could be stolen and in the possession of someone who has unlimited access and time to try various values.

Device Encryption   Data should be encrypted on the device so that if it does fall into the wrong hands, it cannot be accessed in a usable form without the correct passwords. TPM is discussed later in this chapter and recommended for use on laptops where possible.

Remote Wipe/Sanitation   Many programs, such as Microsoft Exchange Server 2010 or Google Apps, allow you to send a command to a phone that will remotely clear the data on that phone. This process is known as a *remote wipe* and is intended to be used if the phone is stolen or going to another user.

Voice Encryption   Voice encryption can be used with mobile phones and similar devices to encrypt transmissions. This is intended to keep the conversation secure and works by adding cryptography (discussed in the next chapter) to the digitized conversation.

GPS Tracking   Should a device be stolen, GPS (Global Positioning System) tracking can be used to identify its location and allow authorities to find it.

Best Practices for Security

In the preceding sections of this chapter, some of the basics of operating system and application hardening were given. These gave you a good foundation for security, but there are several technologies and practices that you, as a security administrator, should also be aware of to best implement security in your environment. Those are covered in this section, and you should be familiar with them for the exam.

URL Filtering

URL filtering involves blocking websites (or sections of websites) based solely on the URL; restricting access to specified websites and certain web-based applications. This is in contrast to content filters, which block data based on its content rather than where it is coming from. Within Internet Explorer, the Phishing Filter included with IE7 acted as a URL filter. The Phishing Filter was replaced with the SmartScreen Filter with IE8 and subsequent releases.

SmartScreen runs in the background and sends the address of the website being visited to the SmartScreen server, where it is compared against a list kept of phishing and malware sites. If a match is found, a blocking web page appears (in red) and encourages you to not continue on. You can continue to the site (not recommended) or abort the operation. You can control the operations of the SmartScreen Filter in IE from the Safety menu. From here, you can toggle it on/off, report an unsafe site, and check to see if a site is in the database. Figure 7.5 shows the results of a check that did not find any threats.

FIGURE 7.5   A website that does not appear in the URL filter list

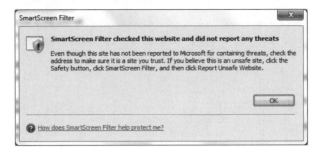

Content Inspection

Instead of relying on a website to be previously identified as questionable, as URL filtering does, content inspection works by looking at the data coming in. Within the most recent versions of Internet Explorer, content filtering can be configured using Content Advisor. In Exercise 7.5, I'll show you how to configure content filtering in Internet Explorer.

EXERCISE 7.5

Configuring Web Filtering

In Internet Explorer, content inspection is done by Content Advisor. This can be turned on and configured by following these steps:

1.   Within Internet Explorer, choose Internet Options from the Tools menu.

2.   Click the Content tab.

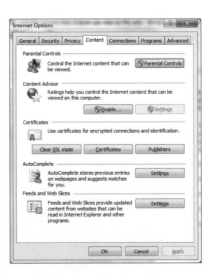

3. Click Enable beneath Content Advisor. The UAC (User Account Control) will prompt you to continue; click Yes. The Content Advisor dialog box will appear.

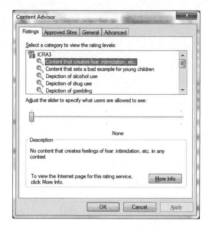

4. For each of the categories that appear in the box, use the slider to choose a setting. Options include None, Limited, Some, and Unrestricted. Definitions of what will appear for each setting are shown in the bottom portion of the dialog box.

5. After making a selection for each category, click OK.

6. Click OK again to exit the Internet Options.

Internet content filters, while not included with every operating system by default, are plentiful and can be readily found for any operating system with a simple web search. It is highly recommended that you place content filters on all servers (NAT, proxy, etc.) facilitating client access as well as on the workstations themselves. This provides two levels of security that can keep errant pages out.

Malware Inspection

It is important to stop malware before it ever gets hold of a system. While tools that identify malware when they find it on a system are useful, real-time tools that stop it from ever making it to the system are better. One of those tools available for Windows is Microsoft Security Essentials, and it runs on Windows 7 as well as Windows Vista and Windows XP SP2. You can download it for free from http://www.microsoft.com/security_essentials/.

Once it's installed, and the definition files are current, you can configure it by choosing the Settings tab, as shown in Figure 7.6.

FIGURE 7.6   Configuring Microsoft Security Essentials

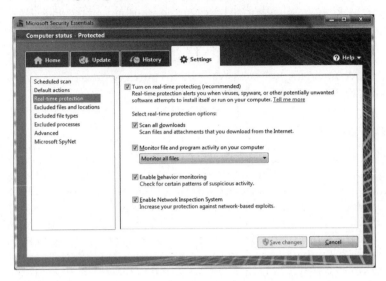

Also note that another free tool from Microsoft is the *Malicious Software Removal Tool*, which helps remove any infection found. An updated version of this tool is released on the second Tuesday of each month and—once installed—it is included, by default, in Microsoft Update and Windows Update. Figure 7.7 shows the opening screen for this tool.

FIGURE 7.7   Running the Microsoft Windows Malicious Software Removal Tool

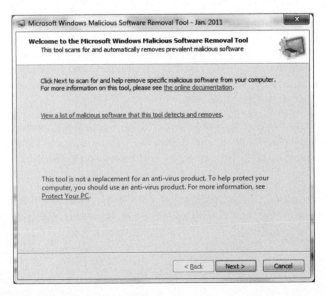

Data Loss Prevention

Data Loss Prevention (DLP) systems monitor the contents of systems (workstations, servers, and networks) to make sure key content is not deleted or removed. They also monitor who is using the data (looking for unauthorized access) and transmitting the data. DLP systems share commonality with Network Intrusion Prevention Systems, discussed in Chapter 3.

One of the best-known DLP systems is MyDLP, an open source solution that runs on most Windows platforms and can be found at `http://www.mydlp.org/`. There are also a large number of commercial programs available for purchase, including Microsoft Forefront (`http://www.microsoft.com/forefront/`).

Data Encryption

Data encryption, mentioned earlier in relation to mobile devices, allows data that has been stolen to remain out of the eyes of the miscreants who did it as long as they do not have the proper passwords. One of the newest security features that is available on only the Ultimate version of Windows 7 and in the Enterprise and Ultimate versions of Vista is *BitLocker*. BitLocker is a *full disk encryption* feature that can encrypt an entire volume with 128-bit encryption. When the entire volume is encrypted, the data is not accessible to someone who might boot another operating system in an attempt to bypass the computer's security.

BitLocker to Go is available only in Windows 7, and it allows you to apply the same technology to removable drives. By encrypting removable hard drives and USB flash drives, you also prevent them from being so meaningful when intercepted by the wrong hands. To illustrate the power of the wrong hands, consider the case study that follows.

 Real World Scenario

The Danger of Unencrypted Data

In March of 2010, Education Credit Management Corp., a Minnesota-based company, reported that a "portable media device" had been stolen from them. While that may seem like a minor occurrence for a large company—someone pilfering a laptop or notebook or other device—such was not to be.

That misappropriated device had the Social Security numbers for 3.3 million students with $9 million in student loans. Their Social Security numbers weren't the only thing in the database, either; they were accompanied by addresses and date-of-birth information as well.

Always consider the harm that could befall those your data represents if it falls into the wrong hands. Armed with that, you should have little difficulty justifying the added cost (dollars and effort) of encryption.

In addition to encrypting the whole disk, encryption can be applied at almost any level: database, individual files, removable media, and so on. Chapter 9 explores EFS (Encrypting File System) and includes an exercise on how to use it to encrypt a file.

Hardware-Based Encryption Devices

In addition to software-based encryption, hardware-based encryption can also be applied. Within the advanced configuration settings on some BIOS configuration menus, for example, you can choose to enable or disable TPM. A *Trusted Platform Module (TPM)* can be used to assist with hash key generation. TPM is the name assigned to a chip that can store cryptographic keys, passwords, or certificates. TPM can be used to protect cell phones and devices other than PCs as well. It can also be used to generate values used with whole disk encryption such as BitLocker. BitLocker can be used with or without TPM. It is much more secure when coupled with TPM (and is preferable) but does not require it.

The TPM chip may be installed on the motherboard; when it is, in many cases it is set to off in the BIOS by default. In Exercise 7.6, you'll look for a TPM chip in Windows Vista. Vista is used as the example here merely because the support for TPM is included with most versions of it, while with Windows 7, that support is limited.

EXERCISE 7.6

Verifying the Presence of a TPM Chip in Windows Vista

The following steps will allow you to verify whether or not a TPM chip is installed on your computer:

1. Within Vista, go to Control Panel and choose Security.

2. Beneath Security, choose BitLocker Drive Encryption.

3. A dialog box will appear. The contents of the box do not matter, but what does matter is a link in the lower-left-hand corner that will read TPM Administration. If this link is there, TPM is installed and active. If you don't see the link but are certain that your computer has such a chip, you may need to boot into your BIOS Setup menu and enable TPM before trying this again.

More information on TPM can be found at the Trusted Computing Group's website: `https://www.trustedcomputinggroup.org/home`.

In addition to TPM, *HSM* (*Hardware Security Module*) is also a cryptoprocessor that can be used to enhance security. HSM is commonly used with PKI systems (discussed in Chapters 8 and 9) to augment security with certification authorities (CAs). As opposed to being mounted on the motherboard as TPMs are, HSMs are traditionally PCI adapters.

Attack Types to Be Aware Of

No chapter would be complete without a few threats to scare you. In this case, there are two worth paying particular attention to: session hijacking and header manipulation. Each is discussed in the sections that follow.

Session Hijacking

The term *session hijacking* is used when the item used to validate a user's session, such as a cookie, is stolen and used by another to establish a session with a host that thinks it is still communicating with the first party. To use an overly simplistic analogy, imagine that you just finished a long cell phone conversation with a family member and then accidentally left your cell phone in the room while stepping outside. If I were to pick up that phone and press redial, the family member would see the caller ID, know that they had just been talking with you, and falsely assume that you were calling back. If I could imitate your voice, I could rattle off numerous nasty comments that would jeopardize the relationship. This same premise could be true if I could fool another host into thinking it was still talking to your computer rather than mine.

Numerous types of attacks utilize session hijacking, including man-in-the-middle and sidejacking. A weakness in a Firefox extension (Firesheep) made news when it became known that an exploit made it possible for public Wi-Fi users to fall prey to this type of attack.

Some of the best ways to prevent session hijacking are to encrypt the sessions, encourage users to log out of sites when finished, and perform secondary checks on the identity of the user. Man-in-the-middle threats were also mentioned in Chapter 4.

Header Manipulation

A *header manipulation* attack uses other methods discussed in this chapter (hijacking, cross-site forgery, etc.) to change values in HTTP headers and falsify access. When used with XSRF, the attacker can even change a user's cookie. Internet Explorer 8 and above include InPrivate Filtering to help prevent some of this. By default, your browser sends information to sites as they need it—think of requesting a map from a site; it needs to know your location in order to give directions. With InPrivate Filtering, you can configure the browser to not share information that can be captured and manipulated.

Figure 7.8 shows the InPrivate Filtering options that can be configured.

FIGURE 7.8   Configuring InPrivate Filtering

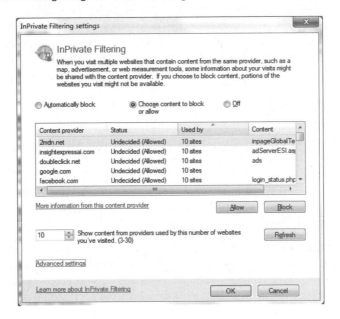

Summary

This chapter introduced you to the concept of hardening operating systems and applications. To secure a network, each of the elements in its environment must be individually evaluated. Remember, your network is no more secure than its weakest link.

The process of making a server or an application resistant to attack is called hardening. One of the major methods of hardening an operating system is to disable any protocols that aren't needed in the system. Keeping systems updated also helps improve security.

The FAT filesystem provides user-level and share-level security. As a result, FAT is largely unsuitable as a filesystem for use in secure environments. NTFS provides security capabilities similar to Unix, and it allows control of individual files using various criteria.

Product updates are often used to improve security and fix errors. The three primary methods of upgrading systems are hotfixes, service packs, and patches. Hotfixes are usually meant as temporary fixes, while service packs usually contain multiple fixes, and patches are used to temporarily fix a program until a permanent fix can be applied.

Application hardening helps ensure that vulnerabilities are minimized. Make sure you run only the applications and services that are needed to support your environment. Attackers can target application protocols. Many of the newer systems offer a rich environment for end users, and each protocol increases your risk.

Directory services allow information to be shared in a structured manner with large numbers of users. These services must be secure in order to prevent impersonation or embarrassment. The more common directory services used are LDAP, AD, X.500, and eDirectory.

Database technologies are vulnerable to attacks because of the nature of the flexibility they provide. Make sure database servers and applications are kept up-to-date. To provide increased security, many environments have implemented multitiered approaches to data access.

Exam Essentials

Be able to describe the process of hardening an operating system.   Make sure all the products used in a network are kept up-to-date with the most current release. Apply service packs and security updates on a regular basis.

Be able to identify the capabilities of the various filesystems used.   Different filesystems have different security capabilities. The least secure is FAT, which provides only share-level and user-level security. Most of the truly networked filesystems provide access down to the individual file or directory level. The method used by Unix allows each individual file to have Read, Write, or Execute permissions for security. The filesystem can be configured when the system is installed. Unix filesystems are considered the most secure for commercial applications.

Know the types of updates used in systems.   The three common methods for updating are hotfixes, service packs, and patches. Hotfixes are usually applied to a system in real time in order to continue operations until a permanent fix can be made. Service packs are groups of updates for a system or application. Service packs typically replace entire programs. Patches are made to systems to solve a problem or to bypass a particular malfunctioning system.

Be able to discuss the weaknesses and vulnerabilities of the various applications that run on a network.   Web, email, and other services present unique security challenges that must be considered. Turn off services that aren't needed. Make sure applications are kept up-to-date with security and bug fixes. Implement these services in a secure manner, as the manufacturer intended; this is the best method for securing applications.

Be able to identify the purpose and common protocols used for directory services.   The most commonly implemented directory service is LDAP. LDAP allows users to globally publish information that they want others to know. This process is done using an LDAP server or service. Other directory services are DNS, AD, eDirectory, and X.500. Most directory services are implemented in a hierarchical manner that allows objects to be uniquely identified.

Review Questions

1. Which of the following terms refers to the process of establishing a standard for security?

   A. Baselining

   B. Security evaluation

   C. Hardening

   D. Methods research

2. You've been chosen to lead a team of administrators in an attempt to increase security. You're currently creating an outline of all the aspects of security that will need to be examined and acted upon. Which of the following terms describes the process of improving security in an NOS?

   A. Common Criteria

   B. Hardening

   C. Encryption

   D. Networking

3. What tool is used in Windows to encrypt an entire volume?

   A. BitLocker

   B. SysLock

   C. Drive Defender

   D. NLock

4. Which filesystem was primarily intended for desktop system use and offers limited security?

   A. NTFS

   B. NFS

   C. FAT

   D. AFS

5. The administrator at MTS was recently fired, and it has come to light that he didn't install updates and fixes as they were released. As the newly hired administrator, your first priority is to bring all networked clients and servers up-to-date. What is a bundle of one or more system fixes in a single product called?

   A. Service pack

   B. Hotfix

   C. Patch

   D. System install

6. Which of the following statements is *not* true?

    A. You should never share the root directory of a disk.

    B. You should share the root directory of a disk.

    C. You should apply the most restrictive access necessary for a shared directory.

    D. Filesystems are frequently based on hierarchical models.

7. Your company does electronic monitoring of individuals under house arrest around the world. Because of the sensitive nature of the business, you can't afford any unnecessary downtime. What is the process of applying a repair to an operating system while the system stays in operation called?

    A. Upgrading

    B. Service pack installation

    C. Hotfix

    D. File update

8. What is the process of applying manual changes to a program called?

    A. Hotfix

    B. Service pack

    C. Patching

    D. Replacement

9. Users are complaining about name resolution problems suddenly occurring that were never an issue before. You suspect that an intruder has compromised the integrity of the DNS server on your network. What is one of the primary ways in which an attacker uses DNS?

    A. Network footprinting

    B. Network sniffing

    C. Database server lookup

    D. Registration counterfeiting

10. LDAP is an example of which of the following?

    A. Directory access protocol

    B. IDS

    C. Tiered model application development environment

    D. File server

11. Your company is growing at a tremendous rate, and the need to hire specialists in various areas of IT is becoming apparent. You're helping to write the newspaper ads that will be used to recruit new employees, and you want to make certain that applicants possess the skills you need. One knowledge area in which your organization is weak is database intelligence. What is the primary type of database used in applications today that you can mention in the ads?

    A. Hierarchical

    B. Relational

    C. Network

    D. Archival

12. The flexibility of relational databases in use today is a result of which of the following?

    A. SQL

    B. Hard-coded queries

    C. Forward projection

    D. Mixed model access

13. You're redesigning your network in preparation for putting the company up for sale. The network, like all aspects of the company, needs to perform the best that it possibly can in order to be an asset to the sale. Which model is used to provide an intermediary server between the end user and the database?

    A. One-tiered

    B. Two-tiered

    C. Three-tiered

    D. Relational database

14. Which of the following is the technique of providing unexpected values as input to an application to try to make it crash?

    A. DLP

    B. Fuzzing

    C. TPM

    D. HSM

15. Which systems monitor the contents of systems (workstations, servers, networks) to make sure key content is not deleted or removed?

    A. DLP

    B. PKM

    C. XML

    D. GSP

16. What is it known as when an attacker manipulates the database code to take advantage of a weakness in it?

    A. SQL tearing

    B. SQL manipulation

    C. SQL cracking

    D. SQL injection

17. If an attacker is able to gain access to restricted directories (such as the root directory) through HTTP, it is known as:

    A. Cross-site forgery

    B. Directory traversal

    C. Root hardening

    D. Trusted platform corruption

18. What is the term used when the item used to validate a user's session, such as a cookie, is stolen and used by another to establish a session with a host that thinks it is still communicating with the first party?

    A. Patch infiltration

    B. XML injection

    C. Session hijacking

    D. DTB exploitation

19. Which of the following involves unauthorized commands coming from a trusted user to the website?

    A. ZDT

    B. HSM

    C. TT3

    D. XSRF

20. Which of the following is the name assigned to a chip that can store cryptographic keys, passwords, or certificates?

    A. ODI

    B. TLC

    C. TPM

    D. RDP

Answers to Review Questions

1. A. Baselining is the process of establishing a standard for security.

2. B. Hardening is the process of improving the security of an operating system or application. One of the primary methods of hardening an OS is to eliminate unneeded protocols.

3. A. BitLocker provides drive encryption and is available with Windows 7 and Windows Vista.

4. C. FAT technology offers limited security options.

5. A. A service pack is one or more repairs to system problems bundled into a single process or function.

6. B. Never share the root directory of a disk if at all possible. Doing so opens the entire disk to potential exploitation.

7. C. A hotfix is done while a system is operating. This reduces the necessity of taking a system out of service to fix a problem.

8. C. A patch is a temporary workaround of a bug or problem in code that is applied manually. Complete programs usually replace patches at a later date.

9. A. DNS records in a DNS server provide insights into the nature and structure of a network. DNS records should be kept to a minimum in public DNS servers. Network footprinting involves the attacker collecting data about the network to devise methods of intrusion.

10. A. Lightweight Directory Access Protocol (LDAP) is a directory access protocol used to publish information about users. This is the computer equivalent of a phone book.

11. B. Relational database systems are the most frequently installed database environments in use today.

12. A. SQL is a powerful database access language used by most relational database systems.

13. C. A three-tiered model puts a server between the client and the database.

14. B. Fuzzing is the technique of providing unexpected values as input to an application to try to make it crash. Those values can be random, invalid, or just unexpected.

15. A. DLP systems monitor the contents of systems (workstations, servers, networks) to make sure key content is not deleted or removed. They also monitor who is using the data (looking for unauthorized access) and transmitting the data.

16. D. SQL injection occurs when an attacker manipulates the database code to take advantage of a weakness in it.

17. B. If an attacker is able to gain access to restricted directories (such as the root directory) through HTTP, it is known as directory traversal.

18. C. Session hijacking occurs when the item used to validate a user's session, such as a cookie, is stolen and used by another to establish a session with a host that thinks it is still communicating with the first party.

19. D. XSRF involves unauthorized commands coming from a trusted user to the website. This is often done without the user's knowledge and employs some type of social networking to pull it off.

20. C. TPM is the name assigned to a chip that can store cryptographic keys, passwords, or certificates. TPM can be used to protect cell phones and devices other than PCs as well.

Chapter

8

Cryptography Basics

THE FOLLOWING COMPTIA SECURITY+ EXAM OBJECTIVES ARE COVERED IN THIS CHAPTER:

✓ **2.8 Exemplify the concepts of confidentiality, integrity and availability (CIA).**

✓ **6.1 Summarize general cryptography concepts.**

  ▪ Symmetric vs. asymmetric

  ▪ Fundamental differences and encryption methods: Block vs. stream

  ▪ Transport encryption

  ▪ Non-repudiation

  ▪ Hashing

  ▪ Key escrow

  ▪ Steganography

  ▪ Digital signatures

  ▪ Use of proven technologies

  ▪ Elliptic curve and quantum cryptography

✓ **6.2 Use and apply appropriate cryptographic tools and products.**

  ▪ WEP vs. WPA/WPA2 and preshared key

  ▪ MD5

  ▪ SHA

  ▪ RIPEMD

  ▪ AES

  ▪ DES

  ▪ 3DES

  ▪ HMAC

- RSA
- RC4
- One-time-pads
- CHAP
- PAP
- NTLM
- NTLMv2
- Blowfish
- PGP/GPG
- Whole disk encryption
- TwoFish
- Comparative strength of algorithms
- Use of algorithms with transport encryption: SSL; TLS; IPSec; SSH; HTTPS

✓ **6.3 Explain the core concepts of public key infrastructure.**

- Certificate authorities and digital signatures: CA; CRLs
- PKI
- Recovery agent
- Public key
- Private key
- Registration
- Key escrow
- Trust models

Cryptography is the art of concealing information. It is the practice of protecting information through encryption and transformation. As data becomes more valuable, and more important, it is an area of high interest to governments and businesses, and, increasingly, to individuals. People want privacy when it comes to their personal and other sensitive information. Corporations want—and need—to protect financial records, trade secrets, customer lists, and employee information. The government uses cryptography to help ensure the safety and well-being of its citizens. Entire governmental agencies have been created to help ensure secrecy, and millions of dollars have been spent trying to protect national secrets and attempting to learn the secrets of other countries.

Individuals who specialize in the development and making of codes are referred to as *cryptographers*. Individuals who specialize in breaking codes are called *cryptanalysts*. Many of these professionals are geniuses with strong backgrounds in math and computer science.

In addition to a brief overview of cryptography, this chapter discusses some of the more common algorithms used, how encryption is used today, Public Key Infrastructure (PKI), and some of the attacks to which cryptographic systems are vulnerable. It also discusses standards, key management, and the key life cycle.

An Overview of Cryptography

Cryptography is a field almost as old as humankind. The first recorded cryptographic efforts occurred 4,000 years ago. These early efforts included translating messages from one language into another or substituting characters. Since that time, cryptography has grown to include a plethora of possibilities.

 You won't be tested on the history of cryptography in the Security+ exam; this information is included primarily for background purposes.

The following sections briefly discuss three categories of cryptography—physical, mathematical, and quantum—as well as code breaking. Quantum cryptography is extremely classified and is relatively new. The other methods discussed are well known and commonly used.

Understanding Non-mathematical Cryptography

Non-mathematical cryptography includes several different approaches. The more common methods involve transposition or substitution of characters or words. Non-mathematical methods also include a method of encryption called *steganography*, which is the science of hiding information within other information, such as within a picture.

> In general, non-mathematical cryptography refers to any method that doesn't alter a value using a mathematical process.

A *cipher* is a method used to encode characters to hide their value. *Ciphering* is the process of using a cipher to encode a message. The three primary types of non-mathematical cryptography, or ciphering methods—substitution, transposition, and steganography—are discussed in the following sections. The hybrid model, which is also discussed, uses one or more methods to accomplish encryption.

> It's important to know that cryptography is always changing in an effort to make algorithms that are more difficult to crack. Not that long ago, single-digit bit encryption was good enough; now triple digits are almost a minimum requirement.

Substitution Ciphers

A *substitution cipher* is a type of coding or ciphering system that changes one character or symbol into another. Character substitution can be a relatively easy method of encrypting information. You may see this method used in a childhood toy such as a decoder ring. For example, let's say you had the following message:

You can do this easily if you put your mind to it.

And here is how the encrypted message read:

You can do qhis zasily if you puq your mind to iq.

Notice in the encrypted example that every instance of *z* is a substitute for *e* and that every instance of *q* is a substitute for *t*. This code, while simple, may prevent someone from understanding the message for a very short period of time.

This type of coding creates two potential problems. Obviously, the system isn't highly secure. In addition, how do you know the *q* isn't really a *q*? Nevertheless, this method has been used in simple codes since time immemorial.

Transposition Ciphers

A *transposition cipher* (also referred to as a *transposition code*) involves transposing or scrambling the letters in a certain manner. Typically, a message is broken into blocks of equal size, and each block is then scrambled. In the simple example shown in Figure 8.1, the characters are transposed by changing the order of the group. In this case, the letters are rotated three places in the message. You could change the way Block 1 is transposed from Block 2 and make it a little more difficult, but it would still be relatively easy to decrypt.

Real World Scenario

Working with rot13

One of the oldest known encoding algorithms is rot13—said by some to be an extension of an algorithm used in the days of Caesar. This simple algorithm rotates every letter 13 places in the alphabet. Thus an *A* becomes an *N*, a *B* becomes an *O*, and so forth. The same rotation of 13 letters that is used to encrypt the message is also used to decrypt the message. Many newsgroups offer a rot13 option that allows you to encrypt/decrypt postings.

See if you can solve these encryptions:

1. Neg snve qrohgf urer Fngheqnl.

2. Gevcyr pbhcbaf ng Xebtre!

3. Gel lbhe unaq ng chmmyrf.

One of the easiest ways to solve rot13 text messages is to take a sheet of paper and write the letters from *A to M* in one column and from *N to Z* in a second. To decipher, replace the letter in the encrypted message with the one that appears beside it in the other column.

Here are the answers:

1. Art fair debuts here Saturday.

2. Triple coupons at Kroger!

3. Try your hand at puzzles.

FIGURE 8.1   A simple transposition code in action

Moon beams are nice.

| Moon | Beams | Are | Nice. | In this example, text is grouped in five-character blocks. |
| on Mo | amsBe | re A | ce.Ni | |

In this example, each character (including the spaces) is moved to the right three positions.

Steganography

Steganography is the process of hiding a message in a medium such as a digital image, audio file, or other file. In theory, doing this prevents analysts from detecting the real message. You could encode your message in another file or message and use that file to hide your message. This type of encryption can be somewhat harder to detect, but it's still breakable.

Steganography is also called *electronic watermarking*. Mapmakers and artists have used watermarking for years to protect copyrights. If an image contains a watermark placed there by the original artist, proving that a copyright infringement has occurred in a copy is relatively easy.

Hybrid Systems

By combining two or more of these methods of non-mathematical cryptography, you can make a pretty good cipher system. These types of systems are widely used, and they're difficult to break using manual methods. Many systems, such as the Enigma machine used during World War II to encode messages between the German command and their U-boats, used a combination of substitution and transposition to make a very sophisticated system.

In Exercise 8.1, I will show you how to encrypt a filesystem in SuSe Linux.

EXERCISE 8.1

Encrypting a File System in Linux

This lab requires access to a server running SuSE Linux Enterprise Server. To encrypt a filesystem, follow these steps:

1. Log in as root and start YaST.

2. Choose System ≻ Partitioner.

3. Answer Yes to the prompt that appears. Select a filesystem and click Edit.

4. Select the Encrypt File System check box and click OK.

Understanding Mathematical Cryptography

Mathematical cryptography deals with using mathematical processes on characters or messages. One of the most common is a function called *hashing*. Hashing refers to performing a calculation on a message and converting it into a numeric hash value. The *hash value* of the example in Figure 8.2 is computed by multiplying each character by 2, adding those results together, and then dividing the sum by 10.

Hashing is discussed in detail in the section "The Science of Hashing" later in this chapter.

FIGURE 8.2   A simple hashing process

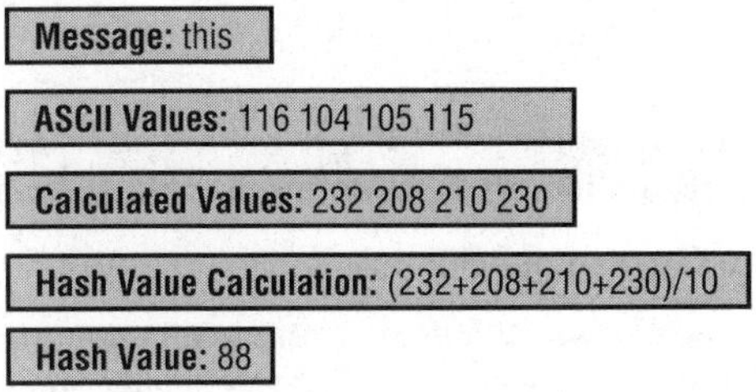

> **Message:** this
>
> **ASCII Values:** 116 104 105 115
>
> **Calculated Values:** 232 208 210 230
>
> **Hash Value Calculation:** (232+208+210+230)/10
>
> **Hash Value:** 88

As you can see, this hash value is a single number. The hash value can't be used to derive the meaning of the message. The number is transmitted with the message to the receiver, and the receiving end uses the same hash function to determine that the message is authentic. If the hash value is different, the message has been altered in some way. This process is also known as performing a *checksum* and helps ensure integrity

This type of hashing is called a *one-way process*. There is no way to reverse the hash and turn the number back into the original message. This method of hashing is used to verify message authenticity, and it may be used in conjunction with one of the other encryption methods previously defined. It's important to note that a one-way hash can't be used to decrypt a message that is used primarily for authenticity verification. Nevertheless, it's considered an encryption process, used primarily to verify the integrity of the message.

As you can imagine, calculating all the numbers in a larger, more complicated message by hand would be cumbersome and time consuming. Computers make hashing a very fast process.

Hashing is used extensively in computer programming. Many early random access file methods used hashing to locate records in a data file.

A *Trusted Platform Module (TPM)* can be used to assist with hash key generation. A TPM is the name assigned to a chip that can store cryptographic keys, passwords, or certificates. The TPM can be used to generate values used with *whole disk encryption* as well as protect cell phones and devices other than PCs.

As discussed in Chapter 7, the Ultimate version of Windows 7 and the Enterprise and Ultimate versions of Vista (as well as Windows Server 2008) include a utility called BitLocker. BitLocker is a *whole disk encryption* (also often called full disk encryption) feature that can encrypt an entire volume with 128-bit encryption. When the entire volume is encrypted, the data is secured should it fall into the wrong hands, even if they try to boot another operating system in an attempt to bypass the computer's security. BitLocker requires two partitions on the OS—one that holds the files needed to boot the system (which cannot be encrypted) and one that holds everything else (which is encrypted).

TPM can be used to authenticate hardware devices; by coupling it with the BIOS, it can identify configuration changes and act accordingly. There is some controversy about TPM, and several countries (such as China and Russia) have banned its deployment. More information on TPM can be found at the Trusted Computing Group's website `https://www.trustedcomputinggroup.org/home`.

In Exercise 8.2, I will show you how to create a hash rule in Windows Server 2008.

EXERCISE 8.2

Hash Rules in Windows Server 2008

This lab requires a test machine (nonproduction) running Windows Server 2008. Note that on a generic 2008 Server with Active Directory, you must access the local security policy slightly differently. Launch an MMC, then choose to add the GPO Editor, and select Local Computer. Everything else will then work the same.

To create a new hash rule, follow these steps:

1. Choose Start ➢ Administrative Tools ➢ Local Security Policy.

2. Expand Software Restriction Policies.

3. Right-click Additional Rules and choose New Hash Rule from the context menu.

4. Click the Browse button and choose the file `hisecws.inf` from the `Templates` folder (this is under `\Winnt\Security\Templates`).

5. Notice the file hash that appears and the file information. Click OK.

6. Notice that the new hash rule is added to the right pane along with the default path rules that appear there.

Working with Passwords

Many password-generation systems are based on a one-way hashing approach. You can't take the hash value and reverse it to guess the password. In theory, this makes it harder to break or decrypt a good password.

Passwords should be as long and as complicated as possible. Most security experts believe a password of 10 characters is the minimum that should be used. If you use only the lowercase letters of the alphabet, you have 26 characters with which to work. If you add the numeric values 0 through 9, you'll get another 10 characters. If you go one step further and add the uppercase letters, you'll then have an additional 26 characters, giving you a total of 62 characters with which to construct a password.

Most vendors recommend that you use nonalphabetic characters such as #, $, and % in your password, and some go so far as to require it.

If you used a 4-character password, this would be 62 ∞ 62 ∞ 62 ∞ 62, or approximately 14 million password possibilities. If you used 5 characters in your password, this would give you 62 to the fifth power, or approximately 920 million password possibilities. If you used a 10-character password, this would give you 62 to the tenth power, or $8.4 \infty 10^{17}$ (a very big number) possibilities. As you can see, these numbers increase exponentially with each position added to the password. The 4-digit password could probably be broken in a fraction of a day, while the 10-digit password would take a bit longer.

If your password used only the 26 lowercase letters from the alphabet, the 4-digit password would have 26 to the fourth power, or 456,000, password combinations. A 5-character password would have 26 to the fifth power, or over 11 million, and a 10-character password would have 26 to the tenth power, or $1.4 \infty 10^{14}$. This is still a big number, but it would take considerably little time to break it.

To see tables on how quickly passwords can be surmised, visit `http://www.lockdown.co.uk/?pg=combi&s=articles`.

Mathematical methods of encryption are primarily used in conjunction with other encryption methods as part of authenticity verification. The message and the hashed value of the message can be encrypted using other processes. In this way, you know that the message is secure and hasn't been altered.

As a security administrator, you should know how to work with hashing within your operating system.

Understanding Quantum Cryptography

Quantum cryptography is a relatively new method of encryption. At one time, its application was limited to laboratory work and possibly to secret governmental applications. This method is based on the characteristics of the smallest particles known.

The process depends on a scientific model called the Heisenberg Uncertainty Principle for security. Part of the Heisenberg Uncertainty Principle basically states that in the process of measuring the results, the results are changed. Werner Heisenberg's early works were published in 1926, and they have been greatly debated by physicists ever since.

Imagine you have a bowl of water and you want to measure the temperature of the water. When you put a thermometer into the water, you change the temperature of the water: The presence of the thermometer makes the temperature of the water rise or drop slightly. In short, the act of measuring the water temperature changes the water temperature, making it impossible to know the true temperature of the water before you measured it.

In quantum cryptography, a message is sent using a series of photons. If the receiver knows the sequence and polarity of the photons, they can decode the message. Otherwise, the photons look like random noise. If someone intercepts the photons, some of the photon positions will change polarity and the message will be altered. This will inform the receiver that someone is listening in on the message. The sender, when informed, can change the pattern and resend the message with a new photon position key. Intercepting the data alters the data and ruins the message.

Figure 8.3 demonstrates this concept. In this example, each photon is polarized in one of several directions. The process of intercepting these photons alters the polarity of some of the photons and makes the message unreadable. This alerts the receiver that an interception activity is occurring. As you can see in this example, the message has been altered as a result of the interception. Each bar in the message is part of the message: The interception changes the polarity of some of the photons (represented by the bars), making the message unreadable.

FIGURE 8.3   Quantum cryptography being used to encrypt a message

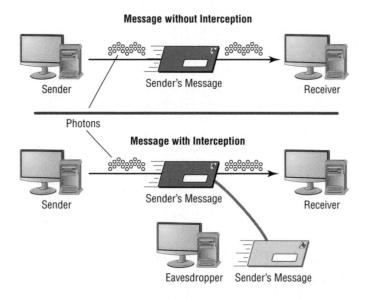

Quantum cryptography has become a solution available for private users, although it's very expensive and has a limited range. It will be interesting to see what the future holds for this technology.

Quantum cryptography is currently implemented using only fiber-optic technology. This technology, when further developed, may make many of the systems now in use obsolete.

Uncovering the Myth of Unbreakable Codes

If time has taught us anything, it is that people frequently do things that other people thought were impossible. Every time a new code or process is invented that is thought to be invincible, someone comes up with a method of breaking it.

The following list includes some common code-breaking techniques:

Frequency Analysis   *Frequency analysis* involves looking at blocks of an encrypted message to determine if any common patterns exist. Initially, the analyst doesn't try to break the code but looks at the patterns in the message. In the English language, the letters *e* and *t* and words like *the*, *and*, *that*, *it*, and *is* are very common. Single letters that stand alone in a sentence are usually limited to *a* and *I*.

A determined cryptanalyst looks for these types of patterns and, over time, may be able to deduce the method used to encrypt the data. This process can sometimes be simple, or it may take a lot of effort.

Algorithm Errors   An *algorithm* is a method or set of instructions used to perform a task or instruction. In computers, algorithms are implemented in programs to perform repetitive operations. Sometimes complex algorithms produce unpredictable results; when discovered, the results can cause the entire encryption algorithm to be compromised. Cryptographic systems may have fundamental flaws in the way they're designed. An error or flaw in either the design or the implementation of the steps can create a weakness in the entire coding system. This weakness may leave a coding system open to decryption regardless of the complexity of the algorithm or steps used to process the codes.

Brute-Force Attacks   *Brute-force attacks* can be accomplished by applying every possible combination of characters that could be the key. For example, if you know that the key is three characters long, then you know that there is a finite number of possibilities that the key could be. Although it may take a long time to find the key, the key can be found.

Although it could take a long time to succeed with a brute-force attack, hackers use programs that run thousands of brute-force trial-and-error attempts in a short period of time.

Exploiting Human Error   Human error is one of the major causes of encryption vulnerabilities. If an email is sent using an encryption scheme, someone else may send it *in the clear* (unencrypted). If a cryptanalyst gets hold of both messages, the process of decoding future messages will be considerably easier. A code key might wind up in the wrong hands, giving insights into what the key consists of. Many systems have been broken as a result of these types of accidents.

A classic example involved the transmission of a sensitive military-related message using an encryption system. Most messages have a preamble that informs the receiver who the message is for, who sent it, how many characters are in the message, the date and time it was sent, and other pertinent information. In this case, the preamble was sent in clear text and this information was also encrypted and put into the message. As a result, the cryptanalysts gained a key insight into the message contents. They were given approximately 50 characters that were repeated in the message in code. This error caused a relatively secure system to be compromised.

Understanding Cryptographic Algorithms

Cryptographic algorithms are used to encode a message from its unencrypted or clear-text state into an encrypted message. The three primary methods of encoding messages are hashing, using symmetric algorithms, and using asymmetric algorithms. The following sections discuss these methods and some of the standards in which they're used.

The Science of Hashing

As we mentioned earlier, *hashing* is the process of converting a message, or data, into a numeric value. The numeric value that a hashing process creates is referred to as a *hash total* or *value*. Hashing functions are considered either one way or two way.

A one-way hash doesn't allow a message to be decoded back to the original value. A two-way hash allows a message to be reconstructed from the hash. Most hashing functions are one way. The primary standards that exist that use the hashing process for encryption are as follows:

Secure Hash Algorithm   The *Secure Hash Algorithm (SHA)* was designed to ensure the integrity of a message. The SHA is a one-way hash that provides a hash value that can be used with an encryption protocol. This algorithm produces a 160-bit hash value. The original SHA was updated to SHA-1. SHA-2 was released several years later and upped the 160 to a 256-bit hash. The new standard is SHA-2, but SHA-1 is still widely used. As of this writing, SHA-3 is in development.

Message Digest Algorithm   The *Message Digest Algorithm (MD)* also creates a hash value and uses a one-way hash. The hash value is used to help maintain integrity. There are several versions of MD; the most common are MD5, MD4, and MD2. MD4 was used by NTLM (discussed below) to compute the NT Hash.

MD5 is the newest version of the algorithm. It produces a 128-bit hash, but the algorithm is more complex than its predecessors and offers greater security. Its biggest weakness is that it does not have strong collision resistance, meaning that attacks such as the Birthday Attack (discussed in Chapter 9) can be used against it.

> Message digests are discussed in detail later in this chapter. The primary thing to know about a message digest is that it's nothing more than text expressed as a single string of digits.

RIPEMD   The *RACE Integrity Primitives Evaluation Message Digest (RIPEMD)* algorithm was based on MD4 and worked with 128 bits. There were questions regarding its security, and it has been replaced by RIPEMD-160, which uses 160-bits. There are versions in existence that use 256 and 320 bits (RIPEMD-256 and RIPEMD-320, respectively), but all versions of RIPEMD remain less popular than SHA-1.

🌐 Real World Scenario

Watch for the Weakest Link

A courier who was responsible for carrying weekly encryption keys took commercial flights that caused him to arrive at his destination on Friday evenings. The courier was obligated to follow certain security methods, including hand-carrying these encryption key units and getting a signature from an authorized signatory at the remote facility. Unfortunately, his flight frequently arrived late at its destination. When this happened, the courier was forced to spend the night in the remote location. On Saturday morning, the courier would go to the facility and hand the key units to the appropriate person.

This process had been going on for several years. The courier often kept the key units in the trunk of his rental car overnight. Unfortunately, one night his car was stolen from the hotel parking lot, and the key units were in the trunk. Luckily, the car was recovered later in the morning, and the trunk had not been opened. This security breach caused the courier to lose his job, and the entire cryptographic system had to have new keys issued worldwide.

As you can see, even if you're extra cautious, sometimes even the safest code isn't safe. Murphy's Law says human error will creep into the most secure security systems.

LANMAN   Prior to the release of Windows NT, Microsoft's operating systems used the LANMAN protocol for authentication. While functioning only as an authentication protocol, LANMAN used LM Hash and two DES keys. It was replaced by the NT LAN Manager (NTLM) with the release of Windows NT.

NTLM   Microsoft replaced the LANMAN protocol with *NTLM (NT LAN Manager)* with the release of Windows NT. NTLM uses MD4/MD5 hashing algorithms. Several versions of this protocol exist (NTLMv1, *NTLMv2*), and it is still in widespread use despite the fact that Microsoft has pointed to Kerberos as being its preferred authentication protocol. While LANMAN and NTLM both employ hashing, they are/were used primarily for the purpose of authentication.

Table 8.1 provides a comparison of each hashing algorithm and its size, as well as the number of rounds commonly associated with each. Blank entries are intentional.

TABLE 8.1   Hashing Algorithms

Algorithm	Size	Rounds
LM Hash	Padding added to send to DES	
MD2	128-bit	18

TABLE 8.1   Hashing Algorithms *(continued)*

Algorithm	Size	Rounds
MD4	128-bit	3
MD5	128-bit	4
NTLM	128-bit	
RIPEMD	160-bit	2
RIPEMD-160	160-bit	3
SHA (aka SHA-0)	160-bit	80
SHA-1	160-bit	80
SHA-2	256-bit	64 or 80
SHA-3 (in development)		

Working with Symmetric Algorithms

Symmetric algorithms require both ends of an encrypted message to have the same key and processing algorithms. Symmetric algorithms generate a secret key that must be protected. A *symmetric key*—sometimes referred to as a secret key or private key—is a key that isn't disclosed to people who aren't authorized to use the encryption system. The disclosure of a private key breaches the security of the encryption system. If a key is lost or stolen, the entire process is breached. These types of systems are common, but the keys require special handling. Figure 8.4 illustrates a symmetric encryption system; in this example, the keys are the same on each end.

FIGURE 8.4   Symmetric encryption system

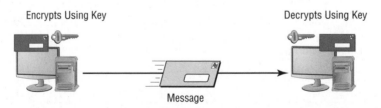

Encrypts Using Key   Decrypts Using Key

Message

Typically, a new key isn't sent across the encrypted channel (if the current key has been compromised, the new key may also be compromised). Keys are sent using an *out-of-band method*: by letter, by courier, or by some other method. This approach may be cumbersome, and it may leave the key subject to human error or social engineering exploitation.

The other disadvantage of a symmetric algorithm is that each person who uses the encryption algorithm must have the key. If you want 50 people to access the same messages, all 50 people must have the key. As you can imagine, it's difficult for 50 people to keep a secret. On the other hand, if you want to communicate with 50 different people in private, you need to know who uses which key. This information can be hard to keep straight—you might spend all your time trying to remember who uses which key.

Encryption methods usually use either a block or stream cipher. As the name implies, with a *block cipher* the algorithm works on chunks of data—encrypting one and then moving to the next. With a *stream cipher*, the data is encrypted a bit, or byte, at a time.

Several successful encryption systems use symmetric algorithms. A strong algorithm can be difficult to break. Here are some of the common standards that use symmetric algorithms:

Data Encryption Standard   The *Data Encryption Standard (DES)* has been used since the mid-1970s. It was the primary standard used in government and industry until it was replaced by AES. It's based on a 56-bit key and has several modes that offer security and integrity. It has become a little dated as a result of advances in computer technology and thus been replaced by AES. For its time, it was one of the best standards available.

Triple-DES   *Triple-DES (3DES)* is a technological upgrade of DES. 3DES is still used, even though AES is the preferred choice for government applications. 3DES is considerably harder to break than many other systems, and it's more secure than DES. It increases the key length to 168 bits.

Advanced Encryption Standard   *Advanced Encryption Standard (AES)* has replaced DES as the current standard, and it uses the Rijndael algorithm. It was developed by Joan Daemen and Vincent Rijmen. AES is now the current product used by U.S. governmental agencies. It supports key sizes of 128, 192, and 256 bits, with 128 bits being the default.

For more information about Rijndael (AES), see its website at `http://csrc.nist.gov/archive/aes/index.html`.

AES256   *AES256* (also often written as AES-256) uses 256 bits instead of 128. This qualifies for U.S. government classification as Top Secret.

CAST   *CAST* is an algorithm developed by Carlisle Adams and Stafford Tavares (hence the name). It's used in some products offered by Microsoft and IBM. CAST uses a 40-bit to 128-bit key, and it's very fast and efficient. Two additional versions, CAST-128 and CAST-256, also exist.

Rivest's Cipher   *RC* is an encryption family produced by RSA laboratories. RC stands for *Rivest's Cipher* or *Ron's Code*. (Ron Rivest is the author of this algorithm.) The current levels are RC4, RC5, and RC6. RC5 uses a key size of up to 2,048 bits. It's considered to be a strong system.

RC4 is popular with wireless and WEP/WPA encryption. It is a streaming cipher that works with key sizes between 40 and 2048 bits and is used in SSL and TLS. It is also popular with utilities used for downloading BitTorrent files since many providers limit the download of these, and by using RC4 to obfuscate the header and the stream, it makes it more difficult for the service provider to realize that they are indeed BitTorrent files being moved about.

Transport encryption and obfuscation are often used interchangeably and are used to refer to encrypting everything from the transport layer up.

Blowfish and Twofish   *Blowfish* is an encryption system produced by Counterpane Systems that performs a 64-bit block cipher at very fast speeds. It is a symmetric block cipher that can use variable-length keys. The original author was Bruce Schneier; he next created *Twofish*, which performs a similar function on 128-bit blocks. The distinctive feature of the latter is that it has a complex key schedule.

International Data Encryption Algorithm   *International Data Encryption Algorithm (IDEA)* was developed by a Swiss consortium. It's an algorithm that uses a 128-bit key. This product is similar in speed and capability to DES, but it's more secure. IDEA is used in Pretty Good Privacy (PGP), a public domain encryption system used by many for email. Currently, ASCOM AG holds the right to market IDEA.

The differentiation between block and stream ciphers applies only to symmetric algorithms.

The Comparative Strength of Algorithms

A great many symmetric encryption algorithms have been mentioned, and it can be difficult keeping all of them straight. Table 8.2 provides an alphabetic list of the symmetric algorithms and should be useful for exam study.

TABLE 8.2   Symmetric Encryption Algorithms

Algorithm	Strength	Mode
AES	128-bit	Block
AES256	256-bit	Block
Blowfish	64-bit	Block
CAST	40-128-bit	Block
DES	56-bit	Block
3DES	168-bit	Block

Algorithm	Strength	Mode
IDEA	128-bit	Block
RC4	Variable	Stream
RC5	128-bit	Block
RC6	128-256-bit	Block
Twofish	128-bit	Block

 By looking at the table, you should readily see that RC4 is the only symmetric encryption option using stream mode.

Working with Asymmetric Algorithms

Asymmetric algorithms use two keys to encrypt and decrypt data. These *asymmetric keys* are referred to as the *public key* and the *private key*. The public key can be used by the sender to encrypt a message, and the private key can be used by the receiver to decrypt the message; what one key does, the other undoes. As you may recall, symmetrical systems require the key to be private between the two parties. With asymmetric systems, each circuit has one key.

The public key may be truly public or it may be a secret between the two parties. The private key is kept private and is known only by the owner (receiver). If someone wants to send you an encrypted message, they can use your public key to encrypt the message and then send you the message. You can use your private key to decrypt the message. The private key is always kept protected. If both keys become available to a third party, the encryption system won't protect the privacy of the message.

Perhaps the best way to think about this system is that it's similar to a safe deposit box. Two keys are needed: The box owner keeps the public key, and the bank retains the second, or private, key. In order to open the box, both keys must be used simultaneously. Figure 8.5 illustrates the two-key method. Notice that in the encryption process, Key 1 is used to encrypt the message and Key 2 is used to decrypt it. In this way, it's harder to break the code unless the private key becomes known.

FIGURE 8.5   A two-key system in use

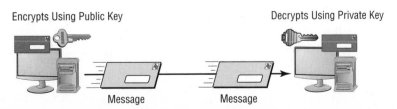

Two-key systems are referred to as *Public Key Cryptography (PKC)*. Don't confuse this with Public Key Infrastructure (PKI), which uses PKC as a part of the process.

The algorithms used in this two-key process are complicated, and several volumes would be needed to explain them thoroughly. In this book, I'll focus primarily on how the two-key process is used. It's implemented in systems such as Public Key Infrastructure (PKI), which is discussed in more detail later in this chapter.

Four popular asymmetric systems are in use today:

RSA   *RSA* is named after its inventors Ron Rivest, Adi Shamir, and Leonard Adleman. The RSA algorithm is an early public-key encryption system that uses large integer numbers as the basis of the process. It's widely implemented, and it has become a de facto standard. RSA works for both encryption and digital signatures, which are discussed later in the chapter. RSA is used in many environments, including Secure Sockets Layer (SSL), and it can be used for key exchange.

Diffie-Hellman   Dr. W. Diffie and Dr. M. E. Hellman conceptualized the *Diffie-Hellman key exchange.* They are considered the founders of the public/private key concept; their original work envisioned splitting the key into two parts. This algorithm is used primarily to send keys across public networks. The process isn't used to encrypt or decrypt messages; it's used merely for the transmission of keys in a secure manner.

Elliptic Curve Cryptography   *Elliptic Curve Cryptography (ECC)* provides similar functionality to RSA. ECC is being implemented in smaller, less-intelligent devices such as cell phones and wireless devices. It's smaller than RSA and requires less computing power. ECC encryption systems are based on the idea of using points on a curve to define the public/private key pair. This process is less mathematically intensive than processes such as RSA.

Palm, Motorola, Cisco, and others have implemented, or are implementing, the ECC system for security. Palm smartphones can now form secure connections to applications running on other systems using wireless or other means. Motorola recently released its new development system for the next generation of cellular phones; this system implements ECC and other protocols as an integral part of the toolkit. You can expect that ECC will be commonly implemented in cellular devices in the near future.

El Gamal   *El Gamal* (often written as ElGamal) is an algorithm used for transmitting digital signatures and key exchanges. The method is based on calculating logarithms. The process used is similar to the Diffie-Hellman key exchange and is based on the characteristics of logarithmic numbers and calculations. The El Gamal algorithm was first published in 1985. The Digital Signature Algorithm (DSA) is based on El Gamal.

Not as many asymmetric algorithms were discussed as symmetric encryption algorithms, but it can still be difficult keeping all of them straight. Table 8.3 provides an alphabetic list of the most popular asymmetric algorithms and should be useful for exam study.

TABLE 8.3 Asymmetric Algorithms

Algorithm	Common Use
Diffie-Hellman	Key agreement
El Gamal	Transmitting digital signatures and key exchanges
Elliptic Curve (ECC)	An option to RSA that uses less computing power and is popular in smaller devices like smart phones
RSA	The most commonly used public key algorithm, it is used for encryption and digital signatures

Wi-Fi Encryption

Encryption on Wi-Fi requires a short discussion of its own. In such an environment, the clients and the access point share the same key, utilizing symmetric encryption, and RC4 was mentioned for this purpose earlier in this chapter. Since all the clients and the access point share the same key, this is known as a *preshared key*.

WEP (Wired Equivalent Privacy) encryption, as discussed in more detail in Chapter 12, was an early attempt to add security but fell short because of weaknesses in the way the encryption algorithms are employed. The Wi-Fi Protected Access (WPA) and Wi-Fi Protected Access 2 (WPA2) technologies were designed to address the core problems with WEP.

WPA couples the RC4 encryption algorithm with TKIP, while WPA2 favors *Counter Mode with Cipher Block Chaining Message Authentication Code Protocol (CCMP)*. CCMP uses 128-bit AES encryption with a 48-bit initialization vector. Chapter 12 focuses solely on wireless and discusses these protocols in greater detail.

Using Cryptographic Systems

A cryptographic system is a system, method, or process that is used to provide encryption and decryption. It may be a hardware, software, or manually performed process. Cryptographic systems exist for the same reasons that security exists: to provide confidentiality, integrity, authentication, non-repudiation, and access control. The following sections discuss these issues within the framework of cryptographic systems.

Confidentiality and Integrity are often lumped with Availability to create the *CIA* model—a popular buzzword du jour.

Confidentiality

One of the major reasons to implement a cryptographic system is to ensure the confidentiality of the information being used. Confidentiality may be intended to prevent the unauthorized disclosure of information in a local network or to prevent the unauthorized disclosure of information across a network. A cryptographic system must do this effectively in order to be of value.

The need to keep records secure from internal disclosure may be just as great as the need to keep records secure from outside attacks. The effectiveness of a cryptographic system in preventing unauthorized decryption is referred to as its *strength*: A strong cryptographic system is difficult to crack. Strength is also referred to as the algorithm's *work factor*: The work factor describes an estimate of the amount of time and effort that would be needed to break a system.

The system may be considered weak if it allows weak keys, has defects in its design, or is easily decrypted. Many systems available today are more than adequate for business and personal use, but they are inadequate for sensitive military or governmental applications.

Integrity

The second major reason for implementing a cryptographic system involves providing assurance that a message wasn't modified during transmission. Modification may render a message unintelligible or, even worse, inaccurate. Imagine the consequences if record alterations weren't discovered in medical records involving drug prescriptions. If a message is tampered with, the encryption system should have a mechanism to indicate that the message has been corrupted or altered.

Integrity can be accomplished by adding information such as redundant data that can be used as part of the decryption process. Figure 8.6 gives a simple example of how integrity can be validated in a message. Notice that data about the message length and the number of vowels in the message are included in the message.

FIGURE 8.6   A simple integrity-checking process for an encrypted message

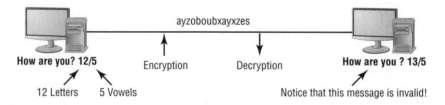

These two additions to the message provide a two-way check on the integrity of the message. In this case, the message has somehow become corrupted or invalidated. The original message had 12 characters; the decrypted message has 13 characters. Of course, the processes used in a real system are much more complicated. The addition of this information could be considered a signature of a sort.

A common method of verifying integrity involves adding a *message authentication code (MAC)* to the message. The MAC is derived from the message and a shared secret key. In Figure 8.6, the MAC is derived from the message, and the originator provides an additional piece of information. This process ensures the integrity of the message. The MAC would be encrypted with the message, adding another layer of integrity checking. From the MAC, you would know that the message came from the originator and that the contents haven't been altered. Figure 8.7 illustrates the MAC value being calculated from the message and included with the message. The receiver also calculates the MAC value and compares it to the value sent in the message. If the values are equal, the message can be assumed to be intact and genuine.

FIGURE 8.7   The MAC value is calculated by the sender and receiver using the same algorithm.

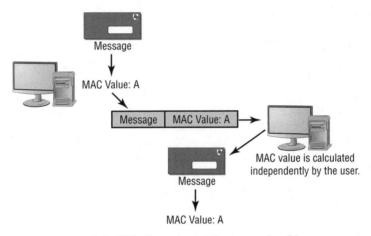

The MAC value is a key, usually derived using a hashing algorithm. The key is normally symmetrical in that the process is accomplished using the same function on both ends of the transmission. *HMAC (Hash-based Message Authentication Code)* is the value (message authentication code) generated in this process. HMAC works with any cryptographic partner, and MD5 and SHA-1 are both popular choices.

Integrity—along with authentication and non-repudiation—is also provided using digital signatures that verify that the originator is who they say they are. The next section discusses digital signatures.

Digital Signatures

A *digital signature* is similar in function to a standard signature on a document. It validates the integrity of the message and the sender. The message is encrypted using the encryption system, and a second piece of information, the digital signature, is added to the message. Figure 8.8 illustrates this concept.

FIGURE 8.8 Digital signature processing steps

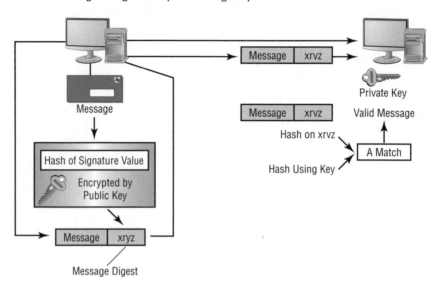

Let's say that the sender in Figure 8.8 wants to send a message to the receiver. It's important that this message not be altered. The sender uses the private key to create a digital signature. The sender then sends the message to the receiver. The receiver uses the public key attached to the message to validate the digital signature. If the values match, the receiver knows the message is authentic.

The digital signature is derived from a hash process known only by the originator. The receiver uses a key provided by the sender—the public key.

The receiver compares the signature area referred to as a *message digest* in the message with the calculated value. If the values match, the message hasn't been tampered with and the originator is verified as the person they claim to be. This process provides message integrity, non-repudiation, and authentication.

Authentication

Authentication is the process of verifying that the sender is who they say they are. This is critical in many applications. A valid message from an invalid source isn't authentic.

One of the common methods of verifying authenticity is the addition of a digital signature. Authenticity can also be established using secret words that have been mutually agreed on in advance. The military has used a series of *one-time pads (OTPs)* that each radio or communications operator could use to verify the authenticity of the sender. An OTP is a type of encryption that has been proven to be impossible to crack if used correctly—with the key as long as the message.

Figure 8.9 illustrates this method. The operator receiving the message challenged the sender using the prescribed pattern. The sender could also challenge the receiver using the same method. In this way, both parties knew they were talking to the right person. These pads were changed either daily or weekly depending on the circumstances. Although it wasn't foolproof, the system was effective and easy to use.

FIGURE 8.9   A one-time pad used for authentication

The authentication letter is obtained below the two-letter pair.

```
A S D F G H J I K L M N Q R Z
B C D L M Q R S T V Z W Z Y S
T Y R U S X Y G Z R M Q S P P
D R D L K M I O P Q S T U V X
```

One-Time Pad

1. Authenticate A S ➤ I authenticate: C

Second operator challenges back to first.

2. Authenticate T Y ➤ I authenticate: R

Both operators checked the card to verify correct response.

A simple process of providing authentication to an organization is the use of code words or key words. For example, you could have a set of code words that instantly identify the person on the other end of a phone conversation.

Two authentication protocols to know for the Security+ exam are PAP and CHAP. These are discussed in the sections that follow.

Password Authentication Protocol

Password Authentication Protocol (PAP) offers no true security, but it's one of the simplest forms of authentication. The username and password values are both sent to the server as clear text and checked for a match. If they match, the user is granted access; if they don't match, the user is denied access. In most modern implementations, PAP is shunned in favor of other, more secure authentication methods.

Challenge Handshake Authentication Protocol

Challenge Handshake Authentication Protocol (CHAP) challenges a system to verify identity. CHAP doesn't use a user ID/password mechanism. Instead, the initiator sends a logon request from the client to the server. The server sends a challenge back to the client. The challenge is encrypted and then sent back to the server. The server compares the value from the client and, if the information matches, grants authorization. If the response fails, the session fails, and the request phase starts over. This handshake method involves a number of steps and is usually automatic between systems.

Non-repudiation

Non-repudiation prevents one party from denying actions they carried out. To use an analogy, imagine coming home to find your house's picture window broken. All three of your kids say they didn't do it, and the babysitter says it must have been broken when she arrived. All the parties who could be guilty are "repudiating" the fact that they did it, and it's their word against common sense. Now, imagine that you had a nanny-cam running and were able to review the tape and see who actually broke it. The tape cancels out their saying they knew nothing about the broken window and offers "non-repudiation" of the facts.

In the electronic world, a similar type of proof can be achieved in a two-key system. The problem is that anyone can claim to be the legitimate receiver, and if they have access to this type of system, they can send you a public key. So although the user would have received the message, you would have no way to verify that the user is really who they say they are and that they're a valid user; you need non-repudiation to verify that someone is who they report to be.

Third-party organizations called *certificate authorities (CAs)* manage public keys and issue certificates verifying the validity of the sender's message. The verifying aspect serves as non-repudiation; a respected third party vouches for the individual. The goal of any effective cryptography system must include non-repudiation. However, the implementation is a little more difficult than the concept.

 The CA process is covered in the section "Using Public Key Infrastructure" in Chapter 9.

Access Control

Access control refers to the methods, processes, and mechanisms of preventing unauthorized access to the systems that do the cryptography. Keys are vulnerable to theft, loss, and human security failings. A key component of access control involves both physical and operational security of these resources.

 Real World Scenario

Non-repudiation and eBay

A few years ago, a young man gained access to his parents' key information on eBay. He managed to successfully win several auctions, and he racked up over a million dollars in charges to his parents' account. The parents (naturally) disputed the bill. eBay invalidated the bids when the deception was discovered. The situation caused a great deal of personal embarrassment for the parents and potentially opened them up to litigation.

The term *access control* is used in many different settings, such as access control lists, access lists, and so on. The important thing to consider is that these techniques are collectively intended to limit access to information.

Key management presents a major challenge with large encryption systems. Keeping the keys in secured areas with limited access by unauthorized personnel is important. If the keys become compromised, the entire system breaks down, no matter how good it is.

Make sure the keys are kept in the highest security areas available to you. Physical keys, such as smart cards, should be immediately erased when they are retired; these keys should also be kept in a secured area for storage. One of the big problems that credit card companies are encountering is the ease with which the encoding on a credit card's magnetic strip can be counterfeited. If you can gain access to an active credit card, the magnetic strip can be duplicated onto a blank card. Make sure all your security devices are kept under tight physical control when they aren't in use.

Key Features

Key escrow addresses the possibility that a third party may need to access keys. Under the conditions of key escrow, the keys needed to encrypt/decrypt data are held in an escrow account (think of the term as it relates to home mortgages) and made available if that third party requests them. The third party in question is generally the government, but could also be an employer if an employee's private messages have been called into question.

A key *recovery agent* is an entity that has the ability to recover a key, key components, or plaintext messages as needed. As opposed to escrow, recovery agents are typically used to access information that is encrypted with older keys. Recovery agents are discussed in more detail in Chapter 9.

Key registration is the process of providing certificates to users, and this function is typically handled by a registration authority (RA) when the load must be lifted from a certificate authority (CA). Both certificate authorities and registration authorities are discussed in Chapter 9.

Trust models exist in PKI implementations and come in a number of types. The four main types of trust models that are used with PKI are bridge, hierarchical, hybrid, and mesh. Chapter 9 goes into detail on PKI trust models.

Understanding Cryptography Standards and Protocols

Numerous standards are available to establish secure services. Some of the standards that will be presented in the following sections have already been discussed in greater detail in earlier chapters. Here I will quickly remind you of them and introduce you to a few more standards.

The movement from proprietary governmental standards toward more unified and global standards is a growing trend that has both positive and negative implications. Higher interoperability between disparate systems will also mean that these standards will be widely utilized. The more the standards are used, the more miscreants will focus on them as they try to break them.

As a security administrator, you have to weigh the pros and cons of the different standards and evaluate them against your organization's needs. The following sections introduce you to the major standards, discuss their focus, and describe how they were developed.

The Origins of Encryption Standards

As mentioned in the beginning of the chapter, early cryptography standards were primarily designed to secure communications for the government and military. Many different standards groups exist today, and they often provide standards that are incompatible with the standards of other groups. These standards are intended to address the specific environments in which these groups work.

The following sections describe key U.S. government agencies, a few well-known industry associations, and public-domain cryptography standards.

The Role of Government Agencies

Several U.S. government agencies are involved in the creation of standards for secure systems. They either directly control specific sectors of government or provide validation, approval, and support to government agencies. We'll look at each of these agencies in the following sections.

National Security Agency

The *National Security Agency (NSA)* is responsible for creating codes, breaking codes, and coding systems for the U.S. government. The NSA was chartered in 1952. It tries to keep a low profile; for many years, the government didn't publicly acknowledge its existence.

The NSA is responsible for obtaining foreign intelligence and supplying it to the various U.S. government agencies that need it. It's said to be the world's largest employer of mathematicians. The NSA's missions are extremely classified, but its finger is in everything involving cryptography and cryptographic systems for the U.S. government, government contractors, and the military.

 The NSA's website is http://www.nsa.gov.

National Security Agency/Central Security Service

The *National Security Agency/Central Security Service (NSA/CSS)* is an independently functioning part of the NSA. It was created in the early 1970s to help standardize and support Department of Defense (DoD) activities. The NSA/CSS supports all branches of the military. Each branch of the military used to have its own intelligence activities. Frequently, these branches didn't coordinate their activities well. NSA/CSS was created to help coordinate their efforts.

 You can find NSA/CSS on the Web at http://www.nsa.gov.

National Institute of Standards and Technology

The *National Institute of Standards and Technology (NIST)*, which was formerly known as the National Bureau of Standards (NBS), has been involved in developing and supporting standards for the U.S. government for over 100 years. NIST has become very involved in cryptography standards, systems, and technology in a variety of areas. It's primarily concerned with governmental systems, and it exercises a great deal of influence on them. NIST shares many of its findings with the security community because business needs are similar to government needs.

NIST publishes information about known vulnerabilities in operating systems and applications. You'll find NIST very helpful in your battle to secure your systems.

 You can find NIST on the Web at http://www.nist.gov.

Industry Associations and the Developmental Process

The need for security in specific industries, such as the banking industry, has driven the development of standards. Standards frequently begin as voluntary or proprietary efforts.

The *Request for Comments (RFC)*, originated in 1969, is the mechanism used to propose a standard. It's a document-creation process with a set of practices. An RFC is categorized as standard (draft or standard), best practice, informational, experimental, or historic.

Draft documents are processed through a designated RFC editor, who makes sure the document meets publication standards. Editors play a key role in the RFC process; they are responsible for making sure proposals are documented properly, and they manage the discussion. The RFC is then thrown open to the computer-user community for comments and critique. This process ensures that all interested parties have the opportunity to comment on an RFC.

The RFC process allows open communications about the Internet and other proposed standards. Virtually all standards relating to the Internet that are adopted go through this process.

Several industrial associations have assumed roles that allow them to address specific environments. The following sections briefly discuss some of the major associations and the specific environments they address.

American Bankers Association

The *American Bankers Association (ABA)* has been very involved in the security issues facing the banking and financial industries. Banks need to communicate with each other in a secure manner. The ABA sponsors and supports several key initiatives regarding financial transactions.

 You can find more information on the ABA at `http://www.aba.com/default.htm`.

Internet Engineering Task Force

The *Internet Engineering Task Force (IETF)* is an international community of computer professionals that includes network engineers, vendors, administrators, and researchers. The IETF is mainly interested in improving the Internet; it's also very interested in computer security issues. The IETF uses working groups to develop and propose standards.

IETF membership is open to anyone. Members communicate primarily through mailing lists and public conferences.

 You can find additional information about the IETF on its website at `http://www.ietf.org`.

Internet Society

The *Internet Society (ISOC)* is a professional group whose membership consists primarily of Internet experts. The ISOC oversees a number of committees and groups, including the IETF.

 You can find a history of ISOC and IETF at `http://www.isoc.org/internet/history/ietfhis.shtml`.

World Wide Web Consortium

The *World Wide Web Consortium (W3C)* is an association concerned with the interoperability, growth, and standardization of the World Wide Web (WWW). It's the primary sponsor of XML and other web-enabled technologies. Although not directly involved in cryptography, the W3C recently published a proposed standard for encryption in XML.

 The W3C's website is located at `http://www.w3.org`.

International Telecommunications Union

The *International Telecommunications Union (ITU)* is responsible for virtually all aspects of telecommunications and radio communications standards worldwide. The ITU is broken into three main groups that are targeted at specific areas of concern: ITU-R is concerned with radio communication and spectrum management, ITU-T is concerned with telecommunications standards, and ITU-D is concerned with expanding telecommunications throughout undeveloped countries. The ITU is headquartered in Switzerland, and it operates as a sponsored agency of the United Nations.

For more information on the ITU, visit `http://www.itu.int/`.

Institute of Electrical and Electronics Engineers

The *Institute of Electrical and Electronics Engineers (IEEE)* is an international organization focused on technology and related standards. Pronounced "I Triple-E," the IEEE is organized into several working groups and standards committees. IEEE is actively involved in the development of PKC, wireless, and networking protocol standards.

You can find information on the IEEE at `http://www.ieee.org`.

Public Domain Cryptography

Public domain cryptography refers to the standards and protocols that emerge from individual or corporate efforts and are released to the general public for use. Public domain structures are developed for many reasons: Developers may merely have a passing interest in something, or they may want to test a new theory.

PGP and RSA are two common public cryptographic initiatives:

Pretty Good Privacy   One of the most successful involves a system called *Pretty Good Privacy (PGP)*. It was developed by Phil Zimmerman, who developed this encryption system for humanitarian reasons. In 1991, he published the encryption system on the Internet. His stated objective was to preserve privacy and protect citizens from oppressive governments. Since its release, PGP has become a de facto standard for email encryption. PGP uses both symmetrical and asymmetrical encryption.

The U.S. government prosecuted Zimmerman for three years because he released PGP. The government claimed he violated U.S. laws prohibiting the exportation of sensitive technology. The government claimed the encryption method supported terrorism and oppression instead of reducing it. The case was finally dropped. PGP has continued to grow in popularity worldwide.

GPG An alternative to PGP that is freeware is *GPG (GNU Privacy Guard)*. It is part of the GNU project by the Free Software Foundation and is interoperable with PGP. Like its alternative, PGP, it is considered a hybrid program since it uses a combination of symmetric and public-key cryptography. This free replacement for PGP can be downloaded, from `http://www.gnupg.org`.

RSA *RSA* provides cryptographic systems to both private businesses and the government. The name RSA comes from the initials of its three founders (Rivest, Shamir, and Adleman). RSA has been very involved in developing Public-Key Cryptography Standards (PKCS), and it maintains a list of standards for PKCS.

Public-Key Infrastructure X.509/Public-Key Cryptography Standards

The *Public-Key Infrastructure X.509 (PKIX)* is the working group formed by the IETF to develop standards and models for the PKI environment. The PKIX working group is responsible for the X.509 standard, which is discussed in the next section.

The *Public-Key Cryptography Standards (PKCS)* is a set of voluntary standards created by RSA and security leaders. Early members of this group included Apple, Microsoft, DEC (now HP), Lotus, Sun, and MIT.

Currently, there are 15 published PKCS standards:

- PKCS #1: RSA Cryptography Standard
- PKCS #2: Incorporated in PKCS #1
- PKCS #3: Diffie-Hellman Key Agreement Standard
- PKCS #4: Incorporated in PKCS #1
- PKCS #5: Password-Based Cryptography Standard
- PKCS #6: Extended-Certificate Syntax Standard
- PKCS #7: Cryptographic Message Syntax Standard
- PKCS #8: Private-Key Information Syntax Standard
- PKCS #9: Selected Attribute Types
- PKCS #10: Certification Request Syntax Standard
- PKCS #11: Cryptographic Token Interface Standard
- PKCS #12: Personal Information Exchange Syntax Standard
- PKCS #13: Elliptic Curve Cryptography Standard
- PKCS #14: Pseudorandom Number Generators
- PKCS #15: Cryptographic Token Information Format Standard

These standards are coordinated through RSA; however, experts worldwide are welcome to participate in the development process.

X.509

The X.509 standard defines the certificate formats and fields for public keys. It also defines the procedures that should be used to distribute public keys. The X.509 version 2 certificate is still used as the primary method of issuing Certificate Revocation List (CRL) certificates. The current version of X.509 certificates is version 3, and it comes in two basic types:

End-Entity Certificate   The most common is the *end-entity certificate*, which is issued by a certificate authority (CA) to an end entity. An *end entity* is a system that doesn't issue certificates but merely uses them.

CA Certificate   The CA certificate is issued by one CA to another CA. The second CA can, in turn, issue certificates to an end entity.

For the exam, remember X.509 v2 for CRL and v3 for certificate.

All X.509 certificates have the following:

- Signature, which is the primary purpose for the certificate
- Version
- Serial number
- Signature algorithm ID
- Issuer name
- Validity period
- Subject name
- Subject public key information
- Issuer unique identifier (relevant for versions 2 and 3 only)
- Subject unique identifier (relevant for versions 2 and 3 only)
- Extensions (in version 3 only)

SSL and TLS

Secure Sockets Layer (SSL) is used to establish a secure communication connection between two TCP-based machines. This protocol uses the handshake method of establishing a session. The number of steps in the handshake depends on whether steps are combined and/or mutual authentication is included. The number of steps is always between four and nine, inclusive, based on who is doing the documentation.

Netscape originally developed the SSL method, which has gained wide acceptance throughout the industry. SSL establishes a session using asymmetric encryption and maintains the session using symmetric encryption.

You can find details on how the SSL process works at http://support.microsoft.com:80/support/kb/articles/Q257/5/91.ASP.

Regardless of which vendor's implementation is being discussed, the steps can be summarized as illustrated in Figure 8.10. When a connection request is made to the server, the server sends a message back to the client indicating that a secure connection is needed. The client sends the server a certificate indicating the capabilities of the client. The server then evaluates the certificate and responds with a session key and an encrypted key. The session is secure at the end of this process.

FIGURE 8.10 The SSL connection process

This session will stay open until one end or the other issues a command to close it. The command is typically issued when a browser is closed or another URL is requested.

As a security administrator, you will occasionally need to know how to configure SSL settings for a website running on your operating system. You should also know that in order for SSL to work properly, the clients must be able to accept the level of encryption that you apply. Modern browsers can work with 128-bit encrypted sessions/certificates. Earlier browsers often needed to use 40- or 56-bit SSL encryption. As an administrator, you should push for the latest browsers on all clients.

VeriSign used a clever advertising strategy that makes this point readily comprehensible: It mailed flyers in a clear bag with the lines, "Sending sensitive information over the Web without the strongest encryption is like sending a letter in a clear envelope. Anyone can see it." This effectively illustrates the need for the strongest SSL possible.

Transport Layer Security (TLS) is a security protocol that expands upon SSL. Many industry analysts predict that TLS will replace SSL in the future. Figure 8.11 illustrates the connection process in the TLS network.

The TLS protocol is also referred to as *SSL 3.1*, but despite its name, it doesn't interoperate with SSL. The TLS standard is supported by the IETF.

FIGURE 8.11 The TLS connection process

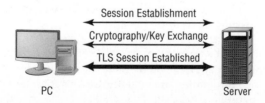

Think of TLS as an updated version of SSL. TLS is based on SSL and is intended to supersede it.

In Exercise 8.3, I will show you how to configure the SSL port in Windows Server 2008.

EXERCISE 8.3

SSL Settings in Windows Server 2008

This lab requires a test machine (nonproduction) running Windows Server 2008. To configure the SSL port setting, follow these steps:

1. Open Internet Information Services Manager by choosing Start ➤ Administrative Tools ➤ Internet Information Services (IIS) Manager.

2. Expand the left pane entries until your website becomes an option. Right-click the website and choose Properties from the context menu.

3. Select the Web Site tab. Check whether the port number for SSL is filled in. If it isn't, enter a number here.

4. Click OK and exit Internet Information Services Manager.

Notice that the SSL port field is blank by default, and any port number can be entered here—this differs from the way some previous versions of IIS worked. The default SSL port is 443; if you enter a number other than that in this field, then clients must know and request that port in advance in order to connect.

Certificate Management Protocols

Certificate Management Protocol (CMP) is a messaging protocol used between PKI entities. This protocol is used in some PKI environments.

XML Key Management Specification (XKMS) is designed to allow XML-based programs access to PKI services. XKMS is being developed and enhanced as a cooperative standard of the World Wide Web Consortium (W3C). XKMS is a standard that is built upon CMP and uses it as a model.

CMP is expected to be an area of high growth as PKI usage grows.

Secure Multipurpose Internet Mail Extensions

Secure Multipurpose Internet Mail Extensions (S/MIME) is a standard used for encrypting email. S/MIME contains signature data. It uses the PKCS #7 standard (Cryptographic Message Syntax Standard) and is the most widely supported standard used to secure email communications.

MIME is the de facto standard for email messages. S/MIME, which is a secure version of MIME, was originally published to the Internet as a standard by RSA. It provides encryption, integrity, and authentication when used in conjunction with PKI. S/MIME version 3, the current version, is supported by IETF.

> S/MIME is defined by RFC 2633. For the exam, know that it's a secure version of MIME used for encrypting email. Know, as well, that it uses asymmetric encryption algorithms for confidentiality and digital certificates for authentication.

Secure Electronic Transaction

Secure Electronic Transaction (SET) provides encryption for credit card numbers that can be transmitted over the Internet. It was developed by Visa and MasterCard.

> SET is most suited for transmitting small amounts of data.

SET works in conjunction with an electronic wallet that must be set up in advance of the transaction. An *electronic* wallet is a device that identifies you electronically in the same way as the cards you carry in your wallet.

Figure 8.12 illustrates the process used in an SET transaction. The consumer must establish an electronic wallet that is issued by the consumer/issuing bank. When the consumer wants to make a purchase, they communicate with the merchant. The wallet is accessed to provide credit/payment information. The merchant then contacts the credit processor to complete the transaction. The credit processor interfaces with the existing credit network. In this situation, the transactions between the issuing bank, the consumer, the merchant, and the credit processor all use SET.

FIGURE 8.12   The SET transaction in process

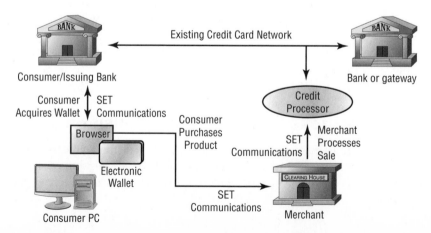

Secure Shell

Secure Shell (SSH) is a tunneling protocol originally used on Unix systems. It's now available for both Unix and Windows environments. The handshake process between the client and server is similar to the process described in SSL. SSH is primarily intended for interactive terminal sessions.

 SSH can be used in place of the older Remote Shell (RSH) utility that used to be a standard in the Unix world. It can also be used in place of rlogin and Telnet.

Figure 8.13 illustrates the SSH connection process. Notice that SSH connections are established in two phases:

Phase 1 The first phase is a secure channel to negotiate the channel connection.

Phase 2 The second phase is a secure channel used to establish the connection.

FIGURE 8.13 The SSH connection-establishment process

Phase 1: Secure Channel Negotiation

Phase 2: Session Establishment

Pretty Good Privacy

Pretty Good Privacy (PGP) is a freeware email encryption system. As mentioned earlier in the chapter, PGP was introduced in the early 1990s, and it's considered to be a very good system. It's widely used for email security.

PGP uses both symmetrical and asymmetrical systems as a part of its process; it is this serial combination of processes that makes it so competent. Figure 8.14 provides an overview of how the various components of a PGP process work together to provide security. During the encryption process, the document is encrypted with the public key and also a session key, which is a one-use random number, to create the ciphertext. The session key is encrypted into the public key and sent with the ciphertext.

Real World Scenario

Securing Unix Interactive Users

You've been asked to examine your existing Unix systems and evaluate them for potential security weaknesses. Several remote users need to access Telnet and FTP capabilities in your network. Telnet and FTP connections send the logon and password information in the clear. How could you minimize security risks for Telnet and FTP connections?

You should consider using a VPN connection between these remote connections and your corporate systems. One workable solution might be to provide SSH to your clients and install it on your Unix servers. Doing so would allow FTP and Telnet connectivity in a secure environment.

On the receiving end, the private key is used to ascertain the session key. The session key and the private key are then used to decrypt the ciphertext back into the original document.

FIGURE 8.14 The PGP encryption system

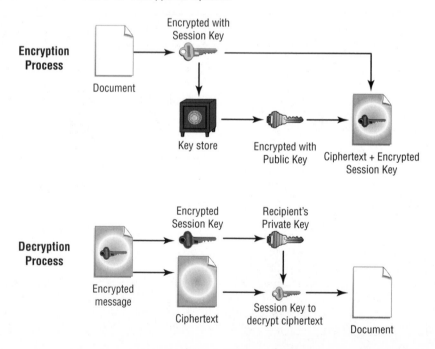

HTTP Secure

Hypertext Transport Protocol over SSL (HTTPS)—also known as Hypertext Transport Protocol Secure—is the secure version of HTTP, the language of the World Wide Web. HTTPS uses SSL to secure the channel between the client and server. Many e-business systems use HTTPS for secure transactions. An HTTPS session is identified by the https in the URL and by a key that is displayed on the web browser.

HTTPS uses port 443 by default.

Secure HTTP

Secure Hypertext Transport Protocol (S-HTTP) is HTTP with message security (added by using RSA or a digital certificate). Whereas HTTPS creates a secure channel, S-HTTP creates a secure message. S-HTTP can use multiple protocols and mechanisms to protect the message. It also provides data integrity and authentication.

S-HTTP is seldom used and defaults to using port 80 (the HTTP port).

IP Security

IP Security (IPSec) is a security protocol that provides authentication and encryption across the Internet. IPSec is becoming a standard for encrypting virtual private network (VPN) channels and is built into IPv6. It's available on most network platforms, and it's considered to be highly secure.

One of the primary uses of IPSec is to create VPNs. IPSec, in conjunction with Layer 2 Tunneling Protocol (L2TP) or Layer 2 Forwarding (L2F), creates packets that are difficult to read if intercepted by a third party. IPSec works at layer 3 of the OSI model.

As a security administrator, it's important for you to know the operations under way on your servers. As an administrator, you need to be able to evaluate operations and performance at all times and be able to establish a baseline of current operations.

The two primary protocols used by IPSec at the bottom layer are *Authentication Header (AH)* and *Encapsulating Security Payload (ESP)*. Both can operate in either the transport or tunnel mode. Protocol 50 is used for ESP, while protocol 51 is used for AH.

You can find the best overview of IPSec and AH/ESP in "An Illustrated Guide to IPsec" by Steve Friedl at http://www.unixwiz.net/techtips/iguide-ipsec.html.

In Exercise 8.4, I will show you how to configure IPSec monitoring on a Windows Vista workstation.

EXERCISE 8.4

Look for Errors in IPSec Performance Statistics

This exercise requires access to a workstation running Windows 7. To configure IPSec monitoring, follow these steps:

1. Open Performance Monitor by pressing the Windows button on the keyboard and typing **R**. Type into the Run box **perfmon.msc** (if the UAC asks you to confirm to continue, click to continue).

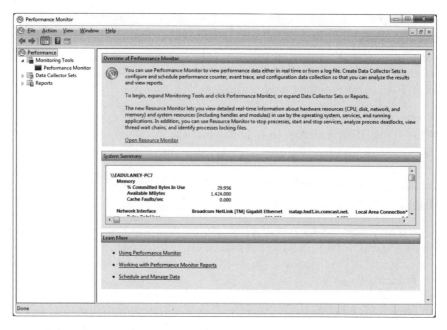

2. Click Performance Monitor.

3. Right-click the graph and choose from the pop-up menu Add Counters.

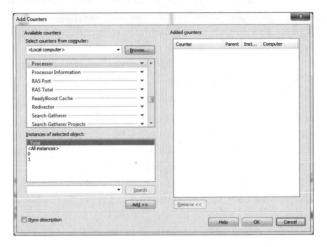

4. For an object, select IPsec IKEv1 IPv4 and expand the options beneath this listing.

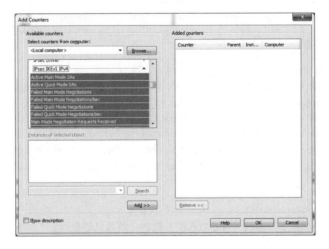

5. Click the Show Description check box to learn what it is able to show you. The descriptions appear in the bottom of the dialog box.

6. Click Add and add the following counters: Failed Main Mode Negotiations and Failed Quick Mode Negotiations.

7. Click OK.

You're now monitoring the failures as they occur. On a properly functioning system, this graph should show no activity. Any activity that appears is indicative of problems since IPSec was last started and should be carefully examined.

Tunneling Protocols

Tunneling protocols add a capability to the network: the ability to create tunnels between networks that can be more secure, support additional protocols, and provide virtual paths between systems. The best way to think of tunneling is to imagine sensitive data being encapsulated in other packets that are sent across the public network. After they're received at the other end, the sensitive data is stripped from the other packets and recompiled into its original form. Tunneling was also discussed in Chapter 2.

The most common protocols used for tunneling are as follows:

Point-to-Point Tunneling Protocol   *Point-to-Point Tunneling Protocol (PPTP)* supports encapsulation in a single point-to-point environment. PPTP encapsulates and encrypts *Point-to-Point Protocol (PPP)* packets. This makes PPTP a favorite low-end protocol for networks. The negotiation between the two ends of a PPTP connection is done in the clear. Once the negotiation is performed, the channel is encrypted. This is one of the major weaknesses of PPTP. A *packet-capture device*, such as a sniffer, that captures the negotiation process can potentially use that information to determine the connection type and information about how the tunnel works. Microsoft developed PPTP and supports it on most of the company's products. PPTP uses port 1723 and TCP for connections.

Layer 2 Forwarding   *Layer 2 Forwarding (L2F)* was created by Cisco as a method of creating tunnels primarily for dial-up connections. It's similar in capability to PPP and shouldn't be used over WANs. L2F provides authentication, but it doesn't provide encryption. L2F uses port 1701 and TCP for connections.

Layer 2 Tunneling Protocol   A few years ago, Microsoft and Cisco agreed to combine their respective tunneling protocols into one protocol: *Layer 2 Tunneling Protocol (L2TP)*. L2TP is a hybrid of PPTP and L2F. It's primarily a point-to-point protocol. L2TP supports multiple network protocols and can be used in networks besides TCP/IP. L2TP works over IPX, SNA, and IP, so it can be used as a bridge across many types of systems. The major problem with L2TP is that it doesn't provide data security: The information isn't encrypted. Security can be provided by protocols such as IPSec. L2TP uses port 1701 and UDP for connections.

Federal Information Processing Standard

The *Federal Information Processing Standard (FIPS)* is a set of guidelines for the United States federal government information systems. FIPS is used when an existing commercial or government system doesn't meet federal security requirements. FIPS is issued by NIST.

Summary

This chapter focused on the basic elements of cryptography and the PKI implementation. There are three primary methods of encryption:

- Symmetric
- Asymmetric
- Hashing

Symmetric systems require that each end of the connection have the same key. Asymmetric systems use a two-key system. In public key cryptography, the receiver has a private key known only to them; a public key corresponds to it, which they make known to others. The public key can be sent to all other parties; the private key is never divulged. Hashing refers to performing a calculation on a message and converting it into a numeric hash value.

There are five main considerations in implementing a cryptography system:

- Confidentiality
- Integrity
- Authentication
- Non-repudiation
- Access control

Confidentiality means that the message retains its privacy. *Integrity* means the message can't be altered without detection. *Authentication* is used to verify that the person who sent the message is actually who they say they are. *Non-repudiation* prevents either the sender or receiver from denying that the message was sent or received. *Access control* is the methods, processes, and mechanisms of preventing unauthorized access to the systems that do the cryptography.

In this chapter, you also learned about the standards, agencies, and associations that are interested in cryptography. Several government agencies have been specifically charged with overseeing security and encryption. The NSA and NIST are both concerned with government encryption standards. NIST is primarily concerned with nonmilitary standards; NSA/CSS is concerned with military applications.

Exam Essentials

Be able to describe the process of a hashing algorithm. Hashing algorithms are used to mathematically derive a key from a message. The most common hashing standards for cryptographic applications are the SHA and MD algorithms.

Know the principles of a symmetric algorithm.   A symmetric algorithm requires that receivers of the message use the same *private key*. Symmetric algorithms can be extremely secure. This method is widely implemented in governmental applications. The private key is changed using out-of-band transmission.

Be able to describe the process of asymmetric algorithms.   Asymmetric algorithms use a two-key method of encryption. The message is encrypted using the public key and decrypted using a second key or private key. The key is derived from the same algorithm.

Know the primary objectives for using cryptographic systems.   The main objectives for these systems are confidentiality, integrity, authentication, and non-repudiation. Digital signatures can be used to verify the integrity and provide non-repudiation of a message.

Understand the process used in PKI.   PKI is an encryption system that utilizes a variety of technologies to provide confidentiality, integrity, authentication, and non-repudiation. PKI uses certificates issued from a CA to provide this capability as well as encryption. PKI is being widely implemented in organizations worldwide.

Review Questions

1. What is the process of deriving an encrypted value from a mathematical process called?

    A. Hashing

    B. Asymmetric

    C. Symmetric

    D. Social engineering

2. During a training session, you want to impress upon users how serious security and, in particular, cryptography is. To accomplish this, you want to give them as much of an overview about the topic as possible. Which government agency should you mention is primarily responsible for establishing government standards involving cryptography for general-purpose government use?

    A. NSA

    B. NIST

    C. IEEE

    D. ITU

3. Assuming asymmetric encryption, if data is encoded with a value of 5, what would be used to decode it?

    A. 5

    B. 1

    C. 1/5

    D. 0

4. You're a member of a consortium wanting to create a new standard that will effectively end all spam. After years of meeting, the group has finally come across a solution and now wants to propose it. The process of proposing a new standard or method on the Internet is referred to by which acronym?

    A. WBS

    B. X.509

    C. RFC

    D. IEEE

5. Mary claims that she didn't make a phone call from her office to a competitor and tell them about developments her company is working on. Telephone logs, however, show that such a call was placed from her phone, and time clock records show she was the only person working at the time. What do these records provide?

    A. Integrity

    B. Confidentiality

    C. Authentication

    D. Non-repudiation

6. Mercury Technical Solutions has been using SSL in a business-to-business environment for a number of years. Despite the fact that there have been no compromises in security, the new IT manager wants to use stronger security than SSL can offer. Which of the following protocols is similar to SSL but offers the ability to use additional security protocols?

   A. TLS

   B. SSH

   C. RSH

   D. X.509

7. MAC is an acronym for what as it relates to cryptography?

   A. Media access control

   B. Mandatory access control

   C. Message authentication code

   D. Multiple advisory committees

8. You've been brought in as a security consultant for a small bicycle manufacturing firm. Immediately you notice that it's using a centralized key-generating process, and you make a note to dissuade them from that without delay. What problem is created by using a centralized key-generating process?

   A. Network security

   B. Key transmission

   C. Certificate revocation

   D. Private key security

9. Which of the following terms refers to the prevention of unauthorized disclosure of keys?

   A. Authentication

   B. Integrity

   C. Access control

   D. Non-repudiation

10. As the head of IT for MTS, you're explaining some security concerns to a junior administrator who has just been hired. You're trying to emphasize the need to know what is important and what isn't. Which of the following is *not* a consideration in key storage?

    A. Environmental controls

    B. Physical security

    C. Hardened servers

    D. Administrative controls

11. What is the primary organization for maintaining certificates called?

   A. CA

   B. RA

   C. LRA

   D. CRL

12. Due to a breach, a certificate must be permanently revoked, and you don't want it to ever be used again. What is often used to revoke a certificate?

   A. CRA

   B. CYA

   C. CRL

   D. PKI

13. Which organization can be used to identify an individual for certificate issue in a PKI environment?

   A. RA

   B. LRA

   C. PKE

   D. SHA

14. Kristin, from Payroll, has left the office on maternity leave and won't return for at least six weeks. You've been instructed to suspend her key. Which of the following statements is true?

   A. In order to be used, suspended keys must be revoked.

   B. Suspended keys don't expire.

   C. Suspended keys can be reactivated.

   D. Suspending keys is a bad practice.

15. What document describes how a CA issues certificates and what they are used for?

   A. Certificate policies

   B. Certificate practices

   C. Revocation authority

   D. CRL

16. After returning from a conference in Jamaica, your manager informs you that he has learned that law enforcement has the right, under subpoena, to conduct investigations using keys. He wants you to implement measures to make such an event run smoothly should it ever happen. What is the process of storing keys for use by law enforcement called?

   A. Key escrow

   B. Key archival

   C. Key renewal

   D. Certificate rollover

17. The CRL takes time to be fully disseminated. Which protocol allows a certificate's authenticity to be immediately verified?

    A. CA

    B. CP

    C. CRC

    D. OCSP

18. Which set of specifications is designed to allow XML-based programs access to PKI services?

    A. XKMS

    B. XMLS

    C. PKXMS

    D. PKIXMLS

19. Which of the following is similar to Blowfish but works on 128-bit blocks?

    A. Twofish

    B. IDEA

    C. CCITT

    D. AES

20. A brainstorming session has been called. The moderator tells you to pull out a sheet of paper and write down your security concerns based on the technologies that your company uses. If your company uses public keys, what should you write as the primary security concern?

    A. Privacy

    B. Authenticity

    C. Access control

    D. Integrity

Answers to Review Questions

1. A. Hashing algorithms are used to derive an encrypted value from a message or word.

2. B. NIST is responsible for establishing the standards for general-purpose government encryption. NIST is also becoming involved in private-sector cryptography.

3. C. With asymmetric encryption, two keys are used—one to encode and the other to decode. The two keys are mathematical reciprocals of each other.

4. C. The Request for Comments (RFC) process allows all users and interested parties to comment on proposed standards for the Internet. The RFC editor manages the RFC process. The editor is responsible for cataloging, updating, and tracking RFCs through the process.

5. D. Non-repudiation offers undisputable proof that a party was involved in an action.

6. A. TLS is a security protocol that uses SSL, and it allows the use of other security protocols.

7. C. A MAC as it relates to cryptography is a method of verifying the integrity of an encrypted message. The MAC is derived from the message and the key.

8. B. Key transmission is the largest problem from among the choices given. Transmitting private keys is a major concern. Private keys are typically transported using out-of-band methods to ensure security.

9. C. Access control refers to the process of ensuring that sensitive keys aren't divulged to unauthorized personnel.

10. A. Proper key storage requires that the keys be physically stored in a secure environment. This may include using locked cabinets, hardened servers, and effective physical and administrative controls.

11. A. A certificate authority (CA) is responsible for maintaining certificates in the PKI environment.

12. C. A Certificate Revocation List (CRL) is created and distributed to all CAs to revoke a certificate or key.

13. B. A local registration authority (LRA) can establish an applicant's identity and verify that the applicant for a certificate is valid. The LRA sends verification to the CA that issues the certificate.

14. C. Suspending keys is a good practice: It disables a key, making it unusable for a certain period of time. This can prevent the key from being used while someone is gone. The key can be reactivated when that person returns.

15. A. The certificate policies document defines what certificates can be used for.

16. A. Key escrow is the process of storing keys or certificates for use by law enforcement. Law enforcement has the right, under subpoena, to conduct investigations using these keys.

17. D. Online Certificate Status Protocol (OCSP) can be used to immediately verify a certificate's authenticity.

18. A. XML Key Management Specification (XKMS) is designed to allow XML-based programs access to PKI services.

19. A. Twofish was created by the same creator of Blowfish. It performs a similar function on 128-bit blocks instead of 64-bit blocks.

20. D. Public keys are created to be distributed to a wide audience. The biggest security concern regarding their use is ensuring that the public keys maintain their integrity. This can be accomplished by using a thumbprint or a second encryption scheme in the certificate or key.

Chapter

9

Cryptography Implementation

As data becomes more valuable and more important, it is an area of high interest to governments, businesses, and increasingly individuals. People want privacy when it comes to their personal and other sensitive information. Corporations want—and need—to protect financial records, trade secrets, customer lists, and employee information. The government uses cryptography to help ensure the safety and well-being of its citizens. Entire governmental agencies have been created to help ensure secrecy, and millions of dollars have been spent trying to protect national secrets and attempting to learn the secrets of other countries.

As always, your primary purpose for reading this book, though, is not just to gain a further understanding of cryptography but to pass CompTIA's Security+ exam. This chapter is written with that goal in mind, and the remaining objectives relevant to cryptography that were not covered in the previous chapter are addressed here.

Using Public Key Infrastructure

The *Public Key Infrastructure (PKI)* is intended to offer a means of providing security to messages and transactions on a grand scale. The need for universal systems to support e-commerce, secure transactions, and information privacy is one aspect of the issues being addressed with PKI.

PKI is a two-key—asymmetric—system with four main components: certificate authority (CA), registration authority (RA), RSA (the encryption algorithm), and digital certificates; the latter two were addressed in the previous chapter and this one focuses more on the former two. Messages are encrypted with a public key and decrypted with a private key. As an example, take the following scenario:

1. You want to send an encrypted message to Jordan, so you request his public key.

2. Jordan responds by sending you that key.

3. You use the public key he sends you to encrypt the message.

4. You send the message to him.

5. Jordan uses his private key to decrypt the message.

Figure 9.1 illustrates this sequence. It allows the two parties to communicate in a secure environment.

The main goal of PKI is to define an infrastructure that should work across multiple vendors, systems, and networks. It's important to emphasize that PKI is a framework and not a specific technology. Implementations of PKI are dependent on the perspective of the software manufacturers that implement it. This has been one of the major difficulties with PKI: Each vendor can interpret the documents about this infrastructure and implement it however they choose. Many of the existing PKI implementations aren't compatible with each other, but this situation should change over the next few years because customers expect compatibility.

FIGURE 9.1 The certificate authority process

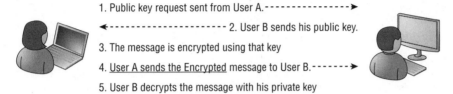

1. Public key request sent from User A.

2. User B sends his public key.

3. The message is encrypted using that key

4. <u>User A sends the Encrypted</u> message to User B.

5. User B decrypts the message with his private key

Most organizations have a PKI policy document that describes the uses for the electronic signing technology. Associated documents that fall under this category often include a confidentiality certificate policy document and a digital signature certificate policy document.

The following sections explain the major functions and components of the PKI infrastructure and how they work in relationship to the entire model.

Under no circumstances should you ever divulge or send your private key. Doing so jeopardizes your guarantee that only you can work with the data and can irreparably damage your security.

Using a Certificate Authority

A *certificate authority (CA)* is an organization that is responsible for issuing, revoking, and distributing *certificates*. A certificate is nothing more than a mechanism that associates the public key with an individual. It contains a great deal of information about the user. Each user of a PKI system has a certificate that can be used to verify their authenticity.

For instance, if Mike wants to send Jeff a private message, there should be a mechanism to verify to Jeff that the message received from Mike is really from Mike. If a third party vouches for Mike and Jeff trusts that third party, Jeff can assume that the message is authentic because the third party says so. Figure 9.2 shows this process happening in a communication between Mike and Jeff; the arrows in this figure show the path between the CA and the person using the CA for verification purposes.

CAs can be either private or public, with VeriSign being one of the best known of the public variety. Many operating system providers allow their systems to be configured as

CA systems. These CA systems can be used to generate internal certificates that are used within a business or in large external settings.

FIGURE 9.2 The certificate authority process

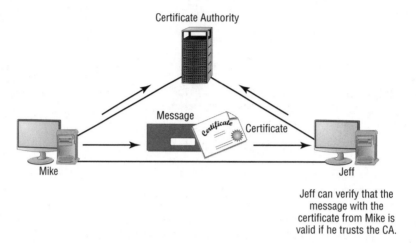

Jeff can verify that the message with the certificate from Mike is valid if he trusts the CA.

The process of providing certificates to users, although effective in helping to ensure security, requires a server. Over time, the server can become overloaded and need assistance. An additional component, the registration authority, is available to help offload work from the CA. Registration authorities are discussed in the next section.

Working with Registration Authorities and Local Registration Authorities

A *registration authority (RA)* offloads some of the work from a CA. An RA system operates as a middleman in the process: It can distribute keys, accept registrations for the CA, and validate identities. The RA doesn't issue certificates; that responsibility remains with the CA. Figure 9.3 shows an RA operating in San Francisco, while the CA is located in Washington, D.C. The Seattle user obtains authorization for the session from the RA in San Francisco. The Seattle user can also use the San Francisco RA to validate the authenticity of a certificate from a Miami user. The arrows between the Seattle user and the RA server represent the certificate request from the remote user. The RA has a communications link with the CA in Washington, D.C. Because the CA in Washington, D.C., is closer, the Miami user will use it to verify the certificate.

A *local registration authority (LRA)* takes the process one step further. It can be used to identify or establish the identity of an individual for certificate issuance. If the user in Seattle needs a new certificate, it would be impractical to fly back to Washington, D.C., to get another one. An LRA can be used to verify and certify the identity of the individual on behalf of the CA. The LRA can then forward authentication documents to the CA to issue the certificate.

FIGURE 9.3 An RA offloading work from a CA

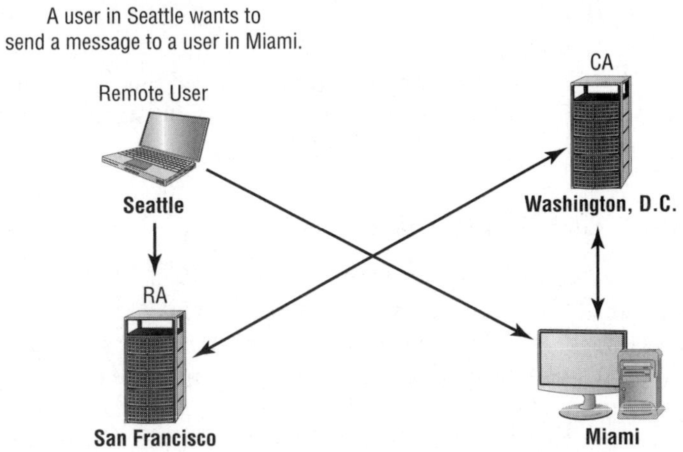

> **TIP** The primary difference between an RA and an LRA is that the latter can be used to identify or establish the identity of an individual.

Figure 9.4 shows this process occurring between an LRA and a CA. The LRA would involve an individual or process to verify the identity of the person needing a certificate. The arrows in Figure 9.4 show the path from the user who requested the certificate (via the LRA) to the CA that issues the certificate and the path from the CA sending the new certificate back to the user.

FIGURE 9.4 The LRA verifying identity for the CA

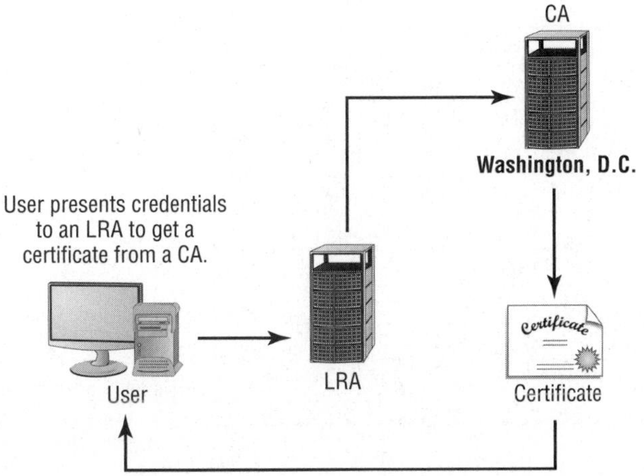

NOTE   The LRA involves the physical identification of the person requesting a certificate.

The next sections provide more detail about certificates and their uses, including validating users, systems, and devices. A certificate also has certain characteristics that will be briefly explained.

Implementing Certificates

Certificates, as you may recall, provide the primary method of identifying that a given user is valid. Certificates can also be used to store authorization information. Another important factor is verifying or certifying that a system is using the correct software and processes to communicate. What good would a certificate be to help ensure authenticity if the system uses an older cryptography system that has a security problem?

The next few sections describe the X.509 certificate structure and some of the more common usages of certification.

X.509

The most popular certificate used is the *X.509* version 3. X.509 is a standard certificate format supported by the International Telecommunications Union (ITU) and many other standards organizations. Adopting a standard certificate format is important for systems to be assured interoperability in a certificate-oriented environment.

The format and contents of a sample certificate are shown in Figure 9.5.

Notice that the certificate contains identifiers of two different algorithms used in the process. In this case, the signature algorithm is Md2RSA, and the digital signature algorithm is sha1. This certificate also has a unique serial number issued by the CA.

FIGURE 9.5   A certificate illustrating some of the information stored

Version	V3
Serial Number	1234 D123 4567 …
Signature Algorithm	Md2RSA
Issuer	Sample Certificate
Valid from:	Thursday, September 8, 2005
Valid to:	Thursday, September 15, 2005
Subject	Mr. Your Name Here, Myco
Public Key	Encrypted Value of Key
Extensions	Subject Type = End Entity
Signature Algorithm Signature	sha1 Encrypted Data

← Digital Signature Area

Fields of a Simple X.509 Certificate

An X.509 certificate has more fields than are illustrated; this example is intended only to give you an overview of what a certificate looks like.

In Exercise 9.1, I'll show you how to view the certificate from a user's perspective.

EXERCISE 9.1

Viewing a Certificate

The following lab will walk through the steps of viewing an existing certificate:

1. Within Internet Explorer 8 or newer, go to the URL https://www.paypal.com. Notice the lock icon that appears in the address bar indicating the secure site.

2. Click the lock icon and a pop-up menu appears.

3. From the pop-up menu, choose View Certificates. By default, the properties will open to the General tab.

4. Click the Details tab and make sure the Show field is set to <All>.

5. Click Issuer to see the values (CN, OU, O, and C) expanded in the lower dialog box. You can do the same with Certificate Policies and the other fields that appear.

6. Click OK to exit the properties box.

Always remember that the purpose of the certificate is to basically bind the public key to the user's identity. When authenticating, certificates can be used to authenticate only the client (*single sided*) or both parties (*dual sided*), the client and server. Aside from the Security+ objectives, no one uses the term *dual-sided certificates*.

Certificate Policies

Certificate policies define what certificates do. A CA can potentially issue a number of different types of certificates: say, one for email, one for e-commerce, and one for financial transactions. The policy might indicate that it isn't to be used for signing contracts or for purchasing equipment. Certificate policies affect how a certificate is issued and how it's used. A CA would have policies regarding the interoperability or certification of another CA site; the process of requiring interoperability is called *cross certification*. The organizations using the certificates also have the right to decide which types of certificates are used and for what purposes. This is a voluntary process in that each organization involved can decide what and how to approve certificate use.

According to the RFC, key usages may be marked as critical or noncritical. This distinction is largely to limit the CA.

The receiving organization can use this policy to determine whether the certificate has come from a legitimate source. Think about it this way: A PKI certificate can be generated any number of ways using any number of servers. The policy indicates which certificates will be accepted in a given application.

Certificate Practice Statements

A *Certificate Practice Statement (CPS)* is a detailed statement the CA uses to issue certificates and implement its policies.

The CA provides the CPS to users of its services. These statements should discuss how certificates are issued, what measures are taken to protect certificates, and the rules CA users must follow in order to maintain their certificate eligibility. The policies should be readily available to CA users.

If a CA is unwilling to provide this information to a user, the CA itself may be untrustworthy, and the trustworthiness of that CA's users should be questioned.

Remember that a CPS is a detailed document used to enforce policy at the CA; a certificate policy pertains not to the CA but to the certificate itself.

Understanding Certificate Revocation

Certificate revocation is the process of revoking a certificate before it expires. A certificate may need to be revoked because it was stolen, an employee moved to a new company, or someone has had their access revoked. A certificate revocation is handled either through a *Certificate Revocation List (CRL)* or by using the *Online Certificate Status Protocol (OCSP)*. A *repository* is simply a database or database server where the certificates are stored.

The process of revoking a certificate begins when the CA is notified that a particular certificate needs to be revoked. This must be done whenever the private key becomes known. The owner of a certificate can request it be revoked at any time, or the request can be made by the administrator.

The CA marks the certificate as revoked. This information is published in the CRL and becomes available using the OCSP. The revocation process is usually very quick; time is based on the publication interval for the CRL. Disseminating the revocation information to users may take longer. Once the certificate has been revoked, it can never be used—or trusted—again.

The CA publishes the CRL on a regular basis, usually either hourly or daily. The CA sends or publishes this list to organizations that have chosen to receive it; the publishing process occurs automatically in the case of PKI. The time between when the CRL is issued and when it reaches users may be too long for some applications. This time gap is referred to as *latency*. OCSP solves the latency problem: If the recipient or relaying party uses OCSP for verification, the answer is available immediately. Currently, this process is under evaluation and may be replaced at some time in the future.

When a key is compromised, a revocation request should be made to the CA immediately. It may take a day or longer for the CRL to be disseminated to everyone using that CA.

Implementing Trust Models

For PKI to work, the capabilities of CAs must be readily available to users. The model that has been shown to this point is the simple trust model. However, the simple trust model may not work as PKI implementations get bigger. Conceptually, every computer user in the world would have a certificate. However, accomplishing this would be extremely complex and would create enormous scaling or growth issues.

Four main types of trust models are used with PKI:

- Hierarchical
- Bridge
- Mesh
- Hybrid

PKI was designed to allow all of these trust models to be created. They can be fairly granular from a control perspective. *Granularity* refers to the ability to manage individual resources in the CA network.

In the following sections, I'll examine each of these models. I'll detail how each model works and discuss its advantages and disadvantages.

Hierarchical Trust Models

In a *hierarchical trust model*—also known as a *tree*—a root CA at the top provides all the information. The intermediate CAs are next in the hierarchy, and they trust only information provided by the root CA. The root CA also trusts intermediate CAs that are in their level in the hierarchy and none that aren't. This arrangement allows a high level of control at all levels of the hierarchical tree.

This might be the most common implementation in a large organization that wants to extend its certificate-processing capabilities. Hierarchical models allow tight control over certificate-based activities.

Figure 9.6 illustrates the hierarchical trust structure. In this situation, the intermediate CAs trust only the CAs directly above them or below them.

Root CA systems can have trusts between them, and there can be trusts between intermediate and leaf CAs. A *leaf CA* is any CA that is at the end of a CA network or chain. This structure allows you to be creative and efficient when you create hybrid systems.

Bridge Trust Models

In a *bridge trust model,* a peer-to-peer relationship exists between the root CAs. The root CAs can communicate with each other, allowing cross certification. This arrangement allows a certification process to be established between organizations or departments. Each intermediate CA trusts only the CAs above and below it, but the CA structure can be expanded without creating additional layers of CAs.

FIGURE 9.6   A hierarchical trust structure

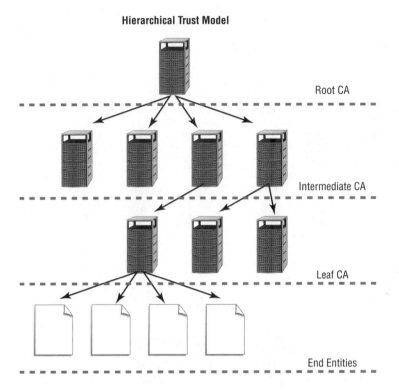

Hierarchical Trust Model

Root CA

Intermediate CA

Leaf CA

End Entities

   Additional flexibility and interoperability between organizations are the primary advantages of a bridge model. Lack of trustworthiness of the root CAs can be a major disadvantage. If one of the root CAs doesn't maintain tight internal security around its certificates, a security problem can be created: An illegitimate certificate could become available to all the users in the bridge structure and its subordinate or intermediate CAs.

   This model may be useful if you're dealing with a large, geographically dispersed organization or you have two organizations that are working together. A large, geographically dispersed organization could maintain a root CA at each remote location; the root CAs would have their own internal hierarchy, and users would be able to access certificates from any place in the CA structure. Figure 9.7 illustrates a bridged structure. In this example, the intermediate CAs communicate only with their respective root CA. All cross certification is handled between the two root CA systems.

Mesh Trust Models

The *mesh trust model* expands the concepts of the bridge model by supporting multiple paths and multiple root CAs. Each of the root CAs shown in Figure 9.8 can cross-certify with the other root CAs in the mesh. This arrangement is also referred to as a *web structure*. Although not shown in the illustration, each of the root CAs can also communicate with the intermediate CAs in their respective hierarchies.

FIGURE 9.7   A bridge trust structure

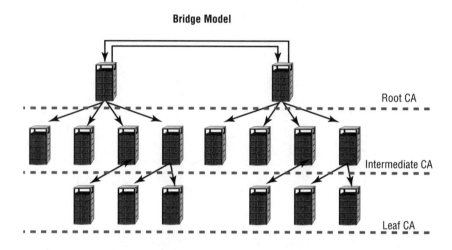

FIGURE 9.8   A mesh trust structure

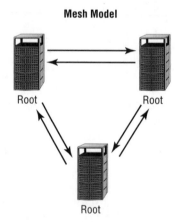

This structure may be useful in a situation where several organizations must cross-certify certificates. The advantage is that you have more flexibility when you configure the CA structures. The major disadvantage of a mesh is that each root CA must be trustworthy in order to maintain security.

Hybrid Trust Model

A *hybrid trust model* can use the capabilities of any or all of the structures discussed in the previous sections. You can be extremely flexible when you build a hybrid trust structure.

The flexibility of this model also allows you to create hybrid environments. Figure 9.9 illustrates such a structure. Notice that in this structure, the single intermediate CA server on the right side of the illustration is the only server that is known by the CA below it. The subordinates of the middle-left CA are linked to the two CAs on its sides. These two CAs don't know about the other CAs, because they are linked only to the CA that provides them a connection. The two intermediate servers in the middle of the illustration and their subordinates trust each other; they don't trust others that aren't in the link.

FIGURE 9.9   A hybrid model

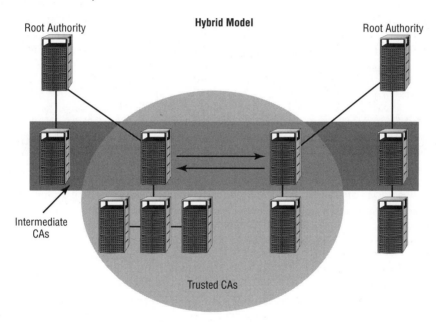

The major difficulty with hybrid models is that they can become complicated and confusing. A user can unintentionally acquire trusts that they shouldn't have obtained. In the example shown in Figure 9.9, a user could accidentally be assigned to one of the CAs in the middle circle. As a member of that circle, the user could access certificate information that should be available only from their root CA. In addition, relationships between CAs can continue long past their usefulness; unless someone is aware of them, these relationships can exist even after the parent organizations have terminated their relationships.

In Exercise 9.2, I'll show you how to back up an EFS certificate. EFS is the Encrypting File System that exists in recent versions of Microsoft operating systems and is used to add cryptographic features to the filesystem. It should be noted that it is not fully supported on all editions of Windows (such as Windows 7 Starter), and the exercise cannot be done on those operating systems. If your operating system supports EFS but it is not enabled, then execute Exercise 9.3.

🌐 **Real World Scenario**

Designing a CA Structure for Your Organization

You've been assigned to implement a CA structure for your organization, which has several large national factories and small remote facilities throughout the country. Some of these facilities have high-speed networks; others have low-speed dial-up capabilities. Your management reports that network traffic is very high, and they don't want to overburden the network with CA traffic. How would you go about implementing this structure?

You should probably install CA systems at each of the major facilities throughout the country. Additionally, you may want to install CAs in key geographic locations where certificate access is needed. You need to establish a procedure to allow certificates to be issued in remote locations, and you also need to implement an RA process in your larger locations. Remote users could receive certificates either by email or by out-of-band methods if network access is limited.

EXERCISE 9.2

Backing Up an EFS Certificate

The EFS allows you to encrypt data and prevent it from being easily seen if stolen. An encryption key is used, and if you lose access to that encryption key, then you can also lose access to the data you encrypted. The following lab will walk through the steps of creating a backup of this certificate:

1. On a Windows 7 or Windows Vista client, click the Start button and type in `certmgr.msc`; then press Enter. When the UAC prompts you to continue, choose to do so. The Microsoft Management Console opens with Certificate Manager.

EXERCISE 9.2 *(continued)*

2. Expand the Personal folder and click Certificates.

3. Select the certificate you want to back up. The EFS certificate will list Encrypting File System under the heading Intended Purposes.

4. Right-click, and on the pop-up menu choose All Tasks ➤ Export.

5. The Certificate Export Wizard will start. Click Next. Choose Yes, Export The Private Key, and click Next.

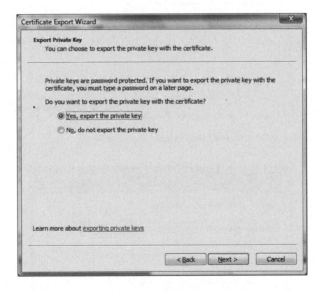

6. Choose Personal Information Exchange, and click Next. Type a password, and click Next.

7. A file will be created to store the certificate. Click Finish to exit.

EXERCISE 9.3

Enable EFS

On some editions/versions of Microsoft Windows, EFS is not enabled by default. The following lab will walk through the steps of enabling EFS on Windows 7 Professional:

1. On a Windows 7 Professional client, click the Start button and type **manage file encryption certificates** (the option will appear in the list of possibilities as you are typing); then press Enter. The Encrypting File System Wizard will appear. Click Next.

2. Choose Create A New Certificate, and click Next.

EXERCISE 9.3 *(continued)*

3. Three choices appear. You can

   - create a self-signed certificate stored on your computer

   - create a self-signed certificate stored on a smart card

   - create a certificate issued by your domain's CA

   Choose to create a self-signed certificate stored on your computer, and click Next.

4. Choose Back Up The Certificate And Key Now. You will need to enter a backup location and enter the password twice.

5. Before clicking Next, click View Certificate to see the details of what was created.

6. Close the properties box and click Next to do the backup. Choose which folders you want to encrypt (the default is All Logical Drives) and click Next. Click Close to exit.

Preparing for Cryptographic Attacks

The ultimate objective of an attack on a cryptographic system is to either decipher the messages or disrupt the network. Cryptographic systems can be susceptible to Denial of Service (DoS) attacks, which were explained in Chapter 4, "Threats and Vulnerabilities."

Ways to Attack Cryptographic Systems

Specific attacks on cryptographic systems can be divided into three types:

Attacking the Key   Key attacks are typically launched to discover the value of a key by attacking the key directly. The keys can be passwords, encrypted messages, or other key-based encryption information. An attacker might try to apply a series of words, commonly used passwords, and other randomly selected combinations to crack a password. A key attack involves trying to crack a key by repeatedly guessing the key value. Most operating system manufacturers provide programming interfaces that allow access to password and encryption subsystems. An attacker can use this access and information to break a password. Remember that passwords are typically generated with a one-way hashing function. The anticipated amount of time it takes to break a password depends on the length of the password and the characters used in the password. Making keys longer and more complicated tends to make key attacks more difficult.

Attacking the Algorithm   The programming instructions and algorithms used to encrypt information are as much at risk as the keys. If an error isn't discovered and corrected by a program's developers, an algorithm might not be able to secure the program. Many algorithms have well-publicized back doors. If a weakness in the programming or model used to develop an algorithm is discovered, a significant security exposure may exist.

 Real World Scenario

WEP (In)Security

A paper was submitted to the Internet community that discussed a theoretical weakness in the algorithm used as the basis for the Wired Equivalent Privacy (WEP) security system. WEP supporters publicly discounted the weakness to the computer community: They indicated that the vulnerability was theoretical and couldn't happen in the real world. Within seven days of their brash statements, they received over a dozen different examples of how to break the WEP system. It is now widely thought that WEP can be broken in as little as five minutes.

Even with increased wireless security, such as WPA2, the network should be considered only as secure as the passphrase, and if a poor eight-character passphrase found directly in the dictionary is used, then it can be cracked in a short amount of time and the network accessed by the crackers.

Intercepting the Transmission   The process of intercepting a transmission may, over time, allow attackers to inadvertently gain information about the encryption systems used by an organization. The more data attackers can gain, the more likely they are to be able to use frequency analysis to break an algorithm. Human error is also a problem in security situations, and it's likely that someone will unintentionally release information that can be used to undermine a security system.

Three Types of Cryptographic Attacks

You should also be aware of the following three types of attacks:

Birthday Attack A *birthday attack* is an example of an attack targeted at the key. It isn't an attack on the algorithm itself, just on the results. A birthday attack is built on a simple premise. If 25 people are in a room, there is some probability that two of those people will have the same birthday. The probability increases as additional people enter the room. It's important to remember that probability doesn't mean that something will occur, only that it's more likely to occur. To put it another way, if I ask if anyone has a birthday of March 9, the odds are 1 in 365 (or 25/365 given the number of students in the room), but if I ask if any student has the same birthday as any other student, the odds of there being a match increase significantly.

Although two people may not share a birthday in every gathering, the likelihood is fairly high, and as the number of people increases, so do the odds that there will be a match. A birthday attack works on the same premise: If your key is hashed, the possibility is that given enough time, another value can be created that will give the same hash value. Even MD5 has been shown to be vulnerable to a birthday attack.

> An easy way to think of a birthday attack is to look at the hashing process in Figure 8.2 in the last chapter. The result of the operation is a value of 88. If the letters *siis* were hashed, they would give the same result even though they differ from the message originally used.

Weak Key Attack *Weak key attacks* are based on the premise that many common passwords are used by lots of people. If the key length is short, the resulting hash value will be easier to guess. Make sure your users use passwords and encryption keys that are hard to guess. You may even want to consider a random-password-generating system. The longer and more complicated a password is, the more difficult it is to successfully launch a weak key attack against it.

 Real World Scenario

Weak Keys in the Military

A security audit performed by the U.S. Air Force uncovered a startling problem with passwords. It discovered that one of the most popular passwords used in several locations was *WWJD*. Upon investigation, they discovered that this was an abbreviation for "What Would Jesus Do." Although the Air Force wasn't trying to suppress religious expression, it sent out a list of unacceptable passwords and, not surprisingly, this was one of them.

Mathematical Attack   *Mathematical attacks* can be focused on the encryption algorithm itself, the key mechanism, or any potential area of weakness in the algorithm. These attacks use mathematical modeling and statistical analysis to determine how the system operates. These types of attacks depend on intercepting large amounts of data and methodically attempting to decrypt the messages using one of the methods previously described.

Understanding Key Management and the Key Life Cycle

Key management refers to the process of working with keys from the time they are created until the time they are retired or destroyed. Key management includes the following stages/areas:

- Centralized versus decentralized key generation
- Key storage and distribution
- Key escrow
- Key expiration
- Key revocation
- Key suspension
- Key recovery and archival
- Key renewal
- Key destruction
- Key usage

 Throughout this discussion, the terms *certificate* and *key* will be used interchangeably. Certificates contain keys that provide security. The process used is the same in either situation.

The term *key life cycle* describes the stages a key goes through during its entire life. You can think of this as a cradle-to-grave situation. By expressing these relationships in the terms of a life cycle, evaluating each phase of a key's use from its creation to its destruction becomes easier. If any aspect of a key's life isn't handled properly, the entire security system may become nonfunctional or compromised.

Key management is one of the main aspects of an effective cryptographic system. Keys, as you may remember, are the unique passwords or passcodes used to encrypt or decrypt messages. You can think of a key as one of the primary components of certificates; this is why these terms are used together. Certificates are used to transport keys between systems.

The following sections compare and contrast centralized and decentralized key generation as well as key storage and distribution. The other aspects of key management are also covered.

Methods for Key Generation

Key generation (the creation of the key) is an important first step in the process of working with keys and certificates. Using certificates is one of the primary methods for delivering keys to end entities. Key length and the method used to create the key also affect the security of the system in use. The security of a key is measured by how difficult it is to break the key. The longer it takes to break the key, the more secure the key is considered to be.

According to RSA, it would take 3 million years and a $10 million budget to break a key with a key length of 1,024 bits. The amount of time it would take to break a 2,048-bit key is virtually incalculable. Of course, these numbers are based on the assumption that the algorithm is secure and no other methods of attack would work to break the algorithm or the key.

 A common method used to generate keys creates very large prime numbers. Computing prime numbers is a laborious process. Most systems use a sophisticated approximation method to calculate prime numbers as opposed to calculating them directly. If the calculation method is flawed, the numbers may not be prime and, consequently, may be easier to determine.

One main thing to consider is where to create the keys. Should they be generated on a central machine or in a decentralized environment? A third method used to generate keys is called the *split generation system*, which is a combination of a centralized and decentralized process. We'll discuss each in the following sections.

Centralized Key Generation

Centralized key generation allows the key-generating process to take advantage of large-scale system resources. Key-generating algorithms tend to be extremely processor intensive. Using a centralized server, this process can be managed with a large single system. However, problems arise when the key is distributed. How can it be transported to end users without compromising security?

Figure 9.10 shows a centralized generation process. In this example, all the physical resources are in a single location, under centralized management control.

Centralized generation has the advantage of allowing additional management functions to be centralized. A major disadvantage is that the key archival and storage process may be vulnerable to an attack against a single point instead of a network. Reliability, security, and archiving can be addressed if the proper systems, procedures, and policies are put into place and followed.

FIGURE 9.10 A centralized key-generating facility

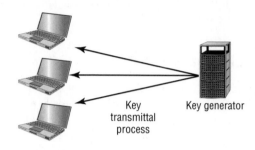

Decentralized Key Generation

Decentralized key generation allows the key-generating process to be pushed out into the organization or environment. The advantage of this method is that it allows work to be decentralized and any risks to be spread. This system isn't vulnerable to a single-point failure or attack. Decentralized generation addresses the distribution issue, but it creates a storage and management issue.

Figure 9.11 demonstrates a decentralized system. In this situation, the loss of any single key-generating system doesn't disrupt the entire network. The RA in the figure refers to a registration authority, and the CA refers to a certificate authority.

FIGURE 9.11 A distributed key-generating system

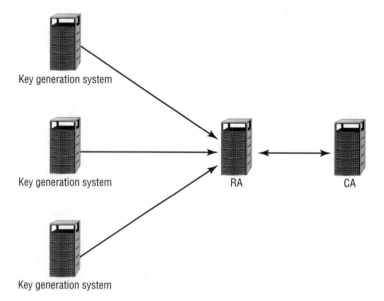

Split-System Key Generation

Many systems, including the PKI system, require the use of a split system. In a split system, the central server generates encryption keys. Digital signature keys are created at the client or in a smart card.

Storing and Distributing Keys

Where and how keys are stored affects how they are distributed. Distributing keys is usually accomplished using a *Key Distribution Center (KDC)*, as used in Kerberos (Microsoft's preferred authentication protocol), or by using a *Key Exchange Algorithm (KEA)*, as in the case of PKI.

In order for Kerberos to function properly, time synchronization must be working correctly. If clocks drift from the correct time, problems can occur with trying to compare time stamps and authenticate.

KDC

A KDC is a single service or server that stores, distributes, and maintains cryptographic session keys. When a system wants to access a service that uses Kerberos, a request is made via the KDC. The KDC generates a session key and facilitates the process of connecting these two systems. The advantage of this process is that once it's implemented, it's automatic and requires no further intervention. The major disadvantage of this process is that the KDC is a single point of failure; if it's attacked, the entire security system could be compromised. Figure 9.12 illustrates the KDC creating a session between two systems.

FIGURE 9.12   The KDC process in a Kerberos environment

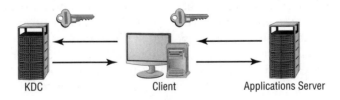

KEA

The KEA process is slightly different from the KDC process. The KEA negotiates a secret key between the two parties; the secret key is a short-term, single-use key intended strictly for key distribution. The KEA process should not be used to transmit both the public and private keys. Figure 9.13 illustrates the KEA process. The KEA session terminates once the key has been successfully transmitted.

FIGURE 9.13   The KEA process

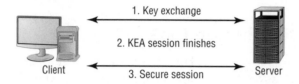

Protecting keys from unauthorized access while making them available for use by authorized personnel is important. The process can utilize physical security measures such as locked cabinets and safes, and it can involve software such as Kerberos and PKI.

 Physical protection methods include physical storage devices that place a key under lock and key. Storage devices include, but aren't limited to, filing cabinets and safes.

Keys as Hardware and Software Devices

Keys can be either hardware devices or software devices. An example of a hardware device would be a smart card. Software keys may be generated by CA-oriented systems such as PKI. Whether they're hardware or software, protecting keys is essential for a security system to operate effectively.

Protecting Private and Public Keys

Protecting keys is a difficult process. Public keys don't require full protection; they require only integrity protection, meaning that they have not been compromised. Private keys, on the other hand, require full protection. The unknowing disclosure of a private key in a symmetrical or public/private key system potentially compromises the system. Armed with a private key, an attacker could read all the communications in the system and also sign information and impersonate the real owner. This fraudulent signature could be difficult to repudiate. The following section briefly discusses private key protection and key server protection, which are both essential for good security.

Physically, private keys should be kept under close supervision. If possible, multiple keys should be required to open the storage facility, and the two keys should never be stored together. If two different people are responsible for storing the keys, both of them must consent and be present for the storage facility to be opened.

Using Key Servers

Key servers also pose potential security problems, both from an access control perspective and from a physical access perspective. If a fault is introduced into the system, a resulting *core dump* (also known as a *memory dump*) may leave the key information in a core dump file. A sophisticated attacker could use the core dump to get key information.

Most private-key security failures can be traced back to physical security or human errors. Make sure that private keys are well guarded and secure.

> Under no circumstances should you ever divulge or send your private key. Doing so jeopardizes your guarantee that only you are able to work with the data and may irreparably damage your security.

Using Key Escrow

A *key escrow* system stores keys for the purpose of law enforcement access. If a criminal investigation is under way, law enforcement agents with a search warrant have the right to access and search records within the scope of the warrant. In general, the key archival system will provide the access needed. Key escrow is listed separately because the usage is important to a law enforcement investigation.

> *Key escrow* refers to both a process and an organization or system that stores keys for access at a later date.

One of the proposed methods of dealing with key escrow involves the storage of key information with a third party, referred to as a *key escrow agency*. This agency would provide key information only when ordered by a court. In general, key escrow is handled by the key archival system.

> In an early encryption system offered by the NSA for civilian use, the NSA would have acted as the key escrow agency. The system was called *Clipper*, and it wasn't widely accepted by industry. The key escrow controversy surrounding it was one of the chief reasons cited for its lack of acceptance. More recently, law enforcement and national security officials have asked for similar capabilities in the interest of national safety but have met with significant resistance (see http://www.nytimes.com/2010/09/27/us/27wiretap.html?_r=2 for an example).

Key escrow systems can also be a part of the key recovery process. Several government agencies are attempting to implement regulations requiring mandated key escrow, which would allow law enforcement agencies to investigate a key escrow user without their knowledge. Many individuals and organizations view this as an invasion of their privacy, and they're fighting the use of mandated key escrow on the basis that it violates personal freedom. The key escrow process is covered in more detail in the section "Recovering and Archiving Keys," later in this chapter.

The FBI and other national agencies are rumored to use keystroke logging software—often delivered as a Trojan horse—for bypassing encryption. One of the best known of these programs was Magic Lantern, but today CIPAV is their collection tool of choice.

Identifying Key Expiration

A key expiration date identifies when a key is no longer valid. Normally, a key is date stamped, meaning it becomes unusable after a specified date. A new key or certificate is normally issued before the expiration date.

Keys with expiration dates work similarly to credit cards that expire. Usually, the card issuer sends another card to the cardholder before the expiration date.

Most applications that are key enabled or certificate enabled check the expiration date on a key and report to the user if the key has expired. PKI gives the user the opportunity to accept and use the key.

Revoking Keys

Keys are revoked when they are compromised, the authentication process has malfunctioned, people are transferred, or other security risks occur. Revoking a key keeps it from being misused. A revoked key must be assumed to be invalid or possibly compromised.

The credit card analogy is applicable here too. Consider a credit card that was stolen from a customer. This card, for all intents and purposes, is a certificate. A retailer could take its chances and accept the card, or it could verify that the card is accurate by running the card through a card verification machine to check its status. If the card has been reported stolen, the credit card authorization process will decline the charge.

Systems such as PKI use a CRL to perform a check on the status of revoked keys. Revocations are permanent. Once a certificate is revoked, it can't be used again; a new key must be generated and issued.

Suspending Keys

A *key suspension* is a temporary situation. If an employee were to take a leave of absence, the employee's key could be suspended until they came back to work. This temporary suspension would ensure that the key wouldn't be usable during their absence. A suspension might also occur if a high number of failed authentications or other unusual activities were occurring. The temporary suspension would give administrators or managers time to sort out what is happening.

Determining the status of suspended keys is accomplished by checking with the certificate server or by using other mechanisms. In a PKI system, a CRL would be checked to determine the status of a certificate. This process can occur automatically or manually. Most key or certificate management systems provide a mechanism to report the status of a key or certificate.

Key management systems use the same general process when checking the status of keys. The Security+ exam distinguishes between status checking for suspension and revocation. The major difference is that a revoked key can't be used again, whereas the status of a suspended key can be changed to allow the key to be used again. Once a key is revoked, a new key is required.

Recovering and Archiving Keys

One of the problems with a key-based system is that older information, unless processed with a new key, may become inaccessible. For example, if you have a two-year-old file on your system and it's still encrypted, will you remember which key was used to encrypt it two years ago? If you're like most people, you won't. If you can't decrypt the data, it's useless.

To deal with this problem, archiving old keys is essential: Any time a user or key generator creates and issues a key, the key must also be sent to the key archive system or to a *key recovery agent*. Archiving is most easily done on a server that offers secure storage. Older keys can be stored and retrieved when necessary. Figure 9.14 illustrates this relationship with a CA. This server requires strong physical security and at least the same security as the key-generating system.

FIGURE 9.14   The key archival system

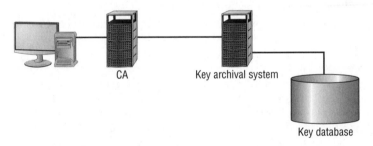

A key recovery agent (KRA), on the other hand, is an entity that has the ability to recover a key, key components, or plaintext messages as needed. Three examples of implementing a KRA into the process can be found at `http://csrc.nist.gov/krdp/exa.html`.

Key recovery is an important part of an encryption system. Information that is stored using older keys will be inaccessible using a new key. Key recovery allows you to access information that is encrypted with older keys. For example, key recovery could be used to retrieve information from an ex-employee. Three different factors must be considered when implementing a key archival system:

Current Keys *Current keys* are the keys in use at the present time. They haven't been revoked. In the event that a current key becomes lost, destroyed, or damaged, you need a way to recover the key so that data loss doesn't occur. A smart card can also become damaged, and a method must be established to reload the card with key information.

If the current key isn't recoverable, all information that was encrypted using it will be unavailable. This type of data loss could be expensive. Some newer systems allow the creation of "virtual" smart cards that can be used temporarily to initialize a new card. This card would generally be good only for a short period of time, such as during a work shift.

This process should be relatively easy for administrators to manage because people do forget to bring their authentication devices to work from time to time.

Previous Keys   *Previous keys* have recently expired and are no longer current. An employee who comes to work today may not know that a key rollover has occurred until they try to open yesterday's email. Depending on what's in the email, this could be a disaster. Many newer systems keep copies of recent keys in a key store on the system; this key store may contain the last two or three keys. If a local key store isn't provided, a key restoration process will be required from the archive system. Again, this may involve manual intervention by administrators.

Archived Keys   Archived keys were mentioned earlier. You should expect that older messages will be needed from time to time. This is especially true in a situation where litigation is involved; during the discovery phase of litigation, all records, correspondence, and memoranda must be presented to attorneys when subpoenaed. Failure to comply will result in sanctions from the court. Imagine that you had to access all the emails and files from a particular department for the last five years; it would be a very labor-intensive undertaking if you didn't have an archive system.

Many recovery and archive systems use the *M of N Control* method of access. This method, simply stated, says that in order to access the key server if *n* number of administrators have the ability to perform a process, *m* number of those administrators must authenticate for access to occur. This may require the administrators' physical presence.

 It's important to remember that your key archival system contains the complete history of all the keys that have been issued by your system. This information might also include all the current keys in use. Gaining access to this server would be the equivalent of discovering the Rosetta stone of your organization. An attacker with this information would have full and unrestricted access to every bit of data in your network.

Renewing Keys

Key renewal defines the process of enabling a key for use after its scheduled expiration date. A key would be reissued for a certain time in this situation. This process is called a *key rollover*. In most cases, the rollover of keys occurs for a given time frame. What would happen, however, if an organization found itself in a situation where a key rollover must not occur? Many systems include means to prevent rolling keys over.

In general, key rollovers are a bad practice and should not be performed except in the direst of situations. The longer a key is used, the more likely it is to be compromised. It is always better to renew keys than to do a key rollover.

If an earthquake occurred in your area and your building was inaccessible for two weeks, you would want to allow the existing keys to be used until higher-priority matters could be resolved when you went back to your building. In a natural disaster, a key roll-over could add an inordinate amount of stress to an already very stressful situation.

 Real World Scenario

What Do You Do about Forgetful Programmers?

You work as a network administrator for a software development company. The president of the company has been reading the newspapers, and he has recently become concerned about industrial espionage. Specifically, he wants to implement a system that will require the use of smart cards for access and authentication by all employees.

Your company has used employee badges for a number of years, and now you'll be upgrading to a newer technology. You've noticed that your software developers work very long hours and sometimes forget to bring their badges to work. This hasn't been much of a problem because you've been able to issue temporary badges when they needed them. How could you deal with an employee who leaves his smart card at home?

You could implement a system that allows a virtual smart card to be created for short periods of time. The employee's supervisor or a security staff member could call your smart desk to authorize the release of a virtual smart card. You would need to make sure that only trusted individuals could authorize or initiate this process.

Destroying Keys

Key destruction is the process of destroying keys that have become invalid. For example, an electronic key can be erased from a smart card. In older mechanical key systems, keys were physically destroyed using hammers.

Many symmetrically based encryption systems use a dedicated device to carry the key for the encryption. This key would be physically delivered to the site using the encryption system. Old keys would be recovered and destroyed.

 Always remember that symmetric encryption uses the same key to encrypt and decrypt the data (a primary weakness being that you have to share the key with others). Asymmetric encryption uses two keys: one to encrypt and another to decrypt the data.

Whether you're using physical keys or software-oriented key systems, old keys must be destroyed in a manner that ensures they don't fall into unauthorized hands.

Identifying Key Usage

During the time when the key is not being revoked, suspended, renewed, or destroyed, it is being used. *Key usage* is simply the use (and management) of public and private keys for encryption. While the topic appears as an objective on the exam, there is nothing additional to know here that is not addressed elsewhere in this chapter.

 Real World Scenario

Selling the Company's Old Computers

You've been asked to verify that the computers your company has liquidated are ready to be sold. What steps should you take to verify that unauthorized access to information doesn't occur?

You need to be concerned about two issues in this case. First, you need to make sure all corporate records, software, and other sensitive information are removed from the system. Second, you need to make sure any special access devices or encryption systems have been removed. Encryption systems that use key-based models may store keys in hidden areas of the disks. As a general practice, the disks on systems that are sold as surplus should be completely zeroed out (sometimes called zeroisation or zeroization); doing so prevents any sensitive information from being released inadvertently.

Summary

PKI is a system that has been widely implemented to provide encryption and data security in computer networks. It's being implemented globally by both governmental agencies and businesses. The major components of a PKI system include the certificate authority, the registration authority (which could be local), and certificates. The most common certificate implemented in PKI is X.509 v3.

The three cryptographic attacks covered in this chapter are mathematical, weak key, and birthday attacks. In mathematical attacks, mathematical methods are used to find ways to break an algorithm and decrypt a message. The birthday attack is based on the probability that patterns and common events become more likely as collections get larger. The weak key attack exploits either poorly chosen passwords or flaws in the password encryption algorithm.

Appropriate key storage is critical to maintaining a secure environment. Keys should be stored on hardened systems under close physical control. Keys can be stored in physical cabinets or on servers. Security storage failures are usually the result of human error. Distributing keys and transporting keys can present security challenges. Private keys should never be sent through the communications network; out-of-band transmission should be used to transport or distribute them. If an existing key has been compromised, the new key will be just as compromised. Public keys are intended for circulation; however, steps must be taken to protect their integrity.

A key expires when it reaches the end of its life cycle. Typically, this is a date-driven event. An expired key may be reissued using a rollover process, but generally this is considered a bad practice. The longer a key is used, the more likely it is to be broken. When a key or certificate has been identified as corrupt, compromised, or lost, it can be revoked. A CRL informs all of the end users and CAs that the certificate has been revoked. Once a key is revoked, it can no longer be used. Keys are suspended to disable them for a period of time. Suspension may occur because the key holder has become ill or has taken time off. A key can be unsuspended and reused.

Key destruction is the process of rendering a key unusable. Physical keys must be physically destroyed. Software keys and smart card keys should have their key files erased to prevent them from being used.

Exam Essentials

Know the trust models used in PKI. PKI provides the ability to use hierarchical, bridged, meshed, and hybrid models for trust. A CA hierarchy, or tree, is broken into subcomponents. The subcomponents are called root authorities, intermediate CAs, and leaf CAs.

Know the primary attack methods used against cryptographic systems. The primary attacks against cryptographic systems are birthday attacks, mathematical attacks, and weak key attacks.

Identify the stages in a key/certificate life cycle. A life cycle involves the generation, distribution, protection, archiving, recovery, and revocation of a key or certificate. Each of these aspects of key management must be considered to provide an effective and maintainable security process.

Know the purpose of key escrow. Key escrow allows law enforcement or other authorized governmental officials to access keys to conduct investigations. A key escrow agency or agent is a third party that is trusted to provide this service. A key archival system would normally be able to accomplish this task.

Explain the purpose of key renewal and destruction. Key renewal isn't a recommended practice. However, sometimes it may be necessary to renew a key in order to continue to use a system for a short time. The longer keys or certificates are used, the more vulnerable they are to decryption. Key destruction is an important part of physical control. When a physical key is retired, it should be physically destroyed. When a software key is retired, it should be erased and zeroed out to prevent inadvertent disclosure.

Review Questions

1. PKI (Public Key Infrastructure) is a key-asymmetric system utilizing how many keys?
   A. One
   B. Two
   C. Three
   D. Four

2. A certificate authority (CA) is an organization that is responsible for issuing, revoking, and distributing:
   A. Tokens
   B. Licenses
   C. Certificates
   D. Tickets

3. A registration authority (RA) can do all the following except:
   A. Distribute keys
   B. Accept registrations for the CA
   C. Validate identities
   D. Give recommendations

4. The primary difference between an RA and _____ is that the latter can be used to identify or establish the identity of an individual.
   A. MLA
   B. STR
   C. BSO
   D. LRA

5. The most popular certificate used is version 3 of:
   A. X.509
   B. B.102
   C. C.409
   D. Z.602

6. The process of requiring interoperability is called:
   A. Cross examination
   B. Cross certification
   C. Cross scoping
   D. Cross marking

7. A Certificate Practice Statement (CPS) is a detailed statement the CA uses to issue certificates and _____ of the CA.

   A. Implement policies

   B. Control processes

   C. Regulate actions

   D. Complete processes

8. Certificate revocation is the process of revoking a certificate before it:

   A. Is renewed

   B. Becomes public

   C. Reuses a value

   D. Expires

9. Which of the following is not one of the four main types of trust models used with PKI?

   A. Hierarchical

   B. Bridge

   C. Custom

   D. Mesh

   E. Hybrid

10. Which of the following refers to the ability to manage individual resources in the CA network?

   A. Regulation

   B. Granularity

   C. Management

   D. Restricting

11. A hierarchical trust model is also known as a:

   A. Bush

   B. Branch

   C. Tree

   D. Limb

12. In a bridge trust model, a _____ to _____ relationship exists between the root CAs.

   A. Parent, child

   B. Peer, peer

   C. Father, daughter

   D. Sister, parent

13. The mesh trust model is also known as what?

A. Web structure

B. Car model

C. Web redemption

D. Corrupt system

14. Key management includes all of the following stages/areas except:

A. Centralized versus decentralized key generation

B. Key storage and distribution

C. Key locking

D. Key escrow

E. Key expiration

15. Key destruction is the process of destroying keys that have become:

A. Invalid

B. Expired

C. Ruined

D. Outdated

16. Public Key Infrastructure (PKI) is a first attempt to provide all the aspects of security to messages and transactions that have been previously discussed. It contains four components including:

A. Certificate Authority (CA), Registration Authority (RA), RSA, and digital certificates

B. Certificate Authority (CA), RSA, Document Authority (DA), and digital certificates

C. Document Authority (DA), Certificate Authority (CA), and RSA

D. Registration Authority (RA), RSA, and digital certificates

17. Which of the following is responsible for issuing certificates?

A. Registration authority (RA)

B. Certificate authority (CA)

C. Document authority (DA)

D. Local registration authority (LRA)

18. In a bridge trust model, each intermediate CA trusts only those CAs that are:

A. Above and below it

B. Above it

C. Below it

D. On the same level

19. Which of the following is an attack against the algorithm?

    A. Birthday attack

    B. Weak key attack

    C. Mathematical attack

    D. Registration attack

20. One disadvantage of decentralized key generation is:

    A. It depends on key escrow.

    B. It is more vulnerable to single point attacks.

    C. There are more risks of attacks.

    D. It creates a storage and management issue.

Answers to Review Questions

1. B. PKI (Public Key Infrastructure) is a key-asymmetric system utilizing two keys.

2. C. A certificate authority (CA) is an organization that is responsible for issuing, revoking, and distributing certificates.

3. D. A registration authority (RA) can distribute keys, accept registrations for the CA, and validate identities. It cannot give recommendations.

4. D. The primary difference between an RA and LRA is that the LRA can be used to identify or establish the identity of an individual.

5. A. The most popular certificate used is version 3 of X.509.

6. B. The process of requiring interoperability is called cross certification.

7. A. A Certificate Practice Statement (CPS) is a detailed statement the CA uses to issue certificates and implement policies of the CA.

8. D. Certificate revocation is the process of revoking a certificate before it expires.

9. C. The four main types of trust models used with PKI are hierarchical, bridge, mesh, and hybrid. Custom is not one of the main PKI trust models.

10. B. Granularity refers to the ability to manage individual resources in the CA network.

11. C. A hierarchical trust model is also known as a tree.

12. B. In a bridge trust model, a peer-to-peer relationship exists between the root CAs.

13. A. The mesh trust model is also known as a web structure.

14. C. Key management includes centralized versus decentralized key generation, key storage and distribution, key escrow, and key expiration. Key locking is not a part of key management.

15. A. Key destruction is the process of destroying keys that have become invalid.

16. A. Public Key Infrastructure (PKI) contains four components: certificate authority (CA), registration authority (RA), RSA, and digital certificates.

17. B. The certificate authority (CA) is responsible for issuing certificates.

18. A. In a bridge trust model, each intermediate CA trusts those CAs that are above and below it.

19. C. A mathematical attack is an attack against the algorithm.

20. D. A disadvantage of decentralized key generation is the storage and management issue it creates.

Chapter 10

Physical and Hardware-Based Security

THE FOLLOWING COMPTIA SECURITY+ EXAM OBJECTIVES ARE COVERED IN THIS CHAPTER:

✓ **2.6 Explain the impact and proper use of environmental controls.**

- HVAC
- Fire suppression
- EMI shielding
- Hot and cold aisles
- Environmental monitoring
- Temperature and humidity controls
- Video monitoring

✓ **3.6 Analyze and differentiate among types of mitigation and deterrent techniques.**

- Physical security: Hardware locks; Mantraps; Video surveillance; Fencing; Proximity readers; Access list

✓ **4.2 Carry out appropriate procedures to establish host security.**

- Hardware security: Cable locks; Safe; Locking cabinets

✓ **5.2 Explain the fundamental concepts and best practices related to authentication, authorization, and access control.**

- Biometrics

This chapter will help you understand the importance of physical security measures such as access controls, physical barriers, and biometric systems. It also covers the environment your systems need in order to be safe and operational. This chapter also discusses securing the network, and looks at security zones and partitioning.

Physical security measures prevent your systems from being accessed in unauthorized ways, primarily by preventing an unauthorized user from physically touching a system or device. Most networked systems have developed high levels of sophistication and security from outside intruders. However, these systems are generally vulnerable to internal attacks, sabotage, and misuse. If an intruder has physical access to your systems, you should never consider them to be secure.

Implementing Access Control

Access control is a critical part of physical security. Systems must operate in controlled environments in order to be secure. These environments must be, as much as possible, safe from intrusion. Computer system consoles can be a vital point of vulnerability because many administrative functions can be accomplished from the system console. These consoles, as well as the systems themselves, must be protected from physical access. Two areas that help increase access control and make a system secure are physical barriers and biometrics, both of which are discussed in the following sections.

Physical Barriers

A key aspect of access control involves *physical barriers*. The objective of a physical barrier is to prevent access to computers and network systems. The most effective physical barrier implementations require that more than one physical barrier be crossed to gain access. This type of approach is called a *multiple barrier system*.

Ideally, your systems should have a minimum of three physical barriers:

- The external entrance to the building, referred to as a *perimeter*, which is protected by burglar alarms, external walls, *fencing*, surveillance, and so on. This should be used with an *access list*, which should exist to specifically identify who can enter a facility and can be verified by a guard or someone in authority.

- A locked door protecting the computer center; you should also rely on such items as *ID badges*, fobs, or keys to gain access.

- The entrance to the computer room itself. This should be another locked door that is carefully monitored. While you try to keep as many intruders out with the other two barriers, many who enter the building could be posing as someone they are not—heating technicians, representatives of the landlord, and so on. Although these pretenses can get them past the first two barriers, they should still be stopped by the locked computer room door.

Each of these entrances can be individually secured, monitored, and protected with alarm systems. Figure 10.1 illustrates this concept.

 Proximity reader is a catchall term for any ID or card reader capable of reading *proximity cards*. Proximity cards go by a number of different titles but are really just RFID (radio frequency identification) cards that can be read when close to a reader and never need to truly touch anything. The readers work with 13.56 MHz smart cards and 125 kHz proximity cards and can open turnstiles, gates, and any other physical security safeguards once the signal is read.

FIGURE 10.1 The three-layer security model

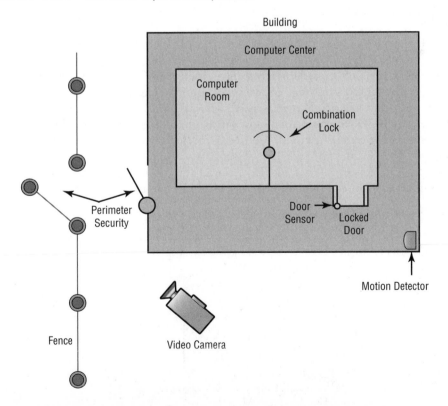

Although these three barriers won't always stop intruders, they will potentially slow them down enough that law enforcement can respond before an intrusion is fully developed. Once inside, a truly secure site should be dependent on a *physical token* or biometrics for access to the actual network resources.

Physical tokens are anything that a user must have on them to access network resources and are often associated with devices that enable the user to generate a one-time password authenticating their identity. SecurID, from RSA, is one of the best-known examples of a physical token, and information on it can be found at http://www.rsa.com/node.aspx?id=1156.

No matter how secure you think your system is, you'll never be able to stop everyone. But your goal is to stop most attempts and, at the very least, slow down the most sophisticated. As an analogy, the front door of your home may contain a lock and a deadbolt. This minimal security is enough to convince most burglars to try somewhere less secure. A professional who is bent on entering your home, however, could always take a chain saw or similar tool to the door.

Mantraps

High-security installations use a type of intermediate access control mechanism called a *mantrap* (also occasionally written as *man-trap*). Mantraps require visual identification, as well as authentication, to gain access. A mantrap makes it difficult for a facility to be accessed in number because it allows only one or two people into the facility at a time. It's usually designed to physically contain an unauthorized, potentially hostile person until authorities arrive. Figure 10.2 illustrates a mantrap. Notice in this case that the visual verification is accomplished using a security guard. A properly developed mantrap includes bulletproof glass, high-strength doors, and locks. In high-security and military environments, an armed guard, as well as *video surveillance*, would be placed at the mantrap. After a person is inside the facility, additional security and authentication may be required for further entrance.

FIGURE 10.2   A mantrap in action

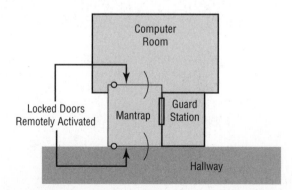

Some mantraps even include scales to weigh the person. While the weight can be used to help identify a person, often the scales are used to make certain no one is sneaking in. If the weight of the scale appears too high, an officer can check to make sure two people haven't crowded in and are attempting to quickly bypass security.

Perimeter Security

Perimeter security, whether physical or technological, is the first line of defense in your security model. In the case of a physical security issue, the intent is to prevent unauthorized access to resources inside a building or facility.

The network equivalent of physical perimeter security is intended to accomplish for a network what perimeter security does for a building. How do you keep intruders from gaining access to systems and information in the network through the network?

In the physical environment, perimeter security is accomplished using locks, doors, surveillance systems, and alarm systems. This isn't functionally any different from a network, which uses border routers, intrusion detection systems, and firewalls to prevent unauthorized access. Figure 10.3 illustrates the systems used to prevent network intrusion.

Few security systems can be implemented that don't have weaknesses or vulnerabilities. A determined intruder can, with patience, overcome most security systems. The task may not be easy, and it may require careful planning and study; however, a determined adversary can usually figure out a way. This is why deterrent factors are so important.

FIGURE 10.3   Network perimeter defense

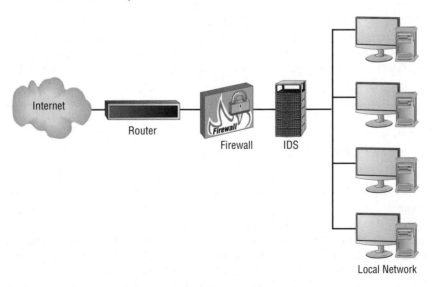

If you want to deter intruders from breaking into your building, you can install improved door locks, coded alarm systems, and magnetic contacts on doors and windows. Remember that you can't always keep an intruder out of your building; however, you can make an intrusion riskier and more likely to be discovered if it happens.

Don't overlook the obvious. Adding a security guard to the front door will go a long way toward keeping an intruder out.

 Real World Scenario

Circumventing Security

Recently, a small business noticed that the level of network traffic seemed to be very high in the late evening and early morning. The business couldn't find a network-related reason why this was happening. Upon investigation, the security consultant found that a part-time employee had established a multiuser game server in his office. The game server was set to turn on after 10:00 p.m. and turn off at 5:30 a.m. This server was hidden under a desk, and it supported around 30 local game players. The part-time employee didn't have a key to the building, so an investigation was conducted to determine how he gained access to the building after hours. The building had electronic locks on its outside entrances, and a pass card was needed to open the doors. However, the door locks were designed to automatically unlock when someone was leaving the building.

The investigation discovered that the employee and a friend had figured out a way to slide a piece of cardboard under one of the external doors, which activated the door mechanisms and unlocked the doors. The intruders took advantage of this weakness in the doors to gain access after hours without using a passcard and then used the server to play games in his office.

Hardware Security

Hardware security involves applying physical security modifications to secure the system(s) and prevent them from leaving the facility. Don't spend all your time worrying about intruders coming through the network wire and overlook the obvious need for physical security.

Adding a *cable lock* between a laptop and a desk prevents someone from picking it up and walking away with a copy of your customer database. Every laptop case I am aware of includes a built-in security slot in which a cable lock can be added to prevent it from easily being removed from the premises, like the one shown in Figure 10.4.

When it comes to desktop models, adding a lock to the back cover can prevent an intruder with physical access from grabbing the hard drive or damaging the internal components. The lock that connects through that slot can also go to a cable that then connects to a desk or other solid fixture to keep the entire PC from being carried away. An example of this type of configuration is shown in Figure 10.5.

FIGURE 10.4   A cable in the security slot keeps the laptop from easily being removed.

FIGURE 10.5   A cable can be used to keep a desktop machine from easily being taken.

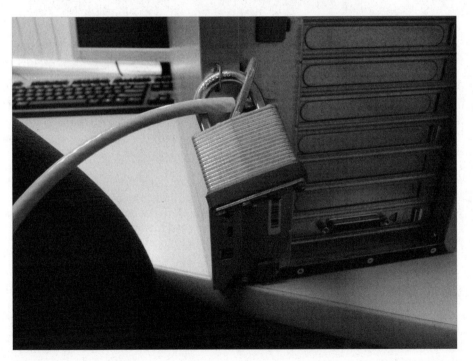

In addition to running a cable to the desk, you can also choose to run an end of it up to the monitor if theft of peripherals is a possibility. An example of this is shown in Figure 10.6.

FIGURE 10.6 If theft of equipment is a possibility, run one end of the cable from the monitor to the desktop machine through the hole in the work desk.

You should also consider using *safes* and *locking cabinets* to protect backup media, documentation, and any other physical artifacts that could do harm if they fell into the wrong hands. Server racks should lock the rack-mounted servers into the cabinets to prevent someone from simply pulling one and walking out the front door with it.

 While this discussion is on physical security, don't overlook encryption as a means of increasing data security should a desktop or laptop machine be stolen. You can also consider removing the hard drives in areas that are difficult to monitor and forcing all data to be stored on the network.

Security Zones

A *security zone* is an area in a building where access is individually monitored and controlled. A large network, such as a big physical plant, can have many areas that require restricted access. In a building, floors, sections of floors, and even offices can be broken down into smaller areas. These smaller zones are referred to as security zones. In the physical environment, each floor is broken into separate zones. An alarm system that identifies a zone of intrusion can inform security personnel about an intruder's location in the building; zone notification tells security where to begin looking when they enter the premises.

The concept of security zones is as old as security itself. Most burglar alarms allow the creation of individual zones within a building or residence; these zones are then treated separately by the security staff. In a residence, it would be normal for the bedroom to be assigned a zone of its own so movement here can occur while other parts of the house may be set on a motion detector.

In Exercise 10.1, we'll walk through the evaluation of your environment.

EXERCISE 10.1

Security Zones in the Physical Environment

As a security administrator, you'll need to evaluate your workplace and think of physical zones that should exist in terms of different types of individuals who might be present. If your workplace is already divided into zones, forget that this has been done and start from scratch. Answer the following questions:

1. What areas represent the physical dimension of your workplace (buildings, floors, offices, and so on)?

2. Which areas are accessible by everyone from administrators to visitors? Can a visitor ever leave the reception area without an escort, and if so, to go where (restroom, break room, and so forth)?

3. In what areas are users allowed to move about freely? Are you certain that no visitors or guests could enter those areas?

4. What areas are administrators allowed to enter that users can't? Server room? Wiring closets? How do you keep users out and verify that only administrators enter?

5. Are wall jacks, network access, or Wi-Fi available in areas where visitors are located?

6. Do other areas need to be secured for entities beyond the user/administrator distinction (such as groups)?

Once you're armed with this information, you should look for ways to address the weaknesses. You should evaluate your environment routinely to make certain the zones that exist within your security plan are still relevant. Always start from scratch and pretend that no zones exist; then verify that the zones that do exist are the same as those you've created from this exercise.

The networking equivalent of a security zone is a network security zone. They perform the same function. If you divide a network into smaller sections, each zone can have its own security considerations and measures—just like a physical security zone. Figure 10.7 illustrates a larger network being broken down into three smaller zones. Notice that the first zone also contains a smaller zone where high-security information is stored. This arrangement allows layers of security to be built around sensitive information. The division of the network is accomplished by implementing virtual LANs (VLANs) and instituting demilitarized zones (DMZs).

FIGURE 10.7 Network security zones

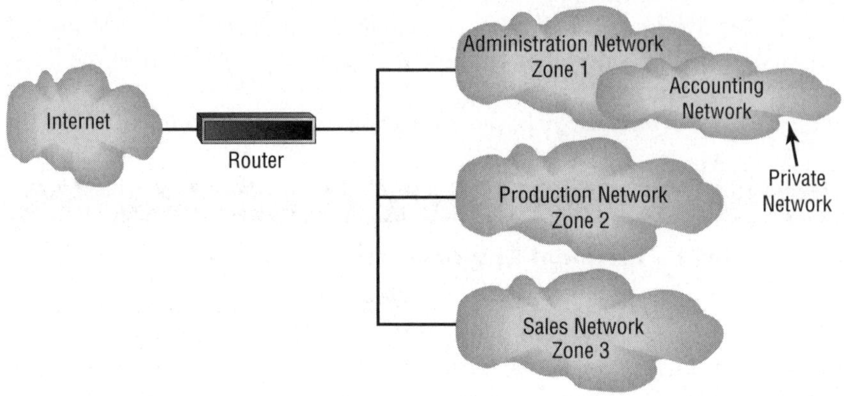

Partitioning

Partitioning a network is functionally the same as partitioning a building. In a building, walls exist to direct pedestrian flow, provide access control, and separate functional areas. This process allows information and property to be kept under physical lock and key.

Through partitioning, you can isolate one entity from another. That entity can be physical (one room can be shut from another in a building) or logical (those who can access one set of data cannot access another). This discussion will elaborate on the possibilities partitioning provides.

Partitions can be either temporary or permanent structures.

Hallways in an office building are usually built differently from internal office space. Hallways are usually more flame resistant, and they're referred to as *fire corridors*. These corridors allow people in the building to escape in the event of a fire. Fire corridor walls go from the floor to the ceiling, whereas internal walls can stop before they reach the ceiling (most office buildings have a false ceiling in them to hold lighting, wiring, and plumbing).

Network partitioning accomplishes the same function for a network as physical partitioning does for a building. Buildings have physical walls, whereas network partitioning involves the creation of private networks within larger networks. Partitions can be isolated from each other using routers and firewalls.

Therefore, while the network systems are all connected using wire, the functional view is that of many smaller networks. Figure 10.8 shows a partitioned network. It's important to realize that unless a physical device (such as a router) separates these partitioned networks, all the signals are shared across the wire. This device accomplishes the same function as a hallway or locked door—from a purely physical perspective.

Partitioning and security zones are essentially interchangeable. Typically, partitioning is more narrowly focused than zones, but this need not always be the case. In a typical installation, a zone would encompass one floor, while a partition would include one room.

FIGURE 10.8   Network partitioning separating networks from each other in a larger network

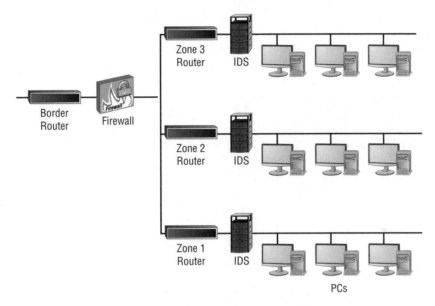

 Real World Scenario

Installing Biometric Devices

You've been asked to solve the problem of people forgetting the smart cards that give them access to the computer center. Hardly a day goes by that a company employee doesn't forget to bring their card. This can cause a great deal of disruption in the workplace because someone has to constantly reissue smart cards. The company has tried everything it can think of short of firing people who forget their cards. What could you recommend to the company?

Investigate whether biometric devices (such as hand scanners) or number access locks can be used in lieu of smart cards for access. These devices will allow people who forget their smart cards to enter areas that they should be able to access.

Biometrics

Biometric systems use some kind of unique biological trait to identify a person, such as fingerprints, patterns on the retina, and handprints. Some of the devices that are used are hand scanners, retinal scanners, facial recognition applications, and keystroke recognition programs, which can be used as part of the access control mechanisms. These devices should be coupled into security-oriented computer systems that record all access attempts. They should also be under surveillance in order to prevent individuals from bypassing them.

These technologies are becoming more reliable, and they will become widely used over the next few years. Many laptops sold now have a fingerprint reader built in. The costs associated with these technologies have fallen drastically in recent years. One of the best independent sources of information on development in the field of biometrics is BiometricNews.net, where you can find links to publications and their blog.

 Real World Scenario

Evaluating Your Security System

You've been asked to evaluate your building's security system. The president chose you because you understand computers, and after all, these new alarm systems are computerized.

In evaluating the environment, you notice that there is a single control panel for the whole building. A few motion detectors are located in the main hallway. Beyond that, no additional security components are installed.

This situation is fairly normal in a small building. You could recommend enhancing the system by adding motion detectors in each major hallway. You could also install *video monitoring* (also known as surveillance) cameras, such as closed-circuit television (CCTV), at all the entrances. Most security/surveillance CCTV cameras have PTZ (Pan, Tilt, and Zoom) capabilities to and can often do so based on sound or motion. You should also consider recommending they upgrade the perimeter security by adding contact sensors on all the doors and ground-floor windows.

Always evaluate the building from a multi-tiered approach. Incorporate as many different elements as you can where needed: perimeter security, security zones, and surveillance.

Maintaining Environmental and Power Controls

The location of your computer facility is critical to its security. Computer facilities must be placed in a location that is physically possible to secure. Additionally, the location must have the proper capabilities to manage temperature, humidity, and other environmental factors necessary to the health of your computer systems. The following sections look at environmental and power systems.

Environmental Monitoring

Many computer systems require *temperature and humidity control* for reliable service. The larger servers, communications equipment, and drive arrays generate considerable amounts of heat; this is especially true of mainframe and older minicomputers. An environmental system for this type of equipment is a significant expense beyond the actual computer system costs. Fortunately, newer systems operate in a wider temperature range. Most new systems are designed to operate in an office environment.

If the computer systems you're responsible for require special environmental considerations, you'll need to establish cooling and humidity control. Ideally, systems are located in the middle of the building, and they're ducted separately from the rest of the *HVAC* (Heating, Ventilation, and Air Conditioning) system. It's a common practice for modern buildings to use a zone-based air conditioning environment, which allows the environmental plant to be turned off when the building isn't occupied. A computer room will typically require full-time environmental control.

Environmental systems should be monitored to prevent the computer center's humidity level from dropping below 50 percent. Electrostatic damage is likely to occur when humidity levels get too low.

Humidity control prevents the buildup of static electricity in the environment. If the humidity drops much below 50 percent, electronic components are extremely vulnerable to damage from electrostatic shock. Most environmental systems also regulate humidity; however, a malfunctioning system can cause the humidity to be almost entirely extracted from a room. Make sure that environmental systems are regularly serviced.

Environmental concerns also include considerations about water and flood damage as well as fire suppression. Computer rooms should have fire and moisture detectors. Most office buildings have water pipes and other moisture-carrying systems in the ceiling. If a water pipe bursts (which is common in minor earthquakes), the computer room could become flooded. Water and electricity don't mix. Moisture monitors would automatically kill power in a computer room if moisture were detected, so the security professional should know where the water cutoffs are located.

Fire, no matter how small, can cause damage to computer systems. Apart from the high heat, which can melt or warp plastics and metals, the smoke from the fire can permeate the computers. Smoke particles are large enough to lodge under the read/write head of a hard disk, thereby causing data loss. In addition, the fire-suppression systems in most buildings consist of water under pressure, and the water damage from putting out even a small fire could wipe out an entire data center.

Fire suppression is discussed further in this chapter in the section by the same name, "Fire Suppression."

The three critical components of any fire are heat, fuel, and oxygen. If any component of this trilogy is removed, a fire isn't possible. Most fire-suppression systems work on this concept.

Power Systems

Computer systems are susceptible to power and interference problems. A computer requires a steady input of AC power to produce reliable DC voltage for its electronic systems. *Power systems* are designed to operate in a wide band of power characteristics; they help keep the electrical service constant, and they ensure smooth operations.

 Real World Scenario

Simple Things Can Have Huge Consequences

Water can come from anywhere, and you need to be prepared when it does. Several years ago, a business had a state-of-the-art server room on the top floor of its building. The room was climate controlled and a true thing of beauty. Directly above the server room was the roof, and on the roof was the bank of air conditioners for the six-floor building. Over the course of one extremely hot weekend, the drain lines for the condensation from the air conditioners clogged. The lines filled with water and then burst, and the water came through the roof into the attic. Once in the attic, all the water worked its way to the lowest spot and created a hole in the ceiling—directly above the servers. Everything was fried in a short period of time.

As far-fetched as it sounds, such things happen all the time. When they do, you need to be ready with backups—backup tapes, backup servers, backup monitors, and so on.

Major fluctuations in AC power can contribute to a condition known as *chip creep*. With creep, unsoldered chips slowly work their way loose and out of a socket over time.

The following products solve most electrical line problems:

Surge Protectors   *Surge protectors* protect electrical components from momentary or instantaneous increases (called *spikes*) in a power line. Most surge protectors shunt a voltage spike to ground through the use of small devices called *metal oxide varistors (MOVs)*. Large-scale surge protectors are usually found in building power supplies or at power-feed points in the building. Portable surge protectors can be purchased as part of an extension cord or power strip but are often good for only one good hit. If subsequent surges occur, the surge protector may not prevent them from being passed through the line to the computer system. Surge protectors are passive devices, and they accomplish no purpose until a surge occurs.

Power Conditioners   *Power conditioners* are active devices that effectively isolate and regulate voltage in a building. They monitor the power in the building and clean it up. Power conditioners usually include filters, surge suppressors, and temporary voltage regulation. They can also activate backup power supplies. Power conditioners can be part of the overall building power scheme; it's also common to see them dedicated strictly to computer rooms.

Backup Power   *Backup power* is generally used in situations where continuous power is needed in the event of a power loss. These types of systems are usually designed for either short-term, as in the case of a battery backup system, or long-term uses, as in an *uninterruptible power supply (UPS)*. UPS systems generally use batteries to provide short-term power. Longer-term backup power comes from power generators that frequently have their own power-loss-sensing circuitry. Power generators kick in if a power loss is detected, and they provide power until disabled. The generators require a short amount of time to start providing power, and the battery backup systems provide time for the generators to come online. Most generator systems don't automatically turn off when power is restored to a building—they're turned off manually. This is necessary because it's common for several false starts to occur before power is restored from the power grid.

Most power generators are either gas or diesel operated, and they require preventive maintenance on a regular basis. These systems aren't much use if they don't start when needed or they fail because no oil is in the motor. Newer systems are becoming available that are based on fuel cell technology; they will probably be very reliable and require less maintenance.

EMI Shielding

Shielding refers to the process of preventing electronic emissions from your computer systems from being used to gather intelligence and preventing outside electronic emissions from disrupting your information-processing abilities. In a fixed facility, such as a computer center, surrounding the computer room with a *Faraday cage* can provide electronic shielding. A Faraday cage usually consists of an electrically conductive wire mesh or other conductor woven into a "cage" that surrounds a room. The conductor is then grounded. Because of this cage, few electromagnetic signals can either enter or leave the room, thereby reducing the ability to eavesdrop on a computer conversation. In order to verify the functionality of the cage, radio frequency (RF) emissions from the room are tested with special measuring devices.

 Electromagnetic interference (EMI) and *radio frequency interference (RFI)* are two additional environmental considerations. Motors, lights, and other types of electromechanical objects cause EMI, which can cause circuit overload, spikes, or electrical component failure. Making sure that all signal lines are properly shielded and grounded can minimize EMI. Devices that generate EMI should be as physically distant from cabling as is feasible because this type of energy tends to dissipate quickly with distance.

Figure 10.9 shows a motor generating EMI. In this example, the data cable next to the motor is picking up the EMI. This causes the signal to deteriorate, and it might eventually cause the line to be unusable. The gray area in the illustration is representative of the interference generated by the motor.

FIGURE 10.9 Electromagnetic interference (EMI) pickup in a data cable

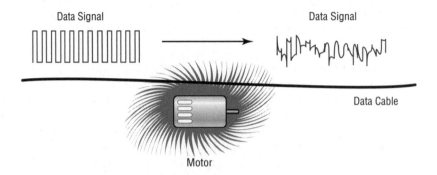

RFI is the byproduct of electrical processes, similar to EMI. The major difference is that RFI is usually projected across a radio spectrum. Motors with defective brushes can generate RFI, as can a number of other devices. If RF levels become too high, it can cause the receivers in wireless units to become deaf. This process is called *desensitizing,* and it occurs because of the volume of RF energy present. This can occur even if the signals are on different frequencies.

Figure 10.10 demonstrates the desensitizing process occurring with a wireless access portal (WAP). The only solutions in this situation would be to move the devices farther apart or to turn off the RFI generator.

In 1985, Dutch researcher Wim van Eck proposed that it is possible to eavesdrop on CRT and LCD displays by detecting their electromagnetic emissions. Known as *Van Eck phreaking,* this problem/possibility has been in the news recently because of potential problems with electronic voting machines. Commonly associated countermeasures recommended by TEMPEST include shielding.

FIGURE 10.10 RF desensitization occurring as a result of cellular phone interference

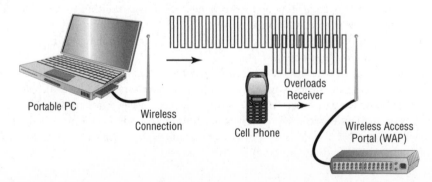

Project TEMPEST

TEMPEST is the name of a project commenced by the U.S. government in the late 1950s. TEMPEST was concerned with reducing electronic noise from devices that would divulge intelligence about systems and information. This program has become a standard for computer systems certification. *TEMPEST shielding protection* means that a computer system doesn't emit any significant amounts of EMI or RFI. For a device to be approved as a TEMPEST, it must undergo extensive testing, done to exacting standards that the U.S. government dictates. Today, control zones and white noise are used to accomplish the shielding. TEMPEST-certified equipment frequently costs twice as much as non-TEMPEST equipment.

Hot and Cold Aisles

In server rooms, there are often multiple rows of servers located in racks. The rows of servers are known as aisles, and they can be cooled as *hot aisles* and *cold aisles*. With a hot aisle, hot air outlets are used to cool the equipment, while with cold aisles, cold air intake is used to cool it. Combining the two, you have cold air intake from below the aisle and hot air outtake above it, providing constant circulation.

It is important that the hot air exhausting from one aisle of racks not be the intake air pulled in by the next row of racks, or overheating will occur. Air handlers must move the hot air out, while cold air, usually coming from beneath a raised floor, is supplied as the intake air. Figure 10.11 shows an example of a hot and cold aisle design.

FIGURE 10.11   Example of a hot and cold aisle design

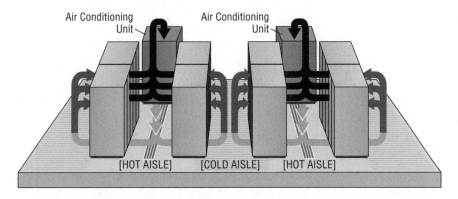

Fire Suppression

Fire suppression is a key consideration in computer-center design. Fire suppression is the act of actually extinguishing a fire versus preventing one. Two primary types of fire-suppression systems are in use: fire extinguishers and fixed systems.

Fire Extinguishers

Fire extinguishers are portable systems. The selection and use of fire extinguishers is critical. Four primary types of fire extinguishers are available, classified by the types of fires they put out: A, B, C, and D. Table 10.1 describes the four types of fires and the capabilities of various extinguishers.

TABLE 10.1   Fire Extinguisher Ratings

Type	Use	Retardant Composition
A	Wood and paper	Largely water or chemical
B	Flammable liquids	Fire-retardant chemicals
C	Electrical	Nonconductive chemicals
D	Flammable metals	Varies, type specific

A type K extinguisher that is marketed for use with cooking oil fires can also be found in stores. In actuality, this is a subset of class B extinguishers.

Several multipurpose types of extinguishers combine extinguisher capabilities in a single bottle. The more common multipurpose extinguishers are A-B, B-C, and ABC.

The recommended procedure for using a fire extinguisher is called the *PASS method*: pull, aim, squeeze, and sweep. Fire extinguishers usually operate for only a few seconds—if you use one, make sure you don't fixate on a single spot. Most fire extinguishers have a limited effective range of from three to eight feet.

A major concern with electrical fires is that they can reoccur quickly if the voltage isn't removed. Make sure you remove voltage from systems when a fire occurs.

Most fire extinguishers require an annual inspection. This is a favorite area of citation by fire inspectors. You can contract with services to do this on a regular basis: They will inspect or replace your fire extinguishers according to a scheduled agreement.

Fixed Systems

Fixed systems are usually part of the building systems. The most common fixed systems combine fire detectors with fire-suppression systems, where the detectors usually trigger either because of a rapid temperature change or because of excessive smoke. The fire-suppression system uses either water sprinklers or fire-suppressing gas. Water systems work with overhead nozzles, as illustrated in Figure 10.12. These systems are the most common method in modern buildings. Water systems are reliable, relatively inexpensive, and require little maintenance.

FIGURE 10.12   Water-based fire-suppression system

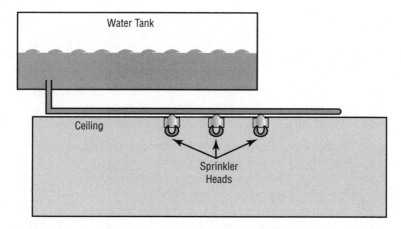

The one drawback to water-based systems is that they cause extreme damage to energized electrical equipment such as computers. These systems can be tied into relays that terminate power to computer systems before they release water into the building.

Gas-based systems were originally designed to use carbon dioxide and later halon gas. Halon gas isn't used anymore because it damages the ozone layer; environmentally acceptable substitutes are now available, with FM200 being one of the most common. The principle of a gas system is that it displaces the oxygen in the room, thereby removing this necessary component of a fire.

Evacuate the room immediately in the event of a fire. Gas-based systems work by removing oxygen from the fire, and this can suffocate anyone in the room as well.

The major drawback to gas-based systems is that they require sealed environments to operate. Special ventilation systems are usually installed in gas systems to limit air circulation when the gas is released. Gas systems are also expensive, and they're usually implemented only in computer rooms or other areas where water would cause damage to technology or other intellectual property.

Summary

In this chapter, I covered the key elements of physical security and the environment. Physical security measures include access controls, physical barriers, and environmental systems. Environmental considerations include electrical, fire-suppression, and interference issues.

Security models must be concerned with physical security, security zones, partitioning, and the communications infrastructure. You should take a multilayered approach when you implement a security model.

Exam Essentials

Know the various aspects of physical security.   Physical security involves mechanisms to provide access control, physical barriers, and authentication systems such as biometric systems.

Be able to describe the types of access control methods used in physical security.   The primary methods of access control include perimeter security, security zones, physical barriers, and identification systems. These systems, when implemented in layers, make it harder for an intruder to gain access. Physical access methods should also include intrusion detection systems such as video surveillance in order to monitor the activities when they occur. This helps security professionals manage the threat and make changes when necessary.

Be able to discuss the various aspects of environmental systems and functions.   Environmental systems include heating, air conditioning, humidity control, fire suppression, and power systems. All of these functions are critical to a well-designed physical plant.

Know the purposes of shielding in the environment.   Shielding primarily prevents interference from EMI and RFI sources. Most shielding is attached to an effective ground, thereby neutralizing or reducing interference susceptibility.

Be able to describe the types of fire-suppression systems in use today.   Fire-suppression systems can be either fixed or portable. Portable systems usually are fire extinguishers. Fixed systems are part of the building, and they're generally water based or gas based. Gas-based systems are usually found only in computer rooms or other locations where water-based systems would cause more damage than is warranted. Gas systems work only in environments where airflow can be limited; they remove oxygen from the fire, causing the fire to go out. Water systems usually remove heat from a fire, causing the fire to go out.

Review Questions

1. Which component of physical security addresses outer-level access control?

    A. Perimeter security

    B. Mantraps

    C. Security zones

    D. Locked doors

2. You've been drafted for the safety committee. One of your first tasks is to inventory all the fire extinguishers and make certain the correct types are in the correct locations throughout the building. Which of the following categories of fire extinguisher is intended for use on electrical fires?

    A. Type A

    B. Type B

    C. Type C

    D. Type D

3. Which of the following won't reduce EMI?

    A. Physical shielding

    B. Humidity control

    C. Physical location

    D. Overhauling worn motors

4. You're the administrator for MTS. You're creating a team that will report to you, and you're attempting to divide the responsibilities for security among individual members. Similarly, which of the following access methods breaks a large area into smaller areas that can be monitored individually?

    A. Zone

    B. Partition

    C. Perimeter

    D. Floor

5. Which of the following is equivalent to building walls in an office building from a network perspective?

    A. Perimeter security

    B. Partitioning

    C. Security zones

    D. IDS systems

6. After a number of minor incidents at your company, physical security has suddenly increased in priority. No unauthorized personnel should be allowed access to the servers or workstations. The process of preventing access to computer systems in a building is called what?

    A. Perimeter security

    B. Access control

    C. Security zones

    D. IDS systems

7. Which of the following is an example of perimeter security?

    A. Chain link fence

    B. Video camera

    C. Elevator

    D. Locked computer room

8. You're the leader of the security committee at ACME. After a move to a new facility, you're installing a new security monitoring system throughout. Which of the following best describes a motion detector mounted in the corner of a hallway?

    A. Perimeter security

    B. Partitioning

    C. Security zone

    D. IDS system

9. Which technology uses a physical characteristic to establish identity?

    A. Biometrics

    B. Surveillance

    C. Smart card

    D. CHAP authenticator

10. The process of reducing or eliminating susceptibility to outside interference is called what?

    A. Shielding

    B. EMI

    C. TEMPEST

    D. Desensitization

11. You work for an electronics company that has just created a device that emits less RF than any competitor's product. Given the enormous importance of this invention and of the marketing benefits it could offer, you want to have the product certified. Which certification is used to indicate minimal electronic emissions?

    A. EMI

    B. RFI

    C. CC EAL 4

    D. TEMPEST

12. Due to growth beyond current capacity, a new server room is being built. As a manager, you want to make certain that all the necessary safety elements exist in the room when it's finished. Which fire-suppression system works best when used in an enclosed area by displacing the air around a fire?

   A. Gas based

   B. Water based

   C. Fixed system

   D. Overhead sprinklers

13. Type K fire extinguishers are intended for use on cooking oil fires. This type is a subset of which other type of fire extinguisher?

   A. Type A

   B. Type B

   C. Type C

   D. Type D

14. Proximity readers work with which of the following? (Choose all that apply.)

   A. 15.75 fob card

   B. 14.32 surveillance card

   C. 13.56 MHZ smart card

   D. 125 kHz proximity card

15. In a hot and cold aisle system, what is the typical method of handling cold air?

   A. It is pumped in from below raised floor tiles.

   B. It is pumped in from above through the ceiling tiles.

   C. Only hot air is extracted and cold air is the natural result.

   D. Cold air exists in each aisle.

16. If RF levels become too high, it can cause the receivers in wireless units to become deaf. This process is called:

   A. Clipping

   B. Desensitizing

   C. Distorting

   D. Crackling

17. RFI is the byproduct of electrical processes, similar to EMI. The major difference is that RFI is usually projected across which of the following?

   A. Network medium

   B. Electrical wiring

   C. Radio spectrum

   D. Portable media

18. For physical security, what should you do with rack-mounted servers?

    A. Run a cable from them to a desk.

    B. Lock each of them into the cabinet.

    C. Install them in safes.

    D. Use only Type D, which incorporates its own security.

19. Which of the following is a method of cooling server racks in which hot air and cold are both handled in the server room?

    A. Hot/cold vessels

    B. Hot and cold passages

    C. Hot/cold walkways

    D. Hot and cold aisles

20. Which of the following is a high-security installation that requires visual identification, as well as authentication, to gain access?

    A. Mantrap

    B. Fencing

    C. Proximity reader

    D. Hot aisle

Answers to Review Questions

1. A. The first layer of access control is perimeter security. Perimeter security is intended to delay or deter entrance into a facility.

2. C. Type C fire extinguishers are intended for use in electrical fires.

3. B. Electrical devices, such as motors, that generate magnetic fields cause EMI. Humidity control won't address EMI.

4. A. A security zone is a smaller part of a larger area. Security zones can be monitored individually if needed. Answers B, C, and D are examples of security zones.

5. B. Partitioning is the process of breaking a network into smaller components that can each be individually protected. This is analogous to building walls in an office building.

6. B. Access control is the primary process of preventing access to physical systems.

7. A. Perimeter security involves creating a perimeter or outer boundary for a physical space. Video surveillance systems wouldn't be considered a part of perimeter security, but they can be used to enhance physical security monitoring.

8. C. A security zone is an area that is a smaller component of the entire facility. Security zones allow intrusions to be detected in specific parts of the building.

9. A. Biometrics is a technology that uses personal characteristics, such as a retinal pattern or fingerprint, to establish identity.

10. A. Shielding keeps external electronic signals from disrupting operations.

11. D. TEMPEST is the certification given to electronic devices that emit minimal RF. The TEMPEST certification is difficult to acquire, and it significantly increases the cost of systems.

12. A. Gas-based systems work by displacing the air around a fire. This eliminates one of the three necessary components of a fire: oxygen.

13. B. Type K fire extinguishers are a subset of Type B fire extinguishers.

14. C, D. Proximity readers work with 13.56 MHz smart card and 125 kHz proximity cards.

15. A. With hot and cold aisles, cold air is pumped in from below raised floor tiles.

16. B. If RF levels become too high, it can cause the receivers in wireless units to become deaf and is known as desensitizing. This occurs because of the volume of RF energy present.

17. C. RFI is the byproduct of electrical processes, similar to EMI. The major difference is that RFI is usually projected across a radio spectrum. Motors with defective brushes can generate RFI, as can a number of other devices.

18. B. Server racks should lock the rack-mounted servers into the cabinets to prevent someone from simply pulling one and walking out the front door with it.

19. D. Hot and cold aisles is a method of cooling server racks in which hot air and cold are both handled in the server room.

20. A. High-security installations use a type of intermediate access control mechanism called a mantrap. Mantraps require visual identification, as well as authentication, to gain access. A mantrap makes it difficult for a facility to be accessed in number because it allows only one or two people into the facility at a time.

Chapter

11

Security and Vulnerability in the Network

THE FOLLOWING COMPTIA SECURITY+ EXAM OBJECTIVES ARE COVERED IN THIS CHAPTER:

✓ **1.2 Apply and implement secure network administration principles.**

- Rule-based management
- Port security
- 802.1X
- Flood guards
- Loop protection
- Prevent network bridging by network separation
- Log analysis

✓ **3.6 Analyze and differentiate among types of mitigation and deterrent techniques.**

- Manual bypassing of electronic controls: Failsafe/secure vs. failopen
- Monitoring system logs: Event logs; Audit logs; Security logs; Access logs
- Port security: MAC limiting and filtering; 802.1X; Disabling unused ports
- Security posture: Initial baseline configuration; Continuous security monitoring; remediation
- Reporting: Alarms; Alerts; Trends
- Detection controls vs. prevention controls: Camera vs. guard

✓ **3.7 Implement assessment tools and techniques to discover security threats and vulnerabilities.**

- Vulnerability scanning and interpret results

- Tools: Vulnerability scanner

- Assessment types: Risk; Threat; Vulnerability

- Assessment technique: Baseline reporting; Code review; Determine attack surface; Architecture; Design reviews

✓ **3.8 Within the realm of vulnerability assessments, explain the proper use of penetration testing versus vulnerability scanning.**

- Penetration testing: Verify a threat exists; Bypass security controls; Actively test security controls; Exploiting vulnerabilities

- Vulnerability scanning: Passively testing security controls; Identify vulnerability; Identify lack of security controls; Identify common misconfiguration

- Black box

- White box

- Gray box

Much of this book has focused on individual security problems and solutions. Viruses, for example, are problems and antivirus software is the solution. When evaluating something as large as a network, however, you can't focus on just one item at a time. Those intent on attacking the network will scan it for any and every problem they can find and then ascertain the best way to inflict harm. To counter these approaches, security administrators need to find—and respond to—problems before attackers can.

Network Security Threats

Network threats involve many facets of the network and organization. You've seen that your systems and information are susceptible to attacks and disruption based on internal, external, and design factors in the systems you support. Ensuring that your systems and applications are kept up-to-date and making sure your security procedures are in place and followed meticulously can minimize many of these threats. Most of the exploitation attacks that occur to programs (be it Microsoft Exchange, sendmail, or any other) are fixed by the developer as soon as they're discovered, if not shortly thereafter. As an administrator, you must apply fixes and patches immediately after they have been thoroughly tested in a lab environment; doing so makes it harder for attackers to learn about your systems and exploit known weaknesses.

CERT Coordination Center

One of the organizations that tracks and reports security problems is the CERT Coordination Center (CERT/CC). CERT/CC is a part of the Software Engineering Institute (SEI) at Carnegie Mellon University. SEI is a federally funded research institution with a strong emphasis on computer security–related topics. CERT/CC provides interesting perspectives on the growth of computer-related incidents but stopped making numbers available several years ago since "attacks against Internet-connected systems have become so commonplace that counts of the number of incidents reported provide little information with regard to assessing the scope and impact of attacks."

CERT/CC provides a great deal of current threat analysis and future analysis in the computer security area. The website for CERT/CC is http://www.cert.org.

In the past, the computer industry hasn't taken the issue of computer security as seriously as it should. This attitude has caused a great deal of frustration on the part of users and administrators who are attempting to protect assets. The important thing to remember is that until recently, many software manufacturers have only paid lip service to the problem of operating system and application vulnerabilities. This leaves it to the administrator to be more proactive and identify their own weaknesses before they become problems.

 According to the Internet Storm Center (`http://isc.sans.org`), a computer connected to the Internet has an average of 5 minutes before it falls under some form of attack.

A penetration test is the best way to tell what services are really running on your system. *Penetration testing* involves trying to get access to your system from an attacker's perspective. Typically, you perform this test from a system on the Internet and try to see if you can break in or, at a minimum, get access to services running on your system.

Just short of penetration testing is *vulnerability testing.* In a vulnerability test, you typically run a software program that contains a database of known vulnerabilities against your system to identify weaknesses. You should consider obtaining a vulnerability scanner and running it across your network. A *vulnerability scanner* is a software application that checks your network for any known security holes; it's better to run one on your own network before someone outside the organization runs it against you. Some of the most well-known vulnerability scanners are Nessus (`http://www.nessus.org/ nessus/`) and Retina (`http://www.eeye.com/Retina`).

Both penetration testing and vulnerability scanning are addressed in the sections that follow. Also addressed are the issues of ethical hacking and various types/techniques of assessment.

Penetration Testing

As mentioned, the goal of penetration testing is to simulate an attack and look for holes that exist in order to be able to fix them. After the testing is done, the usual next step is to create a report detailing the finding and the risk of each along with suggestions for correction/mitigation. Regardless of the software used, or type of testing conducting, the steps to performing this include the following:

Verify a Threat Exists   You need to find the threats that the system is vulnerable to. This can include such things as open ports, unpatched software, weak passwords, and so on.

Bypass Security Controls   Check to see if it is possible to get around the security that you think is there. Standard security features that should stop an attacker include such things as intrusion detection systems, and you want to see if it is possible to enter the system without getting caught by the IDS.

Actively Test Security Controls   Security controls need to be constantly tested to verify that they catch/stop what they should. Even the slightest weakness can leave a hole through which an attacker can gain access and then begin looking for other accounts or holes that they can exploit further.

In the pursuit of infinitely creating acronyms, if the IDS works with wireless networks by scanning the air for unauthorized access points, it is known as WIDS (wireless intrusion detection system). If it can also take countermeasures, then instead of being IPS, it is known as WIPS (wireless intrusion prevention system). In fact, the National Institute of Standards and Technology (NIST) moved to a new naming convention for IDS/IPS. NIST combined the two acronyms into IDPS as the functionality of these systems greatly overlap. More can be learned about IDPS by visiting http://csrc.nist.gov/publications/nistpubs/800-94/SP800-94.pdf.

Exploit Vulnerabilities   Once a vulnerability is found, it is imperative to ascertain the extent to which it can be exploited. Will it allow only guest access, or is there a way it can be misused to allow root permission?

Vulnerability Scanning

Vulnerability scanning involves looking for weaknesses in networks, computers, or even applications. While the definition is much like that of penetration testing, there is usually one large difference: Penetration testing involves trying a number of things, while vulnerable scanning typically involves running a single program: a *vulnerability scanner.* The vulnerability scanner may be a port scanner (such as Nmap: http://nmap.org/), a network enumerator, a web application, or even a worm, but in all cases it runs tests on its target against a gamut of known vulnerabilities.

While Retina and Nessus are two of the better known vulnerability scanners, SAINT and OpenVAS (which was originally based on Nessus) are also widely used. Regardless of the tool, there are five major tasks necessary in using them that CompTIA wants you to know for the Security+ exam:

Passively Testing Security Controls   The vulnerability scanner can test the security controls without doing any actual harm. It looks only for the openings that are there and reports them back to you. As such, its testing is considered to be passive as opposed to active.

Interpreting Results   Once the results are found, they need to be interpreted. What, for example, does it mean that port 31337 is open (a popular user of this port is Back Orifice, discussed in Chapter 4)? Most of the vulnerability scanning programs, and in particular the commercial ones, interpret the results of their findings and deliver a report that can be shared with management.

Identifying Vulnerability   Just knowing that the port is open means little unless you can associate it with the vulnerability tied to it. For example, port 23 being open is a problem since it is commonly associated with Telnet.

Identifying Lack of Security Controls   Looking for weaknesses in security controls is well and good, but just as important is identifying areas where there are no controls in place. You want to know not just what is weak, but what is missing altogether.

Identifying Common Misconfigurations   All too often, problems are introduced when perfectly good applications and services are improperly configured. Those misconfigurations can allow more users to access an application than should, cause the application to crash, or introduce any of a number of other security concerns. In Exercise 11.1, I'll show you how to view the resultant set of policy in Windows 7.

<hr />

EXERCISE 11.1

Viewing the Resultant Set of Policy

Configuration settings occur at any number of places: They are set for a computer, they are set for a user, they are set for a local workstation, they are set for the domain, and so on. Often one of the big unknowns is which set of configuration settings takes precedence and which is overridden. It is possible to ascertain this on a Windows 7 workstation by following these steps:

1.   Click Start, and enter **RSOP.MSC**. This will start the Resultant Set of Policy management console.

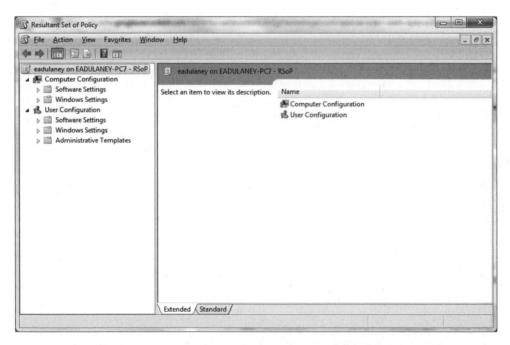

2.   Expand Windows Settings beneath Computer Configuration. Expand Security Settings and choose Account Policies and then Password Policy.

EXERCISE 11.1 *(continued)*

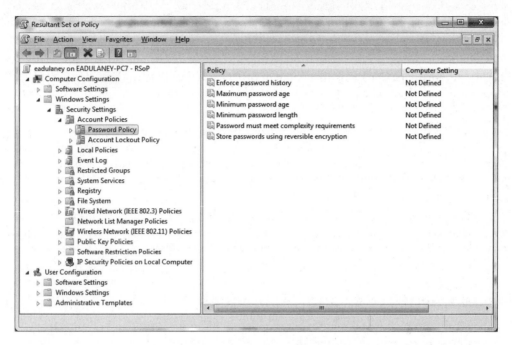

3. The values that are set here are the ones that are overriding all others. Make any changes you deem necessary; then exit the RSoP console.

Ethical Hacking

There are essentially three ways to approach penetration testing and vulnerability scanning, and the analogy of a box is used with each. In all cases, what a security administrator should attempt to do is identify vulnerabilities that exist in a system for which they have authorization—thus known as *ethical hacking*—but the way they approach it will differ. Here are the three most commonly recognized approaches taken in ethical hacking undertakings:

Black Box In *black box* testing, the administrator acts as if they have no prior knowledge of the network. They do not know what safeguards are in place, systems used, or any related information. They act as if they are an attacker from the outside with no familiarity of the system and look for an opening. In some circles, black box testing is also known as *blind* testing.

When conducting a black box test, traditionally only a bare minimum number of administrators are told that it is being done. In this way, others are not tipped off and able to act in a way other than what they would under normal circumstances.

White Box   At the opposite end of the spectrum from black box testing lays *white box* testing. Here, the ethical hacker begins from the premise of knowing something about the network and systems in place—just as a malicious insider would. They try to find a weakness armed with information about the source code, the routing, and so on, and this is also occasionally referred to as *full disclosure* testing.

Typical advantages of a white box attempt include reduced time and money since they are already starting with knowledge they would otherwise have to gain. Usually, technical support, human resources, and management need to be involved in a white box attempt in order to have the information needed to start.

Gray Box   Between black box and white box testing lies *gray box* testing (often written as *grey* box), also known as *partial disclosure* testing. Using this approach, the usual scenario trying to be re-created is that an outsider is working in conjunction with an insider who has given them some information. Because an insider is involved, a big question this approach addresses is what can an insider get to?

In all situations, the ideal contribution expected from the ethical hacker is the identification of problems and subsequent solutions for them. A number of certifications above Security+ are available in this field, and one worth considering if you have additional interests in this area is from EC-Council (`http://www.eccouncil.org`).

Assessment Types and Techniques

Chapter 1 discussed risk and focused on it in detail. From the standpoint of measuring security and vulnerability in the network, you need to focus on three things:

Risk   What is the actual danger under consideration? This is the likelihood of an attack being successful.

Threat   What are the likely causes associated with the risk? These are the means and source of the potential attack.

Vulnerability   Where is the system weak? Identify the flaws, the holes, the areas of exposure, and perils.

A number of generic techniques can prove useful in looking for risk, threat, and vulnerability, and this section looks at many of those. The following discussions focus on baseline reporting, code review, determining attack surface, architecture, and design review.

Baseline Reporting

The term *baseline reporting* became popular with legislation such as Sarbanes-Oxley, which requires IT to provide internal controls that reduce the risk of unauthorized transactions. As the name implies, baseline reporting checks to make sure things are operating status quo, and change detection is used to alert when modifications are made. A changes-from-baseline report can be run to quickly pinpoint security rule breaches.

This is often partnered with gap analysis to measure the controls at a particular company against industry standards. One tool popular for baseline reporting is CA Policy and Configuration Manager (`http://www.ca.com/`).

Code Review

The purpose of *code review* is to look at all custom written code for holes that may exist. The review needs to also examine changes that the code—most likely in the form of a finished application—may make: configuration files, libraries, and the like. During this examination, look for threats such as opportunities for injection to occur (SQL, LDAP, code, etc.), cross-site request forgery, and authentication.

Code review is often conducted as a part of gray box testing. Looking at source code can often be one of the easiest ways to find weaknesses within the application. Simply reading the code is known as *manual assessment*, while using tools to scan the code is known as *automated assessment*.

Determine Attack Surface

The *attack surface* of an application is the area of that application that is available to users—those who are authenticated and more importantly those who are not. As such, it can include the services, protocols, interfaces, and code. The smaller the attack surface, the less visible the application is to attack, and the larger the attack surface, the more likely it is to become a target. The goal of attack surface reduction (ASR) is to minimize the possibility of exploitation by reducing the amount of code and limiting potential damage. The potential damage can be limited by turning off unnecessary functions, reducing privileges, limiting entry points, and adding authentication requirements.

The attack surface concept can extend beyond an application to anywhere that problems may exist, and the word preceding it merely changes to identify the scope, for example: network attack surface, organization attack surface, and the like.

Architecture

An *architectural approach to security* involves using a control framework to focus on the foundational infrastructure. This approach is popular with security regulatory standards as well as compliance standards (such as ISO). One example of this approach is Cisco's SAFE (http://www.cisco.com/en/US/netsol/ns954/index.html).

The Security Control Framework is the backbone of SAFE, and unification is the underlying key (rather than a silo approach) to the security. By being modular, it can incorporate all parts of the network, including the WAN, the extranet, the Internet, and the intranet.

Design Review

The *design review* assessment examines the ports and protocols used, the rules, segmentation, and access control. It is recommended that you review the different models for information access control (Biba, Bell-LaPadula, and so on, discussed in Chapter 6).

Secure Network Administration Principles

To keep the network safe, there are a number of basic principles that you can apply. This section looks at a number of these, many of which have been discussed in passing in previous chapters since nothing exists as a silo. The topics include rule-based management, port security, working with 802.1X, flood guards, loop protection, preventing network bridging, and log analysis.

Rule-Based Management

Rule-based management, also known as *label-based* management, defines conditions for access to objects. The access is granted to the object based on both the object's sensitivity label and the user's sensitivity label. Most software packages that allow you to implement rule-based management divide correlation rules into two categories, system rules and custom rules, with the former being predefined out-of-the-box settings.

With all rules, an action must be defined. That action is triggered when conditions are/aren't met. Rule-based management, along with other forms of access control, was discussed in Chapter 5.

Port Security

Port security involves the Coast Guard keeping our seaports safe from terrorism. Not really. In the realm of IT, port security works at level 2 of the OSI model and allows an administrator to configure switch ports so that only certain MAC addresses can use the port. This is a common feature on both Cisco's Catalyst as well as Juniper's EX Series switches and essentially differentiates so-called dumb switches from managed (or intelligent) switches. Similarly, Dynamic ARP Inspection (DAI) works with these and other smart switches to protect ports from ARP spoofing.

Three areas of port security that CompTIA wants you to be familiar with for the Security+ exam are discussed here:

MAC Limiting and Filtering   Limit access to the network to MAC addresses that are known, and filter out those that are not. Even in a home network, you can implement MAC filtering with most routers and typically have an option of choosing to only allow computers with MAC addresses that you list or only deny computers with MAC addresses that you list.

 If you don't know a workstation's MAC address, use `ipconfig /all` to find it in the Windows-based world (it is listed as *physical address*) and use `ifconfig` in Unix/Linux.

MAC filtering is not foolproof, and a quick look in a search engine will turn up tools that can be used to change the MAC address and help miscreants circumvent this control.

802.1X   This is discussed in the following section, but adding port authentication to MAC filtering takes security for the network down to the switch port level and increases your security exponentially.

Disable Unused Ports   All ports not in use should be disabled. Otherwise, they present an open door for an attacker to enter.

Working with 802.1X

The IEEE standard 802.1X defines port-based security for wireless network access control. As such, it offers a means of authentication and defines the Extensible Authentication Protocol (EAP) over IEEE 802, discussed in Chapter 12, and is often known as *EAP over LAN* (EAPOL). The biggest benefit of using 802.1X is that the access points and the switches do not need to do the authentication but instead rely on the authentication server to do the actual work.

Flood Guards and Loop Protection

A *flood guard* is a protection feature built into many firewalls that allow the administrator to tweak the tolerance for unanswered login attacks. By reducing this tolerance, it is possible to reduce the likelihood of a successful DoS attack.

If a resource—inbound or outbound—appears to be overused, then the flood guard kicks in. With many Cisco firewalls, you can configure the same protection you apply at an upper level to be inherited by children as well in order to protect subgroups and devices.

Loop protection is a similar feature that works in layer 2 switching configurations and is intended to prevent broadcast loops. When configuring it in most systems, you can choose to disable broadcast forwarding and protect against duplicate ARP requests (those having the same target protocol address). The *Spanning Tree Protocol (STP)* is intended to ensure loop-free bridged Ethernet LANs. It operates at the data link layer and makes sure there is only one active path between two stations.

Preventing Network Bridging

Network bridging occurs when a device has more than one network adapter card installed and the opportunity presents itself for a user on one of the networks to which the device is attached to jump to the other. While multiple cards have been used in servers for years (known as multihomed hosts), it is not uncommon today to find multiple cards in laptops (wired and wireless) and the bridging to occur without the user truly understanding what is happening.

To prevent network bridging, you can configure your network such that when bridging is detected, you shut off/disable that jack. You can also create profiles that allow for only one interface.

At a micro level, you can configure workstations to disable connections not used. In Windows 7, for example, this is accomplished by choosing Start ➤ Control Panel ➤ Network And Internet ➤ Network Sharing Center and then clicking Change Adapter Settings. Right-clicking a connection will allow you to choose to disable that connection, as shown in Figure 11.1.

It is not uncommon for a network bridge to appear in the Network Sharing Center. If it does appear, you will want to delete it. Windows Internet Connection is often pointed to as a cause of unintended bridging and should be disabled.

FIGURE 11.1 Disabling a connection in Windows 7

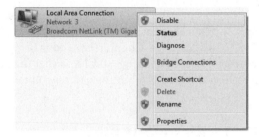

Log Analysis

Log analysis is crucial to identifying problems that occur related to security. As an administrator, you have the ability to turn on logging at many different locations and levels. The next step, however, is the most important—what you do with the log information collected. Far too many administrators turn on logging and then fail to properly (if ever) analyze what they collect because it is a lot of information and a lot of work.

A number of programs are available that can automate the log analysis, such as those from ManageEngine (`http://www.manageengine.com/it-compliance-suite.html`).

Not only do you need to collect and analyze the logs, but you also need to store them for a time in the future when you want to compare what is happening now to then (baselining). They should be stored in a format that you can quickly access and understand without having to convert them to a document each time you want to look at them.

Mitigation and Deterrent Techniques

Among the risk strategies that can be pursued, and that were discussed in Chapter 1, are mitigation and deterrence. This section looks at various techniques for implementing those strategies, including manual bypassing of electronic controls, monitoring system logs, security posture, reporting, and detection/prevention controls.

Manual Bypassing of Electronic Controls

It is always possible for something to crash, be it an application, a system, a safeguard, or almost anything else. When it does fail—either through a crash or someone bypassing the expected control path—there are two states that it can fail in: *failsafe* (secure) or *failopen* (not secure).

When using failsafe, the application stops all work, reports an error, and closes out/exits. Think of circuit breakers in your home; if they suspect anything might be wrong, they flip and stop all current from going through the circuit. In the case of the application, this will leave you frustrated and cursing because you have to start the application over, but it offers a level of security that the alternative will not.

 Real World Scenario

A Failopen Example

Assume that you have written an application that allows an administrator to enter a dozen usernames and password values. The application creates new user accounts for the dozen new users, sets their parameters to the standard new user settings, gives them the passwords you created, and exits. This fantastic application allows you to bypass the need to manually create the accounts or stay logged in for a long period of time at administrator level while you do this. What happens when your application crashes because one of the usernames contains a control character that you mistakenly entered?

To protect the system and its data, it would be far better if the application were not allowed to crash in a failopen state. This situation happens all too often, however, when *rapid application development (RAD)* is the software methodology employed since it favors rapid prototyping over extensive planning. One of the goals of *User Acceptance Testing (UAT)* is to review the software and sign off on it before accepting it and the risks it produces.

The alternative, known as failopen, is for the application to stop running and let you know that it encountered the unexpected character. You can slap your forehead, realize the mistake you made, enter what the character is supposed to be at a prompt, and the application will pick back up where it left off, continuing the process. The problem with this scenario is that when the application crashes, it stays running at the elevated privileges needed to make the changes and is susceptible to an attacker breaking out of it in order to do harm.

The choice of states to fail in is relevant not only to applications you create but also to firewalls (when the control fails, is all traffic blocked or allowed?), databases, and network appliances.

Monitoring System Logs

Log analysis was mentioned earlier in this chapter, and there are four logs that exist on most systems that CompTIA especially expects you to have knowledge of. These are event logs, security logs, access logs and audit logs. Before discussing them, however, it is important that you know how to use the main tool for this purpose that's included with most versions of Windows.

In Exercise 11.2, I'll show you how to view the *event logs* in Event Viewer.

View the Event Logs

Event Viewer has been the primary tool included with Windows for viewing log files for quite some time. The following exercise will walk through using this tool on a Windows 7 workstation:

1. Click Start ➤ Control Panel ➤ Administrative Tools ➤ Event Viewer.

2. Expand Windows Logs and choose System.

EXERCISE 11.2 *(continued)*

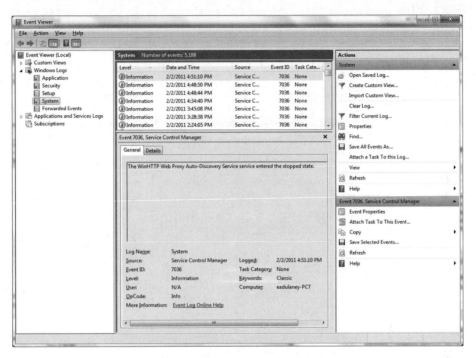

3. Click the heading for the Level field. This will alphabetize the list by the level type and should put Error messages above Information and other such messages.

EXERCISE 11.2 *(continued)*

4. Click an error message and read the details explaining it in the bottom part of the dialog box. If there is insufficient room in the bottom portion of the dialog box to read all of the details, double-clicking the event will open the properties for the event in a separate dialog box.

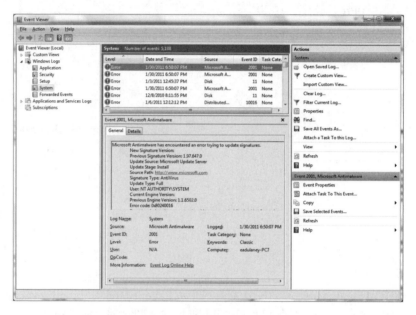

5. Click the link Event Log Online Help. A dialog box should appear asking if you want to send information across the Internet and displaying the information that will be sent. Click Yes.

6. Your browser will access the Microsoft TechNet site and display any other details about the event, including how to resolve it.

7. Exit the browser and exit Event Viewer.

The options within Event Viewer allow you to perform such actions as save the log file (.evt, .txt, or .csv format), open saved logs, filter the log file, and see/change properties. By clicking Properties, you can change the variables shown in Figure 11.2. The default is that the log files are overwritten as space is needed (the maximum size reached), but automatic archiving can be configured as well as the need for the administrator to manually clear logs.

FIGURE 11.2 Properties for the System log

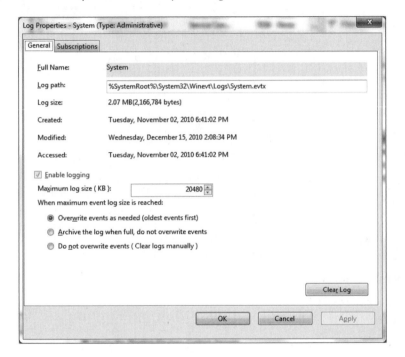

Security Logs/Access Logs

The Security Logs are accessed beneath Windows Logs in Event Viewer, and each event is preceded by either a key (audit success) or a lock (audit failure). For this log, it is recommended that you change the Maximum Log Size entry to as large as you can afford and select Do Not Overwrite Events. Each time you audit the log entries (at least weekly is recommended), choose to manually clear the file once you are certain there are no alarms you should respond to. In Windows, the Access log is the same as the Security log, since it documents who logged on and off of the system. I cannot stress enough that you should look at these logs periodically and not just when something goes wrong.

In the latest versions of Event Viewer, when looking at an event, you can configure a task to run in association with it, as shown in Figure 11.3. This can be used, for example, with a successful logon.

FIGURE 11.3 Assign a task to run with an event

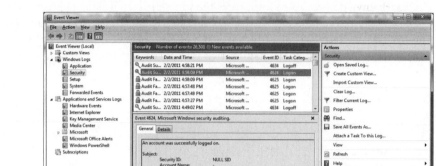

Clicking Attach Task To This Event brings up the Create Basic Task Wizard, as shown in Figure 11.4. Actions can be one of three things: start a program, send an email (useful for an unsuccessful login attempt), or display a message.

FIGURE 11.4 Creating the task

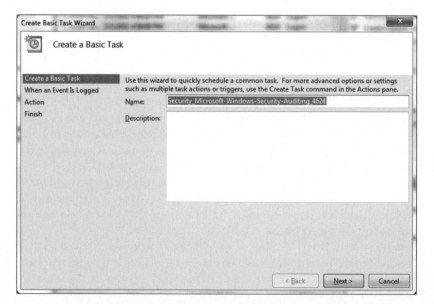

While this does not prevent the need for a more robust notification system, it does work well in small network environments.

 Once you've created a task, you can edit it within Task Scheduler (on the Administrative Tools menu).

Audit Logs

The log files created by crucial network services such as DNS need to be routinely examined regularly. The DNS service, when running on Windows Server 2008, for example, writes entries to the log file that can be examined using Event Viewer. Just as you set the size and overwrite options for the Security Log object, you should take those same actions for the DNS Server logs as well.

A firewall, whether software or hardware, often creates log files the same as most other services do when enabled. Given the importance of the firewall and its purpose, you should hold the entries written to those logs in high esteem and evaluate them regularly. You can create these log files anywhere a firewall is running, from a workstation to an appliance.

Most antivirus programs also create log files when they run that you should regularly check. You want to verify not only that the program is running but also that the definition file(s) being used is current. Pay attention to the viruses that are found and deleted/quarantined, as well as any files that are being skipped.

Security Posture

The *security posture* is the approach a business takes to security. This runs the entire gamut from the planning phase to implementation and everything in between: hardware, software, settings, and so on. An analogy for a security posture is an attitude—the attitude for how you value and view such things as company credit card numbers, client information, and such.

Some companies will perform a security posture assessment for you and report on such items as your vulnerabilities, weaknesses, and exposure to internal/external exploitation. In this regard, the security posture assessment is very much like a vulnerability test. Items it needs to include are discussed here:

Initial Baseline Configuration   The starting point needs to always be documented and used as the basis from which to begin making changes. Most evaluations include an examination of access controls, cryptography controls, integrity/auditing/monitoring controls, privacy policy, application standards, security policies, and configuration management.

Continuous Security Monitoring   Taking a snapshot of the situation at a moment in time fails to give sufficient authority, and it is important to always monitor the current environment.

Remediation   It is not enough to identify problems; you must also identify the solutions to those problems and act on them. This should include a subsequent follow-up to verify that the problem has been resolved.

Reporting

One item ubiquitous in every workplace is the report. Almost every department generates its own reports and uses what they find as a dashboard for action. The IT and Security departments are no different.

When it comes to analyzing or sharing security report information with others, you want to focus on three key areas: alarms, alerts, and trends. We'll explore each of these individually.

Alarms   Alarms are indications of a problem currently going on; think of a siren sounding when someone kicks in the door to a home. These are conditions that you must respond to right now. Alarm rates can indicate trends that are occurring, and after you solve the problem, you need to look for indications that the condition may not be isolated.

Alerts   Slightly below alarms are alerts; these are issues that you need to pay attention to but are not bringing the system to its knees at this very moment (think of them as tornado watches instead of tornado warnings). In Event Viewer, for example, system events are identified as either errors, information, or warnings. While errors are the most critical, the others need attention as well to keep them from eventually becoming errors.

Trends   Trends indicate where problems are occurring. By focusing on trends, you can identify weaknesses in your system and areas where you need to devote more resources to head off future problems.

Detection/Prevention Controls

One of the easiest ways to detect and prevent problems is to let people know that they are being monitored. In the online world, you can do this with messages that appear during login, regular communications, and so on. Not to be overlooked, however, is the physical world. Monitoring here can be done by either cameras or guards.

The *camera versus guard* debate is an old one and one that you must come to a conclusion on for your own environment. The benefit of a camera (a *closed-circuit television*, or *CCTV*) is that it is always running and can record everything it sees—creating evidence that can be admissible in court if necessary. On the other hand, it is stationary, lacks any sort of intelligence, is possible to be avoided, and needs someone to monitor the feed or review the tape (which many times does not happen until a problem has been discovered) to be effective.

The benefit of a guard is that the person can move about, apply intelligence to situations, and collect evidence. The guard, however, is not always recording, can be avoided, and can have more down time.

Where possible, you can combine guards with cameras to create a potent deterrent. The cameras can send signals to a room where they are monitored by a guard capable of responding to a situation when a need arises.

Summary

This chapter focused on issues related to your network's vulnerabilities and ways to identify/prevent them. We looked at penetration testing, as well as vulnerability scanning. The topic of ethical hacking was introduced, along with secure network principles and mitigation and deterrent techniques.

Penetration testing involves trying to get access to your system from an attacker's perspective. In a vulnerability test, you typically run a software program—a vulnerability scanner—that contains a database of known vulnerabilities against your system to identify weaknesses.

One of the approaches a security administrator can use to identify vulnerabilities that exist in a system for which they have authorization is known as ethical hacking. There are three approaches to this: black box, white box, and gray box.

Secure networking principles include rule-based management, port security, working with 802.1X, flood guards, loop protection, preventing network bridging, and log analysis.

Mitigation and deterrence techniques include manual bypassing of electronic controls, monitoring system logs, security posture, reporting, and detection/prevention controls.

Exam Essentials

Be able to describe penetration testing.   Penetration testing involves trying to get access to your system from an attacker's perspective.

Be able to differentiate between black, white, and gray box testing.   Black box testing assumes no prior knowledge about the network, while white box testing assumes that it is an insider (with knowledge) who may be trying to do harm. Gray box testing falls between the two extremes and works under the assumption that an outsider is able to access information from an insider. All three are methods of approaching ethical hacking.

Know the purpose of code review.   The purpose of code review is to look at all custom written code for holes that may exist. The review needs to also examine changes that the code—most likely in the form of a finished application—may make: configuration files, libraries, and the like.

Be able to define an attack surface.   The attack surface is the area available to users—those who are authenticated and, more importantly, those who are not. As such, it can include the services, protocols, interfaces, and code. The smaller the attack surface, the less visible the application is to attack, and the larger the attack surface, the more likely it is to become a target.

Know the difference between failsafe and failopen.   There are two states that an application can fail in. In a failsafe mode, the crash leaves the system secure. In a failopen state, the crash leaves the system exposed (not secure).

Review Questions

1. In which type of testing do you begin with the premise that the attacker has no knowledge of the network?

   A. Black box

   B. White box

   C. Gray box

   D. Green box

2. Which IEEE standard is often referred to as EAP over LAN?

   A. 802.1E

   B. 802.1Z

   C. 802.1Y

   D. 802.1X

3. Which log visible in Event Viewer shows successful and unsuccessful login attempts in Windows 7?

   A. System

   B. Security

   C. Audit

   D. Application

4. During what process do you look at all custom written applications for holes that may exist (in the form of the finished application, configuration files, libraries, and so on)?

   A. Network bridging

   B. Design review

   C. Code review

   D. Remediation

5. What are the two states that an application can fail in?

   A. Dependable

   B. Failsafe

   C. Failopen

   D. Assured

6. You want to implement MAC filtering on a small network but do not know the MAC
    address of a Linux-based workstation. Which command-line tool can you run on the
    workstation to find the MAC address?

    A. `ifconfig`

    B. `ifconfig /show`

    C. `ipconfig`

    D. `ipconfig /all`

7. Which of the following is a protection feature built into many firewalls that allow the
    administrator to tweak the tolerance for unanswered login attacks?

    A. MAC filter

    B. Flood guard

    C. MAC limiter

    D. Security posture

8. The goal of _____ is to minimize the possibility of exploitation by reducing the amount of
    code and limiting potential damage.

    A. EAPOL

    B. EAP

    C. ASR

    D. 802.1X

9. Which Windows workstation feature is accused of—sometimes inadvertently—making net-
    work bridging possible and introducing security concerns?

    A. Internet Connection Sharing

    B. Windows Firewall

    C. Network Address Translation

    D. Dynamic Naming Service

10. Which of the following is a software application that checks your network for any known
    security holes?

    A. Logic bomb

    B. Log analyzer

    C. Vulnerability scanner

    D. Design reviewer

11. In which type of testing do you begin with the premise that the attacker has inside knowl-
    edge of the network?

    A. Black box

    B. White box

    C. Gray box

    D. Green box

12. Rule-based management defines conditions for access to objects and is also known as:

   A. Distributed management

   B. Management by objective

   C. Role-based management

   D. Label-based management

13. Nessus is a tool that performs which security function?

   A. Vulnerability scanning

   B. Penetration testing

   C. Ethical hacking

   D. Loop protection

14. The approach a business takes to security is known as its:

   A. Rule-based management

   B. Network bridging

   C. Security posture

   D. Assessment technique

15. Which of the following is the area of an application that is available to users—those who are authenticated and more importantly those who are not?

   A. Exposed liability

   B. Attack surface

   C. Security weakness

   D. Susceptible claim

16. You want to implement MAC filtering on a small network but do not know the MAC address of a Windows-based workstation. Which command-line tool can you run on the workstation to find the MAC address?

   A. `ifconfig`

   B. `ifconfig /show`

   C. `ipconfig`

   D. `ipconfig /all`

17. Your manager has purchased a program intended to be used to find problems during code review. The program will read the code and look for any possible bugs or holes. What type of assessment is this known as?

   A. Mechanized

   B. Automated

   C. Programmed

   D. Manual

18. What checks to make sure that things are operating status quo and that change detection is used to alert when modifications are made?

A. Baseline reporting

B. Code review

C. Attack surfacing

D. Risk analysis

19. In which type of testing do you begin with the premise that an outsider attacker is being fed some knowledge from someone inside the network?

A. Black box

B. White box

C. Gray box

D. Green box

20. Which of the following involves trying to get access to your system from an attacker's perspective?

A. Loop recon

B. Flood gating

C. Vulnerability scanning

D. Penetration testing

Answers to Review Questions

1. A. With black box testing, you begin with the premise that the attacker has no knowledge of the network.

2. D. The IEEE standard 802.1X is often referred to as EAP over LAN. It defines port-based security for wireless network access control.

3. B. The Security log in Windows 7 (as well as in all versions of Windows) shows successful and unsuccessful login attempts and can be viewed with Event Viewer.

4. C. During a code review, you look at all custom written applications for holes that may exist (in the form of the finished application, configuration files, libraries, and the like).

5. B, C. There are two states that an application can fail in. In a failsafe mode, the crash leaves the system secure. In a failopen state, the crash leaves the system exposed (not secure).

6. A. The command `ifconfig` will show the MAC address on the Linux or Unix-based workstation.

7. B. A flood guard is a protection feature built into many firewalls that allow the administrator to tweak the tolerance for unanswered login attacks. By reducing this tolerance, it is possible to reduce the likelihood of a successful DoS attack.

8. C. The goal of attack surface reduction (ASR) is to minimize the possibility of exploitation by reducing the amount of code and limiting potential damage.

9. A. ICS—Internet Connection Sharing—is accused of (sometimes inadvertently) making network bridging possible and introducing security concerns.

10. C. A vulnerability scanner is a software application that checks your network for any known security holes.

11. B. With white box testing, you begin with the premise that the attacker has inside knowledge of the network.

12. D. Rule-based management, also known as label-based management, defines conditions for access to objects.

13. A. Nessus is one of the better-known vulnerability scanners.

14. C. The security posture is the approach a business takes to security.

15. B. The attack surface of an application is the area of an application that is available to users—those who are authenticated and more importantly those who are not.

16. D. The command `ipconfig /all` will show the MAC address as the physical address.

17. B. Simply reading the code is known as manual assessment, while using tools to scan the code is known as automated assessment.

18. A. Baseline reporting checks to make sure that things are operating status quo and that change detection is used to alert when modifications are made.

19. C. With gray box testing, you begin with the premise that an outsider attacker is being fed some knowledge from someone inside the network.

20. D. Penetration testing involves trying to get access to your system from an attacker's perspective.

Chapter

12

Wireless Networking Security

THE FOLLOWING COMPTIA SECURITY+ EXAM OBJECTIVES ARE COVERED IN THIS CHAPTER:

✓ **1.6 Implement wireless network in a secure manner.**

- WPA
- WPA2
- WEP
- EAP
- PEAP
- LEAP
- MAC filter
- SSID broadcast
- TKIP
- CCMP
- Antenna Placement
- Power level controls

✓ **3.4 Analyze and differentiate among types of wireless attacks.**

- Rogue access points
- Interference
- Evil twin
- War driving
- Bluejacking
- Bluesnarfing
- War chalking
- IV attack
- Packet sniffing

Wireless systems, plainly put, are systems that don't use wires to send information but rather transmit data through the air. The growth of wireless systems creates several opportunities for attackers. These systems are relatively new, they use well-established communications mechanisms, and they're easily intercepted.

This chapter discusses the various types of wireless systems that you'll encounter and mentions some of the security issues associated with this technology. Specifically, the systems deal with Wireless Transport Layer Security (WTLS), the IEEE 802 wireless standards, WPA2, WEP/WAP applications, and the vulnerabilities that each presents.

Working with Wireless Systems

The days of coax running through the room are past. More and more, we are moving to an environment where wireless is *the* networking topology of choice. To make that environment successful, and to pass the CompTIA exam, you need to understand the 802.11 standards that are applicable, as well as the technologies—the implementations of those standards—in use today.

This section looks at the protocols you need to know, as well as the transport layer implementation.

IEEE 802.11*x* Wireless Protocols

The *IEEE 802.11x* family of protocols provides for wireless communications using radio frequency transmissions. The frequencies in use for 802.11 standards are the 2.4GHz and the 5GHz frequency spectrum. Several standards and bandwidths have been defined for use in wireless environments, and—with the exception of 802.11a—tend to be compatible with each other:

802.11   The *802.11* standard defines wireless LANs transmitting at 1Mbps or 2Mbps bandwidths using the 2.4GHz frequency spectrum and using either frequency-hopping spread spectrum (FHSS) or direct-sequence spread spectrum (DSSS) for data encoding.

802.11a   The *802.11a* standard provides wireless LAN bandwidth of up to 54 Mbps in the 5GHz frequency spectrum. The 802.11a standard also uses orthogonal frequency division multiplexing (OFDM) for encoding rather than FHSS or DSSS.

802.11b   The *802.11b* standard provides for bandwidths of up to 11 Mbps (with fall-back rates of 5.5, 2, and 1 Mbps) in the 2.4GHz frequency spectrum. This standard is also called *Wi-Fi* or *802.11 high rate*. The 802.11b standard uses only DSSS for data encoding.

802.11g   The *802.11g* standard provides for bandwidths of up to 54 Mbps in the 2.4GHz frequency spectrum. While able to obtain faster speeds, it also suffers from the same inter-ference problems inherent with 802.11b—having to share the spectrum with other devices using that frequency.

802.11i   The *802.11i* standard provides for security enhancements to the wireless standard with particular focus on authentication. The standard is often referenced as WPA2, the name given it by the Wi-Fi Alliance.

802.11n   The *802.11n* standard provides for bandwidths of up to 300 Mbps in the 5GHz frequency spectrum (it can also communicate at 2.4GHz for compatibility). The advantage of this standard is that it offers higher speed and a frequency that does not have as much interference.

Most of the time, a wireless access point will work with more than one 802.11 standard. In Figure 12.1, for example, the Dell Wireless WLAN Card Utility shows that most of the networks this client is able to pick up a signal from are using 802.11b, 802.11g, and 802.11n.

FIGURE 12.1   A number of wireless networks are found, and most are using more than one 802.11 standard

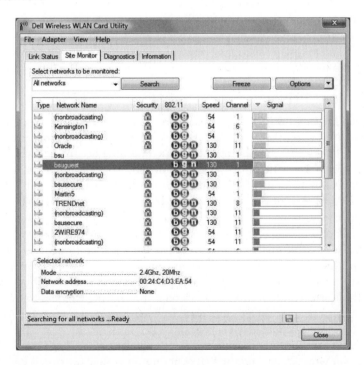

Three technologies are used to communicate in the 802.11 standard and provide backward compatibility with 802.11b:

Direct-Sequence Spread Spectrum   *Direct-sequence spread spectrum (DSSS)* accomplishes communication by adding the data that is to be transmitted to a higher-speed transmission. The higher-speed transmission contains redundant information to ensure data accuracy. Each packet can then be reconstructed in the event of a disruption.

Frequency-Hopping Spread Spectrum   *Frequency-hopping spread spectrum (FHSS)* accomplishes communication by hopping the transmission over a range of predefined frequencies. The changing or hopping is synchronized between both ends and appears to be a single transmission channel to both ends.

Orthogonal Frequency Division Multiplexing   *Orthogonal frequency division multiplexing (OFDM)* accomplishes communication by breaking the data into sub-signals and transmitting them simultaneously. These transmissions occur on different frequencies or sub-bands.

The mathematics and theories of these transmission technologies are beyond the scope of this book.

WEP/WAP/WPA/WPA2

Wired Equivalent Privacy (WEP) was intended to provide basic security for wireless networks, while wireless systems frequently use the Wireless Application Protocol (WAP) for network communications. Over time, WEP has been replaced in most implementations by WPA and WPA2. The following sections briefly discuss these terms and provide you with an understanding of their relative capabilities.

Wired Equivalent Privacy

Wired Equivalent Privacy (WEP) is a wireless protocol designed to provide privacy equivalent to that of a wired network. WEP is implemented in a number of wireless devices, including PDAs and cell phones. WEP is vulnerable because of weaknesses in the way the encryption algorithms (RC4) are employed. These weaknesses allow the algorithm to potentially be cracked in as few as five minutes using available PC software. This makes WEP one of the more vulnerable protocols available for security.

As an example, the initialization vector (IV) that WEP uses for encryption is 24-bit, which is quite weak and means that IVs are reused with the same key. By examining the repeating result, it is easy for miscreants to crack the WEP secret key; this is known as an *IV attack*. To put it in perspective, the attack happens because the algorithm used is RC4, the IV is too small, the IV is static, and the IV is part of the RC4 encryption key.

Figure 12.2 shows the configuration settings on a very simple wireless router and sums up the situation best: The only time to use WEP is when you must have compatibility with older devices that do not support new encryption.

To make the encryption stronger, *Temporal Key Integrity Protocol (TKIP)* was employed. This places a 128-bit wrapper around the WEP encryption with a key that is based on such things as the MAC address of your machine and the serial number of the packet. TKIP was designed as a backward-compatible replacement to WEP and could use all existing hardware. Without the use of TKIP, WEP—as mentioned earlier in this chapter—is considered weak. It is worth noting, however, that even TKIP has been broken.

FIGURE 12.2   Wireless security settings for a simple router

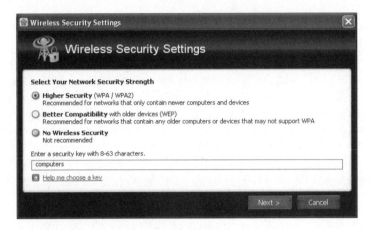

Wireless Application Protocol

The Wireless Application Protocol (WAP) is the technology designed for use with wireless devices. WAP has become a standard adopted by many manufacturers, including Motorola and Nokia. WAP functions are equivalent to TCP/IP functions in that they're trying to serve the same purpose for wireless devices. WAP uses a smaller version of HTML called *Wireless Markup Language (WML)*, which is used for Internet displays. WAP-enabled devices can also respond to scripts using an environment called *WMLScript*. This scripting language is similar to Java, which is a programming language.

The ability to accept web pages and scripts produces the opportunity for malicious code and viruses to be transported to WAP-enabled devices. No doubt this will create a new set of problems, and antivirus software will be needed to deal with them.

WAP systems communicate using a WAP gateway system, as depicted in Figure 12.3. The gateway converts information back and forth between HTTP and WAP as well as encodes and decodes between the protocols.

FIGURE 12.3   A WAP gateway enabling a connection to WAP devices by the Internet

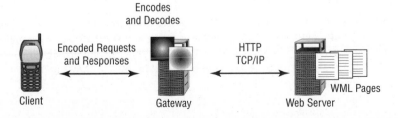

This structure provides a reasonable assurance that WAP-enabled devices can be secured. If the interconnection between the WAP server and the Internet isn't encrypted, packets between the devices may be intercepted (which is referred to as *packet sniffing*), creating a potential vulnerability. This vulnerability is called a *gap in the WAP* (the security concern that exists when converting between WAP and SSL/TLS) and was prevalent in versions of WAP prior to 2.0.

Wi-Fi Protected Access and WPA2

The *Wi-Fi Protected Access (WPA)* and Wi-Fi Protected Access 2 (WPA2) technologies were designed to address the core problems with WEP. These technologies were created to implement the 802.11i standard. The difference between WPA and WPA2 is that the former implements most—but not all—of 802.11i in order to be able to communicate with older wireless cards (which might still need an update through their firmware in order to be compliant) and it used the RC4 encryption algorithm with TKIP, while WPA2 implements the full standard and is not compatible with older cards.

WPA also mandates the use of TKIP, while WPA2 favors *Counter Mode with Cipher Block Chaining Message Authentication Code Protocol (CCMP)*. CCMP uses 128-bit AES encryption with a 48-bit initialization vector. With the larger initialization vector, it increases the difficulty in cracking and minimizes the risk of replay.

As a simplified timeline useful for exam study, think of WEP as coming first. It was fraught with errors and WPA (with TKIP) was used as an intermediate solution, implementing a portion of the 802.11i standard. The final solution—a full implementation of the 802.11i standard—is WPA2 (with CCMP).

Wireless Transport Layer Security

Wireless Transport Layer Security (WTLS) is the security layer of the Wireless Application Protocol, discussed in the section "WEP/WAP/WPA/WPA2." WTLS provides authentication, encryption, and data integrity for wireless devices. It's designed to utilize the relatively narrow bandwidth of these types of devices and is moderately secure. WTLS provides reasonable security for mobile devices, and it's being widely implemented in wireless devices.

Wireless Transport Layer Security provides an encrypted and authenticated connection between a wireless client and a server. WTLS is similar in function to TLS, but it uses a lower bandwidth and less processing power. It's used to support wireless devices, which don't yet have extremely powerful processors.

Figure 12.4 illustrates WTLS as part of the WAP environment. WAP provides the functional equivalent of TCP/IP for wireless devices. Many devices, including newer cell phones and PDAs, include support for WTLS as part of their networking protocol capabilities.

Communication between a WAP handset and WAP server is protected by WTLS. Once on the Internet, a connection is typically protected by the Secure Socket Layer (SSL), an Internet standard for encrypting data between points on the network.

FIGURE 12.4   WTLS used between two WAP devices

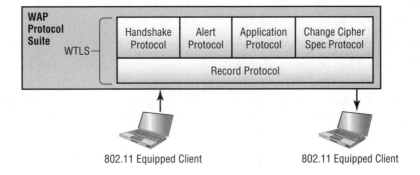

Understanding Mobile Devices

Mobile devices, including smartphones, e-readers, tablet computers, and personal digital assistants (PDAs), are popular. Many of these devices use either RF signaling or cellular technologies for communication. Figure 12.5, for example, shows an Amazon Kindle looking for wireless networks.

FIGURE 12.5   Wireless scanning is done by a wide variety of devices such as the Kindle.

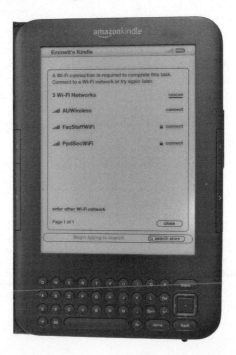

If the device uses the Wireless Application Protocol (WAP), the device in all likelihood doesn't have security enabled. Several levels of security exist in WAP:

Anonymous Authentication   This allows virtually anyone to connect to the wireless portal.

Server Authentication   This requires the workstation to authenticate against the server.

Two-Way (Client and Server) Authentication   This requires both ends of the connection (client and server) to authenticate to confirm validity.

Many new wireless devices are also capable of using certificates to verify authentication. Figure 12.6 shows a mobile systems network; this network uses both encryption and authentication to increase security.

FIGURE 12.6   A mobile environment using WAP security

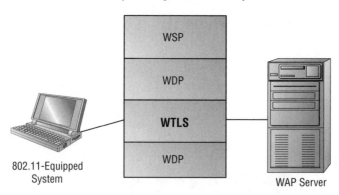

Security is managed at the WTLS layer.

802.11-Equipped System

WAP Server

The following are the technologies used to provide services between the devices:

Wireless Session Protocol (WSP)   This manages the session information and connection between the devices.

Wireless Transaction Protocol (WTP)   This provides services similar to TCP and UDP for WAP.

Wireless Datagram Protocol (WDP)   This provides the common interface between devices.

Wireless Transport Layer Security (WTLS)   This is the security layer of the Wireless Application Protocol.

Wireless Access Points

It does not take much to build a wireless network. On the client side, you need a wireless network interface card (NIC) in place of the standard wired NIC. On the network side, you need something to communicate with the clients.

The primary method of connecting a wireless device to a network is via a wireless portal. A *wireless access point* (commonly just called an access point or AP) is a low-power transmitter/receiver, also known as a *transceiver*, which is strategically placed for access. The portable device and the access point communicate using one of several communications protocols, including *IEEE 802.11* (also known as Wi-Fi).

Wireless communications, as the name implies, don't use wires as the basis for communication. Most frequently, they use a portion of the *radio frequency (RF)* spectrum called *microwave*. Wireless communication methods are becoming more prevalent in computing because the cost of the transmitting and receiving equipment has fallen drastically over the last few years. Wireless also offers mobile connectivity within a campus, a building, or even a city. Most wireless frequencies are shared frequencies in that more than one person may be using the same frequency for communication.

Figure 12.7 illustrates a wireless portal being used to connect a computer to a company network. Notice that the portal connects to the network and is treated like any other connection used in the network.

Wireless communications, although convenient, can also be less than secure. While many APs now ship with encryption turned on, you will still want to verify that this is the case with your network. In Figure 12.1, it is possible to see that bsu and bsuguest are not utilizing security. Figure 12.8 shows a received packet from an unsecure network, while Figure 12.9 shows the information received from a network that has security enabled. Notice the list of protocols in the lower half of Figure 12.9.

FIGURE 12.7   Wireless access portal and workstation

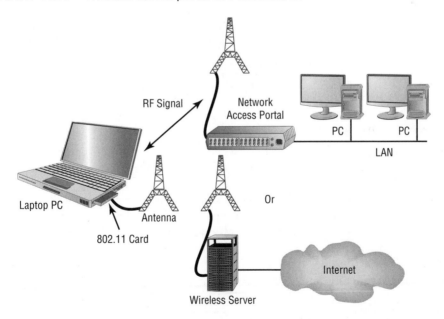

FIGURE 12.8   Data from an unsecure network

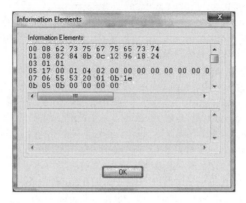

FIGURE 12.9   Data from a secure network

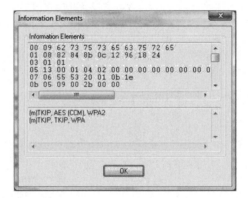

Antenna Placement

Antenna placement can be crucial in allowing clients to reach the access point. There isn't any one universal solution to this issue, and it depends on the environment in which the access point is placed. As a general rule, the greater the distance the signal must travel, the more it will attenuate, but you can lose a signal quickly in a short space as well if the building materials reflect or absorb the signal. You should try to avoid placing access points near metal (which includes appliances) or near the ground. In the center of the area to be served and high enough to get around most obstacles is recommended. On the chance that the signal is actually traveling too far, some access points include *power level controls* that allow you to reduce the amount of output provided.

Real World Scenario

Estimating Signal Strength

One of the most troublesome aspects of working with wireless networks is trying to compute the strength of the signal between the wireless AP and the client(s). It's often joked that a hacker can stand outside a building and tap into your network but a user within the building can't get a strong enough signal to stay on the network.

Think of the signal in terms of any other radio signal—its strength is reduced significantly by cinderblock walls, metal cabinets, and other barriers. The signal can pass through glass windows and thin walls with no difficulty.

When you're laying out a network, it's highly recommended that you install a strength meter on a workstation—many are free to download—and use it to evaluate the intensity of the signal you're receiving. If the signal is weak, you can add additional APs and repeaters to the network, just as you would on a wired network.

A great source for information on RF power values and antenna can be found on the Cisco site at

```
http://www.cisco.com/en/US/tech/tk722/tk809/
technologies_tech_note09186a00800e90fe.shtml
```

MAC Filtering

Most APs offer the ability to turn on *MAC filtering*, but it is off by default. The MAC address is the unique identifier that exists for each network card (part of the hexadecimal address identifies the manufacturer, and the other part acts as a serial number). In the default stage, any wireless client that knows the values looked for can join the network. When MAC filtering is used, the administrator compiles a list of the MAC addresses associated with the users' computers and enters those. When a client attempts to connect, and other values have been correctly entered, an additional check of the MAC address is done. If the address appears in the list, the client is allowed to join; otherwise it is forbidden from so doing. On a number of wireless devices, the term *network lock* is used in place of MAC filtering, and the two are synonymous.

The weakness with MAC filtering is that the MAC address is a value that a miscreant could spoof in order to gain entry. By making it look as if their illegitimate host is a legitimate host, they will pass through the filter and be allowed access.

In Exercise 12.1, I'll show you how to change the order of preferred networks in Windows Vista. Preferred networks are limited in Windows 7 and Windows Vista to networks that you have successfully connected to.

EXERCISE 12.1

Change the Order of Preferred Networks

Most wireless clients are able to receive signals from, and connect to, more than one wireless network. If one wireless network is not available, the connection will often drop down to the next in this list, and thus it is important to have the wireless networks on the client in the order in which you want them to attempt connection. The following exercise will allow changes to this order:

1. On a Windows Vista client click the Windows button, type **Network and Sharing Center** into the search bar, and press Enter.

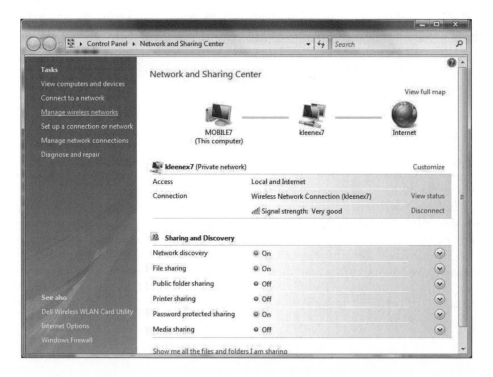

EXERCISE 12.1 *(continued)*

2. Choose Manage Wireless Networks.

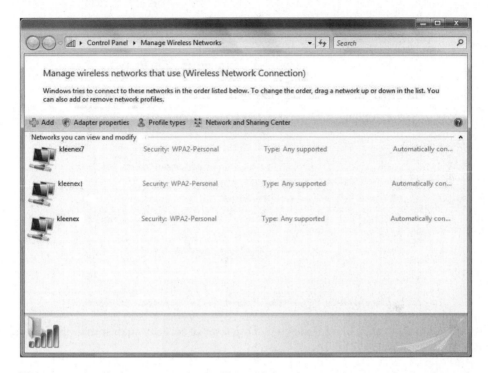

3. Click any network that appears in the list, and drag it up or down to change the order of the preferred networks.

4. Exit out of Manage Wireless Networks.

5. Exit the Network and Sharing Center.

Extensible Authentication Protocol

Extensible Authentication Protocol (EAP) provides a framework for authentication that is often used with wireless networks. Among the five EAP types adopted by the WPA/WPA2 standard are EAP-TLS, EAP-PSK, EAP-MD5, and two that you need to know for the exam: LEAP and PEAP. Figure 12.10 shows that the configuration information on a WLAN card is using EAP-TTLS; this is a form of EAP-TLS that adds tunneling (Extensible Authentication Protocol—Tunneled Transport Layer Security).

FIGURE 12.10 Using EAP-TTLS on a wireless network

By adding the tunneling, TTLS adds one more layer of security against man-in-the-middle attacks or eavesdropping.

Lightweight Extensible Authentication Protocol

Lightweight Extensible Authentication Protocol (LEAP) was created by Cisco as an extension to EAP but is being phased out in favor of PEAP. Because it is a proprietary protocol to Cisco and created only as a quick fix for problems with WEP, it lacks native Windows support.

LEAP requires mutual authentication to improve security but is susceptible to dictionary attacks. It is considered a weak EAP protocol, and Cisco does not currently recommend using it.

An excellent white paper on wireless LAN security from Cisco that discusses LEAP architecture can be found at http://www.cisco.com/en/US/prod/collateral/wireless/ps5678/ps430/ps4076/prod_white_paper09186a00800b469f_ps4570_Products_White_Paper.html.

Protected Extensible Authentication Protocol

Protected Extensible Authentication Protocol (PEAP) was created by Cisco, RSA, and Microsoft. It replaces LEAP and there is native support for it in Windows (which previously favored EAP-TLS) beginning with Windows XP. There is support for it in all Windows operating systems since then, including Windows Vista and Windows 7.

While many consider PEAP and EAP-TTLS to be similar options, PEAP is more secure since it establishes an encrypted channel between the server and the client.

> The same Cisco white paper on wireless LAN security discussing LEAP outlines the PEAP authentication process and can be found at http://www.cisco.com/en/US/prod/collateral/wireless/ps5678/ps430/ps4076/prod_white_paper09186a00800b469f_ps4570_Products_White_Paper.html.

Wireless Vulnerabilities to Know

Wireless systems are vulnerable to all the different attacks that wired networks are vulnerable to. However, because these protocols use radio frequency signals for *data emanation*, they have an additional weakness: All radio frequency signals can be easily intercepted. To intercept 802.11*x* traffic, all you need is a PC with an appropriate 802.11*x* card installed. Many networks will regularly broadcast their name (known as an *SSID broadcast*) to announce their presence. Simple software on the PC can capture the link traffic in the wireless AP and then process this data in order to decrypt account and password information.

> One method of "protecting" the network that is often recommended is to turn off the SSID broadcast. The access point is still there and can still be accessed by those who know of it, but it prevents those who are just scanning from finding it. This should be considered a *very* weak form of security because there are still other ways, albeit a bit more complicated, to discover the presence of the access point besides the SSID broadcast.

In Exercise 12.2, I'll show you how to configure Windows Vista to connect to a network not broadcasting an SSID.

EXERCISE 12.2

Configure a Wireless Connection Not Broadcasting

To configure the client to connect to a network even if the SSID is not broadcasting, follow these steps:

1. On a Windows Vista client, right-click the network icon and choose Connect To A Network.

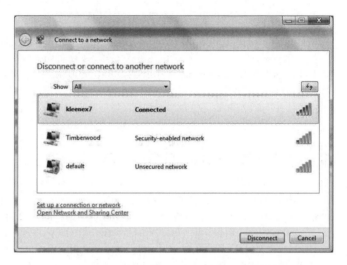

2. Right-click the network you are connected to and choose Properties.

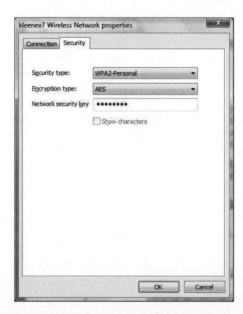

EXERCISE 12.2 *(continued)*

3.   Choose the Connection tab and check the box Connect Even If The Network Is Not Broadcasting.

4.   Click OK.

5.   Exit from the Connect To A Network dialog box.

An additional aspect of wireless systems is the *site survey*. Site surveys involve listening in on an existing wireless network using commercially available technologies. Doing so allows intelligence, and possibly data capture, to be performed on systems in your wireless network.

The term *site survey* initially meant determining whether a proposed location was free from interference. When used by an attacker, a site survey can determine what types of systems are in use, the protocols used, and other critical information about your network. It's the primary method used to gather data about wireless networks. Virtually all wireless networks are vulnerable to site surveys.

If wireless portals are installed in a building, the signals will frequently radiate past the inside of the building, and they can be detected and decoded outside the building using inexpensive equipment. The term *war driving* refers to driving around town with a laptop looking for APs that can be communicated with. The network card on the laptop is set to promiscuous mode, and it looks for signals coming from anywhere. After intruders gain access, they may steal Internet access or corrupt your data.

Once weaknesses have been discovered in a wireless network, *warchalking* (referenced by CompTIA as two words: "war chalking") can occur. Warchalking involves those who discover a way into the network leaving signals (often written in chalk) on, or outside, the premise to notify others that the vulnerability is there. The marks can be on the sidewalk, the side of the building, a nearby signpost, and so on and resemble those shown in Figure 12.11. Figure 12.12 shows an example of what would be present for an open node.

FIGURE 12.11   The warchalking symbols

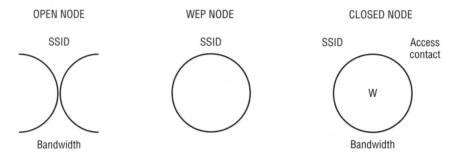

FIGURE 12.12   An example of an open node symbol

Weak encryption was an issue with earlier access points, but most of the newer wireless controllers use special ID numbers (SSID) and must be configured in the network cards to allow communications. However, using ID number configurations doesn't necessarily prevent wireless networks from being monitored, and one particularly mischievous undertaking involves taking advantage of *rogue access points*. Any wireless access point added to your network that has not been authorized is considered a rogue.

The rogue may be added by an attacker, or could have been innocently added by a user wanting to enhance their environment—the problem with the user doing so is that there is a good chance they will not implement the security you would, and this could open the system for a man-in-the-middle attack or *evil twin attack*. An evil twin attack is one in which a rogue wireless access point poses as a legitimate wireless service provider to intercept information users transmit.

Educate and train users about the wireless network and the need to keep it secure, just as you would train and educate them about any other security topic. They may think there is no harm in them joining any wireless network they can find as they travel, such as those shown in Figure 12.13, but you should question whether the administrators for *Where the party at* really have the best interest of your company data at heart.

FIGURE 12.13   An example of some questionable wireless networks available for users to connect to

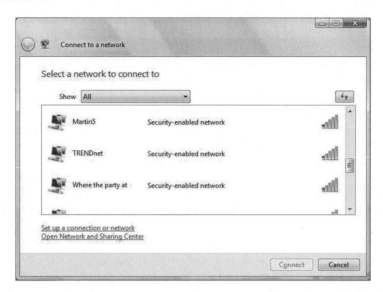

Be sure to change the default settings on all wireless devices. Never assume that a wireless connection is secure. The emissions from a wireless portal may be detectable through walls and for several blocks from the portal. Interception is easy to accomplish, given that RF is the medium used for communication. Newer wireless devices offer data security, and you should use it. You can set newer APs and wireless routers to non-broadcast in addition to configuring WPA2 and a higher encryption level.

With the popularity of Bluetooth on the rise, two additional vulnerabilities have been added: *bluejacking* and *bluesnarfing*. Bluejacking is the sending of unsolicited messages (think spam) over the Bluetooth connection. While annoying, it is basically considered harmless. Bluetooth is often used for creating personal area networks (PANs), and most Bluetooth devices come with a factory default PIN that you will want to change to more secure values.

Bluesnarfing is the gaining of unauthorized access through a Bluetooth connection. This access can be gained through a phone, PDA, or any device using Bluetooth. Once access has been gained, the attacker can copy any data in the same way they would with any other unauthorized access.

The Bluetooth standard has addressed weaknesses in the technology, and it continues to get more secure. One of the simplest ways to secure Bluetooth devices is to not set their attribute to Discoverable.

Summary

Wireless systems are becoming increasingly popular and standardized. The most common protocol implemented in wireless systems is WAP. The security layer for WAP is WTLS. WAP is equivalent to TCP/IP for wireless systems.

The standards for wireless systems are developed by the IEEE. The most common standards are 802.11, 802.11a, 802.11b, 802.11i, 802.11g, and 802.11n. These standards use the 2.4GHz or 5GHz frequency spectrum with the exception of 802.11i which is a security standard often referred to as WPA2. Several communications technologies are available to send messages between wireless devices.

Wireless networks are vulnerable to site surveys. Site surveys can be accomplished using a PC and an 802.11x card. The term *site survey* is also used in reference to detecting interference in a given area that might prevent 802.11x from working.

There are a number of security standards for wireless networking, with WEP (Wired Equivalent Privacy) being the first widely used. It was fraught with errors and replaced in most implementations by WPA (Wi-Fi Protected Access), which used TKIP. This was an intermediate solution that implemented only a portion of the 802.11i standard. The final solution—a full implementation of the 802.11i standard—is WPA2, which uses CCMP.

Vulnerabilities exist because of weaknesses in the protocols. As an example, WEP is vulnerable because of weaknesses in the way the encryption algorithms are employed; the initialization vector (IV) that WEP uses for encryption is 24-bit and IVs are reused with the same key. By examining the repeating result, it is easy for miscreants to crack the WEP secret key, known as using an IV attack.

Mobile devices use either RF signaling or cellular technologies for communication. If the device uses WAP, several levels of security exist: anonymous authentication (anyone can connect), server authentication (the workstation must authenticate against the server), and two-way authentication (both the client and server must authenticate with each other).

Exam Essentials

Know the protocols and components of a wireless system.   The backbone of most wireless systems is WAP. WAP can use WEP to provide security in a wireless environment. WTLS is the security layer of WAP. WAP and TCP/IP perform similarly.

Know the hardware used in a wireless network.   The wireless access point (AP) sits on the wired network and then acts as the router for the wireless clients. Most of the time, a wireless access point will work with more than one 802.11 standard. Wireless clients, using a wireless NIC card, connect to the access point.

Know the capabilities and limitations of the 802.11x network standards.   The current standards for wireless protocols are 802.11, 802.11a, 802.11b, and 802.11g. The 802.11n standard is undergoing review and isn't yet a formal standard.

Know the vulnerabilities of wireless networks.   The primary method of gaining information about a wireless network is a site survey. Site surveys can be accomplished with a PC and an 802.11 card. Wireless networks are subject to the same attacks as wired networks.

Know the wireless security protocols.   The 802.11i standard is often referenced as WPA2. It is an enhancement to earlier standards such as WEP (Wired Equivalent Privacy) and WPA (Wi-Fi Protected Access), which were much weaker.

Review Questions

1. Which protocol is mainly used to enable access to the Internet from a mobile phone or PDA?

   A. WEP

   B. WTLS

   C. WAP

   D. WOP

2. Which protocol operates on 2.4GHz and has a bandwidth of 1 Mbps or 2 Mbps?

   A. 802.11

   B. 802.11a

   C. 802.11b

   D. 802.11g

3. You're outlining your plans for implementing a wireless network to upper management. Suddenly, a paranoid vice president brings up the question of security. Which protocol was designed to provide security to a wireless network and can be considered equivalent to the security of a wired network?

   A. WAP

   B. WTLS

   C. WPA2

   D. IR

4. Which of the following is a primary vulnerability of a wireless environment?

   A. Decryption software

   B. IP spoofing

   C. A gap in the WAP

   D. Site survey

5. Which of the following is synonymous with MAC filtering?

   A. TKIP

   B. Network lock

   C. EAP-TTLS

   D. MAC secure

6. Which of the following 802.11 standards is often referenced as WPA2?

   A. 802.11a

   B. 802.11b

   C. 802.11i

   D. 802.11n

7. Which of the following 802.11 standards provides for bandwidths of up to 300 Mbps?

   A. 802.11n

   B. 802.11i

   C. 802.11g

   D. 802.11b

8. An IV attack is usually associated with which of the following wireless protocols?

   A. WEP

   B. WAP

   C. WPA

   D. WPA2

9. Which type of encryption does CCMP use?

   A. EAP

   B. DES

   C. AES

   D. IV

10. Which encryption technology is associated with WPA?

    A. TKIP

    B. CCMP

    C. WEP

    D. LDAP

11. Which of the following is not one of the three transmission technologies used to communicate in the 802.11 standard?

    A. DSSS

    B. FHSS

    C. VITA

    D. OFDM

12. What is the size of the initialization vector (IV) that WEP uses for encryption?

    A. 6-bit

    B. 24-bit

    C. 56-bit

    D. 128-bit

13. Which of the following is a script language WAP-enabled devices can respond to?

    A. WXML

    B. Winsock

    C. WIScript

    D. WMLScript

14. Which of the following authentication levels with WAP requires both ends of the connection to authenticate to confirm validity?

A. Relaxed

B. Two-way

C. Server

D. Anonymous

15. Which of the following manages the session information and connection between wireless devices?

A. WSP

B. WPD

C. WPT

D. WMD

16. Which of the following provides services similar to TCP and UDP for WAP?

A. WTLS

B. WDP

C. WTP

D. WFMD

17. Which of the following authentication levels with WAP allows virtually anyone to connect to the wireless portal?

A. Relaxed

B. Two-way

C. Server

D. Anonymous

18. If the interconnection between the WAP server and the Internet isn't encrypted, packets between the devices may be intercepted. What is this vulnerability known as?

A. Packet sniffing

B. Minding the gap

C. Middle man

D. Broken promise

19. WAP uses a smaller version of HTML for Internet displays. This is known as:

A. DSL

B. HSL

C. WML

D. OFML

20. What is the size of the wrapper TKIP places around the WEP encryption with a key that is based on such things as the MAC address of your machine and the serial number of the packet?

    A.   128-bit

    B.   64-bit

    C.   56-bit

    D.   12-bit

Answers to Review Questions

1. C. Wireless Application Protocol (WAP) is an open international standard for applications that use wireless communication.

2. A. 802.11 operates on 2.4GHZ. This standard allows for bandwidths of 1 Mbps or 2 Mbps.

3. C. Wi-Fi Protected Access 2 (WPA2) was intended to provide security that's equivalent to the security on a wired network and implements elements of the 802.11i standard.

4. D. A site survey is the process of monitoring a wireless network using a computer, wireless controller, and analysis software. Site surveys are easily accomplished and hard to detect.

5. B. The term *network lock* is synonymous with MAC filtering.

6. C. The WPA2 standard is also known as 802.11i.

7. A. The 802.11n standard provides for bandwidths of up to 300Mbps.

8. A. An IV attack is usually associated with the WEP wireless protocol.

9. C. CCMP uses 128-bit AES encryption.

10. A. The encryption technology associated with WPA is TKIP.

11. C. The three technologies available for use with the 802.11 standard are DSSS (direct-sequence spread spectrum), FHSS (frequency-hopping spread spectrum), and OFDM (orthogonal frequency division multiplexing). VITA (Volunteer Income Tax Assistance) is not a wireless transmission technology.

12. B. The initialization vector (IV) that WEP uses for encryption is 24-bit.

13. D. WAP-enabled devices can respond to scripts using an environment called WMLScript.

14. B. Two-way authentication requires both ends of the connection to authenticate to confirm validity.

15. A. WSP (Wireless Session Protocol) manages the session information and connection between wireless devices.

16. C. The Wireless Transaction Protocol (WTP) provides services similar to TCP and UDP for WAP.

17. D. Anonymous authentication allows virtually anyone to connect to the wireless portal.

18. A. If the interconnection between the WAP server and the Internet isn't encrypted, packets between the devices may be intercepted and this is known as packet sniffing.

19. C. WAP uses a smaller version of HTML called Wireless Markup Language (WML) for Internet displays.

20. A. TKIP places a 128-bit wrapper around the WEP encryption with a key that is based on such things as the MAC address of your machine and the serial number of the packet.

Chapter
13

Disaster Recovery and Incident Response

THE FOLLOWING COMPTIA SECURITY+ EXAM OBJECTIVES ARE COVERED IN THIS CHAPTER:

✓ **2.3 Execute appropriate incident response procedures.**

- Basic forensic procedures: Order of volatility; Capture system image; Network traffic and logs; Capture video; Record time offset; Take hashes; Screenshots; Witnesses; Track man hours and expense

- Damage and loss control

- Chain of custody

- Incident response: first responder

✓ **2.5 Compare and contrast aspects of business continuity.**

- Business impact analysis

- Removing single points of failure

- Business continuity planning and testing

- Continuity of operations

- Disaster recovery

- IT contingency planning

- Succession planning

✓ **2.7 Execute disaster recovery plans and procedures.**

- Backup / backout contingency plans or policies

- Backups, execution, and frequency

- Redundancy and fault tolerance: Hardware; RAID; Clustering; Load balancing; Servers

- High availability

- Cold site, hot site, warm site

- Mean time to restore, mean time between failures, recovery time objectives and recovery point objectives

As a security professional, you must strive not only to prevent losses but also to make contingency plans for recovering from any losses that do occur. This chapter deals with the crucial aspects of business continuity and vendor support from an operations perspective. It also looks at incident response and the basic forensic procedures you would be familiar with. A solid grasp of these concepts will help you prepare for the exam because they appear in multiple objectives. It will also help you become a more proficient and professional security team member. The process of working with, helping to design, and maintaining security in your organization is a tough job. It requires dedication, vigilance, and a sense of duty to your organization.

Understanding Business Continuity

One of the oldest phrases still in use today is "the show must go on." Nowhere is that more true than in the world of business, where downtime means the loss of significant revenue with each passing minute. Business continuity is primarily concerned with the processes, policies, and methods that an organization follows to minimize the impact of a system failure, network failure, or the failure of any key component needed for operation—essentially, whatever it takes to ensure that the business continues, that the show does indeed go on.

Business continuity planning (BCP) is the process of implementing policies, controls, and procedures to counteract the effects of losses, outages, or failures of critical business processes. BCP is primarily a management tool that ensures that *critical business functions (CBF)* can be performed when normal business operations are disrupted.

Critical business functions refer to those processes or systems that must be made operational immediately when an outage occurs. The business can't function without them, and many are information intensive and require access to both technology and data.

Two of the key components of BCP are *business impact analysis (BIA)* and *risk assessment*. BIA is concerned with evaluating the processes, and risk assessment is concerned with evaluating the risk or likelihood of a loss. Evaluating all the processes in an organization or enterprise is necessary in order for BCP to be effective.

You need only a passing knowledge of business continuity issues for the Security+ exam. If you plan on taking the Project+ exam, also from CompTIA, you will need a more thorough knowledge of the topics.

Undertaking Business Impact Analysis

Business impact analysis is the process of evaluating all the critical systems in an organization to determine impact and recovery plans. The BIA isn't concerned with external threats or vulnerabilities; this analysis focuses on the impact a loss would have on the organization.

The key components of a BIA include the following:

Identifying Critical Functions   To identify critical functions, a company must ask itself, "What functions are necessary to continue operations until full service can be restored?" This identification process will help you establish which systems must be returned to operation in order for the business to continue. In performing this identification, you may find that a small or overlooked application in a department may be critical for operations. Many organizations have overlooked seemingly insignificant process steps or systems that have prevented BCP from being effective. Every department should be evaluated to ensure that no critical processes are overlooked.

Prioritizing Critical Business Functions   When business is continued after an event, operations must be prioritized as to essential and nonessential functions. If the organization makes resources available to the recovery process, these resources may be limited. Further, in a widespread outage, full operation may not be possible for some time. What would happen, for example, if your data communications services went down? You can usually establish temporary services, but you probably won't be able to restore full network capability. You should be clear about which applications or systems have priority for the resources available. Your company may find itself choosing to restore email before it restores its website.

Calculating a Time Frame for Critical Systems Loss   How long can the organization survive without a critical function? Some functions in an organization don't require immediate action; others do. Which functions must be reestablished and in what time frame? If your business is entirely dependent on its web presence and is e-commerce oriented, how long can the website stay inoperable? Your organization may need to evaluate and attempt to identify the maximum time that a particular function can be unavailable. This dictates the contingencies that must be made to minimize losses from exceeding the allowable period.

Estimating the Tangible and Intangible Impact on the Organization   Your organization will suffer losses in an outage. These losses will be of a tangible nature, such as lost production and lost sales. Intangible losses will also be a factor. For example, will customers lose faith in your service? Your discovery of these effects can greatly increase the company's realization of how much a loss of service will truly cost.

A thorough BIA will accomplish several things for your organization:

- The true impact and damage that an outage will cause will be visible.
- Understanding the true loss potential may help you in your fight for a budget.
- Perhaps most important, the process will document which business processes are being used, the impact they have on the organization, and how to restore them quickly.

The BIA will have some power in the organization as the costs of an outage become known. People buy insurance not because they intend to have an accident but in case they do. A BIA can help identify what insurance is needed in order for the organization to feel safe.

Utilities

Basic utilities such as electricity, water, and natural gas are key aspects of business continuity. In the vast majority of cases, electricity and water are restored—at least on an emergency basis—fairly rapidly. The damage created by blizzards, tornadoes, and other natural disasters is managed and repaired by utility companies and government agencies. Other disasters, such as a major earthquake or hurricane, can overwhelm these agencies, and services may be interrupted for quite a while. When these types of events occur, critical infrastructure may be unavailable for days, weeks, or even months.

 Real World Scenario

The Importance of Utilities

When the earthquake of 1989 occurred in San Francisco, California, portions of the city were without electricity, natural gas, and water for several months. Entire buildings were left unoccupied because the infrastructure was badly damaged. This damage prevented many businesses whose information systems departments were located in those buildings from returning to operation for several weeks. Most of the larger organizations were able to shift the processing loads to other companies or divisions.

When you evaluate your business's sustainability, realize that disasters do indeed happen. If possible, build infrastructures that don't have a *single point of failure* or connection. After the September 11, 2001, terrorist attack on the World Trade Center (WTC), several ISPs and other companies became nonfunctional because the WTC housed centralized communications systems and computer departments. If you're the administrator for a small company, it is not uncommon for the single point of failure (SPOF) to be a router/gateway. The best way to remove an SPOF from your environment is to add in redundancy.

Consider the impact of weather on your *contingency plans*. What if you needed to relocate your facility to another region of the country? How would you get personnel there? What personnel would be relocated? How would they be housed and fed during the time of the crisis? You should consider these possibilities in advance. Although the likelihood that a crippling disaster will occur is relatively small, you still need to evaluate the risk.

 The year 2005 was the year of the natural disaster. Starting with the tsunami that hit parts of Asia a few days before the start of the year and continuing through Hurricane Katrina that hit Louisiana and other parts of the South, it seemed as if there was a nonstop juggernaut of adversity underfoot. Many a business will never be able to recover from those catastrophes, while many paused for a short period of time and then were back up and running again. The difference, in many cases, was the contingency preparation that had been done beforehand. Having a plan in place before a catastrophe happens can significantly decrease your downtime.

Real World Scenario

Formulating Business Continuity Plans

As a security administrator, you'll need to think through a way to maintain business continuity should a crisis occur. Imagine your company is in each of the following three scenarios:

Scenario 1   Your company is in the business of monitoring criminal offenders who are under electronic house arrest nationwide. Every offender wears an anklet that wirelessly communicates with a device in their home. The home device communicates to your site in real time over phone lines by calling a toll-free number to report if the offender is in or out of the home; you alert local authorities immediately if someone isn't in compliance. The number of offenders, and the number of home devices that call your center, is in the tens of thousands. How could business be maintained if the trunk line for the toll-free phone carrier were disrupted in the middle of the night? How could you verify offender compliance if the problem took hours to correct?

Scenario 2   You're the administrator for a small educational company that delivers certification exams locally. The exams are downloaded the night before and delivered throughout the day as students—who have registered over the Internet—arrive. You show up at 8:00 a.m. on Friday, knowing that there are more than 20 exams to be administered that were downloaded Thursday night. What you find, however, is that someone has broken into the testing room and trashed all the workstations and monitors. Some of those coming to take the exams are driving from far away. How will you approach the situation?

Scenario 3   You're the database administrator for a large grocery chain. When you leave on Wednesday, there are no problems. When you arrive on Thursday—the day a new sale starts—you learn that the DSL lines are down. They went down before the local stores could download the new prices. All scanned goods will ring up at the price they were last week (either sale or regular) and not at current prices. The provider says it's working on the DSL problem but can't estimate how long repairs will take. How do you approach the problem?

Just like in the real world, there are no right or wrong answers for these scenarios. However, they all represent situations that have happened and that administrators planned for ahead of time.

There are several ways to accomplish this, including implementing redundant technology, fault-tolerant systems, and RAID. A truly redundant system won't utilize just one of these methods but rather some aspect of all of them. The following sections address these topics in more detail.

As an administrator, you should always be aware of problems that can occur and have an idea of how you'll approach them. It's impossible to prepare for every emergency, but you can plan for those that could conceivably happen.

High Availability

High availability refers to the process of keeping services and systems operational during an outage. In short, the goal is to provide all services to all users, where they need them, and when they need them. With high availability, the goal is to have key services available 99.999 percent of the time (also known as *five nines availability*).

Redundancy

Redundancy refers to systems that are either duplicated or that *fail over* to other systems in the event of a malfunction. *Fail-over* refers to the process of reconstructing a system or switching over to other systems when a failure is detected. In the case of a server, the server switches to a redundant server when a fault is detected. This allows service to continue uninterrupted until the primary server can be restored. In the case of a network, this means processing switches to another network path in the event of a network failure in the primary path.

> Fail-over systems can be very expensive to implement. In a large corporate network or e-commerce environment, a fail-over might entail switching all processing to a remote location until your primary facility is operational. The primary site and the remote site would synchronize data to ensure that information is as up-to-date as possible.

Many operating systems, such as Linux, Windows Server 2008, and Novell Open Enterprise Server, are capable of *clustering* to provide fail-over capabilities. Clustering involves multiple systems connected together cooperatively (which provides *load balancing*) and networked in such a way that if any of the systems fail, the other systems take up the slack and continue to operate. The overall capability of the server cluster may decrease, but the network or service will remain operational.

> To appreciate the beauty of clustering, contemplate the fact that this is the technology upon which Google is built. Clustering not only allows the company to have redundancy, but it also offers it the ability to scale as demand increases.

Figure 13.1 shows the clustering process in a network. In this cluster, each system has its own data storage and data-processing capabilities. The system that is connected to the network has the additional task of managing communication between the cluster and its users. Many clustering systems allow all the systems in the cluster to share a single disk system. In either case, reliability is improved when clustering technologies are incorporated in key systems.

Most ISPs and network providers have extensive internal fail-over capability to provide high availability to clients. Business clients and employees who are unable to access information or services tend to lose confidence. The trade-off for reliability and trustworthiness, of course, is cost: Fail-over systems can become prohibitively expensive. You'll need to carefully study your needs to determine whether your system requires this capability.

FIGURE 13.1   Server clustering in a networked environment

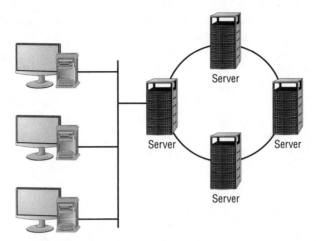

For example, if your environment requires a high level of availability, your servers should be clustered. This will allow the other servers in this network to take up the load if one of the servers in the cluster fails.

Fault Tolerance

Fault tolerance is primarily the ability of a system to sustain operations in the event of a component failure. Fault-tolerant systems can continue operation even though a critical component, such as a disk drive, has failed. This capability involves over-engineering systems by adding redundant components and subsystems.

Fault tolerance can be built into a server by adding a second power supply, a second CPU, and other key components. Several manufacturers (such as HP, Unisys, and IBM) offer fault-tolerant servers; these servers typically have multiple processors that automatically fail over if a malfunction occurs.

In addition to fault-tolerant servers, you can have fault-tolerant implementations such as Tandem, Stratus, and HP. In these settings, multiple computers are used to provide the 100 percent availability of a single server.

There are two key components of fault tolerance you should never overlook: spare parts and electrical power. *Spare parts* should always be readily available to repair any system-critical component if it should fail. The redundancy strategy N+1 means that you have the number of components you need, plus one to plug into any system should it be needed. For example, a small company with five standalone servers that are all the same model should have a power supply in a box nearby to install in any one of the servers should there be a failure. (The redundancy strategy 1+1 has one spare part for every component in use.)

Since computer systems cannot operate in the absence of electrical power, it is imperative that fault tolerance be built into your electrical infrastructure as well. At a bare minimum, an *uninterruptible power supply (UPS)*—with surge protection—should accompany every server and workstation. That UPS should be rated for the load it is expected to carry in the event of a power failure (factoring in the computer, monitor, and any other device connected to it) and be checked periodically as part of your preventive maintenance routine to make sure the battery is operational. You will need to replace the battery every few years to keep the UPS operational.

A UPS will allow you to continue to function in the absence of power for only a short duration. For fault tolerance in situations of longer duration, you will need a *backup generator.* Backup generators run off of gasoline, propane, natural gas, or diesel and generate the electricity needed to provide steady power. While some backup generators can come on instantly in the event of a power outage, most take a short time to warm up before they can provide consistent power, and thus you will find that you still need to implement UPSs within your organization.

Redundant Array of Independent Disks

Redundant Array of Independent Disks (RAID) is a technology that uses multiple disks to provide fault tolerance. There are several designations for RAID levels.

RAID stands for not only *Redundant Array of Independent Disks* but also *Redundant Array of Inexpensive Disks.* While the latter term has lost its popularity, you might still encounter it in some texts.

The most commonly implemented RAID levels are as follows:

RAID Level 0   RAID 0 is *disk striping.* It uses multiple drives and maps them together as a single physical drive. This is done primarily for performance, not for fault tolerance. If any drive in a RAID 0 array fails, the entire logical drive becomes unusable.

RAID Level 1   RAID 1 is *disk mirroring.* Disk mirroring provides 100 percent redundancy because everything is stored on two disks. If one disk fails, another disk continues to operate. The failed disk can be replaced, and the RAID 1 array can be regenerated. This system offers the advantage of 100 percent data redundancy at the expense of doubling the storage requirements. Each drive keeps an exact copy of all information, which reduces the effective storage capability to 50 percent of the overall storage. Some implementations of disk mirroring are called *disk duplexing (duplexing* is a less-commonly used term). The only difference between mirroring and duplexing is one more controller card. With mirroring, one controller card writes sequentially to each disk. With duplexing, the same data is written to both disks simultaneously. Disk duplexing has much faster write performance than disk mirroring. Many hardware implementations of RAID 1 are actually duplexing, but they are still generally referred to as mirrors.

The data is intact in a RAID 1 array if either one of the two drives fails. After the failed drive is replaced with a new drive, you remirror the data from the good drive to the new drive to re-create the array.

RAID Level 3   RAID 3 is *disk striping with a parity disk*. RAID 3 arrays implement fault tolerance by using striping (RAID 0) in conjunction with a separate disk that stores parity information. *Parity information* is a value based on the value of the data stored in each disk location. This system ensures that the data can be recovered in the event of a failure. The process of generating parity information uses the arithmetic value of the data binary. This process allows any single disk in the array to fail while the system continues to operate. The failed disk is removed, a new disk is installed, and the new drive is then regenerated using the parity information. RAID 3 is common in older systems, and it's supported by most Unix systems.

RAID Level 5   RAID 5 is *disk striping with parity* and is one of the most common forms of RAID in use today. It operates similarly to disk striping, as in RAID 0. The parity information is spread across all the disks in the array instead of being limited to a single disk, as in RAID 3. Most implementations require a minimum of three disks and support a maximum of 32.

These four types of RAID drives, or arrays, are illustrated in Figure 13.2.

FIGURE 13.2   The four primary RAID technologies used in systems

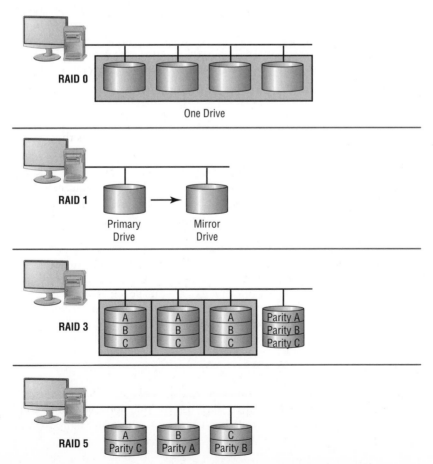

A RAID 5 array can survive the failure of any one drive and still be able to function. It can't, however, survive the failure of multiple drives.

You aren't required to know the current RAID capabilities for the Security+ exam. They are presented here primarily for your knowledge. They are commonly used in highly reliable systems.

RAID levels 0, 1, 3, and 5 are the ones most commonly implemented in servers today, with RAID 5 having largely replaced RAID 3 in newer systems. When two levels are combined for a more potent solution, the numbers simply move into double digits representing the two RAID levels combined. For example, combining RAID 1 with RAID 0 is now called RAID 10 (or, RAID 0+1 in older documentation). Combining RAID 1 with RAID 5 is now known as RAID 15, and so on.

RAID levels are implemented either in software on the host computer or in the disk controller hardware. A RAID hardware-device implementation will generally run faster than a software-oriented RAID implementation because the software implementation uses the system CPU and system resources. Hardware RAID devices generally have their own processors, and they appear to the operating system as a single device.

You must do a fair amount of planning before you implement RAID. Within the realm of planning, you must be able to compute the number of disks needed for the desired implementation.

Disaster Recovery

Disaster recovery is the ability to recover system operations after a disaster. A key aspect of disaster-recovery planning is designing a comprehensive backup plan that includes backup storage, procedures, and maintenance. Many options are available to implement disaster recovery. The following sections discuss backups and the disaster-recovery plan.

It's important to recognize that during a recovery, it may not always be necessary to immediately bring all systems and services back up. Critical systems should be the priority; extraneous services (such as an informational website for the public) can often be of lesser priority and attended to after everything else is up and running.

Types of Backups

Backups are duplicate copies of key information, ideally stored in a location other than the one where the information is currently stored. Backups include both paper and computer records. Computer records are usually backed up using a backup program, backup systems, and backup procedures.

🌐 Real World Scenario

How Many Disks Does RAID Need?

As a security administrator, you must determine how many RAID disks you'll need. Compute how many disks will be needed for each scenario or the amount of storage capacity you'll end up with (answers appear at the end of each scenario).

Scenario 1   Your company has standardized on 500GB disks. A new server will go online next month to hold the data files for a new division; the server will be disk-duplexed and needs to be able to store 800 GB of data. How many drives should you order?

Disk duplexing is the same as disk mirroring except there is also a second controller. Fifty percent of the overall storage capacity must be used for RAID, so you must purchase four 500GB drives. This will give you excess data capacity of 200 GB.

Scenario 2   Your primary server is currently running four 300GB disks in a RAID 5 array. Storage space is at a premium, and a purchase order has just been approved for four 500GB disks. Still utilizing a RAID 5 array, what is the maximum data storage space this server will be able to host?

The solution that will generate the most data storage capacity is to install all eight drives (the four current ones and the four new ones) into the server. The array must use the same size storage on each drive; thus all eight drives will appear as if they are 300GB drives. Under this scenario, 2100 GB can be used for data storage and 300 GB will be used for parity.

Scenario 3   Access speed is of the utmost importance on the web server. You want to purchase some fast 300GB hard drives and install them in a RAID 0 array. How many drives will you need to purchase to host 900 GB of data?

RAID 0 doesn't perform any fault tolerance and doesn't require any extra disk space. You can obtain 900 GB of data by using three disks.

The primary starting point for disaster recovery involves keeping current backup copies of key data files, databases, applications, and paper records available for use. Your organization must develop a solid set of procedures to manage this process and ensure that all key information is protected—steps that we will walk through later in this chapter. A security professional can do several things in conjunction with system administrators and business managers to protect this information. It's important to think of this problem as an issue that is larger than a single department.

As much as we live in an electronic age, it seems almost impossible to get rid of all paper. For a number of reasons, some paper documents must be retained and carefully stored. The following are examples of key paper records that should be archived:

- Board minutes
- Board resolutions

- Corporate papers
- Critical contracts
- Financial statements
- Incorporation documents
- Loan documents
- Personnel information
- Tax records

This list, while not comprehensive, gives you a place to start when you evaluate your archival requirements. Most of these documents can be easily converted into electronic form. However, keeping paper copies is strongly recommended because some government agencies don't accept electronic documentation as an alternative to paper documentation. Be sure to store the paper documents in a secure location where environmental conditions conducive to preserving paper are maintained. Storage facilities specifically intended for this purpose can be found in most large cities after the documents outgrow your closets.

Computer files and applications should also be backed up on a regular basis. Here are some examples of critical files that should be backed up:

- Applications
- Appointment files
- Audit files
- Customer lists
- Database files
- Email correspondence
- Financial data
- Operating systems
- Prospect lists
- Transaction files
- User files
- User information
- Utilities

Again, this list isn't all inclusive, but it provides a place to start.

In most environments, the volume of information that needs to be stored is growing at a tremendous pace. Simply tracking this massive growth can create significant problems.

An unscrupulous attacker can glean as much critical information from copies as they can from the original files. Make sure your storage facilities are secure, and it is a good idea to add physical security to the backup media as well.

You might need to restore information from backup copies for any number of reasons. Some of the more common reasons are listed here:

- Accidental deletion
- Applications errors
- Natural disasters
- Physical attacks
- Server failure
- Virus infection
- Workstation failure

Types of Storage Mechanisms

The information you back up must be immediately available for use when needed. If a user loses a critical file, they won't want to wait several days while data files are sent from a remote storage facility. Several types of storage mechanisms are available for data storage. These include the following:

Working Copies   *Working copy backups*—sometimes referred to as *shadow copies*—are partial or full backups that are kept at the computer center for immediate recovery purposes. Working copies are frequently the most recent backups that have been made.

Typically, working copies are intended for immediate use. They are usually updated on a frequent basis.

> Working copies aren't usually intended to serve as long-term copies. In a busy environment, they may be created every few hours.

Many filesystems used on servers include *journaling*. A journaled file system (JFS) includes a log file of all changes and transactions that have occurred within a set period of time (such as the last few hours). If a crash occurs, the operating system can check the log files to see which transactions have been committed and which ones have not.

This technology works well and allows unsaved data to be written after the recovery, and the system is usually successfully restored to its pre-crash condition.

Onsite Storage   *Onsite storage* usually refers to a location on the site of the computer center that is used to store information locally. Onsite storage containers are available that allow computer cartridges, tapes, and other backup media to be stored in a reasonably protected environment in the building.

> As time goes on, tape is losing its popularity as a medium for backups to other technologies. The Security+ exam, however, is a bit dated and still considers tape the ideal medium.

Onsite storage containers are designed and rated for fire, moisture, and pressure resistance. These containers aren't *fireproof* in most situations, but they are *fire rated*: A fireproof container should be guaranteed to withstand damage regardless of the type of fire or temperature, whereas fire ratings specify that a container can protect the contents for a specific amount of time in a given situation.

If you choose to depend entirely on onsite storage, make sure the containers you acquire can withstand the worst-case environmental catastrophes that could happen at your location. Make sure, as well, that they are in locations where you can easily find them after the disaster and access them (near exterior walls, on the ground floor, and so forth).

 General-purpose storage safes aren't usually suitable for storing electronic media. The fire ratings used for safes generally refer to paper contents. Because paper does not catch fire until 451° Fahrenheit, electronic media are typically ruined well before paper documents are destroyed in a fire.

Offsite Storage *Offsite storage* refers to a location away from the computer center where paper copies and backup media are kept. Offsite storage can involve something as simple as keeping a copy of backup media at a remote office, or it can be as complicated as a nuclear-hardened high-security storage facility. The storage facility should be bonded, insured, and inspected on a regular basis to ensure that all storage procedures are being followed.

Determining which storage mechanism to use should be based on the needs of the organization, the availability of storage facilities, and the budget available. Most offsite storage facilities charge based on the amount of space you require and the frequency of access you need to the stored information.

 While it is easy to see the need for security at any location where your files are stored, don't overlook the need for security during transportation as well.

Crafting a Disaster-Recovery Plan

A *disaster-recovery plan*, or scheme, helps an organization respond effectively when a disaster occurs. Disasters may include system failure, network failure, infrastructure failure, and natural disaster. The primary emphasis of such a plan is reestablishing services and minimizing losses.

In a smaller organization, a disaster-recovery plan may be relatively simple and straightforward. In a larger organization, it may involve multiple facilities, corporate strategic plans, and entire departments. In either case, the purpose is to develop the means and methods to restore services as quickly as possible and to protect the organization from unacceptable losses in the event of a disaster.

A major component of a disaster-recovery plan involves the access and storage of information. Your backup plan for data is an integral part of this process. The following sections address backup plan issues and backup types. They also discuss developing a backup plan, recovering a system, and using alternative sites. These are key components of a disaster-recovery plan: They form the heart of how an organization will respond when a critical failure or disaster occurs.

Understanding Backup Plan Issues

When an organization develops a *backup plan* for information, it must be clear about the value of the information. A backup plan identifies which information is to be stored, how it will be stored, and for what duration it will be stored. You must look at the relative value of the information you retain. To some extent, the types of systems you use and the applications you support dictate the structure of your plan.

Let's look at those different systems and applications:

Database Systems   Most modern database systems provide the ability to globally back up data or certain sections of the database without difficulty. Larger-scale database systems also provide transaction auditing and data-recovery capabilities.

For example, you can configure your database to record in a separate file each addition, update, deletion, or change of information that occurs. These transaction or audit files can be stored directly on archival media, such as magnetic tape cartridges. In the event of a system outage or data loss, the audit file can be used to roll back the database and update it to the last transactions made.

Figure 13.3 illustrates the auditing process in further detail. In this situation, the audit file is directly written to a DAT tape that is used to store a record of changes. If an outage occurs, the audit or transaction files can be rolled forward to bring the database back to its most current state. This recovery process brings the database current to within the last few transactions. Although it doesn't ensure that all the transactions that were in process will be recovered, it will reduce potential losses to the few that were in process when the system failed.

FIGURE 13.3   Database transaction auditing process

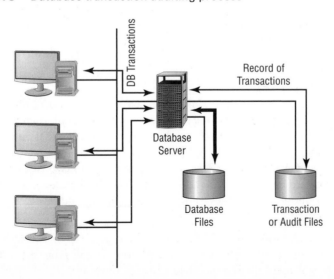

Most database systems contain large files that have only a relatively few records updated in relation to the number of records stored. A large customer database may store millions of records—however, only a few hundred may be undergoing modification at any given time.

User Files   Word processing documents, spreadsheets, and other user files are extremely valuable to an organization. Fortunately, although the number of files that people retain is usually large, the number of files that change after initial creation is relatively small. By doing a regular backup on user systems, you can protect these documents and ensure that they're recoverable in the event of a loss. In a large organization, backing up user files can be an enormous task. Fortunately, most operating systems date-stamp files when they're modified. If backups that store only the changed files are created, keeping user files safe becomes a relatively less-painful process for an organization.

Many organizations have taken the position that backing up user files is the user's responsibility. Although this policy decision saves administrative time and media, it isn't a good idea. Most users don't back up their files on a regular basis—if at all. With the cost of media being relatively cheap, including the user files in a backup every so often is highly recommended.

Applications   Applications such as word processors, transaction systems, and other programs usually don't change on a frequent basis. When a change or upgrade to an application is made, it's usually accomplished across an entire organization. You wouldn't necessarily need to keep a copy of the word processing application for each user, but you should keep a single up-to-date version that is available for download and reinstallation.

Some commercial applications require each copy of the software to be registered with a centralized license server. This may present a problem if you attempt to use a centralized recovery procedure for applications. Each machine may require its own copy of the applications for a recovery to be successful.

Knowing the Backup Types

The frequency at which you do backups should be based on the amount of data you are willing to lose. If you do backups only weekly (never recommended), then you could lose up to a week's worth of data. Similarly, if you do them every day, the most data you should be able to lose is 24 hours' worth.

Regardless of the frequency at which you back up, three methods exist to back up information on most systems. The difference between them is in the data they include, and this has an impact on the amount of time it takes to perform the backup and any restore operations that may later be required:

Full Backup   A *full backup* is a complete, comprehensive backup of all files on a disk or server. The full backup is current only at the time it's performed. Once a full backup is made, you have a complete archive of the system at that point in time. A system shouldn't be in use while it undergoes a full backup because some files may not get backed up. Once the system goes back into operation, the backup is no longer current. A full backup can be a time-consuming process on a large system.

 During a full backup, every single file on the system is copied over, and the archive bit on each file is turned off.

Incremental Backup   An *incremental backup* is a partial backup that stores only the information that has been changed since the last full or the last incremental backup. If a full backup were performed on a Sunday night, an incremental backup done on Monday night would contain only the information that changed since Sunday night. Such a backup is typically considerably smaller than a full backup. Each incremental backup must be retained until a full backup can be performed. Incremental backups are usually the fastest backups to perform on most systems, and each incremental backup tape is relatively small.

 An incremental backup backs up only files that have the archive bit turned on. That is how it can identify which files have changed or been created. At the conclusion of the backup, the archive bit is turned off for all the files that were included in the backup.

Differential Backup   A *differential backup* is similar in function to an incremental backup, but it backs up any files that have been altered since the last full backup; it makes duplicate copies of files that haven't changed since the last differential backup. If a full backup were performed on Sunday night, a differential backup performed on Monday night would capture the information that was changed on Monday. A differential backup completed on Tuesday night would record the changes in any files from Monday and any changes in files on Tuesday. As you can see, during the week each differential backup would become larger; by Friday or Saturday night, it might be nearly as large as a full backup. This means the backups in the earliest part of the weekly cycle will be very fast, and each successive one will be slower.

 A differential backup backs up only files that have the archive bit turned on. At the conclusion of the backup, the archive bit is left on for those files so they are then included again in the next backup.

When these backup methods are used in conjunction with each other, the risk of loss can be greatly reduced, but you can never combine incremental and differential backups in the same set. One of the major factors in determining which combination of these three methods to use is time—ideally, a full backup would be performed every day. Several commercial backup programs support these three backup methods. You must evaluate your organizational needs when choosing which tools to use to accomplish backups.

Almost every stable operating system contains a utility for creating a copy of configuration settings necessary to reach the present state after a disaster. In Windows 7, for example, this is accomplished with an Automated System Recovery (ASR) disk. Make certain you know how to do an equivalent operation for the operating system you are running.

As an administrator, you must know how to do backups and be familiar with all the options available to you. In Exercise 13.1, I'll show you how to perform a backup in SuSE Linux.

EXERCISE 13.1

Create a Backup in SuSE Linux

This exercise assumes the use of SuSE Linux Enterprise Server. While backups are available in all Linux distributions, SuSE simplifies this task (and most administrative tasks as well) by including the YaST (Yet another Setup Tool) interface.

1. Log in as root and start YaST.

2. Choose System and System Backup.

3. Click Profile Management and choose Add; then enter a name for the new profile, such as **fullsystemback**.

4. Click OK.

5. Enter a backup name (using an absolute path such as /home/mybackup.tar), and make certain the archive type is set to a tar variety. Then click Next.

6. At the File Selection window, leave the default options and click Next.

7. Leave the Search Constraints at the defaults and click OK.

8. At the main YaST System Backup dialog box, click Start Backup. After several minutes of reading packages, the backup will begin.

Developing a Backup Plan

Several common models are used in designing backup plans. Each has its own advantages and disadvantages. Numerous methods have been developed to deal with archival backup; most of them are evolutions of the three models discussed here:

Grandfather, Father, Son Method   The *Grandfather, Father, Son method* is based on the philosophy that a full backup should occur at regular intervals, such as monthly or weekly. This method assumes that the most recent backup after the full backup is the son. As newer backups are made, the son becomes the father, and the father, in turn, becomes the grandfather. At the end of each month, a full backup is performed on all systems. This backup is stored in an offsite facility for a period of one year. Each monthly backup replaces the monthly backup from the previous year. Weekly or daily incremental backups are performed and stored until the next full backup occurs. This full backup is then stored offsite and the weekly or daily backup tapes are reused (the January 1 incremental backup is used on February 1, and so on).

This method ensures that in the event of a loss, the full backup from the end of the last month and the daily backups can be used to restore information to the last day. Figure 13.4 illustrates this concept: The annual backup is referred to as the grandfather, the monthly backup is the father, and the weekly backup is the son. The last backup of the month becomes the archived backup for that month. The last backup of the year becomes the annual backup for the year. Annual backups are usually archived; this allows an organization to have backups available for several years and minimizes the likelihood of data loss. It's a common practice for an organization to keep a minimum of seven years in archives.

FIGURE 13.4   Grandfather, Father, Son backup method

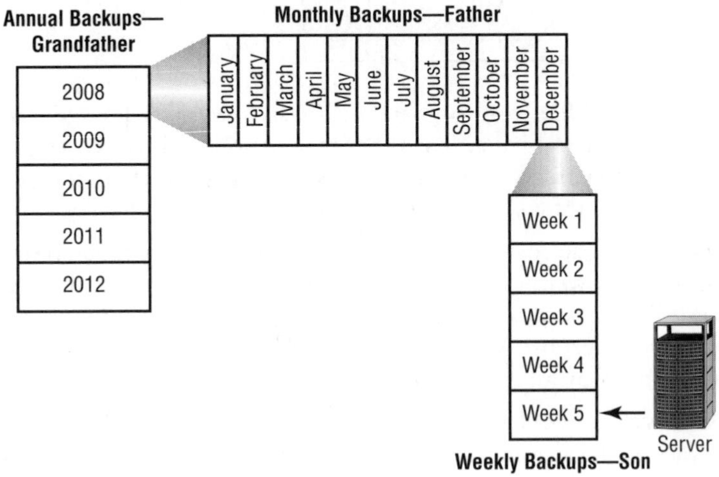

The last full backup of the year is permanently retained. This ensures that previous years' information can be recovered if it's needed for some reason.

The major difficulty with this process is that a large number of tapes are constantly flowing between the storage facility and the computer center. In addition, cataloging daily and weekly backups can be complicated. It can become difficult to determine which files have been backed up and where they're stored.

Full Archival Method   The *Full Archival method* works on the assumption that any information created on any system is stored forever. All backups are kept indefinitely using some form of backup media. In short, all full backups, all incremental backups, and any other backups are permanently kept somewhere.

This method effectively eliminates the potential for loss of data. Everything that is created on any computer is backed up forever. Figure 13.5 illustrates this method. As you can see, the number of copies of the backup media can quickly overwhelm your storage capabilities. Some organizations that have tried to do this have needed entire warehouses to contain their archival backups.

FIGURE 13.5 Full Archival backup method

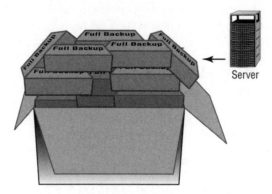

Think about the number of files your organization has: How much storage media would be required to accomplish full archiving? The other major problem involves keeping records of what information has been archived. For these reasons, many larger companies don't find this to be an acceptable method of keeping backups.

Backup Server Method The costs of disk storage and servers have fallen tremendously over the past few years. Lower prices have made it easier for organizations to use dedicated servers for backup. The *Backup Server method* establishes a server with large amounts of disk space whose sole purpose is to back up data. With the right software, a dedicated server can examine and copy all the files that have been altered every day.

Figure 13.6 illustrates the use of backup servers. In this instance, the files on the backup server contain copies of all the information and data on the APPS, ACCTG, and DB servers. The files on the three servers are copied to the backup server on a regular basis; over time, this server's storage requirements can become enormous. The advantage of this method is that all backed-up data is available online for immediate access.

FIGURE 13.6 A backup server archiving server files

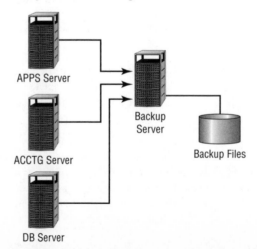

This server can be backed up on a regular basis, and the backups can be kept for a specified period. If a system or server malfunctions, the backup server can be accessed to restore information from the last backups performed on that system.

Backup servers don't need overly large processors; however, they must have large disk and other long-term storage media capabilities. Several software manufacturers take backup servers one additional step and create hierarchies of files: Over time, if a file isn't accessed, it's moved to slower media and may eventually be stored offline. This helps reduce the disk storage requirements, yet it still keeps the files that are most likely to be needed for recovery readily available.

Many organizations utilize two or more of these methods to back up systems. The issue becomes one of storage requirements and retention requirements. In establishing a backup plan, you must ask users and managers how much backup (in terms of frequency, size of files, and so forth) is really needed and how long it will be needed.

 Make sure you obtain input from all who are dealing with governmental or regulatory agencies. Each agency may have different archival requirements, and compliance violations can be expensive. Both HIPAA and Sarbanes-Oxley are affecting—and driving—archival and disposal policies around the nation.

Recovering a System

When a system fails, you'll be unable to reestablish operation without regenerating all of the system's components. This process includes making sure hardware is functioning, restoring or installing the operating systems, restoring or installing applications, and restoring data files. It can take several days on a large system. With a little forethought, you may be able to simplify the process and make it easily manageable.

When you install a new system, make a full backup of it before any data files are created. If stored onsite, this backup will be readily available for use. If you've standardized your systems, you may need just one copy of a base system that contains all the common applications you use. The base system can usually be quickly restored, which allows for reconnection to the network for restoration of other software. Many newer operating systems now provide this capability, and system restores are very fast.

Figure 13.7 demonstrates this process further. Notice that the installation CDs are being used for the base OS and applications.

When the base system has been restored, data files and any other needed files can be restored from the last full backup and any incremental or differential backups that have been performed. The last full backup should contain most of the data on the system; the incremental backup or differential backups contain the data that has changed since the full backup.

Many newer operating systems, such as Windows Server 2008, allow you to create a model user system as a disk image on a server; the disk image is downloaded and installed when a failure occurs. This method makes it easier for administrators to restore a system than it would be to do it manually. It's all well and good to know how to make backups and the importance of doing so. There will come a time, however, when a recovery—the whole reason for disaster planning—will be necessary. As an administrator, you must be ready for this event and know how to handle it.

FIGURE 13.7 System regeneration process for a workstation or server

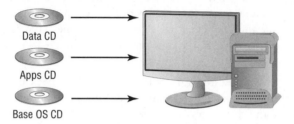

Data CD

Apps CD

Base OS CD

In Exercise 13.2, I'll show you how to use Automated System Recovery with Windows Server 2008.

EXERCISE 13.2

Use Automated System Recovery in Windows Server 2008

In this exercise, you'll use the backup utility included with Windows Server 2008 to create an ASR backup:

1. Start the backup utility by choosing Start ➢ All Programs ➢ Accessories ➢ System Tools ➢ Backup.

2. Choose the Automatic System Recovery Wizard.

3. Walk through the wizard and answer the questions appropriately. When you finish, you'll create the backup set first and a floppy second. The floppy contains files necessary to restore system settings after a disaster.

An important recovery issue is to know the order in which to progress. If a server is completely destroyed and must be re-created, ascertain which applications are the most important and should be restored before the others. Likewise, which services are most important to the users from a business standpoint and need to be available? Conversely, which are nice but not necessary to keep the business running? The answers will differ for every organization, and you must know them for yours.

Backout vs. Backup

While most attention deservedly is on backups, never overlook the need for a *backout* plan. A backout is a reversion from a change that had negative consequences. It could be, for example, that everything was working fine until you installed a service pack on a production machine, and then services that were normally available no longer are. The backout, in this instance, would revert the system to the state it was before the service pack was applied.

While backout plans can include uninstalling service packs, hotfixes, and patches, they can also include reversing a migration, using previous firmware, and so on. A key component to creating such a plan is identifying what events will trigger your implementing the backout.

Planning for Alternate Sites

Another key aspect of a disaster-recovery plan is to provide for the restoration of business functions in the event of a large-scale loss of service. You can lease or purchase a facility that is available on short notice for the purpose of restoring network or systems operations. These are referred to as *alternate* or *backup sites*.

Another term for *alternate site* is *alternative site;* the terms are often used interchangeably.

If the power in your local area were disrupted for several days, how would you reestablish service at an alternate site until primary services were restored? Several options exist to do this; I'll briefly present them here. None of these solutions are ideal, but they are always considered to be significantly less costly—in terms of time—to implement than the estimated time of bringing your original site back up to speed. They are used to allow you to get your organization back on its feet until permanent service is available. An alternative site can be a hot site, a warm site, or a cold site:

Hot Site   A hot site is a location that can provide operations within hours of a failure. This type of site would have servers, networks, and telecommunications equipment in place to reestablish service in a short time. Hot sites provide network connectivity, systems, and preconfigured software to meet the needs of an organization. Databases can be kept up-to-date using network connections. These types of facilities are expensive, and they're primarily suitable for short-term situations. A hot site may also double as an offsite storage facility, providing immediate access to archives and backup media.

A hot site is also referred to as an *active backup model.*

Many hot sites also provide office facilities and other services so that a business can relocate a small number of employees to sustain operations.

Given the choice, every organization would choose to have a hot site. Doing so is often not practical, however, on the basis of cost.

Warm Site   A *warm site* provides some of the capabilities of a hot site, but it requires the customer to do more work to become operational. Warm sites provide computer systems and compatible media capabilities. If a warm site is used, administrators and other staff will need to install and configure systems to resume operations. For most organizations, a warm site could be a remote office, a leased facility, or another organization with which yours has a reciprocal agreement.

Another term for a warm site/reciprocal site is *active/active model.*

Warm sites may be for your exclusive use, but they don't have to be. A warm site requires more advanced planning, testing, and access to media for system recovery. Warm sites represent a compromise between a hot site, which is very expensive, and a cold site, which isn't preconfigured.

An agreement between two companies to provide services in the event of an emergency is called a *reciprocal agreement.* Usually, these agreements are made on a best-effort basis: There is no guarantee that services will be available if the site is needed. Make sure your agreement is with an organization that is outside your geographic area. If both sites are affected by the same disaster, the agreement is worthless.

Cold Site   A *cold site* is a facility that isn't immediately ready to use. The organization using it must bring along its equipment and network. A cold site may provide network capability, but this isn't usually the case; the site provides a place for operations to resume, but it doesn't provide the infrastructure to support those operations. Cold sites work well when an extended outage is anticipated. The major challenge is that the customer must provide all the capabilities and do all the work to get back into operation. Cold sites are usually the least expensive to put into place, but they require the most advanced planning, testing, and resources to become operational—occasionally taking up to a month to make operational.

Almost anywhere can be a cold site; if necessary, users could work out of your garage for a short time. Although this may be a practical solution, it also opens up risks that you must consider. For example, while you're operating from your garage, will the servers be secure should someone break in?

Herein lies the problem. The likelihood that you'll need any of these facilities is low—most organizations will never need to use these types of facilities. The costs are usually based on subscription or other contracted relationships, and it's difficult for most organizations to justify the expense. In addition, planning, testing, and maintaining these facilities is difficult; it does little good to pay for any of these services if they don't work and aren't available when you need them.

One of the most important aspects of using alternative sites is documentation. To create an effective site, you must have solid documentation of what you have, what you're using, and what you need in order to get by.

Management must view the disaster-recovery plan as an integral part of its business continuity planning (BCP). Management must also provide the resources needed to implement and maintain an alternative site after the decision has been made to contract for the facilities.

 Real World Scenario

Some Protection Is Better than None—Or Is It?

You've been tasked with the responsibility of developing a recovery plan for your company to have in place in a critical infrastructure failure. Your CEO is concerned about the budget and doesn't want to invest many resources in a full-blown hot site.

Several options are available to you in this situation. You need to evaluate the feasibility of a warm site, a cold site, or a reciprocal agreement with another company. The warm site and cold site options will cost less than a hot site, but they will require a great deal of work in the event of a failure. A reciprocal site may be a good alternative to both, if a suitable partner organization can be found. You may want to discuss this possibility with some of your larger vendors or other companies that may have excess computer capacity. No matter which direction you recommend, you should test and develop procedures to manage the transition from your primary site to an offsite facility.

Incident Response Policies

Incident response policies define how an organization will respond to an incident. These policies may involve third parties, and they need to be comprehensive. The term *incident* is somewhat nebulous in scope; for our purposes, an incident is any attempt to violate a security policy, a successful penetration, a compromise of a system, or any unauthorized access to information. This includes system failures and disruption of services in the organization.

It's important that an incident response policy establish at least the following items:

- Outside agencies that should be contacted or notified in case of an incident
- Resources used to deal with an incident
- Procedures to gather and secure evidence
- List of information that should be collected about an incident
- Outside experts who can be used to address issues if needed
- Policies and guidelines regarding how to handle an incident

According to CERT, a *Computer Security Incident Response Team (CSIRT)* can be a formalized or ad hoc team. While you can toss a team together to respond to an incident after it arises, investing time in the development process can make an incident more manageable. Many decisions about dealing with an incident will have been considered in advance.

Incidents are high-stress situations; therefore, it's better to simplify the process by considering important aspects in advance. If civil or criminal actions are part of the process, evidence must be gathered and safeguarded properly.

Let's say you've just discovered a situation where a fraud has been perpetrated internally using a corporate computer. You're part of the investigating team. Your incident response policy lists the specialists you need to contact for an investigation. Ideally, you've already met the investigator or investigating firm, you've developed an understanding of how to protect the scene, and you know how to properly deal with the media (if they become involved).

Your policies must also clearly outline who needs to be informed in the company, what they need to be told, and how to respond to the situation. Incidents should include not only intrusions but also attempts.

Understanding Incident Response

Forensics refers to the process of identifying what has occurred on a system by examining the data trail. It involves an analysis of evidence found in computers and on digital storage media. *Incident response*, on the other hand, encompasses forensics and refers to the process of identifying, investigating, repairing, documenting, and adjusting procedures to prevent another incident. Simply put, an *incident* is the occurrence of any event that endangers a system or network. We need to discuss responses to two types of incidents: internal incidents and incidents involving law enforcement professionals. Figure 13.8 illustrates the interlocked relationship of these processes in an incident response. Notice that all the steps, including the first step, are related. Incidents are facts of life. You want to learn from them, and you want your organization to learn from them.

It's a good idea to include the procedures you'll generally follow in an *incident response plan (IRP)*. The IRP outlines what steps are needed and who is responsible for deciding how to handle a situation. The Computer Science department at Carnegie Mellon pioneered this process.

FIGURE 13.8 Incident response cycle

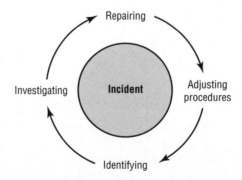

Law enforcement personnel are governed by the rules of evidence, and their response to an incident will be largely out of your control. You need to carefully consider involving law enforcement before you decide that you do not want to handle the situation without them. There is no such thing as dropping charges. Once they begin, law enforcement professionals are required to pursue an investigation.

The term *incident* has special meanings in different industries. In the banking and financial areas, it's very specific and involves something that includes the loss of money. You wouldn't want to call a hacker attempt an *incident* if you were involved in a bank network because this terminology would automatically trigger an entirely different type of investigation.

The next five sections deal with the phases of a typical incident response process. The steps are generic in this example. Each organization will have a specific set of procedures that will generally map to these steps.

An important concept to keep in mind when working with incidents is the *chain of custody*, which covers how evidence is secured, where it is stored, and who has access to it. When you begin to collect evidence, you must keep track of that evidence at all times and show who has it, who has seen it, and where it has been. The evidence must always be within your custody, or you're open to dispute about whether it has been tampered with. It is highly recommended that a log book be used to document every access and visuals (pictures and video) recorded to show how the evidence is secured.

Step One: Identifying the Incident

Incident identification is the first step in determining what has occurred in your organization. An internal or external attack may have been part of a larger attack that has just surfaced, or it may be a random probe or scan of your network.

An event is often an IDS-triggered signal. Operations personnel will determine if an *event* becomes an *incident*. An easy way to think of the two is that an event is anything that happens, while an incident is any event that endangers a system or network.

Many IDSs trigger false positives when reporting incidents. False positives are events that aren't really incidents. Remember that an IDS is based on established rules of acceptance (deviations from which are known as *anomalies*) and attack signatures. If the rules aren't set up properly, normal traffic may set off the analyzer and generate an event. Be sure to double-check your results because you don't want to declare a false emergency.

One problem that can occur with manual network monitoring is overload. Over time, a slow attack may develop that increases in intensity. Manual processes typically will adapt, and they may not notice the attack until it's too late to stop it. Personnel tend to adapt to changing environments if the changes occur over a long period of time. An automated monitoring system, such as an IDS, will sound the alarm when a certain threshold or activity level occurs.

When a suspected incident pops up, *first responders* are those who must ascertain whether it truly is an incident or a false alarm. Depending on your organization, the first responder may only be the main security administrator or could consist of a team of network and system administrators.

After you've determined that you indeed have an incident on your hands, you need to consider how to handle it. This process, called *escalation*, involves consulting policies, consulting appropriate management, and determining how best to conduct an investigation into the incident. Make sure that the methods you use to investigate the incident are consistent with corporate and legal requirements for your organization. Bring your Human Resources and Legal departments into the investigation early, and seek their guidance whenever questions involving their areas of expertise appear.

A key aspect, often overlooked by system professionals, involves information control. When an incident occurs, who is responsible for managing the communications about the incident? Employees in the company may naturally be curious about a situation. A single spokesperson needs to be designated. Remember, what 1 person knows, 100 people know.

 Real World Scenario

The Email Incident

You're the administrator of a small network. This network has an old mail server that is used for internal and external email. You periodically investigate log and audit files to determine the status of your systems and servers. Recently, you noticed that your email log file has been reporting a large number of undeliverable or bounced emails. The addresses appear to be random. Upon examining the email system, you notice that the outbound mail folder seems to be sending mail every second. A large number of files are being sent. After inspecting the workstations in the business, you determine that several of them have out-of-date antivirus software. How should you handle this situation?

For starters, you may have one or more viruses or worms in your system. This type of virus sounds like a Simple Mail Transfer Protocol (SMTP) virus, and a virus can gain access to the address directory and propagate itself using SMTP.

You should investigate why the antivirus software is out-of-date, upgrade these systems as appropriate, and add server-based and mail-server virus-protection capabilities to your network.

Step Two: Investigating the Incident

The process of investigating an incident involves searching logs, files, and any other sources of data about the nature and scope of the incident. If possible, you should determine whether this is part of a larger attack, a random event, or a false positive. False positives are common in an IDS environment and may be the result of unusual traffic in the network. It may be that your network is being pinged by a class of computer security students to demonstrate the return times, or it may be that an automated tool is launching an attack.

It is sad but true: One reason administrators don't put as much security on networks as they could is because they do not want to have to deal with the false positives. While this is a poor excuse, it is still often used by administrators. As a security administrator, you must seek a balance between being overwhelmed with too much unneeded information and knowing when something out of the ordinary is occurring. It is an elusive balance that is easier to talk about than find, but it's one you must strive for.

You might find that the incident doesn't require a response if it can't be successful. Your investigation might conclude that a change in policies is required to deal with a new type of threat. These types of decisions should be documented, and if necessary, reconfigurations should be made to deal with the change.

 Real World Scenario

What If the Intrusion Is Now?

Suppose a junior administrator rushes into your office and reports that an alert just notified him that the guest user account has logged in remotely. A suspected attack is occurring this very moment. What should you do?

You should respond to an attack that's occurring at this moment the same way you would respond to one that happened before you knew about it. You need to determine what the account is doing and try to figure out who the attacker is and where they're coming from. As you collect any information, you should treat it as evidence and keep careful watch over it.

Although collecting as much information as possible is important, no one can be blamed for trying to protect their data. *Damage and loss control* are critical; you need to minimize the impact of the incident. While it may be admirable to catch a crook deleting your data, if you can keep the data from being deleted, you will stand a much better chance of still being employed tomorrow. As soon as it becomes apparent that data is at risk, you should disconnect the user. Catching a bad guy is a noble task, but the security of the data should be considered paramount.

Step Three: Repairing the Damage

One of your first considerations after an incident is to determine how to restore access to resources that have been compromised. Then, of course, you must reestablish control of the system. Most operating systems provide the ability to create a disaster-recovery process using distribution media or system state files.

After a problem has been identified, what steps will you take to restore service? In the case of a DoS attack, a system reboot may be all that is required. Your operating system manufacturer will typically provide detailed instructions or documentation on how to restore services in the event of an attack.

If a system has been severely compromised, as in the case of a worm, it might not be possible to repair it. It may need to be regenerated from scratch. Fortunately, antivirus software packages can repair most of the damage done by the viruses you encounter. But what if you come across something new? You might need to start over with a new system. In that case, you're highly advised to do a complete disk drive format or repartition to ensure that nothing is lurking on the disk, waiting to infect your network again.

 Real World Scenario

The Virus That Won't Stop

A virus recently hit a user in your organization through an email attachment. The user updated all the programs in his computer and also updated his antivirus software; however, he's still reporting unusual behavior in his computer system. He's also receiving complaints from people in his email address book because he's sending them a virus. You've been asked to fix the problem.

The user has probably contracted a worm that has infected the system files in his computer. You should help him back up his user files to removable media. Then, completely reformat his drives and reinstall the operating system and applications. After you've replaced these, you can install new antivirus software and scan the entire system. When the scan is complete, help the user reinstall data files and scan the system again for viruses. This process should eliminate all viruses from system, application, and data files.

 Just as every network, regardless of size, should have a firewall, it should also be protected by antivirus software that is enabled and current. ClamAV is an open source solution once available only for Unix-based systems that is now available for most operating systems.

Step Four: Documenting and Reporting the Response

During the entire process of responding to an incident, you should document the steps you take to identify, detect, and repair the system or network. This information is valuable; it needs to be captured in case an attack like this occurs again. The documentation should be accessible by the people most likely to deal with this type of problem. Many help-desk software systems provide detailed methods you can use to record procedures and steps. These types of software products allow for fast access.

If appropriate, you should report/disclose the incident to legal authorities and CERT (www.cert.org) so that others can be aware of the type of attack and help look for proactive measures to prevent this from happening again. At the CERT site, you can find detailed steps to take to recover after your computer has been compromised; this is located at http://www.cert.org/tech_tips/win-UNIX-system_compromise.html.

You might also want to inform the software or system manufacturer of the problem and how you corrected it. Doing so might help them inform or notify other customers of the threat and save time for someone else.

 Real World Scenario

How Incident Response Plans Work

Emergency management (EM) personnel routinely stage fake emergencies to verify that they know what they should do in the event of an actual emergency. For example, if you live in a town with a train track that is routinely used by railcars carrying toxic chemicals, it isn't uncommon for EM personnel to stage a fake spill every couple of years. Those organizing the practice won't tell those responding what type of spill it is, or the severity of it, until they arrive at the scene. The organizers monitor and evaluate the responses to see that they're appropriate and where they can be improved.

Responding to security incidents requires the same type of focus and training. You should plan a fake incident at your site, inform all those who will be involved that it's coming, and then evaluate their response. You should evaluate the following items:

1. Was the evidence gathered and chain of custody maintained?

2. Did the escalation procedures follow the correct path?

3. Given the results of the investigation, would you be able to find and prosecute the culprit?

4. What was done that should not be done?

5. What could be done better?

Practice makes perfect, and there is no better time to practice your company's response to an emergency than before one really occurs.

Step Five: Adjusting Procedures

After an incident has been successfully managed, it's a worthwhile step to revisit the procedures and policies in place in your organization to determine what changes, if any, need to be made.

Answering simple questions can sometimes be helpful when you're resolving problems. The following questions might be included in a policy or procedure manual:

- How did the policies work or not work in this situation?

- What did we learn about the situation that was new?

- What should we do differently next time?

These simple questions can help you adjust procedures. This process is called a *post-mortem*, and it's the equivalent of an autopsy.

Forensics from the Security+ Perspective

The five steps outlined here will help in all incident response situations. For the exam, however, a number of procedures and topics that CompTIA wants you to be aware of are relevant to a forensic investigation. It is strongly recommended that you familiarize yourself with these as you prepare for the exam.

Act in Order of Volatility   When dealing with multiple issues, address them in order of volatility (OOV); always deal with the most volatile first. Volatility can be thought of as the amount of time you have to collect certain data before that window of opportunity is gone. Naturally, in an investigation, you want to collect everything, but some data will exist longer than others and you cannot possibly collect all of it once. As an example, the order of volatility in an investigation may be RAM, hard drive data, CDs/DVDs, printouts.

Capture System Image   A system image is a snapshot of what exists. Capturing an image of the operating system in its exploited state can be helpful in revisiting the issue after the fact to learn more about it. As an analogy, think of germ samples that are stored in labs after major outbreaks so scientists can revisit them later and study them further.

Document Network Traffic and Logs   Look at network traffic and logs to see what information you can find there. This information can be useful in identifying trends associated with repeated attacks.

Capture Video   Capture any relevant video you can. Video can later be analyzed in individual frames manually as well as run through a number of programs that can create indices of the contents.

Record Time Offset   It is quite common for workstation times to be off slightly from actual time, and that can happen with servers as well. Since a forensic investigation is usually dependent on a step-by-step account of what has happened, being able to follow events in the correct time sequence is critical. Because of this, it is imperative to record the time offset on each affected machine during the investigation. One method of assisting with this is to add an entry to a log file and note the time this was done and the time associated with it on the system.

Take Hashes   It is important to collect as much data as possible to be able to illustrate the situation, and hashes must not be left out of the equation. The NIST (National Institute of Standards and Technology) maintains a National Software Reference Library (NSRL). One of the purposes of the NSRL is to collect "known, traceable software applications" through their hash values and store them in a Reference Data Set (RDS). The RDS can then be used by law enforcement, government agencies, and businesses to determine which files are important as evidence in criminal investigations. More information on the RDS can be found at http://www.nsrl.nist.gov/.

Capture Screenshots   Just like video, capture all relevant screenshots for later analysis. One image can often parlay the same information that it would take hundreds of log entries to equal.

Talk to Witnesses   It is important to talk to as many witnesses to what happened as possible and as soon as possible. Over time, details and reflections can change, and you want to collect their thoughts before they do. If at all possible, document as much of the interview as you can with the video recorders, digital recorders, or whatever recording tools you can find.

Track Man Hours and Expenses   Make no mistake about it; an investigation is expensive. Track total man-hours and expenses associated with the investigation and be prepared to justify them if necessary to superiors, a court, or insurance agents.

Succession Planning

Succession planning outlines those internal to the organization who have the ability to step into positions when they open. By identifying key roles that cannot be left unfilled and associating internal employees who can step into those roles, you can groom those employees to make sure they are up to speed when it comes time for them to fill those positions.

Reinforcing Vendor Support

Software vendors and hardware vendors are necessary elements in the process of building systems and applications. The costs associated with buying preconfigured software, hardware, and services are usually less than building them yourself. Unfortunately, this makes you dependent on a vendor's ability to stay in business.

The following sections discuss service-level agreements and code escrow. These agreements help you protect yourself in the event that a software vendor goes out of business or you have a dispute with a maintenance provider for your systems.

Service-Level Agreements

A *service-level agreement (SLA)* is an agreement between you or your company and a service provider, typically a technical support provider. SLAs are also usually part of network availability and other agreements. They stipulate the performance you can expect or demand by outlining the expectations a vendor has agreed to meet. They define what is possible to deliver and provide the contract to make sure what is delivered is what was promised.

Some SLAs may put you in a vendor-dependent position that can potentially open up your data to eyes that should not see it. Consider a medical practice that must grant an application vendor full access to all patient records in the spirit of being able to maintain the application. Just as with any other contract, you must carefully scrutinize the SLA and make certain you are not unintentionally opening your organization to harm. Running it past the company's legal department and your superior is always a good practice.

Quite often, SLAs exist even within a company. They serve the same purpose within departments of a company as they do between a vendor and a supplier.

SLAs are also known as *maintenance contracts* when referring to hardware or software.

If a vendor promises to provide you with a response time of four hours, this means it will have someone involved and dedicated to resolving any difficulties you encounter—either a service technician in the field or a remote diagnostic process occurring on your system—within that time frame. In either case, the customer has specific remedies that it can demand from the vendor if the terms of an SLA aren't met.

Most computer manufacturers offer a variety of SLA levels. Some can guarantee support in hours, whereas others may require days. Different levels of coverage and different response times usually have different costs associated with them. A 4-hour service agreement will typically cost much more than a 24-hour or 48-hour agreement. An SLA should also stipulate how long the repair will take once the support process has been activated: Having a service technician on site in four hours won't do much good if it takes two weeks to get a replacement for a defective part.

Make sure that you understand the scope and terms of your SLAs; periodically review them to verify that the performance criteria match your performance needs. Doing so can help prevent frustration and unanticipated disruptions from crippling your organization. The following are key measures in SLAs:

Recovery Time Objectives   The *recovery time objective (RTO)* is the maximum amount of time that a process or service is allowed to be down and the consequences still considered acceptable. Beyond this time, the break in business continuity is considered to negatively affect business. The RTO is agreed on during the business impact analysis (BIA) creation.

Mean Time between Failures   The *mean time between failures (MTBF)* is the measure of the anticipated incidence of failure for a system or component. This measurement determines the component's anticipated lifetime. If the MTBF of a cooling system is one year, you can anticipate that the system will last for a one-year period; this means you should be prepared to replace or rebuild the system once a year. If the system lasts longer than the MTBF, your organization receives a bonus. MTBF is helpful in evaluating a system's reliability and life expectancy.

Mean Time to Restore   The *mean time to restore (MTTR)* is the measurement of how long it takes to repair a system or component once a failure occurs (this is often also referenced as *mean time to repair*). In the case of a computer system, if the MTTR is 24 hours, this tells you it will typically take 24 hours to repair it when it breaks.

> While MTTR is considered a common measure of maintainability, be careful when evaluating it because it doesn't typically include the time needed to acquire a component and have it shipped to your location. I once worked with a national vendor who thought MTTR meant mean time to respond. A technician would show up on site within the time the contract called for but would only begin to look at the problem and make a list of any needed supplies as well as get coffee. Make sure the contract agreements spell out exactly what you want.

Most SLAs stipulate the definitions of these terms and how they apply to the agreement. Make sure you understand how these terms are used and what they mean to the vendor.

 Real World Scenario

Should I Buy the Computer Store's SLA for My New Laptop?

You just purchased that new laptop you've been eyeing at the computer store. The store you bought it from is a large, national computer and software retailer. When you purchased the laptop, the salesperson worked hard to sell you an extended warranty agreement. Was it a good deal?

You should evaluate the SLA offered by the computer store and compare it to the manufacturer's warranty and service options. Many retail computer stores can't repair laptops in house, and they send most of them to the manufacturer for all but the simplest service. On the other hand, most laptop manufacturers offer a variety of service options, including 24-hour delivery of replacement systems. You should verify the length of time it will take to have the store repair your laptop before you purchase an SLA. In some situations, a store's repair program is more expensive and slower than a manufacturer's repair program.

Code Escrow Agreements

Code escrow refers to the storage and conditions of release of source code provided by a vendor. For example, a code escrow agreement would stipulate how source code would be made available to customers in the event of a vendor's bankruptcy.

If you contract with a software developer to perform a customized programming effort, your contract may not give you the right to access and view the source code this vendor creates. If you want changes made to the program's functionality, you will be required to contract with the developer or integrator who installed it to perform those changes. This practice is common in application software projects, such as setting up accounting systems.

 In recent years, a number of software companies have been forced to close their doors because of trying economic times. In many cases, the software they sold has become *orphanware*—existing without support of any type.

If the vendor ceases operations, you won't be able to obtain the source code to make further changes unless your agreement stipulates a code escrow clause. Unfortunately, this situation effectively makes your investment a dead-end street. Make sure your agreements provide you with either the source code for projects you've had done or a code escrow clause to acquire the software if the company goes out of business.

Summary

In this chapter, you learned about the many aspects involved in the operations of a secure environment. You studied business continuity and vendor support. Business continuity planning is the process of making decisions about how losses, outages, and failures are handled within an organization. Business impact analysis (BIA) includes evaluating the critical functions of the organization. This information is used to make informed decisions about how to deal with outages should they occur.

The issue of reliable service from utility companies, such as electricity and water, should be evaluated as part of your disaster recovery process. Addressing potential problems as part of your business decision making can prevent unanticipated downtime.

High-availability systems usually provide fail-over capabilities. These systems can use redundant components or fault-tolerant technologies. Clustering is a method of using multiple systems to ensure continuous operations in the event of server failure. One of the most common methods of improving fault tolerance is to utilize RAID devices for disk storage.

Disaster recovery is the process of helping your organization prepare for recovery in the event of an unplanned situation, and it's a part of your organization's business continuity plans.

Vendors can provide support and services to an organization. SLAs set a benchmark for expected performance when needed. Service performance and reliability are measured by MTBF and MTTR. Vendors that provide software or programming support should have code escrow agreements to ensure that software can be maintained if the vendor ceases doing business.

The process of dealing with a security problem is called incident response. An incident response policy should clearly outline what resources, individuals, and procedures are to be involved in the event of an incident.

Exam Essentials

Understand the aspects of disaster recovery.   Disaster recovery is concerned with the recovery of critical systems in the event of a loss. One of the primary issues is the effectiveness of backup policies and procedures. Offsite storage is one of the more secure methods of protecting information from loss.

Know the types of backups that are typically performed in an organization.   The three backup methods are full, incremental, and differential. A full backup involves the total archival of all information on a system. An incremental backup involves archiving only information that has changed since the last backup. Differential backups save all information that has changed since the last full backup.

Be able to discuss the process of recovering a system in the event of a failure.   A system recovery usually involves restoring the base operating systems, applications, and data files. The operating systems and applications are usually either restored from the original distribution media or from a server that contains images of the system. Data is typically recovered from backups or archives.

Be able to discuss the types of alternative sites available for disaster recovery.   The three types of sites available for disaster recovery are hot sites, warm sites, and cold sites. Hot sites typically provide high levels of capability, including networking. Warm sites may provide some capabilities, but they're generally less prepared than a hot site. A cold site requires the organization to replicate critical systems and all services to restore operations.

Be able to describe the needed components of an incident response policy.   The incident response policy explains how incidents will be handled, including notification, resources, and escalation. This policy drives the incident response process, and it provides advance planning to the incident response team.

Understand the basics of forensics.   Forensics is the process of identifying what has occurred on a system by examining the data trail. It involves an analysis of evidence found in computers and on digital storage media. When dealing with multiple issues, address them in order of volatility: Capture system images as a snapshot of what exists, look at network traffic and logs, capture any relevant video/screenshots/hashes, record time offset on the systems, talk to witnesses, and track total man-hours and expenses associated with the investigation.

Review Questions

1. Which plan or policy helps an organization determine how to relocate to an emergency site?

    A.   Disaster-recovery plan

    B.   Backup site plan

    C.   Privilege management policy

    D.   Privacy plan

2. Although you're talking to her on the phone, the sound of the administrative assistant's screams of despair can be heard down the hallway. She has inadvertently deleted a file that the boss desperately needs. Which type of backup is used for the immediate recovery of a lost file?

    A.   Onsite storage

    B.   Working copies

    C.   Incremental backup

    D.   Differential backup

3. You're trying to rearrange your backup procedures to reduce the amount of time they take each evening. You want the backups to finish as quickly as possible during the week. Which backup system backs up only the files that have changed since the last backup?

    A.   Full backup

    B.   Incremental backup

    C.   Differential backup

    D.   Backup server

4. Which backup system backs up all the files that have changed since the last full backup?

    A.   Full backup

    B.   Incremental backup

    C.   Differential backup

    D.   Archival backup

5. You're a consultant brought in to advise MTS on its backup procedures. One of the first problems you notice is that the company doesn't utilize a good tape-rotation scheme. Which backup method uses a rotating schedule of backup media to ensure long-term information storage?

    A.   Grandfather, Father, Son method

    B.   Full Archival method

    C.   Backup Server method

    D.   Differential Backup method

6. Which site best provides limited capabilities for the restoration of services in a disaster?

   A. Hot site

   B. Warm site

   C. Cold site

   D. Backup site

7. You're the head of information technology for MTS and have a brother in a similar position for ABC. The companies are approximately the same size and are located several hundred miles apart. As a benefit to both companies, you want to implement an agreement that would allow either company to use resources at the other site should a disaster make a building unusable. What type of agreement between two organizations provides mutual use of their sites in the event of an emergency?

   A. Backup-site agreement

   B. Warm-site agreement

   C. Hot-site agreement

   D. Reciprocal agreement

8. The process of automatically switching from a malfunctioning system to another system is called what?

   A. Fail safe

   B. Redundancy

   C. Fail-over

   D. Hot site

9. You've been brought in as a temporary for FRS, Inc. The head of IT assigns you the task of evaluating all servers and their disks and making a list of any data not stored redundantly. Which disk technology isn't fault tolerant?

   A. RAID 0

   B. RAID 1

   C. RAID 3

   D. RAID 5

10. Which agreement outlines performance requirements for a vendor?

   A. MTBF

   B. MTTR

   C. SLA

   D. BCP

11. Your company is about to invest heavily in an application written by a new startup. Because it is such a sizable investment, you express your concerns about the longevity of the new company and the risk this organization is taking. You propose that the new company agree to store its source code for use by customers in the event that it ceases business. What is this model called?

   A. Code escrow

   B. SLA

   C. BCP

   D. CA

12. Which of the following would normally *not* be part of an incident response policy?

   A. Outside agencies (that require status)

   B. Outside experts (to resolve the incident)

   C. Contingency plans

   D. Evidence collection procedures

13. Which of the following is the measure of the anticipated incidence of failure for a system or component?

   A. CIBR

   B. AIFS

   C. MTBF

   D. MTTR

14. With high availability, the goal is to have key services available 99.999 percent of the time. What is this availability also known as?

   A. Five nines

   B. Three nines

   C. Perfecta

   D. Trifecta

15. Which of the following outlines those internal to the organization who have the ability to step into positions when they open?

   A. Succession planning

   B. Progression planning

   C. Emergency planning

   D. Eventuality planning

16. What is another name for working copies?

   A. Functional copies

   B. Running copies

   C. Operating copies

   D. Shadow copies

17. What is the maximum number of drive failures a RAID 5 array can survive from and still be able to function?

    A. 0

    B. 1

    C. 2

    D. More than 2

18. The only difference between mirroring and which of the following is the addition of one more controller card?

    A. Additioning

    B. Duplexing

    C. Failing over

    D. Sanctifying

19. Which redundancy strategy has one spare part for every component in use?

    A. 1+1

    B. JWDO

    C. JIT

    D. Rollovers

20. With five nines availability, the total amount of downtime allowed per year is:

    A. 4.38 hours

    B. 526 minutes

    C. 52.65 minutes

    D. 5.26 minutes

Answers to Review Questions

1. A. The disaster-recovery plan deals with site relocation in the event of an emergency, natural disaster, or service outage.

2. B. Working copies are backups that are usually kept in the computer room for immediate use in recovering a system or lost file.

3. B. An incremental backup backs up files that have changed since the last full or partial backup.

4. C. A differential backup backs up all the files that have changed since the last full backup.

5. A. The Grandfather, Father, Son backup method is designed to provide a rotating schedule of backup processes. It allows for a minimum usage of backup media, and it still allows for long-term archiving.

6. B. Warm sites provide some capabilities in the event of a recovery. The organization that wants to use a warm site will need to install, configure, and reestablish operations on systems that may already exist at the warm site.

7. D. A reciprocal agreement is between two organizations and allows one to use the other's site in an emergency.

8. C. Fail-over occurs when a system that is developing a malfunction automatically switches processes to another system to continue operations.

9. A. RAID 0 is a method of spreading data from a single disk over a number of disk drives. It's used primarily for performance purposes.

10. C. A service-level agreement (SLA) specifies performance requirements for a vendor. This agreement may use MTBF and MTTR as performance measures in the SLA.

11. A. Code escrow allows customers to access the source code of installed systems under specific conditions, such as the bankruptcy of a vendor.

12. C. A contingency plan wouldn't normally be part of an incident response policy. It would be part of a disaster-recovery plan.

13. C. Mean time between failures (MTBF) is the measure of the anticipated incidence of failure for a system or component.

14. A. With high availability, the goal is to have key services available 99.999 percent of the time (also known as five nines availability).

15. A. Succession planning outlines those internal to the organization who have the ability to step into positions when they open.

16. D. Working copies are also known as shadow copies.

17. B. A RAID 5 array can survive the failure of any one drive and still be able to function. It can't survive the failure of multiple drives.

18. B. The only difference between mirroring and duplexing is one more controller card.

19. A. The redundancy strategy 1+1 has one spare part for every component in use.

20. D. With five nines availability, the total amount of downtime allowed per year is 5.26 minutes.

Chapter

14

Security-Related Policies and Procedures

THE FOLLOWING COMPTIA SECURITY+ EXAM OBJECTIVES ARE COVERED IN THIS CHAPTER:

✓ **2.2 Carry out appropriate risk mitigation strategies.**

- Implement policies and procedures to prevent data loss or theft

✓ **5.2 Explain the fundamental concepts and best practices related to authentication, authorization, and access control.**

- Least privilege
- Separation of duties
- Time of day restrictions
- Mandatory vacations
- Job rotation

✓ **5.3 Implement appropriate security controls when performing account management.**

- Mitigates issues associated with users with multiple account/roles
- Account policy enforcement: Password complexity; Expiration; Recovery; Length; Disablement; Lockout
- Group based privileges
- User assigned privileges

Policies are one of those things that employees love to complain about; it's common for people to look at them as restrictions on what they cannot do. While restrictions are inherent in policies, you should define to employees not only what can't be done but also what can. By outlining what can and can't be done as related to particular issues, the company can protect itself—as well as its employees—from gaps that can result from a lack of knowledge, a misunderstanding, or almost any other reason.

This chapter looks at policies that a company must have in order to survive, as well as those that it should have in order to make life easier. It also discusses auditing and account enforcement—all areas that can (and should) be governed by policies. It's important to remember, however, that you can have the perfect policies in place, but they will be useless unless they are available and understood by all of those to whom they apply.

Policies You Must Have

Policies can govern just about any facet of the workplace and employment. You can, in fact, have so many policies that you introduce paralysis among employees for fear of violating one. Depending on the size of your organization, you may be able to function with only a few, or you may need several hundred. Regardless of that number, the policies discussed in this section apply to security for all organizations and include data loss/theft, least privilege, separation of duties, time of day restrictions, mandatory vacations, and job rotation. Some of these were discussed in passing in previous chapters as they related to other topics, but all are covered in adequate depth for the Security+ exam here.

When creating policies, never think that you have to start with a blank slate. You can find a plethora of example policies online and modify them for your organization. The SANS Institute has a wonderful collection of security-related templates available at http://www.sans.org/security-resources/policies/.

Data Loss/Theft Policies

Closely tied to *data loss prevention (DLP)*, a *data loss policy* outlines the responsibilities associated with data. A common policy typically begins with wording to the effect

"Dulaney Enterprises is not responsible for any data loss and/or damages..." and contains phrases stating that data loss can be caused by users, human error, security breaches, and so on. These statements are there to protect the company in the event a user loses data and tries to place blame.

The policies then usually include statements along the lines of steps that are in place (in very generic terms) to prevent data from being lost under most circumstances. While it may seem as if the statements contradict each other, the beginning of the policy is intended to flag that there is no 100 percent foolproof way of preventing data from being deleted or modified, and the end flags that the company will do everything it can to reduce the odds of the loss occurring accidentally or intentionally.

Not intended to be confusing, some monitoring packages include settings under the heading of "Data Loss Policy." In those packages, you typically configure options to prevent data loss from occurring—for example, not allowing users to access reports that were run by others. When a user does attempt to access data not owned by them, an alert would be sent to you, a warning would be sent to the user, an entry would be made to the Event log, or a dialog box would ask the user why they are attempting this action (to which they may answer something like "the VP of Sales told me to"). You can then choose the correct course of action for the situation.

A data theft policy defines what constitutes sensitive data and applies protection to it. For example, with Cisco Security Agent, data defined under the data theft policy disables clipboard access so a user can't cut and paste it into something else. It also prevents unauthorized access to the data (logging attempts) and is really a subset of data loss policies.

Least Privilege

The concept of least privilege was mentioned in Chapter 2 and is a simple one: When assigning permissions, give users only the permissions they need to do their work and no more. The biggest benefit to following this policy is the reduction of risk. The biggest headache with following this policy is trying to deal with users who may not understand it. A manager, for example, may assert that he should have more permissions than those who report to him, but giving those permissions to him also opens up all the possibilities for inadvertently deleting files, crippling accounts, and so on.

Access creep is the term used when users accrue more access than they need. While it can happen as a result of small responsibilities here and there, it can also happen when employees change roles or departments. This additional access ability opens up weaknesses that increase risk.

A least privilege policy should exist and be enforced throughout the enterprise. Users should have only the permissions and privileges needed to do their jobs and no more. ISO standard 27002 (which updates 17799) sums it up well: "Privileges should be allocated to individuals on a need-to-use basis and on an event-by-event basis, i.e. the minimum requirement for their functional role when needed." Adopting this as the policy for your organization is highly recommended.

Separation of Duties

Almost every operating system in use today employs the concept of differentiation between users and groups at varying levels. As an example, there is always a system administrator (SA) account which has godlike control over everything: root in Unix/Linux, admin (or a deviation of it) in Windows, administrator in Apple OS X, supervisor in Novell NetWare, and so on. Once you move beyond that user, you move to administrative accounts, then regular users, and all the way down to restricted accounts, which can barely do more than log in.

As a security administrator, you need to use that as a baseline and then go beyond that and make certain that you have as many different levels of permissions and privileges as possible. At a minimum, you should do the following:

- Separate the SA account from regular accounts. *Never* log in as the SA and use the system to perform routine functions. Use the SA account only to do those operations that require those privileges.

- Limit the SA account to as small a group as possible.

- Separate the audit and logging responsibilities from the SA.

Again, using the ISO standard as an example, it recommends the segregation of duties and separation of environments as a way to reduce the likelihood of misuse of systems or information (either intentional or accidental).

Time of Day Restrictions

One of the easiest policies to enforce is time of day restrictions. Almost every operating system—server and workstation—allows you to configure when an account can have access to the system. While it may seem pedantic, it can increase the security of the system significantly. For example, if you are the administrator for an office, and workers use the systems only from 8:00 a.m. to 5:00 p.m. Monday through Friday, then you can configure their accounts to allow access only from 7:00 a.m. to 6:00 p.m. (offering an extra hour at each end for work they need to do outside of normal) on those days and not allow access outside of those parameters. What you have accomplished by making the accounts valid for only 55 hours each week is to prevent them from being used by attackers the other 113 hours. As simple as it is, it is also effective.

Restrictions can be applied as policies for groups or users in Active Directory, set locally, or set through a number of add-on packages. Exercise 14.1 walks through restricting the time of day settings for a user on a Windows 7 workstation.

EXERCISE 14.1

Creating a Time of Day Restriction

In this exercise, we will create a time of day restriction on a Windows 7 workstation for a regular user; such restrictions cannot be placed on an administrative account. To create the restriction, follow these steps:

1. From the Start menu, choose Control Panel ➢ User Accounts And Family Safety ➢ Parental Controls.

2. Choose a standard user, and then click Time Limits beneath Windows Settings.

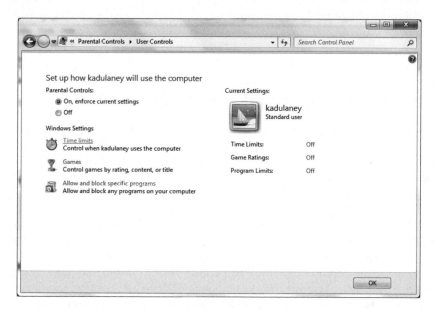

3. Click and drag the cursor in the blocks to restrict access so the account can use the computer only from 7:00 a.m. to 6:00 p.m. Monday through Friday.

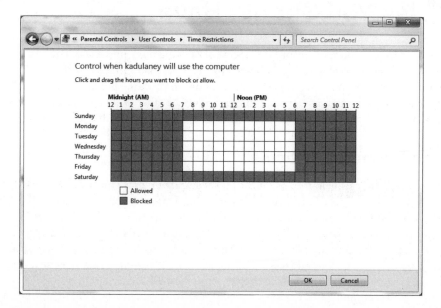

EXERCISE 14.1 *(continued)*

4. Click OK.

5. Click OK again to exit the User Controls.

6. Exit Control Panel.

Mandatory Vacations and Job Rotation

A policy of mandatory vacations should be implemented in order to assist in the prevention of fraud. While a mandatory vacation can have health benefits for employees as well, it provides an opportunity to see what they truly do and look for any improper (including illegal) acts. It is not uncommon for an organization to conduct an audit of activities while an employee is on vacation. Making the possibility of such an action transparent can be a deterrent in and of itself.

Job rotation policies exist for the same reason but are much more extreme than mandatory vacations. By moving an employee through the organization, you disrupt much of their ability to conduct fraud. The larger the organization is, the easier it is to do job rotation, but it still places a significant burden on those involved because of the training that must take place.

While both of these policies provide redundancy in skills and decrease opportunities for illegal activities, they will always be difficult to implement in small companies.

Policies You Should Have

The policies and procedures your organization uses have a huge impact on your ability to manage a secure environment. Although your primary role isn't that of policy maker, you need to understand two critical areas to succeed: human resource policies and certificate policies. These are should-haves as opposed to must-haves because while an organization can survive without them, it will find the environment much more manageable in their presence.

Human Resource Policies

Human resource policies help the organization set standards and enforce behaviors. From a security perspective, this is critical. As a security administrator, you won't generally be making policy decisions, but you have an impact on how policies are developed and enforced.

Human resource policies that consider security requirements will make your job easier. If the people the company hires are trustworthy, internal security problems will diminish. This will free up resources to address other aspects of the business that need attention. In the following sections, we'll look at each type of personnel security policy.

Hiring Policies

Hiring policies define how individuals are brought into an organization. They also establish the process used to screen prospective employees for openings. Your organizational hiring policies should establish expectations for both the interviewer and the prospective employee.

Most organizations that work with the government have mandatory drug-testing requirements. Experience and studies have shown that drug users have a tendency to perform inconsistently, have higher incidents of theft, and are vulnerable to social engineering or compromises such as blackmail.

Your organization should also investigate references, college degrees, certifications, and any other information that is provided as part of the screening process. Security professionals should be screened more thoroughly than many other employees. A special trust is being imparted to security professionals, and this trust should be given only to people who are worthy of it.

Policies should exist to define how users are added to a company's network when hired. Those policies should dictate who can add a new account as well as who can formally request one. They should also define who approves access to the system and the levels of access granted to initial accounts.

Termination Policies

Termination policies involve more than simply firing a person. Your organization needs to have a clear process for informing affected departments about voluntary and involuntary terminations. When an employee leaves a company, their computer access should be discontinued immediately.

If an involuntary termination occurs, you should back up the system they use as well as any files on servers before the termination occurs. Terminations are emotional times; if information is archived before the termination, there is less chance that critical records will be lost if the employee does something irrational. Most people won't do anything unusual, but you're better safe than sorry.

In many cases, ex-employees find themselves with time on their hands. That time could be spent trying to hurt the company that hurt them—through social engineering or other means. Your job is to make certain they can't use that time to find weaknesses in your system and cause harm.

Make sure your termination policies mandate that the appropriate staff is notified when a termination is about to occur so that accounts can be disabled, systems backed up, and any other measures taken that are deemed appropriate. Other accounts may be arguable, but you must always disable a privileged user account in the event of that user's termination.

Many times, a termination policy includes the clause that, upon termination, a former employee must be escorted at all times while performing post-termination activities (cleaning out their desk, hauling items to their car, and so on).

While it is easy to think of hiring and termination when it comes to HR issues, don't forget to consider what lies between the two. Policies govern the time of employment as well and shouldn't be limited to only hiring and firing.

Ethics Policies

Ethics is perhaps best described as the personnel or organizational rules governing how interactions, relationships, and dealings occur. Ethics affect business practices, are the basis of laws, and are highly subjective. An *ethics policy* is the written policy governing accepted organizational ethics.

Many organizations define ethical behavior and the consequences of not behaving in an ethical manner. Most professional organizations have adopted codes of ethics or conduct for their members; in many cases, a violation of these ethics laws will result in suspension, expulsion, or censure by the organization.

One organization, the Computer Professionals for Social Responsibility (CPSR), has created the "Ten Commandments of Computer Ethics" in conjunction with the Computer Ethics Institute (CEI). These commandments (as found on the website `http://cpsr.org/ issues/ethics/cei/`) are listed here:

- Thou shalt not use a computer to harm other people.

- Thou shalt not interfere with other people's computer work.

- Thou shalt not snoop around in other people's computer files.

- Thou shalt not use a computer to steal.

- Thou shalt not use a computer to bear false witness.

- Thou shalt not copy or use proprietary software for which you have not paid.

- Thou shalt not use other people's computer resources without authorization or proper compensation.

- Thou shalt not appropriate other people's intellectual output.

- Thou shalt think about the social consequences of the program you are writing or the system you are designing.

- Thou shalt always use a computer in ways that ensure consideration and respect for your fellow humans.

This list, as you can see, outlines computer usage and ethical behavior for computer professionals. The commandments establish a code of behavior and trust that is important for security and computer-security professionals. This list is a good place to start in the development of both a personnel ethics code and an organizational ethics code, and I would encourage you to consult RFC 1087, which is focused on ethics and the Internet, as well.

It is highly recommended that the ethics policy you craft also discusses gifts. In some organizations, all gifts are strictly prohibited out of fear they will lead to reciprocity ("you gave me a cruise, now I will give you our company's account"). In other organizations, employees are allowed to receive gifts from vendors as long as they are not valued above a certain dollar amount.

Privacy and Compartmentalized Information Policies

Privacy policies for corporate information are essential. You must clearly state what information can and can't be disclosed. Privacy policies must also specify who is entitled to ask for information within the organization and what types of information are provided to employees.

 The process of establishing boundaries for information sharing is called *compartmentalization.* It's a standard method of protecting information.

Your policies must clearly state that employees should have no expectations of privacy. Employers are allowed to search desks, computers, files, and any other items brought into the building. Your policy should also state that emails and telephone communications can be monitored and that monitoring can occur without the employee's permission or knowledge. Many employees wrongly assume they have a right to privacy when in fact they don't. By explicitly stating your policies, you can avoid misunderstandings and potentially prevent employees from embarrassing themselves.

Need-to-Know Policies

Need-to-know policies allow people in an organization to withhold classified or sensitive information from others in the company. The more people have access to sensitive information, the more likely it is that this information will be disclosed to unauthorized personnel. A need-to-know policy isn't intended to prohibit people from accessing information they need; it's meant to minimize unauthorized access.

 Closely related to need-to-know policies are data classifications. This topic was addressed in Chapter 6.

Many naturally curious individuals like to gain sensitive information just for the fun of it. No doubt you've known someone who is a gossip—they will tell everybody the secrets they know. This can prove embarrassing to the organization or the people in the organization.

 The need-to-know section of most policies usually contains a statement to the effect of "Data containing any confidential information shall be readily identified and treated as confidential."

Social Media Policies

Many organizations are encouraging employees to participate in social media in order to help promote the business. Unfortunately, this can open a legal can of worms, and a policy should be in place for employees to understand what they can and cannot do and say. As an example, if a paid employee is using Twitter to send out messages, then the law interprets those messages as advertising and the same rules governing advertising apply. If trade secrets are released, then they are considered to be no longer protected.

Employees need to be aware of rules restricting private company information and that this applies especially where social media are concerned. They need to know that client information must be kept private (no tweeting that a client is acting like a baby) and that those messages they send have the potential to live on the Internet forever.

It is highly recommended that a social media policy exist for every organization and members of IT meet with legal counsel to draft such a policy.

Conducting Background Investigations

Background investigations potentially involve more than checking references. A good background investigation should include credit history and criminal-record checks as well as information about work experience and education. These checks must be done with the permission of the employee or prospective employee. Keep in mind that refusing to agree to this type of investigation doesn't mean that the individual has a problem in their background; it may mean that they value their privacy.

It's a good idea for employees who deal with sensitive information, such as security professionals, to have a thorough background investigation. This ensures that employees are who they say they are and have the education they say they do. A background check should weed out individuals who have misrepresented their background and experiences.

Certificate Policies

The advent of e-commerce has created a grave concern about trust. How does a customer know that they're working with a legitimate supplier? How does a retailer know they're dealing with a legitimate customer? One of the major problems facing e-commerce providers, as well as other businesses, is fraud. Fraud, theft, and other illegal transactions cost businesses billions of dollars a year.

Certificate policies aren't part of the Security+ exam. They are, however, an important aspect of an overall security program and are presented here for your consideration. All you need to know about certificates for the Security+ exam can be found in Chapters 8 and 9.

There are ways to minimize if not eliminate the losses that organizations and individuals face. One method entails the use of digital certificates and certificate policies.

Certificates allow emails, files, and other transactions to be signed by the originator. This digital signing process usually carries close to the same weight as a hand signature. Using digital signatures allows business transactions to occur in a manner that provides a level of trust between the parties involved.

One of the most common certificates in use today is the X.509 certificate. It includes encryption, authentication, and a reasonable level of validity. A certificate issued by a valid certificate authority is valid in almost all cases; exceptions are few and far between. Most e-commerce providers accept the X.509 certificate or equivalent technologies.

Certificate policies refer to organizational policies regarding the issuing and use of certificates. These policies have a huge impact on how an organization processes and works with certificates.

A certificate policy needs to identify the following:

- Which certificate authorities (CAs) are acceptable

- How certificates are used

- How certificates are issued

An organization must also determine whether to use third-party CAs, such as VeriSign, or create its own CA systems. In either case, the policies have implications about trust and trusted transactions.

A *trusted transaction* occurs under the security policy administered by a trusted security domain. Your organization may decide that it can serve as its own trusted security domain and that it can use third-party CAs, thus allowing for additional flexibility. Third-party CAs are usually accredited. However, the process of getting an internal CA accredited is difficult and requires compliance with the policies and guidelines of the accrediting organization.

Transactions require the involvement of a minimum of two parties. In the CA environment, the two primary parties are identified as the *subscriber* and the *relying party*. The subscriber is the individual who is attempting to present the certificate that proves authenticity. The relying party is the person receiving the certificate. The relying party is dependent on the certificate as the primary authentication mechanism. If this certificate comes from a CA, the CA is known as the *third party*. The third party is responsible for providing assurance to the relying party that the subscriber is genuine. Figure 14.1 illustrates these relationships between the parties.

FIGURE 14.1   Parties in a certificate-based transaction

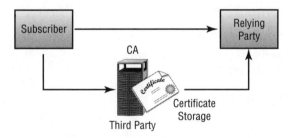

If a dispute occurs, these terms will be used to identify all the parties in the transaction. Your certificate policies should clearly outline who the valid subscribers and third parties are in any transactions. These policies provide your organization with a framework to identify parties, and they provide the rules detailing how to conduct transactions using e-commerce, email, and other electronic media.

The practices or policies that an organization adopts for the certificate process are as important as the process that uses them. Your organization needs to develop practices and methods for dealing with certificate validity, expiration, and management. These policies tend to become extremely complicated. Most CAs require a *Certificate Practice Statement (CPS)*, which defines certificate issue processes, record keeping, and subscribers' legal acceptance of the terms of the CPS.

The CA should also identify certificate expiration and revocation processes. The CA must clearly explain the certificate revocation list (CRL) and CRL dissemination policies.

Security Controls for Account Management

Privilege management involves making decisions about what information is accessed, how it's accessed, and who is authorized to access it. Unlike hardware access control, these concerns deal with policy and implementation issues. Additionally, the issue of auditing is a key factor: You should ensure that your organization doesn't provide more access or privileges than individuals need to do their work.

The following sections cover user and group roles, auditing, and access control. Each of these considerations can be used to form an effective and coherent privilege management process. These processes allow users to gain access to the information they need, to be denied access to information they don't need, and to effectively gain access to system resources.

User and Group Role Management

The process of user, group, and role management involves recognizing how work is accomplished in an organization. Most organizations have a high number of standardized tasks that can be accomplished without a great deal of privileged information, but some departments may routinely work with sensitive information about the organization or its customers. A clear set of rules specifying and limiting access can make the job of managing the process much simpler.

 Real World Scenario

Dealing with Differing Access Needs

XYZ has departments that are involved in sales, finance, manufacturing, vendor relations, and customer relations. Each of these departments has different information needs.

The Sales department may not need to access all of the company's financial information. However, someone in Manufacturing might need that information. The job of establishing the various privilege levels in a company can become complicated. Some individuals may need to view certain information but should be prohibited from changing it, whereas other individuals may need to update that same information.

There is always a fine balance that you must strive for when dealing with access control. This can easily be one of the biggest everyday headaches that a security administrator must contend with.

In a company of several dozen employees, establishing access control can be difficult, but in a company of thousands, establishing access control at an individual level on *user-assigned privileges* can be overwhelming. If each individual needs different access capabilities, thousands of access rules are required.

 Most operating systems allow you to organize users into groups with similar access needs so that you can more easily manage an otherwise cumbersome access puzzle. Individuals, and even other groups, can then be embedded into top-layer groups known as *security groups*.

Employing *group-based privileges*, a security group can have predefined access capabilities associated with it. In this way, you can develop a comprehensive security model that addresses the accessibility needs of everyone in an organization. Figure 14.2 illustrates the group process. In this example, most individuals are placed into one of two departmental groups. The top user in the picture has access only to accounting applications on the ACCTG server, the middle user has access to both, and the bottom user has access only to the APPS server. Departmental groups access information based on established needs and predefined access.

FIGURE 14.2 Security grouping

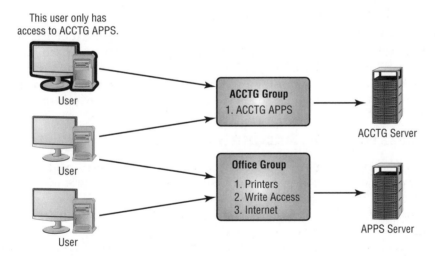

Each department may have different access capabilities. In some cases, different roles within a department have different needs. Although you may want a supervisor to have access to information about a department's performance, you may not want a clerical worker to have that same access. It comes down to an issue of trust, experience, and need.

The process of making decisions about privilege is important. It must be clear and unambiguous to be effective. In the case of a highly centralized environment, a single department or person is responsible for making decisions about access that affect the entire organization. In a decentralized environment, decision making is spread throughout the organization.

The people who are the most aware of the security needs should control the decision-making process. This process can involve everyone in the organization.

 Many operating systems automatically replicate or send changes in access throughout an organization. A single change in a user's access may inadvertently give them access to sensitive information. Careful study of privileges is needed for an effective security policy.

Granting Temporary Access

From time to time, individuals may need special access to information that they wouldn't normally be given. For example, an office or clerical person might need to gather information for a special report. Specialized access should be granted only for the period of time during which they need the access. A separate account with these special privileges is usually the best way to manage these types of situations. When the special project is finished, the account can be disabled or deleted. This ensures that privileges don't become associated permanently with a user or a department. Security professionals who ensure that only authorized access occurs can monitor special accounts to reduce the potential for a security violation to occur.

Granting Administrator Access

Systems administrators are also subject to privilege issues. If an organization has multiple servers, it may not want administrators to have access to all the servers for administrative purposes. In larger organizations, company-wide access could create a serious security risk. As a rule, you should grant administrative access only to specific systems and possibly grant it only at specific times. Again, doing so limits a company's exposure to security violations.

Users with Multiple Accounts/Roles

As mentioned when discussing least privilege, of particular concern is users who have multiple accounts and/or act in multiple roles. An example of this is any administrator who has an account they use for administrative purposes and one they use when performing another role (editor, author, etc.). In most organizations, it is not possible to not have a number of users who operate in multiple capacities. The key then becomes education and policies.

Education is needed to show why employees should use the elevated accounts only when necessary and to make them understand the security risks inherent in operating at those levels. Policies are needed to put into action and enforce the common sense that these users should possess. The policy should be understood—and signed off on—by those operating in this group.

Auditing

Auditing is the process of ensuring that policies, procedures, and regulations are carried out in a manner consistent with organizational standards. A periodic security audit of *user access and rights review* can help determine whether privilege-granting processes are appropriate and whether computer usage and escalation processes are in place and working. Think of an auditor as a consultant charged with helping to ensure that procedures are followed.

An auditor who is doing a good job should pull no punches and should offer concrete suggestions on how to improve. These suggestions may pertain to areas of improvement in contingency planning, to security and access problems, or to physical control issues. The information an auditor provides is extremely valuable; acting on it can save your organization time and aggravation. You may not like the results of the audit, but they can be used as a valuable tool to help improve the organization.

Many will argue over the correct steps to go through when performing an audit. The specifics may differ, but the following general steps should always be undertaken: Plan for the audit, conduct the audit, evaluate the results, communicate the results and needed changes, and follow up.

The following sections discuss the need to verify that users are given appropriate permissions to accomplish the work they're assigned.

Privilege Auditing

Privilege audits verify that accounts, groups, and roles are correctly assigned and that policies are being followed. An audit should verify that access is established correctly, security is in place, and policies are effective. A privilege audit might entail a complete review of all accounts and groups to ensure that they're correctly implemented and up-to-date.

The problems associated with the transfer of an individual in an organization are common. When a personnel transfer occurs, the transferred user needs to be removed from old groups. Failing to do so can result in *privilege creep* (also known as *access creep*, referenced earlier), which occurs when an individual accidentally gains a higher level of access than they would normally be entitled to or need.

Usage Auditing

Usage auditing verifies that systems and software are used appropriately and consistently with organizational policies. A usage audit may entail physically inspecting systems, verifying software configurations, and conducting other activities intended to prove that resources are being used appropriately.

A major concern (although not primarily a security concern) is the issue of installed software and licensing. Illegal use of unlicensed software can carry stiff penalties. Examining systems on a periodic basis verifies that only the software an organization is licensed to use is installed.

From a security perspective, some software is more vulnerable to exploitation than other software. If vulnerable software is installed, it may create a backdoor or other unauthorized usage problem. Periodically inspecting systems to ensure that software updates and patches are current and that only approved software is installed is a good idea.

Usage audits also examine network usage. Is your network being used for illicit purposes? Is pornography present in your environment? Any number of other problems may also be discovered. By performing audits, you can help deter potentially embarrassing or even illegal activities from occurring in your environment.

Escalation Auditing

Escalation audits help ensure that procedures and communications methods are working properly in the event of a problem or issue. Escalation is primarily focused on the issue of gaining access to decision makers in a time of crisis. These types of audits test your organization to ensure that it has the appropriate procedures, policies, and tools to deal with any problems in the event of an emergency, catastrophe, or other need for management intervention.

Disaster recovery plans, business continuity plans, and other plans are tested and verified for accuracy. These types of plans require constant care or they become dated and ineffective. An audit can help ensure that all bases are covered and that your plans have a high likelihood of success when needed.

A good way to determine if your escalation audits are working is to test them. Many organizations develop scenarios to verify that mechanisms are in place to deal with certain situations. If the president of the organization is out of town or unavailable, who has the authority to make a decision about transitioning to an alternative site? If such issues can be worked out in advance, they're much less difficult to deal with in emergencies.

 Real World Scenario

Performing a Usage Audit

Your company has undergone its umpteenth reorganization. Many people have been moved to new positions within the new organizational chart. You've been asked to verify that users can access the information they need to perform their jobs. You also need to make sure that any inappropriate access is removed.

To successfully complete your assignment, you'll need to inspect every user account and group to verify which user accounts belong to which groups. You also need to verify that each group has the appropriate access to the servers and other resources needed to accomplish their assignments.

In many newer systems, you can accomplish this by inspecting the access groups that users belong to and by adding or deleting user accounts as appropriate. If you're using a network that doesn't support security groups, you'll need to modify the access rights of each account individually.

COBIT (Control Objectives for Information and related Technology) is a framework, or set of best practices, that can be used to help with the audit process. The current version is COBIT 5, and information on it can be found at http://www.isaca.org/Knowledge-Center/COBIT/.

Administrative Auditing

One of the most overlooked components of an audit involves administrative elements. It is important to document the procedures undertaken during the *classification of information* (classifying information was discussed in Chapter 6) and who is involved in this process. You must also document who is involved in investigations, when it is suspected that something is awry, and the procedures they follow—known as *due diligence.*

This section of the audit should also address *change management*—the structured approach that is followed to secure the company's assets. Details here should include the controls that are in place to prevent unauthorized access to, and changes of, all IT assets. Among the assets you must be able to demonstrate appropriate controls on are all those related to *personally identifiable information (PII).* PII exists within your databases for all users, customers, vendors, and contacts and includes such things as their phone number, address, credit card number, employee status, and so on. In general, any attribute of any person is considered PII and is thus subject to privacy protection—and liability—issues.

Auditing and Log Files

One operation you will need to perform when working with log files if you are going to evaluate entries from security applications is carefully monitoring their size. In some operating systems, the files are allowed to grow indefinitely (until the drive runs out of space), while in others the size is fixed and older entries are overwritten by new ones. Most Windows Server-based operating systems, for example, set the Security log to a maximum size and overwrite the file as needed.

If you are running Windows 2008, it is recommended that you start Event Viewer and right-click the Security Log object. Choose Properties from the pop-up menu, change the Maximum Log Size entry to as large as you can afford, and select Do Not Overwrite Events. Each time you audit the log entries (at least weekly is recommended), choose to manually clear the file once you are certain there are no alarms you should respond to.

The log files created by crucial network services such as DNS need to be routinely examined regularly. The DNS service, when running on Windows Server 2008 for example, writes entries to the log file that can be examined using Event Viewer. Just as you set the size and overwrite options for the Security Log object, you should take those same actions for the DNS Server logs as well.

A firewall, whether software or hardware, often creates log files the same as most other services when enabled. Given the importance of the firewall and its purpose, the entries written to those logs should be held in high esteem and evaluated regularly. These log files can be created anywhere a firewall is running, from a workstation to an appliance.

In Exercise 14.2, we will look at the firewall log settings in Windows 7 and turn them on.

EXERCISE 14.2

Turning On Windows 7 Firewall Logs

Firewall logging is not on by default in Windows 7. In this exercise, we will turn on logging on a Windows 7 workstation. To start the logging, follow these steps:

1. From the Start menu, choose Control Panel ➢ System And Security ➢ Windows Firewall.

2. Click Advanced Settings.

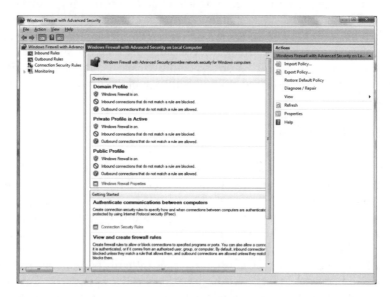

3. Right-click Windows Firewall With Advanced Security On Local Computer and choose Properties.

EXERCISE 14.2 *(continued)*

4. Click Customize beneath Logging to open the Customize Logging Settings For The Domain Profile dialog box.

5. Change the setting for Log Dropped Packets to Yes; this will log why and when the packet was dropped. Note that you can also elect to change the setting on Log Successful Connections, but that can create quite a few more entries and you'll need to check the log files more often; it logs why and when the connection was allowed.

6. Change the Size Limit from the default of 4,096 KB to 8,192 KB. Note that this value is limited to sizes between 1 and 32,767 KB.

7. Click OK. Events, as they occur, can now be found in Event Viewer beneath Applications And Services Logs (choose Windows, and then choose Windows Firewall With Advanced Security).

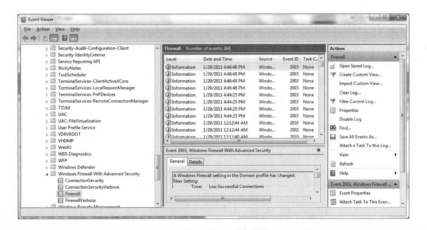

Most antivirus programs also create log files when they run that should be regularly checked. You want to verify not only that the program is running but also that the definition file(s) being used is current. Pay attention to the viruses that are found and deleted/quarantined, as well as any files that are being skipped.

You should regularly check log files from every antivirus program running, from the workstation to the server, and you can educate users on how to routinely examine their own log files. With Sophos Anti-Virus, for example, users right-click the icon that appears in their taskbar and choose Open Sophos Anti-Virus from the pop-up menu. Next, they click Configure Sophos Anti-Virus and choose View Log. Changes to the default logging settings are made by choosing Configure Log and tweaking the settings that appear in the dialog box shown in Figure 14.3.

FIGURE 14.3   Configuring logging with Sophos Anti-virus

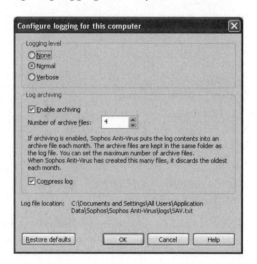

Reporting to Management

An audit should always conclude with a report to management. This report should outline any organizational strengths and weaknesses as they existed at the time of the audit. The audit should also explain any violations of policy, recommendations for improvement, and recommendations for the organization overall. This report is a vital part of the process, and it provides a mechanism that can be used to develop corrective action plans and updated policies.

There must always be one person who can gain access when things go awry. Not that long ago, a rogue network administrator in San Francisco was charged with resetting the passwords on all the city's fiber switches and routers, making them inaccessible to administrators. With all other administrators lacking the permission needed to change the passwords, the city was unable to control the backbone.

Account Policy Enforcement

The account policy determines the security parameters regarding who can and cannot access the system. As has been mentioned before, there is a fine line between lax security (which keeps users happy) and stringent security. When you impose stringent security—long passwords that must be changed every few days and accounts locked as soon as wrong entries are given, you create unhappy users who will often start jeopardizing the very security you are trying to create by writing down values on slips of paper that can fall in the wrong hands.

In this section, we will look at the best practices related to key components of account policy enforcement that you need to know for the exam. These include the issues of password length and complexity, password expiration, password recovery, and finally, password disablement and lockout.

Password Length and Complexity

The more difficult a user's password is, the more difficult it becomes for a miscreant to break it and log in as that user, and the more difficult it becomes, as well, for the user to remember it. Thus you need to obtain a fine balance between the two extremes.

Eight characters (upper and lowercase) are generally considered the minimum for password length, and most systems today encourage the use of at least one non-alpha character—punctuation, special characters, numbers, and so on. On Windows-based systems, the password value can be set to 0 to not require passwords. The current default values, as of the release of Windows 7, is seven characters on domain controllers and 0 on stand-alone servers.

Windows 7, through the Local Security Policy (which is overridden by Group Policy values on a domain controller) allows you to choose to enable password complexity, as shown in Figure 14.4.

FIGURE 14.4   Enabling password complexity in Windows 7

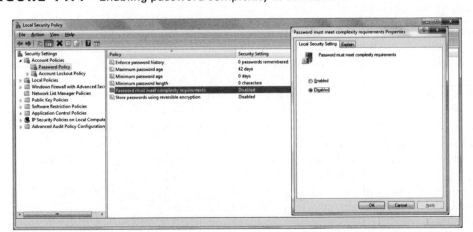

Choosing this option requires passwords to meet the following requirements:

- They cannot contain the user's account name or parts of the user's full name that exceed two consecutive characters.

- They must be at least six characters long.

- They have to contain characters from at least three of the following four sets:

    - A-Z

    - a-z

    - 0-9

    - Non-alpha characters (!, $, #, %, etc.)

Password Expiration

Every password must expire because the longer the same value is used, the more likely it is to be broken. Ninety days is acceptable for many organizations, but Microsoft often recommends setting this to 42 days if you want to enforce strong password usage throughout the organization. For more information on this topic, go to http://technet.microsoft.com/en-us/library/cc875814.aspx.

To keep users from changing their password to the same value as the old one, or to one they used the last time around, you should enable password history. Most Microsoft OSs allow you to set this to a number between 0 (disabled) and 24. For the best security, set this to 24 so that 24 unique passwords must be used by any given user before they can begin to reuse them.

Along with the expiration date, you should configure a minimum number of days that can exist between password changes. If this setting is disabled or set too low, users can immediately change new passwords to other values—something a hacker may want to do. It is recommended this not be set to anything lower than 2 days.

Password Recovery

One of the certainties in life is that users will occasionally forget their password. This often occurs shortly after they've changed it from one value to another, but it can often occur after a long weekend. Since a user's password isn't stored on most operating systems (only a hash value is kept), most operating systems allow the administrator to change the value for a user who has forgotten theirs. This new value allows the user to log in and then immediately change it to another value that they can (hopefully) remember.

If it is the administrator's password that is forgotten, then you can use the reset disk available with most operating systems (including Windows 7) to reset this value.

If the forgotten password is not the login password but rather one set in BitLocker, then you can use the BitLocker Recovery Password Viewer for Active Directory Users and Computers tool. This tool can be downloaded from the Microsoft Download Center (http://www.microsoft.com/downloads/en/default.aspx).

Password Disablement and Lockout

When a user will be gone from a company for a while (maternity leave, for example), their account should be disabled until they return. When a user will be gone from a company forever (termination), their account should be removed from the system immediately.

 If there is the possibility that the terminated employee may come back as a contractor, then consider suspending the account as opposed to removing it. This action is preferable since Relative Identifiers (RIDs) are not reused after they are deleted.

In between the two extremes lies the need to lock an account. This occurs when a user is attempting to log in but giving incorrect values; locking this account is necessary to prevent a would-be attacker from repeatedly guessing at password values until they find a match. You can configure the lockout policies at the local level on the workstation (Local Security Policy) as well as at the domain level (Group Policies), and the values you configure are the same:

Account Lockout Duration   When the system locks the account, this is the duration before it is unlocked. With Windows, this value can range from 0 minutes to 99,999 minutes. Setting it to 0 does not disable the feature but rather requires an administrator to explicitly unlock the account before it can be used again.

Account Lockout Threshold   This setting determines how many incorrect attempts a user can give before the account is locked. This value can range from 0 to 999 failed attempts. If it is set at 0, the account will never be locked out. Note that attempts to enter values at the password-protected screensaver count just the same as attempts to log in after the system has booted and Ctrl+Alt+Delete has been pressed.

Reset Account Lockout Counter After   This is the number of minutes to wait between counting failed login attempts as being part of the same batch of attempts. For example, Account Lockout Threshold may be set to 3 to lock the account after three bad tries, but this value can be set to 5 so that if the user tries once and then waits more than five minutes to try again, they have another three attempts before the account is locked. The values here can range from 0 to 99,999 minutes. This value can be set (or have meaning) only if the Account Lockout Threshold is set, and the reset time must be less than or equal to the Account Lockout Duration.

Summary

Policies exist to govern relationships. Those relationships exist between two parties, with one of them usually being the company or a representative of it. Policies that all organizations should have include data loss/theft, least privilege, separation of duties, time of day restrictions, mandatory vacations, and job rotation.

Human resource policies define all the key relationships between the employee, the organization, and the information they use. These policies dictate the expectations between all the parties involved. They should be comprehensive, and they should have a huge impact on security expectations.

Understanding how certificate policies affect certificate usage requires a clear understanding of the parties involved in a transaction. The subscriber is the presenter of a certificate. The relying party depends on the subscriber or a third party to verify authenticity. A CA should have a clear set of practices (a CPS) to define how business activities are conducted.

Auditing and account enforcement are also areas that can be governed by policies. Privilege management involves making decisions regarding user and group roles, sign-on procedures, how information is accessed and used, auditing, and access control methods. Privilege management is one of the key components of an effective security policy.

Exam Essentials

Define the elements of a security policy.   The security policy sets the internal expectations of how situations, information, and personnel are handled. These policies cover a wide range of the organization. Most policies in an organization affect the security policy.

Understand least privilege.   Least privilege states that when assigning permissions, give users only the permissions they need to do their work and no more. The biggest benefit to following this policy is the reduction of risk.

Define the various types of policies that affect security efforts in an organization.   The major policies that affect security are human resources and certificate policies. Human resource policies describe expected behavior and other policies concerning employees.

Know how to deal with users having multiple roles.   Users who have multiple accounts and/or act in multiple roles, such as an administrator who has an account for administrative purposes and one for performing another role, require attention and education. Users need to understand why they should use the elevated accounts only when necessary and the security risks inherent in operating at those levels.

Be able to describe the purpose of an audit.   An audit is the process of testing and verifying the effectiveness of policies and procedures in an organization. A security audit may include evaluating privileges, systems usage, and escalation. The final product of an audit is the report to management, which outlines the results of the audit and pinpoints areas that need improvement.

Review Questions

1. Which policy dictates how an organization manages certificates and certificate acceptance?

   A. Certificate policy

   B. Certificate access list

   C. CA accreditation

   D. CRL rule

2. You're giving hypothetical examples during a required security training session when the subject of certificates comes up. A member of the audience wants to know how a party is verified as genuine. Which party in a transaction is responsible for verifying the identity of a certificate holder?

   A. Subscriber

   B. Relying party

   C. Third party

   D. Omni registrar

3. MTS is in the process of increasing all security for all resources. No longer will the legacy method of assigning rights to users as they're needed be accepted. From now on, all rights must be obtained for the network or system through group membership. Which of the following groups is used to manage access in a network?

   A. Security group

   B. Single sign-on group

   C. Resource sharing group

   D. AD group

4. Which process inspects procedures and verifies that they're working?

   A. Audit

   B. Business continuity plan

   C. Security review

   D. Group privilege management

5. Which ISO standard states: "Privileges should be allocated to individuals on a need-to-use basis and on an event-by-event basis, i.e. the minimum requirement for their functional role when needed"?

   A. 27002

   B. 27102

   C. 20102

   D. 20112

6. On a NetWare-based system, which account is equivalent to the administrator account in Windows?

    A. Auditor

    B. Supervisor

    C. Root

    D. Master

7. Which type of policy would govern whether employees can engage in practices such as taking gifts from vendors?

    A. Termination policy

    B. Endowment policy

    C. Ethics policy

    D. Benefit policy

8. Which of the following occurs under the security policy administered by a trusted security domain?

    A. Positive inspection

    B. Confident poll

    C. Voucher session

    D. Trusted transaction

9. A periodic security audit of which of the following can help determine whether privilege-granting processes are appropriate and whether computer usage and escalation processes are in place and working?

    A. Event logs

    B. User account and ldp settings

    C. User access and rights review

    D. System security log files

10. Which Windows Firewall events are logged by default in Windows 7?

    A. Dropped packets

    B. Successful connections

    C. Both dropped packets and successful connections

    D. Neither dropped packets nor successful connections

11. Which audits help ensure that procedures and communications methods are working properly in the event of a problem or issue?

    A. Communication

    B. Escalation

    C. Selection

    D. Preference

12. Most CAs require what to define certificate issue processes, record keeping, and subscribers' legal acceptance of terms?

    A. CPS

    B. DAC

    C. SRC

    D. GPM

13. Which of the following is one of the most common certificates in use today?

    A. X.733

    B. X.50

    C. X.509

    D. X.500

14. People in an organization can withhold classified or sensitive information from others in the company when governed by what type of policy?

    A. Nondisclosure

    B. Suppression

    C. Need-to-know

    D. Revelation

15. The process of establishing boundaries for information sharing is called:

    A. Disassociation

    B. Compartmentalization

    C. Isolation

    D. Segregation

16. Which policies define how individuals are brought into an organization?

    A. Service policies

    B. Continuity policies

    C. Pay policies

    D. Hiring policies

17. A policy of mandatory vacations should be implemented in order to assist in:

    A. The prevention of fraud

    B. Identifying employees no longer needed

    C. Reducing insurance expenses

    D. Enforcing privilege management

18. On a Linux-based system, which account is equivalent to the administrator account in Windows?

    A. Auditor

    B. Supervisor

    C. Root

    D. Master

19. Which of the following is the basic premise of least privilege?

    A. Always assign responsibilities to the administrator who has the minimum permissions required.

    B. When assigning permissions, give users only the permissions they need to do their work and no more.

    C. Regularly review user permissions and take away one that they currently have to see if they will complain or even notice that it is missing.

    D. Do not give management more permissions than users.

20. Which policy defines what constitutes sensitive data and applies protection to it?

    A. Classification

    B. BCP

    C. Data review

    D. Data theft

Answers to Review Questions

1.   A. A certificate policy dictates how an organization uses, manages, and validates certificates.

2.   C. The third party is responsible for assuring the relying party that the subscriber is genuine.

3.   A. A security group is used to manage user access to a network or system.

4.   A. An audit is used to inspect and test procedures within an organization to verify that those procedures are working and up-to-date. The result of an audit is a report to management.

5.   A. The ISO standard 27002 (which updates 17799) states: "Privileges should be allocated to individuals on a need-to-use basis and on an event-by-event basis, i.e. the minimum requirement for their functional role when needed."

6.   B. The supervisor user in NetWare is equivalent to the administrator user in Windows.

7.   C. An ethics policy is the written policy governing accepted organizational ethics.

8.   D. A trusted transaction occurs under the security policy administered by a trusted security domain. Your organization may decide that it can serve as its own trusted security domain and that it can use third-party CAs, thus allowing for additional flexibility.

9.   C. A periodic security audit of user access and rights review can help determine whether privilege-granting processes are appropriate and whether computer usage and escalation processes are in place and working.

10.   D. By default, Windows Firewall in Windows 7 logs neither dropped packets nor successful connections. Logging occurs only when one or both of these are turned on.

11.   B. Escalation audits help ensure that procedures and communications methods are working properly in the event of a problem or issue.

12.   A. Most CAs require a Certificate Practice Statement (CPS), which defines certificate issue processes, record keeping, and subscribers' legal acceptance of the terms of the CPS.

13.   C. One of the most common certificates in use today is the X.509 certificate. It includes encryption, authentication, and a reasonable level of validity.

14.   C. People in an organization can withhold classified or sensitive information from others in the company when governed by need-to-know policies.

15.   B. The process of establishing boundaries for information sharing is called compartmentalization.

16.   D. Hiring policies define how individuals are brought into an organization. They also establish the process used to screen prospective employees for openings.

17. A. A policy of mandatory vacations should be implemented in order to assist in the prevention of fraud.

18. C. The root user in Linux is equivalent to the administrator user in Windows.

19. B. The basic premise of least privilege is: When assigning permissions, give users only the permissions they need to do their work and no more.

20. D. A data theft policy defines what constitutes sensitive data and applies protection to it.

Chapter

15

Security
Administration

This chapter differs from all others in this book in that it does not begin with a list of Security+ objectives that are covered in it, because there are none. There are also no exam essentials or study questions at the end either.

The purpose behind the inclusion of this chapter is far grander. It is all well and good to have objectives that suggest you know what access control is, what hot and cold aisles are, and so on, but being able to implement what you truly need on a daily basis to be a security administrator can be something altogether different. In an academic setting, I've run across dozens of individuals who can get a perfect score on every exam they take but are unable to deal with the day-to-day realities of the job.

The true purpose of this chapter is to attempt to summarize in one location the main topics you need to know to be a security administrator. It is included at the back of the book in the hope that you refer to it and read it more thoroughly after you've become certified and need to know how to do the job as opposed to how to pass the exam.

Security Administrator's Troubleshooting Guide

CompTIA's Security+ certification is often seen as the first step on the ladder toward becoming the ultimate security professional. While most people would not necessarily label Security+ an easy rung by any measure, the step up that follows—acting as a security professional—is often an even bigger one. Whether the act of achieving Security+ certification proves to be a significant challenge or a minor hurdle, the most important part of achieving this (or any) certification is putting what you learn into practice. Unless you can soundly demonstrate the skills and expertise that a certification implies, you should not boast of it on your resume or elsewhere, because too much is at stake. Furthermore, by putting your obtained knowledge into practice, you will be expanding your abilities to the next level of achievement.

While it is not possible to offer a troubleshooting guide that fits every operating system and every implementation, you'll find that the administrative information this chapter provides will be helpful for troubleshooting most environments. You should also relish the fact that Security+ is a vendor-neutral certification and does not require you to know how to troubleshoot every operating system.

The arena of security certifications is fairly delineated into foundational certifications and high-level certifications. While a handful of moderate-level certifications do exist, they don't seem to have gained serious footing (such as recognition) in the IT industry.

So, in order to move on from Security+ certification to high-level certifications such as CISSP, SSCP, CEH, Cisco Security, and Microsoft Security, you need to know more than just concepts and theories of security. You need to be able to apply what you know and troubleshoot problems as they arise.

 In addition to those upper-level security certifications mentioned, CompTIA has announced that they are creating a higher-level security certification as well. The new certification, CompTIA Advanced Security Practitioner (CASP) is targeted for the administrator with 10 years of practice in IT, 5 of which have involved hands-on security experience.

Before you embark on the recommendations presented here, you should take several precautionary steps:

1. Discuss your actions with your supervisor and/or the security administrator.

2. Thoroughly read and understand all of the policies you are required to adhere to as an employee.

3. Obtain and maintain copies of these policies so you can review them and double-check yourself often.

 If there are any written policies or direct instructions that preclude your participation in any of the activities discussed here, *do not attempt them*.

Failing to take these precautionary steps could result in performing actions that are against company policy, that violate your assigned privileges, or that may actually be criminal activities. You are responsible for the results of your own actions.

Getting Started

The Security+ certification contains mainly concepts and theories; the actual implementation of these will vary greatly from one organization to another. You will need to learn how these concepts and theories are put into practice in your company. There is significantly more information about security than any single book or certification exam can contain. So you'll need to do the reading and research to learn about the technologies, software, hardware, and procedures you encounter. This is an important step because without a complete understanding of implemented solutions, you won't know how to adapt and apply these generic recommendations.

Creating a Home Lab

Knowing how to do something doesn't mean you should do it. You have been assigned a certain job description that entails a specific set of work tasks and related privileges and permissions. You should not attempt to exceed your assigned authority. If it is not your job, then *it is not your job*. You can learn anything you want, but without authorization, you cannot do anything you want—at least, not at work.

If you want to be able to experiment and implement anything, you should create your own personal lab environment at home. Although you could always submit requests and suggestions to the appropriate personnel, if you want to gain hands-on experience, you'll need to find another avenue to explore and develop your new security skills. A home lab is the best place to start. Even if your home lab is just one underpowered system with an old modem, it is enough to start the learning process.

Your lab could consist of a small network of physical machines or a single high-end machine running a virtual operating system (OS) emulator system, such as VMware or Microsoft's Virtual Server. Then, when you can't implement something at work, you can do it at home. Unless you are the security administrator for your employer, it is doubtful you'll be able to implement many of the security recommendations covered in this chapter.

VMware Player allows you to work in multiple environments on one system. For more information go to http://www.vmware.com/products/player/.

In the Workplace

In some cases, the actions you take, although motivated by good intentions and dictated by sound security concepts, can be perceived as unethical, abnormal, suspicious, antisocial, a breach of security, and even criminal. Think before you act. Consider the effects your actions will produce. Ponder how others will perceive you if they notice your actions. If you are seen peeking around a corner, you might be perceived as spying or trying to hide something. If you are caught looking at network traffic, you can be perceived as a hacker. If you are caught in an area where you are not assigned to work, you can be perceived as a thief or trespasser. Remember, even when you're doing good, without proper permission and authority your actions can be perceived as unethical and criminal.

If you value your job, then keep communication open with your superiors and the security administration. Often they will be supportive of your desire to learn and improve yourself, which is especially the case when your new skills will benefit the organization directly. However, pushing too far, overstepping your limits, or encroaching on another person's boundaries or areas of responsibility can have negative consequences. These can range from minor verbal warnings to job termination or even criminal prosecution. When in doubt, don't. Instead, be proactive and ask for help and guidance from those in your organization with the authority and the know-how.

Not only should you always seek permission, it is highly recommended that you get permission in writing.

Which OS Should You Use?

There is at least one dark secret that everyone in the IT industry has been keeping from you: No operating system—not Windows, not Unix, not Novell, not Sun, not Linux, not even Mac OS—can be fully and completely secured. Therefore, given enough time and resources, every network, every system, and every file can be compromised. While it is true that some solutions and systems offer more security than others, each product, hardware, or software has its own share of problems and issues. Every technological security mechanism has a fault, flaw, oversight, weakness, workaround, or maximum strength that can be overcome. Therefore, picking the "right" OS is not the whole solution—especially because anyone can be an attacker. Modern-day attack tools are powerful, and they don't necessarily require a high level of sophistication from the attacker (hence the terms *script kiddie* and *ankle biter*).

Creating a Security Solution

Security breaches can arise from a myriad of vectors, including external intruders, internal attackers, misguided insiders, contractors, malicious code, accidents, and oversights. A complete security solution does not stop all attacks, but it reduces the possibility that attacks will be successful and strives to detect any attempts.

This solution requires that you take the following steps:

- Create, maintain, and use a written security policy.
- Make informed technology choices.
- Make your best effort to secure your OS using IT technology.
- Deploy multiple overlapping layers of defense.
- Consider protection for confidentiality, integrity, and availability.
- Implement stronger authentication to support realistic accountability.
- Secure your personnel through training.
- Secure the physical environment.
- Watch for the inevitable security breach attempt.
- Be prepared to respond to incidents.
- Maintain that security is a never-ending process.
- Keep in mind that protections should prevent, then deter, then deny, then detect, then delay.

In the sections that follow, these and many other security concepts are explored and their application discussed.

Access Control Issues

Access control is the scheme or mechanism used to control who is granted access to what within the environment as a whole. You should recall that there are three primary options for this:

- Discretionary Access Control (DAC)
- Mandatory Access Control (MAC)
- Role-Based Access Control (RBAC)

What is the access control scheme used in your work environment?

If you don't already know what scheme is used at your office, think about it before asking your network administrator (NA) or security administrator (SA). First, does the office use standard, off-the-shelf operating systems for both client and servers, such as Microsoft, Linux, and Apple? If so, then it is more likely you work in a DAC environment. Second, do you work in an environment where clearances and classifications are used? If so, that is a direct indication of MAC. If you are a private-sector company, then the answer is probably DAC. If you are a government agency or even a government contractor, then the answer is probably MAC.

You might discover that few, if any, environments are completely RBAC based. When RBAC is used at all, it is for those areas of the organization that have a high rate and frequency of staff changes.

If you think you've figured it out, take the time to verify your conclusion. Then discuss with the NA or SA why that specific scheme is used. You might learn some unique perspectives on your organization or discover how the company's decision-making process works.

Accountability Concerns

Accountability is the process of holding individuals responsible for their actions. In the IT world, we want to hold employees accountable for the actions of their user accounts. In order to do this, the entire accountability process must be supportable in a court of law. The ultimate test of how well your security works is if you are able to criminally prosecute someone because of your organization's strong accountability infrastructure. That infrastructure must be able to be explained and proven to a jury so that there remains no reasonable doubt about its reliability. If a defense attorney can reveal a weakness in your accountability infrastructure, then the evidence of a user account performing illegal actions may not be sufficient to prove that a specific human was controlling that user account at that time.

There are five steps of accountability:

1. Identification
2. Authentication
3. Authorization

4. Auditing

5. Accountability

Among the items in this list, authorization stands out as appearing repeatedly throughout this chapter, because so many mechanisms and methodologies exist that govern the processes granting and restricting access to resources.

Auditing

An excellent security principle for you to follow to protect your assets is to lock everything down and then watch them as if they were not locked down. If you secure every asset to the best of your abilities, using your available technologies and your available budget, and then watch for the inevitable breach or attempt to breach, you make your deployed security even better. Locking down an asset and then walking away doesn't mean it won't be attacked; it just means you won't know when it is attacked. And you won't know an attack was successful until you return and notice damage or loss. All too often, administrators fail to look at logs until something goes wrong.

You should consider auditing, monitoring, logging, and watching all forms of security. They actually prevent many attacks from being attempted in the first place, and they detect any attempt that is made to breach security. Most forms of auditing should be announced to all entities trying to gain entry into your secured environment, the computer network as well as the physical building. You should notify anyone trying to enter your environment that only authorized personnel are allowed to enter, that all actions are recorded and monitored, and that any violation of security policy or law will be prosecuted. This type of sign or banner should be clearly visible at every entry point of your building and at every logon or access point on your public and private IT systems.

Auditing prevents casual attacks and detects intentional attacks. But auditing by itself is not enough. Your audit logs need to be protected against tampering and loss. This protection is required while the log is open and active as well as when it is closed and stored on backup media. Your best choice for storage media for auditing is a write once, read many (WORM) device. WORM devices are designed so that once data is written to them, it cannot be altered by any means short of physical destruction of the storage device itself. If you want your audit logs to be 100 percent accurate, to have perfect integrity, and to be supportable in court, WORM devices are your *only* choice. Other forms of storage devices allow written data to be altered. If that is even possible, a good defense attorney can cast doubt on the reliability and integrity of the audit details. Your WORM devices should be of sufficient capacity to collect audit logs for a reasonable amount of time. Remember that you must protect your WORM devices from theft and physical damage.

You should review your audit logs regularly both by automated means (such as a security auditor or an IDS tool) and by human means. Look for abnormalities or specific violations of security policy. Each incident should be investigated. As you discover issues or weaknesses, take action to prevent reoccurrence or future exploitation.

Audit logs should be backed up and retained—not just for a few months or years, but indefinitely. You never know how far back malicious events reach until they are discovered and investigated. If your retention policy allows for backups to be destroyed after only six months, you could easily be destroying essential evidence against internal and external attackers. This might require a separate backup system for audit logs so that the amount of physical space required to maintain all audit logs does not become too significant of a burden.

Authentication Schemes

No matter which access control scheme you use (DAC, MAC, and so forth), the basic two-step process to log into the network is always required. Every authorized user has (or should have) their own user account. To use the IT system, the user must first login. The two-step login process is for you as a claimant to claim an identity (identification) and then prove that you are responsible for that identity (authentication). There are at least three important aspects to this two-step process that require investigation:

- Number and type of factors
- Client, server, or mutual authentication
- Mechanism of authentication protection

Authentication Factors

The number and type of factors reflect the strength of the authentication process. Remember that there are three basic types of authentication factors:

- Type 1 (something you know)
- Type 2 (something you have)
- Type 3 (something you are)

Only a single factor is needed for identification because you only need to claim a single identity. But when it comes to authentication, more and different is always better (and here better means stronger).

Type 1 All Type 1 (something you know) examples are the same no matter what they are called. They are just long or short strings of characters typed onto a keyboard from memory. No matter how many passwords are used, multiple passwords are ultimately no stronger than any single password by itself. This is due to the nature of the password-cracking attack. The same attack can crack (or, more specifically, discover) any password of any type of any length. Yes, longer and more complex passwords will take more time and more processing power, but this does not change the fact that the same attack tool and methodology works against every single example of a Type 1 factor.

Type 2   Type 2 (something you have) factors start to offer a greater level of variety even within this single-factor concept. A smart card is different from a token device. At the least, they are different enough that two different attack tools and methodologies must be used to successfully break them.

Type 3   Type 3(something you are) factors, commonly known as biometrics, are even more varied than Type 2 factors. A fingerprint scanner is different from a palm scanner, which is different from a retina scanner, which is different from a voice recognition system, and so on. Just about every biometric characteristic (each using a different body part) is practically a factor type in and of itself. Thus, multiple Type 3 factors of different body parts are much stronger than dozens or hundreds of passwords. Each and every biometric reader works differently and thus requires a unique attack tool and methodology.

The higher the number and the more varied the form of authentication factors, the stronger the resulting authentication becomes. The ultimate purpose of authentication is to prevent unauthorized people from logging on to another person's user account. This prevention must be so strong that it will hold up in court. A single password is not supportable because of its numerous weaknesses. Using just a password as your authentication mechanism is as secure as locking a screen door on a submarine. However, a long, complex password combined with a smart card and a fingerprint scan may be supportable in court.

If you are not already using at least two-factor authentication, then seek it out. For your company as a whole, migrating up to two or more factors will be a significant expense. But you might be allowed to add multifactor authentication to your user account at your desktop or notebook without forcing it companywide. The simplest two-factor system is to use a long and complex password as one factor and a fingerprint scanner as the second factor. Your administrator can add a scanner to any system with an open USB port. USB smart card readers are another option if you employ public certificate authority (CA) certificates rather than attempting to deploy your own private internal CA trust structure.

If you are not allowed to include additional factors, then take full advantage of the password length and complexity supported by your environment. We provide some stronger password recommendations in the section "Making Stronger Passwords," later in this chapter.

Mutual Authentication

Even with strong multifactor authentication, it is important to know just who is authenticating to whom. Most logons are client authentications. This means that the client (or, more specifically, the user) proves their identity to the system or environment they want to gain entry or access to. Unfortunately, this one-sided authentication process leaves open significant opportunities for spoofing and misdirection.

Logon spoofing has become a serious problem, especially over the Internet. If you are unable to verify the system you are connecting to, then it is possible that it is not what it claims to be. Numerous spoofing attacks have taken place in the last few years in which attackers create real-looking but fake websites of banks, auction sites, e-commerce sites, and even charity sites. These fake sites then fool visitors into "logging on" when all that is really happening is the user's logon credentials are being recorded (stolen) so that the attackers can log on as victims on the actual sites. This action has been called identity theft, impersonation, masquerading, and phishing. No matter what it is labeled, it is avoidable simply by requiring that all logons be mutual.

In mutual authentication both the client and the server must adequately prove their identity to each other before a logon session is started. You need to actively seek out mutual authentication solutions whenever possible. Within your company's private network, mutual authentication may not be necessary. But for any communication occurring outside of your company-controlled LAN, mutual authentication should be considered a requirement.

Another form of authentication is server authentication—when a server proves its identity to the client but does not require the client to return the favor. Many Internet sites and even some ISPs (broadband and wireless) use server authentication.

The best recommendation is to employ mutual authentication whenever it is available. This provides protection for both partners in a communication and will help reduce identity theft, impersonation, masquerading, and phishing attacks.

Authentication Protection

When it comes to authentication, consider the protection of the logon credentials as they travel from the client to the authentication server. This notion is called *authentication protection* or *authentication encryption*. It is simply a mechanism that serves as a transport and as a security barrier for the identification and authentication factors.

There are many forms of authentication protection. Some, such as CHAP, are used mainly on remote access connections. Others, like Kerberos or NTLM, are used on private network connections. Still others, such as certificates, are suited for larger or more distributed environments.

In every case, authentication systems and clients are designed to negotiate the highest level of common authentication security between them. However, some forms of network attacks can subvert this process, causing the systems to use a lower security mechanism that can be easily broken by an eavesdropper. Whenever possible, disable all of the lower forms of authentication protection on a system that are not used or required. Obviously, you'll need to test such changes thoroughly. Many legacy applications or systems might still exist on large networks that are unable to use more modern and secure methods of authentication.

Backup Management

If there is something you can take from real estate success and apply to security success, it is this: *location, location, location*. Now, you might want to change that to *backup, backup, backup*, but even keeping the original still stresses an important point. Backups are your only insurance against data loss. Without a backup, it is impossible to restore data. However, even the best backups are worthless if you do not protect them against damage or loss in the event of an intrusion, incident, or disaster. Thus, off-site storage of backups is essential. A backup site should be far enough away from the main site that it is not affected by the same disaster. You need to understand your organization's backup strategy and do your best to support it; ensure that every bit of data that is important to the company is ultimately stored on a server that is included in the regular backup system of the network. It is not enough to make your own local backup; you need to let the company backup system protect the company data. If you make local backups for personal data or in-progress projects, that should be seen as a supplement protection, not as a primary protection.

Baselining Security

Using security baselines is an administrative tool to ensure that all systems within your environment have the same basic security elements. Think of security baselines as the absolute minimum security that a system must be in compliance with in order to connect to and communicate with the LAN. Any system falling below the baseline threshold should be removed from production until it can be properly resecured.

A security baseline is a subjective thing between one organization and another. Baseline parameters need to be defined as part of your security policy. The baseline can be a written policy document, it can be implemented via a configuration tool, or it can be imposed via an installation/deployment system (such as image clones of a secured original).

Your best effort for establishing or defining a baseline lies in a full understanding of your operating system, business goals, and the vulnerabilities, threats, and risks of your environment. To get started on creating a security baseline, seek out existing public baseline recommendations. Use these as a seed to generate your own customized version. Every OS vendor provides "how to secure this OS" documents, numerous security product vendors provide them, and many third-party security watch groups (grassroots, commercial, and governmental) provide them as well. A few Internet searches should produce more than sufficient results. Some great keywords to search with include the name of your selected OS along with *security policy*, *system hardening*, *how to secure*, *security baselines*, and *security recommendations*.

 The SANS policy site is a good first stop for information on using security baselines (http://www.sans.org/resources/policies).

As previously mentioned, no one operating system is significantly better or worse than any other. So pick the one you are most familiar with and have the most knowledge and experience with. The more you already know about an OS, the less you have to learn. As all of the lockdown or hardening guides will tell you, keeping the system updated and imposing the principle of least privilege are your two best efforts.

After a security baseline is established, you will need to regularly reassess the security state of every system. Time and change can result in the lowering of security. To prevent such a diminishment, you need to be proactive in testing the security of each and every system on a periodic basis. Any system failing to meet baseline requirements should be taken offline, corrected, and verified before being returned to the operating environment.

It should also be a point of procedure that after every security incident, no matter how minor, every system involved should be reassessed. If any system cannot be given a clean bill of health (that is, returned to baseline security levels or better), it should be reconstituted. Any system that has experienced a full-blown intrusion, rootkit deposit, Trojan horse attack, or malware infection should be reconstituted.

Reconstitution is the act of completely purging hardware of all software elements and then reinstalling the entire system from original media or from trusted backups. The purpose of reconstitution is to reestablish the trustworthiness of a compromised system. If a serious compromise occurs, there is no way to fully verify that all aspects of the compromise are removed or thwarted. Thus, reconstitution removes all traces of possible corruption and rebuilds a new trustable system.

Certificate Management

Certificates are currently the top-shelf method of proving identity. However, it is important to stress that identity proof (such as authentication) is the *only* purpose of certificates. Certificates in no way provide proof of reliability, trustworthiness, compatibility, or benevolence of an entity. The only proof provided by a certificate is the identity of that entity. It is a separate and distinct choice to trust in an entity once you know who it is. Certificates are used as the primary means of identity proof on the Internet for e-commerce and resource download sites. However, too many people associate having a certificate with some type of proof of goodness. This is an absolutely incorrect assumption.

A simple understanding of what certificates are and how they are created can easily dispel this misguided notion. Certificates are issued by CAs after they prove the identity of the requesting subject. The identity is proven through various means, which could be as simple as sending an email to a given email address or checking with public records that a business exists at a specific address and is able to be contacted via a specific phone number. That's it; the CA verifies the identity details of a subject and nothing else.

Further proof: Have you ever downloaded an update from a well-known vendor who proved their identity with a digital certificate only to have that update crash your system? Enough said.

To gain the most from certificate security troubleshooting, follow these guidelines:

- Stop assuming certificates prove trustworthiness.

- Consider why you would want to trust each specific entity whose identity is proven by a CA.

- Consider why you trust the CAs that you do (review the trusted roots list in your web browser to see which CAs you are trusting already).

- Choose to make the same selection for this certificate in the future only when you are denying acceptance or trust of an entity.

- When asked to retrust an entity, reconsider.

- If any utility questions any aspect of a certificate, such as the common name (CN) on the certificate not matching the claimed name of a site, *deny acceptance of the certificate*.

- Obtain your own certificate from a reputable CA, such as VeriSign. But don't settle for a free or email-only certificate; obtain a certificate that validates more than just a working email inbox.

- Require mutual certificate-based authentication from all Internet sites whenever available.

- Make sure your client tools update their Certificate Revocation Lists (CRLs) before each check of a received certificate.

Certificates themselves cannot currently be spoofed or stolen after use. However, this security does not mean that fake certificates don't exist or that abuse doesn't occur. You need to be vigilant at inspecting certificates and assume the worst even when accepting the identity from a trusted CA.

Communications Security

Communications security is an ever-expanding branch of IT security and one that is often not given the respect and attention it truly deserves. Communications security encompasses all the means by which data can enter or leave your otherwise private LAN. Even with a strongly secured LAN, weak communications security can bring it all crashing down. Each pathway by which data can move is yet another route through which malware can gain entry and intrusions can take place. In the realm of remote access, several areas fall in this category and demand specific attention: wireless, remote control/remote shell, and VPN.

Remote access is the broad collection of mechanisms that allow external entities to interact with an internal closed environment. These can vary greatly in regard to speed and breadth of access. But even a trickle of data can be used to infiltrate an apparent fortress. Consider how the Grand Canyon was carved through solid rock by just running water. You need to be aware of every flow of data that penetrates the boundaries of your private LAN and fully control each and every bit of data moving across such a gateway.

Preauthentication

One of the most important steps in securing your LAN against malicious events performed over remote access links is to erect a first-stage defense. A first-stage remote access defense is a separate authentication system for remote access that preauthenticates all connections before they are allowed to interact with the LAN itself. These preauthentication systems serve as domain controllers for remote access connections. Thus, if the remote access user fails to properly authenticate to the first-stage defense barrier, they cannot even approach the internal domain controllers or servers on the LAN.

These preauthentication systems make full network attacks from remote links much more difficult. Without them, a remote access attack can directly affect any aspect of the internal LAN. Thus, a successful remote-access-based attack can affect all users. However, with a preauthentication system, most attacks, even initially successful ones, are prevented from gaining access to the private LAN. If the preauthentication system is disabled, then no communication is allowed from any remote access link. The preauthentication system serves as a dead-man switch for all remote access links. It protects the core private LAN. Keep in mind that it is better to lose remote access capabilities than it is to lose the entire private LAN.

You can use preauthentication systems for any form of remote access that connects into a private LAN. These systems include broadband, VPN, wireless, satellite, remote control, and remote shell. You need to know what forms of remote access are needed and how to deploy a preauthentication system to provide that additional layer of protection for the rest of your LAN.

Preauthentication systems can sometimes offer connection filtering. Connection filtering allows for restrictions to be placed on remote access links. These can include the type of OS used, the protocols supported, the user accounts involved, the time of day, the logical addressing of the client, the LAN systems the remote client is allowed to communicate with, and even the content of the communication. The use of connection filtering can reduce an otherwise full-network-access remote link to a limited-functionality, single-purpose link. This filtering greatly reduces the potential for exploitation.

Another important aspect of remote access to consider is that even with the best security on the remote access link itself, if the remote client is compromised, it could lead to the compromise of the LAN. Remote clients can be compromised by malware, theft, or physical intrusion of their storage location. In most cases, the locations where remote access clients reside are much less secure than the physical location of the LAN. Remote access clients also typically use the same system for personal activities and Internet access. These are risky behaviors that can lead to security breaches. You should use a remote access client only to connect securely to the LAN. You should not use a remote access client for any other purpose—especially not for personal Internet access.

Remote Control/Remote Shell

Remote control is the ability to manipulate a remote computer system without having to be physically present at its keyboard. This allows your local keyboard, monitor, and mouse to be used as the interface I/O devices for the remotely controlled system. This mechanism greatly eases administration because numerous systems can be managed from a single workstation. However, it also generally reduces security. Your ability to control a system remotely means that a hijacker or intruder can do so as well.

Remote shell tools are similar to remote control tools except that they are limited to command-line or text-only interaction. Common examples of this include Telnet and Secure Shell (SSH). Telnet should be avoided completely because it offers no security or encryption. Telnet can be deployed securely within a Secure Sockets Layer (SSL) tunnel, but doing so is often too involved for most situations, especially since SSH can be easily installed and offers greater protection than Telnet via SSL. SSH provides encryption for both authentication and data communications.

If you will be using remote control/remote shell tools, enable and require any and all security features available for the product employed. Limit the use of remote control tools over the Internet. Limit who can use these tools, and monitor when and why they are used.

Virtual Private Networks

VPN security is usually a factor of solution selection and configuration. There are three widely used VPN protocols:

- Point-to-Point Tunneling Protocol (PPTP)
- Layer 2 Tunneling Protocol (L2TP)
- Internet Protocol Security (IPSec)

PPTP is often considered a default to use if you are communicating with systems that don't support L2TP or IPSec. If you don't need it for this purpose, you should avoid PPTP because of the vulnerabilities and weak encryption it employs. You should use L2TP alone (without IPSec) when a link is involved in the VPN, which usually means the remote client is connecting to an ISP, and then establishing the VPN link across the resultant pathway. IPSec should be employed if broadband connections are present throughout the pathway between the LAN VPN server and the remote client.

Always enable only the strongest authentication and data encryption supported; avoid using preshared keys and relying on unique session keys and certificates. While the client is connected to the VPN, prevent any other form of communication from occurring over the Internet link. Force periodic reauthentication during the VPN session to check for and prevent hijacking.

Directory Services Protection

As a network user, you can do little to improve or change the security of the directory services deployed. However, you *can* ensure that you don't become a tool for an attacker bent on compromising your organization's security by following these guidelines:

- Ensure that your client is using the most secure form of authentication encryption supported by both your client and the authentication servers.
- Use encrypted software and protocols whenever possible, even for internal communications.
- Change your password according to the company's password policy.
- Use a 16+ character password that is unique for each account.
- Never write your password down, or if you do, divide it up into several pieces and store each in a different secure location (such as a home safe, a gun cabinet, a chemical supply locker, or safety deposit box).
- Never share your password or your logon session with another person; this includes your friends, spouse, and children.

- Consider moving away from passwords, where possible, to stronger authentication such as biometrics, two-factor authentication, smart cards, and so on.
- Verify that your client always interacts with an authentication server during the network logon process and does not use cached credentials.
- Every single time, just before you log on to the network, double-check that a hardware keystroke catcher has not been surreptitiously installed.
- Allow all approved updates and patches to be installed onto your client.
- Ensure that all company data is copied back to a central file server before disconnecting from a logon session.
- Back up any personal data onto verified removable media.
- Never walk away from a logged-on workstation.
- Employ a password-protected screensaver.
- Don't use auto-logon features.
- Be aware of who is around you (and may be watching you) when you log on and when you work with valuable data.
- Never leave a company notebook, cell phone, or PDA in a position where it can be stolen or compromised while you are away from the office. Cable locks should be used to keep notebooks securely in place whenever you are offsite.

The protection of a directory service is based on the initial selection of network operating system and its deployment infrastructure. After these foundational decisions are made, you need to fully understand the technologies employed by your selected directory services system and learn how to make the most functional, yet secure, environment possible. This will usually require the addition of third-party security devices, applications, services, and solutions.

Disaster Planning

Disaster recovery planning and business continuity planning are also an important part of a complete security solution. As an employee, you might not have any involvement in these plans whatsoever. If that's the case, realize that keeping the details of these plans from the general population of employees is in and of itself a security precaution. The disaster recovery plan and business continuity plan can be used for malicious purposes if they get into the wrong hands. It is common practice to give only relevant portions of the plans to just those specific individuals who are responsible for carrying out sections of the larger plan when an emergency actually occurs.

If you happen to be a person with responsibilities within one of these plans, be sure you keep this information confidential. Always work from the latest and most up-to-date version of the plan. Also, be sure you are fully versed in the steps of the plan long before an emergency occurs. You want to be able to respond by instinct when the pressure is on—don't wait until an actual event to read all the fine print.

Regardless of whether you have a part in the recovery or continuity plans, you do have a responsibility to yourself and your fellow employees in the event of emergencies. Your responsibility is to assist with anything that will reduce harm and loss of life. This includes knowing how to perform CPR and the Heimlich maneuver, knowing how to use a fire extinguisher, being familiar with multiple escape routes, and more. Your first priority in a disaster is to get everyone to safety. Then you can consider how to minimize losses to the organization.

Documenting Your Environment

When it comes to troubleshooting, documentation might sound mundane and superfluous, but it is a vital aspect of a complete, functioning, and successful security endeavor. With good exhaustive documentation, everything about an environment, from good to bad, will be recorded for future inspection. So, as a budding security expert, you need the following:

- Document everything, including your actions, your discoveries, and your results.

- Get every instruction, request, or order in writing.

- Always get "official authority" to perform some action in writing, especially if the action without that authority would be a security breach or a crime.

- Always document your communications as well as changes to hardware and software.

  If something is related to security in any way, it needs to be documented.

Email Issues

If malware is one of your biggest security concerns (as it should be), then you need to consider email. It's the most common delivery mechanism used to deposit malware into your secured environment. Email is also often the bearer of hoaxes, spam, phishing, and social engineering attacks. Unfortunately, Internet-based email will always be subject to attack (as well as a means to wage attacks). Internet email delivery is performed in clear text with few means to prevent eavesdropping, alterations, delay, interceptions, and so forth. Currently, the only option is to use a client-side encryption scheme, such as PGP and S/MIME. But they offer security only for messages between other users of the same tool. Thus, most messages are still sent in the clear without any form of protection.

Email security is a product of reducing its functionality and modifying user behavior. As for functionality, secure email is email that does not execute mobile code, nor does it interpret and display HTML. Consider not allowing attachments to reach your clients; strip them off at the firewall. However, this will greatly reduce the ease of data exchange many rely on daily. Spam-filtering services should be added to your email delivery system, if they are not already part of your antivirus solution and your ISP's email services. All inbound email should be quarantined until scanned. Email servers should be deployed as separate systems from all other services on the LAN. As for user-behavior modification, teach your users the following rules:

- Don't open any attachments from unknown entities.
- If you receive an attachment from a known entity, contact them to verify that they intended to send it.
- Don't send any attachments to anyone; use a true file exchange system instead, such as Secure FTP (SFTP), yousendit.com, or hushmail.com.
- If attachments are needed, set up a separate account for sending and receiving them (Gmail is a great tool for that).
- Never click links sent via email.
- Never believe what you read in an email message without confirming it with a third-party source.
- Set up one email address for business communications, a second for personal communications, and a third for all other forms of communication.
- Use only your third email address when registering with a website or handing out your contact information to others. Only after they prove trustworthy should you hand out one of your two primary email addresses.
- Don't blindly follow any instructions included in an email; hoaxes are common.
- Report all suspicious activities or messages to the security administrator.
- Don't attempt to unsubscribe from spam; it's just a ruse to get you to verify that the email address used is valid, and it will encourage more spam.
- Learn to use client-side black lists and white lists.
- Never reveal personal data to anyone via email because phishing attacks are prevalent and con artists are trying to steal your identity.
- Don't forward malicious email to others.
- Report fraud, abuse, spoofing, and spam to the proper authorities (such as spoof@ebay.com and spoof@paypal.com).

As you can see, most of the security benefits with email communication arise from user behavior modification. User behavior modification is often an important part of the overall security infrastructure. However, it cannot operate alone; actual technical security mechanisms and physical access controls must be used to enforce security policy. User behavior modification combines awareness, training, and education. Your goal with user behavior modification is to encourage people to buy into the company's security stance. The more people understand and believe in a security mechanism, the more likely they will uphold it and work within its confines. Without it, people will find ways to get around, subvert, or disable the security mechanism. This concept of user behavior modification applies to every aspect of security, not just email communication security.

File-Sharing Basics

Many work tasks require exchanging files regularly. Unfortunately, the most convenient method of exchange is to attach them to email, which is a problematic issue (see the discussion in the preceding section). So, if security is important and file exchange is essential for productivity, a secure method of exchanging files is needed. There are several secure file-exchange solutions available that either add security to the standard FTP solution or are built on more proprietary technology.

When deploying a file-sharing system, here are some important security ideas to keep in mind:

- Don't use plain FTP.
- Use a file transfer client that employs both authentication and data transfer encryption.
- Don't allow anonymous access for both reading and writing; allow it for only one or the other.
- Use a separate system for writing from anonymous Internet users.
- Monitor file size and usage quota limits.
- Don't allow users to employ the same logon credentials as their domain logons.
- Regularly scan all files on the sharing system for malware.
- Don't enable execution privileges for file-sharing visitors.
- Don't store confidential, private, proprietary, or other forms of highly valuable data on a server that allows remote or anonymous users to exchange files.
- Regularly back up all files stored in the file-sharing server.
- Periodically check that your file-sharing server has not become an underground illegal file-exchange repository.
- Consider setting a maximum file size of 10 MB (or whatever is reasonably appropriate for the types of files shared).
- Consider requiring that all files be uploaded in an archived state (via a ZIP, RAR, or ARJ compression/archiving tool).
- Consider requiring that all files be password locked.
- Consider requiring that all files be encrypted.

A file-sharing system can be a method to prevent email from being used as a malware carrier. However, file sharing itself is not a 100 percent secure option either. Taking the proper precautions will help reduce the likelihood of abuse.

Working with IDSs and Honey Pots

Intrusion detection systems (IDSs) can be outstanding security assets, but it is important not to rely too heavily on them. There are numerous drawbacks to IDS solutions that are often downplayed to the detriment of those implementing them. An IDS is only as good as its programming and detection mechanism. Also, like an antivirus solution, an IDS needs to have its signature database regularly updated and its engine patched. An IDS will not detect all attacks (not detecting an attack is known as a false negative). Nor will all IDS alerts be for actual malicious events (this is known as a false positive). It might be necessary to have a staff member monitor the IDS and investigate every alert produced.

The following warnings and suggestions will help you get the most out of an IDS:

- IDS systems can be hindered by switched networks if not deployed properly. This includes either deploying the IDS off the mirror or audit port of the switch or deploying remote sensors in every disparate network segment.

- An IDS or a sensor should be located in every subnet and in every security zone, including the subnet on the other side of your most external firewall (such as on the Internet link itself).

- A network IDS should be deployed as a separate stand-alone system to give it full access to the processing and storage capabilities of the host.

- IDS systems should not be configured to retaliate against intrusions or attacks; at most, a malicious session should be disconnected.

Often the use of an IDS will warrant the discussion of what to do about a discovered intruder. Initially there are two options: disconnect or watch and learn. Disconnect stops the attack from continuing. Watching and learning often involves a honey pot or padded cell environment. Such environments raise the issue of enticement versus entrapment. Discuss this issue with your legal department because the specifics and ramifications are complex.

The intrusion detection systems of a few years back suffered greatly. Those days of relying on basic devices have gone by the wayside, and it is common today to see them marketed as intrusion detection and prevention systems (IDPS).

Incident Handling

Incident handling often means a criminal investigation. Whenever a criminal activity is suspected, back away from the environment, leave it as is, and contact law enforcement. Unless you are instructed by law enforcement to perform actions to gather evidence, do not do anything. Your actions in looking for, collecting, or analyzing evidence can be easily thrown out of court. This inadmissibility is due to your lack of official training in forensic investigations, your conflict of interest, and the likelihood that you will violate the rules of evidence and/or the chain of custody.

Internet Common Sense

In light of the security recommendations discussed so far, you should already have a good grasp of the obvious when it comes to Internet communications. But just so you don't forget anything, here is a rundown of the guidelines that you should instruct your users to adhere to:

- Never share personal data with a website.
- Be careful what you reveal about yourself in chat rooms, via messaging, on discussion boards, to surveys, and so forth.
- Be suspicious of whom you interact with over the Internet until you have absolute proof of their identity and trustworthiness.
- Make e-commerce purchases only from trusted sites (such as sites with a reputation of protecting their users/visitors).
- Use temporary credit card numbers to make online purchases.
- Keep an eye on the domain name in the URL you visit; if it turns into an IP address, a large decimal number, or a strange two-letter country code site, you may have been redirected.
- Use encrypted communications whenever possible.
- Make sure Transport Layer Security (TLS) is enabled on your browser (it's the even more secure replacement for SSL).
- If the URL prefix is not `https`, then it is not a secure connection.
- Encrypted does not mean you cannot be attacked—it just means the attack will come to you over the encrypted link.
- Don't allow unknown sites to download mobile code to your system.
- Don't allow unsigned code to download or execute.
- Allow signed code from only well-trusted sites to execute.
- Don't allow third-party cookies.
- Limit the use of first-party cookies to trusted sites and then only to those sites that actually require them.
- Keep your client utilities updated and patched.
- Don't download data from unknown sites.
- Use only downloaded data from trusted sites after verifying the integrity of the download.

- Remember that you are probably being watched by an unknown malicious entity while you surf the Internet. Act as if someone is always watching and monitoring you.

- Be aware that not everything that seems like a threat at first is real. Fake antivirus remedies and hoaxes have been growing in number.

- Don't leave Internet connections open and active when you are not actively using your computer.

- Social engineering, spoofing, phishing, and hoaxes can all take place via computer communications such as email and chat and on the Web—watch out!

Think of the Internet as a necessary evil that must be controlled in order to get beneficial tasks accomplished. It is like electricity, which provides uncountable benefits to our lives, but if we lose control of it, the results can include electrocution and property damage through fire. The Internet is a powerful tool that can cause serious harm to your organization and your personal lives if not managed properly. So don't use the Internet without proper protection and awareness.

Key Management Conventions

When working with any form of cryptography, using reasonable key management techniques helps maximize security and minimize potential breaches. Ultimately, key management depends on the deployed cryptosystem product. Thus, know what you are buying and exactly what it does and does not offer.

Based on that, here are some tips to make the most out of what you have (at least in terms of encryption):

- If a PKI system is used, have one public/private key pair set to use for session management and encryption and a second set for identity proof.

- Always use a new and unique public/private key pair set when requesting a new certificate.

- Attempt to renew certificates before they expire in order to maintain existing trust relationships.

- If you are concerned that existing trust relationships might be problematic, allow your current certificate to expire or ask the CA to revoke it.

- Store symmetric and asymmetric keys separately.

- Use a password- or biometrics-locked removable storage medium to store and transport your keys (for example, USB drive or smart card).

- When available, use key escrow database systems for keys involved in stored data encryption.

- Never store keys for identity proof in a key escrow database.

- Be aware of the length of assigned lifetime to keys and certificates.

- Be prepared to renew or reissue keys and certificates after they expire.

- Regularly purge your software to remove copies or caches of both current and expired keys—your current keys should be stored only on a removable media.

- Don't leave active keys or certificates on portable systems.

- Never store the removable media used for key storage in the same luggage or carryall as the device for which it is used.

- Purge all keys that have expired.

- Always check the revocation status of keys and certificates before acceptance or use.

- When a key or certificate will be unused or dormant for seven days or more, request a key/certificate suspension to temporarily "disable" them.

- Ensure that some form of M of N Control is employed on key recovery as well as key/certificate generation and issuance.

- Use session keys only once.

- Generate new session keys at the beginning of each session.

- When available, use a one-time pad form of encryption for highly valuable transmissions.

- Try to make the work function/work factor of a key just barely exceed the length of time the protected data will be valuable.

- Each time a key is reused, consider its useful lifetime or work function/factor reduced by a factor of 2.

- Whenever a compromise of the trust structure, secured server, secured client, or storage media is suspected, destroy all keys and certificates and obtain new ones.

- Never share your keys or certificates with anyone.

- Never encrypt and transmit data as is that is received or extracted from an outside source.

- Never rely on static keys or certificates for protection on truly valuable assets.

As you can see, for the most part, improving your key management tactics is a matter of common sense and a healthy dose of paranoia.

Preventing Common Malicious Events

If you don't know what you are up against, then you don't know how to prepare. "Know your enemy" is an admonishment from Sun Tzu that all security administrators should heed. If you are fully versed in the tools and techniques of your opponents, then you can be well prepared to stave off their attacks. We're sure you've heard the phrase "ethical hacking." It is a flashy marketing phrase for security assessment or penetration testing. Ultimately, it refers to using cracker/attacker techniques and tools to test the security of your environment. But before you can perform ethical hacking, you must have two things:

- Thorough knowledge and skill in cracker/attacker techniques and tools

- Written approval from the owner/manager/administrator of the target network

Study is the best way to obtain knowledge and skill in cracker/attacker techniques and tools. You have four options to accomplish this:

- Learn what you can as you stumble upon relevant materials at work or on the Internet.
- Read relevant books, study guides, and self-paced courses.
- Attend online or computer-based training (CBT) classes.
- Attend instructor-led training.

The first of these options is the cheapest, but it's the least effective. The last option is the most expensive, but it's the most direct route to accomplishing the goal of being well versed in cracker/attacker techniques and tools. If you are serious about learning more about ethical hacking, several official certifications are available, such as Certified Ethical Hacker (CEH) from the EC Council (`www.eccouncil.org`) or the SysAdmin, Audit, Network, Security (SANS) and Global Information Assurance Certification (GIAC) (`www.sans.org` and `www.giac.org`) line of security certification pathways.

After you have a basic foundation of cracker/attacker techniques and tools, you then have to perform self-imposed continuing education, which involves the following:

- Setting up a lab where you can perform attack/defend activities safely. I recommend two books: *Build Your Own Security Lab* by Michael Gregg (Wiley, 2008) and *Professional Penetration Testing* by Thomas Wilhelm (Syngress, 2009).
- Finding a partner to learn and experiment with. You could turn the attack/defend activities into a competition.
- Watching security topic mailing lists and discussion groups.
- Watching major OS, software, and hardware vendor websites.
- Reading about any new vulnerability, exploit, or attack that appears in technical news.
- Endeavoring to learn how and why attacks and exploits function.
- Investigating the vulnerabilities and weaknesses addressed in newly released patches and updates.

Ethical security experts all agree: Never perform any attack activity against any system without written authorization from the owner of that system. Approval is your get-out-of-jail-free card. It is your protection from prosecution and job loss. If you want to experiment with an attack or exploit, do it only in your private lab. Never perform attack or exploit testing over the Internet. If you don't own and control the system, you don't have the legal authority to do what you want on that system. So obtain approval.

Constructing a Line of Defense

After you recognize the vulnerabilities and threats a system faces, you can begin to construct your lines of defense. In a corporate environment, the basics of defense should already be in place. If not, you need to make some strong recommendations to those with the authority to make network security decisions.

Of the basic prevention mechanisms available, here are the items deemed essential for every system:

- Firewall
- Antivirus
- Antispyware
- Anti-adware
- Email filtering

A few of the latest editions of antivirus solutions have combined capabilities that encompass all of these features in a single product (or at least a single suite of products from the same company). Every client and every server in a network should have these security mechanisms installed, configured, and maintained. Depending on the size of your network and available security budget, you should also consider an intrusion detection system to watch for the things these five foundational filtering/scanning tools might miss.

If you have systems that do not have these basic security tools present, then obtain permission to get them installed.

Types of Attacks

But your security protections can't stop there. As you'll see in the following list, there are many forms of attacks and threats that require your focused attention.

Denial-of-Service   These attacks come in two major forms: flaw exploitation and traffic generation. You can protect against flaw-exploitation DoS attacks by applying vendor-supplied patches and updates as well as by installing firewalls and other traffic-filtering tools. Traffic-generation DoS attacks are not as easy to stop. They require detection and network traffic filtering. It is usually possible to block such attacks from entering your network, but you'll have to convince an upstream network (such as an ISP) to filter out the malicious traffic as well. Otherwise, your communication pipeline might be consumed with the bogus attack traffic and thus be unable to support your legitimate communications.

Backdoor Attacks   Backdoors are popular because they allow easy access into a computer or network device without having to deal with the authentication systems protecting them. Some backdoors are left in accidentally by the vendor but are usually patched quickly by a vendor update. If the backdoor is a known user account and/or admin or configuration password, then you need to make sure that the accounts are renamed and a strong password defined. Other backdoors are deposited by hackers or various forms of malicious code, such as Trojan horses. If your security perimeter is working properly and you are actively watching for attacks, depositing backdoors or other malicious code is made significantly more difficult.

Spoofing   Spoofing, as described earlier, is faking information. Common spoofing attacks use email source addresses, packet source addresses, and system MAC addresses. While it is not possible to stop all spoofing attacks, you can eliminate a great number with a few simple actions. Your network traffic filters and email filters should be configured to check for source spoofing in network packets and emails, respectively. If a packet or message is leaving your private LAN, then it cannot have a valid source address from the Internet. Conversely, if a packet or message is entering your private LAN from the Internet, then it cannot have a valid source address from the LAN. These types of filters are known as egress (exiting) and ingress (entering) filters. They need to be configured on every border system.

Reverse Lookups and White/Black Lists   Using reverse lookups and white/black lists also allows you to limit spoofing attacks. Reverse lookups check to see if a source MAC address, IP address, or email address is real, currently in use, and from the expected location before allowing traffic to enter or leave. White lists and black lists are filters that have lists of addresses that are known to be either legitimate and trustworthy or illegitimate and malicious. All addresses on a white list are trusted and are allowed to pass with little interference, whereas all addresses on a black list are either blocked outright or subject to greater levels of inspection before being allowed to pass. Black lists can result in a form of DoS if benign addresses are placed on the black list accidentally. This threat is something to watch for; be prepared to verify and rectify list entries when necessary.

Man-in-the-Middle, Replay, and Session Hijacking Attacks   These are thwarted by several means: complex packet sequencing rules, time stamps in session packets, periodic mid-session reauthentication, mutual authentication, the use of encrypted communication protocols, and spoof-proof authentication mechanisms (such as certificates). Whenever possible, use only modern OSs that are fully updated. Also, attempt to limit your out-of-LAN communications to encrypted sessions verified with certificates.

Antivirus Protection

The appearance of malicious code is at an all-time high, and it will only get worse. As more and more countries, cities, and population groups move into the Internet age, many people are learning how to program. Inevitably, human nature leads some of these new programmers to the dark side, and they become the authors of malicious code. Your job is to erect sufficient barriers to the malware threat to prevent any and all breaches.

The best initial protection against malicious code is antivirus software. However, these packages are not perfect. Even properly managed and fully updated antivirus scanners can still overlook 4 percent of known viruses. This oversight means that you cannot rely on a single scan to provide realistic protection; you need to scan everywhere. It is highly recommended that you employ at least three different antivirus vendors' scanning solutions in your environment.

However, *never install two antivirus products on the same computer!* Install one product on all clients, a second product on all internal servers, and a third product on all border systems. In this manner, every bit of data entering or leaving your environment is scanned at least twice, if not three times, thus reducing the likelihood of missing a known virus from 4 percent to .16 percent (4 percent of 4 percent) or 0.0064 percent (4 percent of 4 percent of 4 percent).

Every antivirus product should scan data as it enters the computer, as it leaves the computer, as data is written to the hard drive, as data is read from the hard drive, and as data is used in memory. Plus, on a weekly or biweekly basis, you should scan every file on every drive. Yes, this will affect your system's performance, but in most cases a small reduction in performance is worth the trade-off for greatly improved malware protection.

Automate the downloading of virus signature databases, but restrict and control the deployment of engine updates. Virus signature database updates have rarely been the cause of problems, but delaying the deployment of the signature database can result in undetected infections. Most modern antivirus solutions offer a staged deployment controller for updates. A single server should poll the public website for antivirus updates two to four times a day. Then, that server should be the host that provides the updates to all other internal systems. This deployment controller usually allows you to make signature database updates immediately available while quarantining all other forms of updates. After updates are tested and verified, you can release the ones that you want deployed.

Users should be trained to avoid malware and risky behavior. You should issue the following warnings to users:

- Don't download anything from the Internet.
- Never install any unapproved software.
- Don't bring in storage media from outside.
- Don't leave removable media in drives.
- Don't boot with removable media connected to a computer.
- Stay away from private or noncommercial sites.
- Always type links into a browser; never click on them from emails or documents.
- Don't accept certificates from unknown CAs.
- Never trust an entity just because you know the CA that issued their certificate.

Consider deploying a sheep-dip system for precleaning removable media before use on your LAN. A *sheep-dip system* is a stand-alone machine that is used solely to scan portable storage devices for malware before they are used on secured LANs. The sheep-dip system needs to be manually updated several times a day with signature database updates because it is air-gapped from the rest of the network. Every device that can store data must be checked by the sheep-dip system before it is connected to the LAN. This scrutiny needs to include cell phones, PDAs, audio/video players, digital cameras, USB drives, floppies, and CD/DVDs.

Each time a vendor releases a new version of its product, upgrade to it. Well, don't rush and do this immediately in a knee-jerk fashion. Give the new version a few months of "public" testing before making the migration. This testing lets others discover and experience the growing pains of new solutions. You can learn and benefit from earlier adaptors. Plus, always thoroughly test new software before deployment. This testing applies to any code, including new versions of software, engine patches, function upgrades, and even signature and pattern database updates. The newer the technology, the more likely it will provide reliable protection against newer malware attacks.

Making Stronger Passwords

Passwords are the most common form of authentication; at the same time, they are the weakest form of authentication. Password attacks have become ubiquitous. Reliance solely on passwords is not true security. At least four attack methods are used to steal or crack passwords. All of them involve *reverse hash matching*. This is the process of stealing the hash of a password directly from an authentication server's account database or plucking out-of-network traffic and then reverse-engineering the original password. Reverse-engineering, in this case, is done by taking potential passwords, hashing them, and then comparing the stolen hash with the potential password hash. If a match is found, then the potential password is probably the actual password.

 Even if the potential password is not the actual password, if it happens to produce the same hash, it will be accepted by the authentication system as the valid password.

There are four password-cracking or -guessing attacks, which we'll discuss in the next sections.

Dictionary

These attacks generate hashes to compare by using prebuilt lists of potential passwords. Often these lists are related to a person's interests, hobbies, education, work environment, and so forth. Dictionary attacks are remarkably successful against non-security professionals.

Brute Force

Brute-force attacks generate hashes based on generated passwords. A brute-force attack tries every valid combination for a password, starting with single characters and adding characters as it churns through the process. Brute-force attacks are always successful, given enough time. Fortunately, brute-force attacks against strong passwords eight characters long can take up to three years.

Hybrid

These attacks take the base dictionary list attack and perform various single-character and then multiple-character manipulations on the base passwords. This includes adding numbers or replacing letters with numbers or symbols. Hybrid attacks are often successful against even security professionals who think they are being smart by changing *a* to @ and *o* to *0* and adding the number *12* to the end of the name of their favorite movie character.

Rainbow Tables

The really worrisome tool for password attacks is called a *rainbow table*. Traditionally, password crackers hashed each potential password and then performed an Exclusive Or (XOR) comparison to check it against the stolen hash. The hashing process is much slower than the XOR process, so 99.99 percent of the time spent cracking passwords was actually spent generating hashes. So, a new form of password cracking was developed to remove the hashing time from the cracking time. Massive databases of hashes are created for every potential password, from single characters on up, using all keyboard characters (or even all ASCII 255 characters). Currently, a rainbow table for cracking Windows OS passwords is available that contains all the hashes for passwords that contain from 1 to 14 characters using any keyboard character. That database is 64 GB in size, but it can be used in an attack to crack a password in less than three hours—meaning that all Windows OS passwords of 14 characters or fewer are worthless.

To protect yourself from this threat, change all of your Windows OS and network passwords to a minimum of 16 characters. Or, if you get approval from your security administrator, start using one or more additional authentication factors (biometrics, smart cards, etc.)

Another protection is the addition of a *salt* to the password before it is hashed. Most modern and secure OSs employ salts. The purpose of a salt is to thwart easy hash cracking and prebuilt hash databases. Often the salt is the SID of the user account; thus a 40-character (or so) phrase is added to a, say, 12-character password to create a 52-character entity that is then hashed. An attacker may be able to learn the salt value, especially if it is the SID, but it still stops all of the easy attack methods. The use of salts forces a true real-time brute force approach to cracking hashes, thus allowing OSs to once again provide real protection for passwords (assuming the password is complex and long to begin with).

Use as many different types of characters as possible, including lowercase letters, uppercase letters, numbers, and symbols. Change your password frequently, at least every 30–45 days if not more often. Never reuse a previous password, and never use the same password for more than one account. Don't use password-storage tools, whether software or hardware. However, if you have to juggle so many passwords that a management tool is essential, then make sure the passwords are stored with strong encryption and the lock on the tool is stronger than the best password it is storing.

Managing Personnel

Personnel management is a security concept that focuses on minimizing the vulnerabilities, threats, and risks that people themselves bring to an organization. Ultimately, people are the last line of defense for your company's assets. There are many mechanisms imposed to help improve personnel security, such as separation of duties, the principle of least privilege, acceptable use policies, job reviews, mandatory vacations, and even exit interviews.

You need to be aware of these controls and learn how to do your job within the boundaries that they dictate. Here are some important recommendations for management:

- Know exactly which privileges you are assigned.

- Don't attempt to exceed your assigned authority.

- Know which actions require multiple people to work together, and then attempt them only with the correct number of admins.

- If you discover that you have a privilege or capability that you should not have, report it.

- Never perform any activity that is unethical or illegal, even if not doing so will cost you the petty respect of your peers and/or your job.

- Watch out for conflicts of interest and make them known to the security administrator when they occur.

- The person who configures a system should not be the auditor.

- The person who designs a system should not be the tester.

- Log on with your admin account only when you actually need that level of access.

- Log on as a normal user account for your daily activities.

- Limit the use of admin accounts over the network; try to use them directly at the console/terminal to reduce the risk of eavesdropping.

Be aware of all of the policies that govern your behavior. Knowing what you are responsible for makes it much easier to comply. Ignorance is never a valid excuse when a violation occurs.

Keeping Physical Security Meaningful

It is difficult to overstress the importance of physical security. Physical security is controlling who can and cannot gain physical proximity to assets. It is a form of access control: defining who has access and to where and who doesn't have access. Without physical access control, there is no security. Every technological security control can be overcome with the right tools or enough time. Even cryptography will fail eventually. Brute-force attacks are always successful, given enough time. But time itself is becoming an ever smaller relative value with the onset of massive parallel distributed processing. For example, with the services of `distributed.net` or its competitors, 10,000 computing hours can be harnessed in an hour of real time.

Two of the scariest issues today in terms of physical security are bootable portable OSs and hardware-based keystroke loggers. A bootable portable OS on a USB drive (or a DVD or CD) can fully bypass any OS-enforced security because it doesn't allow the host OS to load! Without the host OS, no security is actually being enforced. In fact, the only security remaining is file- or drive-based encryption. Thus, an attacker can make copies of encrypted files and then take them elsewhere to break the encryption at their leisure.

Hardware-based keystroke loggers are another security nightmare. As mentioned earlier, these gadgets are available for well under $100 and are designed to be unobtrusive to even the most observant of users. A few seconds to plant, a few seconds to extract days later, and presto! The attacker now has possession of your password-based logon credentials and anything else you might have. Your only protections are multifactor authentication and strong physical security.

To prevent the compromise of technological security, you must use good physical security. As an employee of any organization, it is part of your job to be aware and be suspicious.

To assist with the physical security of the company's facilities, here are some suggestions:

- Make sure that every time you unlock and open a door, you then close and relock it before you walk away.
- If you discover an unlocked door that should be locked, report it immediately.
- If you discover that a door's locking mechanism has been damaged or tampered with, report it immediately.
- If you discover a door propped open when it should be closed and locked, report it immediately.
- Regularly take notice of whether windows are closed and locked; report any changes.
- Regularly look at the security cameras in the area, and report any changes to their direction, if they become obstructed, or if they become damaged.
- Get to know the faces of as many of your fellow employees as possible so you can spot outsiders or intruders.
- If you see any suspicious activity, especially by personnel you do not recognize, report it.
- Don't hold open locked doors that require each person to self-authenticate.
- Never allow anyone into a secured environment who does not have their authentication credentials, even if you think you know them.
- Keep your keys, smart cards, and other access devices under your complete control at all times, especially when away from work.
- Never grant access to a secured area to anyone who is not specifically authorized to be in that area, including your family and friends.
- Don't help strangers if it involves violating company security procedures; it could be a social engineering attack attempt.
- Regularly check the inspection tags on fire extinguishers, detectors, and sprinkler systems, and report any expired tags.
- Never install equipment or computer hardware, especially wireless devices, without specific written authorization.
- Watch for roof leaks, window leaks, or bathroom overflows and report them.
- Avoid touching computer equipment or electronic devices until you have grounded yourself; static electricity can build up in any low-humidity environment, not just during the winter.
- Don't run any device that might overheat and start a fire.
- Never store or place combustible materials near electronic equipment, especially near electrical distribution points or heat exhaust fans.

Reporting actual malicious activity will be rewarded and encouraged. However, if you become the squeaky wheel and most of your reports turn out to be false positives, you may get a reprimand or a strong encouragement to mind your own business. So, be sure that what you are reporting is worth reporting and that you're not just being a nosy neighbor.

Securing the Infrastructure

Defense in depth should always be the guiding principle when designing the security of an entire LAN. Start with the location of your most important, valuable, and essential assets. From that location, design multiple overlapping layers of security. Each layer should provide some aspect of deterrence, denial, detection, and delay as appropriate for the value of the assets being protected.

Here are some good ideas for developing and deploying a solid and secure network infrastructure:

- Every inbound or outbound communication stream should be monitored and filtered by a firewall.
- Firewalls should be deployed between different departments, security levels, and geographically distant subnets.
- Firewalls should be configured with a basic deny by default and allow by explicit necessary exception.
- When possible, deploy firewalls with packet filtering, application filtering, session filtering, and stateful inspection filtering capabilities.
- Firewalls should be deployed as stand-alone network appliances.
- Software firewalls should be deployed on all internal systems, clients, and servers.
- All internal user interaction with the Internet should be controlled through a proxy server.
- All internal clients should be assigned an RFC 1918 IP address and their access to the Internet supported through a NAT system.
- The proxy server should automatically block known malicious sites.
- The proxy server should cache often-accessed sites to improve performance.
- Routers should be configured to prevent unauthorized modifications to routing tables.
- All network devices should be stored/located in locked rooms or cabinets to prevent unauthorized physical interaction.
- Hubs should be replaced with switches.
- Switches should be configured to watch for ARP and MAC flooding attacks.
- Switches should be used to block sniffing attacks.
- Switch configuration should be protected.
- Wireless networks should be avoided. If they are used, they should be configured to use the highest level of encryption you can support.
- Infrared and Bluetooth should be avoided; wires are always more secure and more reliable, and they have greater throughput.
- Modem-based remote access should be avoided.
- Remote access should be properly secured (see the discussion in the section "Communications Security" earlier in this chapter).

- Standard telephone systems should be replaced with a securable PBX or Voice over IP (VoIP) system.
- Audit phone usage.
- VPN usage should be limited.
- VPNs should always have the strongest authentication and data encryption available.
- Network IDSs should be deployed throughout the environment.
- Host-based IDSs should be deployed on mission-critical systems or identified common attack targets.
- Regularly monitor the health and performance of the network.
- Watch for traffic direction, load, and performance trends.
- Build in sufficient growth capacity in every important area of IT productivity. Monitor the consumption of this extra capacity.
- Realize that the compromise of a workstation can result in the compromise of the entire LAN.
- Provide clients with reasonable security that supports the security of servers.
- Avoid the use of mobile devices that interact with the LAN.
- Restrict the type of data that can be stored on mobile devices.
- Treat mobile devices as an attack and malware entry point.
- Always run cables in shielding conduits.
- If multiple copper cables are run through the same conduit, use cables with significantly different twists per inch and use STP instead of UTP.
- Don't run communication cables and power cables in the same conduit.
- Avoid running any type of cable near an EMI or RFI source.
- Use higher-grade cables than what is currently needed for your networking performance levels.
- Use fiber-optic cables if possible.
- Regularly inspect every cable run for tampering or damage.
- Replace any cable that shows wear or damage.
- Use the shortest cable runs possible.
- Use power conditioners for every network device.

Proper infrastructure planning is essential to long-term success of company security policy. Security should be designed from the beginning rather than being imposed after the fact. However, most of us don't get to make the choice of when security is considered, so we must do the best we can with what we are given. Even if it's late in the game to impose security, take the time to plan out the security strategy before starting the implementation.

Working with Security Zones

Even in a purely discretionary access control environment, security zones are important. Security zones are a form of classification. Basically, a security zone is a designation of which portions of the company-controlled IT are accessible to which types of users. You will have at least three user types to deal with: employees, nonemployee business contacts, and external users. These easily lend themselves to the three standard security zones of intranet, extranet, and DMZ, respectively.

In addition to the basic ideas covered in the Security+ content, here are a few considerations:

- Never place the only copy of data or other resources into the DMZ or extranet.
- Regularly back up all data present in the DMZ and extranet.
- Never grant access to external entities into the intranet.
- Audit and monitor all activities in all security zones.
- Erect strong security barriers between each security zone.
- Public and anonymous access in a DMZ does not mean anything goes—detect and block attacks in every zone.
- Whenever possible, deploy the DMZ so that it has *no* connection whatsoever with your intranet or extranet.
- Consider co-location or site hosting at an ISP for your DMZ.

Understanding and respecting these three groups are important for a strong security endeavor. Different forms of security, different levels of access, and different types of data are present in each security zone. Making a mistake and placing the wrong element into a zone can have disastrous consequences. In the company security policy and in the deployed infrastructure, it's essential to set clear definitions of what each security zone will entail.

Social Engineering Risks

Social engineering is quickly becoming a predominant attack method against technically savvy security environments. While no technology is foolproof, some forms of IT protection, such as encryption, are becoming so difficult to penetrate that it is in the interest of the assailant to find a weaker point of attack. The weakest point of any secured environment is the people who work and interact with that environment. Often, if an attacker can compromise someone on the inside, they can get around the protections that prevent a direct external attack. *Rubber hose attack* is the nickname for going directly to people to convince them to give you access to what is otherwise too secured to break into.

While rubber hose attacks are sensationalized on television and in the movies, most often they are more benign in nature and less noticeable. In fact, most victims of successful attacks are unaware that they were ever considered a target. This form of attack is called *social engineering.* Social engineering involves a con artist running a scam on unsuspecting people to gain access or privilege the attacker would otherwise be unable to obtain. Social engineering attacks exploit human nature, and thus everyone is vulnerable.

Unfortunately, there are no technical security controls that will directly affect, prevent, block, or deter social engineering attacks. Understanding that you are a potential target for social engineering attacks is the best defense against such attacks. Watching out for abnormal, strange, or slightly confusing events, communications, or interactions will often reveal elements of social engineering. Social engineering can take place face-to-face, over the phone, via email, or via a website. Never take anything for granted—verify, verify, verify.

A sure sign of a social engineering attack is when someone asks you to perform an action that is a violation of security policy or that seems unethical or questionable. Never reveal private, confidential, proprietary, or valuable data to anyone via phone, email, the Web, or even face-to-face without absolutely verifying their identity. In most cases, asking for proof of identity will scare away the social engineering attacker. When anything that is slightly odd occurs, report it to your security administrator immediately.

System Hardening Basics

No computer is ever without vulnerabilities. It is not possible to make a fully secured, impenetrable system. However, it is possible to make a system so secure that most attacks will fail and those that don't will be noticed before significant damage is done. Fully hardening a system is beyond the scope of this chapter, but the foundations of system hardening are well within your grasp.

System hardening has many facets, but one core and overriding principle to follow is this: If you don't need it, get rid of it. By eliminating all but the bare essentials needed to accomplish your work tasks, you remove numerous vulnerabilities and avenues of attack. Any active process that is not actually being used is simply increasing the complexity of the environment and expanding your attack surface.

The attack surface is the conceptual idea of the area exposed to potential attackers. A nonhardened system is said to have a larger attack surface than a hardened one because more exposed vulnerabilities exist for the attacker to target. Your job is to understand your systems thoroughly enough to know what is essential and what is extraneous.

One obvious place to start removing the chaff from a computer system is to examine its services. After you think you know which services are extraneous, you need to test them one by one. Here is the basic process:

1. Perform a systemwide backup (an image-level backup is preferred for complete recovery ability).

2. Disable a single service.

3. Reboot the system.

4. Verify that the service is not functioning.

5. Test all required features, functions, and capabilities, both locally and on the network.

6. If all are working as needed, leave this service disabled and repeat the process, starting with step 2, for another service.

7. If all are not working as needed, reenable this service, reboot, and start again with step 2 for another service.

Obviously, this process will take considerable time because there are often dozens of services on basic systems to consider. However, as you learn more about the services themselves and the system you are managing, this process can be truncated greatly. You'll soon recognize which services can be disabled without negative consequences, and thus you won't need to test every service change.

This "keep it only if you need it" mentality should be applied to every aspect of your computer, from hardware to software. Don't install or keep installed any hardware device that is not used on a regular basis, especially if it is an internal device. Keep external devices, such as USB devices or other automatically installable connection devices, disconnected and powered off until they are actually needed.

As for software, be careful about installing anything new, especially if it is from the Internet. Go out of your way to verify the source identity and reliability before downloading. Then check the file for authenticity and integrity before you launch it. This action often requires you to check the filename, time/date stamps, exact file size, hash value, and certificate/digital signature.

Install only software you actually need and will regularly use. If you find yourself often "test-driving" new software and then removing it later, consider creating a test-drive system, which can be a completely separate physical computer or just a virtual computer in a VirtualBox, VMware, or Virtual Server environment. A test-drive system provides you with two security improvements. First, it greatly reduces the risk of installing malicious code onto your primary system. Second, it prevents you from cluttering your primary system with unneeded, useless software. Even if you elect to uninstall software, it often leaves traces of itself in the form of Registry entries, data folders, configuration files, and shortcuts. These orphaned items clutter the system, can eventually cause performance and storage problems, and might be increasing your attack surface. Each time you test-drive new software, just delete the virtual machine file and create a new one for the next program down the road.

Review all of the software utilities and add-ons that come with the OS. If you don't need them, remove them or prevent them from loading. Disable all unneeded protocols.

When you've completed the hardware/software weight-loss program, take a complete inventory of the resultant system and create an image-level backup. This image-level backup will serve as your road map should you ever need to reconstitute the computer in the event of a major catastrophe. Securing new systems is always a long and involved process. But through detailed documentation and good backup solutions, rebuilding, duplicating, or improving a secured system is much simpler the next time.

Once you know what you are left with, you need to perform more research to learn about the strengths and weaknesses of every aspect of the OS, active services, employed protocols, and installed software. After you know the vulnerabilities, methods, and tools of attacks, along with the resultant risks, you can take steps to reduce the risks by implementing safeguards and countermeasures.

Securing the Wireless Environment

The wireless network is not and never will be secure. Use wireless only when absolutely necessary. If you must deploy a wireless network, here are some tips to make some improvements to wireless security:

- Change the default SSID.
- Disable SSID broadcasts.
- Disable DHCP or use reservations.
- Use MAC filtering.
- Use IP filtering.
- Use the strongest security available on the wireless access point.
- Change the static security keys on a two- to four-week basis.
- When new wireless protection schemes become available (and reasonably priced), consider migrating to them.
- Limit the user accounts that can use wireless connectivity.
- Use a preauthentication system, such as RADIUS.
- Use remote access filters against client type, protocols used, time, date, user account, content, and so forth.
- Use IPSec tunnels over the wireless links.
- Turn down the signal strength to the minimum needed to support connectivity.
- Seriously consider removing wireless from your LAN.

Wireless discussions sometimes include mobile devices, which are not 802.11 wireless networking devices themselves but instead are specialized services providing limited Internet connectivity to cell phones, PDAs, and pocket PCs. These devices often use WAP or an equivalent communication protocol suite. Unfortunately, providers are required by the Communications Assistance for Law Enforcement Act of 1994 (CALEA) to make wiretaps possible on all forms of communications offered regardless of the technologies employed (requiring a search warrant for actual use, of course).

Therefore, if you want security over a wireless mobile device, your handheld device and the server you ultimately communicate with must have their own encryption scheme rather than relying on that provided by the provider's service.

You should be aware that malicious entities could be actively seeking to eavesdrop on all of your communications. In addition to personally imposed encryption for handheld devices, be careful of what is actually discussed or communicated over your mobile devices. Even if someone can't grab the information while in transit, it is possible they can look over your shoulder at your screen or be within earshot of your voice. There are many ways to collect data; in order to be secure, you need to be aware of all of them and provide protection against all of them.

Summary

This chapter provided an overview of security from the standpoint of using it in the real world as opposed to exam study. It was intended to be an administrator's reference for use after you've passed the exam and are in the thick of the profession. The content contained within is not what you want to study for the exam—the other 14 chapters fulfilled that purpose—but rather what you want to read after the pride in acing the Security+ test has faded a bit.

Appendix

A

About the Companion CD

IN THIS APPENDIX:

✓ What You'll Find on the CD

✓ System Requirements

✓ Using the CD

✓ Troubleshooting

What You'll Find on the CD

The following sections are arranged by category and summarize the software and other goodies you'll find on the CD. If you need help with installing the items provided on the CD, refer to the installation instructions in the section "Using the CD" later in this appendix.

Some programs on the CD might fall into one of these categories:

Shareware programs are fully functional, free, trial versions of copyrighted programs. If you like particular programs, register with their authors for a nominal fee and receive licenses, enhanced versions, and technical support.

Freeware programs are free, copyrighted games, applications, and utilities. You can copy them to as many computers as you like—for free—but they offer no technical support.

GNU software is governed by its own license, which is included inside the folder of the GNU software. There are no restrictions on distribution of GNU software. See the GNU license at the root of the CD for more details.

Trial, demo, or evaluation versions of software are usually limited either by time or by functionality (such as not letting you save a project after you create it).

Sybex Test Engine

The CD contains the Sybex Test Engine, which includes the Assessment Test and all of the chapter review questions in electronic format, as well as the bonus exams located only on the CD.

Electronic Flashcards

These handy electronic flashcards are just what they sound like. One side contains a question, and the other side shows the answer.

PDF of the Glossary

We have included an electronic version of the Glossary in `.pdf` format. You can view the electronic version of the book with Adobe Reader.

Connecting For Those with the Deluxe Edition

If you purchased the Deluxe Edition of this book, in addition to additional bonus exams and flashcards, we have included a number of valuable tools:

Security Simulation Engine   We have included a limited version of a security simulation engine to allow you to walk through the configuration procedures for several utilities without needing to jeopardize a production system.

Tutorial Videos   We have included 43 minutes of short Camtasia-captured videos on security-related topics to illustrate concepts with which you may not otherwise have hands-on access to.

Additional Bonus PDFs   We have also included a number of bonus appendices, located on the CD in PDF format. These include a list of common acronyms, some additional lab exercises and study tools, and a PDF on cabling.

System Requirements

Make sure your computer meets the minimum system requirements shown in the following list. If your computer doesn't match up to most of these requirements, you may have problems using the software and files on the companion CD. For the latest and greatest information, please refer to the ReadMe file located at the root of the CD-ROM.

- A PC running Microsoft Windows 2000, Windows NT4 (with SP4 or later), Windows Me, Windows XP, Windows Vista, or Windows 7
- An Internet connection
- A CD-ROM drive

Using the CD

To install the items from the CD to your hard drive, follow these steps:

1. Insert the CD into your computer's CD-ROM drive. The license agreement appears.
2. Read the license agreement, and then click the Accept button if you want to use the CD.

The CD interface appears. The interface allows you to access the content with just one or two clicks.

Windows users: The interface won't launch if you have AutoRun disabled. In that case, click Start ➤ Run (for Windows Vista or Windows 7, Start ➤ All Programs ➤ Accessories ➤ Run). In the dialog box that appears, type `D:\Start.exe`. (Replace *D* with the proper letter if your CD drive uses a different letter. If you don't know the letter, see how your CD drive is listed under My Computer.) Click OK.

Troubleshooting

Wiley has attempted to provide programs that work on most computers with the minimum system requirements. Alas, your computer may differ, and some programs may not work properly for some reason.

The two likeliest problems are that you don't have enough memory (RAM) for the programs you want to use and you have other programs running that are affecting the installation of a program or how it runs. If you get an error message such as "Not enough memory" or "Setup cannot continue," try one or more of the following suggestions and then try using the software again:

Turn off any antivirus software running on your computer. Installation programs sometimes mimic virus activity and may make your computer incorrectly believe that it's being infected by a virus.

Close all running programs. The more programs you have running, the less memory is available to other programs. Installation programs typically update files and programs, so if you keep other programs running, installation may not work properly.

Have your local computer store add more ram to your computer. This is, admittedly, a drastic and somewhat expensive step. However, adding more memory can really help the speed of your computer and allow more programs to run at the same time.

Customer Care

If you have trouble with the book's companion CD-ROM, please call the Wiley Product Technical Support phone number at (800) 762-2974. Outside the United States, call +1 (317) 572-3994. You can also contact Wiley Product Technical Support at http:// sybex.custhelp.com. John Wiley & Sons will provide technical support only for installation and other general quality-control items. For technical support on the applications themselves, consult the program's vendor or author.

To place additional orders or to request information about other Wiley products, please call (877) 762-2974.

Glossary

3DES   Also known as Triple Digital Encryption Standard (DES). A symmetric block cipher algorithm used for encryption.

802.1X   The IEEE standard that defines port-based security for wireless network access control. It offers a means of authentication and defines the Extensible Authentication Protocol (EAP) over IEEE 802, and it is often known as EAP over LAN (EAPOL).

A

AAA   Acronym for three key areas of security: Authentication, Authorization, and Accounting.

acceptable use policy (AUP)   Agreed-upon principles set forth by a company to govern how the employees of that company may use resources such as computers and Internet access.

access attack   An attack aimed at gaining access to resources.

access control   The means of giving or restricting user access to network resources. Access control is usually accomplished through the use of an access control list (ACL).

access control list (ACL)   A table or data file that specifies whether a user or group has access to a specific resource on a computer or network.

access point (AP)   The point at which access to a network is accomplished. This term is often used in relation to a wireless access point (WAP).

accountability   Being responsible for an item. The administrator is often accountable for the network and the resources on it.

accounting   The act of keeping track of activity. Most often, this term is used to refer to tracking users' interactions with network resources via log files that are routinely scanned and checked.

acknowledgment (ACK)   A message confirming that a data packet was received. Acknowledgment is a TCP function and occurs at the Transport layer of the Open Systems Interconnection (OSI) and TCP/IP models.

active response   A response generated in real time.

active sniffing   Involves an attacker gaining access to a host in the network through a switch and logically disconnecting it from the network.

activity   Any action a user undertakes.

Address Resolution Protocol (ARP)   Protocol used to map known IP addresses to unknown physical addresses.

AD-IDS   Anomaly-detection intrusion detection system. An AD-IDS works by looking for deviations from a pattern of normal network traffic.

administrative policies   A set of rules that govern administrative usage of a system.

administrator   The user who is accountable and responsible for the network.

Advanced Encryption Standard (AES)   A FIPS publication that specifies a cryptographic algorithm for use by the U.S. government. *See also* Federal Information Processing Standard (FIPS).

adware   Software that gathers information to pass on to marketers or that intercepts personal data such as credit card numbers and makes them available to third parties.

AES256   An implementation of Advanced Encryption Standard (AES) that uses 256-bit encryption.

alert   A notification that an unusual condition exists and should be investigated.

algorithm   The series of steps/formulas/processes that is followed to arrive at a result.

analyzer   The component or process that analyzes the data collected by the sensor.

annualized loss expectancy (ALE)   A calculation that is used to identify risks and calculate the expected loss each year.

annualized rate of occurrence (ARO)   A calculation of how often a threat will occur. For example, a threat that occurs once every five years has an annualized rate of occurrence of 1/5, or 0.2.

anomaly detection   The act of looking for variations from normal operations (anomalies) and reacting to them.

anonymous authentication   Authentication that doesn't require a user to provide a username, password, or any other identification before accessing resources.

antivirus   A category of software that uses various methods to prevent and eliminate viruses in a computer. It typically also protects against future infection. *See also* virus.

antivirus engine   The core program that runs the virus-scanning process.

antivirus software   Software that identifies the presence of a virus and is capable of removing or quarantining the virus.

AP   *See* access point (AP).

appliance   A freestanding device that operates in a largely self-contained manner.

Application layer   The seventh layer of the Open Systems Interconnection (OSI) model. This layer deals with how applications access the network and describes application functionality, such as file transfer, messaging, and so on.

application programming interface (API)   An abstract interface to the services and protocols provided by an operating system.

armored virus A virus that is protected in a way that makes disassembling it difficult. The difficulty makes it "armored" against antivirus programs that have trouble getting to, and understanding, its code.

ARO *See* annualized rate of occurrence (ARO).

ARP *See* Address Resolution Protocol (ARP).

ARP table The table that the Address Resolution Protocol uses. Contains a list of known IP addresses and their associated physical addresses. The table is cached in memory so that ARP lookups don't have to be performed for frequently accessed addresses. *See also* Media Access Control (MAC).

asset Any resource of value that you want to secure and protect.

asymmetric algorithm An algorithm that utilizes two keys.

asymmetric encryption Encryption in which two keys must be used. One key is used to encrypt data, and the other is needed to decrypt the data. Asymmetric encryption is the opposite of symmetric encryption, where a single key serves both purposes.

attack Any unauthorized intrusion into the normal operations of a computer or computer network. The attack can be carried out to gain access to the system or any of its resources.

audit files Files that hold information about a resource's access by users.

auditing The act of tracking resource usage by users.

auditors Individuals involved in auditing log and security files.

AUP *See* acceptable use policy (AUP).

authenticating the evidence Verifying that the logs and other resources collected are legitimate. This technique can be useful in verifying that an attack has occurred.

authentication The means of verifying that someone is who they say they are.

Authentication Header (AH) A header used to provide connectionless integrity and data origin authentication for IP datagrams and to provide protection against replays.

availability The ability of a resource to be accessed, often expressed as a time period. Many networks limit users' ability to access network resources to working hours, as a security precaution.

B

back door (backdoor) An opening left in a program application (usually by the developer) that allows additional access to data. Typically, these are created for debugging purposes and aren't documented. Before the product ships, the back doors are closed; when they aren't closed, security loopholes exist.

backup   A usable copy of data made to media. Ideally, the backup is made to removable media and stored for recovery should anything happen to the original data.

backup plan   A documented plan governing backup situations.

backup policy   A written policy detailing the frequency of backups and the location of storage media.

BCP   *See* business continuity planning (BCP).

Bell-LaPadula model   A model designed for the military to address the storage and protection of classified information. This model is specifically designed to prevent unauthorized access to classified information. The model prevents the user from accessing information that has a higher security rating than they are authorized to access. It also prevents information from being written to a lower level of security.

best practices   A set of rules governing basic operations.

BGP   *See* Border Gateway Protocol (BGP).

BIA   *See* Business Impact Analysis (BIA).

Biba model   A model similar in concept to the Bell-LaPadula model but more concerned with information integrity (an area the Bell-LaPadula model doesn't address). In this model, there is no write up or read down. If you're assigned access to top-secret information, you can't read secret information or write to any level higher than the level to which you're authorized. This model keeps higher-level information pure by preventing less-reliable information from being intermixed with it.

biometric device   A device that can authenticate an individual based on a physical characteristic.

biometrics   The science of identifying a person by using one or more of their features. The feature can be a thumbprint, a retinal scan, or any other biological trait.

BIOS   The basic input/output system for an IBM-based PC. It is the firmware that allows the computer to boot.

birthday attack   A probability method of finding collision in hash functions.

Blowfish   A type of symmetric block cipher created by Bruce Schneier.

boot sector   Also known as the Master Boot Record (MBR). The first sector of the hard disk, where the program that boots the operating system resides. It's a popular target for viruses.

Border Gateway Protocol (BGP)   An ISP protocol that allows routers to share information about routes with each other.

border router   A router used to translate from LAN framing to WAN framing.

bot   An automated software program (network robot) that collects information on the Web. In the malicious form, a bot is a compromised computer being controlled remotely.

brute force attack   A type of attack that relies purely on trial and error and tries all possible combinations.

buffer overflow attack   A type of denial of service (DoS) attack that occurs when more data is put into a buffer than it can hold, thereby overflowing it (as the name implies).

business continuity planning (BCP)   A contingency plan that allows a business to keep running in the event of a disruption to vital resources.

business impact analysis (BIA)   A study of the possible impact if a disruption to a business's vital resources were to occur.

C

CA   *See* certificate authority (CA).

CAC   *See* common access card (CAC).

Carlisle Adams Stafford Tavares (CAST)   A type of symmetric block cipher defined by RFC 2144.

CC   *See* Common Criteria (CC).

CCRA   *See* Common Criteria Recognition Agreement (CCRA).

CCTV   *See* closed-circuit television (CCTV).

central office   The primary office from which most resources extend.

CERT   *See* Computer Emergency Response Team (CERT).

certificate   A digital entity that establishes who you are and is often used with e-commerce. It contains your name and other identifying data.

certificate authority (CA)   An issuer of digital certificates (which are then used for digital signatures or key pairs). A certificate authority is occasionally referred to as a certification authority.

certificate policies   Policies governing the use of certificates.

Certificate Practice Statement (CPS)   The principles and procedures employed in the issuing and managing of certificates.

certificate revocation   The act of making a certificate invalid.

Certificate Revocation List (CRL)   A list of digital certificate revocations that must be regularly downloaded to stay current.

chain of custody   The log of the history of evidence that has been collected.

Challenge Handshake Authentication Protocol (CHAP)   A protocol that challenges a system to verify identity. CHAP is an improvement over Password Authentication Protocol (PAP) in which one-way hashing is incorporated into a three-way handshake. RFC 1334 applies to both PAP and CHAP.

change documentation   Documentation required to make a change in the scope of any particular item. In the realm of project management, a change document is a formal document requiring many signatures before key elements of the project can be modified.

checkpoint   A certain action or moment in time that is used to perform a check. It allows a restart to begin at the last point the data was saved as opposed to from the beginning.

checksum   A hexadecimal value computed from transmitted data that is used in error-checking routines.

cipher   *See* cryptographic algorithm.

circuit switching   A switching method where a dedicated connection between the sender and receiver is maintained throughout the conversation.

CIRT   *See* Computer Incident Response Team (CIRT).

Clark-Wilson model   An integrity model for creating a secure architecture.

clear text   Unencrypted text that can be read with any editor.

client   The part of a client/server network where the computing is usually done. In a typical setting, a client uses the server for remote storage, backups, or security (such as a firewall).

client/server network   A server-centric network in which all resources are stored on a file server and processing power is distributed among workstations and the file server.

closed-circuit television (CCTV)   A surveillance camera used for physical-access monitoring.

clustering   A method of balancing loads and providing fault tolerance.

code escrow   The storage and conditions for release of source code provided by a vendor, partner, or other party.

cold site   A physical site that has all the resources necessary to enable an organization to use it if the main site is inaccessible (destroyed). Commonly, plans call for turning to a cold site within a certain number of hours after the loss of the main site.

collection of evidence   The means and orderly fashion by which evidence is collected, identified, and marked.

collusion   An agreement between individuals to commit fraud or deceit.

Common Access Card (CAC)   A standard identification card used by the Department of Defense (DoD) and other employers. It is used for authentication as well as identification.

Common Criteria (CC)   A document of specifications detailing security evaluation methods for IT products and systems.

Common Criteria Recognition Agreement (CCRA)   A set of standards, formerly known as the Mutual Recognition Agreement (MRA), that defines Evaluation Assurance Levels (EALs).

Common Gateway Interface (CGI)   An older form of scripting that was used extensively in early web systems.

companion virus   A virus that creates a new program that runs in place of an expected program of the same name.

compartmentalization   Standards that support a nonhierarchical security classification.

Computer Emergency Response Team (CERT)   A team of experts who respond to computer security incidents.

Computer Incident Response Team (CIRT)   A team of experts who respond to a security incident. The CIRT acronym is growing in popularity and quickly replacing CERT.

confidentiality   Assurance that data remains private and no one sees it except for those expected to see it.

configuration management   The administration of setup and changes to configurations.

connectionless   Type of communications between two hosts that have no previous session established for synchronizing sent data. The data isn't acknowledged at the receiving end. This method can allow data loss. Within the TCP/IP suite, the User Datagram Protocol (UDP) is used for connectionless communication.

connection-oriented   Type of communications between two hosts that have a previous session established for synchronizing sent data. The receiving PC acknowledges the data. This method allows for guaranteed delivery of data between PCs. Within the TCP/IP suite, TCP is used for connection-oriented communications.

cookie   A plain-text file stored on your machine that contains information about you (and your preferences) and is used by a server.

CPS   *See* Certificate Practice Statement (CPS).

cracker   *See* hacker.

critical business functions   Functions on which the livelihood of the company depends.

CRL   *See* Certificate Revocation List (CRL).

cross-site requires forgery (XSRF)   A form of web-based attack in which unauthorized commands are sent from a user that a website trusts.

cryptanalysis   The study and practice of finding weaknesses in ciphers.

cryptanalyst   A person who does cryptanalysis.

cryptographer   A person who participates in the study of cryptographic algorithms.

cryptographic algorithm   A symmetric algorithm, also known as a cipher, used to encrypt and decrypt data.

cryptography   The field of mathematics focused on encrypting and decrypting data.

custodian   An individual responsible for maintaining the data, and the integrity of it, within their area.

cyclic redundancy check (CRC)   An error-checking method in data communications that runs a formula against data before transmission. The sending station then appends the resultant value (called a checksum) to the data and sends it. The receiving station uses the same formula on the data. If the receiving station doesn't get the same checksum result for the calculation, it considers the transmission invalid, rejects the frame, and asks for retransmission.

D

DAC   *See* discretionary access control (DAC).

data integrity   A quality that provides a level of confidence that data won't be jeopardized and will be kept secret.

Data Link layer   The second layer of the Open Systems Interconnection (OSI) model. It describes the physical topology of a network.

data loss prevention (DLP)   Any systems that identify, monitor, and protect data to prevent it from unauthorized use, modification, or destruction.

data packet   A unit of data sent over a network. A packet includes a header, addressing information, and the data itself.

data repository   A centralized storage location for data, such as a database.

data source   Where data originates.

datagram   An OSI Layer 3, User Datagram Protocol (UDP) packet descriptor.

DDoS attack   *See* Distributed Denial of Service (DDoS) attack.

decryption   The process of converting encrypted data back into its original form.

default gateway   The router to which all packets are sent when the workstation doesn't know where the destination station is or when it can't find the destination station on the local segment.

demilitarized zone (DMZ)   An area for placing web and other servers outside the firewall, therefore, isolating them from internal network access.

Denial of Service (DoS) attack   A type of attack that prevents any users—even legitimate ones—from using a system.

destination port number   A portion of a complete address of a PC to which data is being sent from a sending PC. The port portion allows for the demultiplexing of data to be sent to a specific application.

detection   The act of noticing an irregularity as it occurs.

DHCP   *See* Dynamic Host Configuration Protocol (DHCP).

dictionary attack   The act of attempting to crack passwords by testing them against a list of dictionary words. With today's powerful computers, an attacker can combine one of many available automated password-cracking utilities with several large dictionaries or "wordlists" and crack huge numbers of passwords in a matter of minutes. Any password based on any dictionary word is vulnerable to such an attack.

differential backup   A type of backup that includes only new files or files that have changed since the last full backup. Differential backups differ from incremental backups in that they don't clear the archive bit upon their completion.

Diffie-Hellman   An asymmetric standard for exchanging keys. This cryptographic algorithm is used primarily to send secret keys across public networks. The process isn't used to encrypt or decrypt messages; it's used merely for the transmission of keys in a secure manner.

digital signature   An asymmetrically encrypted signature whose sole purpose is to authenticate the sender.

directory   A network database that contains a listing of all network resources, such as users, printers, groups, and so on.

directory service   A network service that provides access to a central database of information, which contains detailed information about the resources available on a network.

direct-sequence (DS)   A method of communication between wireless receivers.

direct-sequence spread spectrum (DSSS)   A communications technology that is used to communicate in the 802.11 standard.

disaster recovery   The act of recovering data following a disaster that has destroyed it.

disaster recovery plan (DRP)   A plan outlining the procedure by which data is recovered after a disaster.

discretionary access control (DAC)   A method of restricting access to objects based on the identity of the subjects or the groups to which they belong.

disk mirroring   Technology that keeps identical copies of data on two disks to prevent the loss of data if one disk faults.

disk striping   Technology that enables writing data to multiple disks simultaneously in small portions called stripes. These stripes maximize use by having all the read/write heads working constantly. Different data is stored on each disk and isn't automatically duplicated (this means disk striping in and of itself doesn't provide fault tolerance).

disk striping with parity   A fault-tolerance solution of writing data across a number of disks and recording the parity on another. In the event any one disk fails, the data on it can be re-created by looking at the remaining data and computing parity to figure out the missing data.

Distributed Denial of Service (DDoS) attack   A derivative of a DoS attack in which multiple hosts in multiple locations all focus on one target to reduce its availability to the public. *See* Denial of Service (DoS) attack.

DLP   *See* Data Loss Prevention (DLP).

DMZ   *See* demilitarized zone (DMZ).

DNS server   Any server that performs address resolution from a DNS fully qualified domain name (FQDN) to an IP address. *See also* Domain Name Service (DNS), Internet Protocol (IP).

DNS zone   An area in the DNS hierarchy that is managed as a single unit. *See also* Domain Name Service (DNS).

DoD Networking Model   A four-layer conceptual model describing how communications should take place between computer systems. The four layers are Process/Application, Host-to-Host, Internet, and Network Access.

domain   Within the Internet, a group of computers with shared traits and a common IP address set. A domain can also be a group of networked Windows computers that share a single SAM database. *See also* Security Accounts Manager (SAM).

Domain Name Service (DNS)   The network service used in TCP/IP networks that translates hostnames to IP addresses. *See also* Transmission Control Protocol/Internet Protocol (TCP/IP).

DoS attack   *See* Denial of Service (DoS) attack.

DRP   *See* disaster recovery plan (DRP).

DS   *See* direct-sequence (DS).

dual-homed host   A host that resides on more than one network and possesses more than one physical network card.

dumb terminal   A keyboard and monitor that send keystrokes to a central processing computer (typically a mainframe or minicomputer) that returns screen displays to the monitor. The unit has no processing power of its own, hence the moniker "dumb."

Dumpster diving   Looking through trash for clues—often in the form of paper scraps—to find users' passwords and other pertinent information.

duplexed hard drives   Two hard drives to which identical information is written simultaneously. A dedicated controller card controls each drive. Used for fault tolerance, and is known as RAID 1.

duplicate servers   Two servers that are identical, for use in clustering.

Dynamic Host Configuration Protocol (DHCP)   A protocol used on a TCP/IP network to send client configuration data, including IP address, default gateway, subnet mask, and DNS configuration, to clients. DHCP uses a four-step process: Discover, Offer, Request, and Acknowledgement. *See also* default gateway, Domain Name Service (DNS), Transmission Control Protocol/Internet Protocol (TCP/IP).

dynamic packet filtering   A type of firewall used to accept or reject packets based on their contents.

dynamic routing   The use of route-discovery protocols to talk to other routers and find out what networks they are attached to. Routers that use dynamic routing send out special packets to request updates from the other routers on the network as well as to send their own updates.

dynamically allocated port   A TCP/IP port that is not constantly used but accessed by an application when needed.

E

EAL   *See* Evaluation Assurance Level (EAL).

EAP   *See* Extensible Authentication Protocol (EAP).

eavesdropping   Any type of passive attack that intercepts data in an unauthorized manner—usually in order to find passwords. Cable sniffing, wiretapping, and man-in-the-middle attacks are eavesdropping attacks.

ECC   *See* elliptic curve cryptography (ECC).

EF   *See* exposure factor (EF).

electromagnetic interference (EMI)   The interference that can occur during transmissions over copper cable because of electromagnetic energy outside the cable. The result is degradation of the signal.

elliptic curve cryptography (ECC)   A type of public key cryptosystem that requires a shorter key length than many other cryptography systems (including the de facto industry standard, RSA).

EMI   *See* electromagnetic interference (EMI).

Encapsulating Security Payload (ESP)   A header used to provide a mix of security services in IPv4 and IPv6. ESP can be used alone or in combination with the IP Authentication Header (AH).

encoding   The process of translating data into signals that can be transmitted on a transmission medium.

Encrypting File System (EFS)   A feature in NTFS on Windows-based operating systems that allows for filesystem-level encryption to be applied.

encryption   The process of converting data into a form that makes it less likely to be usable to anyone intercepting it if they can't decrypt it.

encryption key   A string of alphanumeric characters used to decrypt encrypted data.

enticement   The process of luring someone.

entrapment   The process of encouraging an attacker to perform an act, even if they don't want to do it.

enumeration   An attempt to gain information about a network by specifically targeting network resources, users and groups, and applications running on the system.

escalation   The act of moving something up in priority. Often, when an incident is escalated, it's brought to the attention of the next-highest supervisor. *See also* privilege escalation.

Evaluation Assurance Level (EAL)   A level of assurance, expressed as a numeric value, based on standards set by the Common Criteria Recognition Agreement (CCRA).

event   Any noticeable action or occurrence.

exposure factor (EF)   A calculation of how much data (or other assets) could be lost from a single occurrence. If all the data on the network could be jeopardized by a single attack, the exposure factor is 100 percent.

Extensible Authentication Protocol (EAP)   An authentication protocol used in wireless networks and point-to-point connections.

external threat   A threat that originates from outside the company.

extranet   Web (or similar) services set up in a private network to be accessed internally and by select external entities, such as vendors and suppliers.

extrusion   Examining data leaving a network for signs of malicious traffic.

F

fail-over/failover   The process of reconstructing a system or switching over to other systems when a failure is detected.

fail-over device   A device that comes online when another fails.

fail-over server   A hot-site backup system in which the fail-over server is connected to the primary server. A heartbeat is sent from the primary server to the backup server. If the heartbeat stops, the fail-over system starts and takes over. Thus, the system doesn't go down even if the primary server isn't running.

false positive   A flagged event that isn't really an event and has been falsely triggered.

Faraday cage   An electrically conductive wire mesh or other conductor woven into a "cage" that surrounds a room and prevents electromagnetic signals from entering or leaving the room through the walls.

fault-resistant network   A network that is up and running at least 99 percent of the time or that is down less than 8 hours a year.

fault tolerance   The ability to withstand a fault (failure) without losing data.

fault-tolerant network   A network that can recover from minor errors.

Federal Information Processing Standard (FIPS)   An agreed-upon standard published under the Information Technology Management Reform Act. The secretary of commerce approves the standards after they're developed by the National Institute of Standards and Technology (NIST) for federal computer systems.

File Transfer Protocol (FTP)   TCP/IP and software that permit transferring files between computer systems and utilize clear-text passwords. Because FTP has been implemented on numerous types of computer systems, files can be transferred between disparate computer systems (for example, a personal computer and a minicomputer). *See also* Transmission Control Protocol/Internet Protocol (TCP/IP).

fire suppression   The act of stopping a fire and preventing it from spreading.

firewall   A combination of hardware and software that protects a network from attack by hackers who could gain access through public networks, including the Internet.

footprinting   The process of systematically identifying the network and its security posture. This is typically a passive process.

forensics   In terms of security, the act of looking at all the data at your disposal to try to figure out who gained unauthorized access and the extent of that access.

frequency-hopping spread spectrum (FHSS)   A communications technology used to communicate in the 802.11 standard. FHSS accomplishes communication by hopping the transmission over a range of predefined frequencies.

FTP   *See* File Transfer Protocol (FTP).

FTP proxy   A server that uploads and downloads files from another server on behalf of a workstation.

full backup   A backup that copies all data to the archive medium.

full distribution   An information classification stating that the data so classified is available to anyone.

G

Gramm-Leach-Bliley Act   A government act containing rules on privacy of consumer finance information.

Grandfather, Father, Son   One of the most popular methods of backup tape rotation. Three sets of tapes are rotated in this method. The most recent backup after the full backup is the Son. As newer backups are made, the Son becomes the Father, and the Father, in turn, becomes the Grandfather. At the end of each month, a full backup is performed on all systems. This backup is stored in an off-site facility for a period of one year. Each monthly backup replaces the monthly backup from the previous year. Weekly or daily incremental backups are performed and stored until the next full backup occurs. This full backup is then stored off site, and the weekly or daily backup tapes are reused.

H

hacker   Generally used to refer to someone who gains access to a system, software, or hardware without permission. Also can be called a cracker.

handshake   The process of agreeing to communicate and share data. TCP uses a three-way handshake to establish connections, and part of this process can be exploited by certain types of attacks.

hardening   The process of making an entity, usually an operating system, more secure by closing known holes and addressing known security issues.

hash/hashing   The process of transforming characters into other characters that represent (but are not) the originals. Traditionally, the results are smaller and more secure than the original.

hash value   A single number used to represent an original piece of data.

Health Insurance Portability and Accountability Act (HIPAA)   An act that addresses security and privacy of health-related data.

high availability   A clustering solution to provide resource reliability and availability.

hijacking (TCP/IP hijacking)   *See* man-in-the-middle attack.

HIPAA   *See* Health Insurance Portability and Accountability Act (HIPAA).

hoax   Typically an email message warning of something that isn't true, such as the outbreak of a new virus. The hoax can send users into a panic and cause more harm than the virus.

honeypot (also known as Honey pot)   A bogus system set up to attract and slow down a hacker. A honeypot can also be used to learn of the hacking techniques and methods that hackers employ.

host   Any network device with a TCP/IP network address.

host-based IDS (HIDS)   An intrusion detection system that is host based. The alternative is network based.

host-based IPS (HIPS)   An intrusion prevention system that is host based. To prevent the intrusion, it must first detect it (thus making it a superset of HIDS) and then act accordingly.

hostile code   Any code that behaves in a way other than in the best interest of the user and the security of data.

host-to-host   Describes communication that occurs between hosts.

hot fix/hotfix   Another word for a patch. When Microsoft rolls a bunch of hotfixes together, they become known as a service pack.

hot site   A location that can provide operations within hours of a failure.

HTTP   *See* Hypertext Transfer Protocol (HTTP).

HTTPS   *See* Hypertext Transfer Protocol over SSL.

HVAC   A common acronym for Heating, Ventilation, and Air Conditioning.

Hypertext Markup Language (HTML)   A set of codes used to format text and graphics that will be displayed in a browser. The codes define how data will be displayed.

Hypertext Transfer Protocol (HTTP)   The protocol used for communication between a web server and a web browser.

Hypertext Transfer Protocol over SSL   Also known as HTTPS and HTTP Secure. A combination of HTTP with Secure Sockets Layer (SSL) to make for a secure connection. It uses port 443 by default.

I

IAB   *See* Internet Architecture Board (IAB).

IANA   *See* Internet Assigned Numbers Authority (IANA).

ICMP   *See* Internet Control Message Protocol (ICMP).

ICMP attack   An attack that occurs by triggering a response from the Internet Control Message Protocol (ICMP) when it responds to a seemingly legitimate maintenance request. *See also* Internet Control Message Protocol (ICMP).

identification and authentication (I&A)   A two-step process of identifying a person (usually when they log on) and authenticating them by challenging their claim to access a resource.

IDS   *See* intrusion detection system (IDS).

IEEE   *See* Institute of Electrical and Electronics Engineers, Inc. (IEEE).

IEEE 802.10 LAN/MAN Security   A series of guidelines dealing with various aspects of network security.

IEEE 802.11   A family of protocols that provides for wireless communications using radio-frequency transmissions.

IEEE 802.11 Wireless LAN   Defines the standards for implementing wireless technologies such as infrared and spread-spectrum radio.

IETF   *See* Internet Engineering Task Force (IETF).

IGMP   *See* Internet Group Management Protocol (IGMP).

illicit server   An application/program that shouldn't be there but is operating on the network, and one that is commonly used to gain unauthorized control by allowing someone to bypass normal authentication. NetBus is one of the best-known examples of an illicit server.

IM   *See* instant messaging (IM).

IMAP   *See* Internet Message Access Protocol (IMAP).

incident   An attempt to violate a security policy, a successful penetration, a compromise of a system, or unauthorized access to information.

incident response   How an organization responds to an incident.

incident response plan (IRP)   A policy that defines how an organization will respond to an incident.

incident response team (IRT)   Also known as a Computer Security Incident Response Team (CSIRT). The group of individuals responsible for responding when a security breach has occurred.

incremental backup   A type of backup in which only new files or files that have changed since the last full backup or the last incremental backup are included. Incremental backups clear the archive bit on files upon their completion.

information classification   The process of determining what information is accessible to what parties and for what purposes.

information classification policies   Written policies detailing dissemination of information.

information destruction policies   Policies that define how information is destroyed when it has reached the end of its useful life.

Information Flow model   A model concerned with all the properties of information flow, not just the direction of the flow.

information policies   Policies governing the various aspects of information security. Information policies include access, classifications, marking and storage, and the transmission and destruction of sensitive information. The development of information policies is critical to security.

information retention A designation of how long data is retained and any other significant considerations about information.

information security Security practices applied to information.

infrastructure The hardware and software necessary to run your network.

infrastructure security Security on the hardware and software necessary to run your network.

instant messaging (IM) Immediate communication that can be sent back and forth between users who are currently logged on. From a security standpoint, there are risks associated with giving out information via IM that can be used in social engineering attacks; in addition, attachments sent can contain viruses.

Institute of Electrical and Electronics Engineers, Inc. (IEEE) An international organization that sets standards for various electrical and electronics issues.

Integrated Services Digital Network (ISDN) A telecommunications standard that is used to digitally send voice, data, and video signals over the same lines.

integrity *See* data integrity.

interception The process of covertly obtaining information not meant for you. Interception can be an active or passive process.

internal information Information intended to remain within an organization.

internal threat A threat that arises from within an organization.

International Data Encryption Algorithm (IDEA) An algorithm that uses a 128-bit key. This product is similar in speed and capability to Digital Encryption Standard (DES), but it's more secure. IDEA is used in Pretty Good Privacy (PGP).

International Organization for Standardization (ISO) The standards organization that developed the Open Systems Interconnection (OSI) model. This model provides a guideline for how communications occur between computers.

International Telecommunications Union (ITU) Organization responsible for communications standards, spectrum management, and the development of communications infrastructures in underdeveloped nations.

Internet A global network made up of a large number of individual networks that are interconnected and use TCP/IP. *See also* Transmission Control Protocol/Internet Protocol (TCP/IP).

Internet Architecture Board (IAB) The committee that oversees management of the Internet. It's made up of two subcommittees: the Internet Engineering Task Force (IETF) and the Internet Research Task Force (IRTF). *See also* Internet Engineering Task Force (IETF) and Internet Research Task Force (IRTF).

Internet Assigned Numbers Authority (IANA)   The organization responsible for governing IP addresses. `http://www.iana.org`.

Internet Control Message Protocol (ICMP)   A message and management protocol for TCP/IP. The Ping utility uses ICMP. *See also* Ping, Transmission Control Protocol/Internet Protocol (TCP/IP).

Internet Engineering Task Force (IETF)   An international organization that works under the Internet Architecture Board to establish standards and protocols relating to the Internet. *See also* Internet Architecture Board (IAB).

Internet Group Management Protocol (IGMP)   A protocol used for multicasting operations across the Internet.

Internet layer   The network layer responsible for routing, IP addressing, and packaging.

Internet Message Access Protocol (IMAP)   A protocol with a store-and-forward capability. It can also allow messages to be stored on an email server instead of downloaded to the client.

Internet Protocol (IP)   The protocol in the TCP/IP suite responsible for network addressing. *See also* Transmission Control Protocol/Internet Protocol (TCP/IP).

Internet Research Task Force (IRTF)   An international organization that works under the Internet Architecture Board to research new Internet technologies. *See also* Internet Architecture Board (IAB).

Internet service provider (ISP)   A company that provides direct access to the Internet for home and business computer users.

Internet Society (ISOC)   A professional membership group composed primarily of Internet experts. It oversees a number of committees and groups, including the Internet Engineering Task Force (IETF).

intranet   Web (or similar) services set up in a private network to be accessed internally only.

intrusion   The act of entering a system without authorization to do so.

intrusion detection system (IDS)   Tools that identify and respond to attacks using defined rules or logic. An IDS can be network based or host based.

intrusion detector   The item/application performing intrusion detection. *See also* intrusion detection system (IDS).

IP proxy   A server that acts as a go-between for clients accessing the Internet. All communications look as if they originated from a proxy server because the IP address of the user making a request is hidden. Also known as Network Address Translation (NAT).

IP Security (IPSec) A set of protocols that enable encryption, authentication, and integrity over IP. IPSec is commonly used with virtual private networks (VPNs) and operates at Layer 3.

IP spoofing An attack during which a hacker tries to gain access to a network by pretending their interface has the same network address as the internal network.

ISP *See* Internet service provider (ISP).

J

JavaScript A programming language that allows access to system resources of the system running the script. These scripts can interface with all aspects of an operating system just like programming languages, such as the C language.

journaling The ability of a filesystem to use a log file of all changes and transactions that have occurred within a set period of time (for example, the last few hours). If a crash occurs, the operating system can look at the log files to see what transactions have been committed and which ones have not.

K

Kerberos An authentication scheme that uses tickets (unique keys) embedded within messages. Named after the three-headed guard dog that stood at the gates of Hades in Greek mythology.

key/certificate life cycle The time during which the processes of a key or certificate take place.

key distribution center (KDC) An organization/facility that generates keys for users.

key escrow agency An agency that stores keys for the purpose of law-enforcement access.

Key Exchange Algorithm (KEA) A method of offering mutual authentication and establishing data encryption keys.

key generation The act of creating keys for use by users.

key suspension The temporary deferment of a key for a period of time (such as for a leave of absence).

Keyed-Hash Message Authentication Code (HMAC) "A mechanism for message authentication using cryptographic hash functions" per the draft of the Federal Information Processing Standard (FIPS) publication. Addressed in RFC 2104.

L

latency   The wait time between the call for an action or activity and the actual execution of that action.

lattice   The concept that access differs at different levels. Often used in discussion with the Biba and Bell-LaPadula models as well as with cryptography to differentiate between security levels based on user/group labels.

Layer 2 Forwarding (L2F)   A tunneling protocol often used with virtual private networks (VPNs). L2F was developed by Cisco.

Layer 2 Tunneling Protocol (L2TP)   A tunneling protocol that adds functionality to the Point-to-Point Protocol (PPP). This protocol was created by Microsoft and Cisco and is often used with virtual private networks (VPNs).

Lightweight Directory Access Protocol (LDAP)   A set of protocols that was derived from X.500 and operates at port 389.

limited distribution   Describes information that isn't intended for release to the public. This category of information isn't secret, but it's private.

Link Control Protocol (LCP)   The protocol used to establish, configure, and test the link between a client and PPP host. *See also* Point-to-Point Protocol (PPP).

local area network (LAN)   A network that is restricted to a single building, group of buildings, or even a single room. A LAN can have one or more servers.

local registration authority (LRA)   An authority used to identify or establish the identity of an individual for certificate issuance.

logic bomb   Any code that is hidden within an application and causes something unexpected to happen based on some criteria being met. For example, a programmer could create a program that always makes sure his name appears on the payroll roster; if it doesn't, then key files begin to be erased.

logs and inventories   Tools used to help an organization know what is happening to its systems and assets. System logs tell what is happening with the systems in the network. Inventories refer to both the physical assets and the software assets a company owns.

M

M of N Control method   A rule stating that in order to access the key server if n number of administrators have the ability to perform a process, m number of those administrators must authenticate for access to occur. M of N Control may involve physical presence.

MAC   *See* Media Access Control (MAC), Mandatory Access Control (MAC), and message authentication code (MAC).

MAC address   The address that is either assigned to a network card or burned into the network interface card (NIC). PCs use MAC addresses to keep track of one another and keep each other separate.

macro virus   A software exploitation virus that works by using the macro feature included in many applications.

malicious code   Any code that is meant to do harm.

Mandatory Access Control (MAC)   A security policy wherein labels are used to identify the sensitivity of objects. When a user attempts to access an object, the label is checked to see if access should be allowed (that is, whether the user is operating at the same sensitivity level). This policy is "mandatory," because labels are automatically applied to all data (and can be changed only by administrative action), as opposed to "discretionary" policies that leave it up to the user to decide whether to apply a label.

man-in-the-middle attack   An attack that occurs when someone/something that is trusted intercepts packets and retransmits them to another party. Man-in-the-middle attacks have also been called TCP/IP hijacking in the past.

mantrap   A device, such as a small room, that limits access to one or a few individuals. Mantraps typically use electronic locks and other methods to control access.

mathematical attack   An attack focused on the encryption algorithm itself, the key mechanism, or any potential area of weakness in the algorithm.

mean time between failure (MTBF)   The measure of the anticipated incidence of failure of a system or component.

mean time to repair (MTTR)   The measurement of how long it takes to repair a system or component once a failure occurs.

Media Access Control (MAC)   A sublayer of the Data Link layer of the Open Systems Interconnection (OSI) model that controls the way multiple devices use the same media channel. It controls which devices can transmit and when they can transmit.

message authentication code (MAC)   A common method of verifying integrity. The MAC is derived from the message and a secret key.

message digest   The signature area within a message.

Message Digest Algorithm (MDA)   An algorithm that creates a hash value. The hash value is also used to help maintain integrity. There are several versions of MD; the most common are MD5, MD4, and MD2.

Microsoft Challenge Handshake Authentication Protocol (MSCHAP)   An implementation of the Challenge Handshake Authentication Protocol (CHAP) common in Microsoft's Windows-based operating systems. The latest version, and the only one supported in Windows Vista, is MSCHAPv2.

misuse-detection IDS (MD-IDS)   A method of evaluating attacks based on attack signatures and audit trails.

modification attack   An attack that modifies information on your system.

multicasting   Sending data to more than one address.

multi-factor   The term employed anytime more than one factor must be considered.

multipartite virus   A virus that attacks a system in more than one way.

N

NAT   Network Address Translation. *See* IP proxy.

National Computing Security Center (NCSC)   The agency that developed the Trusted Computer System Evaluation Criteria (TCSEC) and the Trusted Network Interpretation Environmental Guideline (TNIEG).

National Institute of Standards and Technology (NIST)   An agency (formerly known as the National Bureau of Standards [NBS]) that has been involved in developing and supporting standards for the U.S. government for over 100 years. NIST has become involved in cryptography standards, systems, and technology in a variety of areas. It's primarily concerned with governmental systems, where it exercises a great deal of influence.

National Security Agency (NSA)   The U.S. government agency responsible for protecting U.S. communications and producing foreign intelligence information. It was established by presidential directive in 1952 as a separately organized agency within the Department of Defense (DoD).

need-to-know   A method of information dissemination based on passing information only to those who need to know it.

network   A group of devices connected by some means for the purpose of sharing information or resources.

Network Access Control (NAC)   The set of standards defined by the network for clients attempting to access it. Usually, NAC requires that clients be virus free and adhere to specified policies before allowing them on the network.

Network Address Translation (NAT)   *See* IP proxy.

network attached storage   Storage, such as hard drives, attached to a network for the purpose of storing data for clients on the network. Network attached storage is commonly used for backing up data.

network-based IPS (N-IPS)   An intrusion prevention system that is network based. To prevent the intrusion, it must first detect it (thus making it a superset of IDS), and then act accordingly.

Network Control Protocol (NCP)   The protocol Point-to-Point Protocol (PPP) employs for encapsulating network traffic.

Network File System (NFS)   A protocol that enables users to access files on remote computers as if the files were local.

network interface card (NIC)   A physical device that connects computers and other network equipment to the transmission medium.

Network Interface layer   The lowest level of the TCP/IP suite; it is responsible for placing and removing packets on the physical network.

Network layer   The third layer of the OSI model, it is responsible for logical addressing and translating logical names into physical addresses. This layer also controls the routing of data from source to destination as well as the building and dismantling of packets. *See also* Open Systems Interconnection (OSI) model.

Network Operations Center (NOC)   A single, centralized area for network monitoring and administrative control of systems.

network operating system (NOS)   The software enabling networking; NOS can be on a LAN or WAN.

network sniffer   A device that has access to the signaling on the network cable.

network-based IDS (N-IDS)   An approach to an intrusion detection system (IDS), it attaches the system to a point in the network where it can monitor and report on all network traffic.

network-based IPS (N-IPS)   *See* host-based IPS (H-IPS).

nonessential service   A service that isn't necessary to keep the server operating at the expected level in its expected role.

Noninterference model   A model intended to ensure that higher-level security functions don't interfere with lower-level functions.

non-repudiation   Verifying (by whatever means) that data was seen by an intended party. It makes sure they received the data and can't repudiate (dispute) that it arrived.

notification   The act of being alerted to an event.

notification policies   A set of rules about what triggers notification.

NSA   *See* National Security Agency (NSA).

O

off-site storage   Storing data off the premise, usually in a secure location.

one-tier model   A model in which the database and applications exist on the same system.

one-time pad Words added to values during authentication. The message to be encrypted is added to this random text before hashing.

on-site storage Storing backup data at the same site as the servers on which the original data resides.

Open Shortest Path First (OSPF) A link-state routing protocol used in IP networks.

Open Systems Interconnection (OSI) model A model defined by the ISO to categorize the process of communication between computers in terms of seven layers. The seven layers are Application, Presentation, Session, Transport, Network, Data Link, and Physical. *See also* International Organization for Standardization (ISO).

operational security Security as it relates to how an organization does things (operates).

operator The person primarily responsible for the intrusion detection system (IDS).

OS hardening The process of applying all security patches and fixes to an operating system to make it as secure as possible.

out-of-band method A way to transmit the encryption key by using a method other than the one used to transmit the data. The key value is sent by letter, by courier, or by some other separate means.

OVAL An acronym for Open Vulnerability and Assessment Language, it is a community standard for system analysis that focuses on testing, analyzing, and reporting.

owner The person responsible for the current existence of a resource.

P

packet filtering A firewall technology that accepts or rejects packets based on their content.

packet switching The process of breaking messages into packets at the sending router for easier transmission over a WAN.

pad A number of characters often added to data before an operation such as hashing takes place. Most often unique values, known as one-time pads, are added to make the resulting hash unique.

partitioning The process of breaking a network into smaller components that can be individually protected.

passive detection A type of intruder detection that logs all network events to a file for an administrator to view later.

passive response A nonactive response, such as logging. Passive response is the most common type of response to many intrusions. In general, passive responses are the easiest to develop and implement.

Password Authentication Protocol (PAP)   One of the simplest forms of authentication. Authentication is accomplished by sending the username and password to the server and having them verified. Passwords are sent as clear text and, therefore, can be easily seen if intercepted.

password guessing   Attempting to enter a password by guessing its value.

password history   A list of passwords that have already been used.

PAT   *See* Port Address Translation (PAT).

patch   A fix for a known software problem.

penetration   The act of gaining access.

perimeter security   Security set up on the outside of the network or server to protect it.

personal electronic device (PED)   Any electronic device transported by a user. Examples include smartphones, electronic book readers, and music players.

personally identifiable information (PII)   Information that can be uniquely used to identify, contact, or locate a single person. Examples include social security number, driver's license number, fingerprints, and handwriting.

PGP   *See* Pretty Good Privacy (PGP).

phage virus   A virus that modifies and alters other programs and databases.

phishing   A form of social engineering in which you simply ask someone for a piece of information that you are missing by making it look as if it is a legitimate request. Commonly sent via email.

phreaker   Someone who abuses phone systems, as opposed to data systems.

physical access control   Control access measures used to restrict physical access to the server(s).

physical barrier   An object, such as a locked door, used to restrict physical access to network components.

Physical layer   The first layer of the OSI model; controls the functional interface. *See also* Open Systems Interconnection (OSI) model.

physical port   On a computer, an interface where you can connect a device.

physical security   Security that guards the physical aspects of the network.

Ping   A TCP/IP utility used to test whether another host is reachable. An Internet Control Message Protocol (ICMP) request is sent to the host, which responds with a reply if it's reachable. The request times out if the host isn't reachable.

ping of death   A large Internet Control Message Protocol (ICMP) packet sent to overflow the remote host's buffer. A ping of death usually causes the remote host to reboot or hang.

plain old telephone service (POTS)   Standard telephone service, as opposed to other connection technologies like Digital Subscriber Line (DSL).

point-to-point   Network communication in which two devices have exclusive access to a network medium. For example, a printer connected to only one workstation is using a point-to-point connection.

Point-to-Point Protocol (PPP)   A full-duplex line protocol that supersedes Serial Line Internet Protocol (SLIP). It's part of the standard TCP/IP suite and is often used in dial-up connections.

Point-to-Point Tunneling Protocol (PPTP)   An extension to Point-to-Point Protocol (PPP) that is used in virtual private networks (VPNs). An alternative to PPTP is L2TP.

policies   Rules or standards governing usage. These are typically high level in nature.

polymorphic   An attribute of some viruses that allows them to mutate and appear differently each time they crop up. The mutations make it harder for virus scanners to detect (and react) to the viruses.

port   Some kind of opening that allows network data to pass through.

Port Address Translation (PAT)   A means of translating between ports on a public and private network. Similar to Network Address Translation (NAT), which translates addresses between public and private.

port scanner   The item (physical or software) that scans a server for open ports that can be taken advantage of. Port scanning is the process of sending messages to ports to see which ones are available and which ones aren't.

postmortem   Anything that occurs "after the fact," such as an audit or review.

Post Office Protocol (POP)   An email access program that can be used to retrieve email from an email server.

Post Office Protocol Version 3 (POP3)   The protocol used to download email from an SMTP email server to a network client. *See also* Simple Mail Transfer Protocol (SMTP).

POTS   *See* plain old telephone service (POTS).

power conditioner   A device that "conditions" the electrical supply to take out spikes and surges.

power system   A device that provides electrical power.

PPP   *See* Point-to-Point Protocol (PPP).

PPTP   *See* Point-to-Point Tunneling Protocol (PPTP).

Presentation layer   The sixth layer of the OSI model; responsible for formatting data exchange, such as graphic commands, and converting character sets. This layer is also responsible for data compression, data encryption, and data stream redirection. *See also* Open Systems Interconnection (OSI) model.

preservation of evidence   The process of controlling access to evidence within chain-of-custody measures, often by placing it in a controlled-access area with a single custodian responsible for all access.

Pretty Good Privacy (PGP)   An implementation of RSA encryption. *See also* RSA.

privacy   A state of security in which information isn't seen by unauthorized parties without the express permission of the party involved.

Private Branch Exchange (PBX)   A system that allows users to connect voice, data, pagers, networks, and almost any other application into a single telecommunications system. A PBX system allows an organization to be its own phone company.

private information   Information that isn't for public knowledge.

private key   An asymmetric encryption technology in which both the sender and the receiver have different keys. A public key is used to encrypt messages and the private key is used to decrypt them. *See also* public key.

private network   The part of a network that lies behind a firewall and isn't "seen" on the Internet. *See also* firewall.

privilege audit   An audit performed to verify that no user is accessing information, or able to access information, beyond the security level at which they should be operating.

privilege escalation   The result when a user obtains access to a resource they wouldn't normally be able to access. Privilege escalation can be done inadvertently, by running a program with Set User ID (SUID) or Set Group ID (SGID) permissions or by temporarily becoming another user (via su or sudo in Unix/Linux or RunAs in Windows). It can also be done purposefully by an attacker seeking full access.

process list   The list of processes currently running on a system.

promiscuous mode   A mode wherein a network interface card (NIC) intercepts all traffic crossing the network wire and not just the traffic intended for it.

protocol analyzer   A software and hardware troubleshooting tool that is used to decode protocol information to try to determine the source of a network problem and to establish baselines.

protocols   Standards or rules.

proxy   A type of firewall that prevents direct communication between a client and a host by acting as an intermediary. *See also* firewall.

proxy cache server   An implementation of a web proxy. The server receives an HTTP request from a web browser and makes the request on behalf of the sending workstation. When the response comes, the proxy cache server caches a copy of the response locally. The next time someone makes a request for the same web page or Internet information, the proxy cache server can fulfill the request out of the cache instead of having to retrieve the resource from the Web.

proxy firewall   A proxy server that also acts as a firewall, blocking network access from external networks.

proxy server   A type of server that makes a single Internet connection and services requests on behalf of many users.

public information   Information that is publicly made available to all.

public key   A technology that uses two keys—a public key and a private key—to facilitate communication. The public key is used to encrypt a message to a receiver. *See also* private key.

Public Key Cryptography Standards (PKCS)   A set of voluntary standards created by RSA security and industry security leaders.

Public Key Infrastructure (PKI)   A two-key encryption system wherein messages are encrypted with a private key and decrypted with a public key.

Public Key Infrastructure X.509 (PKIX)   The Internet Engineering Task Force (IETF) working group developing standards and models for the Public Key Infrastructure (PKI) environment. The most current version is v3.

public network   The part of a network outside a firewall that is exposed to the public. *See also* firewall.

public key system   An encryption system employing a key that is known to users beyond the recipient.

Q

quantum cryptography   Cryptography based on changing the polarity of a photon. Quantum cryptography makes the process of interception difficult because any attempt to intercept the message changes the value of the message.

R

radio frequency (RF)   The part of the radio spectrum that a device uses.

radio frequency interference (RFI)   The byproduct of electrical processes, similar to electromagnetic interference. The major difference is that RFI is usually projected across a radio spectrum.

RADIUS   *See* Remote Authentication Dial-In User Service (RADIUS).

RAID   *See* Redundant Array of Independent (or Inexpensive) Disks (RAID).

RAID levels   The different types of RAID, such as RAID-0, RAID-1, and so on.

RBAC   *See* role-based access control (RBAC).

RC5   *See* Rivest Cipher 5 (RC5).

Redundant Array of Independent (or Inexpensive) Disks (RAID)   A configuration of multiple hard disks used to provide fault tolerance, should a disk fail, or gains in efficiency. Different levels of RAID exist.

registration authority (RA)   An organization that offloads some of the work from a certificate authority (CA). An RA system operates as a middleman in the process. The RA can distribute keys, accept registrations for the CA, and validate identities. The RA doesn't issue certificates; that responsibility remains with the CA.

relying party   The person receiving a certificate.

remote access protocol   Any networking protocol that is used to gain access to a network over public communication links.

remote access server (RAS)   A computer that has one or more modems installed to enable remote connections to the network.

Remote Authentication Dial-In User Service (RADIUS)   A mechanism that allows authentication of dial-in and other network connections. RADIUS is commonly used by Internet service providers (ISPs) and in the implementation of virtual private networks (VPNs).

replay attack   Any attack where the data is retransmitted repeatedly (often fraudulently or maliciously). In one such possibility, a user can replay a web session and visit sites intended only for the original user.

replication   The process of copying directory information to other servers to keep them all synchronized.

repository   A database or database server where the certificates are stored.

repudiation attack   An attack in which the intruder modifies information in a system.

Request for Comments (RFC)   A document-creation process and a set of practices that originated in 1969 and is used for proposed changes to Internet standards.

response   How you react to an event.

restricted information   Information that isn't made available to all and to which access is granted based on some criteria.

retrovirus   A virus that attacks or bypasses the antivirus software installed on a computer.

reverse DNS   Using an IP address to find a domain name rather than using a domain name to find an IP address (normal DNS). Pointer (PTR) records are used for the reverse lookup, and often reverse DNS is used to authenticate incoming connections.

reverse engineering   The process of re-creating the functionality of an item by first deciding what the result is and then creating something from scratch that serves the same purpose.

revocation   The process of canceling credentials that have been lost or stolen (or are no longer valid). With certificates, revocation is accomplished with a Certificate Revocation List (CRL).

RIP   *See* Routing Information Protocol (RIP).

risk analysis   An evaluation of each risk that can be identified. Each risk should be outlined, described, and evaluated on the likelihood of it occurring.

risk assessment   An evaluation of how much risk you and your organization are willing to take. An assessment must be performed before any other actions—such as how much to spend on security in terms of dollars and manpower—can be decided.

Rivest Cipher 5 (RC5)   A cipher algorithm created by Ronald Rivest (for RSA) and known for its speed. It works through blocks of variable sizes using three phases: key expansion, encryption, and decryption.

roaming profile   A profile downloaded from a server at each logon. When a user logs out at the end of the session, changes are made and remembered for the next time the user logs on.

rogue server   An active Dynamic Host Configuration Protocol (DHCP) server that has been added to the network and is now leasing addresses to users instead of them obtaining an address from your server.

role-based access control (RBAC)   A type of control wherein the levels of security closely follow the structure of an organization. The role the person plays in the organization (accountant, salesman, and so on) corresponds to the level of security access they have to data.

rootkit   Software program that has the ability to obtain root-level access and hide certain things from the operating system.

route   The path to get to the destination from a source.

route cost   The number of router hops between the source and the destination in an internetwork.

router   A device that connects two or more networks and allows packets to be transmitted and received between them. A router determines the best path for data packets from source to destination.

routing   A function of the Network layer that involves moving data throughout a network. Data passes through several network subnetworks using routers that can select the path the data takes. *See also* router.

Routing Information Protocol (RIP)   A distance-vector route discovery protocol used by Internetwork Packet Exchange (IPX) and Internet Protocol (IP). IPX uses hops and ticks to determine the cost for a particular route. *See also* Internetwork Packet Exchange (IPX).

routing table   A table that contains information about the locations of other routers on the network and their distance from the current router.

RSA   One of the providers of cryptography systems to industry and government. RSA stands for the initials of the three founders of RSA Security Inc.: Rivest, Shamir, and Adleman. RSA maintains a list of standards for Public Key Cryptography Standards (PKCS).

Rule Set-Based Access Control (RSBAC)   An open-source access control framework for the Linux kernel that uses access control modules to implement Mandatory Access Control (MAC).

S

SAM   *See* Security Accounts Manager (SAM).

sandbox   A set of rules used when creating a Java applet that prevents certain functions when the applet is sent as part of a web page.

scanning   The process that attackers use to gather information about how a network is configured.

screened host   A router that is in front of a server on the private network. Typically, this server does packet filtering before reaching the firewall/proxy server that services the internal network.

secret key   *See* private key.

Secure Electronic Transaction (SET)   A protocol developed by Visa and MasterCard for secure credit card transactions. The protocol is becoming an accepted standard by many companies. SET provides encrypted credit card numbers over the Internet, and it's most suited to small amounts of data transmission.

Secure Hash Algorithm (SHA)   A one-way hash algorithm designed to ensure the integrity of a message.

Secure Hypertext Transfer Protocol (S-HTTP)   A protocol used for secure communications between a web server and a web browser.

Secure Shell (SSH)   A replacement for `rlogin` in Unix/Linux that includes security. `rlogin` allowed one host to establish a connection with another with no real security being employed; SSH replaces it with `slogin` and digital certificates.

Secure Sockets Layer (SSL)   A protocol that secures messages by operating between the Application layer (HTTP) and the Transport layer.

Secure WLAN Protocol (SWP)   A method of securing wireless networks that is beginning to gain momentum and acceptance.

Security Accounts Manager (SAM)   A database within Windows NT–based operating systems that contains information about all users and groups and their associated rights and settings within a domain.

security audit   An audit of the system (host, network, and so on) for security vulnerabilities and holes.

security log   A log file used in Windows NT to keep track of security events specified by the domain's audit policy.

security policies   Rules set in place by a company to ensure the security of a network. These may include how often a password must be changed or how many characters a password should be.

security professionals   Individuals who make their living working with computer security.

security token   A piece of data that contains the rights and access privileges of the token bearer as part of the token.

security zone   A method of isolating a system from other systems or networks.

segment   A unit of data transmission found at the Transport layer of the Open Systems Interconnection (OSI) model and used by TCP.

sensor   A device that collects data from the data source and passes it on to the analyzer.

separation of duties   A set of policies designed to reduce the risk of fraud and prevent other losses in an organization.

sequence number   A number used to determine the order in which parts of a packet are to be reassembled after the packet has been split into sections.

Serial Line Internet Protocol (SLIP)   An older protocol that was used in early remote-access environments. SLIP was originally designed to connect Unix systems together in a dial-up environment, and it supports only serial communications.

server   A computer that provides resources to the clients on the network.

server and client configuration   A network in which the resources are located on a server and accessed by clients.

server authentication   A process that requires the workstation to authenticate against the server.

service   An item that adds functionality to a network by providing resources or doing tasks for other computers.

service account   An account created on a server for a user to perform special services, such as a backup operator, an account operator, and a server operator.

service-level agreement (SLA)   An agreement that specifies performance requirements for a vendor. This agreement may use mean time before failure (MTBF) and mean time to repair (MTTR) as performance measures in the SLA.

service pack   Operating system updates from Microsoft.

session key   The agreed-upon (during connection) key used between a client and a server during a session. This key is generated by encrypting the server's digital ID (after validity has been established). The asymmetric key pair is then used to encrypt and verify the session key that is passed back and forth between client and server during the length of the connection.

Session layer   The fifth layer of the OSI model. It determines how two computers establish, use, and end a session. Security authentication and network naming functions required for applications occur here. The Session layer establishes, maintains, and breaks dialogs between two stations. *See also* Open Systems Interconnection (OSI) model.

SHA   *See* Secure Hash Algorithm (SHA).

share-level security   A network security method that assigns passwords to individual files or other network resources (such as printers) instead of assigning rights to network resources to users. The passwords are then given to all users that need access to these resources. All resources are visible from anywhere in the network, and any user who knows the password for a particular network resource can make changes to it.

shoulder surfing   Watching someone when they enter their username/password/ sensitive data.

S-HTTP   *See* Secure Hypertext Transfer Protocol (S-HTTP).

signal   Transmission from one PC to another. A signal could be a notification to start a session or end a session.

signal encoding   The process whereby a protocol at the Physical layer receives information from the upper layers and translates all the data into signals that can be transmitted on a transmission medium.

signaling method   The process of transmitting data across the medium. Two types of signaling are digital and analog.

signed applet   An applet that doesn't run in the Java sandbox and has higher system access capabilities. Signed applets aren't usually downloaded from the Internet but are provided by in-house or custom programming efforts.

Simple Mail Transfer Protocol (SMTP)   A protocol for sending email between SMTP servers.

Simple Network Management Protocol (SNMP)   The management protocol created for sending information about the health of the network-to-network management consoles.

single loss expectancy (SLE)   The cost of a single loss when it occurs. This loss can be a critical failure, or it can be the result of an attack.

single sign-on (SSO)   A relationship between the client and the network wherein the client is allowed to log on one time, and all resource access is based on that logon (as opposed to needing to log on to each individual server to access the resources there).

site survey   A generic site survey involves listening in on an existing wireless network using commercially available technologies. A wireless site survey, or wireless survey, is the process of planning and designing a wireless network, in particular an 802.11.

SLIP   *See* Serial Line Internet Protocol (SLIP).

SMTP   *See* Simple Mail Transfer Protocol (SMTP).

SMTP relay   A feature designed into many email servers that allows them to forward email to other email servers. While the ability to act as a relay exists to allow networks to grow, the possibility exists for rogue servers to also participate.

smurf attack   An attack in which large volumes of ICMP echo requests (pings) are broadcast to all other machines on the network and in which the source address of the broadcast system has been spoofed to appear as though it came from the target computer. When all the machines that received the broadcast respond, they flood the target with more data than it can handle.

snapshot backup   A method of performing backups that creates a compressed file of a database as it exists at the moment, without taking the users offline. A snapshot backup can take the place of other backups. It's often run on mirrored servers, but the snapshot captures only the most recent version of files.

sniffer   A physical device that listens in (sniffs) on network traffic and looks for items it can make sense of. There is a legitimate purpose for these devices: Administrators use them to analyze traffic. However, when they're used by sources other than the administrator, they become security risks.

sniffing   Analyzing data to look for passwords and anything else of value. Sniffing is also known as wiretapping, eavesdropping, and a number of other terms (packet sniffing, network sniffing, and so on).

SNMP   *See* Simple Network Management Protocol (SNMP).

snooping   Looking through files in hopes of finding something interesting.

social engineering   An attack that uses others by deceiving them. It does not directly target hardware or software, but instead targets and manipulates people.

socket   The primary method used to communicate with services and applications such as the Web and Telnet. The socket is a programming construct that enables communication by mapping between ports and addresses.

software exploitation   An attack launched against applications and higher-level services.

spam Unwanted, unsolicited email sent in bulk.

spike A momentary or instantaneous increase in power over a power line.

spoofing attack An attempt by someone or something to masquerade as someone else.

spyware Software programs that work—often actively—on behalf of a third party.

SSH *See* Secure Shell (SSH).

SSL *See* Secure Sockets Layer (SSL).

state table A firewall security method that monitors the status of all the connections through the firewall.

stateful packet filtering Inspections that occur at all levels of the network and provide additional security using a state table that tracks every communications channel.

static Address Resolution Protocol (ARP) table entry An entry in the Address Resolution Protocol (ARP) table that a user adds manually when a PC will be accessed often.

static routing A method of routing packets where the router's routing table is updated manually by the network administrator instead of automatically by a route discovery protocol.

stealth port A port that is open but might not be obvious (invisible to those who don't know it exists). Trojan horses often exploit them.

stealth virus A virus that attempts to avoid detection by masking itself from applications.

steganography The science of hiding information within other information, such as a picture.

strength The effectiveness of a cryptographic system in preventing unauthorized decryption.

subscriber An individual who is attempting to present a certificate proving authenticity.

surge protector A device that protects electrical components from momentary or instantaneous increases (called spikes) in a power line.

switched A network that has multiple routes to get from a source to a destination. Switching allows for higher speeds.

SWP *See* Secure WLAN Protocol (SWP).

symmetrical keys The keys used when the same key encrypts and decrypts data.

SYN flood A Denial of Service attack in which the hacker sends a barrage of spoofed SYN packets. The receiving station tries to respond to each SYN request for a connection, thereby tying up all the resources. All incoming connections are rejected until all current connections can be established.

system architecture Documents that provide you with the blueprint of your organization's software and hardware infrastructure.

T

tap   A type of connection that directly attaches to a cable.

TCP   *See* Transmission Control Protocol (TCP).

TCP ACK attack   An attack that begins as a normal TCP connection and whose purpose is to deny service. It's also known as a TCP SYN flood.

TCP sequence attack   An attack wherein the attacker intercepts and then responds with a sequence number similar to the one used in the original session. The attack can either disrupt a session or hijack a valid session.

TCP SYN flood   *See* TCP ACK attack.

TCP wrapper   A low-level logging package designed for Unix systems.

TCP/IP   *See* Transmission Control Protocol/Internet Protocol (TCP/IP).

TCP/IP hijacking   An attack in which the attacker commandeers a TCP session from a legitimate user after the legitimate user has achieved authentication, thereby removing the need for the attacker to authenticate himself.

teardrop attack   A DoS attack that uses large packets and odd offset values to confuse the receiver and help facilitate a crash.

Telnet   A protocol that functions at the Application layer of the OSI model, providing terminal emulation capabilities. *See also* Open Systems Interconnection (OSI) model.

Temporal Key Interchange/Integrity Protocol (TKIP)   A wrapper that works with wireless encryption to strengthen WEP implementations. It was designed to provide more secure encryption than the notoriously weak Wired Equivalent Privacy (WEP).

Terminal Access Controller Access-Control System (TACACS)   An authentication system that allows credentials to be accepted from multiple methods, including Kerberos. The TACACS client/server process occurs in the same manner as the Remote Authentication Dial-In User Service (RADIUS) process.

terminal emulator   A program that enables a PC to act as a terminal for a mainframe or a Unix system.

termination policy   A clear process of informing affected departments of a voluntary or involuntary termination.

test account   An administrator-created account for confirming the basic functionality of a newly installed application, for example. The test account has equal rights to accounts that will use the new functionality. It's important to use test accounts instead of administrator accounts to test new functionality. If an administrator account is used, problems related to user rights might not manifest themselves because administrator accounts typically have full rights to all network resources.

TFTP   *See* Trivial File Transfer Protocol (TFTP).

thin client   Systems that don't provide any disk storage or removable media on their workstations.

third party   A party responsible for providing assurance to the relying party that a subscriber is genuine.

threat   Any perceivable risk.

three-tier model   A system that effectively isolates the end user from the database by introducing a middle-tier server.

time to live (TTL)   A field in an IP packet that indicates how many routers the packet can cross (hops it can make) and how long it takes before it's discarded. TTL is also used in Address Resolution Protocol (ARP) tables to indicate how long an entry should remain in the table.

TLS   *See* Transport Layer Security (TLS).

token   A piece of data holding information about the user. This information can contain group IDs, user IDs, privilege level, and so on.

TPM   *See* trusted platform module (TPM).

Traceroute   *See* Tracert.

Tracert   The command-line utility that shows the user every router interface a packet passes through on its way to a destination.

trailer   A section of a data packet that contains error-checking information.

transceiver   A device that allows the network interface card (NIC) to connect to the network.

transmission   Sending packets from the PC to the server. The transmission can occur over a network cable, wireless connection, or other medium.

Transmission Control Protocol (TCP)   The protocol found at the Host-to-Host layer of the Department of Defense (DoD) model. This protocol breaks data packets into segments, numbers them, and sends them in order. The receiving computer reassembles the data so that the information is readable for the user. In the process, the sender and the receiver confirm that all data has been received; if not, it's resent. TCP is a connection-oriented protocol. *See also* connection-oriented.

Transmission Control Protocol/Internet Protocol (TCP/IP)   The protocol suite developed by the Department of Defense (DoD) in conjunction with the Internet. It was designed as an internetworking protocol suite that could route information around network failures. Today it's the de facto standard for communications on the Internet.

transmission media   Physical cables and/or wireless technology across which computers are able to communicate.

Transport layer   The fourth layer of the OSI model. It's responsible for checking that the data packet created in the Session layer was received. If necessary, it also changes the length of messages for transport up or down the remaining layers. *See also* Open Systems Interconnection (OSI) model.

Transport Layer Security (TLS)   A protocol whose purpose is to verify that secure communications between a server and a client remain secure. Defined in RFC 2246.

Triple-DES (3DES)   A symmetric block cipher algorithm used for encryption.

Trivial File Transfer Protocol (TFTP)   A UDP-based protocol similar to FTP that doesn't provide the security or error-checking features of FTP. *See also* File Transfer Protocol (FTP).

Trojan horse   Any application that masquerades as one thing in order to get past scrutiny and then does something malicious. One of the major differences between Trojan horses and viruses is that Trojan horses tend not to replicate themselves.

Trust List   A list of objects signed by a trusted entity. Also known as a Certificate Trust List (CTL).

Trusted Platform Module (TPM)   A method of utilizing encryption and storing the passwords on a chip. The hardware holding the chip is then needed to unencrypt the data and make it readable.

TTL   *See* time to live (TTL).

tunneling   The act of sending data across a public network by encapsulating it into other packets.

two-factor authentication   Using two access methods as a part of the authentication process.

two-tier model   A model in which the client PC or system runs an application that communicates with a database that is running on a different server.

U

UDP   *See* User Datagram Protocol (UDP).

Uniform Resource Locator (URL)   A way of identifying a document on the Internet. It consists of the protocol used to access the document and the domain name or IP address of the host that holds the document; for example, http://www.sybex.com.

uninterruptible power supply (UPS)   A device that can provide short-term power, usually by using batteries.

uptime   The amount of time a particular computer or network component has been functional.

URL *See* Uniform Resource Locator (URL).

usage policies Defined policies governing computer usage.

user The person who is using a computer or network or a resource.

User Datagram Protocol (UDP) The protocol at the Host-to-Host layer of the TCP/IP Department of Defense (DoD) model, which corresponds to the Transport layer of the OSI model. Packets are divided into datagrams, given numbers, sent, and put back together at the receiving end. UDP is a connectionless protocol. *See also* connectionless, Open Systems Interconnection (OSI) model.

user-level security A type of network security in which user accounts can read, write, change, and take ownership of files. Rights are assigned to user accounts, and each user knows only their own username and password—which makes this the preferred method for securing files.

user management policies Defined policies that detail user management.

V

virtual LAN (VLAN) Local area network (LAN) that allows users on different switch ports to participate in their own network separate from, but still connected to, the other stations on the same or a connected switch.

virtual link A link created by using a switch to limit network traffic.

virtual private network (VPN) System that uses the public Internet as a backbone for a private interconnection (network) between locations.

virus A program intended to damage a computer system. Sophisticated viruses are encrypted and hide in a computer, and might not appear until the user performs a certain action or until a certain date. *See also* antivirus.

volume The loudness of a sound, or the portion of a hard disk that functions as if it were a separate hard disk.

W

WAN *See* wide area network (WAN).

war driving Driving around with a laptop looking for open wireless access points with which to communicate.

warm site A site that provides some capabilities in the event of a disaster. The organization that wants to use a warm site will need to install, configure, and reestablish operations on systems that might already exist in the warm site.

weak key   A cipher hole that can be exploited.

weak key attack   An attack that looks for cipher holes.

web proxy   A type of proxy that is used to act on behalf of a web client or web server.

web server   A server that holds and delivers web pages and other web content using HTTP. *See also* Hypertext Transfer Protocol (HTTP).

WEP   *See* Wired Equivalent Privacy (WEP).

wide area network (WAN)   A network that crosses local, regional, and/or international boundaries.

Wi-Fi   *See* Wireless Fidelity (Wi-Fi).

Wi-Fi protected access (WPA)   Security protocol developed by the Wi-Fi Alliance to protect wireless networks and surpass what WEP offered. There are two versions, WPA and WPA2, with the latter being the full implementation of the security features.

Windows socket   A Microsoft API used to interact with TCP/IP.

Wired Equivalent Privacy (WEP)   A security protocol for 802.11b (wireless) networks that attempts to establish the same security for them as would be present in a wired network.

wireless access point   A wireless bridge used in a multipoint radio frequency (RF) network.

wireless bridge   A bridge that performs all the functions of a regular bridge but uses RF instead of cables to transmit signals.

Wireless Fidelity (Wi-Fi)   A wireless network operating in the 2.4 Ghz or 5 Ghz range.

wireless local area network (WLAN)   A local area network that employs wireless access points (WAPs) and clients using the 802.11 standards.

wireless portal   The primary method of connecting a wireless device to a network.

wireless technologies   Technologies employing wireless communications.

Wireless Transport Layer Security (WTLS)   The security layer of the Wireless Applications Protocol (WAP). WTLS provides authentication, encryption, and data integrity for wireless devices.

work factor   An estimate of the amount of time and effort that would be needed to break a system.

workgroup   A specific group of users or network devices, organized by job function or proximity to shared resources.

working copy   The copy of the data currently in use on a network.

workstation   A computer that isn't a server but is on a network. Generally, a workstation is used to do work, whereas a server is used to store data or perform a network function.

World Wide Web Consortium (W3C)   An association concerned with interoperability, growth, and standardization of the World Wide Web (WWW). This group is the primary sponsor of XML and other web-enabled technologies.

worm   A program similar to a virus. Worms, however, propagate themselves over a network. *See also* virus.

WPA   *See* Wi-FI protected access (WPA).

X

X.500   The International Telecommunications Union (ITU) standard for directory services in the late 1980s. The standard was the basis for later models of directory structure, such as Lightweight Directory Access Protocol (LDAP).

XSRF   *See* cross-site request forgery (XSRF).

Z

zombie   Any system taking directions from a master control computer. Zombies are often utilized in distributed denial of service (DDoS) and botnet attacks.

zone   An area in a building where access is individually monitored and controlled.

Index

E

I

N

O

The Absolute Best CompTIA Security+ Book/CD Package on the Market!

Get ready for your CompTIA Security+ certification with the most comprehensive and challenging sample tests anywhere!

The Sybex Test Engine features:

- All the review questions, as covered in each chapter of the book
- Challenging questions representative of those you'll find on the real exam
- Two Practice Exams available only on the CD
- An Assessment Test to narrow your focus to certain objective groups.

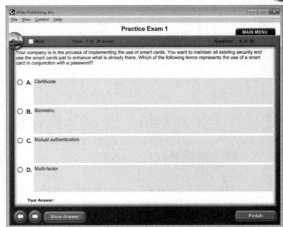

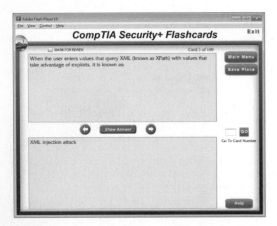

Use the Electronic Flashcards to jog your memory and prep last-minute for the exam!

- Reinforce your understanding of key concepts with these hardcore flashcard-style questions.

Use the Glossary for instant reference:

- Search through the PDF of the Glossary to find key terms you'll need to be familiar with for the exam.

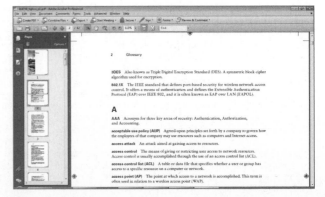